Imagining Society

Second Edition

As a global academic publisher, Sage is driven by the belief that research and education are critical in shaping society. Our mission is building bridges to knowledge—supporting the development of ideas into scholarship that is certified, taught, and applied in the real world.

Sage's founder, Sara Miller McCune, transferred control of the company to an independent trust, which guarantees our independence indefinitely. This enables us to support an equitable academic future over the long term by building lasting relationships, championing diverse perspectives, and co-creating social and behavioral science resources that transform teaching and learning.

Imagining Society

An Introduction to Sociology

Second Edition

Catherine Corrigall-Brown

The University of British Columbia

FOR INFORMATION:

2455 Teller Road
Thousand Oaks, California 91320
E-mail: order@sagepub.com

1 Oliver's Yard
55 City Road
London, EC1Y 1SP
United Kingdom

Unit No 323–333, Third Floor, F-Block
International Trade Tower
Nehru Place, New Delhi—110 019
India

18 Cross Street #10–10/11/12
China Square Central
Singapore 048423

Printed in the United States of America.

Library of Congress Cataloging-in-Publication Data

Names: Corrigall-Brown, Catherine, author.

Title: Imagining society : an introduction to sociology / Catherine Corrigall-Brown, The University of British Columbia.

Description: Second edition. | Los Angeles : SAGE, [2024] | Includes bibliographical references and index.

Identifiers: LCCN 2023047095 (print) | LCCN 2023047096 (ebook) | ISBN 9781071917138 (paperback) | ISBN 9781071917152 (epub)

Subjects: LCSH: Sociology.

Classification: LCC HM585 .C674 2024 (print) | LCC HM585 (ebook) | DDC 301--dc23/eng/20231102

LC record available at https://lccn.loc.gov/2023047095

LC ebook record available at https://lccn.loc.gov/2023047096

Acquisitions Editor: Erica DeLuca

Content Development Editor: Cassie Carey

Production Editor: Aparajita Srivastava

Copy Editor: Diana Breti

Typesetter: diacriTech

Cover Designer: Scott Van Atta

Marketing Manager: Jennifer Haldeman

This book is printed on acid-free paper.

24 25 26 27 28 10 9 8 7 6 5 4 3 2 1

BRIEF CONTENTS

DETAILED CONTENTS

USING YOUR SOCIOLOGICAL IMAGINATION

PREFACE

I remember signing up for my first sociology class. I needed one more course to complete my schedule in my first year of university and my mother suggested that I take sociology. Even though I had never heard of sociology and did not know what it would entail, I took the class. I was forever changed.

That course fundamentally altered the way I think about the world around me. Sociology provided me with a lens through which to study and understand our complex society. I learned that, although we all have a lifetime of experiences within society, the importance of that society is often hard to understand because we are so immersed in it. Sociology helped me see how society shaped my life and the world around me.

By teaching sociology for many years, I have had the pleasure of helping students discover their sociological imagination, the key lens we use to understand the connection between individuals and society. It is a delight to see them start to use the theories, ideas, and research in our discipline to help make sense of the world around them. We can use these ideas to answer pressing questions such as, "Why is there poverty?" "Why do men and women earn different amounts of money?" "How do race and ethnicity shape our lives?" and "How does social change happen?" This book aims to bring sociology to life.

ORGANIZATION OF THIS BOOK

As the systematic study of human society, sociology covers a lot of ground. This book is divided into four sections. **Part I** introduces the sociological imagination, the process of socialization, how we learn to fit into society and develop a sense of identity, and the role of deviance in society. **Part II** focuses on social inequality, a core area of sociology. This section examines social class, social status, race, ethnicity, gender, and sexuality. Understanding how inequalities between people arise, perpetuate, and can be reduced is fundamental to sociology and is a primary theme of this book. **Part III** assesses several core institutions of society, including the media, family, education, work, and health. Sociology as a discipline encourages us to understand how individual choices can be structured or limited by larger social forces. Institutions are one such force that can shape the kind of lives we lead and larger patterns of social inequality.

We end the book by examining social change. There is much inequality in society and a myriad of social problems in the United States and around the world. In **Part IV** we learn about the role of the state, social movements, and other avenues for creating social change. It is certainly possible to make a more equal and just world. In fact, social change is a constant phenomenon that has helped us to address many social problems. The diversity of people in your sociology class is a testament to how society can change and become more equal, but much more can be done. To conclude this book we will learn about social change, which hopefully will ignite your sociological imagination.

KEY FEATURES

Each chapter includes the following features to enhance student comprehension and offer avenues of learning beyond the classroom.

Learning Objectives. Learning objectives help students focus on concepts they will learn throughout the chapter.

Readings. Excerpts from books or articles written by the founders of the discipline and today's top sociologists illuminate the concepts and theories in the text. These readings highlight the discipline's roots as well as its current foci and findings. Critical thinking questions, which follow every reading, facilitate further thought and help you apply the reading's main concepts. The readings incorporated in the text enable students to see how concepts and ideas have their origins in the work of our founding sociologists and how the concepts of our discipline are being applied.

Using Your Sociological Imagination Activities. Each chapter also includes activities that help you connect the theories and ideas of sociology to your life. For example, what can you learn about socialization by looking at the toys you played with as a child? How can comparing your grandparents' education with your own help you understand the larger social changes in educational attainment in the United States? What do the curricula of your high school classes tell you about the values of society and how they are changing? How are protest events depicted in the media and how does this portrayal shape how you think about protesters? This type of hands-on learning and engagement with the concepts in the class can help students to practice using their sociological imagination in a way that feels more relevant to daily life.

Methods in Depth. This book has Methods in Depth sections in each chapter to help illustrate how sociologists actually *do* research. Instead of having a chapter on methods isolated from the substantive areas being studied, methods are presented throughout the book to show how sociologists engage in the research process to better understand the core questions in sociology. Each chapter examines a study in detail and then considers all the issues that come up in the research process. By the end of the text, students will have been introduced to all the major qualitative and quantitative methods and will see how they are used by sociologists.

Summary. To help reinforce students' understanding of the content, a short summary can be found at the end of each chapter.

Key Terms. A list of key terms in alphabetical order is provided at the end of each chapter. You can find a full glossary in the back of the book.

For Further Reading. Additional readings are provided at the end of each chapter for students interested in learning more about any of the topics covered in this book.

DIGITAL RESOURCES

Teaching Resources

This text includes an array of instructor teaching materials designed to save you time and to help you keep students engaged. To learn more, visit sagepub.com or contact your SAGE representative at sagepub.com/findmyrep.

ACKNOWLEDGMENTS

My sociological imagination has been shaped by the many wonderful professors who taught me at the University of Victoria, Western University, and the University of California, Irvine. My students and colleagues at the University of British Columbia have helped build on this foundation and deepened my interest and enjoyment of sociology. They have all shaped my understanding of and fascination with the discipline, which I hope to pass on to future sociology students.

I am indebted to the wonderful people at SAGE who have helped this project come to fruition. They have deftly guided this project through its many stages, and their hard work is much appreciated. I also join SAGE in thanking the following reviewers for their comments on the manuscript:

Wendy Brame, Briar Cliff University
Derrick M. Bryan, Morehouse College
Jennifer Dabbs, Lubbock Christian University
Aneliese Dar, University of North Carolina, Greensboro
Sarah B. Donley, Jacksonville State University
Glenn Eichel, University of Maine
Kristi Hagen, Chippewa Valley Technical College
Shantelle Holts, Tidewater Community College
Eric Jorrey, Central Ohio Technical College
Mark Killian, Whitworth University
Kim MacInnish, Bridgewater State University
Gudmundur Oddsson, University of Akureyri, Iceland
Dina Radeljas, Mohawk Valley Community College
Bryan K. Robinson, University of Mount Union
Karl Smith, University of Maryland, Eastern Shore
Kimberly Touches, Centenary University
Roberta Villalón, St. John's University
Adria Welcher, Morehouse College
Stephen Zehr, University of Southern Indiana

Most important, I thank my wonderful husband, Steve Weldon, for his endless support of this project and all my work. I also gratefully acknowledge my parents, Melodie and Hans, for their encouragement, and my sister, Sarah, for her inspiration.

This book is dedicated to my son, Leo. He was born into a challenging world but one that is filled with possibilities. May it become more equal and just as he grows.

ABOUT THE AUTHOR

Catherine Corrigall-Brown is professor and head of sociology at the University of British Columbia in Vancouver. Her research focuses on social movements and protest, particularly examining what keeps individuals involved in activism over time, framing, and identity. She is the author of five books, including *Patterns of Protest*, published with Stanford University Press, and *Keeping the March Alive*, published with New York University Press. She has published more than 50 articles, book chapters, and review essays. These works have appeared in journals such as *Social Forces, Mobilization, American Behavioral Scientist*, the *International Journal of Comparative Sociology, Sociological Perspectives, Social Movement Studies,* and the *Canadian Review of Sociology*. This research was funded by grants from the National Science  Foundation (U.S.) and the Social Sciences and Humanities Research Council (Canada). She has served as chair of the Social Movement and Collective Behavior Section of the American Sociological Association. She is currently a deputy editor of *Mobilization,* the premiere social movements journal. She was awarded the Killam Faculty Teaching Prize in 2017 and the Outstanding Teaching Award from the Canadian Sociological Association in 2022. She received the Early Investigator Award for best early career scholar from the Canadian Sociological Association in 2013.

UNDERSTANDING SOCIETY

deberarr/iStockPhoto

THE SOCIOLOGICAL IMAGINATION

LEARNING OBJECTIVES

1. Identify and understand the difference between society and culture.

2. Describe the concept of the sociological imagination, particularly the connection between personal troubles and public issues.

3. Explain the three core foci of sociology: social inequality, social institutions, and social change.

4. Explain and give examples of the three core aims of sociology.

5. Assess how Durkheim's study of suicide illustrates the connection between the individual and society.

6. Discuss the main ways that sociologists study society and the parts of the research process.

7. Compare qualitative and quantitative research methods, highlighting the benefits and challenges of each approach.

Auguste Comte first coined the word "sociology." He believed that this new discipline had the potential to bring together all the sciences and to improve society. Comte was, in part, inspired to create this new area of study because he lived in a period of rapid social change (1798–1857). Industry was replacing agriculture as a way of life, democracies were emerging from monarchies, and populations were migrating from the countryside to the cities. To make sense of this immense social change, Comte sought to understand how society worked, as well as the effect of these larger processes on society and the people living in it.

Before and after Comte, individuals from all disciplines have been interested in explaining how society operates and why it sometimes does not work as well as we think it could. For example, philosophers as far back as Socrates and Plato considered what makes a good society. But sociology is different from this type of philosophical thought. In fact, the definition of sociology is that it is the systematic study of human society. This definition begs the question, "What is society?"

SOCIETY AND CULTURE

Society is the largest-scale human group that shares a common geographic territory and common institutions. Societies are not necessarily the same as states. In fact, many states contain several different societies. For example, the United Kingdom is said to contain four distinct societies: England, Northern Ireland, Scotland, and Wales.

Society is based on and requires social interaction among its members. These interactions can occur in a variety of settings and on many different levels, such as in neighborhoods, schools, or workplaces. Such connections are important because they create shared understandings and are the basis of continued cooperation among the members of a society. These interactions also work to socialize newcomers, either those who emigrated from other parts of the world or young people who are learning how to behave within our society. Through this socialization we teach others the written and unwritten rules and values of our society. We also use this interaction between members to monitor and regulate each other, making sure that we all follow society's rules and expectations.

Interactions within society happen in patterned ways; for example, most people go to the same coffee shop every morning and have the same conversation with the barista. The routines, expectations, and behaviors in these interactions are established over time so that ongoing cooperation between people is possible (Charon, 2012). Imagine if you replied to the barista's question, "How are you?" with a long story about your new sociology course or your indecision about whether to go on another date with someone. He would probably be quite surprised at your unusual behavior in this situation because the routine is that you simply say, "Fine, thank you." By responding in an unexpected way, you challenge the common expectations of how this social interaction should take place. The fact that most interactions in society are predictable establishes a common set of understandings of how our society works and how we are supposed to behave in it.

It is important to note that these patterns can change over time. When the COVID-19 pandemic became a global concern in 2020, it shaped our behavior in many different domains. Obviously, it had serious implications for our health and the health of our communities. However, the implications reached many other parts of society. Consider the interaction with the barista just discussed. Even this innocuous conversation was quite different in December 2020 than it was a year before. By December 2020, you would have been wearing a mask while talking to a masked barista. There would have been plexiglass in front of you as you were encouraged to pay with a credit card so as to minimize touching surfaces. And, you could not sit in the coffee shop to drink your latte. In fact, you were expected to move out of the store quickly and not engage in any casual conversation about the weather with the staff as you may have done the year before. This example illustrates how social interactions are patterned, but also how these patterns change and evolve over time.

Harold Garfinkel (1991) was interested in the unexamined ways that we follow the rules of our society. He argued that people unknowingly create and re-create the rules of society every day and that we do not really see or understand these rules until they are broken. Individuals are constantly interacting with one another, guided by a set of expectations regarding how they should act in a given situation. However, we are not always able to articulate, or even notice, these rules because we take them for granted. To examine these accepted ways of producing order in society, Garfinkel developed what he called breaching experiments. In a breaching experiment, the researcher breaks a social rule to reveal the unrecognized way that all individuals cooperate to maintain the smooth social interactions and social order. Garfinkel—or, more often, his graduate students—would break a social rule and then see how people reacted. By creating disorder, he hoped to demonstrate how social order is usually maintained.

In one experiment, Garfinkel instructed his students to act as guests in their parents' homes during their holiday visit. The students were to be excessively polite, ask permission to use the restroom, and pretend not to know the people in the household. By behaving like strangers, the students undermined the expectations of how children should act toward their parents. Students reported that parents were upset and confused by the behavior—some were even quite angry at being treated so formally. What would your parents think if you acted this way toward them?

Garfinkel also did many experiments in grocery stores. He had students take items from other people's carts. Shoppers initially assumed that a mistake had been made. Perhaps the students thought the cart was their own? However, the students told the other shoppers that they simply found it easier to take items from another cart instead of walking up and down the aisles. This behavior is not explicitly forbidden— grocery stores have no signs telling you not to take things from someone else's cart—and the items had not yet been purchased. However, the shoppers often were angry at having their carts raided.

Socially awkward behaviors can inspire sociologists to ask what we consider normal or acceptable behaviors. The TV show *Ted Lasso* follows a U.S. football coach who moves to the UK to coach a soccer team. The humor comes from Ted's inability to understand the culture and rules of both the UK and soccer.

27th Annual SAG Awards/Getty Images for WarnerMedia/Getty Images

Although many people find encounters with rule breakers frustrating, it is a long-standing part of comedy. The TV show *Ted Lasso* is based on the way that the main character, Ted, does things that break social norms because, as an American, he does not understand the cultural practices of the British. He is constantly friendly and chatty, is always very upbeat, and bakes cookies for his boss. The humor in the show comes from his inability to pick up on the social cues from people around him. Television shows such as *The Big Bang Theory, Arrested Development, Bob's Burgers,* and *The Office* are also based on the humor in seeing other people break social rules. When Tina Belcher from *Bob's Burgers* does something unusual, such as refusing to give a customer space to decide on their order and instead inching closer and closer, we find it humorous because social rules dictate that servers give their customers space and time to decide on their meal. It is only by breaking the social rule, or seeing others do so, that we can see what the social rule is and why following it makes society run smoothly.

Interactions in society are shaped by culture. Culture is a system of behaviors, beliefs, knowledge, practices, values, and materials. Cultures shape how we behave and the physical elements of our society. Our culture affects a myriad of elements of our lives, from how we set up cities to how we dress. It is clear from this definition that culture is contested: We certainly do not all agree on how we should act or what we should believe. There can be important distinctions between the dominant culture and subcultures or countercultures.

The dominant culture can impose its values, beliefs, and behaviors on a given society because of its political and economic power. Think about the human-interest stories discussed on *The View* or *Good Morning America.* They tend to be of interest to the people with a lot of money or power: how to decorate a home, what to wear, or which products to buy. These stories are based on the values of the dominant culture—that it is important to look attractive and fashionable, own an impressive house, and own lots of things. There are many people who disagree with these foci in our culture. A counterculture is a group that rejects certain elements of the dominant culture. For example, anticonsumerist groups are countercultural. They reject our society's dominant focus on the importance of acquiring and consuming mass amounts of products to show our status and worth.

The hit musical *Hamilton* brings together the high culture realm of theater with the popular culture sphere of rap music and modern dance. *Hamilton's* playwright, Lin Manuel Miranda, wrote another musical combining these high and popular culture elements called *In the Heights*.

Bruce Glikas/Bruce Glikas/FilmMagic/Getty Images

Subcultures also differ from the dominant culture, but they do not necessarily oppose it the way that countercultures do. For example, minor differences in occupational groups can create subcultures. Lawyers' daily routines, interests, and style of dress might differ significantly from those of plumbers. Students involved in fraternities or sororities, those on sports teams, and those in theater programs might also be quite different from each other in their behaviors and dress. However, they do not necessarily oppose the values or behaviors of the other groups.

Culture is often divided into high and popular culture. When people say that someone is cultured, they tend to mean that the person participates in **high culture**, the culture of a society's elite. In general, this type of culture may be difficult to appreciate without having been taught to enjoy and understand it. **Popular (or low) culture** is the culture of the majority. In the world of music, opera and classical music are high culture, while rap and pop are popular culture. In literature, classic novels and plays (think Austen or Shakespeare) are high culture; science fiction, fantasy, or romance novels are popular culture (*The Hunger Games, Harry Potter, Twilight,* or Jenny Han's novels).

THE SOCIOLOGICAL IMAGINATION

In American society, most people believe that individuals shape their own destiny. To a certain extent, this is true; we, as individuals, make decisions every day that shape the kind of life we lead. For example, you made decisions about whether to attend university or college, how hard to work in your classes, where to live while attending school, and what type of summer job you want. But, of course, many factors influence these decisions.

C. Wright Mills, the author of *The Sociological Imagination*, is pictured here. Using the social imagination, we can see how society can shape our individual experiences and how our own biographies are related to larger historical processes.

Archive Photos/Getty Images

Let's examine your decision about a summer job. If your parents are willing and able to help pay for your education, you might not need to work in the summer or you might choose to take an unpaid internship, which would be impossible if you needed to pay your own tuition. In this way, your individual choice of whether you work and what type of job you get is, to some degree, structured by the wealth and support of your parents.

We might be interested in how your individual choices are constrained because this might shape later outcomes. For example, students who have completed an unpaid internship might find it easier to get a good job after graduation because they will have gained skills and social contacts while interning. Students who have wealthy parents (and therefore do not need a summer job) are more likely than other students to have the time and resources to do an internship, which can perpetuate inequality in society over time.

This example illustrates how individual choices (sometimes called "agency") are structured in society. We can make decisions, but our choices are often shaped or limited by larger social forces such as our family, our social class, the economy, the education system, and gender norms. Many sociologists have tried to make sense of this complicated relationship between an individual's agency and society's constraints. Karl Marx famously said, "[People] make their own history, but they do not make it as they please; they do not make it under self-selected circumstances, but under circumstances existing already, given and transmitted from the past" (in Tucker, 1978, p. 595).

Getting to Know: C. Wright Mills (1916–1962)

- As a child, he once wrapped his arms and legs around a telephone pole for many hours to protest attending a school he didn't like. His father tried to remove him but was unsuccessful.

- He often arrived at Columbia University on a roaring BMW motorcycle, dressed in plaid shirts, old jeans, and work boots that stood in sharp contrast to the gray flannel suits worn by his colleagues.

- He was a public intellectual whose work offered a scathing critique of American society, foreign policy, and an academic culture that promoted disinterested observations of society.

- His *Letter to the New Left* (1960) argued that young intelligentsia—university students—have the potential to bring about radical social change. This letter, as well as his book *The Power Elite* (1956), inspired many of the leaders and organizations of the vibrant student movement that erupted in 1960s America.

C. Wright Mills (1959/2000) also tried to tackle these complicated issues with what he called the sociological imagination. Mills called on us to try to see the connections between our individual lives and the larger society in which we live. He argued that we can only understand our own lives and biographies if we understand the larger history of our society. Once we make these connections, we will be able to see the relationship between our personal troubles (problems that we face as individuals) and larger public issues (social problems that arise in society).

READING: FROM *THE SOCIOLOGICAL IMAGINATION*

C. Wright Mills

First published in 1959, Mills's The Sociological Imagination is one of the most widely read sociology books of all time. The sociological imagination is at the core of sociology. The following excerpt from Chapter 1 of the book discusses the links between personal troubles and public issues. When reading this chapter, consider how Mills encourages us to see connections between our own lives and larger social structures.

Nowadays men often feel that their private lives are a series of traps. They sense that within their everyday worlds, they cannot overcome their troubles, and in this feeling, they are often quite correct: what ordinary men are directly aware of and what they try to do are bounded by the private orbits in which they live; their visions and their powers are limited to the close-up scenes of job, family, neighbourhood; in other milieux, they move vicariously and remain spectators. And the more aware they become, however vaguely, of ambitions and of threats which transcend their immediate locales, the more trapped they seem to feel.

Underlying this sense of being trapped are seemingly impersonal changes in the very structure of continent-wide societies. The facts of contemporary history are also facts about the success and the failure of individual men and women. When a society is industrialized, a peasant becomes a worker; a feudal lord is liquidated or becomes a businessman. When classes rise or fall, a man is employed or unemployed; when the rate of investment goes up or down, a man takes new heart or goes broke. When wars happen, an insurance salesman becomes a rocket launcher; a store clerk, a radar man; a wife lives alone; a child grows up without a father. Neither the life of an individual nor the history of a society can be understood without understanding both.

Yet men do not usually define the troubles they endure in terms of historical change and institutional contradiction. The well-being they enjoy, they do not usually impute to the big ups and downs of the societies in which they live. Seldom aware of the intricate connection between the patterns of their own lives and the course of world history, ordinary men do not usually know what this connection means for the kinds of men they are becoming and for the kinds of history-making in which they might take part. They do not possess the quality of mind essential to grasp the interplay of man and society, of biography and history, of self and world. They cannot cope with their personal troubles in such ways as to control the structural transformations that usually lie behind them.

Surely it is no wonder. In what period have so many men been so totally exposed at so fast a pace to such earthquakes of change? That Americans have not known such catastrophic changes as have the men and women of other societies is due to historical facts that are now quickly becoming "merely history." The history that now affects every man is world history. Within this scene and this period, in the course of a single generation, one-sixth of mankind is transformed from all that is feudal and backward into all that is modern, advanced, and fearful. Political colonies are freed; new and less visible forms of imperialism installed. Revolutions occur; men feel the intimate grip of new kinds of authority. Totalitarian societies rise, and are smashed to bits—or succeed fabulously. After two centuries of ascendancy, capitalism is shown up as only one way to make society into an industrial apparatus. After two centuries of hope, even formal democracy is restricted to a quite small portion of mankind. Everywhere in the underdeveloped world, ancient ways of life are broken up and vague expectations become urgent demands. Everywhere in the overdeveloped world, the means of authority and of violence become total in scope and bureaucratic in form. Humanity itself now lies before us, the super-nation at either pole concentrating its most coordinated and massive efforts upon the preparation of World War III.

The very shaping of history now outpaces the ability of men to orient themselves in accordance with cherished values. And which values? Even when they do not panic, men often sense that older ways of feeling and thinking have collapsed and that newer beginnings are ambiguous to the point of moral stasis. Is it any wonder that ordinary men feel they cannot cope with the larger worlds with which they are so suddenly confronted? That they cannot understand the meaning of their epoch for their own lives? That—in defence of selfhood—they become morally insensible, trying to remain altogether private men? Is it any wonder that they come to be possessed by a sense of the trap?

It is not only information that they need—in this Age of Fact, information often dominates their attention and overwhelms their capacities to assimilate it. It is not only the skills of reason that they need—although their struggles to acquire these often exhaust their limited moral energy.

What they need, and what they feel they need, is a quality of mind that will help them to use information and to develop reason in order to achieve lucid summations of what is going on in the world and of what may be happening within themselves. It is this quality, I am going to contend, that journalists and scholars, artists and publics, scientists and editors are coming to expect of what may be called the sociological imagination.

1

The sociological imagination enables its possessor to understand the larger historical scene in terms of its meaning for the inner life and the external career of a variety of individuals. It enables him to take into account how individuals, in the welter of their daily experience, often become falsely conscious of their social positions. Within that welter, the framework of modern society is sought, and within that framework the psychologies of a variety of men and women are formulated. By such means the personal uneasiness of individuals is focused upon explicit troubles and the indifference of publics is transformed into involvement with public issues.

The first fruit of this imagination—and the first lesson of the social science that embodies it—is the idea that the individual can understand his own experience and gauge his own fate only by locating himself within his period, that he can know his own chances in life only by becoming aware of those of all individuals in his circumstances. In many ways it is a terrible lesson; in many ways a magnificent one. We do not know the limits of man's capacities for supreme effort or willing degradation, for agony or glee, for pleasurable brutality or the sweetness of reason. But in our time, we have come to know that the limits of "human nature" are frighteningly broad. We have come to know that every individual lives, from one generation to the next, in some society; that he lives out a biography, and that he lives it out within some historical sequence. By the fact of his living he contributes, however minutely, to the shaping of this society and to the course of its history, even as he is made by society and by its historical push and shove.

The sociological imagination enables us to grasp history and biography and the relations between the two within society. That is its task and its promise. To recognize this task and this promise is the mark of the classic social analyst. And it is the signal of what is best in contemporary studies of man and society.

No social study that does not come back to the problems of biography, of history, and of their intersections within a society has completed its intellectual journey. Whatever the specific problems of the classic social analysts, however limited or however broad the features of social reality they have examined, those who have been imaginatively aware of the promise of their work have consistently asked three sorts of questions:

1. What is the structure of this particular society as a whole? What are its essential components, and how are they related to one another? How does it differ from other varieties of social order? Within it, what is the meaning of any particular feature for its continuance and for its change?
2. Where does this society stand in human history? What are the mechanics by which it is changing? What is its place within and its meaning for the development of humanity as a whole? How does any particular feature we are examining affect, and how is it affected by, the historical period in which it moves? And this period—what are its essential features? How does it differ from other periods? What are its characteristic ways of history-making?
3. What varieties of men and women now prevail in this society and in this period? And what varieties are coming to prevail? In what ways are they selected and formed, liberated and repressed, made sensitive and blunted? What kinds of "human nature" are revealed in the conduct and character we observe in this society in this period? And what is the meaning for "human nature" of each and every feature of the society we are examining?

Whether the point of interest is a great power state or a minor literary mood, a family, a prison, a creed—these are the kinds of questions the best social analysts have asked. They are the intellectual pivots of classic studies of man in society—and they are the questions inevitably raised by any mind possessing the sociological imagination. For that imagination is the capacity to shift from one perspective to another—from the political to the psychological; from examination of a single family to comparative assessment of the national budgets of the world; from the theological school to the military establishment; from considerations of an oil industry to studies of contemporary poetry. It is the capacity to range from the most impersonal and remote transformations to the most intimate features of the human self—and to see the relations between the two. Back of its use there is always the urge to know the social and historical meaning of the individual in the society and in the period in which he has his quality and his being.

That, in brief, is why it is by means of the sociological imagination that men now hope to grasp what is going on in the world, and to understand what is happening in themselves as minute points of the intersections of biography and history within society. In large part, contemporary man's self-conscious view of himself as at least an outsider, if not a permanent stranger, rests upon an absorbed realization of social relativity and of the transformative power of history. The sociological imagination is the most fruitful form of this self-consciousness. By its use men whose mentalities have swept only a series of limited orbits often come to feel as if suddenly awakened in a house with which they had only supposed themselves to be familiar. Correctly or incorrectly, they often come to feel that they can now provide themselves with adequate summations, cohesive assessments, comprehensive orientations. Older decisions that once appeared sound now seem to them products of a mind unaccountably dense. Their capacity for astonishment is made lively again. They acquire a new way of thinking, they experience a transvaluation of values: in a word, by their reflection and by their sensibility, they realize the cultural meaning of the social sciences.

2

Perhaps the most fruitful distinction with which the sociological imagination works is between "the personal troubles of milieu" and "the public issues of social structure." This distinction is an essential tool of the sociological imagination and a feature of all classic work in social science.

Troubles occur within the character of the individual and within the range of his immediate relations with others; they have to do with his self and with those limited areas of social life of which he is directly and personally aware. Accordingly, the statement and the resolution of troubles properly lie within the individual as a biographical entity and within the scope of his immediate milieu—the social setting that is directly open to his personal experience and to some extent his willful activity. A trouble is a private matter: values cherished by an individual are felt by him to be threatened.

Issues have to do with matters that transcend these local environments of the individual and the range of his inner life. They have to do with the organization of many such milieux into the institutions of a historical society as a whole, with the ways in which various milieux overlap and interpenetrate to form the larger structure of social and historical life. An issue is a public matter: some value cherished by publics is felt to be threatened. Often there is a debate about what that value really is and about what it is that really threatens it. This debate is often without focus if only because it is the very nature of an issue, unlike even widespread trouble, that it cannot very well be defined in terms of the immediate and everyday environments of ordinary men. An issue, in fact, often involves a crisis in institutional arrangements, and often too it involves what Marxists call "contradictions" or "antagonisms."

In these terms, consider unemployment. When, in a city of 100,000, only one man is unemployed, that is his personal trouble, and for its relief we properly look to the character of the man, his skills, and his immediate opportunities. But when in a nation of 50 million employees, 15 million men are unemployed, that is an issue, and we may not hope to find its solution within the range of opportunities open to any one individual. The very structure of opportunities has collapsed. Both the correct statement of the problem and the range of possible solutions require us to consider the economic and political institutions of the society, and not merely the personal situation and character of a scatter of individuals.

Consider war. The personal problem of war, when it occurs, may be how to survive it or how to die in it with honour; how to make money out of it; how to climb into the higher safety of the military apparatus; or how to contribute to the war's termination. In short, according to one's values, to find a set of milieux and within it to survive the war or make one's death in it meaningful. But the structural issues of war have to do with its causes; . . . with its effects upon economic and political, family and religious institutions, with the unorganized irresponsibility of a world of nation-states.

Consider marriage. Inside a marriage a man and a woman may experience personal troubles, but when the divorce rate during the first four years of marriage is 250 out of every 1,000 attempts, this is an indication of a structural issue having to do with the institutions of marriage and the family and other institutions that bear upon them.

Or consider the metropolis—the horrible, beautiful, ugly, magnificent sprawl of the great city. For many upper-class people, the personal solution to "the problem of the city" is to have an apartment with private garage under it in the heart of the city, and 40 miles out, a house by Henry Hill, garden by Garrett Eckbo, on a hundred acres of private land. In these two controlled environments—with a small staff at each end and a private helicopter connection—most people could solve many of the problems of personal milieux caused by the facts of the city. But all this, however splendid, does not solve the public issues that the structural fact of the city poses. What should be done with this wonderful monstrosity? Break it all up into scattered units, combining residence and work? Refurbish it as it stands? Or, after evacuation, dynamite it and build new cities according to new plans in new places? What should those plans be? And who is to decide and to accomplish whatever choice is made? These are structural issues; to confront them and to solve them requires us to consider political and economic issues that affect innumerable milieux.

In so far as an economy is so arranged that slumps occur, the problem of unemployment becomes incapable of personal solution. In so far as war is inherent in the nation-state system and in the uneven industrialization of the world, the ordinary individual in his restricted milieu will be powerless—with or without psychiatric aid—to solve the troubles this system or lack of system imposes upon him. In so far as the family as an institution turns women into darling little slaves and men into their chief providers and unweaned dependents, the problem of a satisfactory marriage remains incapable of purely private solution. In so far as the overdeveloped megalopolis and the overdeveloped automobile are built- in features of the overdeveloped society, the issues of urban living will not be solved by personal ingenuity and private wealth.

What we experience in various and specific milieux, I have noted, is often caused by structural changes. Accordingly, to understand the changes of many personal milieux we are required to look beyond them. And the number and variety of such structural changes increase as the institutions within which we live become more embracing and more intricately connected with one another. To be aware of the idea of social structure and to use it with sensibility is to be capable of tracing such linkages among a great variety of milieux. To be able to do that is to possess the sociological imagination.

Reading Questions

1. What does Mills mean by, "Neither the life of an individual nor the history of a society can be understood without understanding both"? How could you understand your own life better by knowing more about history? How do individual biographies shape history? Think of a concrete example of this connection between individual biography and larger social history.
2. What do the terms *personal troubles* and *public issues* mean?
3. How could we understand the issues of gender inequality, poverty, and crime as either a personal trouble or public issue? How does labelling these problems a personal trouble or a public issue shape the kinds of solutions we might propose?

Mills, C. W. (1959). *The sociological imagination.* Oxford University Press. Reprinted with permission from Oxford University Press.

USING YOUR SOCIOLOGICAL IMAGINATION:
COVID-19 AND THE OPIOID CRISIS AS PERSONAL TROUBLES OR PUBLIC ISSUES

The sociological imagination encourages us to understand how problems can be seen as personal troubles or public issues. In this activity, we consider how we can understand two issues, COVID-19 and the opioid epidemic, as personal troubles or as public issues.

1. First, let's consider these two problems as personal troubles and as public issues. How can we think of COVID-19 as a personal trouble, related to the personal circumstances of individuals? How is it a public issue, related to larger institutions and structures of society? Consider how the opioid crisis and drug-related deaths can be seen as personal troubles or public issues.
2. Search online for "COVID-19" and "Opioid Crisis." When you read newspaper articles about these two issues, do the articles tend to focus on them as personal troubles or public issues? Are these two social problems equally likely to be seen in each of these ways? Why or why not?
3. How much coverage and discussion has there been of each of these two social problems in the past two years? (Consider both in the news and among your family and friends.) Why might one of these issues be discussed more than the other?
4. Figure 1.1 shows the number of opioid overdose deaths reported to the U.S. National Center for Health Statistics between 2015 and 2023. Figure 1.2 shows the number of deaths per week in the U.S. due to COVID-19 from 2020 to 2023. Are you surprised to see the number of deaths from opioids in this period? Why do you think that the opioid deaths received so much less attention than COVID-19 in the media and in the community? How is this related to our understanding of these issues as personal trouble or public issues?
5. Why do you think that the government response to COVID-19 (including shutting down parts of the economy and schools) was so much more aggressive than the response to opioid deaths? What types of policies could the government enact if they were as focused on addressing drug-related deaths?

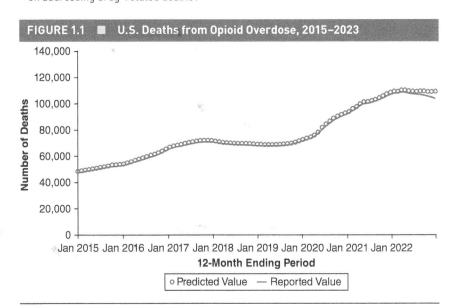

FIGURE 1.1 ■ U.S. Deaths from Opioid Overdose, 2015–2023

Source: National Center for Health Statistics (n.d.). *Provisional Drug Overdose Death Counts.* Centers for Disease Control. Retrieved May 12, 2023, from https://www.cdc.gov/nchs/nvss/vsrr/drug-overdose-data.htm

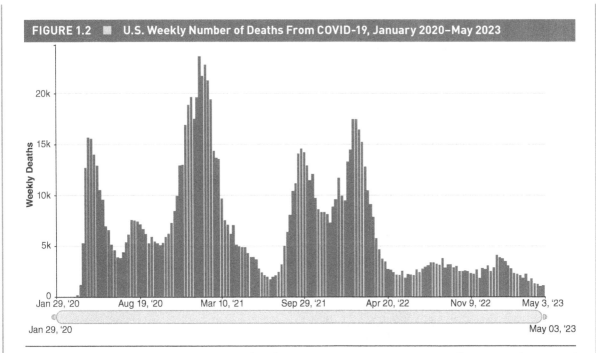

FIGURE 1.2 ■ U.S. Weekly Number of Deaths From COVID-19, January 2020–May 2023

Source: Centers for Disease Control and Prevention. (2023). *COVID Data Tracker Weekly Review.* https://www.cdc.gov/coronavirus/2019-ncov/covid-data/covidview/index.html

THREE CORE FOCI OF SOCIOLOGY

As we learned earlier, sociology is the systematic study of human society. Sociologists can study a wide variety of things; in fact, almost anything in human society can be examined with a sociological perspective. However, most of sociology focuses on three core areas: the study of social inequality, the role of social institutions, and the study of social change.

Social Inequality

The study of social inequality is at the core of sociology. Generally, inequality is the gap between the advantaged and disadvantaged in society. More precisely, inequality is based on the "differences between people . . . that are *consequential* for the lives they lead, most particularly for the rights and opportunities they exercise and the rewards or privileges they enjoy" (Grabb, 2006, p. 2; emphasis in original). People differ from one another in an almost infinite number of ways. For example, humans have different eye colors, are different heights, and write with either their right or left hand (or both). Although these are all differences among people, they are not particularly consequential in a person's life. Differences that are more important, and that have been the basis of most sociological inquiry, include social class, gender, race, and ethnicity. These topics have been of interest to sociologists since the beginning of the discipline. More recently, sociologists—and society in general—are starting to see the importance of other differences, such as sexual orientation, age, immigration status, and disability status. All these differences can be very important for the lives that individuals lead.

Characteristics such as gender, race, or age can shape the rights, opportunities, rewards, or privileges that individuals enjoy. Examples include the right to vote and the opportunity to attend college. Women were not afforded the right to vote in federal elections in the United States until 1920 and Native Americans were not fully enfranchised and able to vote in all states until 1957. Therefore, being female or Native American had important consequences for the political rights granted to these individuals. Rewards and privileges include access to good jobs and safe housing. We know, for example, that Americans who are of a lower social class are much less likely than those in a higher class to live in a safe neighborhood with good amenities (such as parks and schools nearby).

Inequality between people exists in all societies. When sociologists look at inequality, they are interested in several key questions: Why does inequality exist? How is inequality generated, maintained, and reproduced? What are the implications of inequality? How can inequality be reduced? These and other important questions form the basis of the sociological study of inequality.

Although the existence of inequality is universal, the type and amount differ across societies and over time. Different societies exhibit varying levels of inequality, with some societies being much more equitable than others. For example, the traditional caste system in India, which makes it almost impossible for people to move out of the social status of their birth, is much more unequal than modern American society. Inequality also increases and decreases within a single society. Even India's rigid caste system has been challenged over time. The Indian government passed legislation to fight the discrimination experienced by the lowest caste group, the Dalits. There has also been a rise in marriage between castes, which was historically unthinkable but has reduced prejudice and inequality between groups. In fact, India now has relatively high representation of the lowest class in elected office, showing how inequality can change over time. Finally, inequality is based on different factors across societies: Some societies have a lot of racial inequality but little class differentiation, while others have little racial inequality but strict class hierarchies.

Many people wonder if our society is becoming more or less equal. This question is extremely difficult to answer because it depends on the kind of inequality being examined and on the measures used. For simplicity's sake, we will examine income and assess whether inequality based on this factor is increasing or decreasing across social class, race, and gender groups.

There is a great deal of evidence that class inequality is increasing in the United States. We can see this trend if we compare the richest 20% of families with the poorest 20%. In an equal society, each group would earn 20% of the society's entire income. We know that this is certainly not the case, since there are some people who are much richer than others in this country. Class inequality has been increasing rapidly since the late 1960s. In 2006 the top 20% of Americans earned more than 14 times as much as the bottom 20%. Just 14 years later, in 2020, the top 20% were making 17.4 times the income of the bottom 20% (Shrider, Kollar, Chen, and Semega, 2021).

The growing divide between America's rich and poor does not tell the whole story of inequality in this country. Inequality between racial and ethnic groups illustrates the complexity of the issue. Let's compare earnings of individuals who self-categorize as White, Black, Hispanic, or Asian. In 1973 Black people made 60 cents for every dollar made by a White person and Hispanic people earned 77 cents for every dollar earned by a White person, on average. By 2020 this had remained relatively stagnant for Blacks (61 cents) but had declined for Hispanics (74 cents; Shrider et al., 2021). Asian Americans, however, have increased their earnings relative to Whites (from 114% in 1987 to 126% in 2020). Thus, racial and ethnic inequality has either risen, declined, or remained stagnant, depending on the group examined.

Some inequality is declining over time. For example, income inequality based on gender has diminished in a pronounced way in the past 60 years. In 1959 American women working full time made 61% of what their male counterparts did. This number increased to 82% by

2020 (U.S. Department of Labor, 2020). In other words, women went from making 61 cents for every dollar a man made to 82 cents per dollar. These examples show the challenges of assessing changing inequality. The task would be even more difficult if we looked beyond simple income to wealth inequality or educational and work opportunities. It is no surprise, then, that so many sociologists are concerned with such an important and challenging topic.

In addition to measuring and assessing social inequality, sociologists often study why and how inequality persists. We know that all societies have inequality. But why is this the case? How does inequality endure? How can it be reduced? This book examines all these questions. In particular, we will learn more about inequality that arises from social class, race, ethnicity, and gender.

Social Institutions

Social institutions are the norms, values, and rules of conduct that structure human interactions. Institutions are not just physical places or buildings. They are also the social arrangements for how things are done. For example, the institution of education is not just a school or classroom, but is also a set of larger arrangements that organize how people will be educated and what they will learn. There are five core institutions in modern American society: the family, education, religion, the economy, and government. Other institutions, such as the mass media, medicine, science, and the military, are also important parts of American society.

Institutions are standardized ways of doing something. In institutions, actions become regularized, patterned, and reproduced. When you consider education, you might think of your specific teachers, your class experience, or the schools you attended. Such details are certainly important aspects of your education. However, the institution of education is far more than these parts. It is based on the routine and patterned ways that education is delivered and assessed. For example, the material that you learned in elementary and high school was not simply the choice of your teachers. The institution of education sets a curriculum and decides that all students in 9th grade will read Shakespeare's *Romeo and Juliet*. Our education system is also based on teaching students from roughly 8:30 a.m. to 3:00 p.m., 5 days a week for 10 months of the year. All these routines are established by the institution of education in the United States and structure how education functions across states and in the country as a whole.

Institutions are important because they generally help society run smoothly. They do so, in part, by socializing us and teaching us the rules of our society. When you first go to school, you learn that you must sit quietly in class and raise your hand when you want to speak. These rules are important and help later schooling and other social interactions function. Imagine if everyone just wandered around the room during your college classes—the result would certainly be a chaotic environment and make it impossible to learn.

However, institutions can also serve a negative function by maintaining and reinforcing inequality. In fact, one of the main reasons that inequality tends to persist is the role of social institutions. Because standardized patterns of behavior become routine, they can reinforce some of the differences between people. For example, if your college has very high tuition, students of lower social classes might not be able to attend. In this way, the institution and decisions about tuition rates are partly responsible for people from lower social classes being less likely to get the degrees that would allow them to increase their social standing over time.

Institutions can also be an avenue for social change. We know that individuals from lower social classes are much less likely to get a university or college degree than those from higher social classes. Many social programs instituted by the U.S. government have tried to address this imbalance. The Servicemen's Readjustment Act (commonly known as the G.I. Bill), passed in

1944, included a program that helped World War II veterans receive postsecondary education by paying their full tuition and living expenses to attend college or trade schools. The idea was that helping soldiers get an education would help them return to civilian life. From 1944 to 1949, nearly 9 million veterans received close to $4 billion from this program. This program vastly increased the educational attainment of this group of young people. However, it should be noted that White male veterans were more able to take advantage of the bill. African American and female veterans faced discrimination in applying to this program; as a result, these groups had less-dramatic outcomes from this legislation (Berman, 2015).

Social Change

Social change is the third core area of sociology. As we have seen, sociologists examine how social institutions can perpetuate inequality or create social change. If society is based on interactions among people, it can change just as people do.

One major institution in modern American society that has changed greatly is religion. Secularization—the process of a religion losing its authority over individuals and social life in general—is a frequently discussed social change. Core founders of sociology, such as Karl Marx, Max Weber, and Émile Durkheim, all argued that the modernization of society would inevitably coincide with a decline in religiosity. Karl Marx was quite happy about this shift: He thought that religion was an opiate of the masses, something that just dulled our pain and senses so that we would not resist the great social inequality that we experience in our lives. Durkheim was more likely to lament the decline of religion; he thought religion was an important part of the glue that holds individuals together in society. Weber looked at how new rational systems, such as science and bureaucracies, would make religious answers to questions less relevant (Collins, 1994). These examples illustrate how sociologists have always been interested in religion's role in society while also highlighting that your perspective on religion is related to the theoretical lens you use to study it. (We will learn much more about these three sociologists throughout this book.)

Statues of the Ten Commandments outside of government buildings are frequent sites of contentious legal battles in the United States. Courts often find that these statues violate the principle of separation between church and state. Think about government institutions where you grew up. Did they adhere to this secular ideal?

Jana Birchum/Getty Images

The study of secularization seeks to explain how, why, and when religious values, practices, and institutions lose their power in modern society. It is certainly true that religion is currently less integral to many functions of American society than it was in the past. For example, many schools were once run by religious institutions. You can still attend a religious school, but most schools in the United States are now operated by the state and are nonreligious. Religious institutions were also once the main provider of charitable and welfare services, running orphanages, food banks, and hospitals. Now, many different groups perform such functions. Many religious institutions are still involved with these activities and raise money for these causes, but the control of these services rests mostly in the hands of the state or private foundations.

Religiosity (the measure of how religious a person is) is declining somewhat in the United States. In 1992, 58% of Americans said that religion was a very important part of their life. This number had declined to 49% by 2021 (Gallup, 2021). This decline is typical of the general secularization occurring across North America and Europe. However, some sociologists have questioned whether it is a universal trend or just a tendency in a certain set of countries that also share other characteristics, such as level of development.

In fact, religiosity is increasing in many parts of the world. Between 1950 and 2020, the number of Catholics in the world doubled from fewer than 500 million to more than 1.36 billion (National Catholic Register, 2022). There has also been a dramatic increase in the spread of evangelical Protestantism, which now has 700 million adherents worldwide (Bibby, 2011).

The discussion of religion's changing role illustrates several key elements in the study of sociology. Religion is an important institution in society. It provides norms, values, and rules of conduct for individuals and helps to structure human interactions. Religion's changing role shows the larger social transformations that are at the heart of the study of sociology. Finally, the changing nature of religion depends on the social context in which it is examined. Comparing across countries or religions highlights how the trends of rising or declining religiosity is context dependent.

THREE CORE AIMS OF SOCIOLOGY

Sociologists aim to do three main things: They try to see general themes in everyday life. They seek to assess critically what seems familiar and common sense. And they examine how individuals both shape society and are shaped by society.

Everyone has a lifetime of experiences in society. From all these experiences, we can generalize how society functions and how people behave in it. However, sometimes this familiarity can be a challenge—it can be difficult to study society because it is all around us. It is like a fish trying to study water. However, sociology, as the systematic study of human society, pushes us to make sense of all our experiences and what we see around us and to come up with general ideas of how society functions.

In *Invitation to Sociology,* Peter Berger (1963) calls on us to see the general in the particular. Put another way, sociologists should look for general patterns in particular people's experiences. We may know some women who are very successful in large companies and who have a great deal of responsibility in their jobs, but we see that most CEOs and senators are men. This information suggests that there is a general pattern of women being less likely than men to hold positions of power. We can now ask ourselves why this might be the case: Is it that fewer women choose to enter business or politics, or is there discrimination in these professions? Through systematic study, we can answer these types of questions.

READING: "BODY RITUAL AMONG THE NACIREMA"

Horace Miner

The following reading from Horace Miner helps us with this first core aim of sociology. In this article, Miner describes the Nacirema culture. He outlines the Naciremas' rituals, customs, and practices and encourages us to see the general themes in particular experiences. Remember how Berger (1963) also called on us to see the strange in the familiar. He said that the first wisdom of sociology is that things are not what they seem. When we travel to other countries, we expect to have some sort of culture shock—to see people eating different food, performing different customs, and wearing different clothing. Berger said that, when we study our own society, it should also be a culture shock minus the geographic displacement. In other words, the sociologist travels at home, with shocking results. Miner's article illustrates how we can work to see the strange in the familiar when confronted with a society and culture (even our own).

The anthropologist has become so familiar with the diversity of ways in which different peoples behave in similar situations that he is not apt to be surprised by even the most exotic customs. In fact, if all of the logically possible combinations of behaviour have not been found somewhere in the world, he is apt to suspect that they must be present in some yet undescribed tribe. This point has, in fact, been expressed with respect to clan organization by Murdock (1949: 71). In this light, the magical beliefs and practices of the Nacirema present such unusual aspects that it seems desirable to describe them as an example of the extremes to which human behaviour can go.

Professor Linton first brought the ritual of the Nacirema to the attention of anthropologists 20 years ago (1936: 326), but the culture of this people is still very poorly understood. They are a North American group living in the territory between the Canadian Cree, the Yaqui, and Tarahumare of Mexico, and the Carib and Arawak of the Antilles. Little is known of their origin, although tradition states that they came from the east. According to Nacirema mythology, their nation was originated by a culture hero, Notgnihsaw, who is otherwise known for two great feats of strength—the throwing of a piece of wampum across the river Pa-To-Mac and the chopping down of a cherry tree in which the Spirit of Truth resided.

Nacirema culture is characterized by a highly developed market economy which has evolved in a rich natural habitat. While much of the people's time is devoted to economic pursuits, a large part of the fruits of these labours and a considerable portion of the day are spent in ritual activity. The focus of this activity is the human body, the appearance and health of which loom as a dominant concern in the ethos of the people. While such a concern is certainly not unusual, its ceremonial aspects and associated philosophy are unique.

The fundamental belief underlying the whole system appears to be that the human body is ugly and that its natural tendency is to debility and disease. Incarcerated in such a body, man's only hope is to avert these characteristics through the use of the powerful influences of ritual and ceremony. Every household has one or more shrines devoted to this purpose. The more powerful individuals in the society have several shrines in their houses and, in fact, the opulence of a house is often referred to in terms of the number of such ritual centres it possesses. Most houses are of wattle and daub construction, but the shrine rooms of the more wealthy are walled with stone. Poorer families imitate the rich by applying pottery plaques to their shrine walls.

While each family has at least one such shrine, the rituals associated with it are not family ceremonies but are private and secret. The rites are normally only discussed with children, and then only during the period when they are being initiated into these mysteries. I was able, however, to establish sufficient rapport with the natives to examine these shrines and to have the rituals described to me.

The focal point of the shrine is a box or chest which is built into the wall. In this chest are kept the many charms and magical potions without which no native believes he could live.

These preparations are secured from a variety of specialized practitioners. The most powerful of these are the medicine men, whose assistance must be rewarded with substantial gifts. However, the medicine men do not provide the curative potions for their clients, but decide what the ingredients should be and then write them down in an ancient and secret language. This writing is understood only by the medicine men and by the herbalists who, for another gift, provide the required charm.

The charm is not disposed of after it has served its purpose, but is placed in the charm-box of the household shrine. As these magical materials are specific for certain ills, and the real or imagined maladies of the people are many, the charm-box is usually full to overflowing. The magical packets are so numerous that people forget what their purposes were and fear to use them again. While the natives are very vague on this point, we can only assume that the idea in retaining all the old magical materials is that their presence in the charm-box, before which the body rituals are conducted, will in some way protect the worshipper.

Beneath the charm-box is a small font. Each day every member of the family, in succession, enters the shrine room, bows his head before the charm-box, mingles different sorts of holy water in the font, and proceeds with a brief rite of ablution. The holy waters are secured from the Water Temple of the community, where the priests conduct elaborate ceremonies to make the liquid ritually pure.

In the hierarchy of magical practitioners, and below the medicine men in prestige, are specialists whose designation is best translated [as] "holy-mouth-men." The Nacirema have an almost pathological horror of and fascination with the mouth, the condition of which is believed to have a supernatural influence on all social relationships. Were it not for the rituals of the mouth, they believe that their teeth would fall out, their gums bleed, their jaws shrink, their friends desert them, and their lovers reject them. They also believe that a strong relationship exists between oral and moral characteristics. For example, there is a ritual ablution of the mouth for children which is supposed to improve their moral fibre.

The daily body ritual performed by everyone includes a mouth-rite. Despite the fact that these people are so punctilious about care of the mouth, this rite involves a practice which strikes the uninitiated stranger as revolting. It was reported to me that the ritual consists of inserting a small bundle of hog hairs into the mouth, along with certain magical powders, and then moving the bundle in a highly formalized series of gestures.

In addition to the private mouth-rite, the people seek out a holy-mouth-man once or twice a year. These practitioners have an impressive set of paraphernalia, consisting of a variety of augers, awls, probes, and prods. The use of these objects in the exorcism of the evils of the mouth involves almost unbelievable ritual torture of the client. The holy-mouth-man opens the client's mouth and, using the above-mentioned tools, enlarges any holes which decay may have created in the teeth. Magical materials are put into these holes. If there are no naturally occurring holes in the teeth, large sections of one or more teeth are gouged out so that the supernatural substance can be applied. In the client's view, the purpose of these ministrations is to arrest decay and to draw friends. The extremely sacred and traditional character of the rite is evident in the fact that the natives return to the holy-mouth-men year after year, despite the fact that their teeth continue to decay. . . .

The medicine men have an imposing temple, or *latipso*, in every community of any size. The more elaborate ceremonies required to treat very sick patients can only be performed at this temple. These ceremonies involve not only the thaumaturge but a permanent group of vestal maidens who move sedately about the temple chambers in distinctive costume and headdress.

The *latipso* ceremonies are so harsh that it is phenomenal that a fair proportion of the really sick natives who enter the temple ever recover. Small children whose indoctrination is still incomplete have been known to resist attempts to take them to the temple because "that is where you go to die." Despite this fact, sick adults are not only willing but eager to undergo the protracted ritual purification, if they can afford to do so. No matter how ill the supplicant or how grave the emergency, the guardians of many temples will not admit a client if he cannot give a rich gift to the custodian. Even after one has gained admission and survived the ceremonies, the guardians will not permit the neophyte to leave until he makes still another gift.

The supplicant entering the temple is first stripped of all his or her clothes. In every-day life the Nacirema avoids exposure of his body and its natural functions. Bathing and excretory acts are performed only in the secrecy of the household shrine, where they are ritualized as part of the body-rites. Psychological shock results from the fact that body secrecy is suddenly lost upon entry into the *latipso*. A man, whose own wife has never seen him in an excretory act, suddenly finds himself naked and assisted by a vestal maiden while he performs his natural functions into a sacred vessel. This sort of ceremonial treatment is necessitated by the fact that the excreta are used by a diviner to ascertain the course and nature of the client's sickness. Female clients, on the other hand, find their naked bodies are subjected to the scrutiny, manipulation, and prodding of the medicine men.

Few supplicants in the temple are well enough to do anything but lie on their hard beds. The daily ceremonies, like the rites of the holy-mouth- men, involve discomfort and torture. With ritual precision, the vestals awaken their miserable charges each dawn and roll them about on their beds of pain while performing ablutions, in the formal movements of which the maidens are highly trained. At other times they insert magic wands in the supplicant's mouth or force him to eat substances which are supposed to be healing. From time to time the medicine men come to their clients and jab magically treated needles into their flesh. The fact that these temple ceremonies may not cure, and may even kill, the neophyte in no way decreases the people's faith in the medicine men.

There remains one other kind of practitioner, known as a "listener." This witch-doctor has the power to exorcise the devils that lodge in the heads of people who have been bewitched. The Nacirema believe that parents bewitch their own children. Mothers are particularly suspected of putting a curse on children while teaching them the secret body rituals. The counter-magic of the witch-doctor is unusual in its lack of ritual. The patient simply tells the "listener" all his troubles and fears, beginning with the earliest difficulties he can remember. The memory displayed by the Nacirema in these exorcism sessions is truly remarkable. It is not uncommon for the patient to bemoan the rejection he felt upon being weaned as a babe, and a few individuals even see their troubles going back to the traumatic effects of their own birth.

In conclusion, mention must be made of certain practices which have their base in native esthetics but which depend upon the pervasive aversion to the natural body and its functions. There are ritual fasts to make fat people thin and ceremonial feasts to make thin people fat. Still other rites are used to make women's breasts larger if they are small, and smaller if they are large. General dissatisfaction with breast shape is symbolized in the fact that the ideal form is virtually outside the range of human variation. A few women afflicted with almost inhuman hypermammary development are so idolized that they make a handsome living by simply going from village to village and permitting the natives to stare at them for a fee.

Reference has already been made to the fact that excretory functions are ritualized, routinized, and relegated to secrecy. Natural reproductive functions are similarly distorted. Intercourse is taboo as a topic and scheduled as an act. Efforts are made to avoid pregnancy by the use of magical materials or by limiting intercourse to certain phases of the moon. Conception is actually very infrequent. When pregnant, women dress so as to hide their condition. Parturition takes place in secret, without friends or relatives to assist, and the majority of women do not nurse their infants.

Our review of the ritual life of the Nacirema has certainly shown them to be a magic-ridden people. It is hard to understand how they have managed to exist so long under the burdens which they have imposed upon themselves. But even such exotic customs as these take on real meaning when they are viewed with the insight provided by Malinowski when he wrote (1948: 70):

> Looking from far and above, from our high places of safety in the developed civilization, it is easy to see all the crudity and irrelevance of magic. But without its power and

guidance early man could not have mastered his practical difficulties as he has done, nor could man have advanced to the higher stages of civilization.

References

Linton, Ralph. (1936). *The study of man*. D. Appleton-Century.

Malinowski, Bronislaw. (1948). *Magic, science, and religion*. Free Press.

Murdock, George P. (1949). *Social structure*. Macmillan.

Reading Questions

1. What group is Horace Miner really talking about in this classic article? (Hint: What is "Nacirema" spelled backwards?)
2. Miner mentions several interesting elements of Nacirema culture. What is he referring to when he talks about shrine rooms, charm-boxes, holy-mouth-men, mouth-rites, the *latipso*, and the listener?
3. Miner says that the Nacirema feel that the "human body is ugly and that its natural tendency is to debility and disease" and that this group has a "pervasive aversion to the natural body and its functions." Do you think this is true? What evidence could you find to support or contradict these claims?
4. What is the main point of this article? How does this article help you develop a more critical sociological perspective, particularly an ability to see the strange in the familiar?

Miner, H. (1956). Body ritual among the Nacirema. *American Anthropologist, 58*(3), 503–507.

ÉMILE DURKHEIM AND SOCIAL FACTS

The final goal of sociology is to understand the dual process of how we shape society and how society shapes us. People create institutions in society in many ways, such as by passing laws and electing leaders who decide how institutions will run. The institutions then influence individuals and the structure of society. Émile Durkheim's famous study of suicide illustrates this relationship.

Although Comte coined the term *sociology*, no universities offered courses or did research in sociology during his lifetime. Émile Durkheim, who was born in France in 1858, was one of the original proponents of creating a field of sociology that would have a significant presence at universities. He argued that sociology would be different from philosophy, a popular discipline at the time, because it would focus on empirical research. He claimed that sociology was distinct from psychology, another well-established discipline of the period, because this new discipline would prioritize the social over the individual. To help establish sociology as a discipline, Durkheim created *L'Année Sociologique,* an annual review of French sociology that became the country's most influential publication of its kind. He also wrote several significant books and other documents using the sociological perspective and method he was advocating, including *The Division of Labor in Society* (1893/1960), *The Rules of the Sociological Method* (1895), *Suicide* (1897/1951), and *The Elementary Forms of Religious Life* (1912/2008).

Getting to Know: Émile Durkheim (1858–1917)

- Durkheim was part of the Army of Justice, a group of intellectuals who fought what they considered the unfair execution of a French captain accused of treason.

- Durkheim's early death was attributed to his "loss of spirit and well-being" after his son's death in World War I.

- Durkheim wrote three of sociology's most influential works (*Suicide*, *The Rules of Sociological Method*, and *The Division of Labour in Society*) within a 5-year period.

- Durkheim did not make it into the École Normale Supérieure until his third attempt.

For Durkheim, sociology was a unique discipline because it was based on the study of **social facts**, the external social structures, norms, and values that shape individuals' actions. As Durkheim (1897/1951, pp. 37–38) explained, the "sociological methods as we practice it rests wholly on the basic principle that social facts must be studied as things, that is, as realities external to the individual." He believed that society is something more than just a group of individuals and the individual in society is "dominated by a moral reality greater than himself" (p. 38).

The Study of Suicide

To illustrate his concept of social facts and the way the sociological method could work, Durkheim conducted a study of suicide. The topic was chosen deliberately. At first glance, suicide seems like an obviously individual act; a person's choice to take his own life is often explained in terms of the person's own psychology. For example, we often think that people die from suicide because they are depressed or unhappy. Although Durkheim acknowledged that psychology might matter, he argued that psychology alone cannot explain suicide. "Admittedly," he wrote, "under similar circumstances, the [unwell man] is more apt to commit suicide than the well man; but he does not necessarily do so because of his condition" (Durkheim, 1897/1951, p. 81). He asked the following question: If suicide is strictly an individual psychological decision, why are suicide rates different for men and women, for Protestants and Catholics, and across countries? These differences can be explained only by social facts, elements of society that are beyond the individual.

Durkheim began his study not by looking at an individual's decision to die from suicide but by comparing the rates of suicide across groups of people. This systematic study of suicide led him to argue that there are four types of suicide that differ based on the level of integration or regulation in a society. Societies differ in their level of individual integration. In societies with extremely low levels of integration, individuals commit egoistic suicide, whereas in societies with extremely high levels of integration, they commit altruistic suicide. Societies also differ in their level of regulation, the degree of external constraint on individuals. When regulation is excessively low, individuals commit anomic suicide; when it is excessively high, they commit fatalistic suicide. Durkheim thus argued that the conditions of society are so powerful that they influence even this most personal decision for individuals.

Durkheim believed that the best parts of individuals—their morals, values, and sense of purpose—come from society. When individuals do not feel integrated into society, that condition can lead to egoistic suicide. Being a part of society can give our lives meaning, and participating in religion is one way that many people derive such meaning. Despite this important potential function, not all religions are equally effective at integrating individuals. For example, Durkheim found that Protestants were much more likely than Catholics to die from suicide, even though both religions prohibit and condemn suicide with equal fervor. He argued that this difference was partly because the Protestant Church is less effective than the Catholic Church at integrating its members. Protestantism focuses on individual faith, and adherents are encouraged to read and interpret the Bible on their own. Catholicism, however, places more emphasis on participating in church activities that are run by a clearly defined hierarchy of leaders. This feature encourages Catholics to interact with one another and to rely on the church to interpret religious teachings for them, both of which increase the amount of social interaction between members as well as the integration they feel.

In order to support this argument, Durkheim compared countries that were mostly Protestant (Prussia, Denmark, and Saxony) with those that were mostly Catholic (Spain, Portugal, and Italy). He found that the average suicide rate in the Protestant countries was 190 per million persons, whereas it was only 58 per million persons in the Catholic countries (Durkheim, 1897/1951, p. 152). The larger social context of Protestantism was associated with a suicide rate more than four times as high as the social context of Catholicism. However, some might argue that other differences between these countries might account for the different suicide rates. To test this claim, Durkheim compared suicide rates across regions of Switzerland, a country with both Catholic and Protestant areas. Even within this one country, the suicide rate of Protestants was four to five times higher than that of Catholics (p. 155). These data support Durkheim's argument that those who are less integrated are more likely to die from suicide and some religions are more effective at integrating their adherents than others.

Although a lack of integration in society can lead to suicide, Durkheim argued that excessively integrated societies can also have high suicide rates. Highly integrated societies can include cults in which some adherents commit mass suicide. For example, there was a mass suicide of 39 Heaven's Gate members in California in 1997. Terrorists who martyr themselves for a cause are also examples of how being excessively integrated into a society, so much so that a person thinks only about the group's needs, can be associated with suicide.

According to Durkheim, levels of regulation in society are also associated with suicide. In a society with very little regulation, individuals can begin to feel "anomic," a term Durkheim used to refer to a feeling of rootlessness or normlessness. When the rules and regulations of society are weak or unclear, individuals feel free to do anything they please. Although this freedom sounds good, a lack of regulation can reduce an individual's feeling of meaning and connection to others. Durkheim argued that a lack of regulation can occur in either good times, such as economic booms, or bad times, such as economic depressions. Any temporary disruption in the social order makes the collectivity unable to exercise its authority over the individual. In these times, the old rules and standards for behavior no longer apply, but new rules and standards have not yet been created. This situation can lead to anomic suicide.

The final type of suicide discussed by Durkheim, fatalistic suicide, occurs when there is excessive regulation in society. Durkheim named this type of suicide but did not spend much time discussing it in his work. He did say, however, that it occurs among "persons with futures pitilessly blocked and passions violently choked by oppressive discipline" (1897/1951, p. 276). For example, an enslaved person might commit suicide because she feels she has no other option and her life is totally controlled by another.

USING YOUR SOCIOLOGICAL IMAGINATION
SUICIDE IN THE UNITED STATES

Can we still use Durkheim's insights to understand suicide rates today? Figure 1.3 shows suicide rates in the United States by gender and age. Table 1.1 lists countries by their level of religiosity and suicide rates. Examine the data and answer the following questions.

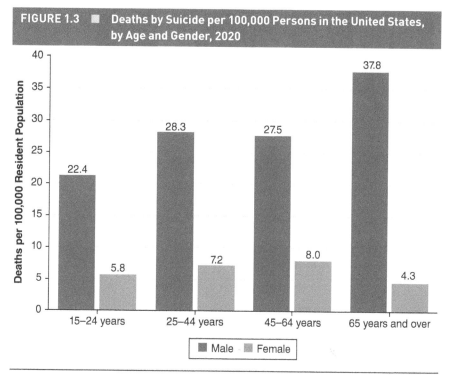

FIGURE 1.3 ■ Deaths by Suicide per 100,000 Persons in the United States, by Age and Gender, 2020

Source: Centers for Disease Control and Prevention. (2022). *Changes in suicide rates—United States, 2019 and 2020.* https://www.cdc.gov/mmwr/volumes/71/wr/mm7108a5.htm#T1_down

TABLE 1.1 ■ Suicide Rates and Religiosity by Country, 2019

Country	Religiosity (%)	Suicide Rate (per 1,000 residents)
Philippines	79	2.54
India	76	12.91
Guatemala	75	6.23
Brazil	69	6.41
Ireland	63	8.90
United States	61	14.51
Chile	54	8.04

Country	Religiosity (%)	Suicide Rate (per 1,000 residents)
Canada	49	10.34
Israel	44	5.15
France	30	9.65
Japan	29	12.24
Russia	28	21.6

Sources: Religiosity: Adapted from Pelham, Brett, and Zsolt Nyiri. (2008, 3 July). "In more religious countries, lower suicide rates: Lower suicide rates not a matter of national income." https://www.gallup.com/poll/1086 25/more-religious-countries-lower-suiciderates.aspx (2005 Data); Suicide Rate: World Health Organization. (2019). *Suicide rates.* https://www.who.int/data/gho/data/themes/mental-health/suicide-rates

1. How are gender and age related to suicide rates? How does Durkheim's theory about certain social conditions leading to suicide explain the suicide rates among American men and women in different age groups?
2. How is religiosity related to suicide rates across countries? Would Durkheim be surprised that countries that are more religious tend to have lower levels of suicide? Why or why not? How would he explain this relationship?
3. In general, countries that are very religious have low levels of suicide and countries that are not very religious have higher levels. But Israel has a relatively low rate of suicide given its low level of religiosity, and India has a relatively high rate of suicide given its high rate of religiosity. How can you explain these unusual cases? Can you use Durkheim's theory? Why or why not?

The brilliance of Durkheim's study is in the way it shows how a phenomenon that is generally thought of as purely psychological, the decision to die from suicide, is shaped by the structure of the society in which a person lives. In other words, by examining the integration and regulation in a society, we can predict its suicide rate. Or, when examining groups of people, we can predict who will be more likely and who will be less likely to die from suicide based on the propensity of their group to be integrated into or regulated by society. For example, Durkheim compared the suicide rates of men and women and found that men are more likely to die from suicide, in part because they tend to be less integrated into society. In the same way, he found that unmarried individuals are more likely to commit suicide because they are less integrated into families.

Durkheim's work, though highly influential, has sparked criticism and debate. Some later researchers argue that there is a logical error in the research: Durkheim explained microlevel individual behavior (the act of suicide) with macrolevel country statistics (suicide rates). Despite this potential problem, the work illuminates the connection between individuals and the society in which they live, which is at the heart of sociology.

Women in Early Sociology

It is not surprising that the founding figures of sociology were male. This reflects the fact that sociology as a discipline emerged in a time when women were not able to attain higher education and were expected to focus on family roles instead of engaging in paid work. Because of this, feminist scholars have argued that sociology has traditionally been organized around men—their experiences and their interests (Seidman, 2008). In essence, men have been both the subjects and the authors of sociology, and the experiences of women have been (largely) ignored until recently (Smith, 1987).

Despite their underrepresentation, there have been a few trail-blazing women active in early sociology. Harriet Martineau (1802–1876) is often called the first female sociologist. Jane Addams (1860–1935) was also an important early female sociologist. When we learn about the foundations of our discipline, it is important to consider the people from all backgrounds who made it what it is today.

Getting to Know: Harriet Martineau (1802–1876)

- Harriet's childhood experience was marked by increasing deafness that required her to use an ear trumpet (the precursor to the cochlear implant) as an adult. Her writing was some of the first to engage with issues related to disability. At 32, Harriet wrote an essay, *Letters to the Deaf* (1834), that detailed the social isolation, health care challenges, and stigma experienced by people with a hearing impairment.

- Social norms of 19th-century England prevented Martineau from attending university, so she committed herself to intense self-directed study at home.

- She translated and condensed Auguste Comte's *Cour de philosophie positive*, which significantly facilitated the introduction of positivist sociology to the United States.

- Harriet's book, *How to Observe Morals and Manners* (1838), is ground-breaking as the first foundational text on sociological methods and discussed topics such as class, forms of religion, and types of suicide long before "founding fathers" Karl Marx, Émile Durkheim, and Max Weber.

Hulton-Deutsch/Hulton-Deutsch Collection/Corbis via Getty Images

Getting to Know: Jane Addams (1860–1935)

- One of the first applied sociologists who co-founded (with friend Ellen G. Starr) and resided in the famous Hull House in Chicago, a social settlement that sought to improve conditions of residents in Chicago's industrial districts by offering kindergarten classes, club meetings, and in later years, social services such as a library, employment bureau, and art gallery.

- She was known as a strong advocate for progressive reforms that would improve the lives of marginalized people including immigrants, Black Americans, the working class, women, and children.

- Adams was the first woman to be awarded an honorary degree from Yale University in 1910.

- She was a committed feminist who championed women's suffrage and a pacifist who publicly opposed the Spanish-American War and World War I.

- Addams was awarded the Nobel Peace Prize in 1931.

Library of Congress Prints and Photographs Division

IS SOCIOLOGY JUST COMMON SENSE?

Because we all live within society, it is sometimes hard to see how there could be much to learn in sociology. Can't we just use our own experiences to make sense of the social world? Isn't sociology really just common sense? Randall Collins (1992), a well-known sociologist, notes that obvious social questions may not have obvious or simple answers. Sociology's greatest strength, he argues, is precisely its potential for moving past the superficial observation of everyday life and finding the fundamental social processes hidden beneath.

For example, many people wonder what makes a romantic couple compatible. Common sense tells us that opposites attract. However, it also tells us that birds of a feather flock together. If both axioms are common sense and are based on our lived experiences, how can we decide which idea is the better explanation of compatibility? Much systematic research has been conducted in sociology to answer just this question, and this research comes to a clear consensus that, although it may seem like opposites attract, most couples share similar characteristics. In fact, the homophily principle structures social relationships of every type, including marriage, friendship, and work relationships. Most people have personal networks that are very homogeneous, which is partly why most romantic partners are similar to one another. They are most likely to be similar in race and ethnicity, with age, religion, education, and occupation following, in roughly that order. In addition, couples are also most often similar in terms of their attitudes and values.

There are many reasons why most people romantically couple with and marry people who are like them. The most important reason is simple geography. Most people have more contact with those who are like them. For example, one of the main reasons that people tend to date and marry others of similar age is because of the age-based structure of schooling. The fact that schools group ages together into classrooms induces homophily. As many people meet romantic partners and select mates while they are attending school and are most likely to meet and interact with others of their age group in these settings, it is not surprising that they are most likely to choose a partner in their age group.

Partners are also most likely to come from the same social class. This is, in part, because our social class often determines the neighborhood where we grow up and live. People with more money and higher status occupations tend to live in more expensive neighborhoods, where other upper-class people live. They are also more likely to attend elite private schools, where they meet others of their social class. And they are more likely to work in fields such as law, business, or medicine, where other people of their class also work. These social networks bring people of the same class into contact with one another and provide opportunities to create friendships.

The finding that most relationships, be they romances, friendships, or acquaintances, tend to occur between people who are similar can be very important for understanding how society works. If people tend to know others like themselves, they might be less likely to be open to or tolerant of people who are different from them. It also might limit the amount and diversity of information people receive because they are generally just in contact with people who have the same opinions and experiences. Considering what we think we know about society and examining it in a systematic way can help us to better understand the world around us. This is what sociology is all about.

How Would Different Disciplines Study Your Classroom?

One way to think about how sociology is distinct as a discipline is to compare it with other academic areas of study. For example, how would a sociologist study your classroom? How might an engineer, biologist, historian, or psychologist study it differently?

According to the homophily principle, friends and romantic partners tend to have similar interests and to come from similar backgrounds. These friends at Coachella share an interest in music and fashion (particularly a love of cowboy hats) and probably come from similar ethnic and class backgrounds. What similarities and dissimilarities can you find between you and your friends?

Presley Ann/Getty Images for Coachella

An engineer might be interested in the classroom's acoustics and whether those sitting in the back can hear the professor. She might also study the airflow, the materials used for the furniture or fixtures, and the insulation. A biologist would be much less interested in these issues and would probably focus on the students' genetic diversity, the other organic material in the room (hopefully not bugs or rodents), and the spread of bacteria from person to person.

A historian would be more similar to a sociologist than would either the engineer or biologist, but he would still study very different elements of the classroom. He might be interested in the growth of universities over the past 100 years, the history of a school, and perhaps larger histories of migration that brought the students in this classroom to this particular area. Psychologists may be interested in the how students process information and learn the material in the class or how they made the decision to take this particular course.

Although sociologists share some of these interests (e.g., like the historians, they are also interested in migration patterns, and like the psychologists, they are interested in why a student took the class), they would be much more likely to emphasize the three core foci of sociology. Sociologists might ask, "Who is in this classroom and who is not?" They would examine how men and women, different ethnicities and religions, and different social classes are represented in the classroom, and they would try to understand the social processes that make some people more likely to attend college than others. They would also be interested in how the institution of education shapes young people: Who decides what material is covered in your education? What material is not covered? How does going to college socialize us? Finally, when examining social change, a sociologist might ask how the university has changed. Do different types of people attend today than attended in the past? Are different subjects taught? How does the relationship between the university and other institutions in society change over time? Although all the disciplines have important and interesting questions to ask about this classroom, each has a particular and distinct perspective for making sense of the world.

Who is in this classroom and who is not? To what extent does this photo depict the ethnic, class, and gender makeup of your college or university?

iStockphoto.com/monkeybusinessimages

The Role of Theory

Sociologists systematically study the social world, including the events, interactions, and institutions in our society. When they do this, they develop theories in an attempt to explain why things work as they do. A theory is a way to explain different aspects of society and to create hypotheses. Hypotheses are testable propositions about society. These hypotheses are very important. In order for theories to be useful, they should allow for hypotheses that can be subjected to empirical observation and testing. For example, we might have a theory that a person's gender is related to their income. To test this theory, we set out a hypothesis. We could have a hypothesis that men make more than women in a specific job, such as high school teaching. In order to test this theory, we would need a set of research methods that would see if this hypothesis has support in empirical data (that is coming up next!).

Theories vary in their scope and scale. Macro-level theories focus on large-scale issues and large groups of people. For example, we might have theories about why countries go to war, explaining patterns of global migration, or why there are changes in marriage rates over time. These are all theories concerned with large-scale trends and issues in society. We also might have micro-level theories, which focus on relationships between individuals and groups. For example, we could look at why some people chose to go into the military, how migration shapes the educational outcomes of children, or the impact of divorce on earnings. These are all focused on similar issues but examine their implications at the individual level.

In order for a theory to be useful, it should help us understand or explain the social world. If a theory does not do a good job of explaining why things are the way they are, we should consider how we might revise that theory so it is more effective at helping us make sense of the world around us. It is also useful for the theory to be able to make predictions, which can assist in making policies that concern the social world.

Many theories are introduced and discussed in this book. Table 1.2 lists the main theories that are discussed in this text and the chapters in which they are introduced.

TABLE 1.2 ■ Theories and Theoretical Perspectives Discussed in This Textbook	
Theory	**Chapter**
Sociological Imagination	1
Structural Functionalism	2
Conflict Theory	2 and 4
Feminist Theory	2 and 6
Symbolic Interactionism	2
Dramaturgical Perspective	2
Social Construction	3
Labelling Theory	3
Thomas Principle	5
Critical Race Theory	5
Intersectionality	6
Rationalization	10
Modernization Theory	12
World Systems Theory	12
World Society Theory	12
Protest Paradigm	14
Framing Theory	14
Resource Mobilization Theory	14
Political Process Theory	14

RESEARCH METHODS: HOW DO SOCIOLOGISTS STUDY SOCIETY?

Sociologists conduct research in a systematic way in order to understand how society operates. They use this information to answer questions about individual behavior and the functioning of society.

When sociologists look at a social issue, one of the first things they do is posit a research question. Research questions focus on the relationship between two (or more) variables. A variable is any construct that can take on different values— that can vary. For example, age can be a variable because people are different ages. There are two main types of variables: independent variables and dependent variables. Independent variables *affect* other variables. By nature, they come before a dependent variable. Dependent variables are *affected by* independent variables. Research questions look at the relationship between independent and dependent variables—how the former affect the latter. For example, if we are asking, "What is the relationship between ethnicity and income?" ethnicity is the independent variable and income is the dependent variable. We are testing to see whether your ethnicity affects how much money you make. We would not expect that the amount of money that you make would change your ethnicity. Once sociologists have a research question and know the variables on which they will focus, they decide on the research method that is most appropriate for answering this question.

Quantitative Research

Sociology and the other social sciences use two major types of research: quantitative and qualitative (although many researchers use both types of methods). Quantitative research focuses on things that can be counted. This research examines how variables relate to one another and tests these relationships with statistical models. For example, a quantitative researcher interested in education might focus on the educational outcomes of different groups of people. They could record the age, sex, and ethnicity of people and their level of education. Then they could use statistical models to generalize about who is more or less likely to get degrees. Quantitative research focuses on measuring social phenomena and on using statistical models to assess the patterns of association among variables. Because these types of techniques require many cases to test for the relationships between variables effectively, quantitative research often must examine relationships at a more general level.

One of the major ways that quantitative research is conducted is with surveys. Survey research involves giving questionnaires to a large number of people to learn about their characteristics, attitudes, or behaviors. The census, collected by the U.S. Census Bureau, is an example of a survey. The census asks people living in the United States about themselves, including their age, gender, and income. We can use these data to examine many types of questions. For example, we can study whether men earn more money than women do, how this discrepancy might differ by education level, and whether it is increasing or decreasing over time. This information is quite important for understanding gender inequality.

Experiments are another major quantitative method. In experiments the researcher looks at the effect of some factor, sometimes called a treatment, on individual behavior. This approach involves comparing two groups: the experimental group and the control group. The experimental group is given the treatment, while the control group is not. If we wanted to understand the effect of money as an incentive for learning, for example, we could bring two groups of students to a lab. We would ask all the students to try to learn a list of words. Half the students would be paid money for each correct word they learned and the other students would receive nothing. Presuming that the students in each group were the same in terms of important characteristics (such as their intelligence), if the students who were told they would be paid for correct answers did better on the task than those not given this incentive, we would conclude that paying students to achieve was a useful way to increase performance. Garfinkel's breaching experiments, discussed earlier in the chapter, are a particular kind of experiment.

Qualitative Research

Qualitative research tends to examine a smaller number of cases in more detail and emphasizes social processes. Instead of focusing on counting phenomena, qualitative researchers often examine the meaning of action for individuals and groups. Sociologists use a variety of qualitative techniques. Two major qualitative methods in sociology are interviewing and participant observation. Interviewing is a qualitative method in which a researcher asks each participant the same set of questions and records participant responses. Interviews allow the researcher to ask questions that require longer answers and to ask follow-up questions to get more detail. For example, interviews might be quite useful for understanding how going to college changes the way young people see themselves. To assess how various elements of university life, such as living in a dorm, taking classes, joining campus groups, and making friends, can shape an individual's identity, you might want to give individuals more time to explain these complicated changes and to ask follow- up questions to probe for more information.

Participant observation (ethnography) is another core qualitative method. The researcher actively engages with a group of individuals and works to understand their lives and experiences through intensive involvement with them over an extended period. For example, if you wanted to understand how young people pick up people in a bar, you might go to the same bar every Saturday night and watch as young people introduce themselves to one another. By observing them, you could see what types of people are the most likely to approach others or be approached. You could also see how couples interact with one another in the context of the bar. Though you could, of course, survey or interview people about their pick-up practices, you could certainly learn additional things by watching these interactions happen in person. In fact, as a researcher you might gain insights that the people had not considered; after all, we might not be the best assessors of our own pick-up techniques.

Content analysis or document coding is also used by sociologists and other social scientists. This involves the systematic coding of documents to answer research questions and can be done in a qualitative or quantitative way. For example, sociologists could look at all newspaper articles written about a key event, such as an election, to understand how people make sense of the event and how this might differ across places and times. We could also code Facebook pages, Twitter, or other social media. Archival documents, like meeting minutes, parliamentary debate, or personal letters, can be systematically coded to answer research questions.

These five core sociological methods are all good ways to understand the social world. No one method is the best method of research. All these techniques are simply tools. Just as it would be ridiculous to argue that a hammer is a better tool than a saw (it depends on whether you want to join things together or cut them in half), it does not make sense to argue which method is the best. Each method is more (or less) useful for understanding different types of phenomena, and it is always good to have as many tools in our toolkit as possible.

Doing Sociology: Making Use of Sociological Methods

The five main sociological methods are useful for answering different types of research questions. If you are interested in studying crime, for example, surveys could help you answer many questions. In the United States, the government conducts a survey of victimization every year as part of the National Crime Victimization Survey. In this survey, individuals are asked a whole series of questions about crime and being a victim of crime. Using these data you could answer research questions such as, "Who is most likely to be a victim of crime?" or "Who is most likely to report a crime to the police?" By comparing results from men and women, older and younger people, those who live in cities with those who live in rural areas, and different ethnic groups, you could better understand who is most likely to experience crime and who is most likely to report that crime to the police when it happens.

Experiments could also help you to better understand crime, albeit by answering different specific questions. An experiment would not be very effective at helping you understand who is most likely to be a victim of a crime because the group of people who you would have come to your laboratory to engage in your experiment would probably not accurately reflect the experiences of the entire American population. However, experiments could help you to answer different types of questions. For example, you could create an experiment to better understand how we perceive different perpetrators of crime. You could tell your research subjects to read a story of a crime, perhaps about a theft of a pair of jeans from a store. They would all read the same story, except half would be told that the thief was a woman and half would be told that the thief was a man. You could then ask each group how serious they considered the crime. Through this type of experiment you could better understand if people see the severity of a crime differently depending on who they think committed it. Are we more likely to see a male perpetrator as a real criminal and a female perpetrator as a casual shoplifter? Would we think differently of a 15-year-old perpetrator as opposed to one who is 50?

Interviews could also be effective ways to understand crime. They are most appropriate for unpacking complex thought processes because the interviewer has longer to talk with the respondent and is able to get answers that are more in-depth. We could use interviews to answer a research question such as, "How do people start to engage in criminal behavior?" To answer this question, we could go to a prison and interview inmates about how they first got involved in crime. By talking with them about how their involvement started, we could better understand how their family background, friends, neighborhood, and other factors did (or did not) relate to their entry into criminal activity. You could, of course, use a survey to ask how inmates got involved in crime, but respondents would then be forced to answer from a set of fixed categories (perhaps you would have a list of five or six reasons they could check off), and you would not be able to ask for more detail about this complex process.

Finally, you could engage in participant observation of crime. If you were interested in how police enforce crime, for example, you could engage in participant observation and ride along with police officers to see how they interact with people who are suspected of committing crimes. Police have a lot of discretion whether to stop people. And even when they stop someone and think that person committed a crime, the police often can decide to give them a warning, give them a ticket, or take them in to the police station and charge them with a crime. How do police officers make these decisions? It would be possible to conduct a survey or interviews of police officers. However, some of these processes are unconscious and may be better observed in real time.

All these methods, as well as other methods used by sociologists, can help us to understand the complex issues surrounding crime and criminality. Each can address slightly different research questions and provide different types of data. In order to really understand any social phenomenon, it is useful to have sociologists working with all these different research techniques and sharing their findings.

Methods in *Imagining Society*

Throughout this book, we will learn about studies using each of these core methods. When you come across these studies in this class and others, think about how the methods used were useful for answering the research question. How might the study be different if another method had been used? We will consider potential challenges or issues that arise in the research process, as well as the benefits and drawbacks of the methods employed. Table 1.3 highlights some of the places in this book where you will find examples of, and discussion of, the main methods sociologists use to study the social world.

TABLE 1.3 ■ Social Research Methods Discussed and Applied in This Text		
Method	**"Methods in Depth" sections**	**Readings**
Survey	Halpern & Perry-Jenkins (Chapter 6) James-Kangal et al. (Chapter 8) Gentrup et al. (Chapter 9) Rooney-Varga et al. (Chapter 12) Ozturk (Chapter 13) McAdam (Chapter 14)	
Experiment	Mayo (Chapter 10) Rooney-Varga et al. (Chapter 12)	Rosenhan (Chapter 3)

Method	"Methods in Depth" sections	Readings
Interviews	Blee (Chapter 2) Brayne (Chapter 3) Bettis (Chapter 4) Gentrup (Chapter 9) McAdam (Chapter 14)	Hochschild (Chapter 10)
Participant Observation	Blee (Chapter 2) Brayne (Chapter 3) Bettis (Chapter 4) Gentrup et al. (Chapter 9)	
Content Analysis/ Document Analysis	Blee (Chapter 2) Stephens-Davidowitz (Chapter 5) Hoewe (Chapter 7) Brothers et al. (Chapter 11)	Pangborn (Chapter 4) Mullen (Chapter 9)

SUMMARY

We began this chapter, and this book, by introducing sociology as a discipline focused on the systematic study of human society. Sociologists focus on three core areas of study: social inequality, social institutions, and social change. When looking at these three areas, sociologists aim to see general themes in everyday life, critically examine the familiar world around them, and understand how society shapes individuals while individuals also shape society. We have begun to better understand these ideas through examining C. Wright Mills's concept of the sociological imagination, Harold Garfinkel's breaching experiments, Horace Miner's article on the Nacirema, and Émile Durkheim's study of suicide. Mills encourages us to connect our own individual biography with the history of society and to see how our personal troubles are connected to larger public issues. Through this lens of the sociological imagination, we can make sense of how society works and how individuals are connected to the society in which they live. Finally, we learned some of the major qualitative and quantitative ways that sociologists conduct research—something that will be highlighted throughout the book.

FOR FURTHER READING

Berger, P. (1963). *Invitation to sociology*. Doubleday.

Collins, R. (1992). *Sociological insight: An introduction to non-obvious sociology* (2nd ed.). Oxford University Press.

Durkheim, É. (1951). *Suicide: A study in sociology*. Free Press. (Original work published 1897)

Kuhn, T. S. (1995). *The structure of scientific revolutions*. University of Chicago Press.

Mills, C. W. (2000). *The sociological imagination*. Oxford University Press. (Original work published 1959)

GLOSSARY

breaching experiments

content analysis

counterculture

culture

dependent variables

dominant culture

experiments

high culture

homophily

hypotheses

independent variables

interviewing

macro-level theories

micro-level theories

participant observation (ethnography)

personal troubles

popular (or low) culture

public issues

qualitative research

quantitative research

religiosity

research questions

secularization

social facts

social inequality

social institutions

society

sociological imagination

sociology

subcultures

survey research

types of suicide

theory

variable

Diversity Studio/iStockPhoto

2

SOCIALIZATION AND SOCIAL INTERACTION

LEARNING OBJECTIVES

1. Explain how Durkheim sees the connection between individuals and society.

2. Define socialization and illustrate how the different theoretical approaches explain this process.

3. Explain socialization as a lifelong process and give examples of how we are socialized over the course of our lives.

4. Explain Goffman's dramaturgical model and outline how this model helps us to understand social interaction.

One of the core concerns of sociology is to understand how individuals are shaped by society. We are socialized over the course of our lives to fit in to society and to follow its rules. This socialization starts early with our parents telling us to share with our siblings or to say "please" and "thank you." It continues as we learn in school how to make friends and be a good student. And it will last throughout our whole lives as we move into new relationships, family roles, occupations, and social groups. This is the process of learning to fit in to society. However, we also sometimes challenge society and its rules. For example, we may dress in an unconventional way, make career or family decisions that are different from what our parents might hope, or join a group that challenges laws or rules with which we do not agree. How can we understand the complex relationship between individuals and society? These connections are the core of this chapter and of sociology itself.

Émile Durkheim is often considered one of the founding figures of sociology. Here he sits, perhaps pondering society.

The History Collection / Alamy Stock Photo

THE INDIVIDUAL AND SOCIETY

Émile Durkheim, whose study of suicide was discussed in Chapter 1, said that society soars above us, exerts a constraining influence on us, and regulates collective activity. At the same time, society enables us to understand the rules that govern social behavior and helps us get along with one another. This chapter examines how we become a member of society through socialization, an important process that both facilitates our existence in society and constrains our actions. We will discuss how we, as individuals, learn to fit into society through socialization, why this process is important, and how it continues throughout our lives.

Durkheim's first published article, excerpted in the following pages, was a review of the German sociologist Albert Schaeffle's *Bau und Leben des Sozialen Körpers: Erster Band* (which roughly translates as "the construction and life of the social body"). Written when Durkheim was 27 years old, the article lays the foundation for his influential theory of society, which he continued to develop over the course of his career. The review begins with a discussion of Jean-Jacques Rousseau's ideas of human nature. A well-known philosopher and political theorist, Rousseau (1712–1778) began his theories of human nature by thinking about what humans would be like before society existed. Rousseau (2011) thought that humans could exist before there were societies and that they would be "happy savages" who did not have language or interact with one another. He asserted that the stage before society existed, between the primitive idea of humans as brute animals and the modern extreme of decadent civilization, was the best stage in human development. He imagined that "nothing is so gentle as man in his primitive state, when placed by nature at an equal distance from the stupidity of brutes and the fatal enlightenment of civil man" (Rousseau, 2011, p. 64). He goes on to say that,

> The more one reflects on it, the more one finds that this state was the least subject to upheavals and the best for man, and that he must have left it only by virtue of some fatal chance happening that, for the common good, ought never to have happened. The example of savages, almost all of whom have been found in this state, seems to confirm that the human race had been made to remain in it always; that this state is the veritable youth of the world; and that all the subsequent progress has been in appearance so many steps toward the perfection of the individual, and in fact toward the decay of the species. (Rousseau, 2011, p. 74)

For Rousseau, society corrupts humans and leads to our decay.

Durkheim fundamentally disagreed with these ideas for several reasons. First, he thought that humans could not exist without society or develop without interaction with other humans. In addition, he argued that society is good for people because it helps them feel connected to one another. In fact, Durkheim's definition of what it means to be human is fundamentally social; he posited that part of what makes us human is our interactions with and dependence on one another. Although Rousseau might have been able to imagine a world of humans before society, Durkheim claimed that it is impossible to have humans without society because society is what *makes* us human.

READING: "REVIEW OF ALBERT SCHAEFFLE'S BAU UND LEBEN DES SOZIALEN KÖRPERS: ERSTER BAND"

Émile Durkheim

The following review written by Émile Durkheim outlines the basis for his theories about the connections between the individual and society. In this article, Durkheim highlights his main assertion that individuals are fundamentally shaped by society. When reading this article, consider how it challenges the dominant view in society that individuals are the "masters of their own fate." How are our individual decisions and actions shaped by larger society?

Society is not a simple collection of individuals, it is an entity which preceded those who comprise it at present and which will survive them, which acts more on them than they on it, which has its own life, own consciousness, own interests and destiny. But what is its nature?
. . .

We are not dealing with man as Rousseau conceived of him—that abstract being, born to solitude, renouncing it only very late and by a sort of voluntary sacrifice, and then only as the issue of a well-deliberated covenant. Every man is, on the contrary, born for society and in a society. What proves this is not only his marvelous aptitude for defining himself within it and, consequently, for uniting himself with it; still more, it is his inability to live in isolation. What remains if, from the sum of our knowledge, our sentiments, and our customs we take away all that comes to us from our ancestors, our masters, and the milieu in which we live? We will have removed at the same time all that makes us truly men. But aside from all that thus reaches us from outside, there is within us, or so it appears, something intimate and personal which is our own creation; this is our ideal. This is, in the final analysis, a world in which the individual reigns supreme and into which society does not penetrate. Doesn't the cult of the ideal presuppose an entirely internal life, a spirit turned inward on itself and detached from other things? Is idealism not at once the most elevated and the most prideful form of egoism? Quite the contrary, there is no more powerful link for uniting men to one another. For the ideal is impersonal; it is the common possession of all mankind. It is toward this dimly glimpsed goal that all the forces of our nature converge. The more we are clearly aware of it, the more we feel that we are in solidarity with each other. This is precisely what distinguishes human society from all others; it alone can be moved by this need for a universal ideal. . . .

IV

There exists a social consciousness of which individual consciousness are, at least in part, only an emanation. How many ideas or sentiments are there which we obtain completely on our own? Very few. Each of us speaks a language which he has not himself created: we find it ready-made. Language is, no doubt, like the clothing in which thought is dressed up. It is not, however, everyday clothing, not flattering to everyone's figure, and not the sort that anyone can wear to advantage. It can adapt itself only to certain minds. Every articulated language presupposes and represents a certain articulation of thought. By the very fact that a given people speaks in its own way, it thinks in its own way. We take in and learn at the same time. Similarly, where do we get both the rules of reasoning and the methods of applied logic? We have borrowed all these riches from the common capital. Finally, are not our resolutions, the judgments which we make about men and about things, ceaselessly determined by public mores and tastes? That is how it happens that each people has its own physiognomy, temperament, and character. That is how it happens that at certain moments a sort of moral epidemic spreads through the society, one which, in an instant, warps and perverts everyone's will. All these phenomena would be inexplicable if individual consciousness were such independent monads.

But how are we to conceive of this social consciousness? Is it a simple and transcendent being, soaring above society? The metaphysician is free to imagine such an indivisible essence deep within all things! It is certain that experience shows us nothing of the sort. The collective mind (*l'esprit collectif*) is only a composite of individual minds. But the latter are not mechanically juxtaposed and closed off from one another. They are in perpetual interaction through the exchange of symbols; they interpenetrate one another. They group themselves according to their natural affinities; they coordinate and systematize themselves. In this way is formed an entirely new psychological being, one without equal in the world. The consciousness with which it is endowed is infinitely more intense and more vast than those which resonate within it. For it is "a consciousness of consciousness" (*une conscience de consciences*). . . .

We can, therefore, affirm that a collective consciousness is nothing but an integrated system, a harmonic consensus. And the law of this organization is the following: each social mass gravitates about a central point and is subject to the action of a directing force which regulates and combines the elementary movements. Schaeffle calls this force authority. The various authorities are subordinated one to another in their turn, and that is how a new life, at once unified and complex, arises out of all the individual activities.

Authority can be represented by a man or by a class or by a slogan. But whatever form it takes, it is indispensable. What would become of individual life without innervation? We would have chaos. Always and everywhere it is faith that provides the force of authority. If we obey when authority commands, it is because we believe in it. Faith can be freely given or imposed; with progress, it will no doubt become more intelligent and more enlightened, but it will never disappear. If, by the use of violence or trickery, it is suffocated for a time, either the society breaks apart or new beliefs are reborn without delay—beliefs less correct and worse than those which preceded them because they are less ripe and not so well tested, because, pressed by the necessity of living, we seize upon the first beliefs to happen along, without examining them. What's more, faith is nothing to be embarrassed about. We cannot know everything or do everything for ourselves; this is an axiom which every day becomes more true. It is, therefore, quite necessary that we address ourselves to someone else, someone more competent. Why stake our honour on being self-sufficient? Why not take advantage of the division of labour?

Authority is, nonetheless, a terrible thing if it is tyrannical. Everyone must be able to criticize it and need submit to it only voluntarily. If the masses are reduced to passive obedience, they will ultimately resign themselves to this humiliating role; they will become, little by little, a sort of inert matter which will no longer resist events, which can be moulded at will, but from which it will no longer be possible to wrest the slightest spark of life. Yet the basis of a people's force is the initiative of the citizens; it is the activity of the masses. Authority directs social life but neither creates it nor replaces it. It coordinates its movements, but presupposes their existence. . . .

A broad-minded individual can, almost at the same time, think one thing and its opposite; but he cannot at once act and abstain from acting. One must choose between two courses of action. It is, therefore, necessary that someone in the society be charged with choosing and deciding. Some authority is no doubt also necessary to coordinate individual intellects and sensitivities. But this authority has no precise organization; it is established here or there according to needs and circumstances. It is, moreover, only consultative. On the other hand, that authority which is charged with guarding the interests of the country is made to command and must be obeyed. That is why it is concentrated at certain determinate points of the territory and belongs only to certain clearly designated persons. In the same way, the principles which regulate collective activity are not indecisive generalizations or vague approximations but positive laws, the formulation of which is sharply delineated once and for all.

However, the role of the public is not purely passive submission: it participates in this activity even though it does not direct it. The laws do not owe their existence to the solitary will of the legislator. They are immanent in society just as the laws of gravity are immanent in physical bodies. The state does not create the former any more than the scientist creates the latter. Law and morality are simply the conditions of collective life; it is, therefore, the people who make them, so to speak, and the people who determine them just by living. The legislator states and formulates them. Moreover, he is not indispensable. If he does not intervene, the law nonetheless exists in the form of custom—half unconscious, it is true, but no less efficacious for that. It loses its precision, not its authority. Moreover, most collective resolutions are directly prepared and almost imposed by public opinion. Once a question becomes the order of the day, opposing sides are organized, engage in battle, and fight for the majority. To be sure, in well-constituted societies, this entire movement, once it arrives on the threshold of social consciousness, stops there. At that point, the organ of the will begins to function. But who cannot see that the matter has already been decided, just as the human will has already been predetermined, by the time that deliberation is cut off? It is the stronger side which triumphs.

But if we concede so large a role to individual wills, will they not impart to the social body all sorts of disordered movements? This fear would be legitimate if egoism was man's only natural sentiment. If everyone pursued only his personal ends, the society would be done for; torn in all directions, it would soon break apart. But at the same time that we love ourselves, we love others. We have a certain sense of solidarity (*Gemeinsinn*) which prevents us from ignoring others and which predisposes us without difficulty to devotion and sacrifice. Of course, if we believe that society is an invention of men, an artificial combination, then there is reason to fear that it will perpetually be torn apart. For so fragile a bond can be broken at any moment.

Man is free, Rousseau said, and yet everywhere he is in chains. If this is true, there is reason to fear that at any moment he will break his chains. But this savage individualism is not part of nature. The real man—the man who is truly a man—is an integral part of a society which he loves just as he loves himself, because he cannot withdraw from it without becoming decadent.

V

Social psychology can ultimately be reduced to the special study of the nervous system: it is a chapter of histology. Schaeffle passes from the tissues to the organs.

Every organ is formed by the combination of five functional tissues. . . . These five elements are combined in different ways and in different proportions, but they are all necessary and are found everywhere. The Church, whose ends are not of this world, still has its economic organization; the shop and the factory have their intellectual lives. . . .

Social life does not take place in the penumbra of the unconscious; everything happens in broad daylight. The individual is not led by instinct; rather, he has a clear conception of the group to which he belongs and the ends which it is appropriate to pursue. He compares, discusses, and yields only to reason. Faith itself is but the free submission of an intellect which comprehends the advantages and the necessity of the division of labour. That is why there is something free and willed about the social organization. Societies are not, to be sure, the product of a contract, and they cannot be transformed from one day to the next. But, on the other hand, they are not the product of a blind necessity, and their history is not a fatal evolution. Consciousness are perpetually open to ideas and, consequently, to change. They can, therefore, escape their first impulse and modify the given direction, or, at any rate, if they persist in the original course, it is because they wished to. Finally, what sets human societies entirely apart is their remarkable tendency toward universality. Animal societies never extend beyond a tiny space, and colonies of a single species always remain distinct, often even enemies. Human societies (*les nations*), on the contrary, become more and more confused with one another; national characteristics, races, and civilizations mix and interpenetrate. Already science, art, and religions have no country. Thus, little by little a new society emerges from all the isolated and distinct groups, a society in which all others will fuse, and which will end by one day including the entire human race.

Reading Questions

1. Durkheim begins his article by stating that society is not simply a collection of individuals; society has "its own life, own consciousness, own interests and destiny." What does he mean by society's consciousness and interests? Give examples of both.
2. Durkheim suggests that individuals have very few ideas that are completely their own. If ideas are not our own, where do they come from?
3. How do ideas become the great truths of science, dogmas of religion, or prescriptions of fashion? How does Durkheim say that these ideas become accepted as true?
4. Where do laws come from, according to Durkheim?

Durkheim, É. (1978). *Émile Durkheim on Institutional Analysis* (M. Traugott, Ed. & Trans.). University of Chicago Press. (Original work published 1885)

SOCIALIZATION

Although Durkheim and Rousseau might have disagreed about what humans would be like without society, they agreed that humans are shaped by their society. Much sociological work is focused on how this process of shaping occurs. How do we learn to fit into society? We gain this knowledge through **socialization,** the lifelong process of learning our society's norms, customs, and ideologies. This process also provides us with the skills necessary for participating in society, thereby helping us both to fit into society and to develop a sense of identity and self.

Socialization is understood differently depending on your theoretical perspective. Sociology has three classic theoretical perspectives that will be used throughout this book: structural functionalism, conflict theory, and symbolic interactionism. Feminist and postmodernist perspectives emerged later in the discipline but are also important lenses through which we can understand the social world.

Structural Functionalism

Structural functionalism, which was particularly popular in the early years of the discipline, is mainly interested in explaining how society functions effectively. Sociologists working within the structural functionalist tradition look at how different structures or institutions in society work together to create consensus and social cohesion. A common analogy, popularized by structural functionalist Herbert Spencer (1820–1903), is that the parts of society are like organs in the human body. Just as the body is made up of various parts that need to function together properly for it to be healthy, the parts of society need to work well together for society to run smoothly. The body's purpose is to survive; therefore, its subsystems (e.g., the respiratory system or central nervous system) need to cooperate to maintain the system. For the structural functionalists, society's purpose is also to survive and reproduce itself. All the subsystems of society (e.g., the family or the education system) must work well together to keep society running smoothly.

Structural functionalists consider socialization an extremely significant part of how society functions effectively. From this perspective, socialization is a top-down process. Children internalize social rules and values through socialization and learn to conform to the **roles** (the behaviors, beliefs, and norms performed in social situations) and expectations of society. This helps them to become a part of society. Talcott Parsons, a prominent structural functionalist who was influenced by Durkheim, discussed the importance of socialization in his book *Family, Socialization, and Interaction Process*. According to Parsons (1955), we must all learn society's rules and values; when we all understand them, there is social conformity and consensus. The more thoroughly members of society accept and adopt the dominant rules and values, the more smoothly society will function.

Conflict Theory

Structural functionalists see socialization as a process that helps to create solidarity and cohesion. However, some sociologists argue that this perspective takes a rather rosy picture of how individuals are socialized into society. They claim that socialization is not always a harmonious process and that fitting into society as it is might not be such a great thing, given the inequality and social problems that exist. **Conflict theory** sees society and socialization in a very different way: Instead of focusing on cohesion as the foundation of society, conflict theorists suggest that human behavior and social relations result from the underlying conflicts that exist between competing groups. Conflict theory was developed by Karl Marx, who understood society as being based on the conflict between social classes—particularly the clash between individuals who own the means of production (capitalists) and those who do not (workers). We will learn more about Marx in Chapter 4, where we discuss social class and status. A common theme in this perspective is that some individuals and groups have more power than others and that the struggle over power is a key element of social life.

Many later sociologists have extended Marx's theory and applied it to conflicts based on social differences beyond class. For example, feminist sociologists focus on gender relations. Feminist theorists argue that, in virtually every society, men (and things associated with men), are held in higher regard than women (Seidman, 2008). And, as a group with social power, men have an interest in maintaining their social privilege over women (Seidman, 2008). In general, feminist theory focuses on **patriarchy**, the system of male domination in society. Feminist theorists argue that patriarchy is at least as important as class inequality in determining a person's power in life. We will learn more about feminist theory, and the different strains of this theory, in Chapter 6 on gender.

It is not surprising that the founding figures of sociology were male. This reflects the fact that sociology as a discipline emerged in a time when women were not able to attend higher education and were expected to focus on family roles instead of on work outside the home. Because of this, feminist scholars argue that sociology has traditionally been organized around men—their experiences and their positions (Seidman, 2008). Men have been both the subjects and the authors of sociology and the experiences of women have been (largely) ignored until recently (D. Smith, 1987). Despite their underrepresentation, there have been a few trailblazing women active in early sociology. Harriet Martineau and Jane Addams were important early female sociologists who were introduced in Chapter 1 of this book.

Both conflict theorists and structural functionalists agree that socialization helps to re-create society as it is now. But whereas structural functionalists see this re-creation as positive, conflict theorists see it as negative. Conflict theorists tend to focus on questions such as, Who has the power to shape how individuals are socialized? How does socializing people to fit into society as it is benefit some groups over others? How does socialization help or hinder social inequality?

Melvin Kohn's (1959) classic study of parental socialization and social class illustrates how conflict theorists might think about socialization. Kohn examined how parental social class shapes the values that parents encourage in their children. He argues that, although most parents agree that children should be taught a general set of values, parents' opinions on the most important values to teach children are shaped by their social class.

Kohn (1959) interviewed 400 families—half from the working class and half from the middle class. He found significant differences when comparing the values emphasized by the mothers from these two groups. Middle-class mothers were more likely to focus on the importance of internal feelings and self-direction. For example, they tended to value empathy, happiness, self-control, and curiosity for both their sons and their daughters. Working-class mothers, however, were more likely to emphasize the importance of values that lead to conformity among their children. For example, neatness and obedience were much more likely to be highly valued by working-class mothers than by middle-class mothers. Working-class mothers also had very different expectations for boys and girls. For boys, they valued school performance and ambition highly; for girls, they tended to emphasize the importance of neatness and good manners.

How do these findings affect our understanding of socialization? A conflict theorist would highlight how the different values could reinforce the preexisting inequality between these two social classes. Valuing curiosity and happiness instead of conformity and obedience has real implications for the types of jobs that these children will be prepared to do. Most professional jobs require ambition and curiosity and could not be done well by someone who is merely obedient. The working-class mothers also perpetuate gender inequality by encouraging their sons to perform well in school and their daughters to be polite. These different traits could certainly lead to different career outcomes for boys and girls.

Symbolic Interactionism

Like structural functionalists, conflict theorists tend to think of socialization as mostly a top-down process. Some sociologists argue, however, that children also learn from one another and from their shared experiences. For example, kids on the playground learn songs and games from one another. Symbolic interactionism examines how socialization is negotiated through our connections with other people. Instead of seeing people as receptacles of socialization (as, some might say, structural functionalists and conflict theorists do), symbolic interactionists claim that we actively participate in our socialization. Furthermore, this group of sociologists does not believe that meanings naturally attach to things. Herbert Blumer (1969) elaborated on this theory in *Symbolic Interactionism: Perspectives and Methods*. In this book, he explains that symbolic interactionism contains three basic premises: humans act toward things based on the meanings they assign to them, the meaning of things is derived or arises from social interactions between people, and individuals use an interpretative process to understand and modify meanings.

Socialization not only teaches us how to interact with one another, but it also helps us develop a sense of self. In fact, sociologists believe that even something as personal as our identity and sense of self comes from others. Our own name and our nicknames are given to us by others; we think of ourselves with words and categories used and created by others; and our identity is assembled and constructed from the reactions of others. Symbolic interactionists are particularly interested in how we develop a sense of self through socialization.

Two important symbolic interactionists who were interested in socialization and the development of self were George Herbert Mead and Charles Horton Cooley. Mead (1934) argued that children develop their sense of self through four stages of role-taking. In the first, or preparatory stage, children learn to use language and other symbols by imitating the significant others in their lives. Significant others are key individuals—primarily parents and, to a lesser degree, older siblings and close friends—on whom young children model themselves. Children in this stage simply copy other people's actions or behaviors. For example, when you smile at a baby, she will often smile back. Babies do not necessarily understand what you are doing or why; they simply imitate your actions. They also mimic their parents by wanting to hold the objects they see their parents using, such as keys or a phone, even though they do not understand how to use such items.

The second stage, in which children pretend to be other people, is called the role-taking stage. Children engage in role-playing games. For example, many children like to play house by performing the role of mother or father. In these roles, they might cook, clean, or care for "children" (dolls).

By about 7 years of age, children move into the third stage, the game stage. Games are different from play because they involve complex rules and require children to take the role of several other people simultaneously. For example, if you are a pitcher in a baseball game, you need to think about what you are doing while simultaneously understanding what the batter, the shortstop, and the catcher are supposed to do. You also have to remember all the rules of the game, such as when a player is allowed to run from base to base, when a player is out, and when an inning is over. Understanding all these roles and rules at once is quite complicated.

What is the child emulating? Where might he have learned this behavior? What other mimicking behaviors have you noticed among small children?

iStockPhoto.com/Anchiy

The COVID-19 pandemic changed social interactions, such as the expectation that people maintain a distance of 6 feet from others when socializing out in public. These ways of interacting seemed very strange at the start of the pandemic but became an accepted "new normal" over time.

iStockPhoto.com/Kirkikis

The final stage involves taking the role of the generalized other. Children in this stage can think of how they generally appear to other people instead of how they appear to one specific significant other, such as a parent or sibling. Do people tend to think of you as shy, smart, or funny? Understanding how a generalized other will think of you requires that you be able to take the perspective of people you may not know well or at all.

Through all these stages, individuals learn about themselves and the society in which they live. This development is not a simple matter of learning a list of rules. Instead, children interact with other people to understand the roles that these other people play, their own roles, and how they should fit into relationships with others. They must negotiate how they see themselves and their place in society through interacting with other people.

Making Sense of COVID-19: Applying the Core Theories

One of the challenges of sociology is seeing social phenomena from different theoretical perspectives. Think of theories as lenses. If you put on sunglasses with purple lenses, the world looks purple. If you change to a pair with green lenses, the same world looks green. When you look at an issue through a structural functionalist lens, you will see it in a different way from the way you would if you were looking through a lens of conflict theory, symbolic interactionism, or feminist theory. For example, the theories would understand the COVID-19 pandemic very differently.

Structural functionalists focus on the role of structures in society and the functions that they serve. These theorists might be particularly interested in the role that major institutions of our society, such as the government, the media, and business, have played in helping us navigate the crisis. Governments, in particular, helped to maintain social order in these changing times by regulating the type and number of social contacts we could have. They also worked to maintain feelings of calm by having press conferences, often at the same time each day, to give us information about the spread of COVID-19 and policies they enacted to help deal with some of the social harms this pandemic caused, such as unemployment and mental health issues. Structural functionalists focus on the ways that we create and maintain social order and consensus, even in times of social change.

Although structural functionalists help us to understand the important role of different structures of society and the ways that they foster cohesion, this theory misses certain things. Conflict theory would offer a different perspective on COVID-19 by focusing on how COVID-19 is rooted in conflict, power, and inequality. What types of people were most likely to become infected by this virus? This is related to larger inequalities that come from class, race, gender, and other dimensions. For example, some people, because of their social class and type of job, were able to work or attend school from home and reduce their risk of being infected by COVID-19. Others, such as grocery store workers, a job with low pay and low status, were not able to work from home, leaving them at higher risk of illness. Conflict theorists might also consider who is most likely to have access to vaccines. For example, why are vaccines more available in richer countries than developing nations?

Feminist theorists would focus on the gendered dimensions of COVID-19. Some recent research has argued that the pandemic resulted in a "she-cession" because women tend to work in industries hit hardest by the pandemic, such as hospitality and food service, retail, education, and health care (Deschamps, 2020). Feminist theorists would examine the effect of the pandemic by gender, focusing on how women may have experienced it differently because of their often larger role in caring for children (who were at home from school) and caring for the elderly (who may have needed additional assistance while in lockdown). Feminist theorists are also interested in how gender might intersect with other types of inequality, such as racial disparities in COVID-19 rates and mortality.

Symbolic interactionists would ask still different questions. These theorists are focused on the interactions that make up social life and the role of symbols. They might examine how COVID-19 has changed dating practices, how people managed social isolation during periods of lockdown, and how rules for social contact affected the way people socialized.

Although these theories are presented as distinct and separate, sociological work often incorporates multiple theories when trying to understand the social world. The best way to understand the social world is to bring these different insights together to make sense of social issues.

Agents of Socialization

Mead's (1934) theory highlights the importance of significant and generalized others in the process of socialization. Other theorists call these various groups of people agents of socialization because they guide us through the process of becoming a member of society and help to shape the people we become. There are many different agents of socialization, but we tend to consider family, peer groups, the education system, mass media, and religion to be the most important. Each of these groups teaches us how we are supposed to behave as adults, to perform different roles, and to function effectively within society and social groups. We sometimes learn from agents of socialization through direct teaching, such as when we learn math or reading in school. However, much socialization takes the form of latent learning, which occurs when we imitate role models, such as the people we see in the media.

Charles Horton Cooley (1902) said that our sense of self is assembled and constructed from the reactions of others. He called this process the looking-glass self. When we look at other people, they act as a mirror that helps us to understand how we appear. In other words, we look to others to better understand who we are.

The idea behind Cooley's theory is that we refine our sense of self in light of other's reactions. In fact, we develop a self-image based on the messages we get from others (as we understand them). This development occurs in three main steps: we imagine how others see us, we imagine how others judge our appearance, and we refine our appearance based on how we interpret such judgments. In other words, our understanding about who we are depends largely on how we see ourselves evaluated by others. Just as we see our physical body reflected in a mirror, we also see our social selves reflected in other people's reactions to us.

It is easy to see how this process might become problematic. Consider a person with an eating disorder. Although this person might be a normal and healthy body weight, she might see herself as overweight and might think that others also see her in this way, even when they do not. Other people are clearly valuable sources of information for us, but we are not always good at reading what they think about us. For example, when people laugh after we say something, we cannot always tell if they are ridiculing us or if they think we just told a funny joke. As a result, we could respond to a false impression of how we appear to others. In addition, it is usually not a good idea to let other people's opinions of us shape how we feel about ourselves.

Cooley's (1902) concept of the looking-glass self has all the key components of the symbolic interactionist perspective. It focuses on how meanings are not naturally attached to things.

It is only through interacting with other people that we are able to attach meanings to things and experiences within society. In addition, this theory is based on the idea that we learn about ourselves through interacting with others in society.

Primary Socialization

Socialization is a lifelong process. In its earliest stage, called **primary socialization**, we learn how to become a member of society by discovering the attitudes, values, and actions that are culturally and socially appropriate. It helps to think of primary socialization as the process by which individuals learn the unwritten rules of a society, such as how to have a conversation. Family members are very important in this primary socialization because they are the first people we encounter in our lives.

Much of what we learn at this stage is not explicitly taught. Instead, it is learned through observation and imitation. For example, no one specifically tells us how far we should stand from other people when we talk with them. We learn this information by observing how our parents and other adults engage in conversations. We might not even be able to say the specific acceptable distance between conversation partners—is it 20 or 30 inches? But we can definitely tell if someone is standing too close or too far away. People who stand too close seem aggressive and rude. People who stand too far away seem uninterested and snobbish. Primary socialization teaches us unwritten rules like these.

Secondary Socialization

Next, we go through **secondary socialization**, in which we learn the appropriate behaviors and attitudes of a subculture within our larger society. For example, secondary socialization could occur when people join a soccer team. When they join this smaller group, they cannot simply apply the rules they learned in primary socialization. They certainly could not seek the kind of nurturing relationship they have with their parents from their team members. Along with having to alter their behavior to fit into this new group, they also need to learn new behaviors that will mark them as a member of the group. For example, they learn how to interact with teammates, do team cheers, wear the uniform, and playfully trash talk the other team. The main difference between primary and secondary socialization is one of scale. Primary socialization refers to the process of becoming a member of larger society, while secondary socialization refers to the process of socializing someone to be a member of a *smaller* group within that society.

Primary and secondary socialization usually occur during the early years of an individual's life. However, as we age, we learn to play new roles. Two types of socialization that occur later in life, when life changes such as entering a new profession or family situation require people to incorporate new roles, are anticipatory socialization and resocialization.

Anticipatory Socialization

Anticipatory socialization refers to the process by which individuals rehearse potential roles that they may expect to take on in the future, such as the role of mother or father, or a new position at work. We can see this in Mead's (1934) theory of the development of the self: Children play at being parents to rehearse for a role they might later perform. We continue to rehearse roles later in life. For example, medical students often practice interacting with patients to learn good bedside manner. Anticipatory socialization gives us a chance to prepare for a new role before we even begin to play it in real life. This way, we are ready for all the behaviors and responsibilities that the role will entail before we are expected to perform it.

Resocialization

People are also sometimes resocialized, whereby they take on new roles and discard former behaviors, attitudes, and values. In **resocialization,** we do not just add a new role to all the other roles we play: We replace an old role with a new one. For example, adults who retire face the prospect of resocialization when they discard their former patterns of working and the identity attached to their occupation and take on the new role of a retiree. Resocialization is sometimes a voluntary process, such as when a person has a religious conversion, emigrates to a new country, or joins the military. Other times individuals are forced to change roles. Involuntary resocialization can include role changes such as leaving prison, being fired, or being forced to enter a rehab facility. A person does not have a choice about whether to enter or leave prison, but he must discard the prisoner role for a new one when he completes his sentence.

The process of resocialization can be difficult, but many things can ease this transition. For example, ex-convicts sometimes live in halfway houses after they leave prison. Instead of having to manage on their own, they are assisted with reintegrating into society by having a structure that helps them to find work, reestablish an independent routine, and organize their time. They replace their old role as a prisoner with a new role as a free member of society.

Helen Rose Fuchs Ebaugh (1988) both experienced and wrote about resocialization. Ebaugh was a Catholic nun who left the order and married later in life. This major transformation led her to think more critically about how people generally transition from one role to another. She argues that changing roles is a common experience in modern society. In earlier societies individuals often spent their whole lives in the same town with one partner, one job, and a very limited set of experiences. Today, people move from city to city, change jobs, partner and then re-partner, and experience a multitude of other social role changes. To understand these changes, Ebaugh interviewed 185 people who were experiencing a wide range of social transformations, such as leaving jail, divorcing, leaving jobs as police officers or doctors, retiring, and evolving sexual identity. Her research illustrated common stages of what she calls the "role exit process." Individuals move from being disillusioned with a particular identity to searching for alternative roles, experiencing a turning point that triggers their decision to exit a past role, and, finally, creating an identity as an "ex." Think about what it means to become an ex-girlfriend or boyfriend. This requires that you shed your old identity (as one half of a couple) and embrace a new role of being an ex. How do we expect exes to act? Will they be happy to see their past partners move on or do we expect that they will be jealous and bitter? The ex role in this context is clearly defined and shapes how people expect you to behave when you leave a relationship. This is why the public is often so skeptical of celebrities who "consciously uncouple" and remain friends after a divorce. They are challenging our taken-for-granted conceptions of what the role of an ex is in this context.

USING YOUR SOCIOLOGICAL IMAGINATION
HOW DO TOYS SOCIALIZE US?

Even things as innocuous as toys are important parts of socialization. You have probably noticed that many children play with gender-specific toys. Playing with dolls, action figures, or other gendered toys is part of how children become socialized into their gender roles. Gender (ideas of femininity and masculinity) are learned. Gender socialization is the process of learning how to behave in a way that is consistent with the gender rules and norms of your society. The play that we engage in as children is an important part of our learning to act in ways that our society deems appropriately masculine or feminine.

For example, playing with Barbies or Disney princesses and superheroes or action figures teaches children something about what a boy or girl should be like in society. Think about what you do with a Barbie or other doll: Usually, you simply dress her up, change her hair, and buy her accessories, such as cars and dream houses. This play reinforces the idea that physical appearance is very important for women and that material goods can help them define and demonstrate who they are. Even the newer versions of Barbie, including Doctor Barbie and Astronaut Barbie, are only distinguishable from the original by clothing and accessories. Apparently, all it takes to be a doctor is a nice lab coat and a stethoscope! Other examples of gendered toys you might have played with include Bratz dolls, Easy Bake Ovens, Cabbage Patch dolls, or My Little Ponies.

What types of clothes do we sell to boys and girls? Girls' shirts often say "Princess," "Smile," and "Happy," and are pink, like the t-shirt of the girl shown here. Boys' shirts often have images of cars or superheroes and are blue, like the shirt of the boy. How do these clothes reinforce ideas of gender in society?

Daniel Dempster Photography / Alamy Stock Photo

What about G.I. Joe, the "real American hero," or superhero figures? Do you dress him and change his hair, as you do with Barbie? No—you cannot even change G.I. Joe's or a superhero's outfit because it is painted on. Instead, these action figures fight with one another, reinforcing the idea that men should be aggressive and strong and that they become heroes by being violent and physically powerful. It is important to note that there is much discussion about Barbie's physical shape being an unrealistic ideal for women (which is certainly true) but little discussion of action figures' physicality, which is also unrealistic (unless you have no neck and an upper body like an upside-down triangle). Toys like Teenage Mutant Ninja Turtles or toy guns also emphasize these sorts of traits for boys.

To see what toys today's children play with, visit websites such as Walmart or Target and then answer the following questions:

1. What are these toys teaching?
2. Are boys and girls encouraged to play with different types of toys? What might be the impact of such encouragement?
3. Do toys that were traditionally gender neutral (such as LEGO) now seem gendered? If so, how?

Socialization in general, and gender socialization in particular, starts very young. However, we are taught and retaught how to act according to our gender throughout our lives. Think about the bath products that you use. Deodorant, shampoo, and razors are the same across brands, but they are marketed to and priced for men and women very differently. Using the following websites as starting points, explore the Internet and your local drugstore to look at these different products and their advertisements.

Product	Men	Women
Deodorant	Old Spice (www.oldspice.com/en)	Secret (www.secret.com)
Shampoo	American Crew (www.americancrew.com)	Herbal Essences (www.herbalessences.com)
Razors	Gillette (www.gillette.com)	Schick Quattro (https://www.schick.com/pages/womens-landing-page)

Now answer these questions:

1. How are these products marketed to men and women differently?
2. What could these products and advertisements be teaching us about the ways women and men should act?
3. What products, if any, did you find that do not follow gender stereotypes?

Methods in Depth: The Socialization of Women in the Hate Movement

Racist activism and White supremacy have a long history in the United States. However, it is not just an historical issue. The Southern Poverty Law Center (2021) estimates that there are 733 racist groups currently operating in the United States and that racist groups are present in all states. The White supremacist marches in Charlottesville and other cities in 2017 illustrate the salience of these issues.

Research Question

How do people become involved in these groups? Kathleen Blee argues that people are not born racist, but that they *learn* racism in racist groups. In this way, these groups socialize members into racist attitudes, behaviors, and social networks. Blee argues that the only way we can confront and disempower organized racism is by understanding how people become a part of it, how it keeps them involved over time, and why (some) people leave.

Methods

Blee's book, *Inside Organized Racism* (2003), is a multimethod analysis of women in the racist movement. She conducted participant observation of racist group events, analyzed documents produced by racist groups, and interviewed 34 women who were active members of racist groups in the United States. This mixed-methods approach allowed Blee to understand how women get involved in the movement and how participating in it can impact these women.

Challenges

One of the most complicated parts of the study was finding women to interview. Organized racism is a challenging group to study because many people who are involved in it do not publicize their engagement. There is no list of members in racist groups that we could access to send out a survey. So, how do we contact members of racist groups and learn about their experiences? Blee began by collecting and reading all magazines, newsletters, websites, and other sources from self-proclaimed racist, anti-Semitic, White supremacist, and other racist groups. She then selected groups from this list. Once she had the smaller sample of groups, she sought to contact women within the groups who identified as racist activists. This is difficult because these women did not have their names written on group documents and tend to be highly suspicious of outsiders. Blee contacted women through either a first contact in the group (a method known as snowball sampling) or through intermediaries (such as parole officers, reporters, attorneys, and others).

This study focuses on women racist activists (instead of racist activists more generally). Blee explains that there were both theoretical and methodological reasons for this decision. Statistically, women are the fastest growing part of the racist movement. Although they had historically been quite a small part of the movement, they now account for up to 50% of new recruits (Blee, 2003). And, most studies about racist activists focus on men (who still make up most of the movement). This means that women are both critically important to study as a growing part of the movement and, so far, not well understood. In addition, Blee highlights a critical methodical reason for focusing on women. As Blee notes in the book, male racist activists would have been much more difficult for her to interview. As she explains, "the intense and conflicting feelings that male racists hold about women, especially women professionals and women outside the racist movement" undermined her ability to contact and interview male activists (p. 204). This highlights the importance of considering one's own position in conducting research—how one's gender, ethnicity, social class, sexuality, or other characteristics shape the research process.

Ethical Issues

A critical ethical issue that arises in studies such as Blee's work on racist women is how to engage with a group with whom you strongly disagree. Usually rapport is key to conducting interview and participant observation research. It is critical for those we study to feel comfortable and understood by the researcher. However, the importance of rapport is based on research with groups with whom we are sympathetic. Blee is careful to note in her book that she was always clear with the women she studied that she did not agree with their racist convictions and that her own views were opposed to theirs. However, she did tell them that she would endeavor to depict them accurately.

Another issue in the study of groups such as White supremacists is the concern that this research would unintentionally give a platform to racist propaganda. Blee highlights how, on the one hand, she wants to describe these groups accurately because it is only through understanding these groups that we can determine how to deal with them and, hopefully, reduce their appeal to certain people. On the other hand, she did not want to create celebrities or icons for the movement. She decided that she would obscure biographical details of the women and their groups, even when they wanted them to be made public, in an attempt not to draw new members or attention to their work. Blee's work on women in racist movements is an innovative and important study of socialization that highlights some of the difficult ethical and methodological issues that come up when researching unsympathetic groups.

AGING AND SOCIALIZATION

As we have discussed, the process of learning how to become a member of society and developing an identity is shaped by the society in which we live. Although it may seem as if growing up is just a natural biological process that remains unchanged over time, the culture and institutions of our society shape this process. The sociological study of aging focuses on both the social aspects of how individuals age and concerns with the general aging of the population. The experience of aging, and moving through the life course, depends on social factors such as changes in public policies and programs, overarching cultural values, and norms. In addition, our understanding of the aging process, and its different stages, has changed over time.

One way that our cultural understanding of aging has changed is in the concept of childhood as a life stage. The historian Steven Mintz (2004) explains that, prior to the 18th century, there was no idea of childhood as a separate period of life— children were just small adults-in-waiting. By the middle of the century, "childhood was increasingly viewed as a separate stage of life that required special care and institutions to protect it" (p. 3). For example, child labor laws emerged to protect children, as a group, from the harsh realities of working in factories. During the 19th century, the growing acceptance of this new ideal of childhood was evident among the middle class. Young people began living in the parental home for longer periods and were expected to obtain more formal schooling. This period also saw an increasing consciousness about young people's emotional and psychological development. These changes culminated in the development of the concept of adolescence around the beginning of the 20th century.

The notion of adolescence as a period between childhood and adulthood, in which young people learn about themselves and form identities, is also a historical invention. Our modern conception of adolescence is that it is a period when young people are rebellious, prone to dramatic displays, and engaging in violent and risky behavior. Think of how television shows such as *Riverdale, The Vampire Diaries, Pretty Little Liars,* or *Euphoria* depict adolescents as impulsive, tempestuous, and emotional. This period is generally thought to be a time of storm and stress for young people (Hall, 1904).

One of the first and most important scholarly works that challenged our current ideas about adolescence as a time of turmoil and stress was *Coming of Age in Samoa* (1928) by anthropologist Margaret Mead (no relation to our friend George Herbert Mead). To see if our Western understanding of adolescence was a natural and biological phenomenon or a social creation, she compared the transition to adulthood in American society with the same period in Samoan society. If young Samoans also experienced adolescence as a time of storm and stress, as Hall (1904) put it, Mead would have additional evidence that such turmoil was simply the natural experience of this period of life. However, if she found that adolescence was not such a stressful period in Samoa, it would lead us to question the assumption that young people are always dramatic, rebellious, and in search of their identity at this stage of their lives.

Margaret Mead (center) poses with two Samoan women. Through her research, Mead found that adolescent Samoan girls were free of the teen angst experienced by Westerners. Think about how teenagers are currently depicted in the Western media: Does the media tend to depict this period as one of stress and anxiety?

Library of Congress Prints and Photographs Division

Mead (1928) engaged in participant observation in three villages in Samoa. She lived in these villages and (with the help of an interpreter) interviewed 68 young women between the ages of 9 and 20. She found that, compared with Western societies, adolescence in Samoa was not a stressful time. She attributed this finding to cultural differences between Samoa and Western countries. Although Mead's book on this research was very popular and generally well received, some argued that she failed to recognize how Samoan society was changing over time, as all societies do. Instead, critics argued that she presented Samoan society as being stagnant. Despite this concern, the research highlights how something that appears natural could be a product of the culture and institutions of society.

Popular movies and television shows often focus on the struggles that young people have when transitioning to adulthood. Television shows such as *Friends, Girls,* and *Master of None* focus on the prolonged period during which young people transition into adulthood. Sociologists have long been interested in how individuals move through life stages and how larger institutions of society can shape these transitions. Frank Furstenberg and his colleagues (Furstenberg, Kennedy, McLoyd, Rumbaut, & Settersten, 2004) focus particularly on the transition to adulthood in modern society. They argue that our ideas about becoming an adult have changed and that these changes are related to larger historical transformations in society.

What does it take to be considered an adult? Do you feel like an adult? Furstenberg et al. argue that there are seven traditional markers of adulthood: completing education, attaining financial independence, working full time, being able to support a family, leaving the parental home, getting married, and having a child. With these markers in mind, a full 65% of American men and 77% of American women had reached adulthood and done all seven of these things by age 30 in 1960. By 2000, though, only 31% of men and 46% of women had completed these steps by that age (Furstenberg et al., 2004).

More-recent data show that young people are certainly staying in the family home longer than they did only 10 years ago. In 1955, 29% of Americans aged 18 to 34 lived in their parent's home. By 2020 a full 52% lived with their parents (Fry, Passel, and Cohn, 2020; see Figure 2.1). Comparing childbearing across time also shows that the transition to adulthood is being delayed (see Figure 2.2). In 1976, 69% of women were mothers by the age of 29. By 2014, only 50% of women had given birth to their first child by that age (see Figure 2.2).

FIGURE 2.1 ■ Young Adults Living at Home, 1900–2020

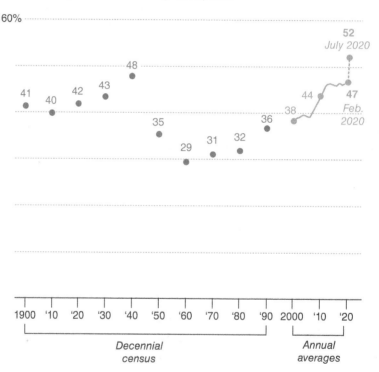

Share of young adults living with parents rises to levels not seen since the Great Depression era

% of 18- to 29-year olds in U.S. living with a parent

Note: "Living with a parent" refers to those who are residing with at least one parent in the household. 1900–1990 shares based on household population.

Source: Pew Research Center analysis of decennial census 1900-1990; Current Population Survey annual averages 2000-2019; 2020 Current Population Survey monthly files (IPUMS). https://www.pewresearch.org/wp-content/uploads/2020/09/ft_2020.09.04_livingwithparents_02.png

It is important to note, however, that our idea of adulthood and what it takes to be considered an adult has changed over time. Although marriage and children were critical markers of adulthood in the 1950s, particularly for women, they are no longer seen this same way. In fact, Furstenberg et al. (2004) found that only slightly more than half of Americans still see marriage and having children as important parts of what makes someone an adult. Markers such as

FIGURE 2.2 ■ Women and Childbirth

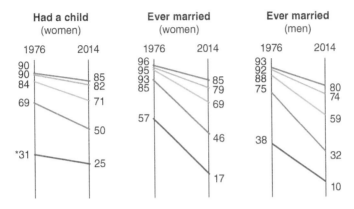

Adults who have ever had a child or married: percentage change from 1976 to 2014

Age —20 to 24 — 25 to 29 —30 to 34 —35 to 39 —40 to 44

Had a child
(women)

1976	2014
90	
90	85
84	82
69	71
	50
*31	25

Ever married
(women)

1976	2014
96	
95	
93	85
85	79
	69
57	46
	17

Ever married
(men)

1976	2014
93	
92	
88	80
75	74
	59
38	32
	10

* 18 to 24 years old for the 1976 data on having had a child.

Source: U.S. Census Bureau, 1976 and 2014 Current Population Survey Annual Social and Economic Supplement for ever married; 1976 and 2014 Current Population Survey, June Supplement for fertility. https://www.census.gov/content/dam/Census/library/publications/2017/demo/p20-579.pdf

moving out of the parental home, completing education, and getting a job remain important components of how we see adulthood in contemporary society, but these transitions are increasingly difficult for individuals to achieve and take longer for them to complete.

Why does the transition to adulthood take longer today than it did in the past? It is easy to argue that this results from the different character of young people today—sometimes people say that young people are simply not working hard enough or are entitled. These explanations see the problem of delayed adulthood as a personal trouble that young people face in modern times. Remember that C. Wright Mills saw personal troubles as problems that affect individuals. However, this delayed adulthood is also a public issue, a problem that exists on a social level and has social causes. For example, programs that helped young people who fought in World War II to attend university, which were discussed in Chapter 1, made college more affordable for a whole cohort of young people. Higher tuition and expenses associated with going to college and the increased cost of housing make it more difficult for young people to become financially independent today. Finally, it takes longer to complete education and secure a full-time, good paying job than it did in the past. For all these reasons, it is simply not true that young people today are at fault for having trouble making a smooth transition to adulthood. Instead, the larger social structure is creating more barriers to this transition and there are fewer programs to assist young people in overcoming barriers.

As stated earlier, aging research is centrally concerned with different phases of the life course and changes in our understanding of these phases. This research also examines the aging of the population and the implications of this aging for society. American society is aging. The U.S. Census Bureau finds that in 2020, for the first time in history, there were more people aged 65 and older than there were children under age 5 (see Figure 2.3).

The fastest growing age group in the United States is seniors. This trend is expected to continue for the next several decades, mainly due to low fertility rates and increasing life

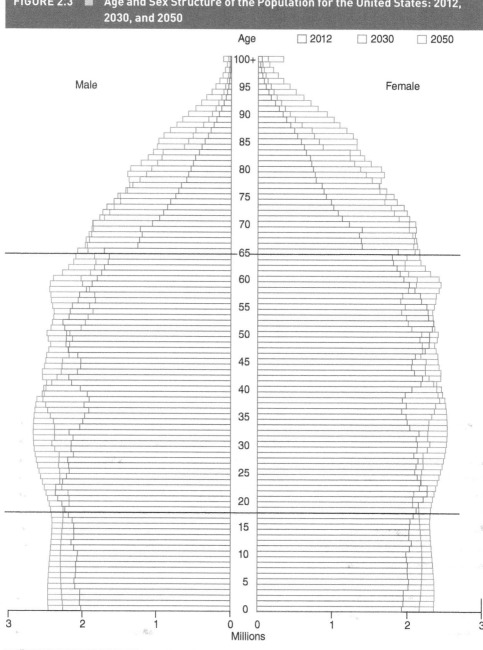

FIGURE 2.3 ■ Age and Sex Structure of the Population for the United States: 2012, 2030, and 2050

Source: US Census Bureau. (2012). *2012 Population Estimates and 2012 National Projections.* https://www.census.gov/data/tables/2012/demo/popproj/2012-summary-tables.html

expectancies. Figure 2.4 shows the age structure of the U.S. population for selected years, and that the percentage of people under the age of 18 is decreasing while the percentage of people in the over-65 age categories is increasing. This data predicts the percentage of the population over the age of 65 and shows that, by 2030, one in five Americans will be a senior. At this time, there will be roughly the same number of seniors as young people under age 18 in the United States. The number of seniors will more than double between 2014 and 2060 (Mather, Jacobsen, & Pollard, 2015).

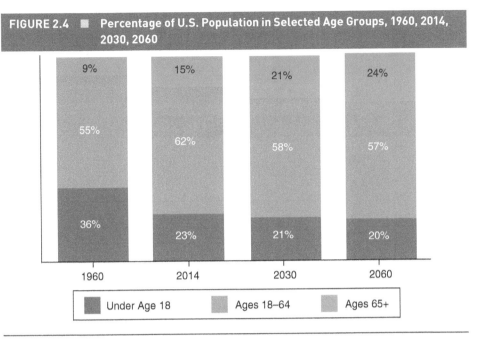

FIGURE 2.4 ■ Percentage of U.S. Population in Selected Age Groups, 1960, 2014, 2030, 2060

Note: Numbers may not sum to 100 due to rounding.

Source: Mather, Mark et al. "Aging in the United States." *Population Bulletin*, Vol. 70, No. 2, December 2015. Population Reference Bureau.

The aging of the population has serious social and economic implications. The growth of the senior portion of the population will have a serious impact on Social Security and Medicare, programs specifically targeted at seniors. For example, Social Security and Medicare will each account for 6% of the GDP by 2050 (see Figure 2.5). With the increased size of the over-65 group, there will also be a decreased proportion of working-age individuals to support social

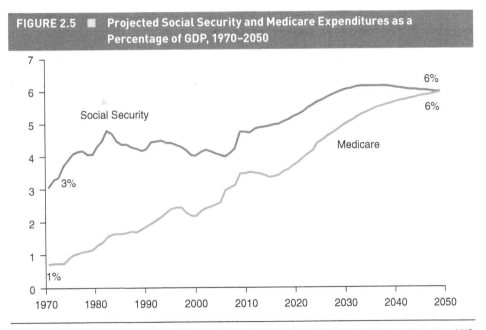

FIGURE 2.5 ■ Projected Social Security and Medicare Expenditures as a Percentage of GDP, 1970–2050

Source: Mather, Mark et al. "Aging in the United States." Population Bulletin, Vol. 70, No. 2, December 2015. Population Reference Bureau.

services. As Figure 2.6 shows, in 1900 there were 13.6 working-age persons for each senior. This number decreased to 4.3 working-age persons per senior in 2014 and is projected to decline further to 2.4 by 2060. This means that there are fewer working-age people paying taxes to support social programs in general, including those for seniors such as Social Security and Medicare (see Figures 2.5 and 2.6).

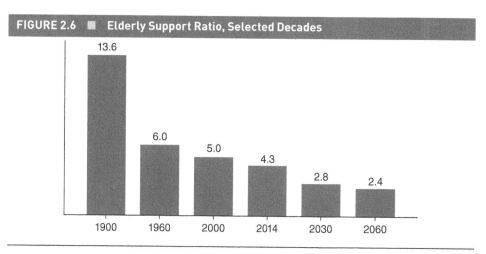

FIGURE 2.6 ■ Elderly Support Ratio, Selected Decades

Note: Elderly support ratio is the number of persons aged 18 to 64 for every person aged 65 or older.

Source: Mather, Mark et al. "Aging in the United States." *Population Bulletin*, Vol. 70, No. 2, December 2015. Population Reference Bureau.

THE PERFORMANCE OF SOCIAL ROLES

An important part of socialization is the process of learning to perform roles. Shakespeare thought a lot about how people play roles in society. In *As You Like It,* he wrote, "All the world's a stage, And all the men and women merely players." Canadian sociologist Erving Goffman (1922–1982) shared this view when he created the dramaturgical perspective, seeing social life as a stage and individuals as actors portraying roles.

Goffman is considered one of the most influential sociologists of the 20th century. He believed that when we meet others, we work to influence their impression of us (Goffman, 1959): We want to manage the impression that we give to others. We can do this by changing our setting or appearance, perhaps selecting our clothing to give off a certain impression. And, this process is iterative: While we try to shape our conversation partner's impression of us, she tries to form the most accurate impression possible. Like other symbolic interactionists, Goffman was interested in how individuals interact with others to create an impression and to gauge the impressions given by others.

Getting to Know: Erving Goffman (1922–1982)

- Erving earned the nickname "the little dagger" from his fellow graduate students due to his constant stream of sarcasm.

- To help alleviate local suspicions that he was a spy while conducting ethnographic research on the small Scottish Island of Unst, Goffman masqueraded as an American interested in agricultural techniques.

- He was an astute stock market analyst and earned two-thirds of his income from royalties and investments.

- Goffman frequently played blackjack in Nevada, and he later trained and worked as a blackjack dealer. Eventually, he became a pit manager at Station Plaza Casino in Las Vegas, where he supervised games and financial transactions.

Goffman also believed that individuals try to smooth out social interaction to make it easier and more comfortable for everyone. To do this we constantly work to avoid embarrassing others or ourselves. For example, if someone slips and falls, we might help them up and then casually say, "The floor is a bit wet; I find it slippery too," so that they feel less embarrassed. The challenge is that the behaviors that are appropriate or least likely to cause embarrassment differ across situations. For example, it is acceptable to yell and sing loudly at a football game but probably not in class. Therefore, we must learn to tailor how we act based on the situation. We must be able to take our stage of action into account when deciding how to behave and then modify our behavior accordingly.

For example, if you have a job interview, you might practice parts of your performance in advance, thinking of how you would answer questions that might be asked. You would certainly think about your clothing and appearance because you want to look like you fit in the new workplace. If everyone wears a suit, perhaps you should too. If the interview is for a creative job, such as at an advertising agency or media company, you would perhaps choose to present a more artistic self with an interesting necklace or funky patterned socks. You manage the impression you give, and the props you use to do so, based on the social situation.

In social interaction, as in the theatre, there is a front stage where we perform. This is where actors work to make a positive impression on others. But there is also a backstage that includes the private places where individuals do not feel they are being watched, with no audience.

The concepts of front stage and backstage are easy to see in many social settings. Think about restaurant workers. How are they different when they are front stage in the restaurant (where they are serving tables for customers) versus backstage (in the kitchen or dishwashing area)? Workers tend to maintain a calm demeanor and a cheerful disposition in the front of the restaurant, while they might complain and joke around backstage. Although we often prepare for the front stage by thinking about what impression we hope to make, we are sometimes caught out of character when someone unexpectedly sees us in our backstage. For example, a customer walking past a restaurant's kitchen to get to the restroom may see the servers in their backstage, perhaps having a drink or complaining about the customers.

During the pandemic, many office workers began working from home. Where is Goffman's front stage and backstage for these workers? How has remote work blurred these boundaries?

iStockPhoto.com/SDI Productions

READING: FROM *THE PRESENTATION OF SELF IN EVERYDAY LIFE*

Erving Goffman

The following reading is from Goffman's most famous book, *The Presentation of Self in Everyday Life* (1959). In this excerpt, Goffman explains the dramaturgical model, which has been very influential in many areas of sociology. As you read the following pages, consider what this theory tells us about social interaction and socialization. How do we learn to interact with others? How is this process like the theatre?

When an individual enters the presence of others, they commonly seek to acquire information about him or to bring into play information about him already possessed. They will be interested in his general socio-economic status, his conception of self, his attitude toward them, his competence, his trustworthiness, etc. Although some of this information seems to be sought almost as an end in itself, there are usually quite practical reasons for acquiring it. Information about the individual helps to define the situation, enabling others to know in advance what he will expect of them and what they may expect of him. Informed in these ways, the others will know how best to act in order to call forth a desired response from him.

For those present, many sources of information become accessible and many carriers (or "sign-vehicles") become available for conveying this information. If unacquainted with the individual, observers can glean clues from his conduct and appearance which allow them to apply their previous experience with individuals roughly similar to the one before them or, more important, to apply untested stereotypes to him. They can also assume from past experience that only individuals of a particular kind are likely to be found in a given social setting. They can rely on what the individual says about himself or on documentary evidence he provides as to who and what he is. If they know, or know of, the individual by virtue of experience prior to the interaction, they can rely on assumptions as to the persistence and generality of psychological traits as a means of predicting his present and future behavior.

However, during the period in which the individual is in the immediate presence of the others, few events may occur which directly provide the others with the conclusive information they will need if they are to direct wisely their own activity. Many crucial facts lie beyond the time and place of interaction or lie concealed within it. For example, the "true" or "real" attitudes, beliefs, and emotions of the individual can be ascertained only indirectly, through his avowals or through what appears to be involuntary expressive behavior. . . .

The expressiveness of the individual (and therefore his capacity to give impressions) appears to involve two radically different kinds of sign activity: the expression that he *gives*, and the expression that he *gives off.* The first involves verbal symbols or their substitutes which he uses admittedly and solely to convey the information that he and the others are known to attach to these symbols. This is communication in the traditional and narrow sense. The second involves a wide range of action that others can treat as symptomatic of the actor, the expectation being that the action was performed for reasons other than the information conveyed in this way. As we shall have to see, this distinction has an only initial validity. The individual does of course intentionally convey misinformation by means of both of these types of communication, the first deceit, the second feigning. . . .

Let us now turn from the others to the point of view of the individual who presents himself before them. He may wish them to think highly of him, or to think that he thinks highly of them, or to perceive how in fact he feels toward them, or to obtain no clear-cut impression; he may wish to ensure sufficient harmony so that the interaction can be sustained, or to defraud, get rid of, confuse, mislead, antagonize, or insult them. Regardless of the particular objective which the individual has in mind and of his motive for having this objective, it will be in his interests to control the conduct of the others, especially their responsive treatment of him.[1] This control is achieved largely by influencing the definition of the situation which the others come to formulate, and he can influence this definition by expressing himself in such a way as to give them the kind of impression that will lead them to act voluntarily in accordance with his own plan. Thus, when an individual appears in the presence of others, there will usually be some reason for him to mobilize his activity so that it will convey an impression to others which it is in his interests to convey. Since a girl's dormitory mates will glean evidence of her popularity from the calls she receives on the phone, we can suspect that some girls will arrange for calls to be made, and Willard Waller's finding can be anticipated:

> It has been reported by many observers that a girl who is called to the telephone in the dormitories will often allow herself to be called several times, in order to give all the other girls ample opportunity to hear her paged.[2]

Of the two kinds of communication—expressions given and expressions given off—this report will be primarily concerned with the latter, with the more theatrical and contextual kind, the nonverbal, presumably unintentional kind, whether this communication be purposely engineered or not. As an example of what we must try to examine, I would like to cite at length a novelistic incident in which Preedy, a vacationing Englishman, makes his first appearance on the beach of his summer hotel in Spain:

> But in any case he took care to avoid catching anyone's eye. First of all, he had to make it clear to those potential companions of his holiday that they were of no concern to him whatsoever. He stared through them, round them, over them—eyes lost in space. The beach might have been empty. If by chance a ball was thrown his way, he looked surprised; then let a smile of amusement lighten his face (Kindly Preedy), looked round dazed to see that there *were* people on the beach, tossed it back with a smile to himself and not a smile *at* the people, and then resumed carelessly his nonchalant survey of space.
>
> But it was time to institute a little parade, the parade of the Ideal Preedy. By devious handlings he gave any who wanted to look a chance to see the title of his book—a Spanish translation of Homer, classic thus, but not daring, cosmopolitan too—and then gathered together his beach-wrap and bag into a neat sand-resistant pile (Methodical and Sensible Preedy), rose slowly to stretch at ease his huge frame (Big- Cat Preedy), and tossed aside his sandals (Carefree Preedy, after all).
>
> The marriage of Preedy and the sea! There were alternative rituals. The first involved the stroll that turns into a run and a dive straight into the water, thereafter smoothing into a strong splashless crawl towards the horizon. But of course not really to the horizon. Quite suddenly he would turn on to his back and thrash great white splashes with his legs, somehow thus showing that he could have swum further had he wanted to, and then would stand up a quarter out of water for all to see who it was.
>
> The alternative course was simpler, it avoided the cold-water shock and it avoided the risk of appearing too high-spirited. The point was to appear to be so used to the sea, the Mediterranean, and this particular beach, that one might as well be in the sea as out of it. It involved a slow stroll down and into the edge of the water—not even noticing his toes were wet, land and water all the same to *him*!—with his eyes up at the sky gravely surveying portents, invisible to others, of the weather (Local Fisherman Preedy).[3]

The novelist means us to see that Preedy is improperly concerned with the extensive impressions he feels his sheer bodily action is giving off to those around him. We can malign Preedy further by assuming that he has acted merely in order to give a particular impression, that this is a false impression, and that the others present receive either no impression at all, or, worse still, the impression that Preedy is affectedly trying to cause them to receive this particular impression. But the important point for us here is that the kind of impression Preedy thinks he is making is in fact the kind of impression that others correctly and incorrectly glean from someone in their midst.

There is one aspect of the others' response that bears special comment here. Knowing that the individual is likely to present himself in a light that is favorable to him, the others may divide what they witness into two parts; a part that is relatively easy for the individual to manipulate at will, being chiefly his verbal assertions, and a part in regard to which he seems to have little concern or control, being chiefly derived from the expressions he gives off. The others may then use what are considered to be the ungovernable aspects of his expressive behavior as a check upon the validity of what is conveyed by the governable aspects. In this a fundamental asymmetry is demonstrated in the communication process, the individual presumably being aware of only one stream of his communication, the witnesses of this stream and one other. For example, in Shetland Isle one crofter's wife, in serving native dishes to a visitor from the mainland of Britain, would listen with a polite smile to his polite claims of liking what he was eating; at the same time she would take note of the rather rapidity with which the visitor lifted his fork or spoon to his mouth, the eagerness with which he passed food into his mouth, and the gusto expressed in chewing the food, using these signs as a check on the stated feelings of the eater. The same woman, in order to discover what one acquaintance (A) "actually" thought of another acquaintance (B), would wait until B was in the presence of A but engaged in conversation with still another person (C). She would then covertly examine the facial expressions of A as he regarded B in conversation with Not being in conversation with B, and not being directly observed by him, A would sometimes relax usual constraints and tactful deceptions, and freely express what he was "actually" feeling about B. This Shetlander, in short, would observe the unobserved observer.

Now given the fact that others are likely to check up on the more controllable aspects of behavior by means of the less controllable, one can expect that sometimes the individual will try to exploit this very possibility, guiding the impression he makes through behavior felt to be reliably informing.[4] . . . A specific illustration may be cited from Shetland Isle. When a neighbor dropped in to have a cup of tea, he would ordinarily wear at least a hint of an expectant warm smile as he passed through the door into the cottage. Since lack of physical obstructions outside the cottage and lack of light within it usually made it possible to observe the visitor unobserved as he approached the house, islanders sometimes took pleasure in watching the visitor drop whatever expression he was manifesting and replace it with a sociable one just before reaching the door. However, some visitors, in appreciating that this examination was occurring, would blindly adopt a social face a long distance from the house, thus ensuring the projection of a constant image. . . .

In everyday life, of course, there is a clear understanding that first impressions are important. When the interaction that is initiated by "first impressions" is itself merely the initial interaction in an extended series of interactions involving the same participants, we speak of "getting off on the right foot" and feel that it is crucial that we do so. . . .

In stressing the fact that the initial definition of the situation projected by an individual tends to provide a plan for the co-operative activity that follows—in stressing this action point of view—we must not overlook the crucial fact that any projected definition of the situation also has a distinctive moral character. It is this moral character of projections that will chiefly concern us in this report. Society is organized on the principle that any individual who possesses certain social characteristics has a moral right to expect that others will value and treat him in an appropriate way. Connected with this principle is a second, namely that an individual who implicitly or explicitly signifies that he has certain social characteristics ought in fact to be what he claims he is. In consequence, when an individual projects a definition of the situation and thereby makes an implicit or explicit claim to be a person of a particular kind, he automatically exerts a moral demand upon the others, obliging them to value and treat him in the manner that persons of his kind have a right to expect. He also implicitly foregoes all claims to be things he does not appear to be[5] and hence foregoes the treatment that would be appropriate for such individuals. The others find, then, that the individual has informed them as to what is and as to what they *ought* to see as the "is."

One cannot judge the importance of definitional disruptions by the frequency with which they occur, for apparently they would occur more frequently were not constant precautions taken. We find that preventive practices are constantly employed to avoid these embarrassments and that corrective practices are constantly employed to compensate for discrediting occurrences that have not been successfully avoided. When the individual employs these strategies and tactics to protect his own projections, we may refer to them as "defensive practices"; when a participant employs them to save the definition of the situation projected by another, we speak of "protective practices" or "tact." Together, defensive and protective practices comprise the techniques employed to safeguard the impression fostered by an individual during his presence before others. It should be added that while we may be ready to see that no fostered impression would survive if defensive practices were not employed, we are less ready perhaps to see that few impressions could survive if those who received the impression did not exert tact in their reception of it.

In addition to the fact that precautions are taken to prevent disruption of projected definitions, we may also note that an intense interest in these disruptions comes to play a significant role in the social life of the group. Practical jokes and social games are played in which embarrassments which are to be taken unseriously are purposely engineered.[6] Fantasies are created in which devastating exposures occur. Anecdotes from the past—real, embroidered, or fictitious—are told and retold, detailing disruptions which occurred, almost occurred, or occurred and were admirably resolved. There seems to be no grouping which does not have a ready supply of these games, reveries, and cautionary tales, to be used as a source of humor, a catharsis for anxieties, and a sanction for inducing individuals to be modest in their claims and reasonable in their projected expectations. The individual may tell himself through dreams of getting into impossible positions. Families tell of the time a guest got his dates mixed and arrived when neither the house nor anyone in it was ready for him. Journalists tell of times when an all-too-meaningful misprint occurred, and the paper's assumption of objectivity or decorum was humorously discredited. Public servants tell of times a client ridiculously misunderstood form instructions, giving answers which implied an unanticipated and bizarre definition of the situation.[7] Seamen, whose home away from home is rigorously he-man, tell stories of coming back home and inadvertently asking mother to "pass the fucking butter."[8] Diplomats tell of the time a near-sighted queen asked a republican ambassador about the health of his king.[9]

To summarize, then, I assume that when an individual appears before others he will have many motives for trying to control the impression they receive of the situation. . . .

Notes

Here I owe much to an unpublished paper by Tom Burns of the University of Edinburgh. He presents the argument that in all interaction a basic underlying theme is the desire of each participant to guide and control the responses made by the others present. A similar argument has been advanced by Jay Haley in a recent unpublished paper, but in regard to a special kind of control, that having to do with defining the nature of the relationship of those involved in the interaction.

Willard Waller, "The Rating and Dating Complex," *American Sociological Review*, 2, 730.

William Sansom, *A Contest of Ladies* (London: Hograth, 1956), 230–31.

The widely read and rather sound writings of Stephen Potter are concerned in part with signs that can be engineered to give a shrewd observer the apparently incidental cues he needs to discover concealed virtues the gamesman does not in fact possess.

This role of the witness in limiting what it is the individual can be has been stressed by Existentialists, who see it as a basic threat to individual freedom. See Jean-Paul Sartre, *Being and Nothingness*, trans. by Hazel E. Barnes (New York: Philosophical Library, 1956].

Goffman, op. cit., pp. 319-27.

Peter Blau, "Dynamics of Bureaucracy" (PhD dissertation, Department of Sociology, Columbia University, forthcoming, University of Chicago Press), pp. 127–29.

Walter M. Beattie, Jr., "The Merchant Seaman" (unpublished MA Report, Department of Sociology, University of Chicago, 1950], p. 35.

Sir Frederick Posonby, *Recollections of Three Reigns* (London: Eyre & Spottiswoode, 1951].

Reading Questions

1. What is Goffman's distinction between expressions that one gives and expressions that one gives off? What is Goffman referring to when he uses the terms "face-to-face interaction," "projective techniques," "defensive practices," and "protective practices/tact"?

   a. Imagine you are about to visit or e-mail your professor to ask a question about an upcoming examformatted by ManiKumar minute ago you give off, how could you ensure that your professor infers that you are a smart student?

   b. Imagine you are preparing for a date that you have been looking forward to for several days. Your goal is to have fun and to ensure that your partner infers that you are a cool person. How might you accomplish this goal?

   c. Is there a difference between how you would act in each situation? Why or why not? Which is the real you?

2. Goffman seems to imply that individuals have considerable control over how others perceive them and that these perceptions are largely the result of face-to-face interactions. What are some other factors that might influence the perceptions others have of you? For example, how might power, inequalities, or history influence a person's perceptions of you?

USING YOUR SOCIOLOGICAL IMAGINATION
PERFORMING THE SELF ONLINE

People present different versions of themselves online (and in different platforms online). Is there a real self? How "real" are these depictions?

CHRIS DELMAS/AFP via Getty Images

Who are we in a social media age? Clara Dollar ponders this question in her essay "My (So Called) Instagram Life" published in the *New York Times* (2017). She describes meeting a man online and the self she displayed in this process:

> "You're like a cartoon character," he said. "Always wearing the same thing every day."
>
> He meant it as an intimate observation, the kind you can make only after spending a lot of time getting to know each other. You flip your hair to the right. You only eat ice cream out of mugs. You always wear a black leather jacket. I know you.
>
> And he did know me. Rather, he knew the caricature of me that I had created and meticulously cultivated. The me I broadcast to the world on Instagram and Facebook. The witty, creative me, always detached and never cheesy or needy.
>
> That version of me got her start online as my social media persona, but over time (and I suppose for the sake of consistency), she bled off the screen and overtook my real-life personality, too. And once you master what is essentially an onstage performance of yourself, it can be hard to break character.

Clara's story unpacks how she presents herself online and the thought that goes into this process. Is this Instagram self her real self? Or is her presentation of self offline (face to face) her real self? And what about the differences across her social media presentations—Facebook, Instagram, Twitter, TikTok? In this activity, consider how you present yourself online and how these different representations relate to Goffman's dramaturgical model.

First, take a look at your online presence. Are you on Facebook, Instagram, Twitter, TikTok, or other social media? If so, answer the following questions about yourself. If you are not on social media, find a celebrity or public figure, look at their various social media profiles, and answer the following questions about this person.

1. How do you (or your celebrity) appear online? How is this the same, or different, from how you are in real life when face to face with someone? Why might there be differences?
2. How can we use Goffman's dramaturgical model to understand the presentation of self online? What is front stage and what is backstage? How might people break character online? What are the impressions given and impressions given off online?
3. Are you (or your celebrity) different across your different profiles? Why are you consistent or different? What does this tell you about the complexity of the self?
4. Some people have fake profiles—profiles on these platforms that are not made under their real names. Why might someone create a fake profile? Does this tell us anything about their sense of self or their identity?

SUMMARY

In this chapter we have learned how socialization helps individuals become members of society. Socialization is important because it is the process of both learning the rules and norms of society and developing a sense of identity. Sociologists from different theoretical traditions look at this process in a variety of ways. Sociologists in the structural functionalist tradition, such as Durkheim and Parsons, tend to focus on how socialization helps society run smoothly and creates social cohesion. Conflict theorists, such as Marx, focus on how socialization may reinforce the inequality in society. Symbolic interactionists, such as George Herbert Mead, Cooley, and Goffman, see socialization as something that is negotiated throughout social life. Socialization is generally understood as a complicated, lifelong process that is shaped by a variety of individuals and institutions. For example, many different agents of socialization, such as the family and peer groups, help to form the people we become as adults. This process is also shaped by the culture and history of our society. Looking at the invention of adolescence and the changing transition to adulthood highlights how our understanding of the way that individuals become adults has changed.

FOR FURTHER READING

Blumer, H. (1969). *Symbolic interactionism: Perspective and method*, Prentice-Hall.

Cooley, C. H. (1902). *Human nature and the social order*, Scribner's.

Goffman, E. (1959). *The presentation of self in everyday life*, Anchor Books.

Mead, G. H. (1934). *Mind, self, and society*, University of Chicago Press.

Parsons, T. (1955). *Family, socialization, and interaction process*, Free Press.

GLOSSARY

agents of socialization

anticipatory socialization

conflict theory

dramaturgical perspective

gender socialization

looking-glass self

patriarchy

primary socialization

resocialization

roles

secondary socialization

significant others

socialization

stages of role-taking

structural functionalism

symbolic interactionism

3 DEVIANCE, LAW, AND CRIME

LEARNING OBJECTIVES

1. Define deviance and the different types of deviance in society.

2. Explain the concept of social construction and the changing social construction of deviance.

3. Discuss the different theories of why people commit crimes, and compare individual and social explanations of crime.

4. Assess how crime rates differ across social groups and the causes of those differences.

5. Explain the different reasons behind punishment in society and the different ways of understanding its use.

People tend to be interested in crime. We seek to understand why people commit mass shootings in schools, how drugs are trafficked across borders, why gangs are prevalent in some cities and not others, and how sexual assault can be addressed on college campuses. It is not surprising that these issues attract our attention—they are large-scale social problems that are difficult to explain. Sociologists have long been fascinated with why people break norms and laws. This chapter examines crime, law, and deviance and asks, Why do people commit crimes? Why do some people deviate from accepted norms of behavior, even though we are all socialized to fit in and follow the rules? How do we deal with people who have engaged in crime in our society?

WHAT IS DEVIANCE?

Deviance is any act that breaks an accepted social standard, from minor misdeeds to serious crimes. Many deviant acts break norms but are not punishable by the state. No person goes to jail for cheating on a spouse, but most people consider adultery to be contrary to an important norm of behavior (i.e., we should be faithful to our romantic partner).

It is also important to note that deviant acts are not always unusual, even though they involve breaking norms. Take the example of jaywalking. Jaywalking certainly breaks both a norm and the law (you can be fined for doing this). However, engaging in this behavior is normal; most people have, at some point, jaywalked. Perhaps you were on a quiet street in the middle of the night and darted across the road. Although doing so might be normal, it still breaks a norm of behavior and is illegal in many situations.

Deviance varies in the severity of public response, perceived harmfulness, and degree of public agreement. Severity of public response refers to the public's reaction to the act, which can range from minor disapproval, such as a scowling look, to severe punishment, such as a prison sentence. Perceived harmfulness is the amount of harm the perpetrator's behavior is thought to have inflicted. An act could be a bit offensive or could cause severe physical pain or death. The degree of public agreement is the extent to which the public agrees that the act is deviant or criminal. Acts such as smoking marijuana may be considered seriously dangerous and deviant by some but dismissed as insignificant minor deviance or not at all deviant by others. However, crimes such as sexual assault or incest are almost universally considered deviant and criminal.

Some acts of deviance are labelled as minor deviance. Acts of minor deviance are not crimes and are generally not seen as particularly harmful to society. Having a tattoo, for example, is not seen (even by your grandmother) as being particularly harmful to society; therefore, the general

In a highly publicized case called Operation Varsity Blues, federal investigators charged actress Lori Loughlin and other celebrities with fraud for bribing officials to admit their children into college. Loughlin was sentenced to two months in federal prison. When you think about criminals, do you tend to think about people such as Loughlin? Why or why not?

UPI/Alamy Stock Photo

public response will be mild. In the United States, no one is sent to jail or fined for having a tattoo. Such acts are seen as minor ways of stepping outside the norms of society.

The next level of deviant acts are lesser crimes—acts that are illegal but are not usually seen as extremely serious violations of social norms. For example, petty theft and speeding are both illegal, but committing these crimes does not tend to carry serious social or legal consequences. Many people have stolen something small when they were children. You probably do not think that someone who stole a candy bar when she was 8 years old is a bad person, even though theft is bad behavior and is illegal. At some point, most people have also driven faster than the legal speed limit and many people have been punished for this act in the form of a speeding ticket. Speeding is illegal; however, this crime's perceived harmfulness and severity of public response is moderate—you certainly get a ticket if you are caught, but you will not be sent to jail or judged harshly by others.

The final category of deviant acts is called consensus crimes. Acts in this group are illegal, perceived to be very harmful to society, and have a high level of public agreement regarding their seriousness. Murder and sexual assault are typically categorized as consensus crimes. They are seen as extremely harmful to society, and most individuals agree that they are very wrong. These crimes carry severe punishments, ranging from long prison sentences to (in some states or countries) capital punishment (legally authorized execution).

One form of deviance that has high social costs and a negative impact on society is white-collar crime. This type of crime often occurs in a work setting and is motivated by monetary gain; it does not involve intentional or direct acts of violence. White-collar crime can be small in scale, such as stealing post-it notes from one's workplace. However, there are also more serious acts, such as those that sparked the 2008 housing market crisis in the United States. White-collar crime is discussed less often and involves less stigma than other types of crimes, even though it has serious social costs. Conflict theorists argue that the reason why these crimes are considered to be less serious is that white-collar criminals usually have more social and economic power and can thus avoid punishments or even prosecution.

SOCIAL CONSTRUCTION

The theory of social construction was developed by Peter L. Berger and Thomas Luckmann (1966). In *The Social Construction of Reality*, they argue that all knowledge is created and maintained by social interactions. When we interact with other people, we reinforce our common knowledge of reality, as well as our understanding of how society is and should be. In this interaction, we also shape each other's definition of the situation.

These ideas might sound familiar. Social construction is based on the symbolic interactionist perspective, discussed in Chapter 2. Remember that the main basis of symbolic interactionist theory is that meanings do not naturally attach to things; we derive meaning and understand our society and our role in it through interacting with other people. Just like the symbolic interactionists Cooley and Mead, Berger and Luckmann argue that we internalize a predefined world. We learn about this world through the process of socialization and interaction with socializing agents, such as our parents and friends.

Berger and Luckmann (1966) explain that social construction is a two-step process. First, people categorize experiences, then act on the basis of this information. Second, they forget the social origins of categories and classifications, seeing them as natural and unchanging. For example, different societies have arbitrarily categorized time in different ways throughout history—from 3- to 19-day weeks. Once we divided time into a 7-day week, as we have in our society, we set up practices such as market days and religious days that function within this configuration. These days become routine as we set up our lives around them—for instance, many of us do not work on the weekends. We have forgotten that the 7-day week is a somewhat random social creation that could be organized in another way. Instead, we see it as a natural and unchangeable way of doing things.

Norms and the Social Construction of Deviance

Our ideas about deviance are socially constructed. Norms are social expectations that guide behavior. The norms we define as important in our society evolve and are different across cultures. Because these norms are always changing, there is nothing natural about what we consider deviant (or even criminal).

For example, in the United States and other countries, attitudes toward the lesbian, gay, bisexual, transgender, or queer/questioning (LGBTQ) community are becoming increasingly tolerant, with laws legalizing same-sex marriage, adoption, and other spousal rights and benefits for gay couples. Sexual activity between consenting persons of the same sex has been legal nationwide in the United States since 2003 (which is relatively recent). By 2015, only 12 years later, all states recognized and licensed marriages between same-sex couples. Despite this legislation, however, there is no federal law in the United States that outlaws discrimination against LGBTQ people. This leaves some people, in some states, without protection from discrimination in employment, housing, and other services based on their sexual orientation and/or gender identity. Furthermore, many countries still consider engaging in homosexual activity highly deviant and punish this behavior with the death penalty (see Figure 3.1). The changing norms around sexuality and gender identity in the United States and around the world illustrate the socially constructed nature of categories and how this can change over time.

FIGURE 3.1 ■ Laws on Criminalization of Homosexuality and Legalization of Gay Marriage by Country, 2020

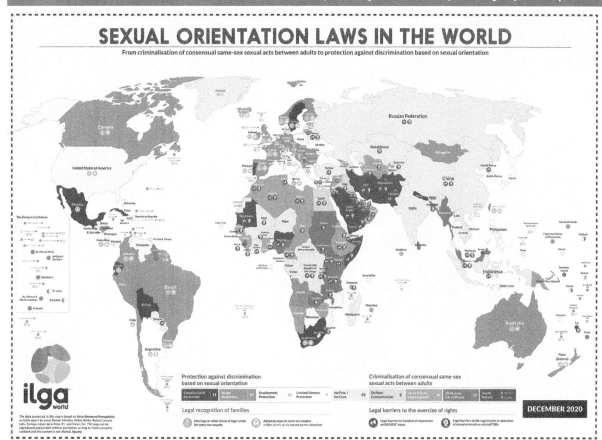

Source: ILGA World: Lucas Ramon Mendos, Kellyn Botha, Rafael Carrano Lelis, Enrique López de la Peña, Ilia Savelev and Daron Tan, *State-Sponsored Homophobia 2020: Global Legislation Overview Update* (Geneva: ILGA, December 2020). https://ilga.org/sites/default/files/downloads/ENG_ILGA_World_map_sexual_orientation_laws_dec2020.png

Émile Durkheim thought about crime and deviance in a very unconventional way. Instead of portraying crime and deviance as a negative force in society, Durkheim (1982) suggested that they are necessary, functional, and even good for a society. He noted that all societies have crime and deviance; that is, there is a normality of crime. In addition, he argued that deviance and crime cannot be eliminated because they are important and functional.

According to Durkheim (1982), deviance has four basic functions. First, it affirms cultural values and norms. When people commit an act of deviance it helps others to understand the rules of society—we know that a rule is important if breaking it is labelled as deviant. In this way, deviance is needed to define and sustain morality in society. Second, society's response to a deviant act helps individuals understand what is right and what is wrong. We cannot learn what is and is not acceptable without illustrations of people breaking rules. Third, responding to deviance helps unite individuals in society. For example, when someone commits a mass murder, other members of society feel shocked and alarmed. Seeing that others feel the same way affirms the severity of the deviance and brings people together. Finally, deviance can encourage social change. Durkheim argued that today's deviant can become tomorrow's beacon of morality. Important leaders of social movements, such as Martin Luther King Jr. and Rosa Parks, were considered deviant in their time because they broke norms. Now they are considered heroes and are recognized for helping to change values and norms in their societies, furthering civil rights for minority groups.

Daytime talk shows such as *Maury, Dr. Phil,* and *Judge Judy* illustrate Durkheim's first three functions of deviance. Many consider the guests on such shows to be deviant— they cheat on their spouses, steal from their parents, or deny being the father of children without DNA tests. The audience members, in the studio and at home, enjoy watching these shows partly because they get to sit in judgment of the people on the stage. By seeing people who are clearly breaking the norms of society, the audience feels a sense of solidarity because they believe that society's norms and rules are clear, and they get satisfaction from knowing that they follow those rules while the guests do not.

Danielle Bregoli, a rapper known as Bhad Bhabie, famously challenged Dr. Phil audience members to a fight when confronted about her deviant behavior.

SMXRF/Star Max/GC Images/Getty Images

Television programs such as Dr. Phil depend on displaying the deviance of their guests for viewers. How would Durkheim argue that this show is functional for society?

Michael Tran/FilmMagic/Getty Images

USING YOUR SOCIOLOGICAL IMAGINATION
THE CHANGING SOCIAL CONSTRUCTION OF DEVIANCE

Even within the same society, individuals have different ideas about what counts as deviance and the seriousness of various deviant acts. Some people's definition of deviance is more influential than others. For example, people who make laws (elected officials) and who enforce those laws (such as police officers) have more power to define deviance in consequential ways. Consider the acts in this list:

- Downloading music without paying
- Cheating on your romantic partner
- Using steroids to improve athletic performance
- Hitting a child as punishment
- Taking a prescription drug, such as Adderall, to stay up late cramming for an exam
- Dating someone from a different ethnic group
- Abstaining from alcohol in any context
- Hitting your spouse

- Getting a tattoo
- Killing someone
- Having sex outside marriage
- Punching someone in a fight
- Driving after drinking alcohol

Answer the following:

1. Rank these acts in terms of their severity. Which ones do you consider to be the most and least serious acts of deviance (or not deviant at all)?
2. Which of these acts are illegal in the United States? Which are legal in the United States but illegal elsewhere?
3. Which acts are now considered less serious than they were in the past? Which are considered more serious?
4. How do different groups of people vary in their attitudes about the seriousness of these acts? How would your grandparents, religious leader, friends, or other people in your life answer these questions differently?
5. How is power related to defining deviance? What groups have more power to define deviance and to make their definitions dominant in society? How is power related to deciding on the punishments for different deviant acts?

WHY ARE PEOPLE DEVIANT?

Scholars have developed many theories to explain why people are deviant or commit crimes. Some of these theories look at individual-level explanations. Most of the theories that sociologists use, however, are based on broader social explanations for an individual's propensity to engage in deviant or criminal behavior.

Individual Explanations of Deviance and Crime

Individual-level explanations of crime generally focus on the deviant or criminal's character (Collins, 1992). The logic behind these explanations is, for example, that thieves steal because they are greedy and murderers kill because they are violent. Some arguments are grounded in biology, such as the theory that criminals are genetically defective, predisposed to crime, or have too much testosterone. The idea that criminals are simply bad people and their deviant propensities come from within generally leads to support for severe punishments, such as the death penalty or long prison sentences. After all, if criminals are just bad apples, nothing can be done to rehabilitate them; therefore, we should reduce the potential harm they can do by removing them from society. However, as Collins notes, there is little empirical evidence to support the claim that more punitive reactions to crime significantly reduce crime rates. We will discuss punishment and its effects later in this chapter.

Social Explanations of Deviance and Crime

Unlike individual explanations, social explanations seek to understand criminal activity as a product of the criminal's environment, particularly how it shapes his actions. Sociologists use a wide variety of these explanations, which originate from the different theoretical perspectives we have discussed in this book.

Strain Theory

Strain theory argues that sometimes an individuals' goals and opportunities for success do not match (Merton, 1949/1957/1968). If, for example, individuals are raised in an abusive family, live in a low-income neighborhood, or lack opportunities to change their social conditions, they may experience strain. An individual might want to earn enough money to be self-sufficient but be unable to get a well-paying job. Thus, he could turn to crime to earn a living.

Subcultural Theory

Subcultural theory focuses on the role of culture in crime. Stanley Cohen (2011) argues that gangs and other criminal organizations are subcultures with different norms and values than the larger culture. As such, we can understand these gangs as a collective adaptation to social conditions and a rejection of the establishment's cultural goals. For example, beating someone up to defend a friend might be seen as both legitimate and necessary within gang subculture.

Elijah Anderson's (1999) famous study, *Code of the Street: Decency, Violence, and the Moral Life of the Inner City,* uses both strain and subcultural theories to explore the street-oriented subculture of American inner cities. Through participant observation, Anderson tries to understand how young minority men living in these areas search for respect and how this search can create the need for aggressive, violent, and criminal behavior. He explains that the consequence of this relentless pursuit of respect is a vicious cycle that begins with the hopelessness and alienation many inner-city youth feel at the hands of joblessness and racism in mainstream culture. As a result, these young men can begin to use violence as a means of gaining respect. This violence, in turn, reinforces the negative perceptions many Whites and middle-class individuals have about the poor people living in these areas, thus legitimating the code of the street in the eyes of minority youth.

Anderson (1999, p. 9) writes that the code's basic requirement is "the display of a certain predisposition to violence" and "mayhem," which may include fighting, exacting revenge, or stealing "trophy" objects (such as clothes or girlfriends). Young men ascribing to the code of the street often use violence and the threat of violence to campaign for respect. In this way, the ability to engage in violence helps you gain respect among your peers on the street even as society at large sees these same actions as negative. He argues that these young men, for example, spend a great deal of time hanging around with their peers on the street, thus making their primary social bonds with their friends rather than their parents.

Consistent with subcultural theory, this important work highlights how the norms and values that groups follow can be quite different, even within the same society, and how the social context can influence behavior. In many ways, it is rational for young minority men living in poor neighborhoods to act violently and criminally if that is what it takes to survive. These same behaviors would be irrational in a middle-class suburban context.

Learning Theory

Developed by Edwin Sutherland (1947), learning theory is an extension of strain and subcultural theories. Sutherland argued that different environments provide opportunities to learn to engage in deviance and crime. The saying, "The best place to learn how to be a criminal is in prison" epitomizes the logic behind learning theory: If people interact with and are exposed to criminals, they learn to engage in criminal behavior. For example, individuals in prison can learn how to engage in criminal behavior simply by interacting with others who have these skills. Sitting in a prison cafeteria might lead to a conversation about how best to steal a car without getting caught or how to justify to oneself that committing crimes is acceptable. This argument is based on ideas about the importance of socialization (see Chapter 2).

Control Theory

Travis Hirschi's (2004) control theory also focuses on social context's role in deviant and criminal behavior. He argues that weak social control can lead individuals to engage in deviant or criminal acts. Several factors can result in weak control. An individual might not have close relationships with her parents, teachers, or peer group. Or individuals can have weak institutional involvement if they are not actively engaged in organizations such as religious institutions, schools, sports teams, or other groups. Finally, individuals can have limited opportunities for success if, for example, there is high unemployment or a lack of access to education where they live. Most people are integrated in these ways and thus are less likely to engage in deviance. This theory might remind you of Durkheim's theory of suicide. Remember, Durkheim argued that individuals who are well integrated into their community and peer groups are less likely to die from suicide, which is arguably an act of deviance because it breaks a social norm.

Labelling Theory

These social explanations of crime focus on why individuals might be more or less likely to commit crimes based on their social environment. Labelling theory (similar to symbolic interactionist theory) explores how we respond to deviant or criminal acts and how this reaction (or label) can either increase or decrease an individual's propensity to engage in further deviance. This theory originated in the work of Howard Becker (1963), who argues that almost all young people engage in deviant behavior but only some are caught. If a young person is apprehended by authorities and is arrested, charged, convicted, and sentenced, her life can be significantly affected in a negative way. It is not the deviant behavior, per se, that leads to the later problems. Instead, being labelled deviant can create a deviant or criminal identity for the young person. Once an individual is labelled a criminal, she may find it difficult to get a job and may turn to illegitimate means, such as crime, to earn a living. Labelling involves a process by which identifying someone as a criminal can produce a self-fulfilling prophecy. Collins (1992) explains how the response to deviance is critical in labelling theory:

> The labelling theory declares that crime is actually created by the process of getting caught. Unlike the previous types of theories that we looked at, the personal characteristics of the individuals, or their social class or ethnic or neighborhood background, is not a crucial point. It is assumed that all sorts of people violate the law. But only some of them get caught, are prosecuted, labelled and all the rest, thereby becoming full-fledged criminals. If criminals who go through the courts and the prisons are so often likely to be disproportionately poor, black, or otherwise fit someone's idea of "social undesirables" or the "socially deprived," it is because these are the types of people who are most likely to be apprehended and prosecuted. (Collins, 1992, p. 99)

In sum, labelling theory posits that, when a person is caught and labelled as a deviant or a criminal, she is stigmatized and viewed as a criminal by others. This situation also creates a process of identity formation—people begin to adopt the identity of deviant. As a result, individuals sometimes change the way they view themselves and engage in deviant or criminal behavior to fulfill this social role or identity.

It is important, from a labelling theory perspective, to differentiate between primary and secondary acts of deviance. Primary deviance includes early, random acts of deviance. This sort of deviance is very common and most people, at some point, have engaged in primary deviant activity. Secondary deviance, however, is much more serious. The result of persistent deviant behavior, it can often cause an individual to organize his life and identity around being deviant.

Take, for example, a young boy who gets in a fight at school. If this were his first act of deviance, labelling theory would encourage us not to label him a deviant or criminal. He did a bad thing, we would say, but he is not a bad kid. But if the boy were arrested for his behavior, others would likely label him a deviant and a bad kid. Over time, it would be hard for him to find a job or other opportunities because everyone knows he is a "bad seed." In this way, it is not so much the act of deviance but how we as a society respond to it that leads to more or less deviance.

Each U.S. state has its own distinct juvenile justice system. However, one of the main tenants of these systems is based on the importance of labelling. In most states, there are limitations placed on public access to juvenile records because of the fear of unnecessary stigmatization that might come from being labelled a criminal or deviant. Court proceedings are also often kept confidential to protect the privacy of young people and to avoid labelling (Public Broadcasting Service, 2018). Keeping a young offender's identity private could help prevent primary deviance from becoming secondary deviance and thus reduce the chance that youthful deviance will lead to a life of crime.

Social explanations generally advocate for rehabilitative punishments and crime prevention by focusing on contextual factors, such as reducing poverty and facilitating access to education and employment. Some of these theories, including labelling theory, shift the emphasis away from the offender and his environment and toward the response to the deviant act. Proponents of labelling theory tend to promote programs that divert young people caught engaging in criminal acts from the courts and into community service to avoid labelling them as a criminal too hastily.

READING: "ON BEING SANE IN INSANE PLACES"

D. L. Rosenhan

D. L. Rosenhan's article illustrates the process of labelling. Rosenhan had eight mentally and physically healthy volunteers admitted to a mental hospital to see how they would be treated once they were labelled insane, as well as how long it would take for them to be labelled sane and released. When you read this article, consider how society applies labels to individuals and why it is sometimes difficult to change a label once it has been applied.

If sanity and insanity exist, how shall we know them?

The question is neither capricious nor itself insane. However much we may be personally convinced that we can tell the normal from the abnormal, the evidence is simply not compelling. It is commonplace, for example, to read about murder trials wherein eminent psychiatrists for the defense are contradicted by equally eminent psychiatrists for the prosecution on the matter of the defendant's sanity. . . .

To raise questions regarding normality and abnormality is in no way to question the fact that some behaviors are deviant or odd. Murder is deviant. So, too, are hallucinations. Nor does raising such questions deny the existence of the personal anguish that is often associated with "mental illness." Anxiety and depression exist. Psychological suffering exists. But normality and abnormality, sanity and insanity, and the diagnoses that flow from them may be less substantive than many believe them to be.

At its heart, the question of whether the sane can be distinguished from the insane (and whether degrees of insanity can be distinguished from each other) is a simple matter: Do the salient characteristics that lead to diagnoses reside in the patients themselves or in the environments and contexts in which observers find them? . . .

Gains can be made in deciding which of these is more nearly accurate by getting normal people (that is, people who do not have, and have never suffered, symptoms of serious psychiatric disorders) admitted to psychiatric hospitals and then determining whether they were discovered to be sane and, if so, how. If sanity of such pseudopatients were always detected, there would be prima facie evidence that a sane individual can be distinguished from the insane context in which he is found. Normality (and presumably abnormality) is distinct enough that it can be recognized wherever it occurs, for it is carried within the person.

If, on the other hand, the sanity of the pseudopatients were never discovered, serious difficulties would arise for those who support traditional modes of psychiatric diagnosis. Given that the hospital staff was not incompetent, that the pseudopatient had been behaving as sanely as he had been outside of the hospital, and that it had never been previously suggested that he belonged in a psychiatric hospital, such an unlikely outcome would support the view that psychiatric diagnosis betrays little about the patient but much about the environment in which an observer finds him.

This article describes such an experiment. Eight sane people gained secret admission to 12 different hospitals. . . .

Pseudopatients and Their Settings

The eight pseudopatients were a varied group. One was a psychology graduate student in his twenties. The remaining seven were older and "established." Among them were three psychologists, a pediatrician, a psychiatrist, a painter, and a housewife. Three pseudopatients were women, five were men. All of them employed pseudonyms, lest their alleged diagnoses embarrass them later. Those who were in mental health professions alleged another occupation in order to avoid the special attentions that might be accorded by staff, as a matter of courtesy or caution, to ailing colleagues. With the exception of myself (I was the first pseudopatient and my presence was known to the hospital administrator and chief psychologist and, so far as I can tell, to them alone), the presence of pseudopatients and the nature of the research program was not known to the hospital staffs.

The settings were similarly varied. In order to generalize the findings, admission into a variety of hospitals was sought. The 12 hospitals in the sample were located in 5 different states on the East and West coasts. Some were old and shabby, some were quite new. Some were research- oriented, others not. Some had good staff–patient ratios, others were quite understaffed. Only one was a strictly private hospital. All of the others were supported by state or federal funds or, in one instance, by university funds.

After calling the hospital for an appointment, the pseudopatient arrived at the admissions office complaining that he had been hearing voices. Asked what the voices said, he replied that they were often unclear, but as far as he could tell they said "empty," "hollow," and "thud." The voices were unfamiliar and were of the same sex as the pseudopatient. The choice of these symptoms was occasioned by their apparent similarity to existential symptoms. Such symptoms are alleged to arise from painful concerns about the perceived meaninglessness of one's life. It is as if the hallucinating person were saying, "My life is empty and hollow." The choice of these symptoms was also determined by the absence of a single report of existential psychoses in the literature.

Beyond alleging the symptoms and falsifying name, vocation, and employment, no further alterations of person, history, or circumstances were made. The significant events of the pseudopatient's life history were presented as they had actually occurred. Relationships with parents and siblings, with spouse and children, with people at work and in school, consistent with the aforementioned exceptions, were described as they were or had been. Frustrations and upsets were described along with joys and satisfactions. These facts are important to remember. If anything, they strongly biased the subsequent results in favor of detecting sanity, since none of their histories or current behaviors were seriously pathological in any way.

Immediately upon admission to the psychiatric ward, the pseudopatient ceased simulating any symptoms of abnormality. In some cases, there was a brief period of mild nervousness and anxiety, since none of the pseudopatients really believed that they would be admitted so easily. Indeed, their shared fear was that they would be immediately exposed as frauds and greatly embarrassed. Moreover, many of them had never visited a psychiatric ward; even those who had nevertheless had some genuine fears about what might happen to them. Their nervousness, then, was quite appropriate to the novelty of the hospital setting, and it abated rapidly.

Apart from that short-lived nervousness, the pseudopatient behaved on the ward as he "normally" behaved. The pseudopatient spoke to patients and staff as he might ordinarily.

Because there is uncommonly little to do on a psychiatric ward, he attempted to engage others in conversation. When asked by staff how he was feeling, he indicated that he was fine, that he no longer experienced symptoms. He responded to instructions from attendants, to calls for medication (which was not swallowed), and to dining-hall instructions. Beyond such activities as were available to him on the admissions ward, he spent his time writing down his observations about the ward, its patients, and the staff. Initially these notes were written "secretly," but as it soon became clear that no one much cared, they were subsequently written on standard tablets of paper in such public places as the dayroom. No secret was made of these activities.

The pseudopatient, very much as a true psychiatric patient, entered a hospital with no foreknowledge of when he would be discharged. Each was told that he would have to get out by his own devices, essentially by convincing the staff that he was sane. The psychological stresses associated with hospitalization were considerable, and all but one of the pseudopatients desired to be discharged almost immediately after being admitted. They were, therefore, motivated not only to behave sanely, but to be paragons of cooperation. That their behavior was in no way disruptive is confirmed by nursing reports, which have been obtained on most of the patients. These reports uniformly indicate that the patients were "friendly," "cooperative," and "exhibited no abnormal indications."

The Normal Are Not Detectably Sane

Despite their public "show" of sanity, the pseudopatients were never detected. Admitted, except in one case, with a diagnosis of schizophrenia,[1] each was discharged with a diagnosis of schizophrenia "in remission." The label "in remission" should in no way be dismissed as a formality, for at no time during any hospitalization had any question been raised about any pseudopatient's simulation. Nor are there any indications in the hospital records that the pseudopatient's status was suspect. Rather, the evidence is strong that, once labelled schizophrenic, the pseudopatient was stuck with that label. If the pseudopatient was to be discharged, he must naturally be "in remission"; but he was not sane, nor, in the institution's view, had he ever been sane.

The uniform failure to recognize sanity cannot be attributed to the quality of the hospitals, for, although there were considerable variations among them, several are considered excellent. Nor can it be alleged that there was simply not enough time to observe the pseudopatients. Length of hospitalization ranged from 7 to 52 days, with an average of 19 days. The pseudopatients were not, in fact, carefully observed, but this failure speaks more to traditions within psychiatric hospitals than to lack of opportunity.

Finally, it cannot be said that the failure to recognize the pseudopatients' sanity was due to the fact that they were not behaving sanely. While there was clearly some tension present in all of them, their daily visitors could detect no serious behavioral consequences—nor, indeed, could other patients. It was quite common for the patients to "detect" the pseudopatient's sanity. During the first three hospitalizations, when accurate counts were kept, 35 of a total of 118 patients on the admissions ward voiced their suspicions, some vigorously. "You're not crazy. You're a journalist, or a professor [referring to the continual notetaking]. You're checking up on the hospital." While most of the patients were reassured by the pseudopatient's insistence that he had been sick before he came in but was fine now, some continued to believe that the pseudopatient was sane throughout his hospitalization. The fact that the patients often recognized normality when staff did not raises important questions.

Failure to detect sanity during the course of hospitalization may be due to the fact that physicians operate with a strong bias toward what statisticians call the type 2 error.[2] This is to say that physicians are more inclined to call a healthy person sick (a false positive, type 2) than a sick person healthy (a false negative, type 1). The reasons for this are not hard to find: it is clearly more dangerous to misdiagnose illness than health. Better to err on the side of caution, to suspect illness even among the healthy.

But what holds for medicine does not hold equally well for psychiatry. Medical illnesses, while unfortunate, are not commonly pejorative. Psychiatric diagnoses, on the contrary, carry with them personal, legal, and social stigmas.[3] It was therefore important to see whether the tendency toward diagnosing the sane insane could be reversed. . . .

The Stickiness of Psychodiagnostic Labels

Beyond the tendency to call the healthy sick—a tendency that accounts better for diagnostic behavior on admission than it does for such behavior after a lengthy period of exposure—the data speak to the massive role of labelling in psychiatric assessment. Having once been labelled schizophrenic, there is nothing the pseudopatient can do to overcome the tag. The tag profoundly colors others' perceptions of him and his behavior. . . .

Once a person is designated abnormal, all of his other behaviors and characteristics are colored by that label. Indeed, that label is so powerful that many of the pseudopatients' normal behaviors were overlooked entirely or profoundly misinterpreted. Some examples may clarify this issue. . . .

As far as I can determine, diagnoses were in no way affected by the relative health of the circumstances of a pseudopatient's life. Rather, the reverse occurred: the perception of his circumstances was shaped entirely by the diagnosis. A clear example of such translation is found in the case of a pseudopatient who had had a close relationship with his mother but was rather remote from his father during his early childhood. During adolescence and beyond, however, his father became a close friend, while his relationship with his mother cooled. His present relationship with his wife was characteristically close and warm. Apart from occasional angry exchanges, friction was minimal. The children had rarely been spanked. Surely there is nothing especially pathological about such a history.

Indeed, many readers may see a similar pattern in their own experiences, with no markedly deleterious consequences. Observe, however, how such a history was translated in the psychopathological context, this from the case summary prepared after the patient was discharged.

> This white 39-year-old male . . . manifests a long history of considerable ambivalence in close relationships, which begins in early childhood. A warm relationship with his mother cools during his adolescence. A distant relationship to his father is described as becoming very intense. Affective stability is absent. His attempts to control emotionality with his wife and children are punctuated by angry outbursts and, in the case of the children, spankings. And while he says that he has several good friends, one senses considerable ambivalence embedded in those relationships also. . . .

All pseudopatients took extensive notes publicly. Under ordinary circumstances, such behavior would have raised questions in the minds of observers, as, in fact, it did among patients. Indeed, it seemed so certain that the notes would elicit suspicion that elaborate precautions were taken to remove them from the ward each day. But the precautions proved needless. The closest any staff member came to questioning those notes occurred when one pseudopatient asked his physician what kind of medication he was receiving and began to write down the response. "You needn't write it," he was told gently. "If you have trouble remembering, just ask me again."

If no questions were asked of the pseudopatients, how was their writing interpreted? Nursing records for three patients indicate that the writing was seen as an aspect of their pathological behavior. "Patient engaged in writing behavior" was the daily nursing comment on one of the pseudopatients who was never questioned about his writing. Given that the patient is in the hospital, he must be psychologically disturbed. And given that he is disturbed, continuous writing must be a behavioral manifestation of that disturbance, perhaps a subset of the compulsive behaviors that are sometimes correlated with schizophrenia.

One tacit characteristic of psychiatric diagnosis is that it locates the sources of aberration within the individual and only rarely within the complex of stimuli that surrounds him.

Consequently, behaviors that are stimulated by the environment are commonly misattributed to the patient's disorder. For example, one kindly nurse found a pseudopatient pacing the long hospital corridors. "Nervous, Mr. X?" she asked. "No, bored," he said.

The notes kept by pseudopatients are full of patient behaviors that were misinterpreted by well-intentioned staff. Often enough, a patient would go "berserk" because he had, wittingly or unwittingly, been mistreated by, say, an attendant. A nurse coming upon the scene would rarely inquire even cursorily into the environmental stimuli of the patient's behavior. Rather, she assumed that his upset derived from his pathology, not from his present interactions with other staff members. Occasionally, the staff might assume that the patient's family (especially when they had recently visited) or other patients had stimulated the outburst. But never were the staff found to assume that one of themselves or the structure of the hospital had anything to do with a patient's behavior. One psychiatrist pointed to a group of patients who were sitting outside the cafeteria entrance half an hour before lunchtime. To a group of young residents, he indicated that such behavior was characteristic of the oral-acquisitive nature of the syndrome. It seemed not to occur to him that there were very few things to anticipate in a psychiatric hospital besides eating.

A psychiatric label has a life and an influence of its own. Once the impression has been formed that the patient is schizophrenic, the expectation is that he will continue to be schizophrenic. When a sufficient amount of time has passed, during which the patient has done nothing bizarre, he is considered to be in remission and available for discharge. But the label endures beyond discharge, with the unconfirmed expectation that he will behave as a schizophrenic again. Such labels, conferred by mental health professionals, are as influential on the patient as they are on his relatives and friends, and it should not surprise anyone that the diagnosis acts on all of them as a self-fulfilling prophecy. Eventually, the patient himself accepts the diagnosis, with all of its surplus meanings and expectations, and behaves accordingly.[4]

Notes

Interestingly, of the 12 admissions, 11 were diagnosed as schizophrenic and 1, with the identical symptomatology, as manic-depressive psychosis. This diagnosis has a more favourable prognosis, and it was given by the only private hospital in our sample. On the relations between social class and psychiatric diagnosis, see A. deB. Hollingshead and F. C. Redlich, *Social Class and Mental Illness: A Community Study* (Wiley, New York, 1958).

T. J. Scheff, *Being Mentally Ill: A Sociological Theory* (Aldine, Chicago, 1966).

J. Cumming and E. Cumming, *Community Men. Health* 1, 135 (1965); A. Farina and K. Ring, *J. Abnorm. Psychol.* 70, 47 (1965); H.E. Freeman and O. G. Simmons, *The Mental Patient Comes Home* (Wiley, New York, 1963); W. J. Johannsen, *Ment. Hygiene* 53, 218 (1969); A. S. Linsky, *Soc. Psychiat.* 5, 166 (1970).

Scheff, *Being Mentally Ill.*

Reading Questions

1. How does the article illustrate labelling theory? How did the diagnosis of "insane" lead to the symptoms observed by the staff?
2. Why does a false positive diagnosis of mental illness generally have more serious repercussions than a false positive diagnosis of physical illness?
3. What is the significance of the fact that many patients, but none of the staff, managed to detect the fake patients?
4. What can this study teach us about why people engage in deviant acts and/or crime? How can it help us to better deal with people labelled deviant?

Rosenhan, D. L. "On Being Sane in Insane Places." American Association for the Advancement of Science. *Science* 19 Jan 1973: Vol. 179, Issue 4070, pp. 250–258.

THE POWER OF THE SITUATION

Let's consider two incidents of gun violence. On June 12, 2016, a shooter killed 49 people and wounded 53 in an attack inside a gay nightclub in Florida. The shooter was identified as a 29-year-old American man born in New York. However, much of the media coverage also reported that his parents were born in Afghanistan and he was raised Muslim. On October 1, 2017, a shooter opened fire on a crowd at a music festival in Las Vegas, killing 58 people and wounding 851. The perpetrator, a 64-year-old American man born in Iowa, was often described in the media as a gambler and a heavy drinker. His race and religion were not often mentioned in the news coverage, although he was White and Christian.

How can we understand these crimes? Why was the coverage of these two crimes so different? Though neither of these men had criminal records, their acts were described in very different ways: as terrorism in the former case and as an individual with addiction problems in the latter case. How might the fact that the second shooter was White and Christian have altered the type of media coverage this act received, particularly the fact that it was not described as a terrorist attack and his ethnicity and religion were not central to the coverage of the shooting?

Two famous experiments have investigated how individuals who often have no history of deviant or criminal behavior can commit crimes, particularly engaging in violent behavior. These experiments rose to prominence after World War II when academics were trying to understand how people with seemingly normal upbringings engaged in heinous activities, such as participating in the genocide in Germany during the Holocaust. Perpetrators sometimes justify their actions by saying that they were simply following orders. In the 1960s Stanley Milgram tested whether individuals are more likely to blindly follow orders from authority figures in certain conditions and, if so, how this behavior affected people's treatment of one another. Ten years later Philip Zimbardo conducted the Stanford Prison experiment, which explored how individuals' behaviors are shaped by the social context and social roles. Let's examine each of these classic experiments.

Milgram's (1963) experiment involved three people: an experimenter (in the role of the authority), a volunteer (in the role of a teacher), and a learner (who was an actor paid by Milgram). The volunteer and the learner/actor drew slips of paper to determine their roles; however, unknown to the volunteer, both slips said "Teacher." The actor would always play the learner role and the volunteer would always be the teacher. Throughout the experiment, the learner/actor and teacher were placed in different rooms so that they could talk to but not see one another. The teacher was instructed to teach the learner/actor a list of word pairs. Each time the learner/actor made a mistake, the teacher was told to give him an electrical shock. The teacher was given a sample shock to get a sense of how strong it felt. After each wrong answer, the teacher was to increase the shock by 15 volts. Of course, though, there were no shocks. The learner/actor set up a tape recorder integrated with the electroshock generator, which played prerecorded sounds for each shock level. Partway through the experiment, after receiving several shocks, the learner/actor began to bang on the wall between him and the teacher. He then began complaining of a heart condition. Finally, there was silence from the learner/actor's room.

As the learner/actor demonstrated increasingly serious signs of distress, most of the teachers wanted to stop the experiment. But the experimenter urged them to go on, saying "The experiment requires that you continue," "It is essential that you continue," and "You have no other choice; you must go on." Milgram and his colleagues thought that most people would not continue to administer the shocks after hearing the distress of the learner/actor, but 65% (26 of 40) of the volunteers in the first set of the experiment administered the final, massive 450-volt shock, though many were very uncomfortable doing so. Milgram concluded that being assigned the role of teacher and having an authority figure giving instructions led many people to administer much stronger shocks than they would have otherwise.

Philip Zimbardo also examined the power of the situation in his research. In the Stanford Prison experiment, Zimbardo (Zimbardo, Maslach, & Haney, 1999) recruited 24 mentally and physically healthy, middle-class, White males with no history of crime or emotional, physical, or social problems. Half of the participants were randomly assigned to the role of prisoner and half to the role of guard. Zimbardo placed these young men in a simulated prison in the basement of Stanford University to see how they would adapt to their assigned roles in this unfamiliar environment.

Zimbardo was astonished by the extent to which the participants adopted their roles. The guards enforced their authority over the prisoners, sometimes engaging in psychological torture. Many prisoners passively accepted the abuse. Those who resisted the guards were harassed by the other prisoners. In fact, the treatment of the prisoners was so dire that two of the prisoners quit the experiment early and the experiment was stopped after only 6 days. As Zimbardo (in Aronson & Aronson, 2011, p. 127) explains, "In less than a week the experience of imprisonment undid (temporarily) a lifetime of learning, human values were suspended, self-concepts were challenged and the ugliest, most base, pathological side of human nature surfaced."

These studies highlight how deviant behaviors are more likely and more severe in certain social settings. Both push us to understand that it is not just that some people are bad but that some situations can make people act in ways contrary to their usual selves. As Zimbardo (in Aronson & Aronson, 2011, p. 128) argues, "Individual behavior is largely under the control of social forces and environmental contingencies rather than personality traits, character, will power or other empirically unvalidated constructs." We thus expect that deviance is more likely in certain situations, such as when individuals enjoy anonymity: In Milgram's study the volunteer is in a separate room from the person he is shocking; in Zimbardo's, the guards wear a uniform and reflective glasses so prisoners cannot see their eyes. How can these studies help us to understand how other acts of violence or aggression happen in our society?

Crime Rates in the United States

Crime has consequences at both the micro-individual level as well as the macro-social level. People who have been victims of crime are clearly affected by their experience; however, the existence of crime in a community can also affect residents' general well-being and health (Pittman, Nykiforuk, Mignone, Mandhane, Becker, & Kozyrskyj, 2012). These serious implications are one reason governments spend large amounts of money trying to prevent and reduce crime.

To this end, governments must know how much and what types of crimes occur in their country. The FBI created the Uniform Crime Reporting (UCR) Program in 1929 to do just this in the United States. This program collects information on murder and manslaughter, forcible rape, robbery, aggravated assault, burglary, larceny-theft, motor vehicle theft, arson, and human trafficking. Law enforcement agencies report arrest data for 22 additional crime categories (U.S. Department of Justice, 2014). These data allow us to see, in Figure 3.2, that violent crime increased until the early 1990s and has been generally decreasing since this time. Figure 3.3 examines property crime and shows the sharp decline in this type of criminal activity over time.

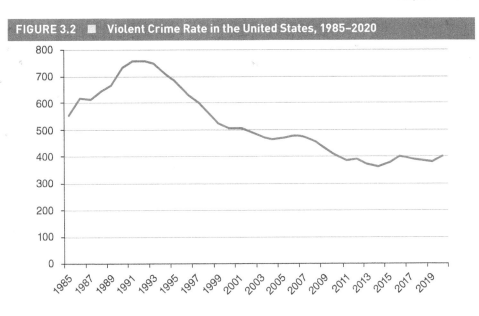

FIGURE 3.2 ■ Violent Crime Rate in the United States, 1985–2020

Source: Federal Bureau of Investigation. Crime Data Explorer. https://cde.ucr.cjis.gov/LATEST/webapp/#/pages/explorer/crime/crime-trend

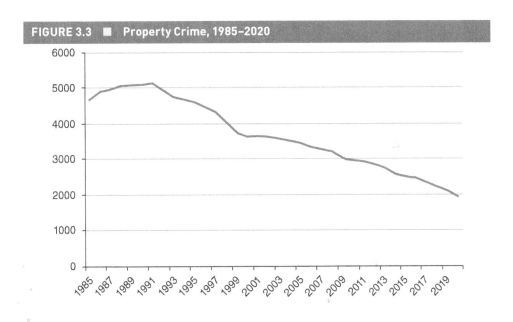

FIGURE 3.3 ■ Property Crime, 1985–2020

Source: Federal Bureau of Investigation. Crime Data Explorer. https://cde.ucr.cjis.gov/LATEST/webapp/#/pages/explorer/crime/crime-trend

Crime Around the World

Comparing crime rates across countries is difficult because laws, police practices, and crime classifications often differ across countries. For example, marijuana possession is legal in the Netherlands, has recently been legalized in Canada and some U.S. states, and can lead to incarceration in other U.S. states.

Murder is reported and tracked in all countries. Because of this, it is a good basis for comparing crime across nations. Figures 3.4 and 3.5 show that most of the Western world has relatively low murder rates compared to other regions. One major explanation for high murder rates is that these rates tend to occur in countries with high levels of poverty, inequality, and discrimination. These differences partly account for the higher murder rates in certain countries. Figure 3.4 shows murder rates across the world in 2019. Figure 3.5 compares the U.S. murder rate with that of some other industrialized countries. We can see that the murder rate in the United States is very high when compared with most European countries, Australia, and Japan, but considerably lower than countries such as South Africa, Brazil, and Mexico.

FIGURE 3.4 ■ World Homicide Rates (Number of Deaths per 100,000 Persons), 2019

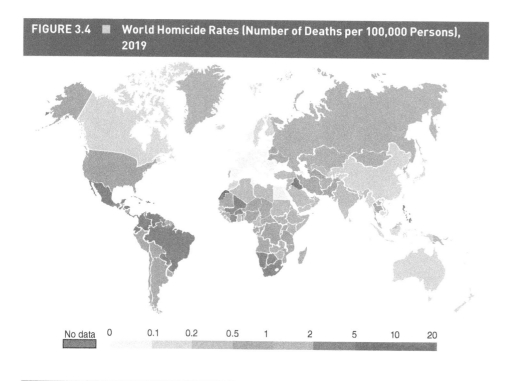

Source: Max Roser and Hannah Ritchie (2013) Homicides. *OurWorldInData.org.* Retrieved from https://ourworldin data.org/homicides

The rate of gun ownership is another explanation given for higher crime rates in certain countries, particularly murder rates. The United States has the highest per capita gun ownership of any country in the world (see Figure 3.6). There are many reasons for this, including different cultural ideas about the role of guns in society and an explicit right to bear arms in the U.S. Constitution, a right that does not exist in many other Western industrialized countries. Consequently, it is simply easier to get a gun in the United States than in most other countries. As outlined in Table 3.1, the rules and steps for getting a gun in America are few compared with other countries.

Table 3.1 shows the rules for purchasing guns in four countries. In the United States, federal law requires only that an adult pass an instant background check to be able to buy a gun. Table 3.1 shows that the United States is an outlier regarding the ease with which individuals can buy guns. In Japan, for example, there are eight quite complex steps in the process of buying a gun,

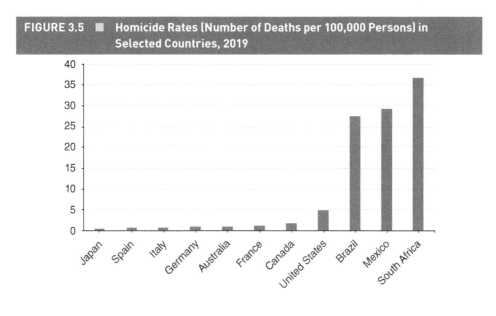

FIGURE 3.5 ■ Homicide Rates (Number of Deaths per 100,000 Persons) in Selected Countries, 2019

Source: Based on data from the United Nations Office on Drugs and Crime, 2019, https://dataunodc.un.org/content/country-list

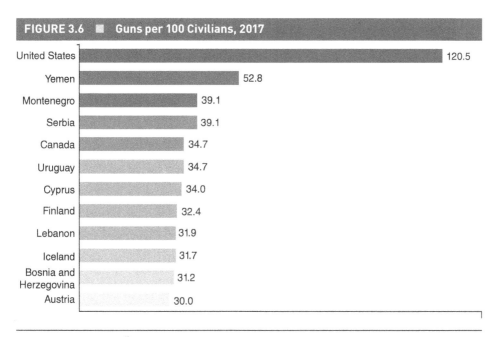

FIGURE 3.6 ■ Guns per 100 Civilians, 2017

Source: Fox, K. (2019). How U.S. gun culture compares with the world. *CNN.* https://www.cnn.com/2017/10/03/americas/us-gun-statistics/index.html

including taking a firearms class, getting a doctor's note describing your mental health and drug use, a police interview, buying and having a gun safe inspected at your home, and having references from family and friends. In part because of these additional steps, there are far fewer guns in Japan and other countries that have longer and more complex approval processes.

TABLE 3.1 ■ Steps to Purchase Guns in the U.S., Canada, Japan, and Australia	
Country	**Steps to Buy a Gun**
United States	Pass an instant background check that considers criminal convictions, domestic violence, and immigration status. (Note: Under federal law, Americans do not need to pass a background check when purchasing from a private seller.) Buy a gun.
Canada	To buy a handgun, prove that you practice at an approved shooting club or range, or show that you are a gun collector. For any gun, complete a safety course and pass both a written and a practical test. Supply two references and list the names of partners you have lived with for the past 2 years, who also must sign the application. Apply for a license, and wait 28 days before processing begins. Pass a background check that considers your criminal record, mental health, addiction and domestic violence history. Buy a gun. If you bought a handgun, register it with the police before taking it home.
Japan	Take a firearm class and pass a written exam, which is held up to three times a year. Get a doctor's note saying you are mentally fit and do not have a history of drug abuse. Apply for a permit to take firing training, which may take up to a month. Describe in a police interview why you need a gun. Pass a review of your criminal history, gun possession record, employment, involvement with organized crime groups, personal debt, and relationships with friends, family, and neighbors. Apply for a gunpowder permit and take a one-day training class and pass a firing test. Those who want to have a gun must apply for a hunting license. Individuals must buy a gun safe and ammunition locker.
Australia	To get a gun, you must show a valid reasons for owning a gun. Must join and regularly attend a hunting or shooting club, and clubs must inform authorities of any inactive members. If not a member of a club, you must document that you are a gun collector. Pass a written and practical test. Pass a review of criminal history, including domestic violence, restraining orders, and arrest history. Family and peers may be interviewed by authorities. Complete a course on safe gun handling and storage. Install safe gun storage. If approved, you can apply for a permit for a specific type of gun and then wait 28 days. Buy a gun.

Source: Adapted from Johncox, C. (2022, May 26). *How easy is it to buy guns in other countries compared to US?* ClickOnDetroit.com. Retrieved June 12, 2023, from https://www.clickondetroit.com/news/national/2022/05/26/how-easy-is-it-to-buy-guns-in-other-countries-compared-to-us/. Data sourced from https://www.nytimes.com/interactive/2018/03/02/world/international-gun-laws.html

When we compare cross-nationally, there is a clear relationship between the number of guns in a society and the amount of violent crime, particularly mass shootings. As Figure 3.7 shows, the more guns there are per capita, the more likely there will be mass shooter incidents. Although the United States comprises about 4% of the world population, it accounts for 31% of the global mass shootings. In addition, gun homicide rates are 25 times higher in the United States than in other high-income countries (see Figure 3.7). Finally, there is the very high rate of gun suicides in the United States. Suicide is the second most common cause of death for Americans between the ages of 15 and 34 and the 10th most common cause of death among all age groups (Centers for

Disease Control and Prevention, 2020). And, of all deaths by firearm in the United States, 54% are gun suicides (Gramlich, 2022). As this example shows, policies such as the rules and regulations around gun ownership differ greatly cross-nationally. Comparing in this way can help us to better understand the ways in which our society is unique and how we might address large-scale social issues, such as gun violence.

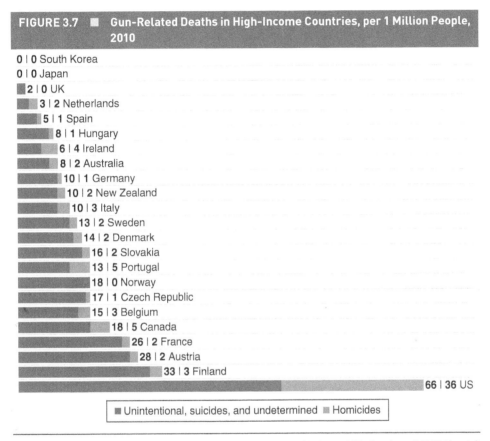

FIGURE 3.7 ■ Gun-Related Deaths in High-Income Countries, per 1 Million People, 2010

0 | 0 South Korea
0 | 0 Japan
2 | 0 UK
3 | 2 Netherlands
5 | 1 Spain
8 | 1 Hungary
6 | 4 Ireland
8 | 2 Australia
10 | 1 Germany
10 | 2 New Zealand
10 | 3 Italy
13 | 2 Sweden
14 | 2 Denmark
16 | 2 Slovakia
13 | 5 Portugal
18 | 0 Norway
17 | 1 Czech Republic
15 | 3 Belgium
18 | 5 Canada
26 | 2 France
28 | 2 Austria
33 | 3 Finland
66 | 36 US

■ Unintentional, suicides, and undetermined   ■ Homicides

Source: Based on data collected in "How US gun culture compares with the world in five charts," CNN, March 9, 2018. https://www.cnn.com/2017/10/03/americas/us-gun-statistics/index.html

Crime Rates by Group

Looking at a country's overall crime rate can allow us to assess whether crime is increasing or decreasing and what types of crimes are most prevalent. However, these overall statistics mask some important differences between groups.

Age

Crime rates vary widely by age of the accused perpetrators. Individuals are most likely to commit crimes between the ages of 25 to 29 (see Figure 3.8). These youth crimes are usually acts of primary deviance and tend to be of low severity, such as minor drug use, shoplifting, and petty theft. In most cases, criminal behavior ends with the onset of adulthood and adult responsibilities. And, after age 60, people are highly unlikely to engage in criminal activity.

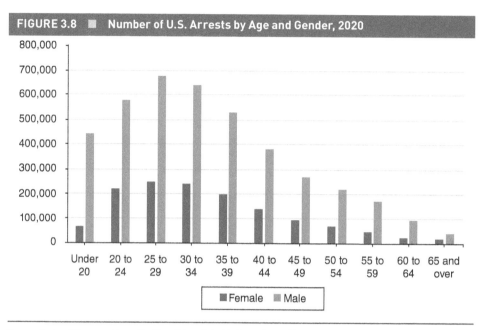

FIGURE 3.8 ■ Number of U.S. Arrests by Age and Gender, 2020

Source: Federal Bureau of Investigation, Crime Data Explorer. https://crime-data-explorer.app.cloud.gov/pages/explorer/crime/arrest

Gender

Crime rates also differ significantly by gender. Women account for only about 25% of people arrested in the United States (see Figure 3.8). The gender imbalance in arrests is most pronounced for violent crimes, such as homicide, where women account for only about one-tenth of the accused. Women tend to be more evenly represented in crimes such as abduction, prostitution, and theft under $5,000.

Race and Ethnicity

Arrest rates are also very different across racial and ethnic groups. Of all those arrested in 2020, 69% were White, 27% were Black, and the remaining 4% were individuals who identify as American Indian, Asian, or Other (UCR, 2019). When one compares this with the national population, where only 12% of the population is Black, for example (Jensen et al., 2021), we can see that there is a massive disparity in arrest rates. It can be quite difficult to explain these disparities. They could be a product of the large economic and educational gaps between racial groups, both of which are associated with crime rates. However, it is also possible that these disparities are related to biased policing. Research finds that at least 70 law enforcement departments in the United States arrest Black people at a rate 10 times higher than the rate of arrests for other racial groups. And a much larger group of police departments arrest Blacks at a rate of around three times higher than other races—in fact more than 1,500 police departments are more than three times as likely to arrest a Black person as they are to arrest a person of another race, despite their relatively smaller percentage of the population (Heath, 2014).

The disparity that exists between the rates of arrests and incarceration across racial and ethnic groups has been the cause of much concern. One concern is the way that police and racialized communities interact. As we have just discussed, there are high numbers of arrests of certain racialized groups, particularly Black men. There are more arrests, in part, because police see the high rates of past arrests in these communities and, as a result, concentrate their policing efforts in these areas and among these groups. As a result, there are more arrests over time—with more police in an area looking for crime among particular groups, the arrest rate will tend to be higher. Other groups, for example Whites, are not monitored or policed at such high rates, which is part of the reason they are less likely to be arrested. Think of the analogue of a speeding ticket—you get a speeding ticket if you speed, but you can only get a ticket if a police officer is sitting on your street to ticket you. If there are more police officers on your street, there will be more speeding tickets given out on your street, even if the rate of speeding is the same on your street as it is on a street where there is no police officer to give a ticket.

This higher surveillance is a part of why there are higher rates of arrest among certain groups, which leads to stereotypes that perpetuate the perceived need for more surveillance and justifies higher arrests. It is also associated with more aggressive policing of certain groups and serious concerns over police brutality. For example, Black Americans are twice as likely as White Americans to be killed by police officers. Young Black men are particularly at risk: Black men between the ages of 15 and 34 are nine times more likely than other groups to be killed by police (Swaine & McCarthy, 2017). These very high rates and concerns over highly publicized incidents in which unarmed Black men have been shot by police has led to the widespread Black Lives Matter campaign, which is discussed in more detail in Chapter 14.

PUNISHMENT

Punishment is the penalty inflicted on someone for committing a transgression. In criminal law, penalties are decided by a judge depending on the severity of the crime. Punishments are a denial of certain privileges, abilities, or rights; in the United States, these can be fines, community service, imprisonment, capital punishment, or restorative justice measures.

USING YOUR SOCIOLOGICAL IMAGINATION
THE CHALLENGE OF COVID-19 IN PRISONS

Before the COVID-19 pandemic, more than two million incarcerated people in U.S. prisons faced overcrowded living conditions and inadequate access to medical care. The COVID-19 pandemic amplified these issues. Incarcerated people were unable to socially distance, leading to mass outbreaks in prisons across the United States. Prison workers, who have frequent contact with people who are incarcerated, quickly spread COVID-19 cases to surrounding communities. Incarcerated people also lacked access to COVID-19 testing and personal protective equipment, crucial measures to prevent viral spread.

COVID-19 data from U.S. prisons are difficult to obtain. Some prisons do not report COVID-19 cases and deaths to the public. Other prisons report inmate deaths from other underlying health conditions, without disclosing whether the patient had COVID-19 before they died. Different nonprofit organizations have created resources for the public with available data on COVID-19 in prisons in order to better assess the spread of COVID-19 in the prison population.

Go to "UCLA Law COVID Behind Bars Data Project" at https://uclacovidbehindbars.org/. Explore the website and answer the following questions.

1. Choose the state where you currently reside. How many cumulative COVID-19 cases have been reported in the state's prisons? How many people have died from COVID-19 in your state's prisons?
2. What are the implications of high rates of COVID-19 within prisons? How does this affect the prison population? How does it affect the community in the surrounding area?

3. How do COVID-19 cases differ by type of prison (state, federal, county jails, ICE detention centers, and state and local youth facilities)?

4. The UCLA Law COVID Behind Bars Data Project suggests decarceration, especially in immigration detention centers, as one strategy to prevent the spread of COVID-19. What is decarceration? How could decarceration impact COVID-19 cases? What other ways could we reduce the COVID-19 rates within prisons?

Why Do We Punish?

Punishment has various functions. Perhaps the most basic is **retribution**. Retribution is based on the idea that a punishment should be comparable to the suffering caused by the crime (i.e., an eye for an eye). The thinking is that a crime upsets society's moral balance. By punishing the criminal in equal measure, this balance and moral order can be restored. Retributive justice must be proportionate to the crime committed so that criminals suffer the pain that they have inflicted on others. A murderer can be executed, but someone who commits robbery should not be. Proponents of retributive justice argue that it can help to satisfy the resentment felt by the victim or victim's family.

The second main function of punishment is **deterrence**, the process of dissuading someone from future wrongdoing by making the cost of punishment outweigh the benefit of committing the crime. Deterrence assumes that offenders conduct a rational cost-benefit analysis before committing an offense. There are two types of deterrence: general and specific. **General deterrence** involves making an example out of deviants to deter others from committing crimes. **Specific deterrence** aims to discourage specific individuals by convincing them that engaging in crime does not benefit them. For example, if an individual is charged with drug trafficking and sentenced to a long prison sentence, he may decide that remaining in the drug trade is not worth the risk of future (and longer) prison terms.

Many people consider the death penalty the ultimate deterrent. The idea is that the high cost of potentially being executed is greater than any benefit from committing a crime. The death penalty was legal in 27 states in 2022. The United States is the only Western country that currently uses the death penalty. Although the death penalty is used in 54 other countries, including China, Iran, North Korea, and Yemen, the United States has the most executions per year (Rogers & Chalabi, 2013). Many people support the death penalty, but others believe that it is morally wrong to kill in any context. Still others worry that some innocent people are executed, which is particularly problematic given the strong evidence of bias, especially racial bias, in capital punishment. For example, studies show that Blacks, and non-Whites more generally, who are convicted of killing Whites are more likely to get the death penalty than Whites who kill other Whites (Paternoster, 2007).

The next major function of punishment is **rehabilitation**, a newer focus of the criminal justice system. Rehabilitation is not simply about punishing criminals but aims to reform, or heal, them and help them reintegrate into society so that they will not reoffend. If you believe, for example, that crime originates from the social environment, rehabilitation might be an appropriate response to deviance. If offenders learn to be deviant, they can learn to be nondeviant. However, rehabilitation is needed to transform the deviant into this new identity. Rehabilitation transforms by motivating constructive improvement on the part of the offender.

Parole, the supervised early release of a prisoner for such things as good behavior, can be thought of as part of rehabilitation. Parole officers work with parolees to help them adjust to life outside prison and to ensure that they do not violate the conditions of their release. If parolees breach those terms, they can be sent back to prison. Probation is a possibility for individuals who are convicted of less serious crimes. These individuals are released into the community under supervision and certain conditions, such as attending and completing a substance abuse program or having a curfew. If the offender does not adhere to these conditions or is rearrested, the probation can be revoked.

Rehabilitation programs work to help reintegrate offenders into society.

iStockphoto.com/SolStock

Punishment is also about societal protection. When we incapacitate criminals, we physically prevent them from committing crimes. For example, when criminals are incarcerated or equipped with electronic monitoring devices, we limit their ability to commit crimes and try to protect other members of society from crime. Incapacitation can include imprisonment, the death penalty, or chemical castration of sex offenders.

Punishment is also used for boundary-setting, education, and norm reinforcement. The logic is that if wrongdoing goes unpunished, citizens will become demoralized and will not respect laws, thus ultimately threatening the moral fabric of society. Historically, societies pursued these goals by holding executions in public. These reinforced the sovereign's power (i.e., the state's power to punish those who violate its laws) in the minds of the people. Punishment thus aided in boundary-setting by illustrating what the population is or is not allowed to do and publicly demonstrating that the state is the ultimate enforcer of laws. A very effective way to increase solidarity in a society is to have its members collectively agree that something is wrong. For example, when people comment on what a monster a high-profile murderer is, they implicitly emphasize the collective opinion that murder is wrong and that those who commit murder are deviant and are outside society's norms. This theory of punishment is consistent with Durkheim's argument about the functions of crime, which include creating solidarity and clarifying social norms.

Finally, punishment can lead to restoration. Offenders restore order by compensating or fixing the injustice caused by their crime. Restorative justice requires that the offender must first admit guilt. Vermont has long had restorative justice programs. These programs aim to promote citizens' ownership of the criminal and juvenile justice systems by involving them directly in the justice process. It also allows the victims and community members to confront the offenders and address their behavior in a constructive manner. Offenders can take responsibility for their actions and be held accountable and learn to accept community-driven consequences for their behavior (Bazemore & Umbreit, 2001).

READING: "THE BODY OF THE CONDEMNED"
Michel Foucault

The following excerpt from Michel Foucault's *Discipline and Punish: The Birth of the Prison* (1995) examines two types of punishment: torture and incarceration. The comparison of the public torture of Robert-François Damiens, who was convicted of attempted murder in the mid-18th century, with the daily routine of inmates in a 19th-century prison illustrates the dramatic changes that have occurred in punishment in Western societies. Foucault also discusses the reasons for these changes and considers how we determine the most humane way to punish a criminal.

On 2 March 1757 Damiens the regicide was condemned "to make the *amende honorable* before the main door of the Church of Paris," where he was to be "taken and conveyed in a cart, wearing nothing but a shirt, holding a torch of burning wax weighing two pounds"; then, "in the said cart, to the Place de Grève, where, on a scaffold that will be erected there, the flesh will be torn from his breasts, arms, thighs and calves with red- hot pincers, his right hand, holding the knife with which he committed the said parricide, burnt with sulphur, and, on those places where the flesh will be torn away, poured molten lead, boiling oil, burning resin, wax and sulphur melted together and then his body drawn and quartered by four horses and his limbs and body consumed by fire, reduced to ashes and his ashes thrown to the winds" (*Pièces originales* . . ., 372–4).

"Finally, he was quartered," recounts the *Gazette d'Amsterdam* of 1 April 1757. "This last operation was very long, because the horses used were not accustomed to drawing; consequently, instead of four, six were needed; and when that did not suffice, they were forced, in order to cut off the wretch's thighs, to sever the sinews and hack at the joints. . . .

"It is said that, though he was always a great swearer, no blasphemy escaped his lips; but the excessive pain made him utter horrible cries, and he often repeated: 'My God, have pity on me! Jesus, help me!' The spectators were all edified by the solicitude of the parish priest of St Paul's who despite his great age did not spare himself in offering consolation to the patient."

Bouton, an officer of the watch, left us his account: "The sulphur was lit, but the flame was so poor that only the top skin of the hand was burnt, and that only slightly. Then the executioner, his sleeves rolled up, took the steel pincers, which had been especially made for the occasion, and which were about a foot and a half long, and pulled first at the calf of the right leg, then at the thigh, and from there at the two fleshy parts of the right arm; then at the breasts. Though a strong, sturdy fellow, this executioner found it so difficult to tear away the pieces of flesh that he set about the same spot two or three times, twisting the pincers as he did so, and what he took away formed at each part a wound about the size of a six-pound crown piece.

"After these tearings with the pincers, Damiens, who cried out profusely, though without swearing, raised his head and looked at himself; the same executioner dipped an iron spoon in the pot containing the boiling potion, which he poured liberally over each wound. Then the ropes that were to be harnessed to the horses were attached with cords to the patient's body; the horses were then harnessed and placed alongside the arms and legs, one at each limb.

"Monsieur Le Breton, the clerk of the court, went up to the patient several times and asked him if he had anything to say. He said he had not; at each torment, he cried out, as the damned in hell are supposed to cry out, 'Pardon, my God! Pardon, Lord.' Despite all this pain, he raised his head from time to time and looked at himself boldly. The cords had been tied so tightly by the men who pulled the ends that they caused him indescribable pain. Monsieur Le Breton went up to him again and asked him if he had anything to say; he said no. Several confessors went up to him and spoke to him at length; he willingly kissed the crucifix that was held out to him; he opened his lips and repeated: 'Pardon, Lord.'

"The horses tugged hard, each pulling straight on a limb, each horse held by an executioner. After a quarter of an hour, the same ceremony was repeated and finally, after several attempts, the direction of the horses had to be changed, thus: those at the arms were made to pull towards the head, those at the thighs towards the arms, which broke the arms at the joints. This was repeated several times without success. He raised his head and looked at himself. Two more horses had to be added to those harnessed to the thighs, which made six horses in all. Without success.

"Finally, the executioner, Samson, said to Monsieur Le Breton that there was no way or hope of succeeding, and told him to ask their Lordships if they wished him to have the prisoner cut into pieces. Monsieur Le Breton, who had come down from the town, ordered that renewed efforts be made, and this was done; but the horses gave up and one of those harnessed to the thighs fell to the ground. The confessors returned and spoke to him again. He said to them (I heard him): 'Kiss me, gentlemen.' The parish priest of St Paul's did not dare to, so Monsieur de Marsilly slipped under the rope holding the left arm and kissed him on the forehead. The executioners gathered round and Damiens told them not to swear, to carry out their task and that he did not think ill of them; he begged them to pray to God for him, and asked the parish priest of St Paul's to pray for him at the first mass. "

Eighty years later, Léon Faucher drew up his rules "for the House of young prisoners in Paris":

Art. 17. The prisoners' day will begin at six in the morning in winter and at five in summer. They will work for nine hours a day throughout the year. Two hours a day will be devoted to instruction. Work and the day will end at nine o'clock in winter and at eight in summer.

Art. 18. *Rising*. At the first drum-roll, the prisoners must rise and dress in silence, as the supervisor opens the cell doors. At the second drum-roll, they must be dressed and make their beds. At the third, they must line up and proceed to the chapel for morning prayer. There is a five-minute interval between each drum-roll.

Art. 19. The prayers are conducted by the chaplain and followed by a moral or religious reading. This exercise must not last more than half an hour.

Art. 20. *Work*. At a quarter to six in the summer, a quarter to seven in winter, the prisoners go down into the courtyard where they must wash their hands and faces, and receive their first ration of bread. Immediately afterwards, they form into work-teams and go off to work, which must begin at six in summer and seven in winter.

Art. 21. *Meal*. At ten o'clock the prisoners leave their work and go to the refectory; they wash their hands in their courtyards and assemble in divisions. After the dinner, there is recreation until twenty minutes to eleven.

Art. 22. *School*. At twenty minutes to eleven, at the drum-roll, the prisoners form into ranks, and proceed in divisions to the school. The class lasts two hours and consists alternately of reading, writing, drawing, and arithmetic.

Art. 23. At twenty minutes to one, the prisoners leave the school, in divisions, and return to their courtyards for recreation. At five minutes to one, at the drum-roll, they form into work-teams.

Art. 24. At one o'clock they must be back in the workshops: they work until four o'clock.

Art. 25. At four o'clock the prisoners leave their workshops and go into the court-yards where they wash their hands and form into divisions for the refectory.

Art. 26. Supper and the recreation that follows it last until five o'clock: the prisoners then return to the workshops.

Art. 27. At seven o'clock in the summer, at eight in winter, work stops; bread is distributed for the last time in the workshops. For a quarter of an hour one of the prisoners or supervisors reads a passage from some instructive or uplifting work. This is followed by evening prayer.

Art. 28. At half-past seven in summer, half-past eight in winter, the prisoners must be back in their cells after the washing of hands and the inspection of clothes in the courtyard; at the first drum-roll, they must undress, and at the second get into bed. The cell doors are closed and the supervisors go the rounds in the corridors, to ensure order and silence (Faucher, 1838, 274–82).

We have, then, a public execution and a timetable. They do not punish the same crimes or the same type of delinquent. But they each define a certain penal style. Less than a century separates them. It was a time when, in Europe and in the United States, the entire economy of punishment was redistributed. It was a time of great "scandals" for traditional justice, a time of innumerable projects for reform. It saw a new theory of law and crime, a new moral or political justification of the right to punish; old laws were abolished, old customs died out. "Modern" codes were planned or drawn up: Russia, 1769; Prussia, 1780; Pennsylvania and Tuscany, 1786; Austria, 1788; France, 1791, Year IV, 1808 and 1810. It was a new age for penal justice.

Among so many changes, I shall consider one: the disappearance of torture as a public spectacle. Today we are rather inclined to ignore it; perhaps, in its time, it gave rise to too much inflated rhetoric; perhaps it has been attributed too readily and too emphatically to a process of "humanization," thus dispensing with the need for further analysis. And, in any case, how important is such a change, when compared with the great institutional trans-formations, the formulation of explicit, general codes and unified rules of procedure; with the almost universal adoption of the jury system, the definition of the essentially corrective character of the penalty and the tendency which has become increasingly marked since the nineteenth century, to adapt punishment to the individual offender? Punishment of a less immediately physical kind, a certain discretion in the art of inflicting pain, a combination of more subtle, more subdued sufferings, deprived of their visible display, should not all this be treated as a special case, an incidental effect of deeper changes?

And yet the fact remains that a few decades saw the disappearance of the tortured, dis-membered, amputated body, symbolically branded on face or shoulder, exposed alive or dead to public view. The body as the major target of penal repression disappeared.

By the end of the eighteenth and the beginning of the nineteenth century, the gloomy fes-tival of punishment was dying out, though here and there it flickered momentarily into life. In this transformation, two processes were at work. They did not have quite the same chronol-ogy or the same raison d' être. The first was the disappearance of punishment as a spectacle. The ceremonial of punishment tended to decline; it survived only as a new legal or adminis-trative practice The use of prisoners in public works, cleaning city streets or repairing the highways, was practiced in Austria, Switzerland, and certain of the United States, such as Pennsylvania. These convicts, distinguished by their "infamous dress" and shaven heads, "were brought before the public. The sport of the idle and the vicious, they often become incensed, and naturally took violent revenge upon the aggressors. To prevent them from returning injuries which might be inflicted on them, they were encumbered with iron collars and chains to which bombshells were attached, to be dragged along while they performed their degrading service, under the eyes of keepers armed with swords, blunderbusses and other weapons of destruction" (Roberts Vaux, *Notices*, 21, quoted in Teeters, 1937–24). This practice was abolished practically everywhere at the end of the eighteenth or the beginning of the nineteenth century. . . .

Punishment, then, will tend to become the most hidden part of the penal process. This has several consequences: it leaves the domain of more or less everyday perception and enters that of abstract consciousness; its effectiveness is seen as resulting from its inevitability, not from its visible intensity; it is the certainty of being punished and not the horrifying spectacle of public punishment that must discourage crime; the exemplary mechanics of punishment changes its mechanisms. . . .

The disappearance of public executions marks therefore the decline of the spectacle; but it also marks a slackening of the hold on the body One no longer touched the body, or at least as little as possible, and then only to reach something other than the body itself. It might be objected that imprisonment, confinement, forced labor, penal servitude, prohibition from entering certain areas, deportation—which have occupied so important a place in modern penal systems—are "physical" penalties: unlike fines, for example, they directly affect the body. But the punishment–body relation is not the same as it was in the torture during public executions. The body now serves as an instrument or intermediary: if one intervenes upon it to imprison it, or to make it work, it is in order to deprive the individual of a liberty that is regarded both as a right and as property. The body, according to this penalty, is caught up in a system of constraints and privations, obligations and prohibitions. Physical pain, the pain of the body itself, is no longer the constituent element of the penalty As a result of this new restraint, a whole army of technicians took over from the executioner, the immediate anatomist of pain: warders, doctors, chaplains, psychiatrists, psychologists, educationalists; by their very presence near the prisoner, they sing the praises that the law needs: they reassure it that the body and pain are not the ultimate objects of its punitive action. . . .

The modern rituals of execution attest to this double process: the disappearance of the spectacle and the elimination of pain. . . .

But a punishment like forced labor or even imprisonment—mere loss of liberty—has never functioned without a certain additional element of punishment that certainly concerns the body itself: rationing of food, sexual deprivation, corporal punishment, solitary confinement. Are these the unintentional, but inevitable, consequence of imprisonment? In fact, in its most explicit practices, imprisonment has always involved a certain degree of physical pain. The criticism that was often leveled at the penitentiary system in the early nineteenth century (imprisonment is not a sufficient punishment: prisoners are less hungry, less cold, less deprived in general than many poor people or even workers) suggests a postulate that was never explicitly denied: it is just that a condemned man should suffer physically more than other men. It is difficult to dissociate punishment from additional physical pain. What would a non-corporal punishment be? . . .

The reduction in penal severity in the last 200 years is a phenomenon with which legal historians are well acquainted. But, for a long time, it has been regarded in an overall way as a quantitative phenomenon: less cruelty, less pain, more kindness, more respect, more "humanity." In fact, these changes are accompanied by a displacement in the very object of the punitive operation. Is there a diminution of intensity? Perhaps. There is certainly a change of objective.

If the penalty in its most severe forms no longer addresses itself to the body, on what does it lay hold? It seems to be contained in the question itself: since it is no longer the body, it must be the soul. The expiation that once rained down upon the body must be replaced by a punishment that acts in depth on the heart, the thoughts, the will, the inclinations. . . .

They are punished by means of a punishment that has the function of making the offender "not only desirous, but also capable, of living within the law and of providing for his own needs"; they are punished by the internal economy of a penalty which, while intended to punish the crime, may be altered (shortened or, in certain cases, extended) according to changes in the prisoner's behavior; and they are punished by the "security measures" that accompany the penalty (prohibition of entering certain areas, probation, obligatory medical treatment), and which are intended not to punish the offence, but to supervise the individual, to neutralize his dangerous state of mind, to alter his criminal tendencies, and to continue even when this change has been achieved During the 150 or 200 years that Europe has been setting up its new penal systems, the judges have gradually, by means of a process that goes back very far indeed, taken to judging something other than crimes, namely, the "soul" of the criminal. . . .

A corpus of knowledge, techniques, "scientific" discourses is formed and becomes entangled with the practice of the power to punish.

References

Faucher, L. (1838). *De la réforme des prisons*. Angé.

Pièces originales et procédures du procès fait à Robert-François Damiens, III. (1757). Chez Pierre-Guillaume Simon.

Teeters, N. K. (1937). *They were in prison*. John C. Winston.

Vaux, R. (1768). *Notices of the original, and successive efforts, to improve the discipline of the prison at Philadelphia*. Kimber and Sharpless.

Reading Questions

1. How did punishment change over time, according to Foucault? How are these changes related to evolving ideas of punishing the body versus punishing the soul?
2. What is the public's role in punishment and how has it changed?
3. What is the purpose of punishment? How did the purpose change from the 18th to the 19th centuries?
4. Who decides and enacts punishment in Foucault's analysis? How is this person/institution related to ideas about why people commit crimes, the function of the criminal justice system, and the reasons for punishment?

Michel Foucault

Bruno de Monès / Roger-Viollet / Grange

Getting to Know: Michel Foucault (1926–1984)

- Michel Foucault was a French philosopher born to a wealthy family in Poitiers, France.

- As a child, Foucault was very close with his sister, who was 2 years his senior. When she started elementary school, Foucault, then 4 years old, received special permission to attend alongside her.

- In high school, Foucault participated in the *concours*, a highly competitive and prestigious nationwide exam in which he placed fourth. His parents wanted to reward him for his success, and Foucault asked for German lessons as a reward for his performance!

- Foucault worked at universities in Tunisia, Sweden, Poland, Germany, Brazil, Canada, and Japan and gave annual lectures at the University of California, Berkeley.

- His favorite meal was a well-made club sandwich with a Coke, which is scandalous to the French.

- He was a founder of the *Groupe d'information sur les prisons*. The group collected and disseminated information about inhumane prison conditions in France.

How Do We Punish?

Individuals who ascribe to individual-level explanations for crime tend to favor harsher punishments, while those who use social explanations tend to support less punitive responses. Regardless of whether the punishments are harsh or lenient, recidivism rates (the rates at which individuals reoffend) are generally quite high. The Bureau of Justice Statistics tracked 404,638 prisoners in 30 states after their release from prison in 2005. They found that, within 4 years of release, more than three-quarters (77%) were rearrested. Of those rearrested, more than half had been arrested by the end of the first year (National Institute of Justice, 2018). This number should make us question how well the current system rehabilitates individuals who have entered the criminal justice system.

Though there are many ways that individuals can be punished for engaging in crime, sending people to prisons is one of the most prevalent. However, the extent to which individuals who break laws are sent to prisons differs greatly across countries. Figure 3.9 shows that the United States has more people in prison than almost any other country. Although the United States makes up only 4% of the world's population, it accounts for more than 19% of the world's prisoners (Fair and Walmsley, 2021). In fact, the United States has 532 people incarcerated per 100,000. This is much higher than Russia (300) and China (119) and even more noticeably higher than Western Europe and Canada (which ranges from 67–116).

This prison boom in the United States began in the 1970s when the number of inmates expanded dramatically from about 100 inmates per 100,000 residents for most of the 20th century to 486 inmates per 100,000 residents by 2004 (Pager, 2007, p. 11).

Prisons are very expensive. American prisons employ more than 700,000 people and cost more than $80 billion annually to maintain (Kyckelhahn, 2015; Slevin, 2005). The cost of imprisoning a person is about $45,771 a year (USA Facts, 2022). The amount that states are spending on corrections has also dramatically increased since the 1980s. U.S. states spent $6.7 billion on corrections in 1985, which increased to $56.6 billion in 2019 (The Sentencing Project, 2021). When we consider the very high rates of recidivism, discussed earlier in this chapter, it is easy to question why we are spending so much money on imprisoning individuals when the rate of returning to crime is so high.

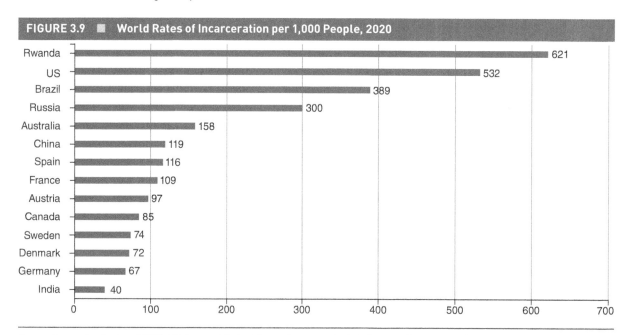

FIGURE 3.9 ■ World Rates of Incarceration per 1,000 People, 2020

Source: Sentencing Project. (2017). *US State and Federal Prison Population, 1925–2015.* https://urrc.tsu.edu/wp-content/uploads/trends-in-us-corrections.pdf; updated data from World Prison Brief. (2023). *World Prison Brief data.* https://www.prisonstudies.org/world-prison-brief-data

Many people argue that one of the reasons that there is such a growth in prisons is because of the **prison industrial complex**: Large numbers of people, including bureaucrats, politicians, private prison companies, and prison employees, have a vested interest in the existence and further expansion of the prison system. The rise of private, for-profit prisons is a particular concern. Because of privatization, these groups may advocate for harsher punishments, which send more people to prisons, or for longer sentences, which keep people in prisons for more time.

Methods in Depth: Big Data, Predictive Policing, and Surveillance

We have seen that there are widespread racial and ethnic disparities in how different groups of people interact with police and the criminal justice system. This is partly a function of higher rates of surveillance in racialized communities. Police surveillance has proliferated since the turn of the 21st century, and this has been facilitated by the growth of big data analytics. Big data refers to the analysis of massive amounts of digital information (sometimes involving tens of millions of unique observations!) that are merged from different sources into one large dataset. The digital nature of big data allows organizations to efficiently share, merge, and quickly analyze millions of observations (Brayne, 2017). The information contained in these datasets facilitates surveillance by identifying high crime areas, which can then be used to direct police activity and resources. However, big data is also increasingly used for predictive policing. Predictive analytics include, for example, using algorithms to determine where future crimes will occur or the people and networks most likely to be involved in gun violence.

Methodology

Sarah Brayne's (2017) research is some of the first to examine how big data is used in predictive policing and whether it amplifies or transforms existing surveillance activities. The research involves a combination of traditional as well as novel methods. Traditional methods include 75 interviews with officers and civilian employees of the Los Angeles Police Department (LAPD), the Los Angeles County Sherriff's Department (LASD), the Joint Regional Intelligence Center (JRIC) of Southern California, and representatives from technology companies (Palantir and PredPol) who design the big data platforms used by the LAPD. Participants in the study include those engaging in crime analysis, police patrolling, criminal investigation, and the provision of criminal and noncriminal activity data to the LAPD. Novel methods include observations on ride-alongs in patrol cars to witness firsthand how big data is used in the field as well as shadowing analysts to reveal how they respond in real time to queries from police and analyze data for patrols.

This combination of methods reveals how big data both amplifies and transforms existing practices. During a ride-along with a police officer, Brayne (2017) found that predictive policing practices included using an officer's experiential knowledge of criminal activity to determine which areas to patrol, and big data analytics provided by PredPol confirmed that these same areas are likely sites of future criminal activity. However, PredPol algorithms also suggested new areas for her and the police officer to visit. The algorithm assumes that once a crime occurs, the immediate surrounding area is also at risk of future crime, facilitating patrols in neighboring areas. The use of ride-alongs provide an important window into how big data is used in the context of predictive policing and expanding surveillance. Interviews and observations related to the Palantir platform reveal how data is now being collected for both a person of interest *and* their social networks. For example, data of a person of interest includes all the people, phone numbers, and addresses he is connected to, as well as their relations to him (sibling, co-worker, etc.). The networks associated with a person of interest can be auto tracked so that police officers receive real-time alerts if they come into contact with any police or government agencies.

Challenges

Brayne's (2017) use of interviews and observations together provide a rich account of how big data operates on the ground to transform policing as well as how it is used to expand surveillance to include larger groups of people and neighborhoods. The use of observations, in particular, functions as a check against interview content. For example, what someone may say in an interview may not accurately reflect what they do in practice. By supplementing interviews with observations, we can get a more accurate account of how big data is generated and used for the purpose of predictive policing and surveillance.

Implications

This research suggests that big data may reproduce existing racial inequalities by increasing surveillance of individuals—and their networks—who reside in low-income and minority communities. Although big data is increasingly used for police surveillance, it is also a potential antidote to racially biased policing because it may hold police accountable for discriminatory practices. More research is needed to better understand how algorithms are produced, as human discretion and bias may be reflected in the type of data that is collected and used for predictive policing and surveillance.

Many employers ask potential new employees whether they have been convicted of a crime. The "Ban the Box" campaign calls for this practice to stop. They argue that, for people to rehabilitate after committing a crime, we need to help facilitate their ability to get jobs and move on with their lives.

Larry French/Getty Images for ColorOfChange.org

SUMMARY

This chapter discussed the different kinds of deviance and crime that exist in society and how these categories are socially constructed. Explanations for deviance can be at the individual level, by looking at a person's biology or personality, or at the social level, by focusing on a person's social environment. Most sociological work in this area focuses on social explanations. We also examined labelling theory and Rosenhan's experiment on the powerful impact of labelling someone a deviant. This chapter explored crime rates around the world, including how these numbers are calculated. We ended by considering punishment's different functions in society and Foucault's famous discussion of changes in punishment.

FOR FURTHER READING

Anderson, E. (1999). *Code of the street*, Norton.

Becker, H. (1963). *Outsiders: Studies in the sociology of deviance*, Free Press.

Downes, D., Rock, P., & McCormick, C. (2013). *Understanding deviance: A guide to the sociology of deviance and rule breaking* ((2nd Canadian ed.) ed.). Oxford University Press.

Foucault, M. (1995). *Discipline and punish: The birth of the prison*, Vintage.

Goffman, E. (1986). *Stigma: Notes on the management of spoiled identity*, Simon and Schuster.

GLOSSARY

consensus crimes

control theory

deterrence

deviance

general deterrence

labelling theory

learning theory

lesser crimes

normality of crime

norms

parole

primary deviance

prison industrial complex

probation

punishment

recidivism rates

rehabilitation

restoration

retribution

secondary deviance

social construction

societal protection

specific deterrence

strain theory

subcultural theory

Uniform Crime Reporting (UCR) Program

white-collar crime

SOCIAL INEQUALITY

Eddie Gerald / Alamy Stock Photo

4 SOCIAL STRATIFICATION AND SOCIAL CLASS

LEARNING OBJECTIVES

1. Describe the main components of Karl Marx's view of social inequality.

2. Explain the relationship between the different classes within capitalism.

3. Analyze the importance of class consciousness and its role in class struggles.

4. Explain and differentiate between Marx's and Weber's understandings of social class.

5. Analyze income and wealth inequality in the United States and assess the level of social mobility over time.

6. Describe how we measure poverty and the ways in which poverty becomes a cycle.

Do you think of yourself as a member of the working class, middle class, upper class, or some other group? If you are like most Americans, you see yourself as middle class. In fact, almost 70% of Americans consider themselves to be middle class (Northwestern Mutual, 2018). This subjective feeling is very important. However, the Pew Research Center finds that, by objective measures, only 50% of Americans fit into the category of middle class (Kochhar & Sechopolos, 2022). What does it mean to be middle class? Why do people choose to describe themselves as members of this class? Why might there be a difference between people's subjective feelings of their class and objective class measures?

In this chapter, we will explore what two of the founders of sociology—Karl Marx and Max Weber—thought about social class. We will also examine the significance of social status and social mobility in the United States. Social class and social status are important because they shape our opportunities, from the neighborhoods we grow up in to the schools we attend and the types of jobs we get. Although most Americans do not think much about the matter of social class, it has many important implications for the kind of life we lead.

CONFLICT THEORY AND KARL MARX

Karl Marx (1818–1883) is one of the most important figures in the development of sociology and, as mentioned in Chapter 2, is the founder of conflict theory. He is also a significant figure outside sociology; his ideas shaped many historical events and are still debated today. Governments espousing Marxist ideology came to power in the Union of Soviet Socialist Republics (USSR, or Soviet Union) in 1922 and the People's Republic of China in 1949. Marx's writings also inspired the rise of many of the world's labor unions and workers' parties, which advocate for workers' rights and safer working conditions.

It may surprise some that Marx's parents were middle class and relatively wealthy. Marx studied at the University of Bonn and the University of Berlin. In 1843 he moved to Paris, where he met Friedrich Engels, with whom he collaborated throughout his life. In 1849, Marx was exiled and moved to London with his family. His work was important as an academic theory and a way of understanding the world. It was also very political and focused on trying to change the world outside academia. For example, he campaigned for socialism and for workers' groups, such as the International Workingmen's Association.

Getting to Know: Karl Marx (1818–1883)

- While he was a student at the University of Bonn, Marx was a member of the Poets' Club and a co-president of the Trier Tavern Club drinking society.

- In university, Marx was in a duel with another student.

- Marx married Jenny von Westphalen, a Prussian baroness, in 1843. Their relationship was controversial because of their different social classes and ethnic origins. They had seven children and, by all accounts, a very happy marriage.

- In 1837, Marx wrote a short novel, a play, and a series of love poems to his wife. All remain unpublished.

Marx argued that the core struggle in all societies is class struggle: conflicts between those who own the means of production (the bourgeoisie, or capitalist) and those who simply own their own labor power (workers, also called the proletariat). He called capitalism—the economic system in which businesses are privately owned and goods are sold on the market for profit—the dictatorship of the bourgeoisie. According to Marx, capitalism is controlled and run by a small group of wealthy business owners. He argued that capitalism, like all previous economic systems, is founded on internal tensions that make it unsustainable. He predicted that capitalism would eventually be replaced by socialism, an alternative economic system featuring collective ownership of the means of production. In socialism, power is held by the working class. Marx referred to this system as the dictatorship of the proletariat or a workers' democracy. He also theorized that socialism would be replaced by communism, a completely classless society (Marx & Engels, 1848).

Marx actively fought for the implementation of socialism, arguing that academics should play an important role in toppling capitalism and causing revolutionary social change. In fact, in the final line of his *Theses on Feuerbach*, a work first published in 1888 and coedited with Engels, Marx writes, "The philosophers have only *interpreted* the world, in various ways. The point, however, is to *change* it" (1888/2004, Thesis 11; emphasis in original). Marx sought to be part of that change by promoting the development of a socialist economic system.

Karl Marx's work encourages us to think critically about how social class shapes our lives and society. And he had a pretty outstanding beard!

Bettmann/Getty Images

Marx's view of the world emphasizes the economy's role in social life. He argued that historical periods are distinguished by the mode of production of goods and services that dominate the time. The mode of production is the system that we use to make things in our society. For example, in early feudalism the nobility owned land, including farms, homes, and villages, and peasants worked the land, mainly using human and animal energy. The mode of production creates the distinctions and relationships between classes in a society. The feudal system led to certain relationships between the nobility and the peasantry. Peasants were tied to land owners, who gave them a place to live and protection in exchange for their labor, and land owners needed peasants to work on their farms and in their homes.

The award-winning South Korean film *Parasite* (2019) depicts the class struggle between the poor Kim family and their wealthy employers, the Parks.

Pictorial Press Ltd / Alamy Stock Photo

CLASS STRUGGLES

Classes, for Marx, are groups of people who play different roles in the productive system. Capitalism has two main classes: the bourgeoisie (capitalists) and the proletariat (workers). The bourgeoisie are the people who own the means of production and property, which is any resource that can be used to produce things of value and to generate wealth. Land is an important type of property because it allows the owner to grow food or raise animals that can be sold. Other types of property include businesses or factories, in which an owner can produce goods such as shoes, clothing, or other products to sell. Thus, the bourgeoisie owns the means of producing more wealth.

The proletariat does not own the means of production. Members of the proletariat own only their capacity to labor (either physically or mentally), which they must sell to the capitalist. Thus, the proletariat must work in the capitalists' factories or on their farms to make a wage (which is a fraction of the profits from the bourgeoisie's sales set by the bourgeoisie) to survive.

Marx argued that classes are relational and are defined by their relationship to both the means of production and to each other. Capitalists cannot exist without workers to labor in their factories; at the same time, workers must have somewhere to sell their labor to make money to survive. However, the relationship between these two groups is coercive by nature: Workers are beholden to the capitalist, who can pay them low wages and give them poor working conditions. Marx argued that capitalism functions and continues to exist through this perpetual exploitation of the worker's labor and subsequent oppression.

Despite the power differentiation between the bourgeoisie and proletariat, the two classes clearly depend on one another. The capitalist cannot have a functioning factory or farm without workers. And the worker needs the capitalist to make a wage in order to live. But the relationship between the two is by nature unequal, which inevitably leads to class struggles. As

Marx (Marx & Engels, 1848, p. 34) describes, "The history of all hitherto existing society is the history of class struggles. Freeman and slave, patrician and plebeian, lord and serf, guild-master and journeyman, in a word, oppressor and oppressed, stood in constant opposition to one another, carried on an uninterrupted, now hidden, now open fight, a fight that each time ended, either in a revolutionary reconstitution of society at large, or in the common ruin of the contending classes." According to Marx, class struggles exist because the classes want different things and have different interests. For example, capitalists want to make as much money as they can from their factories or farms. They must pay wages so that workers will be able to live and return to the workplace over time. However, capitalists want to extract the most surplus value—the excess value that workers produce beyond the cost of their labor—from the workers that they can. Surplus value is the amount of money that capitalists get to keep after paying their workers' wages. It is not surprising that capitalists want as much of this surplus as possible, which means keeping wages low, having workers work quickly, and setting long work hours. As Marx (1867/2000, p. 218) wrote, "The rate of surplus value is . . . an exact expression of the degree of exploitation of labour power by capital, or of the labourer by the capitalist."

Workers and capitalists want very different things. Workers want to make a good wage that allows them to live and support their families, and they want to work under safe conditions and for a reasonable number of hours. These desires can conflict with the capitalist's attempt to make large profits, which could include creating more cost-effective, yet more dangerous, workplaces.

READING: "MANIFESTO OF THE COMMUNIST PARTY"

Karl Marx and Friedrich Engels

Marx wrote many academic books about the problems created by capitalism and a possible socialist future. He was also interested in helping to overthrow capitalism. He worked to help encourage a worker's revolution by explaining the perils of capitalism and the benefits of socialist and communist systems to a wider audience. In 1848, the Communist League commissioned Marx and Engels to write a short pamphlet outlining the problems with capitalism. The following is an excerpt from the result, *The Communist Manifesto.*

Bourgeois and Proletarians 1

In the earlier epochs of history, we find almost everywhere a complicated arrangement of society into various orders, a manifold gradation of social rank. In ancient Rome we have patricians, knights, plebeians, slaves; in the Middle Ages, feudal lords, vassals, guild-masters, journeymen, apprentices, serfs; in almost all of these classes, again, subordinate gradations.

The modern bourgeois society that has sprouted from the ruins of feudal society has not done away with clash antagonisms. It has but established new classes, new conditions of oppression, new forms of struggle in place of the old ones.

Our epoch, the epoch of the bourgeoisie, possesses, however, this distinctive feature: it has simplified the class antagonisms: Society as a whole is more and more splitting up into two great hostile camps, into two great classes directly facing each other: Bourgeoisie and Proletariat.

From the serfs of the Middle Ages sprang the charted burghers of the earliest towns. From these burgesses the first elements of the bourgeoisie were developed.

The discovery of America, the rounding of the Cape, opened up fresh ground for the rising bourgeoisie. The East-Indian and Chinese markets, the colonization of America, trade with the colonies, the increase in the means of exchange and in commodities generally, gave to commerce, to navigation, to industry, an impulse never before known, and thereby, to the revolutionary element in the tottering feudal society, a rapid development.

The feudal system of industry, under which industrial production was monopolized by closed guilds, now no longer sufficed for the growing wants of the new markets. The manufacturing system took its place. The guild-masters were pushed on one side by the manufacturing middle class; division of labor between the different corporate guilds vanished in the face of division of labor in each single workshop.

Meantime the markets kept ever growing, the demand ever rising. Even manufacture no longer sufficed. Thereupon, steam and machinery revolutionized industrial production. The place of manufacture was taken by the giant, Modern Industry, the place of the industrial middle class, by industrial millionaires, the leaders of whole industrial armies, the modern bourgeois.

Modern Industry has established the world market, for which the discovery of America paved the way. This market has given an immense development to commerce, to navigation, to communication by land. This development has, in its turn, reacted on the extension of industry; and in proportion as industry, commerce, navigation, railways extended, in the same proportion the bourgeoisie developed, increased its capital, and pushed into the background every class handed down from the Middle Ages.

We see, therefore, how the modern bourgeoisie is itself the product of a long course of development, of a series of revolutions in the modes of production and of exchange.

Each step in the development of the bourgeoisie was accompanied by a corresponding political advance of that class. An oppressed class under the sway of the feudal nobility, an armed and self-governing association in the medieval commune;[2] here independent urban republic (as in Italy and Germany), there taxable "third estate" of the monarchy (as in France), afterwards, in the period of manufacture proper, serving either the semi-feudal or the absolute monarchy as a counterpoise against the nobility, and, in fact, cornerstone of the great monarchies in general, the bourgeoisie has at last, since the establishment of Modern Industry and of the world market, conquered for itself, in the modern representative State, exclusive political sway. The executive of the modern State is but a committee for managing the common affairs of the whole bourgeoisie.

The bourgeoisie, historically, has played a most revolutionary part.

The bourgeoisie, wherever it has got the upper hand, has put an end to all feudal, patriarchal, idyllic relations. It has pitilessly torn asunder the motley feudal ties that bound man to his "natural superiors," and has left remaining no other nexus between man and man than naked self- interest, than callous "cash payment." It has drowned the most heavenly ecstasies of religious fervour, of chivalrous enthusiasm, of philistine sentimentalism, in the icy water of egotistical calculation. It has resolved personal worth into exchange value, and in place of the numberless indefeasible chartered freedoms, has set up that single, unconscionable freedom—Free Trade. In one word, for exploitation, veiled by religious and political illusions, it has substituted naked, shameless, direct, brutal exploitation.

The bourgeoisie has stripped of its halo every occupation hitherto honored and looked up to with reverent awe. It has converted the physician, the lawyer, the priest, the poet, the man of science, into its paid wage-laborers.

The bourgeoisie has torn away from the family its sentimental veil, and has reduced the family relation to a mere money relation. . . .

The bourgeoisie cannot exist without constantly revolutionizing the instruments of production, and thereby the relations of production, and with them the whole relations of society. Conservation of the old modes of production in unaltered form, was, on the contrary, the first condition of existence for all earlier industrial classes. Constant revolutionizing of production, uninterrupted disturbance of all social conditions, everlasting uncertainty and agitation distinguish the bourgeois epoch from all earlier ones. All fixed, fast-frozen relations, with their train of ancient and venerable prejudices and opinions, are swept away, all new-formed ones become antiquated before they can ossify. All that is solid melts into air, all that is holy is profaned, and man is at last compelled to face with sober senses, his real conditions of life, and his relations with his kind.

The need of a constantly expanding market for its products chases the bourgeoisie over the whole surface of the globe. It must nestle everywhere, settle everywhere, establish connections everywhere. . . .

The bourgeoisie, by the rapid improvement of all instruments of production, by the immensely facilitated means of communication, draws all, even the most barbarian, nations into civilization. The cheap prices of its commodities are the heavy artillery with which it batters down all Chinese walls, with which it forces the barbarians' intensely obstinate hatred of foreigners to capitulate. It compels all nations, on pain of extinction, to adopt the bourgeois mode of production; it compels them to introduce what it calls civilization into their midst, i.e., to become bourgeois themselves. In one word, it creates a world after its own image.

The bourgeoisie has subjected the country to the rule of the towns. It has created enormous cities, has greatly increased the urban population as compared with the rural, and has thus rescued a considerable part of the population from the idiocy of rural life. Just as it has made the country dependent on the towns, so it has made barbarian and semi-barbarian countries dependent on the civilized ones, nations of peasants on nations of bourgeois, the East on the West.

The bourgeoisie keeps more and more doing away with the scattered state of the population, of the means of production, and of property. It has agglomerated population, centralized means of production, and has concentrated property in a few hands. The necessary consequence of this was political centralization. Independent, or but loosely connected provinces, with separate interests, laws, governments, and systems of taxation, became lumped together into one nation, with one government, one code of laws, one national class-interest, one frontier, and one customs-tariff.

The bourgeoisie, during its rule of scarce 100 years, has created more massive and more colossal productive forces than have all preceding generations together. Subjection of Nature's forces to man, machinery, application of chemistry to industry and agriculture, steam navigation, railways, electric telegraphs, clearing of whole continents for cultivation, canalization of rivers, whole populations conjured out of the ground—what earlier century had even a presentiment that such productive forces slumbered in the lap of social labor?

We see then: the means of production and of exchange, on whose foundation the bourgeoisie built itself up, were generated in feudal society. At a certain stage in the development of these means of production and of exchange, the conditions under which feudal society produced and exchanged, the feudal organization of agriculture and manufacturing industry, in one word, the feudal relations of property became no longer compatible with the already developed productive forces; they became so many fetters. They had to be burst asunder; they were burst asunder.

Into their place stepped free competition, accompanied by a social and political constitution adapted to it, and by the economical and political sway of the bourgeois class. . . .

The weapons with which the bourgeoisie felled feudalism to the ground are now turned against the bourgeoisie itself.

But not only has the bourgeoisie forged the weapons that bring death to itself; it has also called into existence the men who are to wield those weapons—the modern working class—the proletarians.

In proportion as the bourgeoisie, i.e., capital, is developed, in the same proportion is the proletariat, the modern working class, developed—a class of laborers, who live only so long as they find work, and who find work only so long as their labor increases capital. These laborers, who must sell themselves piecemeal, are a commodity, like every other article of commerce, and are consequently exposed to all the vicissitudes of competition, to all the fluctuations of the market.

Owing to the extensive use of machinery and to division of labor, the work of the proletarians has lost all individual character, and consequently, all charm for the workman. He becomes an appendage of the machine, and it is only the most simple, most monotonous, and most easily acquired knack, that is required of him. Hence, the cost of production of a workman is restricted, almost entirely, to the means of subsistence that he requires for his maintenance, and for the propagation of his race. But the price of a commodity, and therefore also of labor,[3] is equal to its cost of production. In proportion, therefore, as the repulsiveness of the work increases, the wage decreases. Nay more, in proportion as the use of machinery and division of labor increases, in the same proportion the burden of toil also increases, whether by prolongation of the working hours, by increase of the work exacted in a given time or by increased speed of the machinery, etc.

Modern industry has converted the little workshop of the patriarchal master into the great factory of the industrial capitalist. Masses of laborers, crowded into the factory, are organized like soldiers. As privates of the industrial army they are placed under the command of a perfect hierarchy of officers and sergeants. Not only are they slaves of the bourgeois class, and of the bourgeois State; they are daily and hourly enslaved by the machine, by the overlooker, and, above all, by the individual bourgeois manufacturer himself. The more openly this despotism proclaims gain to be its end and aim, the more petty, the more hateful and the more embittering it is.

The less the skill and exertion of strength implied in manual labor, in other words, the more modern industry becomes developed, the more is the labor of men superseded by that of women. Differences of age and sex have no longer any distinctive social validity for the working class. All are instruments of labor, more or less expensive to use, according to their age and sex.

No sooner is the exploitation of the laborer by the manufacturer, so far, at an end, that he receives his wages in cash, than he is set upon by the other portions of the bourgeoisie, the landlord, the shopkeeper, the pawnbroker, etc.

The lower strata of the middle class—the small tradespeople, shopkeepers, and retired tradesmen generally, the handicraftsmen and peasants—all these sink gradually into the proletariat, partly because their diminutive capital does not suffice for the scale on which Modern Industry is carried on, and is swamped in the competition with the large capitalists, partly because their specialized skill is rendered worthless by new methods of production. Thus the proletariat is recruited from all classes of the population. . . .

But with the development of industry the proletariat not only increases in number; it becomes concentrated in greater masses, its strength grows, and it feels that strength more. The various interests and conditions of life within the ranks of the proletariat are more and more equalized, in proportion as machinery obliterates all distinctions of labor, and nearly everywhere reduces wages to the same low level. The growing competition among the bourgeois, and the resulting commercial crises, make the wages of the workers ever more fluctuating. The unceasing improvement of machinery, ever more rapidly developing, makes their livelihood more and more precarious; the collisions between individual workmen and individual bourgeois take more and more the character of collisions between two classes. Thereupon the workers begin to form combinations (Trades Unions) against the bourgeois; they club together in order to keep up the rate of wages; they found permanent associations in order to make provision beforehand for these occasional revolts. Here and there the contest breaks out into riots.

Now and then the workers are victorious, but only for a time. The real fruit of their battles lies, not in the immediate result, but in the ever-expanding union of the workers. This union is helped on by the improved means of communication that are created by modern industry and that place the workers of different localities in contact with one another. It was just this contact that was needed to centralize the numerous local struggles, all of the same character, into one national struggle between classes. But every class struggle is a political struggle. And that union, to attain which the burghers of the Middle Ages, with their miserable highways, required centuries, the modern proletarians, thanks to railways, achieve in a few years.

This organization of the proletarians into a class, and consequently into a political party, is continually being upset again by the competition between the workers themselves. But it ever rises up again, stronger, firmer, mightier. It compels legislative recognition of particular interests of the workers, by taking advantage of the divisions among the bourgeoisie itself. Thus the ten-hours' bill in England was carried. . . .

The lower-middle class, the small manufacturer, the shopkeeper, the artisan, the peasant, all these fight against the bourgeoisie, to save from extinction their existence as fractions of the middle class. They are therefore not revolutionary, but conservative. Nay more, they are reactionary, for they try to roll back the wheel of history. If by chance they are revolutionary, they are so only in view of their impending transfer into the proletariat, they thus defend not their present, but their future interests, they desert their own standpoint to place themselves at that of the proletariat. . . .

Hitherto, every form of society has been based, as we have already seen, on the antagonism of oppressing and oppressed classes. But in order to oppress a class, certain conditions must be assured to it under which it can, at least, continue its slavish existence. The serf, in the period of serfdom, raised himself to membership in the commune, just as the petty bourgeois, under the yoke of feudal absolutism, managed to develop into a bourgeois. The modern laborer, on the contrary, instead of rising with the progress of industry, sinks deeper and deeper below the conditions of existence of his own class. He becomes a pauper, and pauperism develops more rapidly than population and wealth. And here it becomes evident, that the bourgeoisie is unfit any longer to be the ruling class in society, and to impose its conditions of existence upon society as an overriding law. It is unfit to rule because it is incompetent to assure an existence to its slave within his slavery, because it cannot help letting him sink into such a state, that it has to feed him, instead of being fed by him. Society can no longer live under this bourgeoisie, in other words, its existence is no longer compatible with society.

The essential condition for the existence, and for the sway of the bourgeois class, is the formation and augmentation of capital; the condition for capital is wage-labor. Wage-labor rests exclusively on competition between the laborers. The advance of industry, whose involuntary promoter is the bourgeoisie, replaces the isolation of the laborers, due to competition, by their revolutionary combination, due to association. The development of Modern Industry, therefore, cuts from under its feet the very foundation on which the bourgeoisie produces and appropriates products. What the bourgeoisie, therefore, produces, above all, is its own gravediggers. Its fall and the victory of the proletariat are equally inevitable.

Notes

By bourgeoisie is meant the class of modern Capitalists, owners of the means of social production and employers of wage-labor. By proletariat, the class of modern wage-laborers who, having no means of production of their own, are reduced to selling their labor-power in order to live. [*Engels, English Edition of 1888*]

"Commune" was the name taken, in France, by the nascent towns even before they had conquered from their feudal lords and masters local self-government and political rights as the "Third Estate." Generally speaking, for the economical development of the bourgeoisie, England is here taken as the typical country; for its political development, France. [*Engels, English edition of 1888*]

This was the name given their urban communities by the townsmen of Italy and France, after they had purchased or wrested their initial rights of self- government from their feudal lords. [*Engels, German edition of 1890*]

Subsequently Marx pointed out that the worker sells not his labor but his labor power.

Reading Questions

1. What significant changes occurred with the rise of the bourgeoisie class?
2. What is the relationship between the bourgeoisie and the proletariat?
3. The final stage proposed by Marx and Engels was a communist society without classes. Marx argues that the actions of the bourgeoisie will lead to this change. How does he think that this could happen?

Marx, K., & Engels, F. (1848). Manifesto of the communist party. In K. Marx & F. Engels (Eds.), *Marx/Engels selected works* (Vol. 1, pp. 21–65). Progress.

The Ideology of Capitalism

It seems clear from Marx's discussion that capitalism can create many problems for workers and that the inequality between those who own the means of production and those who own only their labor power can be severe. However, it is also clear that there are many more workers than there are capitalists. Why don't the workers simply rise up and ask for better wages, working conditions, and other benefits? Why don't they start the revolution Marx dreamed about? Marx outlined several reasons for the lack of such an uprising and for the difficulties in uniting to fight oppression.

One of the main reasons that workers do not join together is due to ideology. An ideology is a set of conscious and unconscious ideas or beliefs that govern and guide people's lives. Marx (2000) said that the dominant ideologies in any historical epoch are those of the dominant class in that period: "The ideas of the ruling class are in every epoch the ruling ideas, i.e., the class which is the ruling material force of society, is at the same time its ruling intellectual force" (p. 64).

For those of us who were raised within capitalist societies, it is sometimes hard to see the many ideologies and assumptions on which this system is based. Ideologies such as meritocracy, individualism, progress, expansion, and development are fundamentally intertwined with our economic system, yet they often seem natural and invisible so they end up being accepted by those within the society.

For example, American society has a strong belief in meritocracy, the idea that people will achieve based on their own merit. This ideology supports the idea that wealthy people earned their money from working hard and that those with less money must have not worked as hard or are less deserving. From a Marxist perspective, we can see that this ideology benefits the bourgeoisie by legitimizing the fact that they have money, highlighting

Kylie Jenner appeared on the cover of *Time* magazine labelled as the youngest "self-made millionaire." As the child of wealthy parents and the sister of many wealthy women, such as Kim Kardashian, how "self-made" is Kylie Jenner? How does this headline support our broader ideology of meritocracy?

Araya Doheny/Getty Images for Baby2Baby

the hard work and intelligence it took to get that money, and making it seem that anyone could achieve this status with effort and perseverance. It helps encourage the proletariat (the rest of us) to buy into the system of capitalism because it promotes the belief that we, too, can become rich and successful if we work hard enough. However, this ideology ignores the many other factors that determine one's social position. An individual's social class, which shapes his educational opportunities and social connections, also plays an important role in determining financial and other types of success. Marx would argue that other ideologies, such as individualism and progress, also benefit the dominant class and legitimize the economic and social system as it is.

Marx claimed that workers in capitalism develop a false consciousness, a willingness to believe in ideologies that support the ruling class but are disadvantageous to working-class interests. Ideologies such as individualism and meritocracy support and serve the interests of the dominant class. They blunt the working class's desire to unite and call on capitalists and governments to be more responsive to their needs. Social institutions, such as the education system, mass media, and the family, teach us these ideologies and help to perpetuate them.

One example of an ideology in modern American society that perpetuates capitalism is the ideology of positive thinking. This ideology is the basis of Gwyneth Paltrow's Goop website and Oprah's book club, among other endeavors. Take, for example, the book *The Secret*, a best-selling self-help book by Rhonda Byrne (2006). Based on what Byrne calls the law of attraction, the book claims that positive thinking can create life-changing results, such as increased wealth, health, and happiness. The book has sold almost 20 million copies and has been translated into 52 languages. Here are a few examples of Byrne's advice:

- Money is magnetic energy. You are a magnet attracting to you all things, via the signal you are emitting through your thoughts and feelings. To become a powerful money magnet:

- Be clear about the amount of money you want to receive. State it and intend it! Do not think about how much money you earn, but instead think about how much you want to receive.

- Visualize and imagine yourself spending all the money you want, as though you already have it.

- Speak, act, and think from the mindset of being wealthy now. Eliminate thoughts and words of lack such as "I can't afford it" or "It is too expensive."

- Do whatever it takes for you to feel wealthy.

- Do whatever it takes to feel good. The emotions of joy and happiness are powerful money magnets. Be happy now!)

It is hard to argue that positive thinking is a bad thing: Everyone likes a person with a positive attitude! But is there a danger in these kinds of teachings? First, consider that an ideology that says that individuals can create the wealth they want also encourages us to blame those who are poor for their circumstances. Perhaps they were simply not clear enough about the money they wanted or were not committed enough to this goal? This individual focus also detracts from larger systemic reasons why some people have less than others, including racial or gender inequality, discrimination, and other factors. Second, the idea that we should act as though we are wealthy now without considering our actual financial situation encourages overspending and the accumulation of debt, something that is great for capitalism but not so great for individuals. In fact, this is very dangerous and potentially self-perpetuating for individuals. Once we are in debt, it is very hard to get out. Although Marx surely did not read *The Secret,* the ideologies in this book would concern him because of the way that they support capitalism without considering the impact on workers.

The State and the Class System

For Marx, even the government is simply a tool of capitalism because capitalists use the state to further their own interests. In fact, Marx (1975) says that the state is used to sustain the class system that benefits the ruling class. Consequently, he argues, the state does not reflect the interest of most people, who are the workers. This situation is complicated in a democracy by the fact that the workers have the right to vote. The small group of capitalists must persuade the larger group of workers to accept the concentration of power in the former's hands. This is done, in part, by the capitalist control of ideas through avenues such as the media and school curriculums. Through these mechanisms, the capitalist tries to persuade the workers that the current system is the optimal way of running society and is simply the natural way for things to be organized. However, Marx argued that when these softer ways of convincing people about the benefits of capitalism fail, the ruling class uses more coercive methods, such as the police, military, or the judicial system, to defend this system.

Marx and Engels demonstrated that, far from being inevitable, the current organization of the economy is socially constructed and can be changed. The means of production—in our case, capitalism—determines the resulting social systems, relations, class struggles, and ideologies in society. Marx and Engels argued that all aspects of society, from overarching power structures (i.e., the way the government is run) to daily individual experiences with exploitation (i.e., workers in factories) form as a result of the economic system or means of production.

Are There Just Two Social Classes?

Marx's ideas have formed how many sociologists and others think about social class. However, these ideas have not gone without criticism. Many people argue that there are no longer simply two classes and they criticize Marx for seeing the economic world as such a sharp distinction between capitalists and workers. In some ways, this criticism is unfair. Marx (1907) identified two smaller and, in his opinion, less important class groupings: the petite bourgeoisie and the lumpenproletariat. The petite bourgeoisie (little bourgeoisie) are small-scale capitalists, such as shopkeepers and managers. People in this group do not necessarily sell their labor like proletariats, but neither do they buy the labor of others like the capitalists (Marx & Engels, 1848). Unlike the bourgeoisie, the petite bourgeoisie often work alongside laborers. For example, a petite bourgeoisie who owns a small coffee shop might, like his employees, make coffee. However, the owner of Starbucks, a large bourgeoisie, would not. Because the petite bourgeoisie work alongside their employees, they may know their workers better and be more sympathetic to their concerns. If the coffee shop is too hot or the espresso machine burns the baristas' hands, this may be more quickly noticed and of concern to an owner who also has to work in the store and make coffee than it would be to an owner of a large coffee company who rarely goes into the cafés. However, Marx said that the petite bourgeoisie would disappear over time, mostly because they would eventually fall into the proletariat class.

The lumpenproletariat (translated roughly as slum workers) is the lowest layer of the working class. Marx (1907) says that this class includes beggars, prostitutes, petty criminals, and the chronically unemployed. Marx largely dismissed this group, believing that its members were highly unlikely to join what he hoped would be a workers' revolution.

Keeping Marx's classes in mind, where would a group such as lawyers fit? This occupational group makes a relatively high salary yet does not own the means of production. Under Marx's conceptual framework, they would be considered proletariats. However, some theorists argue that workers such as lawyers are not in the same fundamentally exploitative relationship with capitalists as the proletariat class that Marx discussed.

Economic systems have changed since Marx's time. He wrote in an era of industrial capitalism, when most individuals working in paid labor were employed in manufacturing. Today, however, most people work in other industries. In 2020, 80% of Americans had service jobs (e.g., retail, health, and education) and only 13% worked in the goods-producing sector, including manufacturing, construction, and mining (U.S. Bureau of Labor Statistics, 2021). As you can see, changes in the structure of the economic system complicate Marx's theories of class stratification.

CLASS CONSCIOUSNESS

Class consciousness is a term used in Marxist theory to refer to people's beliefs regarding their social class and class interests. Marx (Marx & Engels, 1848) made a distinction between a class in itself, a category of people with a common relation to the means of production (such as the worker), and a class for itself, a group organized in active pursuit of its own interests (such as unionized workers pushing for better working conditions). Class consciousness is an awareness of what is in the best interests of one's class and is an important precondition for organizing into a class for itself to advocate for class interests.

Marx wanted the working class to develop a class consciousness so that workers could fight for socialism. Class consciousness has also been important in many capitalist societies, such as the United States, in leading to the rise of unions. Unions are organizations of employees who work together to negotiate for their join interests, including pay, benefits, hiring and firing practices, and working conditions. Through a process known as collective bargaining, unions negotiate with the employer on behalf of workers, and they negotiate labor contracts. These actions are a result of a group of people working as a class for itself, with the unions advocating for workers' rights.

Customer service and warehouse workers experienced particularly dangerous and stressful working conditions during the COVID-19 pandemic. In response, many of these workers, including at some Amazon and Starbucks locations, have started to unionize for higher wages and stronger workplace safety protections.

Shannon Finney/Getty Images for SEIU

Trade union density is the percentage of wage earners in a population who are part of a union. Table 4.1 shows this density across time and countries. We can see that there is a wide range in union membership across countries. For example, 91% of workers in Iceland are in a union whereas only one-tenth of workers in the United States are union members.

TABLE 4.1 ■ Trade Union Density, Selected Countries, 1999–2018					
	Percentage of Employees				
Country	1998	2003	2008	2013	2018
Turkey	19	17	11	6	9
Korea	11	11	10	10	.*
United States	13	12	12	11	10
Mexico	17	.	16	14	12
Japan	22	20	18	18	17
Australia	28	23	19	17	14
Canada	29	28	27	27	26
Ireland	41	35	30	31	24
Sweden	81	78	68	68	65
Iceland	88	87	85	89	91

*Cells with a "." denote missing data.

Source: Data from OECD, 2021, "Trade Union Density," OECD Stat (database), https://stats.oecd.org/Index.aspx?Data SetCode=TUD

We can also see that, in general, union density is on the decline. With the exception of Iceland, each country in the sample has seen a drop in union density over the 20-year period. In the United States the decline has been relatively small, only 3%, but it has been consistently quite low. However, the decline in Sweden has been steep (16%), which is notable because the rate of unionization in Sweden has been very high.

Why are unionization rates declining? Comparing rates in Canada and the United States sheds some light on this question. These two countries had similar rates of union membership from 1920 to 1960. However, as you can see from Figure 4.1, the rates have diverged dramatically since that time.

There are many potential reasons for the decrease in American unionization rates. Some people argue that globalization and technological advances have undermined unions. Others claim that the decline in manufacturing has led to fewer union jobs. However, these factors have affected both the United States and Canada, but the latter maintains a relatively high rate of unionization. How can we explain this difference?

In general, American labor laws and public policies have been less supportive of unions than have laws in Canada. For example, several Canadian provinces ban temporary or permanent strike replacement (people who work in place of striking employees, sometimes called scab workers). These laws do not exist in the United States. Also, 28 U.S. states have "right-to-work" laws, which restrict a union's ability to require individual members to pay union dues. These laws make it more difficult for unions to fund their work. Furthermore, the process of creating a

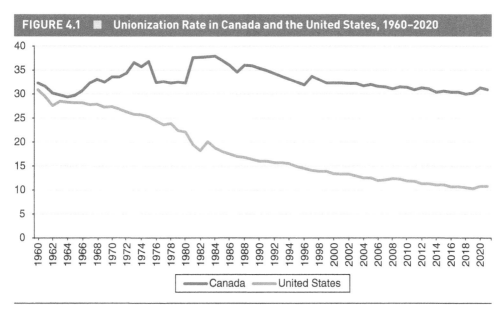

FIGURE 4.1 ■ Unionization Rate in Canada and the United States, 1960–2020

Sources: Statistics Canada. Table 14-10-0132-01 Union status by industry. DOI: https://doi.org/10.25318/1410013201-eng; Statistics Canada. https://www150.statcan.gc.ca/n1/daily-quotidien/170908/dq170908a-eng.htm; Bureau of Labor Statistics, U.S. Department of Labor, The Economics Daily, A look at union membership rates across industries in 2020 at https://www.bls.gov/opub/ted/2021/a-look-at-union-membership-rates-across-industries-in-2020.htm (visited May 10, 2023).; Dunn, M., & Walker, J. (2016, September 1). *Union membership in the United States.* Retrieved May 9, 2023, from https://www.bls.gov/spotlight/2016/union-membership-in-the-united-states/; OECD/AIAS database on Institutional Characteristics of Trade Unions, Wage Setting, State Intervention and Social Pacts (ICTWSS) https://stats.oecd.org/Index.aspx?DataSetCode=TUD#

union is much quicker in Canada. It usually takes only 5 to 10 days, once the employees have signed a petition. The same process can take months or years in the United States.

These examples clearly illustrate how public policies and laws can shape larger structures in society, such as unionization rates. Creating a union is one way for the working class to organize into a class for itself. However, these organizations face challenges, such as ideological barriers presented by the ruling classes and structural impediments enacted by them, such as laws.

Class struggle between workers and capitalists can be overt. When workers strike, create a union, or lead a revolution, they are open and clear about their unhappiness with the power inequality between themselves and capitalists. Marx advocated for overt struggles against the capitalist system. However, workers can also engage in more covert actions to undermine capitalism, capitalists, and their workplaces. As Hollander and Einwohner (2004, p. 545) explain, "Overt resistance is behaviour that is visible and readily recognized by both targets and observers as resistance and, further, is intended to be recognized as such. This category includes collective acts such as social movements . . . as well as individual acts of refusal We use the term *covert resistance* to refer to acts that are intentional yet go unnoticed (and, therefore, unpunished) by their targets, although they are recognized as resistance by other, culturally aware observers."

Imagine that you think your boss or company is treating you badly. Perhaps you are paid a low wage, need to work a lot of unpaid overtime, adjust to changing schedules at the last minute, work in unsafe conditions, or put up with being harassed at work. You have the option of overt resistance, such as forming a union or complaining to your boss's boss, but you fear losing your job or being punished. Instead, you show your unhappiness by engaging in more covert actions. Perhaps you work a little slower than you could or waste time at work. You spend a few extra minutes checking your e-mail or texting friends. Perhaps you undermine your boss by talking about her with coworkers or you do not quite follow the rules—you give customers free refills or you do not wear the proper uniform. You might push this covert resistance so far that you steal from your work by taking extra food or other things. You justify this action by telling yourself that you are just leveling the playing field. This sort of resistance aims at regaining dignity from organizations that violate workers' interests and undermine their autonomy. Have you engaged in any of these activities at work? Are they ever justified? If so, in what context?

MAX WEBER AND THE MULTIPLE BASES OF POWER

Though highly influenced by Marx, Max Weber (1864–1920) took a slightly different approach to thinking about inequality. Born in Prussia, Weber became a faculty member at the University of Berlin and wrote a series of ground-breaking sociological works. His book *The Protestant Ethic and the Spirit of Capitalism* (1905/1958) was translated into English in 1930 by Talcott Parsons (one of the most famous structural functionalists, whom we learned about in Chapter 2). At the time of his death, he was working on *Economy and Society*, which was completed by his wife, Marianne Weber, and published in 1922. *From Max Weber: Essays in Sociology* (1946), edited and translated by H. H. Gerth and C. Wright Mills, remains the most comprehensive collection of Weber's works. (You will remember C. Wright Mill from his theory of the sociological imagination in Chapter 1.) As Gerth and Mills write in their introduction, "The prestige of Max Weber among European social scientists would be difficult to over-estimate. He is widely considered the greatest of German sociologists and has become a leading influence in European and American thought" (in Shimer, 1946, p. 374).

Getting to Know: Max Weber (1864–1920)

- Max Weber's full name is Karl Emil Maximillian Weber. With these two additional names, is it any surprise that he, Karl Marx, and Emile Durkheim became three founding fathers of sociology?

- For Christmas 1876, Weber gave his parents two historical essays he had written: "About the Course of German History, with Special Reference to the Positions of the Emperor and the Pope" and "About the Roman Imperial Period from Constantine to the Migration of Nations." Quite a present from a 12-year-old!

- During his first years as a student at the University of Berlin, Weber spent much of his time "drinking and fencing"—a dangerous combination.

- Weber suffered from depression and insomnia and spent the summer and fall of 1900 in a sanatorium. He described his ongoing ordeal in his autobiography, which was later destroyed by his wife because she feared that public knowledge of his mental illness would tarnish his legacy.

Weber began his theory of social inequality by looking at the distribution of power in society. In *Economy and Society,* he defines power in the following way: "In general, we understand by 'power' the chance of a [person] or of a number of [people] to realize their own will in a communal action even against the resistance of others who are participating in the same action" (cited in Gerth & Mills, 1946, p. 180). Although he agreed with Marx that economic power is very important, Weber argued that many other, noneconomic factors are significant parts of who has power in society and who does not. Ideas and interests that emerge from politics, religion, and other institutions also shape who has power in society. Contrary to Marx, Weber contended that these other types of power are not simply secondary to the economy. He posited that there are three primary bases of power in society: economic class (income, wealth), social status (prestige, honor), and party (political power). For Weber, classes are about power in the economic order, status groups are about power in the social order, and parties are about power oriented toward influencing communal action.

Both Weber and Marx define class based on an individual's relationship to the economy. Classes, for Weber, are groups of people who share a similar position with respect to the ownership of property or goods. They are economic categories developing out of human interaction in a market, a system of competitive exchange whereby people buy and sell things of value in pursuit of profit. According to Weber, a class is a group of people sharing a common situation in this market and, therefore, having common interests. The main division for Weber was between the classes with property and those without. So far, this description sounds very similar to Marx's theory of class, discussed earlier in the chapter. The difference between Marx and Weber lies in the finer details of their ideas about class and the divisions they saw. Weber said that class can be differentiated into the kinds of property and services that an individual can offer in a market. Whereas Marx described two main groups, Weber claimed that there were four classes: large capitalists, small capitalists, specialists, and the working class.

Large capitalists own large factories, farms, or other businesses that employ large numbers of workers; small capitalists (or what Marx called the petite bourgeoisie) own smaller businesses with fewer employees.

Max Weber is one of the core founding fathers of sociology.

Archiv Gerstenberg/ullstein bild/ Getty Images

Specialists, such as doctors, lawyers, and professors, have marketable skills and training that they sell to the capitalist through their labor. The working class, which is similar to Marx's proletariat, are manual laborers. They do not have specialized education or training; therefore, they have less power and freedom in the labor market than specialists do.

Weber's second main basis of power is status. **Status groups** have a style of life based on social honor and prestige that is expressed in our interactions with each other. This kind of recognition can be formal—such as when we refer to a person with a special title or give them a degree to mark their status. The titles "doctor" or "professor" refer to a particular type of education and occupation. These titles cannot be used by people freely who do not have this education or experience. However, status can also be informal, such as when we respect older people even if they have no specific title or position of authority. Social honor may be either positive or negative, in that an individual may be given a high level of social esteem or honor or may be disrespected because she is seen to fall into an undesirable social category.

In general, people of high social class tend to have high status. For example, a CEO of a large company is from the capitalist class and has a lot of status. She is likely to have a lifestyle that involves a large house, designer clothing, and luxury goods. Such people are usually accorded respect and esteem by others. Conversely, those with low social class tend to have low social status. People who work in fast-food restaurants, for example, have a low social class and receive little status or respect in society.

It is important to note, however, that social class and social status do not always correspond. For example, priests, rabbis, and imams have very high social status. They are accorded much distinction and esteem and are deferred to in a variety of social settings, yet they are not necessarily of the upper social class. They are not capitalists who own the means of production; in fact, many of them have very little money. At the other end of the spectrum, plumbers or electricians might make a good salary and be self-employed (making them petite bourgeoisie or bourgeoisie). However, people in these jobs are not generally accorded the respect or status given to religious leaders. Weber's ideas encourage us to think about how social class and social status are distinct constructs and how power in society is multidimensional.

Status groups can be formed from a variety of dimensions. For example, men and women form different status groups. They have distinct styles of life and are accorded different levels of esteem. Sexual orientations, education levels, ethnicities, religions, and neighborhood affiliations could also be status groups. Hence, individuals can be a part of many different status groups but are in only one social class.

Weber's last main dimension of power is party. Parties are organizations that attempt to influence social action and that focus on achieving some goal in the sphere of power. Parties are not simply political parties, such as the Democratic Party or the Republican Party. Parties also include groups aimed at improving specific social problems (e.g., a neighborhood watch or a parent-teacher group), environmental groups (e.g., Greenpeace, World Wildlife Fund) or even sporting and recreation organizations.

As the preceding discussion shows, the theories of Marx and Weber have certain similarities and differences. Are their theories compatible? Which is more useful in helping to understand modern American society?

USING YOUR SOCIOLOGICAL IMAGINATION
SOCIAL STATUS MARKERS

TIMOTHY A. CLARY/AFP via Getty Images

What does it mean to mark your social status? How do you signal to other people the status group to which you belong? There has been a recent rise in high profile scams in which people pretend to be from the upper social class using social status markers. Let's examine

Weber's concept of style of life by looking at cases of two people who successfully pretended to be members of a wealthy status group, in the following videos:

https://www.youtube.com/watch?v=co7WpsrhQT8
   —*Anna Delvey*

https://www.youtube.com/watch?v=lbhsxGSHUc8
   —*Simon Leviev*

Discussion Questions

1. What social status markers do Anna Delvey and Simon Leviev use to convince people that they are upper class? Why do you think Anna and Simon both change their last names when they pretend to be upper class?

2. Are all of these markers purely financial? What other types of markers are not based on money alone? Are there personality traits that are associated with an upper-class lifestyle?

3. Both Anna Delvey and Simon Leviev's deceptions became highly publicized stories. Anna's story was adapted into the TV series *Inventing Anna* (2022), while Simon Leviev was the subject of the documentary *The Tinder Swindler* (2022). Why do you think people are so interested in their stories? What do they tell us about how status is formed in the United States?

Methods in Depth: *Women Without Class* by Julie Bettis

Women Without Class: Girls, Race, and Identity by Julie Bettis (2014) is an ethnographic portrait of working-class White and Mexican American young women. The goal of the book is to learn how these young women experience and understand class differences and how these understandings shaped their perceptions of the possibilities for their futures. It is an examination of how young women learn to perform class and how this can have important consequences for their lives in high school and after.

Methodology

Bettis began her research by interviewing women at a community college in Sacramento, California. Instructors allowed her into their classrooms to find volunteers to be interviewed. She also interviewed students from her university who had come from working-class families, some of whom had transferred from community colleges and who told stories of both the stigma associated with their time at those colleges and the interactional work they performed to conceal it when they could. All these college women spoke at length about how their class background shaped their experiences of college and university.

Despite the importance of these interviews, Bettis became frustrated by the fact that these young women's descriptions of themselves and their high school peers were devoid of context. Although their experiences were relational, clearly defined by the context of the communities from which they came, she could not understand that context because she could not see it for herself. Furthermore, missing from this sample was the experiences of high school students who did not make it to college.

At this point, Bettis expanded her work to find a high school at which she could conduct her research. She conducted 9 months of participant observation in a high school that she calls Waretown High. This research included spending informal time with girls in classrooms and hallways, during lunch hours, at school dances, sports events, club meetings, in coffee shops, at a shopping mall, in the school parking lot, and even in their homes. She came to know more than 60 girls well, about half of whom were Mexican American and half White, and many more as acquaintances. She talked with them about all aspects of their lives, including dating, friendships, school, family, work, and their hopes for the future.

Women Without Class is an ethnography that also relies on interviews. Although there are many ways that we could study social class, ethnography was particularly appropriate for this research. First, by spending time with the young women in this study, Bettis was able to better understand how they saw social class and the divisions in their school. How could we have created a survey, for example, without knowing the types of groups and divisions that existed? Second, the process whereby class emerges is not always apparent or conscious. By observing the dynamics in the school, Bettis is able to see how class emerges through interaction and, later in interviews, she can explore these processes in a more in-depth way. For example, she can observe how different cliques in the school mark their social class with clothing and behaviors; then, later in the interviews, she can ask follow-up questions about those topics. Finally, Bettis makes the theoretical argument that class is relational and situational. It is not just something you have, but something you do. With this theoretical perspective, you would need to study class in a way that you could both observe how it is negotiated between people and see it within a specific context (in this case, the particular high school). As she notes herself, her initial interviews with women at colleges and universities were illuminating but did not allow her to see how young women came to understand class and how different contexts shaped this process (because the women at universities she interviewed came from all different types of high schools).

Challenges

One of the challenges Bettis faced when doing this project was being able to access and talk with different groups of young women at the high school. This high school, like many others, was very clearly delineated by cliques that did not tend to overlap. How do you get access to talk to one group of girls without alienating other groups who you might want to talk with later? Bettis considered this when she first came to the school. She introduced herself as a student from the university (which she was, completing her PhD). She believed that the shared status of student helped the young women see her as an ally (despite the fact that she was 31). She notes that she had to be careful not to try to blend too much and be seen as trying too hard to be like them, which might make her seem phony. She also did not try to adjust her clothes to each group, but rather wore a generic costume that was virtually the same every day. "I wore Levi's (not too baggy, not too tight) and the cheap version ($9.99 at Payless Shoes) of basic brown leather clunky-heeled shoes that were in fashion at the moment. I wore variously colored scoop-necked T-shirts and in the winter an open flannel shirt over them. In an effort to acknowledge my difference and not look like I was trying too hard to fit in, I chose to carry my canvas shoulder bag rather than the backpack that most prep students favored" (Bettis, 2014, p. 20). Though it may seem that this level of attention to small details is silly, Bettis needed to fit in with a variety of different groups of young women and develop rapport, while being genuine, in order to garner the trust needed to conduct the study.

Ethical Issues

Another major issue in this type of study is paying attention to one's own perspective. Bettis discusses how her identity as a White woman might result in research that was "not sensitive to Mexican American culture and racial/ethnic identity, either, on the one hand, by failing to recognize cultural specificity or, on the other hand, by reducing girls to their ethnicity, whereby everything they do can be attributed to and is overdetermined by 'their' culture, ignoring intra-cultural variation" (Bettis, 2014, p. 25). It is important, in all research, to be sensitive to one's own perspective. Although this certainly does not mean that we can only study others just like ourselves, we want to constantly consider how our own background might color how we see and understand the experiences of our research subjects. This can be a challenge both when the research focuses on people very unlike oneself (as you can simplify or stereotype their experiences) or when you study people similar to yourself (as you can assume you understand their experiences without thinking critically about your perspective).

INCOME AND WEALTH INEQUALITY IN THE UNITED STATES

Many sociologists examine inequality in the United States using the concept of socioeconomic status (SES). SES is a measure of an individual's or family's social and economic position relative to others. It is a composite scale that includes measures of income, educational attainment, and occupational prestige. Income refers to any wages, salaries, profits, rents, dividends, or pensions a person receives. Educational attainment is the highest level (grade or degree) a person has completed. Occupational prestige is measured by the educational attainment required, the income earned, and the associated skills of one's job. SES is typically divided into three categories: high, middle, and low.

You can see that SES incorporates ideas about social class and social status, as discussed by Marx and Weber. The concept also makes it possible to deal with some of the disjunctions that sometimes occur between class and status. Recall the earlier example of a plumber. SES can reconcile the apparent contradiction between a plumber's high wages and low occupational status.

One way to think about income inequality in the United States is to look at it over time. Figure 4.2 shows data from a Stanford/Pew study that illustrates how much money you are likely to make as an adult based on how much money your parents make. If your parents are in the bottom 10% of income, Pew predicts that your total family earnings will be $33,900 a year if you are a man and $40,500 a year if you are a woman. If your parents are in the top 10% of earners, Pew predicts that your total family earnings will be $104,700 if you are a man and $118,300 if you are a woman (Pew Trusts, 2015). You will notice here that women are predicted to have higher total family earnings than men. This is interesting given that women make, on average, less than men. This is because women, particularly those who come from the higher earning backgrounds, are more likely to marry and more likely to marry individuals who make more money, giving them a higher total family income.

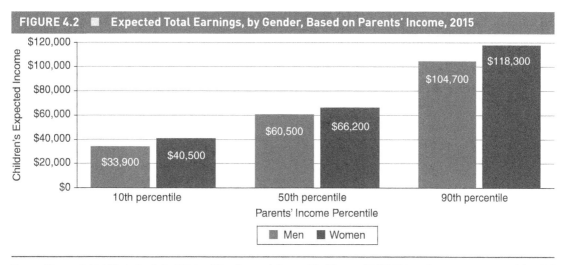

FIGURE 4.2 ■ Expected Total Earnings, by Gender, Based on Parents' Income, 2015

Source: "Economic Mobility in the United States." Pew Research Center, Washington, DC (2015) http://www.pewtrusts.org/~/media/assets/2015/07/fsm-irs-report_artfinal.pdf.

Income inequality is related to, but not the same as, wealth inequality. Wealth inequality refers to the total amount of assets of an individual or household. This could include things like property, stocks, or pensions. Because wealth is passed from one generation to the next, wealth inequality is even more severe in the United States than income inequality.

Figure 4.2 clearly shows income inequality in the United States. The amount of money your parents make is clearly linked to how much we expect you to make as an adult. How concerned should we be about this issue? If there is a lot of social mobility (movement on a stratification system, such as the class system) in the United States, income inequality is less of a problem. If the rich are getting richer because they are working harder and people can move from one class to another through hard work, the gap between the rich and the poor is less concerning.

This idea is an example of an achievement-based stratification system. In this system, people's rank depends on their accomplishments; those who work hard and are diligent achieve high social status or class. Conversely, an ascription-based stratification system determines an individual's rank by her ascribed characteristics (i.e., the features with which she is born). If people of certain ethnicities, religions, or sexes hold certain ranks in society simply because of who they are (not what they have done), they live in an ascription-based system. Apartheid in South Africa was such a system. The minority White population ran the country, while the Black majority was oppressed because of their skin color, and there was no possibility for individuals of any racial category to change location in this system over time.

We are all born with a SES determined by our parents' income, occupational status, and education. But the extent to which a society is achievement or ascription based depends on its level of social mobility. There are two types of social mobility: intergenerational and intragenerational. Intergenerational mobility occurs between generations. Your parents or grandparents might be working class, but perhaps you are middle or upper class. Intragenerational mobility occurs within a single generation. Perhaps your parents were born into the working class but reached the middle class during their lifetime.

Many studies compare social mobility across countries. Some measure intergenerational income elasticity—the statistical relationship between a parent's and a child's economic standings. The higher the number, the less social mobility a society has and the greater the parent's standing features in predicting a child's economic standing. Lower numbers indicate that children's economic standing is the result of their individual talents and capabilities.

Figure 4.3 shows the average number of generations that it would take the children of a low-income family to reach the average income, by country. In the United States, it will take a low-income child, on average, 5 generations to reach the national average income. It is much shorter to make this transition in Denmark, only 2 generations. However, there are a number of countries where there is even less social mobility than in the U.S., such as South Africa and Colombia, where it would take between 9 and 11 generations to move from low to average income. In general, this shows that it is quite hard (and would take quite a long time) to change one's social class in the U.S. This is surprising given the firmly held idea of the American Dream, which is based on the vision of individuals being able to change their position in the social hierarchy by hard work alone.

Given the general idea of the American Dream, how can we account for this relatively low level of social mobility in the United States? As previously stated, each of us grows up in a particular class. The people we know also tend to be in the same class because we live in the same neighborhoods, go to the same schools, or have similar circles of friends. For this reason, it is sometimes hard to truly understand how other people experience social class and inequality.

FIGURE 4.3 ■ Average Number of Generations for Offspring of a Low-Income Family to Reach the Average Income, by Country (2018)

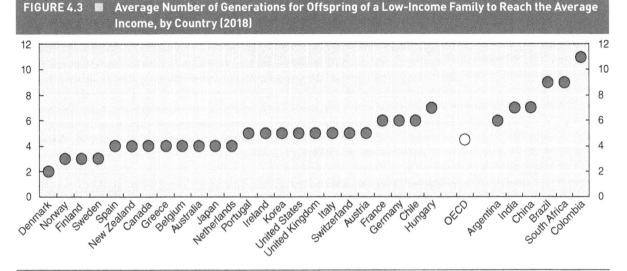

Source: OECD. (2018). *A Broken Social Elevator? How to Promote Social Mobility.* https://doi.org/10.1787/9789264301085-en

READING: RACE, GENDER, AND NEW ESSENTIAL WORKERS DURING COVID-19

NICOLE A. PANGBORN AND CHRISTOPHER M. REA

"Crazy how grocery store workers had no idea they signed up for the draft," Twitter user @ blairsocci noted on March 16, 2020. Around the same time, public health officials across the United States began encouraging Americans to stay at home—with the exception of leaving for "essential activities," like buying groceries—to slow the spread of COVID-19. Since then, store clerks, sanitation workers, bus drivers, and healthcare workers have found themselves among those on the front lines of a pandemic.

Staying home, health experts say, is a means of social distancing—reducing the amount of close physical contact between individuals. Social distancing cuts the number of opportunities for person-to-person transmission, slowing the (inevitable) spread of the virus and lessening the burden on the nation's healthcare system. In order to promote social distancing, by March 24, 2020, all 50 states had recommended or ordered the closure of schools; governors and mayors across the country had ordered restaurants and businesses to switch to takeout and delivery; in-person gatherings, religious services, weddings, and funerals had been cancelled or strongly discouraged; universities had switched to online teaching; and companies all over the world had asked employees to telecommute.

But telecommuting isn't possible for everybody.

As Twitter user @le___RATO put it on March 17, 2020, "S/O [shout-out] to all the taxi drivers/uber driver[s]/train drivers/bus drivers who are still operating. Not everyone has the luxury of working from home."

The idea of social distancing is not new. In early October 1918, during the Spanish Flu pandemic, the city of St. Louis ordered residents to close "all theaters, moving picture shows, schools, pool and billiard halls, Sunday schools, cabarets, lodges, societies, public funerals, open air meetings, dance halls and conventions." The intervention, which remained in effect until December 28 of that year, worked: social distancing successfully reduced the city's excess death rate compared to places like Boston and Philadelphia.

But 100 years later, there is a new dimension to social distancing. Some workers can work from home and continue to receive a paycheck, sheltered from the virus behind their computer screens. Others cannot.

A quick look at some basic data from the U.S. Bureau of Labor Statistics reveals some of these emerging inequalities (Table 1). First, there seems to be a class divide between those who can easily transition to working from home and those who can't: the median monthly earnings of the 64 million Americans in management and professional occupations—people who are now mostly working from home—is more than twice that of the 27 million home health aides, cooks, janitors, childcare providers and other service workers who mostly have to work on-site to earn a paycheck.

BLS Occupational Category	Median Monthly Earnings[1]	Women (%)	Black (%)	Latinx (%)	Employed
More telecommute-friendly					
Management & professional	$5,236	51.8	9.6	10.1	64,218,000
Mixed Sales & office	$3,032	60.6	13.0	17.1	33,370,000
Telecommute-unfriendly					
Service occupations	$2,368	57.6	17.1	25.0	26,978,000
Nat. resources, construct., & maint.	$3,476	5.4	7.7	31.9	14,343,000
Production, trans., & material moving	$2,908	23.0	16.9	23.0	18,628,000
National	**$3,668**	**47.0**	**12.3**	**17.6**	**157,538,000**

Table 1: Characteristics of U.S. occupation groups more- and less-likely to be able to work from home during the COVID-19 pandemic. 86% of workers in management and professional occupations have telecommute-friendly jobs; healthcare professionals are the major exception. 58% of workers in sales and office occupations have telecommute-friendly jobs; retail workers are the major exception. 0% of workers in service; natural resources, construction, and maintenance; and production, transportation, and material moving occupations have telecommute-friendly jobs. Demographic groups with substantial over-representation in an occupational category (> 5 percentage-points above national figures) are shown in red.

Source: labor Force Statistics from the Current Population Survey, U.S. Bureau of Labor Statistics, 2019.

[1]See note on monthly earnings in Table 2.

Second, there are also some important gender-based differences between those who can and cannot easily work from home. Around 60% of workers in sales and office professions—administrative assistants, bank tellers, customer service reps, retail clerks—are women; about 42% of this group hold jobs not amenable to telecommuting. On the other hand, men make up nearly 95% of the 14 million workers in occupations related to natural resources, construction, and maintenance. None of this work is telecommute-friendly; one cannot frame building walls, lay rail track, or repair buses from home.

Third, racial and ethnic differences also emerge. Latinx workers are heavily over-represented in telecommute-unfriendly professions, like construction and automotive repair.

Self-identified "Hispanic or Latino" individuals make up about 18% of the U.S. workforce but fully 36.4% of the 8.3 million construction and extraction workers; nearly 32% of all workers in natural resources, construction, and maintenance occupations as a whole; and fully a quarter of all service workers.

To get an even more finely grained sense of these disparities, we gathered data on occupations specifically designated as "essential" in the recent shelter in place orders issued in the San Francisco Bay Area (Table 2).

Profession	Median Monthly Earnings[1]	Women (%)	Black (%)	Latinx (%)	Employed
Healthcare					
Physicians and surgeons	$9,168	40.8	8.2	7.6	1,098,000
Registered nurses	$4,892	88.9	12.4	7.2	3,242,000
Home health aides	$2,248	88.3	37.2	17.6	2,086,000
Personal care aides	$2,064	85.6	25.1	21.6	1,458,000
Social Service					
Social workers	$3,856	81.9	23.0	14.3	823,000
Childcare workers	$1,980	93.4	17.4	24.6	1,193,000
Consumer Services					
Cashiers	$2,012	71.2	17.9	24.1	3,164,000
First-line retail supervisors	$3,268	45.4	9.5	14.7	3,232,000
Bank tellers	$2,300	84.7	9.9	20.0	294,000
Postal clerks	$3,628	55.1	35.8	6.7	96,000
Laundry and dry-cleaning	$1,960	75.4	25.1	37.9	134,000
Flight attendants	$3,292	81.3	17.5	15.3	110,000
Bus drivers	$2,696	45.3	27.0	15.0	546,000
Taxi drivers and chauffeurs	$2,456	16.8	29.5	23.6	790,000
Food Production & Prep.					
Misc. agricultural workers	$2,232	24.2	2.6	54.0	866,000
Cooks	$2,048	41.7	18.1	36.7	2,031,000
Food prep. Workers	$1,984	59.3	13.2	28.1	1,079,000

Profession	Median Monthly Earnings[1]	Women (%)	Black (%)	Latinx (%)	Employed
Trades					
Auto mechanics	$3,244	1.9	8.7	27.7	880,000
Plumbers	$3,684	2.7	8.4	27.1	637,000
Construction laborers	$2,892	3.5	8.6	46.7	2,051,000
Freight, stock, and material movers	$2,536	21.5	19.8	23.1	2,235,000
First Responders					
Police officers	$4,444	17.6	12.6	17.0	716,000
Firefighters	$4,828	3.3	8.5	11.6	318,000
EMTs and paramedics	$3,648	33.5	10.5	11.5	206,000
Media					
Reporters and correspondents	$5,204	45.1	6.9	9.2	93,000
National	**$3,668**	**47.0**	**12.3**	**17.6**	**157,538,000**

Table 2: Selected "essential" professions exempted from March 16, 2020 "shelter in place" order issued in seven San Francisco Bay Area counties in response to COVID-19 pandemic. Figures are nationally representative. Over-represented demographic groups are color-coded as in Table 1.

Source: Labor Force Statistics from the Current Population Survey, U.S. Bureau of labor Statistics, 2019.

[1]Monthly earnings figures shown are median weekly earnings reported by BLS multiplied by 4. For professions where work is often intermittent and precarious (e.g., cashiers, agricultural workers, construction laborers), this may represent a substantial over-estimate.

Aside from physicians and surgeons, the healthcare professionals on the front lines of the COVID-19 epidemic are overwhelmingly women. So are social service workers, childcare providers, home health aides, and consumer service workers, like retail cashiers, bank tellers, and flight attendants. (Taxi drivers are a notable exception; they are mostly men.) Many of these female-dominated professions put workers at especially high risk of infection: they involve being in close proximity to other people and high probabilities of exposure to the virus.

Men are heavily over-represented in blue-collar work also deemed "essential," but many of these professions are at somewhat lower-risk in the midst of a viral outbreak: construction work, auto repair, and freight, for example, involve lower levels of interaction with the public and fewer chances of disease transmission.

Most workers designated as "essential" earn less money than the national median and are disproportionately likely to be people of color. Despite the fact that about 12% of the workforce identifies as Black and 18% identifies as Latinx, more than half of agricultural workers, over a third of cooks, and nearly 30% of food preparation workers—all designated as "essential" in the recent Bay Area orders—are Latinx, and over a third of postal clerks and 27% of bus drivers identify as Black. These essential employees remain hard at work across the country.

As we mount a national response to the global COVID-19 pandemic, taking account of these demographic differences in work is important. Emergency responses that put particular groups—people of color and women—at higher risk stand on morally shaky ground: there is no reason that one segment of the population ought to bear the brunt of a viral scourge. But early data suggest that this is precisely what is happening. In Michigan, for example, Black Americans make up 14% of the state population but 40% of coronavirus deaths. And in New York City, the coronavirus seems to be twice as deadly for Black and Latinx people compared to whites.

COVID-19 has transformed the world for all of us, but the data make it clear: it is not transforming in the same way for everyone.

Reading Questions

1. What is the relationship between social class, race/ethnicity, gender and the ability to work from home?

2. What are some of the physical, psychological, and emotional challenges that might be particularly prominent for essential workers?
3. This article focuses on working from home. How is this related to your experience as a university or college student? Were you able to work from home during the pandemic? How might this differ across social class, race/ethnicity, and gender?

Pangborn, N. A., & Rea, C. M. (2020, April 16). Race, gender, and new essential workers during COVID-19. *Contexts*. Retrieved June 12, 2023, from https://contexts.org/blog/inequality-during-the-coronavirus-pandemic/

POVERTY

Poverty—a state in which resources (material or cultural) are lacking—is a serious social problem in the world. We can think about this issue in terms of relative poverty, the deprivation of one individual in comparison with another, or absolute poverty, the life-threatening deprivation of an individual. Approximately 1 billion people, or 20% of the global population, live in absolute poverty. Both absolute and relative poverty are important concerns in the United States. People who are homeless or who are unable to buy food, clothing, and other necessities live in absolute poverty. Many more people in America live in a state of precarious housing and employment that is not necessarily life threatening but places them in relative poverty.

USING YOUR SOCIOLOGICAL IMAGINATION
THE POVERTY THRESHOLD

Defining poverty is a challenge because there are different thresholds (such as absolute and relative poverty) and because it is context dependent. The U.S. Census Bureau has an official measure of poverty, which has been used to estimate the national poverty rate since 1959. The federal government creates income thresholds for the poverty rate by tripling the inflation-adjusted cost of a minimum food diet in 1963 and adjusting for family size, composition, and the age of the householder. If you live under these income thresholds, you are considered to live in poverty (see Table 4.2).

TABLE 4.2 ■	Poverty Thresholds (Annual Income) for 2021 by Size of Family and Number of Related Children Under 18 Years								
	Related children under 18 years								
Size of family unit	None	One	Two	Three	Four	Five	Six	Seven	Eight or more
One person (unrelated individual):									
Under age 65	14,097								
Aged 65 and older	12,996								
Two people:									
Householder under age 65	18,145	18,677							
Householder aged 65 and older	16,379	18,606							
Three people	21,196	21,811	21,831						
Four people	27,949	28,406	27,479	27,575					
Five people	33,705	34,195	33,148	32,338	31,843				
Six people	38,767	38,921	38,119	37,350	36,207	35,529			
Seven people	44,606	44,885	43,925	43,255	42,009	40,554	38,958		
Eight people	49,888	50,329	49,423	48,629	47,503	46,073	44,585	44,207	
Nine people or more	60,012	60,303	59,501	58,828	57,722	56,201	54,826	54,485	52,386

Source: https://www.census.gov/data/tables/time-series/demo/income-poverty/historical-poverty-thresholds.html

Let's examine these thresholds and consider how one might be able to live on these amounts of money.

1. Select a family size and composition. For example, you could use your current living situation or the one you plan to have in the future. Using the table, determine the amount of money you need to live above the corresponding poverty threshold. How much money would you need to make per hour (based on a 40-hour week) to pass that threshold?
2. Go online and see what the minimum wage is in your state (https://www.dol.gov/agencies/whd/mw-consolidated).
3. Will working all year and full time at minimum wage allow you to live above the poverty threshold? Could you take a vacation or time off if you or a family member is ill? How

much flexibility will you have in your work? Would you expect to have health benefits for yourself and your family (e.g., dental, sick leave, prescription drugs)?

4. Look up the rent for an apartment or house in your community. Could you afford this rent, along with food and clothing, on the amount of money indicated in the poverty threshold? Is the poverty threshold a reasonable measure of what you would need to survive in your community? Why or why not? How might this be different in a small town or a large city?

5. The poverty threshold is based on the amount of money needed to pay for food, times three. What other expenses are not included? How much do they cost? Are the costs likely to differ depending on your age, gender, and family situation? Why or why not?

The poverty threshold activity demonstrates that living on minimum wage is a real struggle. Almost one in eight Americans lives in poverty, but one's propensity to live in this condition is not equally distributed. Figure 4.4 compares the poverty rate among different groups of Americans.

Figure 4.4 shows the number of people living in poverty and the poverty rate in the country from 1959 until 2019. Although the number of people in poverty has increased since the 1970s, the poverty rate has been relatively consistent, ranging from about 10% to 15% in this period. Poverty rates are very different across groups of people. Women are more likely than men to live in poverty, and poverty rates for women are higher among all age groups than they are for men. Younger people are much more likely than older people to live in poverty. Those who are over 65 have much lower poverty rates than those under the age of 18 (see Figure 4.5). People who live within families are much less likely to live in poverty than those who are single. This last finding is not surprising when you consider that individuals living within families can share expenses

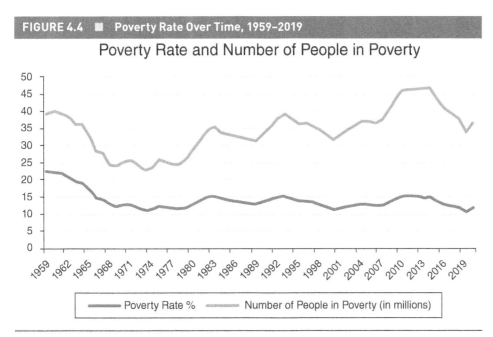

FIGURE 4.4 ■ Poverty Rate Over Time, 1959–2019

Poverty Rate and Number of People in Poverty

Legend: Poverty Rate %   Number of People in Poverty (in millions)

Source: U.S. Census Bureau, Current Population Survey, 1960 to 2021 Annual Social and Economic Supplements (CPS ASEC); Shrider, Emily A., Melissa Kollar, Frances Chen, and Jessica Semega, U.S. Census Bureau, Current Population Reports, P60-273, *Income and Poverty in the United States*: 2020,U.S. Government Publishing Office, Washington, DC, September 2021.

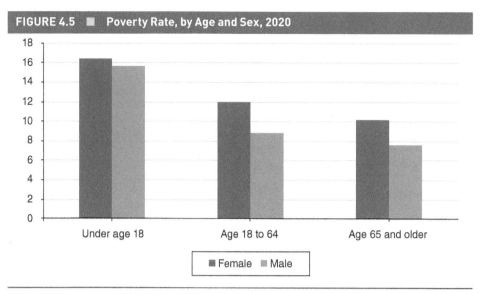

FIGURE 4.5 ■ **Poverty Rate, by Age and Sex, 2020**

Source: U.S. Census Bureau, Current Population Survey, 1960 to 2021 Annual Social and Economic Supplements (CPS ASEC)

(such as rent and car costs) and can rely on one another in times of resource scarcity (such as when one person loses a job or falls ill). And single-parent families have quite high poverty rates, particularly families with a female head of household (see Figure 4.6).

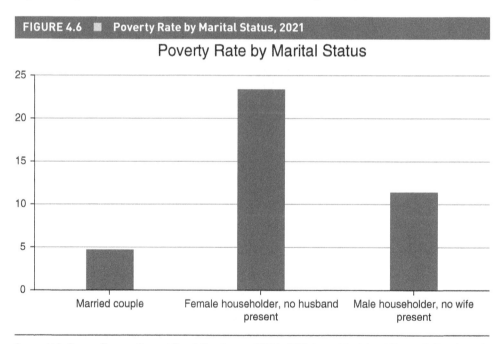

FIGURE 4.6 ■ **Poverty Rate by Marital Status, 2021**

Source: U.S. Census Bureau, Current Population Survey, 1960 to 2021 Annual Social and Economic Supplements (CPS ASEC); Shrider, Emily A., Melissa Kollar, Frances Chen, and Jessica Semega, U.S. Census Bureau, Current Population Reports, P60-273, *Income and Poverty in the United States*: 2020,U.S. Government Publishing Office, Washington, DC, September 2021.

Poverty among the elderly is an interesting example of how social policies affect the lived experiences of individuals. As shown in Figure 4.5, poverty among this group was very high historically until the 1970s. To deal with this extremely important social issue, the federal government passed a series of old age security benefits. These programs started in 1935, when the first limited program of old-age benefits was passed, called the Social Security Act. This legislation was a response to the very high rate of unemployment after the Great Depression and the very high rate of poverty among the elderly. It provided a federally administered system of social insurance for those over age 65, funded by payroll taxes paid by employers and employees. The benefits in this first act applied to only a subset of all workers: just those who worked in commerce or industry. And there were no benefits for spouses or children. By the 1960s, coverage under these programs had expanded and was almost universal; virtually everyone who reached retirement age could receive benefits. In the 1970s and 1980s, additional changes were made to the programs, including cost-of-living increases, so that the benefits could keep up with inflation (Social Security Administration, 2018).

This program vastly reduced poverty among the elderly from around 35% before the 1970s to 15% by 1975; the number now hovers around 9%. These numbers illustrate that Social Security has been very successful at reducing poverty among this group. Think about what programs we could institute to reduce poverty among other at-risk groups, such as children, who still have a poverty rate of about 16%.

The cycle of poverty refers to how poverty tends to perpetuate itself and is therefore likely to continue for an individual or group unless there is some outside intervention. This cycle is perpetuated by such factors as low (or no) income, little education, lack of sufficient housing and other material resources, insufficient social connections, and/or poor health. All these disadvantages compound to create a cycle that is very difficult to break and makes it extremely challenging for individuals to escape poverty.

For example, if you are poor and living on the street, you might be looking for a job. However, a job search is difficult when you do not have an address to put on your résumé, a computer to print a résumé, or clean clothes to wear to an interview. Children who come from poor families might find it hard to get out of this situation because it is difficult for them to do well in school without proper food, clothing, or supplies. In these ways, poverty can be a self-perpetuating cycle.

Poverty is also very inefficient and expensive. If you do not have enough money to pay monthly rent up front, you might pay daily rates at a hotel or motel, which is considerably more expensive. If you cannot afford a car, you might not be able to get to supermarkets. As a result, you would buy groceries in small quantities at a corner store or eat out, which is less efficient and more expensive than cooking at home.

Lunch programs for school children are one way to address the symptoms of poverty (in this case, hunger) among at-risk groups (in this case, children). What other kinds of social programs try to minimize poverty's effects?

iStockphoto.com/SteveDebenport

There are serious consequences to living in poverty. Perhaps the most obvious is that individuals living in poverty tend to have inadequate housing—housing that is unsafe, in poor repair, too small, or temporary. This housing tends to be in neighborhoods with high crime rates, high levels of traffic, few public spaces such as parks, and poor social services such as schools, libraries, or community centers. Moreover, poverty is associated with inadequate nutrition, poor health care, poor physical and mental health, increased stress, and shorter life spans. A large study by the University of Washington shows that there is a 20-year difference in life expectancy between areas of the United States, mostly because of the wealth or poverty of the areas. Certain rich counties in central Colorado have an average life expectancy of 87 years, while the poorest areas of North and South Dakota, particularly on Native American reservations, have a life expectancy of only 66 years (Luscombe, 2017). In fact, about 60% of the differences in life expectancy can be explained by socioeconomic factors alone (Scutti, 2017). This highlights the significance of wealth and poverty as they shape our lives.

SUMMARY

This chapter explores the importance of social class, social status, and inequality in American society. Karl Marx understood social class as being based on an individual's relationship to the means of production: You are either a capitalist who owns the means of production or a worker who owns only your labor power. Max Weber added the importance of social status (the honor and prestige accorded to various groups) to Marx's ideas. Modern American society tends to use SES to talk about social inequality. Based on income, education, and occupational prestige, this concept considers issues of class and status. The chapter also discusses issues of social mobility in the United States, comparing mobility across countries. Finally, we examined the important social issue of poverty in the United States. The activity on poverty thresholds shows how we define poverty and how various groups are more likely or less likely to live in poverty.

FOR FURTHER READING

Ehrenreich, B. (2001). *Nickel and dimed: On (not) getting by in America*, Metropolitan Books.

Gerth, H. H., & Mills, C. W (Eds.). (1946). *From Max Weber: Essays in sociology*. Oxford University Press.

Giddens, A. (1981). *The class structure of advanced societies*, Unwin Hynman.

Marx, K., & Engels, F. (1848). Manifesto of the Communist Party. In K. Marx & F. Engels (Eds.), *Marx/Engels selected works* (Vol. 1, pp. 198–137). Progress.

Tilly, C. (1999). *Durable inequality*, University of California Press.

GLOSSARY

achievement-based stratification system

ascription-based stratification system

bourgeoisie (capitalist)

class consciousness

class struggle

classes

cycle of poverty

false consciousness

ideology

intergenerational income elasticity

lumpenproletariat

meritocracy

mode of production

parties

petite bourgeoisie

poverty

poverty threshold

power

proletariat (worker)

property

social mobility

socioeconomic status (SES)

status groups

surplus value

trade union density

unions

wealth inequality

5 RACE AND ETHNICITY

Rachel Dolezal was the president of the Spokane, Washington, chapter of the National Association for the Advancement of Colored People (NAACP). The NAACP is one of the largest and most well-known groups working for civil rights for African Americans in the United States. It was founded in 1909 by a group that included W. E. B. Du Bois (a well-known sociologist you will hear about later in this chapter). What is interesting about this story is that, although Dolezal had been describing herself as a Black woman, both of her parents are White and of European ancestry (Malkin, 2015). In fact, she does not have any known Black or African ancestry. When this story came out, Dolezal resigned from her job at the NAACP and was dismissed from her position as an instructor in Africana studies at Eastern Washington University. In a November 2015 television interview, Dolezal publicly stated for the first time that she was born White, but that she still identified as Black (Malkin, 2015).

This story incited a heated debate about racial identity. Critics of Dolezal argued that she was engaged in cultural appropriation and fraud in claiming she was Black when she did not have Black ancestry. Dolezal and her supporters argued that her self-identification is genuine, though not based on race or ancestry, and was, in part, based on her close attachment to her four adopted Black siblings. Regardless of your feelings about Dolezal personally, this story highlights the uncomfortable nuances of racial and ethnic identity. Is racial identity about biology or is it about personal self-definition? This question gets to the heart of the differences between race and ethnicity and the ways that society shapes our understanding of these categories.

Rachel Dolezal identifies as a Black woman despite having two parents of White, European ancestry and no known Black or African ancestry. What are the consequences of her identifying in this way for Dolezal, the African American community, and the way society thinks about race?

Ray Tamarra/Getty Images

RACE AND ETHNICITY

The words "race" and "ethnicity" are often used interchangeably in conversation, but there are key distinctions between them. Race is a social distinction based on perceived physical or biological characteristics. For example, we often look at hair texture, eye color, nose shape, or other physical traits to determine a person's racial group. Ethnicity is rooted in cultural differences such as language, religion, and the shared history among people in a group. For example, the ethnic group of Italian Americans may share a language, a cuisine, the Catholic religion, and a common history in Italy and in their migration to the United States.

Traditionally, we thought of race and ethnicity as natural and permanent. This view, known as essentialism, argues that some essential or inherent element makes a person part of a specific racial or ethnic group. From this perspective, each racial or ethnic group contains traits that have been carried from the past to the present with little or no change. As a result, ethnic groups exist because they are based on biological factors (such as similar appearance, skin color, or eye color) and in a territorial location (a region or country). This argument relies on kinship: Members of an ethnic or racial group believe they share characteristics, origins, or sometimes even a blood relationship.

One of the criticisms of essentialism is that it sees race and ethnicity as fixed and permanent. Thus, it cannot account for the ways our ideas of different ethnic groups or races have changed. For example, our idea of who falls under the category of White has changed. In the early settlement of the United States, people who came from Greece and Eastern Europe were not considered White, although they are categorized in this way now. Finnish immigrants in North America were labelled as Asian, a label that has also changed. If race is fixed and essential, how is it possible that our labels of racial groups differ over time and across countries? Most sociologists would argue that these changing definitions occur because race and ethnicity are both socially constructed categories.

Race and Ethnicity as Social Constructions

Our ideas of race and ethnicity are socially constructed. Berger and Luckmann (1966) argue that

> all knowledge, including the most basic, taken-for-granted common sense knowledge of everyday life, is derived from and maintained by social interactions. When people interact, they do so with the understanding that their respective perceptions of reality are related to one another. And, when we are interacting together, our common knowledge of reality becomes reinforced. Through these processes, our ideas of deviance are socially constructed. (p. 55)

Social constructionists argue that racial and ethnic categories are not natural but instead are created within society. For example, many societies categorize people based on their skin color. This choice is rooted in historical contexts such as slavery and colonialism. However, we could just as easily use eye color or height to divide people into groups. Such arbitrary focus on a certain feature highlights how the different physical characteristics perceived to be significant between racial categories hold no intrinsic value and are not rooted in biological differences between groups.

The role of biology in distinguishing between racial and ethnic groups is seriously undermined by the fact that all humanity is 99.9% genetically similar. As the work of Spencer Wells makes clear, genetic testing cannot reveal a person's race. Wells (2002) examined the Y chromosome (the sex chromosome carried by males) and found that all humans alive today share a common male ancestor who lived in East or Southern Africa about 60,000 years ago. In other words, all humans trace their ancestors back to this one man, and apparent differences between people are simply skin deep because all people are separated by only 2,000 generations.

Another reason that the biological basis of race is questionable is that within-group variation is much larger than between-group variation. For example, a person might be categorized as Black but have lighter skin

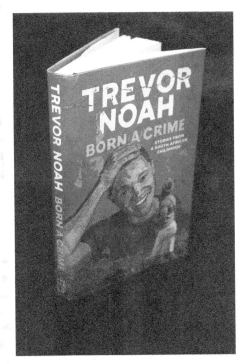

In comedian Trevor Noah's memoir *Born a Crime*, he chronicles his childhood in apartheid South Africa. Trevor spent many of his earliest years indoors, hidden from the government, because his parents were a white Swiss father and black Xhosa mother. Having interracial relationships was illegal and punishable by 5 years in prison. What does Trevor's story reveal about the social construction of race?

John Lamparski/Getty Images

than another person categorized as White. The distinction between white and black categories of skin tone is arbitrary.

Definitions of races have also changed over time and across cultures. We discussed how Americans tend to define race primarily by unchanging physical characteristics and have changed some of our racial categorizations over time. However, in some parts of the world race is not simply a matter of permanent physical features and is seen to be changeable. For example, in Brazil a person's race can change and is intimately connected with her class and social status. Roy (2001, p. 16) explains: "A disproportionate number of dark people are poor, but if a person becomes wealthier, he or she is understood by others to become whiter." In addition, rich non-White and interracial parents in Brazil are more likely than poorer parents to label their children White. This system of racial and ethnic divisions challenges our usual understanding of these categories as being fixed and immutable (impossible to change); it supports the theory that race and ethnicity are shaped by the social context and are socially constructed.

A modern and important lens that sociologists, and other social scientists, have used to understand race is critical race theory. This theoretical tradition was created in the 1980s by Kimberlé Crenshaw and Derrick Bell, who are critical legal studies scholars. Critical race theory is based on four key ideas (Delgado & Stefancic, 2001, p. 9). First, racism is ordinary and not an unusual part of society. What this means is that acts of racism are not, in fact, rare. Instead, we live in a society that is founded on racist ideologies and racism is structurally embedded in our society. Second, racism serves important purposes. Many people benefit from the racial hierarchies that exist in society. And, if we do not recognize how some people benefit from these systems, we cannot change them. Third, race and races are products of social thought and relations and are categories invented by society. In essence, racial and ethnic categories are socially constructed and can change. Finally, critical race theory is founded on the idea of intersectionality. Crenshaw created this concept to argue that every individual brings together a number of different identities and that these all work together to create a person's lived experience. We will discuss the important concept of intersectionality in more detail in Chapter 7.

As a whole, critical race theory pushes us to see how racism is not just about an individual's feelings and attitudes. Instead, racism is a systemic feature of our society. It is very important to understand racism in a systemic way. Seeing it as a public issue, instead of a personal trouble (as Mills would encourage us to do), pushes us to seek larger social solutions to racism and racial inequality. Although it is, of course, important to work to change individual attitudes, we also need to alter larger structures of society, such as the education system, the government, policing, and the media, in order to address racial inequality in society as a whole.

USING YOUR SOCIOLOGICAL IMAGINATION
DEFINING AND CALCULATING RACIAL GROUPS

Many governments around the world conduct a census to systematically collect and record data about the people living within their borders. The earliest censuses were collected in Egypt in about 3,340 BC. The U.S. government has conducted a census every 10 years since 1790, so there have been 23 censuses of the United States as of this writing. The census provides important demographic data about individuals living in the United States. This information is used to plan social services, including health care, education, and transportation. It also enables the government to track population changes and trends.

Censuses in the United States and other countries collect information about racial and ethnic groups. Questions about race and ethnicity are posed in different ways across countries and periods.

Think about how you would identify yourself and then answer the following questions.

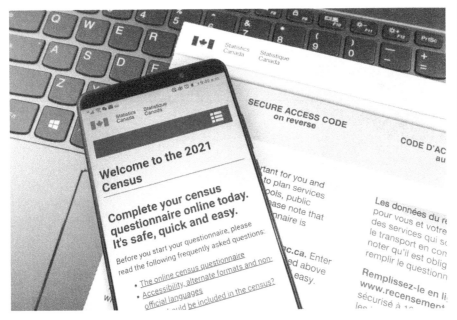

A link to the Canadian Census form.

JHVEPhoto/ Alamy Stock Photo

The U.S. Census form.

Michael Ventura/ Alamy Stock Photo

The Irish Census form.

Radharc Images / Alamy Stock Photo

Please go to the following websites to see the Census questions about race and ethnicity from the United States, Canada, and Ireland:

United States: https://www.pewresearch.org/fact-tank/2014/03/14/u-s-census-looking-at-big-changes-in-how-it-asks-about-race-and-ethnicity/

Canada: Question 17–19 at https://worthwhile.typepad.com/worthwhile_canadian_initi/2013/06/if-canada-used-american-racial-categories.html

Ireland: https://www.cso.ie/en/census/faq/detailedlookatcensusquestions/question14/

1. What do these questions tell us about how these countries think about race and ethnicity? Do these categories make sense? Why are some categories countries, some categories racial or ethnic groups, and other categories regions?

2. You will note that the current censuses allow respondents to define their ethnicity as within two different categories and to combine categories. Why is this option useful? Are there any problems with it?

3. Find a census from a different country online. How does it compare to these three censuses?

4. Some people argue that we should no longer collect information about race and ethnicity in the United States and that we should be a color blind society. Why is it useful (or not useful) to collect information about race and ethnicity? How could we use this information to plan government programs (such as health care, education, pensions, policing), communities, or other things?

The idea of race and ethnicity being socially constructed implies that individuals have a choice over how they construct their racial and ethnic identities. This is true, to some extent. However, some people can choose to highlight certain parts of their ethnicity over others. Who has this choice and who does not?

READING: MIDDLE EASTERN AND NORTH AFRICAN AMERICANS MAY NOT BE PERCEIVED, NOR PERCEIVE THEMSELVES, TO BE WHITE

Neda Maghbouleh, Ariel Schachter, René D. Flores

Among North American and European countries that collect population-level data on race and ethnicity, the United States stands alone in counting Middle Eastern and North African (MENA) individuals as White. This stems from a legal ruling in 1944 that deemed all persons from the MENA region, regardless of their religion, "White by law" alongside European Americans (1–3). This decision has had profound consequences for the collection of sociodemographic data. For one, the U.S. Census currently has no direct way to identify MENA individuals, as they are considered part of the White category by the federal government. However, using small surveys, scholars have found that MENAs may be different in some regards from the White population. They are more likely to live below the poverty line, rent rather than own their homes, and report worse health outcomes, including higher age-adjusted mortality risk and lower birth weights (4–6). In countries that collect data on MENA as racialized minorities or people of color, MENAs report rates of discrimination higher than Whites, and on par with other groups of color (7, 8). Such findings suggest that MENAs' official designation in the United States as White does not correspond to their lived experiences. Nevertheless, given the diversity of the MENA population, composed of 19 different nationalities and 11 ethnicities who arrived and settled across the United States at different time periods, such empirical trends cannot be fully examined without finer-grained Census-level data (9). And because Census definitions of race and ethnicity influence how data are collected in survey research, the federal Office of Management and Budget's decision to continue counting MENA as White in the 2020 Census has the downstream effect of rendering this group invisible in most available survey data.

For most of the United States' history, Hispanics were also not identifiable from the larger White population, despite evidence of discrimination and systematic racialization (10, 11). Nevertheless, in 1970 a group of Hispanic activists, ethnic entrepreneurs, and Census officials came together to create an ethnicity question in the US Census to identify Hispanics (12). For nearly 50 years, MENA activists have similarly called for the creation of a MENA identity category apart from the White category in federal data. In making their case, activists argued that MENA populations are not actually perceived by others in the United States as White. They have suggested that September 11, 2001 (9/11), the War on Terror, and increasingly divisive rhetoric in United States political campaigns further differentiated this group from Whites, leading to discriminatory experiences (13,14). However, due to the invisibility of this population in administrative data, it has been difficult for researchers to empirically test these claims.

The activists' suggestion to the MENA community to "Check it Right, You Ain't White" warrants systematic examination (15). First, it is not clear whether non-MENA Whites think of MENAs as part of the White population or as a separate non-White group (16). MENAs' perceived racial status may shape how Whites treat MENAs in their everyday lives (17,18). There is some evidence that MENA-origin names hold non-White ethnic/racial connotations in the United States, but less is known about the comparative effects of multiple social characteristics, like names, skin tone, and religion, on the classification of MENA people (19). Furthermore, given the significant linguistic, ethnic, and phenotypic heterogeneity of the MENA population, it is unclear who is perceived as MENA by others, and where the boundaries of this panethnic label may lie (20).

Second, it is not clear how MENA individuals will self-identify (21). Identification as White was a conscious effort pursued by prior generations of immigrants to qualify for naturalization and signal their entry into the American mainstream (22–24). The White category may continue to be preferred by certain immigrant generations or specific ethnic, religious, and national groups from the diverse MENA region. For example, in the United States, where White and Christian identities are closely linked, Christian Arab Americans are more likely than Muslim Arab Americans to self-identify as White [25,26]. At the same time, there is evidence that MENA Americans, as a class, face prejudice and discrimination as in the Trump Administration's Executive Orders 13769 (2017) and 13780 (2017–2021), which largely targeted potential migrants of MENA origin [27]. Such racial hostility may trigger reactive ethnicity or ethnic militancy in reaction to perceived discrimination by the mainstream [28,29]. External attacks may increase MENA's internal solidarity and strengthen their identification as MENA [30]. Nevertheless, even if MENA individuals perceive discrimination from others, this does not necessarily mean that they will identify as non-White. Some express worry that identifying as MENA in the Census may result in state surveillance based on alleged national security interests [31]. Others may choose to identify as White as a coping mechanism to deal with perceived racial animosity or even due to different ethnoracial categories or ideologies from their countries of origin [32–34]. It is unclear whether a MENA category is equally appealing to all members of this heterogenous population.

Moreover, MENA individuals may not see identification as a zero-sum decision between MENA and White, and instead choose to identify as both White and MENA. Indeed, similar identification patterns have been observed among descendants of Hispanic and Asian immigrants, whose ultimate position within the United States ethnoracial hierarchy remains uncertain [35].

In response to growing public pressure, the Census Bureau conducted a preliminary internal test in 2015 to examine how MENA populations would react to the addition of a MENA category in Census forms. Based on these internal results, the report recommended a dedicated MENA category separate from the White box on the 2020 US Census. This also would have meant that persons marking both MENA and White would be counted as MENA in the Census' analyses, as this is how persons who mark one White (majority) and one non-White (minority) box are counted [35]. However, in 2018, Census Bureau officials rejected the recommendation to add a MENA category on the grounds that "more research and testing is needed" [36].

We heed the calls for more evidence by empirically examining both sides of this ethnoracial boundary: (1) how Whites and MENAs in the United States perceive the racial status of MENA traits (external categorization), and (2) how MENA American individuals identify themselves (self-identification).

Materials and Methods

In our first experiment focused on external categorization we assessed how both non-MENA, non-Hispanic Whites, and MENAs perceive the racial status of MENA traits. Identifying MENA respondents is not easy or straightforward. Many survey companies in the United States do not explicitly identify MENA individuals. Furthermore, the lack of Census data on this population makes it difficult to develop sampling frames to create nationally representative samples of MENA respondents. Therefore, we turned to online survey platforms to collect nonprobability samples of respondents. Recent evidence suggests that, for online experiments, crowdsource-recruited, nonprobability samples can provide similar results to population-based samples (37, 38). The survey experiments, which were approved by the Institutional Review Board of the Washington University in St. Louis, were implemented in summer 2021. Informed consent was obtained from all respondents (a detailed description of all sampling and survey procedures is in *SI Appendix, Sampling and Survey Procedures*).

First, to understand external classification of MENA individuals by both White and MENA respondents, we used a conjoint, or multidimensional choice, experimental design to simultaneously compare the effects of multiple ethnoracial signals on classification (44–46). Respondents viewed and classified 10 profiles each. Respondents were randomly assigned to either view profiles of immigrants or native-born individuals to control for nativity effects. As is typical in conjoint experiments, all treatments were fully randomized for each profile. While this randomization scheme may lead to some combinations of signals that are more

FIG. 1   ■   Example of Fictitious "Immigrant" Profile Viewed by Respondents in the External Classification Experiment

	Immigrant 1	Immigrant 2
Primary language spoken at home	German	German
Occupation	Lawyer	Real Estate Agent
Ancestors are from	Ethiopia and Lebanon	England and Germany
Name	Claire	Jake
Religion	Christian (Catholic)	Atheist/Agnostic
Skin Color		

likely to be observed outside of the experimental context than others, all are theoretically possible. Our design is based on previous research that uses a conjoint experiment to examine external classification inclusive of the proposed MENA category (47). See *SI Appendix, Text and Questions for External Classification Experiment* for more detailed explanation of the conjoint experiment. The total number of observations for each sample ranges from 3,240 to 4,210.

The key dependent variable was respondents' decisions to classify each hypothetical profile as either MENA, White, or Black. Our profiles of fictitious individuals varied along dimensions chosen to reflect ethnoracial perceptions between White, Black, and MENA categories in the United States, as well as the three largest estimated MENA American subgroupings: Middle Eastern, North African, and non-Arab Iranian (41). We varied given name, religion, language, class (indexed by occupational status), skin color, and family ancestry, employing country-level labels that represent specific regions around the world.

Second, to assess how MENA American individuals identify themselves, we replicated an experiment applied by the US Census in 2015 to examine how MENA individuals self-identify when given a MENA option. We replicated this experiment because the Census data were not available for reanalysis and because this allowed us to look at heterogeneous treatment effects within our sample. We inserted this second experiment in our two surveys of MENA respondents collected via Prolific and Lucid.

The dependent variable was ethnoracial self-identification. Respondents in the control condition were asked: "What is your race or origin?" (9). The response options were: White; Hispanic, Latino, or Spanish origin; Black or African American; Asian; American Indian or Alaska Native; Native Hawaiian or other Pacific Islander; and some other race or origin. Crucially, the control did not include a MENA category but rather, reproduced the White response category provided by the Census, which listed two MENA nationalities, Lebanese and Egyptian, as examples of White subgroups alongside German, Irish, English, and Italian. In turn, respondents in the experimental condition were asked "Which categories describe you?" (9). Critically, a new identity category was added as a response option: Middle Eastern or North African. Nationalities like Lebanese and Egyptian were also no longer listed as examples of White subgroups. They were listed instead as examples of Middle Eastern or North African subgroups. All other category labels were the same as in the control condition.

Individuals were randomly assigned to either the control or the experimental condition. Therefore, our survey experiment assesses the effect of being offered a MENA option on respondents' identification choices. In both treatment and control conditions, respondents were able to check more than one box. Although phrasing of the two questions is different, the Census reported no effect on individuals' responses [9]. We retained the phrasing to ensure replication of the Census experiment. See *SI Appendix*, Table S9 for a randomization check.

Results

First, among both groups of respondents, we found the largest effects with fully MENA ancestries compared to a fully European ancestry. MENA individuals react even more strongly to the ancestry treatments compared to Whites; for example, compared to a fully European ancestry, a fully Arab ancestry (signaled via having only Lebanese and Syrian ancestors) increases the probability that MENA respondents will classify a profile as MENA by 51 percentage points, while it increases the probability that White respondents will classify a profile as MENA by 36 percentage points. (See *SI Appendix*, Fig. S8 for formal comparison of ancestry treatment effects across survey samples.)

Second, MENA and White respondents similarly react to certain cultural traits as a signal of MENA classification. Common MENA names and languages increase classification as MENA by 5 to 20 percentage points among both groups of respondents (see *SI Appendix*, Table S2 for detailed point estimates). We found relatively large effects for language; relative to speaking English, speaking Amharic, Arabic, or Persian increases the probability that a profile is classified as MENA by both respondent groups by 11 to 20 percentage points. Interestingly, neither MENA nor White respondents associate certain occupations with MENA classification. However, relative to profiles marked as Protestant, those described as Atheist/Agnostic, Hindu, Jewish, and Muslim are more likely to be classified as MENA by both MENA and White respondents; the largest religion effects are observed for Muslim, which increases MENA classification by 8 to 11 percentage points. In sum, MENA-related religion, language, and names have a negative effect on White classification, but overall, the effect size for cultural cues is smaller than ancestry cues.

Third, MENA and White respondents substantively differ on how skin color relates to MENA classification. MENA respondents are more likely to classify individuals with light and medium skin tones as MENA over individuals with dark skin tones. In contrast, White respondents associate medium skin tones with MENA classification, but not light skin tones or dark skin tones. Overall, MENA individuals understand MENA as a category that crosscuts a wider array of skin colors, whereas for White respondents MENA exists within a narrower band. See *SI Appendix*, Fig. S9 for a formal comparison of skin color treatment effects by survey sample.

We also examined the extent to which traits associated with the MENA category in the United States are used by MENA and White respondents to mark individuals as not White or Black. As shown in Figs. 3 and 4, MENA and White respondents similarly use MENA traits to exclude individuals from the White and Black categories. For example, fully Arab, North African, and Iranian ancestries reduce the probability that a profile will be classified as White or Black (*SI Appendix*, Table S3). Common MENA names and languages and identifying as Muslim also reduce White and Black classification among both groups of respondents. The negative effect of identification as Muslim on Black categorization is particularly notable, given that one in five American Muslims are Black, highlighting the racialization of Islam as not White or Black [48–51]. White and MENA respondents also recognize that medium and dark skin tones mark someone as not White and as Black, though in general White respondents appear to react more strongly to skin color relative to MENA respondents. See *SI Appendix*, Fig. S10 for a formal comparison of skin color treatment effects on White and Black classification by survey sample.

In *SI Appendix* we analyze the conjoint experiment results with our second MENA sample of respondents collected from Lucid and find small variations in magnitude but substantively similar treatment effects for MENA, White, and Black classification (*SI Appendix*, Figs. S1–S3 and Tables S2 and S3). This successful replication of our findings among MENA respondents suggests that the ethnoracial classification norms we uncovered are not driven by the specific sample selection criteria we used but may be widespread in the United States.

Our results from the external classification experiment show that many non-MENA White and MENA respondents consider MENA cultural and ancestry traits to be non-White ethnoracial markers. Nevertheless, it is still not clear whether MENA respondents would prefer to identify as White-only or in a new MENA category if given the option, which we examined in our second experiment on self-identification.

Treatment Effects for Self-Identification

Results from the self-identification factorial experiment demonstrate that offering a MENA category significantly decreases the rate of MENA individuals who identify as exclusively White. . . [This research] shows that 80% of MENA respondents who were not given a MENA identity option (control group) identified as White and 6% identified as Asian. In addition, 15% of respondents checked "some other race" (SOR).

In contrast, 88% of individuals in the treatment condition identified as MENA when we included both those who identified as only MENA and those who identified as MENA and an additional category. The majority of individuals in the treatment condition, 59%, identified as only MENA. The second most common identification was MENA and White, at 27%. Only 11% identified as exclusively White when offered a specific MENA category. These results show that, when given the option, most MENA respondents self-identify as MENA. As shown in *SI Appendix*, Table S4, a Pearson χ^2 test indicates that the distribution of self-identification is significantly different in the treatment condition—when the MENA identification category was offered—compared to the control condition.

Overall, we found that offering a specific MENA identity category significantly decreases identification as exclusively White among each subgroup, underscoring overall widespread preferences by individuals with MENA ancestry to not identify with just the White category. Effect sizes for each subgroup range from 47 to 65 percentage point decreases in identifying as White-only (*SI Appendix*, Figs. S3–S18). However, our results also point to some heterogeneity in identification patterns among MENA individuals.

First, with respect to ancestry, we found that MENA individuals reject identifying as exclusively White at similar rates (*SI Appendix*, Figs. S13 and S14). This suggests that the MENA grouping, which combines Middle Eastern and North African, is legible to both groups as a distinct category. However, we did observe some variation in identification trends across these two subgroups for other ethnoracial categories. We found that 12% of North African ancestry individuals identify as exclusively Black even when offered a separate MENA category, compared to just 1% of Middle Eastern individuals (*SI Appendix*, Figs. S10 and S11 and Table S6). This finding aligns with expectations that some individuals will continue to identify as Black, as the inclusive definition of MENA we drew upon in this study intentionally brings together persons typically aggregated in Black (e.g., Somali, Sudanese) as well as White (e.g., Iranian, Syrian) Census categories. It may also be the case that some individuals from countries like Morocco or Egypt will consistently identify as Black regardless of labels offered, based on how their phenotypes are perceived in the United States.

Second, we found that respondents who identify as Muslim, along with those identifying as nonreligious, reject Whiteness in favor of the MENA category at higher rates than those who identify as Christian (*SI Appendix*, Table S10). When offered a MENA option, just 6% of Muslim MENAs choose the White-only category versus 25% of Christian MENAs. However, Christian MENAs are also more likely to choose MENA or MENA and White (61%) over White-only when offered a MENA option (*SI Appendix*, Figs. S23–S27). Respondents identifying with other religions (beyond Islam or Christianity) appear to display similar patterns to Christian respondents, though the confidence intervals for this heterogenous group are much wider. Altogether, our findings suggest that Christian and White identities remain linked among MENA Americans. But because a much higher share of post-1965 MENA arrivals are Muslim than previous waves of MENA migration, our findings on religion also suggest that MENA Americans may increasingly prefer the MENA category over White in the future (41).

Next, we interacted treatment assignment with immigrant generation and found that second-generation individuals—the children of immigrants—are significantly more likely to reject identifying as exclusively White compared to both the first generation (foreign-born immigrants) and the third-plus generation (*SI Appendix*, Fig. S21). In addition, the third-plus generation (one or both parents born in the United States) is less likely to identify as only MENA (at just 18%, compared to 76% of second-generation individuals and 60% of first-generation respondents), and more likely to identify as MENA and White (32%, compared to 11% of second generation and 16% of first generation) and only White (25%, compared to 5% of second generation and 13% of first generation) (*SI Appendix*, Figs. S15–S17 and Table S7).

Conclusion and Discussion

Overall, our findings on external classification highlight how ancestry, color, and culture inform an emerging White–MENA boundary. Given pervasive public perceptions of a "majority–minority" future in the United States (35), research has shown that the threat of demographic decline can push Whites to tighten the White category and exclude "ambiguous" Whites and Latinos (63). We expanded this inquiry to show that when categorizing others today, White and MENA people will also distinguish and exclude MENA, an ambiguously White population, from the White category.

With respect to self-identification, we show that when MENA are not offered a MENA label, 80% choose to identify as White. However, when MENA is offered as a category, only 10% continue to exclusively choose White. The majority instead choose MENA, and this appears to be an especially salient single category of choice for second-generation immigrants, MENA Muslims and nonreligious MENAs, those with Middle Eastern (versus North African) ancestry, and those who perceive more discrimination against MENA people. We speculate that the MENA category may therefore represent for some a reactive ethnoracial identity, triggered acutely since the events of September 11, 2001, which led to an increase in state surveillance and public stigmatization of this group. President Donald Trump's anti-immigrant and anti-Muslim rhetoric and policies—exemplified by the Muslim Ban, which curtailed immigration from a list of mostly MENA countries—and the significant backlash to such divisive politics may have hastened MENA peoples' exit from the White box. This seems to contradict expectations that MENA Americans, like conditionally White immigrant generations before them, would seek cover under the White category. Past research has examined how individuals develop identities through interactions with others. European Americans claim ethnic identities that are "symbolic, voluntary, and intermittent"; in contrast, Black Americans' encounters with racial discrimination trigger reactive and oppositional identities (64). Future research should adjudicate whether MENA Americans' ultimate path is more ethnic or racial in character.

At the same time, we found that a sizable minority of individuals with MENA ancestry identify as both White and MENA. This may be linked to a growing number of individuals of mixed MENA–White parentage, especially by the third generation. In addition, some members of the MENA population may understand White and MENA as identities that are cooccurring or nonexclusive with one another. The considerable number of respondents who self-identify as both MENA and White may also reflect how, according to the 2020 Census, more Americans than ever are identifying as multiracial. These heterogeneous findings suggest that the relationship between Whiteness and MENAness is complex and far from settled, which future research should examine.

Importantly, offering MENA as a box reduced the percentage of respondents who chose the single category SOR from 15 to 0. The proportion of the United States population identifying as SOR has grown substantially over time, reaching 49.9 million people in the 2020 Census (65). Our study suggests that adding a MENA category would lead many MENA individuals to reclassify themselves out of SOR to MENA, which would improve the useability of Census data for both administrative and research purposes.

Notes

I. Haney-Lopez, *White By Law: The Legal Construction of Race* (NYU Press, 2006, 1996).

R. Alba, *Ethnic Identity: The Transformation of White America* (Yale University Press, 1992).

A. Jamal, N. Naber, Eds., *Race and Arab Americans Before and After 9/11: From Invisible Citizens to Visible Subjects* (Syracuse University Press, 2008).

N. N. Abuelezam, A. M. El-Sayed, S. Galea, Differences in health behaviors and health outcomes among non-Hispanic Whites and Arab Americans in a population-based survey in California. *BMC Public Health 19*, 892 (2019).

A. M. El-Sayed, M. Tracy, P. Scarborough, S. Galea, Ethnic inequalities in mortality: The case of Arab-Americans. *PLoS One 6*, e29185 (2011).

E. Bakhtiari, Health effects of Muslim racialization: Evidence from birth outcomes in California before and after September 11, 2001. *SSM Popul. Health 12*, 100703 (2020).

Statistics Canada, *Perceptions of discrimination, by visible minority status, General Social Survey.* https://www150.statcan.gc.ca/n1/pub/85-002-x/2018001/article/54913/ tbl/tbl04-eng.htm. Accessed 16 December 2021.

A. Pedersen, K. Dunn, J. Forrest, C. McGarty, Prejudice and discrimination from two sides: How do Middle Eastern Australians experience it and how do other Australians explain it? *J. Pacific Rim Psychol. 6*, 18–26 (2012).

K. Matthews et al., *2015 National Content Test: Race and Ethnicity Analysis Report.* https://www2.census.gov/programs-surveys/decennial/2020/program-management/ final-analysis-reports/2015nct-race-ethnicity-analysis.pdf. Accessed 16 December 2021.

L. Gomez, *Inventing Latinos: A New Story of American Racism* (The New Press, 2020).

D. S. Massey, Racial formation in theory and practice: The case of Mexicans in the United States. *Race Soc. Probl. 1*, 12–26 (2009).

G. C. Mora, *Making Hispanics: How Activists, Bureaucrats, and Media Constructed a New American* (University of Chicago Press, 2014).

W. Hobbs, N. Lajevardi, Effects of divisive political campaigns on the day-to-day segregation of Arab and Muslim Americans. *Am. Polit. Sci. Rev. 113*, 270–276 (2019).

N. Lajevardi, *Outsiders at Home: The Politics of American Islamophobia* (Cambridge University Press, 2020).

J. Krogstad, *Census Bureau explores new Middle East/North Africa category.* https:// www.pewresearch.org/fact-tank/2014/03/24/census-bureau-explores-new-middle-eastnorth-africa-ethnic-category/. Accessed 16 December 2021.

K. Chaney, D. Sanchez, L. Saud, White categorical ambiguity: Exclusion of Middle Eastern Americans from the White racial category. *Soc. Psychol. Personal. Sci. 12*, 593–602 (2020).

R. Nassar, Threat, prejudice, and White Americans' attitudes toward immigration and Syrian refugee resettlement. *J. Race. Ethn. Polit. 5*, 196–220 (2020).

R. Horry, D. Wright, Anxiety and terrorism: Automatic stereotypes affect visual attention and recognition memory for White and Middle Eastern faces. *Appl. Cogn. Psychol. 23*, 345–357 (2008).

S. M. Gaddis, R. Ghoshal, Arab American housing discrimination, ethnic competition, and the contact hypothesis. *Ann. Am. Acad. Pol. Soc. Sci. 660*, 282–299 (2015).

G. C. Mora, D. Okamoto, Boundary articulation and emergent identities: Asian and Hispanic panethnicity in comparison 1970–1980. *Soc. Probl. 67*, 56–76 (2020).

G. Awad, H. Hashem, H. Nguyen, Identity and ethnic/racial self-labeling among Americans of Arab or Middle Eastern and North African descent. *Identity 21*, 115–130 (2021).

M. Hout, J. Goldstein, How 4.5 million Irish immigrants became 40 million Irish Americans: Demographic and subjective aspects of the ethnic composition of White Americans. *Am. Sociol. Rev. 59*, 64–82 (1994).

S. Gualtieri, *Between Arab and White: Race and Ethnicity in the Early Syrian American Diaspora* (University of California Press, 2009).

M. Gordon, *Assimilation in American Life: The Role of Race, Religion, and National Origins* (Oxford University Press, 1964).

K. Joshi, *White Christian Privilege: The Illusion of Religious Equality in America* (NYU Press, 2020).

K. J. Ajrouch, A. Jamal, Assimilating to a White identity: The case of Arab Americans. *Int. Migr. Rev. 41*, 860–879 (2007).

S. Aziz, *The Racial Muslim: When Racism Quashes Religious Freedom* (University of California Press, 2021).

R. D. Flores, "What are the social consequences of immigrant scapegoating by political elites?" in *The Trump Paradox*, R. Hinojosa Ojeda, E. Telles, Eds. (University of California Press, 2021), pp. 214–226.

W. Haller, A. Portes, S. M. Lynch, Dreams fulfilled, dreams shattered: Determinants of segmented assimilation in the second generation. *Soc. Forces 89*, 733–762 (2011).

L. Coser, *The Functions of Social Conflict* (Routledge, 1998, 1956).

K. Beydoun, Boxed in: Reclassification of Arab Americans on the U.S. census as progress or peril. *Loy. U. Chi. L. J. 47*, 693–760 (2016).

J. R. Goldstein, G. Stecklov, From Patrick to John F.: Ethnic names and occupational success in the last era of mass migration. *Am. Sociol. Rev. 81*, 85–106 (2016).

A. Marvasti, Being Middle Eastern American: Identity negotiation in the context of the War on Terror. *Symbolic Interact. 28,* 525–547 (2011).

N. Maghbouleh, *The Limits of Whiteness: Iranian Americans and the Everyday Politics of Race* (Stanford University Press, 2017).

R. Alba, *The Great Demographic Illusion: Majority, Minority, and the Expanding American Mainstream* (Princeton University Press, 2020).

H. Wang, *No Middle Eastern or North African category on 2020 Census, Bureau says.* National Public Radio, 29 January 2018. https://www.npr.org/2018/01/29/581541111/no-middle-eastern-or-north-african-category-on-2020-census-bureau-says. Accessed 16 December 2021.

J. Weinberg, J. Freese, D. McElhattan, Comparing data characteristics and results of an online factorial survey between a population-based and a crowdsource-recruited sample. *Sociol. Sci.* (2014), 10.15195/v1.a19.

K. Mullinix, T. Leeper, J. Druckman, J. Freese, The generalizability of survey experiments. *J. Exp. Political Sci. 2*, 109–138 (2015).

H. Gans, "Whitening" and the changing American racial hierarchy. *Du Bois Rev. 9*, 267–279 (2012).

Moise A. Khayrallah Center for Lebanese Diaspora Studies at North Carolina State University, *The early Lebanese in America: A demographic portrait.* https://lebanesestudies.news.chass.ncsu.edu/2018/11/08/the-early-lebanese-in-america-a- demographic-portrait-1880-1930/. Accessed 16 December 2021.

M. Cumoletti, J. Batalova, *Middle Eastern and North African immigrants in the United States.* https://www.migrationpolicy.org/article/middle-eastern-and-north- african-immigrants-united-states-2016. Accessed 16 December 2021.

S. S. Johfre, A. Saperstein, J. A. Hollenbach, Measuring race and ancestry in the age of genetic testing. *Demography 58*, 785–810 (2021).

W. Roth, B. Ivemark, Genetic options: The impact of genetic ancestry testing on consumers' racial and ethnic identities. *Am. J. Sociol. 124*, 150–184 (2018).

J. Hainmueller, D. Hangartner, T. Yamamoto, Validating vignette and conjoint survey experiments against real-world behavior. *Proc. Natl. Acad. Sci. U.S.A. 112*, 2395–2400 (2015).

A. Schachter, From "different" to "similar": An experimental approach to understanding assimilation. *Am. Sociol. Rev. 81*, 981–1013 (2016).

R. Flores, A. Schachter, Who are the "illegals"? The social construction of illegality in the United States. *Am. Sociol. Rev. 83*, 839–868 (2018).

A. Schachter, R. Flores, N. Maghbouleh, Ancestry, color, or culture? How whites racially classify others in the U.S. *Am. J. Sociol. 126*, 1220–1263 (2021).

B. Mohamed, J. Diamant, *Black Muslims account for a fifth of all U.S. Muslims and about half are converts to Islam*. https://www.pewresearch.org/fact-tank/2019/01/17/ black-muslims-account-for-a-fifth-of-all-u-s-muslims-and-about-half-are-converts- to-islam/. Accessed 16 December 2021.

A. Husain, Moving beyond (and back to) the Black-White binary: A study of Black and White Muslims' racial position in the United States. *Ethn. Racial Stud. 42*, 589–606 (2017).

J. Guhin, Colorblind Islam: The racial hinges of immigrant Muslims in the United States. *Soc. Incl. (Lisboa) 6*, 87–97 (2018).

H. Yazdiha, Toward a Du Boisian framework of immigrant incorporation: Racialized contexts, relational identities, and Muslim American collective action. *Soc. Probl. 68*, 300–320 (2021).

Arab American Institute, *Arab American demographics*. https://www.aaiusa.org/ demographics. Accessed 16 December 2021.

A. Brittingham, G. De la Cruz, *We the People of Arab Ancestry in the United States* (US Census Bureau, 2005).

M. Waters, Ethnic and racial identities of second-generation black immigrants in New York City. *Int. Migr. Rev. 28*, 795–820 (1994).

C. Feliciano, R. Rumbaut, Varieties of ethnic self-identities: Children of immigrants in middle adulthood. *Russell Sage Foundation Journal of the Social Sciences 4*, 26–46 (2018).

T. Jimenez, Affiliative ethnic identity. *Ethn. Racial Stud. 33*, 1756–1775 (2010).

H. Schuman, C. Steeh, L. Bobo, *Racial Attitudes in America: Trends and Interpretations* (Harvard University Press, 1985).

N. Masuoka, Together they become one: Examining the predictors of panethnic group consciousness among Asian Americans and Latinos. *Soc. Sci. Q. 87*, 993–1011 (2006).

A. Portes, R. Rumbaut, *Legacies: The Story of the Immigrant Second Generation* (University of California Press, 2001).

D. Herda, Reactive ethnicity and anticipated discrimination among American Muslims in southeastern Michigan. *J. Muslim Minor. Aff. 38*, 372–391 (2018).

E. Love, *Islamophobia and Racism in America* (NYU Press, 2017).

V. Di Stasio, B. Lancee, S. Veit, R. Yemane, Muslim by default or religious discrimination? Results from a cross-national field experiment on hiring discrimination. *J. Ethn. Migr. Stud. 47*, 1305–1326 (2019).

M. Abascal, Contraction as a response to group threat: Demographic decline and Whites' classification of people who are ambiguously White. *Am. Sociol. Rev. 85*, 298–322 (2020).

M. Waters, "Optional ethnicities: For Whites only?" *Origins and Destinies: Immigration, Race, and Ethnicity in America*, S. Pedraza, R. Rumbaut, Eds. (Wadsworth Press, 1996), pp. 444–454.

N. Jones, R. Marks, R. Ramirez, M. Rios-Vargas, *2020 Census illuminates racial and ethnic composition of the country*. https://www.census.gov/library/stories/2021/08/ improved-race-ethnicity-measures-reveal-united-states-population-much-more- multiracial.html. Accessed 16 December 2021.

Reading Questions

1. Why do the authors claim that discrimination post 9/11 has changed the racial classification of Middle Eastern and North African Americans?

2. How does MENA identification change in the study based on immigration, religion, and experience with discrimination?

3. Many participants in the study identified as both MENA and White. However, the U.S. Census currently does not have a MENA category. Does the box that you would check on the census fully represent your identity? What additional categories would you like to see?

Maghbouleh, N., Schachter, A., & Flores, R. D. (2022, November 7). *Middle Eastern and North African Americans may not be perceived, nor perceive themselves, to be White*. PNAS. Retrieved June 12, 2023, from https://www.pnas.org/doi/full/10.1073/pnas.2117940119

THE CONSEQUENCES OF SOCIAL CONSTRUCTIONS

The theory of social construction highlights the ways that the social categories we consider natural and unchanging, such as race and ethnicity, are in fact socially created. It helps us to understand how the norms, rules, and categories of our society originate and how they can change. Although social constructionists argue that race is not a real thing—that there is no biological basis for racial categories and that they change over time—our social construction of race has real consequences for individuals in society. Being defined as one race or another can shape the type of neighborhood you live in, the job that you are likely to get, and the perceptions that others may have of you.

American sociologist Mary C. Waters introduced the concept of optional ethnicities. She argues that White people in the United States have the ability to select the ethnic label they would like to claim or to claim no ethnic label at all. These White Americans can choose to be seen as a "hyphenated American" (e.g., German-American, Italian-American, Polish-American) or to simply be categorized as "American." For them, claiming an ethnicity is often symbolic. According to Waters, symbolic ethnicity is an individualistic label that has little cost for the individual. In this way, White people can celebrate Oktoberfest or Cinco de Mayo but ignore other ethnic holidays and traditions. Visible minorities, however, do not have this same freedom. They often have no control over the ethnic labels that others assign to them.

How does understanding this Oktoberfest parade through the lens of symbolic ethnicities change how you see this event and others like it? What problems, if any, exist with these displays?

Romy Arroyo Fernandez/NurPhoto/Getty Images

The idea that social constructions have real consequences is called the Thomas principle. According to W. I. Thomas and D. S. Thomas (a husband-and-wife team of sociologists), "If [people] define situations as real, then they are real in their consequences" (Thomas & Thomas, 1928, p. 52). For example, ghosts are not real. But when a little boy cannot sleep at night because he is worried that there are ghosts under his bed, they have real consequences. It does not matter that when you look under the bed, there are no ghosts. Not being able to sleep is a real consequence of a social construction. Far more important, racism is a real consequence of our socially constructed ideas about race. It does not matter that race is not based in biology; our racial categories have important social consequences.

Racism

Racism is a real consequence of our socially constructed ideas about race. It does not matter that race is not based in biology: Our racial categories have important social consequences. Racism is an organized system of race-based group privilege that operates at every level of society and is held together by a sophisticated ideology of race supremacy (Cazenave & Maddern, 1999, p. 42). Racism leads to both privileges and sanctions. Privileges include the White privilege discussed later in this chapter. Sanctions include restrictions and limitations on people in certain racial categories.

Racism against Black Americans has a long history in the United States, including the history of slavery, Jim Crow, segregation, and police violence. Other groups have also faced racism in the United States. For example, in 1882 Congress passed the Chinese Exclusion Act, which suspended the immigration of Chinese laborers for a period of 10 years. It also required every Chinese person traveling in or out of the country to carry a certificate identifying his or her status as a laborer, scholar, diplomat, or merchant. This act was the first in U.S. history to place such broad restriction on immigration and it was entirely targeted to one ethnic group. The Chinese Exclusion Act was not repealed until 1943, and then only in the interest of aiding the morale of an ally in World War II (U.S. Department of State, 2018).

Anti-Asian racism in the United States rose dramatically during the COVID-19 pandemic. After reports of COVID-19 emerged out of Wuhan, China in March 2020, U.S. government officials and news media referred to COVID-19 as the "Chinese Virus," "Wuhan Virus," and "Kung Flu." (Lee, 2020; Viala-Gaudefroy & Lindaman, 2020). These labels invoked centuries-old xenophobic stereotypes of Asian Americans (Gover, Harper, & Langton, 2020). Data from the Federal Bureau of Investigation (FBI) reported that hate crimes among people of Asian descent rose by 73%, from 161 incidents in 2019 to 279 incidents in 2020 (FBI, 2021). However, these numbers are likely an underestimate, as research has found that Asian Americans are the least likely to report hate crimes to authorities compared to members of other racial minorities (Yam, 2021).

An organization called the Stop AAPI Hate Coalition collects data on Asian American and Pacific Islander (AAPI) hate incidents across the United States using community-reported data. From March 19, 2020 to December 31, 2021, the Stop AAPI Hate Coalition (2021) reported 10,905 hate incidents against AAPI persons. The Coalition reported that the majority of incidents consisted of verbal harassment in public spaces, with physical assault as the second largest category. The majority of hate incidents were reported by AAPI women. Both hate crimes and feelings of exclusion are real consequences of racial and ethnic discrimination.

The label for Aunt Jemima syrup has been criticized for its racist depiction of an African American women. This caricature was based on the song "Aunt Jemima" that was performed during a show in which the actors wore blackface. In 2021, in response to complaints from the public about this image, the company revealed a new logo and name for the brand.

To understand the racial and ethnic inequality that occurs in the United States, we can examine how groups vary in terms of education and income. Table 5.1 compares income and education for several ethnic groups (based on how people self-identify on the census). We can see that Asian Americans have the highest incomes, followed by White Americans. Black Americans have the lowest income, making less than half of what Asian Americans make per year and about 63% of what Whites earn, on average.

The original Aunt Jemima bottle, which was created in the late 1940s.

Pictorial Press Ltd / Alamy Stock Photo

The first attempt to "rebrand" the Aunt Jemima label, which was used through 2020.

Pat Canova / Alamy Stock Photo

The new 2021 rebranding of the company's maple syrup, which removes the tie to the problematic image of "Aunt Jemima" and focuses on the origins of the Pearl Milling Company.

Gado Reportage / Alamy Stock Photo

Most people believe that the United States is a meritocracy and, as a result, expect that ethnic groups with high levels of education should have relatively high incomes. This correlation is certainly true for some groups in the table. Asian Americans, for example, have both the highest incomes and highest high school graduation rate. However, Black Americans have relatively high education levels, the third highest after Asian and White Americans. Yet Black Americans have the lowest average income.

There are a variety of explanations for this discrepancy. Some might argue that different ethnic groups are selecting into different types of jobs, with higher or lower pay. However, racism and discrimination are also clearly part of the story. For example, Black physicians make 15% less than White physicians (Marcus, 2017). Among cashiers, more than 70% of Black workers earn less than $15 per hour, whereas only 58% of White workers do (Ruetschlin & Asante-Muhammad, 2015). We can see that, even within the same job, there is a wide discrepancy in average wages depending on one's ethnic origin. This is particularly pronounced among higher paid workers.

TABLE 5.1 ▪ Household Income and Education by Ethnic Group, United States, 2020		
Ethnic Group	**Median Income ($)**	**Bachelor's or Higher Education (percentage)**
Asian	93,759	72.0
White	69,823	44.6
Native Hawaiian and Other Pacific Islander	66,464	30.5
Hispanic or Latino (of any race)	55,658	24.9

(Continued)

TABLE 5.1 ■ Household Income and Education by Ethnic Group, United States, 2020 (*Continued*)		
Ethnic Group	**Median Income ($)**	**Bachelor's or Higher Education (percentage)**
Other race	53,097	n/a
American Indian and Alaska Native	45,476	11.3
Black or African American	43,862	27.7
Average	65,712	39.2

Note: n/a = no number reported.

Sources: U.S. Department of Commerce, Census Bureau, U.S. Census of Population: 1960, Vol. I, Part 1; J.K. Folger and C.B. Nam, Education of the American Population (1960 Census Monograph); Current Population Reports, Series P-20, various years; and Current Population Survey (CPS), Annual Social and Economic Supplement, 1970 through 2020. (This table was prepared October 2020.) https://nces.ed.gov/programs/digest/d20/tables/dt20_104.20.asp

Methods in Depth: Racial Stereotypes and Voting

Research consistently shows that we all have sets of preconceived notions about different groups of people. This does not mean that everyone is a racist or sexist—it just means that we all have some unconscious biases. Knowing this, and understanding how these biases might work, is important because it can help us to better understand our own thinking and, hopefully, help to reduce the ways in which we may, even unintentionally, discriminate or disadvantage certain groups or people.

Research Question

Seth Stephens-Davidowitz (2014) is interested in racial bias. In particular, he is interested in the impact of racial stereotypes and prejudice on human behavior. However, this is a massive topic. So, to get a handle on this issue, he narrowed the scope of his study and focused on how people's ideas about race affected their vote for a presidential candidate, in this case Barack Obama.

Challenges

One of the major challenges of this research is that it is quite difficult to study underlying racial attitudes. First, many of us do not even realize that they hold biased views. This makes it very difficult to ask questions about racial attitudes. Second, most people tend to withhold socially unacceptable attitudes, such as negative feelings toward certain racial groups. The phenomenon in which people who are the subject of research tend to behave or answer in ways that make them appear favorably to researchers is called the social desirability bias. This bias could come, for example, in the form of reporting more open attitudes toward LGBTQ peoples, racial minorities, or women. Or it could be saying that you engage in activities that you think are more socially acceptable— reporting that you make more money than you actually earn or that you do not smoke even if you do. With these issues in mind, how do we know what people's attitudes really are when they may simply be reporting attitudes that they think are more socially acceptable, such as less prejudicial attitudes toward certain racial groups?

Methodology

Stephens-Davidowitz uses a novel approach to studying racial attitudes that could get around both of these methodological issues. He measures the racial attitudes of an area through the percentage of Google search queries that include racially charged language (such as racial slurs).

He compares the percentage of searches with racially charged language with Barack Obama's vote shares, controlling for the vote share of the last Democratic candidate (John Kerry in 2004). Google data are unlikely to suffer from the issue of social desirability—we are online mostly alone at home, which makes it easier to express socially taboo thoughts. In addition, Google is a giant search engine and we can combine information from millions of searches.

Findings

This research found that the percentage of searches using racially charged language was a significant negative predictor of vote share for Obama, meaning that areas with more of these searches also had a lower percentage of people who voted for Obama. Taking into account the number of people who voted Democrat in the previous election, the researcher argues that the overall effect of racial prejudice cost Obama 4% of the national vote in 2008 and 2012. This estimate is 1.5 to 3 times larger than the estimate from surveys examining the same issue. By using this novel form of data, the researcher can navigate one of the most challenging aspects of the research process: how to deal with respondents' tendency to give socially desirable answers. Through better understanding the role of racial attitudes on behavior (such as voting; see Table 5.2), we can begin to address the ways in which prejudicial attitudes of all kinds (including those based on gender, sexuality, religion, disability, and other characteristics) have real and important implications for society.

TABLE 5.2 ■ Timeline of Race and Voting in the United States	
Date	Milestone
1790	The Naturalization Act allowed White men born outside the United States to become U.S. citizens and to vote.
1869	Congress passed the 15th Amendment giving African American men the right to vote.
1887	The Dawes Act granted citizenship to Native Americans who were willing to disassociate themselves from their tribes, making them technically eligible to vote.
1896	Louisiana passed the grandfather clause to keep former slaves and their descendants from voting.
1920	Women were granted the right to vote.
1924	All Native Americans were granted citizenship and the right to vote, regardless of tribal affiliation.
1940	Only 3% of African Americans in the South were registered to vote because of Jim Crow laws (such as literacy tests and poll taxes) designed to keep Blacks from voting.
1943	Chinese immigrants were given the right to citizenship and to vote by the Magnuson Act.
1965	President Johnson signed the Voting Rights Act, barring barriers to political participation by racial or ethnic minorities.

Source: Adapted from the American Civil Liberties Union. https://www.aclu.org/voting-rights-act-major-dates-history.

WHERE DOES PREJUDICE COME FROM?

Prejudice and Discrimination

One of the important consequences of racial and ethnic distinctions is the rise of prejudice and discrimination. Prejudice is a negative attitude toward someone based solely on his membership in a group. If I do not like a person because I think he has an irritating personality, that is not prejudice. However, if I dislike someone because she is Chinese, female, or poor, that is prejudice. Prejudice can lead to discrimination, the negative or positive treatment of someone as a result of his belonging (or being perceived as belonging) in a particular group.

Academic interest in prejudice increased after the atrocities of World War II against certain groups, including Jewish people, people with physical disabilities, and homosexuals. In particular, the extreme implications of anti-Semitism made people around the world ask themselves, "How do people develop prejudice?" and "Who is most likely to develop prejudicial attitudes?" Theodore W. Adorno and his colleagues (1950) wrote some of the earliest research on prejudice. They argued that individuals with a certain personality type, called an authoritarian personality, are more likely to develop prejudicial attitudes. People with this personality tend to use strict or oppressive behavior toward subordinates. They tend to see the world in terms of good and evil and strictly follow rules and orders. Such behavior existed in the concentration camps, where many Nazi officers treated prisoners horrifically. When asked how they could commit such barbaric acts, many stated that they were simply following orders and adhering to the Nazi party's rules. Adorno and his colleagues claim that the authoritarian personality was simply more prevalent among the German population than elsewhere, such as in France or Belgium, which is why the Holocaust was centrally located in Germany.

The idea that someone's personality makes her more likely or less likely to be prejudiced is very appealing. But most sociologists would question how some countries happen to have more (or less) of a certain personality type and how the number of people with this personality trait can rise and fall over time. The World Values Survey is a large international survey that asks citizens of various countries about their lives, values, and political participation. This information allows us to compare the attitudes and behaviors of citizens around the world. Table 5.3 lists, by country, people's responses to one question in the survey: How would you feel about having someone of a different race as a neighbor? Of the countries surveyed, Americans are relatively tolerant of diversity.

If prejudice comes from an inherent personality trait, do nearly seven times as many South Koreans as Americans have this trait? Or does something in South Korean society that does not exist in American society lead to the development of prejudice? Most sociologists would argue that prejudice, and other attitudes, arise from our social context and socialization.

Lawrence Bobo (1983) was one of the first social scientists to examine how social context shapes people's attitudes, particularly prejudice. He argues that prejudice stems from social groups' competition for valued resources or opportunities. This realistic conflict theory makes intuitive sense. It states that when groups want access to the same things, they compete with one another and can have increasingly negative attitudes toward one another. For example, if there are a limited number of good jobs, spaces in universities, or safe neighborhoods in which to live, groups will compete for access to them. Over time, these groups in competition see the others who are vying for similar resources in increasingly negative terms, see clearer boundaries between their own group and other groups, and view their own group as superior.

To test these ideas, Muzafer Sherif and colleagues (Sherif et al., 1961) conducted the Robbers Cave experiment, which involved sending 22 boys aged 11 and 12 to summer camp for 3 weeks. The boys were very similar—they were all healthy, socially well-adjusted, intelligent, White, Protestant, and middle class. One would expect these boys to get along well, since their similarities meant that there was no obvious basis for prejudicial attitudes.

In the first week of camp, the boys were randomly divided into two groups—the Rattlers and the Eagles. The groups lived in cabins far apart and did not interact with each other. Each

TABLE 5.3 ■ Prejudice by Country, 2017–2020	
Country	Percentage who would not like to have people of a different race as their neighbor
Sweden	1.0
Canada[1]	2.5
United States	3.0
Australia	3.9
Germany	4.6
Netherlands	6.3
Chile	6.9
Mexico	11.4
Japan	14.3
Russia	14.7
South Korea	15.2
Nigeria	15.8
China	18.0

1. Canadian data is from the 2006 wave because information on Canadians was not collected in subsequent waves.

Source: Data compiled from World Values Survey data analysis tool, 2017–20 wave, https://www.worldvaluessurvey.org/WVSOnline.jsp

group lived and played together for the week and did regular, fun camp activities: The boys swam and hiked and generally enjoyed their camp experience. Just like any summer camp, the kids in each group formed friendships with one another and developed a group identity.

The second week, the Rattlers and Eagles were introduced to one another. The boys from each group were set to participate in a series of competitions, including tug-of-war and capture-the-flag, to receive a trophy and prizes that the boys strongly desired. These competitions led to severe tensions between the groups. First, the groups exchanged verbal taunts (calling boys in the other group stinkers and braggers—some pretty serious taunts for 1961!). Then, the boys became more aggressive: The Eagles ransacked the Rattlers' cabin; the Rattlers responded by burning the Eagles' flag. The boys developed increasingly negative attitudes toward those in the other group. Within a week two groups of boys who were almost the same on most dimensions—gender, race, religion, class—and who had never previously met had developed intense animosity and preju-dice toward one another. Just as Bobo (1983) had predicted, competition over resources led them to develop prejudice.

After Sherif had created these tensions, he wanted to see how prejudice could be reduced. One popular theory at the time was contact theory (Allport, 1954). This theory argues that increasing contact between antagonistic groups will lead to a growing recognition of similari-ties and will alter stereotypes about the other group, thereby reducing prejudice. To test this theory, Sherif created situations where both groups would encounter one another. For example, the Rattlers and the Eagles started eating in the cafeteria at the same time. However, instead of leading to more positive attitudes between the groups, this change was just an opportunity for each group to express dislike for the other group. The groups sat separately (think of cliques in your high school cafeteria) and started a food fight. More contact between the groups was obviously not enough to reduce the conflict.

Sherif then tried to encourage cooperation between the groups. He created situations where the two groups needed to work together for what he called superordinate goals, things that both groups desired but neither could accomplish alone. For example, the boys all wanted a movie night but had to pool their money to rent the movie. Sherif also intentionally broke the pipe that pumped water into the camp, and all the boys had to cooperate in order to fix it. It was only when the boys worked together to achieve these shared goals that their conflict and prejudice diminished. Look at Figures 5.1 and 5.2 to see how cooperation created more positive attitudes and ties between the groups.

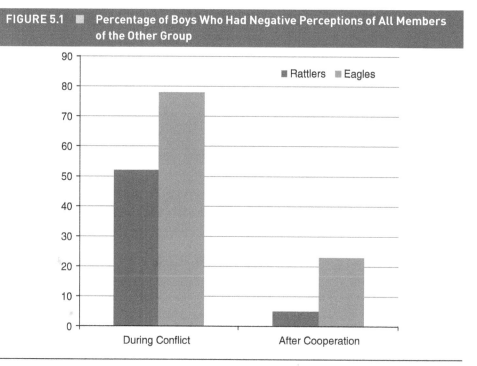

FIGURE 5.1 ■ Percentage of Boys Who Had Negative Perceptions of All Members of the Other Group

Source: Sherif, M., O. J. Harvey, B. J. White, W. Hood, and C. W. Sherif. 1961. *Intergroup Conflict and Cooperation: The Robbers Cave Experiment.* Norman, OK: University Book Exchange.

What does this experiment tell us about how prejudice arises between groups and how we can reduce it? How can we apply these lessons to the real world? First, we see that the social context is very important for creating and reducing prejudice. It was not simply that some boys were more likely to be prejudiced than others, but rather that all boys were more likely to develop prejudicial attitudes in situations of conflict and to reduce those attitudes in situations that required cooperation. This finding sheds light on prejudice in the real world—it can be increased or reduced by changing elements of the social context.

Second, this study lends some support for the realistic conflict theory. When the boys were competing for something that both groups wanted, there were more conflicts and prejudicial attitudes between the groups. This situation is similar to the real world, where ethnic, religious, gender, or other groups often compete for jobs, access to education, or other benefits.

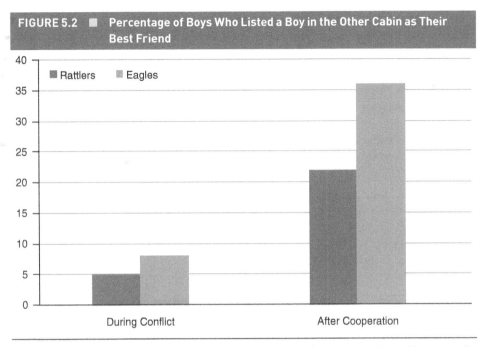

FIGURE 5.2 ■ Percentage of Boys Who Listed a Boy in the Other Cabin as Their Best Friend

Source: Sherif, M., O. J. Harvey, B. J. White, W. Hood, and C. W. Sherif. 1961. *Intergroup Conflict and Cooperation: The Robbers Cave Experiment.* Norman, OK: University Book Exchange.

Third, contact between groups is often not enough to reduce conflict or prejudice. Later research indicates that contact between groups reduces prejudice only when the groups are roughly equal in status, the contact is informal, and the contact permits the disconfirmation of stereotypes. It is also important that the contact involve cooperation, which is the final lesson of this study. Cooperating for the achievement of superordinate goals can lead to increased tolerance and positive attitudes among different groups in society. Think about how these lessons could apply to real-world conflicts between groups. Can we use experiments such as Sherif's to understand, and potentially alleviate, conflict between groups? If so, how?

W. E. B. Du Bois

W. E. B. Du Bois was a critical figure in the founding of sociology, particularly in the United States. He was born in Massachusetts and was a sociologist, civil rights activist, and author. He was a professor of history, sociology, and economics at Atlanta University. Du Bois was prolific over his career and wrote 23 nonfiction books, three autobiographies, and five novels, and edited *The Crisis* (the NAACP's magazine) from 1910 to 1933.

One of Du Bois's most influential books was *The Souls of Black Folks* (1903), which is a collection of 14 essays. This book opens with the following line: "The problem of the twentieth century is the problem of the color line" (p. 1). This central thesis was the basis of much of his life's work, which highlighted the way that racial inequality and injustice prevail in American social and political life. This book also highlights what Du Bois referred to as a double consciousness. A double consciousness is when a person has an identity that feels divided into many parts, which makes it difficult for them to feel that they have a unified sense of self. Du Bois argued that this was a problem for many African Americans when trying to unify the identities of being Black and American. Du Bois argues that this unique identity could be either a handicap, as it had been in the past, or a strength, as it could be in the future. In fact, his work introduces the concept of a hyphenated identity—something that is much discussed in the modern and diverse era, particularly in relation to ideas about multicultur-alism. Du Bois argues, "Henceforth, the destiny of the race could be conceived as leading neither to assimilation nor separatism but to proud, enduring hyphenation" (in Lewis, 1993, pp. 194–195).

One of Du Bois's major contributions was to highlight the importance of studying and understanding the lives and experiences of Blacks in the United States. This was the core of *The Philadelphia Negro* (Du Bois, 1899), an in-depth sociological study of the African American community in Philadelphia based on fieldwork he conducted in 1896–1897. This book was the first scientific study of African Americans and a major early work of American sociology. He also published *The Negro* (1915/2002), a general history of Black Americans, the first of its kind in English. Both books shed light on the experiences of Blacks in the United States and highlight the importance of studying racial inequality.

W. E. B. Du Bois, one of the founders of sociology, used sociological tools to show how society works and to fight racism.

New York Public Library/Science Source

Du Bois's work was not appreciated at the time by the White sociological or larger academic community. According to Arthur Spingarn, a White scholar who was Du Bois's contemporary, Du Bois spent his time "battering his life out against ignorance, bigotry, intolerance, and slothfulness, projecting ideas nobody but he understands, and raising hopes for change which may be comprehended in a hundred years" (Spingarn, quoted by Lewis, 1993, p. 645). Du Bois is now recognized for his critical importance to the rise of sociology in the United States (Morris, 2015). In fact, the highest award given out by the American

Sociological Association is now called the W. E. B. Du Bois Career of Distinguished Scholarship Award.

Du Bois was a pioneer both within and outside academia. He engaged in the sociological study of Blacks in the United States and the major social issues of racism and discrimination, but he also focused his work on creating social change outside of the academy, through social movements and politics. He was a critical figure in the civil rights movement and one of the founders of the NAACP. He was actively involved in the antiwar movement, in support of women's rights, and in labor issues.

Getting to Know: W. E. B. Du Bois (1868–1963)

- The first African American to earn a PhD from Harvard University in 1895.

- Co-founded the National Association for the Advancement of Colored People (NAACP) in 1909.

- One of the leaders of the Harlem Renaissance (1918–1937), a movement to establish the Harlem neighborhood in New York as the epicenter of African American culture. The Harlem Renaissance encouraged the development of African American literature, music, theatre, and visual art that challenged the representation of Black experiences in American culture and cultivated Black pride.

- Helped organize a series of international meetings known as the Pan-African Congress (1919–1927), the goal of which was to end racial discrimination and colonial occupation of the West Indies and African nations.

- Worked as an anti-war and anti-nuclear weapons activist who was Chair of the Peace Information Center (1950), an organization that promoted peace and a global ban on nuclear weapons.

White Privilege

One of the challenges in studying inequality—be it racial, ethnic, class, gender, or other—is that it requires us to examine the disadvantages of various groups in society. This task is difficult because it goes against our society's dominant ideology that we live in a meritocracy, where the smartest and hardest-working people are those who get ahead. How do we reconcile this view with the reality that, based on characteristics individuals do not control (social class, race, gender), some groups have more advantages than others?

Another reason that it is challenging to think about inequality is that it forces us to consider not only the disadvantages that some groups face but also the advantages that accrue to other groups. For example, we cannot think about the disadvantages to the poor without thinking of the advantages our society gives to the rich, the disadvantages to racialized people without thinking of the advantages given to Whites, or the disadvantages given to gays and lesbians without thinking of the advantages given to heterosexuals.

Peggy McIntosh (1988) wrote a fascinating article in which she challenged herself to not only think about the disadvantages that racialized minorities face but also to enumerate the advantages that she, as a White American, experiences in her daily life. She talks about these advantages of White privilege as an invisible knapsack— "an invisible package of unearned assets that I can count on cashing in each day, but about which I was 'meant' to remain oblivious.

White privilege is like an invisible weightless knapsack of special provisions, maps, passports, codebooks, visas, clothes, tools, and blank checks" (p. 1). Here are some examples of the privileges she experiences:

- I can if I wish arrange to be in the company of people of my race most of the time.

- I can be pretty sure that my neighbors will be neutral or pleasant to me.

- I can turn on the TV or open a paper and see people of my race widely represented.

- When I am told about our national heritage or about civilization, I am shown that people of my color made it what it is.

- I can go to a shop and find the music of my race, into a supermarket and find my staple foods, into a salon and find someone who can cut my hair.

- I can do well in a challenging situation without being called a credit to my race.

- I am never asked to speak for all people of my race.

- I can easily buy posters, postcards, picture books, cards, dolls, and toys featuring people of my race.

- I can take a job with an affirmative action employer without having coworkers suspect I got it because of my race.

- I can choose blemish cover or bandages in flesh tone and have them more or less match my skin. (pp. 2–3)

ColorPop cosmetics was recently criticized for releasing a line of makeup where the lighter shades are named "illuminati" and "castle" while the darker shades have names such as "yikes" and "typo." After the outcry from consumers, the company did change the names of the darker shades. However, this naming highlights the often-unexamined messages about the desirability of different racial and ethnic traits in our society.

Liudmila Chernetska/iStockPhoto

IMMIGRATION

The movement of people around the world is central to the process of globalization (see Chapter 12). Although such movement has occurred throughout history, long-distance human migration for permanent settlement has become increasingly common over the past century. The result is a growing intermingling of the world's people, although not all countries receive or welcome migrants to the same degree.

The United States has one of the highest per capita immigration rates in the world, which makes our population very ethnically and culturally diverse. More than 15% of the United States' population, or 50.6 million people, were born outside the United States in 2020 (see Figure 5.3). In contrast, some countries have extremely low foreign-born populations. Only 0.1% of the population of China and 2.2% of the population of Japan, for example, were born outside those countries. The Immigration and Naturalization Act governs immigration policy in the United States. It bases immigration decisions on four main principles: reuniting families, admitting immigrants with skills that are valuable to the U.S. economy, protecting refugees, and promoting diversity.

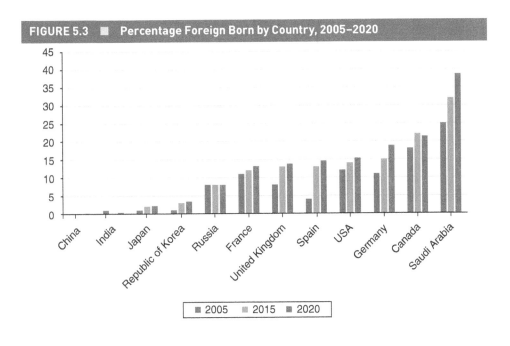

FIGURE 5.3 ■ Percentage Foreign Born by Country, 2005–2020

■ 2005 ■ 2015 ■ 2020

*Numbers represent the International migrant stock as a percentage of the total population, both sexes combined.

Source: United Nations, Department of Economic and Social Affairs, Population Division (2016). International Migration Report 2015: Highlights (ST/ESA/SER.A/375). https://www.un.org/en/development/desa/population/migration/publications/migrationreport/docs/MigrationReport2015_Highlights.pdf; United Nations Department of Economic and Social Affairs, Population Division (2020). International Migration 2020 Highlights (ST/ESA/SER.A/452). https://www.un.org/development/desa/pd/sites/www.un.org.development.desa.pd/files/undesa_pd_2020_international_migration_highlights.pdf

In 2020 the United States admitted 707,362 legal immigrants. Of this group, 17% were family sponsored, 45% were the immediate relatives of U.S. citizens, 21% were employment-based preferences, 4% were part of the Diversity Immigrant Visa program, and 9% were refugees and asylum seekers (U.S. Department of Homeland Security, 2020). Employment-based immigration is based on more than 20 types of visas that are issued for temporary nonimmigrant workers, for example those with extraordinary ability, those who are highly skilled, or diplomatic employees. The Diversity Visa program was created by the Immigration Act of 1990 and works to channel immigrants from countries with low rates of immigration to the United States: Each year 50,000 visas are allocated randomly to nations from countries that have sent fewer than 50,000 immigrants to the United States in the previous 5 years. Each of these different channels of immigration brings different kinds of people with diverse sets of skills and ties to the United States. The decisions made about who to admit and under what conditions are political and have important implications for shaping the character and diversity of the United States. These decisions are related to larger questions about the identity of the United States as a nation and what principles Americans value.

READING: FROM *IMAGINED COMMUNITIES: REFLECTIONS ON THE ORIGIN AND SPREAD OF NATIONALISM*

Benedict Anderson

A nation is a group of people united by a common fate and with a shared national character. Nations are often based on a shared language, ethnicity, and history (Bauer, 1907 in Davis, 1967, p. 150). A nation-state is a group of people who share a physical territory and government, although they may not share an ethnicity, language, or history. The United Sates is a nation-state. It has a common territory made up of a diverse set of peoples from a variety of language, cultural, and ethnic groups. Benedict Anderson argues that nations are based on imagined communities because "the members of even the smallest nation will never know most of their fellow members, meet them, or even hear of them, yet in the minds of each lives the image of their communion." This idea highlights the socially constructed aspect of nations.

In an anthropological spirit, . . . I propose the following definition of the nation: it is an imagined political community—and imagined as both inherently limited and sovereign.

It is *imagined* because the members of even the smallest nation will never know most of their fellow members, meet them, or even hear of them, yet in the minds of each lives the image of their communion.[1] Renan referred to this imagining in his suavely back-handed way when he wrote that "Or l'essence d'une nation est que tous les individus aient beaucoup de choses en commun, et aussi que tous aient oublié bien des choses."[2] With a certain ferocity Gellner makes a comparable point when he rules that "Nationalism is not the awakening of nations to self-consciousness: it *invents* nations where they do not exist."[3] The drawback to this formulation, however, is that Gellner is so anxious to show that nationalism masquerades under false pretenses that he assimilates "invention" to "fabrication" and "falsity," rather than to "imagining" and "creation." In this way he implies that "true" communities exist which can be advantageously juxtaposed to nations. In fact, all communities larger than primordial villages of face-to-face contact (and perhaps even these) are imagined. Communities are to be distinguished, not by their falsity/genuineness, but by the style in which they are imagined. Javanese villagers have always known that they are connected to people they have never seen, but these ties were once imagined particularistically—as indefinitely stretchable nets of kinship and clientship. Until quite recently, the Javanese language had no word meaning the abstraction "society." We may today think of the French aristocracy of the *ancien régime* as a class; but surely it was imagined this way only very late.[4] To the question "Who is the Comte de X?" the normal answer would have been, not "a member of the aristocracy," but "the lord of X," "the uncle of the Baronne de Y," or "a client of the Duc de Z."

The nation is imagined as *limited* because even the largest of them, encompassing perhaps a billion living human beings, has finite, if elastic, boundaries, beyond which lie other nations. No nation imagines itself coterminous with mankind. The most messianic nationalists do not dream of a day when all the members of the human race will join their nation in the way that it was possible, in certain epochs, for, say, Christians to dream of a wholly Christian planet.

It is imagined as *sovereign* because the concept was born in an age in which Enlightenment and Revolution were destroying the legitimacy of the divinely ordained, hierarchical dynastic realm. Coming to maturity at a stage of human history when even the most devout adherents of any universal religion were inescapably confronted with the living *pluralism* of such religions, and the allomorphism between each faith's ontological claims and territorial stretch, nations dream of being free, and, if under God, directly so. The gage and emblem of this freedom is the sovereign state.

Finally, it is imagined as a *community*, because, regardless of the actual inequality and exploitation that may prevail in each, the nation is always conceived as a deep, horizontal comradeship. Ultimately it is this fraternity that makes it possible, over the past two centuries, for so many millions of people, not so much to kill, as willingly to die for such limited imaginings.

These deaths bring us abruptly face to face with the central problem posed by nationalism: what makes the shrunken imaginings of recent history (scarcely more than two centuries) generate such colossal sacrifices? I believe that the beginnings of an answer lie in the cultural roots of nationalism.

Notes

Cf. Seton-Watson, *Nations and States*, p. 5: "All that I can find to say is that a nation exists when a significant number of people in a community consider themselves to form a nation, or behave as if they formed one." We may translate "consider themselves" as "imagine themselves."

Ernest Renan, "Qu'est-ce qu'une nation?" in *Oeuvres Completes*, 1, p. 892. He adds: "tout citoyen français doit avoir oublié la Saint-Barthelemy, les massacres du Midi an XIIIe siècle. Il n'y a pas en France dix familles qui puissent fournir la preuve d'une origine franque . . ."

Ernest Gellner, *Thought and Change*, p. 169. Emphasis added.

Hobsbawm, for example, "fixes" it by saying that in 1789 it numbered about 400,000 in a population of 23,000,000. (See his *The Age of Revolution*, p. 78). But would this statistical picture of the noblesse have been imaginable under the *ancien régime*?

Reading Questions

1. What four features does Anderson use to describe nations?

2. How are nations imagined? Who imagines them? How does the idea of imagined communities relate to the theory of social construction?

3. Anderson quotes Ernest Gellner's statement that nationalism "invents nations where they do not exist." What is nationalism and how does it invent nations?

Anderson, B. (2006). Imagined communities. In *Imagined communities: Reflections on the origin and spread of nationalism* (Rev. ed.; pp. 5–7). Verso.

How Well Doe the United States Integrate Immigrants?

Coming to a new country is challenging. Individuals need to find jobs or enter school, make friends and social connections, learn about how to participate in the political system and how to access social services. The Migrant Integration Policy Index brings together data from countries around the world and measures how well these countries are doing at integrating newcomers along eight dimensions: labor market mobility, family reunion, education, health, political participation, access to permanent residency, access to citizenship, and protection from discrimination. The United States does fairly well on this index, ranking 7th out of the 56 countries measured (see Figure 5.4). Sweden, Finland and Portugal are among the countries that score higher than the United States on this index (Migrant Integration Policy Index, 2019).

FIGURE 5.4 ■ U.S. Ranking and Score on the Migrant Integration Policy Index

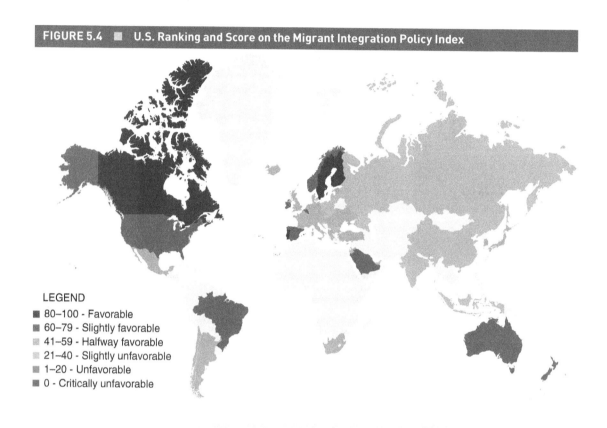

LEGEND
- ■ 80–100 - Favorable
- ■ 60–79 - Slightly favorable
- ▦ 41–59 - Halfway favorable
- ▒ 21–40 - Slightly unfavorable
- ■ 1–20 - Unfavorable
- ■ 0 - Critically unfavorable

USA

2014	
Rank:	**7** out of **56**
MIPEX Score:	**73**

Labor market mobility		69
Family reunion		62
Education		83
Health		79
Political participation		40
Permanent residence		63
Access to nationality		88
Anti-discrimination		97

Source: Migrant Integration Policy Index 2020, Solano, Giacomo and Huddleston, Thomas (2020). Reprinted with permission of the Migration Policy Group, The developer of MIPEX.

There are some dimensions on which the United States is very successful at integrating new-comers. For example, the United States ranks second among all countries in our antidiscrimination protections for immigrants. People in the United States, particularly those in California, enjoy among the strongest laws in the world protecting them from discrimination. However, the U.S. ranks quite low on political participation for newcomers (20 out of 56). This is, in part, because we do not allow even long-time permanent residents voting rights. In many European countries, long-time permanent residents can vote in local or city elections, giving them more access to the political system. We also rank very low on the ability of newcomers to become permanent residents (24 out of 56). Many immigrants have no path to permanent status and some eligible immigrants have second-class status and fewer rights than U.S. citizens.

Immigrants are a vital and important part of American society. These types of indexes high-light the challenges that immigrants face and the many ways that countries can assist immigrants in integrating into a new country.

USING YOUR SOCIOLOGICAL IMAGINATION
AMERICAN CIVICS TEST FOR CITIZENSHIP

One of the last steps when adult immigrants become American citizens is taking a test called the Civics Test, which is a portion of the overall naturalization test. Applicants answer questions orally in English during an interview with a U.S. Citizenship and Immigration Services officer. An applicant must answer six out of the ten questions correctly in order to pass the Civics Test. These questions focus on American government (principles of American democracy, systems of government, rights and responsibilities), American history (the colonial period and independence, the 1800s, recent American history) and integrated civics (geography, symbols, and holidays). Go to the U.S. Citizenship and Immigration Services website (https://my.uscis.gov/prep/test/civics) and do a practice test. Remember that if you were really taking this test you would not have multiple choice answers to select from.

After you have completed the test, answer the following questions:

1. How did you do on this test? Where did you learn the information covered?
2. What kinds of questions and topics are included in the test? How do they emphasize the way that the American government imagines the nation of the United States of America? What, if any, questions would you remove from the test?
3. What other types of questions might you add to the test if you were creating it? What other things do you think that people should know before becoming an American citizen?

SUMMARY

We began this chapter by examining the differences between race and ethnicity. Race is based on perceived physical traits, and ethnicity is based on cultural differences between people. The theory of social construction, introduced by Berger and Luckmann, can help us to understand how we create racial and ethnic categories in our society. The Thomas principle shows how these categories, despite being socially constructed, can have real consequences for individuals. Both theories can be applied to many concepts—such as gender, social class, and sexuality—that we will learn about throughout this book. Through Sherif's experiment we examined how prejudice and discrimination arise in society and how they can be reduced. We also talked about immigration to the United States and concluded by examining the idea of the United States of America as an imagined community.

FOR FURTHER READING

Anderson, B. (2006). *Imagined communities: Reflections on the origin and spread of nationalism*, Verso Books.

Berger, P. L., & Luckmann, T. (1966). *The social construction of reality: A treatise in the sociology of knowledge*, Anchor Books.

Koopmans, R. (2013). Multiculturalism and immigration: A contested field in cross-national comparison. *Annual Review of Sociology, 39*, 147–169.

Waters, M. C. (1990). *Ethnic options: Choosing identities in America*, University of California Press.

GLOSSARY

authoritarian personality	multiculturalism
census	nation
contact theory	nation-state
critical race theory	prejudice
discrimination	race
essentialism	racism
ethnicity	realistic conflict theory
imagined communities	social desirability bias
immigration	symbolic ethnicity
invisible knapsack	Thomas principle

6 GENDER AT THE INTERSECTIONS

LEARNING OBJECTIVES

1. Explain and differentiate between the concepts of sex and gender and illustrate how each is socially constructed.

2. Describe the role of major institutions, such as sports, work, and politics, in perpetuating our ideas of gender and gender inequality.

3. Define feminism and compare the main waves of feminism in the United States.

4. Discuss the concept of intersectionality and how it shapes our experiences of inequality.

5. Describe the growth of research on sexuality over time and the changing ideas of sexuality in society.

How can we tell someone's sex? The International Olympics Committee (IOC), which governs the Olympics, has been struggling with this question. Up until the 1960s, female competitors had to parade, nude, in front of an all-female panel to have their sex verified. At the 1968 Olympics, these physical checks were replaced by tests of chromosome levels. However, these types of checks are both humiliating and ineffective. There is simply not a clear line between female and male in either anatomy or chromosomes (Aschwanden, 2016).

Take Maria Jose Martinez-Patino, a hurdler from Spain. After the chromosomal tests, she was told that she has a 46, XY karyotype—meaning she is genetically male. However, she was also born with insensitivity to testosterone, so she developed as a female. She had no advantage due to testosterone because her body is unable to use it. After this test Maria's sports scholarship was revoked and her records were erased. Maria has classically female anatomy—a vagina and breasts—and has always identified as female. As she says, she always "knew [she] was a woman" (Aschwanden, 2016). This case was pivotal in ending the chromosome tests at the 2000 Olympics, but Olympics officials can still test and examine female athletes who they consider to be suspicious (Aschwanden, 2016). What do these tests tell us about what it means to be a man or woman? Is it simply a matter of anatomy or chromosomes or is it something more?

Transgender athletes also challenge the Olympic Committee's norms around sex- based competition categories. In November 2016, the IOC issued new guidelines that allow athletes who have transitioned their sex to compete without sex reassignment surgery. These new rules make it possible for an athlete who has previously identified as female to compete in the male category without restriction. However, an athlete who has previously identified as male is subject to the following regulations if they want to compete as in the female category: They must have declared a female identity for at least 4 years and they must show that their testosterone levels have remained below a certain level for at least 1 year in order to compete (Aschwanden, 2016). Some applaud these new guidelines for focusing on both biological traits and gender identification and for not forcing individuals to undergo physical surgery in order to qualify. Others question the somewhat arbitrary lengths of time one must identify as female and the basis for the levels of testosterone that are deemed "female." In addition, these rules are still subject to criticism from those who believe that they go too far in allowing athletes to compete in categories into which they were not born. These rules and the complications they bring highlight the blurry lines of sex and gender.

SEX AND GENDER

In Chapters 4 and 5, we learned about the importance of social class, social status, race, and ethnicity as dimensions of inequality. Another major type of inequality that exists in our society is based on the categories of sex and gender. Sex is a biological identity and can be divided into the main categories of male and female. Gender is a social concept referring to the entire array of social patterns we associate with men and women in a society. Gender exists along the continuum of masculinity and femininity. In many ways the difference between sex and gender mirrors the difference between race and ethnicity. Whereas sex and race are based on perceived biological differences, gender and ethnicity are rooted in social and cultural constructions and distinctions.

There are certainly biological differences between men and women. For example, men are, on average, taller than women, and men and women have different reproductive organs. However, neither of these two distinctions is as clear-cut as it seems. Some women are very tall; some men are very short. Some people are born with the sexual organs of both sexes. Despite these issues, assigned sex is based on perceived physical differences. It is important to note, though, that such differences do not explain gender-based social disparities. In effect, the way we expect men to act (what we deem masculine behavior) and women to act (what we deem feminine behavior) is socially constructed. As with ethnicity (see Chapter 5), our ideas of what is acceptable and laudable behavior for men and women are socially created. The clear division between men/women and masculinity/femininity is, at least partly, an illusion.

Thinking of sex as a dichotomy is problematic in several ways, as illustrated by the discussion of athletes at the Olympics. In addition, the existence of middle sex categories challenges the male/female binary. For example, some societies have three genders—men,

Actor Elliot Page came out as transgender in 2020 and was the first transgender person to appear on the cover of *Time* magazine. He has used his journey to help raise awareness about trans issues and equality.

David Livingston/Getty Images

women, and a third group that is variously named. Some African and Native American societies have a group of individuals who they call "manly hearted women." This group is made up of biological females who perform the social role of men in their society; they have the social responsibilities and privileges usually bestowed only on husbands and fathers. Having the wealth to buy a wife bestows the social status of men on these women (Lorber, 1994).

Intersex people, those born with the sexual organs of both sexes, also challenge the male/female binary. Approximately 1% of live births in North America are sexually ambiguous based on their anatomy (Fausto-Sterling, 2000). Between 0.1 and 0.2% of all births are so sexually ambiguous that specialists medically assign a sex to the child. Today, fewer people with ambiguous genitalia are forced to have this surgery—at least until they are old enough to select for themselves—than people were decades ago.

Individuals who are transgender also test our conceptions of sex and gender. There are a variety of different groups of people within this larger community, such as transgender, gender fluid, and agender people. Advocates for individuals within these groups have coined the term transgender (trans) umbrella to encompass the variety of different gender identities and sexual expressions in modern society. The struggles and triumphs of individuals within this community have attracted increased attention recently, due in part to the prominence of transgender characters on shows such as *Pose, Glee, Orange Is the New Black, I am Jazz, Euphoria,* and *Transparent.* Figure 6.1 illustrates the terms and the groups that we can use to understand differences in sex, gender, and sexuality.

FIGURE 6.1 ■ The Gender Unicorn

Source: Trans Student Educational Resources, https://transstudent.org/gender/

Gender as a Social Construction

Recall that social construction, which we learned about in Chapter 3, is a two-step process. First, we classify experiences and act based on these categories. Second, we forget that we have created these divisions and instead see them as natural and unchangeable. When we meet people one of the first things we do is try to place them into previously learned categories. Are they male or female? Old or young? Doing so helps us to understand how we should interact with them. Not knowing how to categorize an individual can make your interactions uncomfortable because the societal norms are unclear.

Learning, understanding, and viewing one another as male and female is a social process. Our parents hold certain ideas about gender-appropriate behavior, which they teach us. Later our teachers help us learn to perform our gender through socialization. Expected behavior is further reinforced within same-sex social circles in school, during a period when boys tend to play with only other boys and girls with only other girls (Kimmel, 2011). The media also informs our sense of gender-appropriate behavior. This process continues in the workplace and our familial roles. Furthermore, social institutions, such as sports, education, and the family, support and perpetuate gender-appropriate behavior.

USING YOUR SOCIOLOGICAL IMAGINATION: SOCIOLOGY AND THE "GENDER REVEAL" PARTY

In 2008, a pregnant woman named Jenna Karvunidis held a gender reveal party to announce the sex of her future child with the color (pink or blue) inside of a cake. She posted about the cake on her blog and gender reveal parties became a viral sensation. Celebrities and social media stars quickly embraced the trend. By 2020, Karvunidis wrote to her followers that she made a mistake and regretted popularizing these parties.

Read Karvunidis's story about why she regrets starting the gender reveal trend (https://www.theguardian.com/lifeandstyle/2020/jun/29/jenna-karvunidis-i-started-gender-reveal-party-trend-regret) and answer the following questions.

1. How did Karvunidis's experience raising children change her ideas about gender?

2. Besides gender reveals, how else are gender roles introduced before a child is born?

3. How do you think early childhood messages about gender may have shaped how you identify today? How did these messages shape your hobbies or academic interests?

4. What issues do gender reveal parties raise for our ideas of sex and gender in society as a whole?

Gender Roles and Performativity

In Chapter 2 we talked about social roles, the sets of connected behaviors, beliefs, and norms that individuals perform in a social situation. Gender roles are the behaviors, beliefs, and norms associated with performing our gender. Gender is not something we are born with, but instead is situationally constructed through individuals' performances. Goffman's (1959) dramaturgical perspective helped us to see how individuals perform roles in our day-to-day lives. We are actors on the stage of life, performing our gender through our clothes, mannerisms, and behaviors. Remember that the front stage is where individuals perform for others, whereas the backstage is where individuals do not need to perform. The front stage, for many individuals, is living up to the expected gender norms, but their backstage reveals a different set of gender displays.

In her influential book *Gender Trouble,* the feminist scholar Judith Butler (1990) argues that all gender is created and sustained through performances. Performativity is "not a singular act, but a repetition and a ritual. [What we take to be an] internal essence of gender is manufactured through a sustained set of acts, posited through the gendered stylization of the body"; what we see as an "internal feature of ourselves is one that we anticipate and produce through certain bodily acts" (pp. xv–xvi). Although it appears that our gender is just a natural part of who we are, Butler argues that we create gender through our actions and interactions.

Butler (1990) argues further that labelling a person as male or female is overly restrictive. A person defined as male, for example, is supposed to possess masculine and heterosexual traits (e.g., be sexually active, aggressive, attracted to females). These characteristics are exhibited as a performance but are not necessarily voluntary. Some men might naturally want to behave this way, but others might find that these behaviors do not reflect their sense of self. In this way, gender does not automatically stem from inherent personality characteristics but is the result of cultural norms and practices that are subsequently reinforced. The concepts of masculine and feminine, therefore, appear to be just as natural as the sex to which they are attached. And deviations, such as homosexuality or the display of opposite-gendered characteristics, are marginalized as being outside normality.

USING YOUR SOCIOLOGICAL IMAGINATION
PERFORMING GENDER IN MUSIC

The media is an important avenue for learning about gender norms—how we should act as men and women and what is feminine and masculine behavior. Music, in particular, is part of how we come to understand the role of men and women in society. However, as we listen to music we rarely think critically about the messages it contains. In this activity, we will investigate examples of music that support a narrow understanding of masculinity and femininity, as well as music that challenges our ideas of men's and women's roles in society.

Find the lyrics and videos to some songs that talk about gender and answer the following questions. (You can obtain lyrics to many songs at www.azlyrics.com and find videos on YouTube.)

1. Find a song that you think reproduces gender stereotypes. How do the lyrics or video for this song reproduce these stereotypes?

2. Find a song that challenges our ideas of gender. How do the lyrics or the video for this song challenge these ideas?

3. What types of music genres or artists are more likely to challenge gender roles and what types are less likely to do so?

4. Why do you think that musicians, record labels, or music sites release gender-stereotypical or gender-challenging music?

Butler (1990) also claims that a focus on sex as a binary (leaving only the options of male or female) encourages us to see other dichotomies in categorizing people. For example, seeing only two sexes leads to an illusion of only two distinct and opposite genders (masculine or feminine) and two distinct and opposite sexualities (heterosexual or homosexual). Instead, she pushes us to think about gender and sexuality as continuums. Although there are certainly men who are very masculine and women who are very feminine, there are also men who are more feminine and women who are more masculine.

Michael Messner (1997) argues that there are many social costs to displaying gender in ways that our society deems inappropriate. Messner particularly focuses on what he calls the costs of masculinity. Though we often concentrate on the costs of being female (e.g., lower pay, discrimination, violence, and others, which we will discuss in more detail later in this chapter), our society also has a very restrictive idea of what it means to be a man. Messner outlines the rules of masculinity. For example, men must avoid anything feminine. Those who like romantic comedies, music written and/or performed by women, or dance cannot share these interests with others for fear of seeming less masculine. Masculinity is also defined by external success (money, fast cars, prestigious jobs). And men are expected to show little emotion and to be aggressive.

These rules for behavior are very limiting for men. Furthermore, men are sanctioned for stepping outside these norms. Men who perform jobs that are considered feminine, such as nurse or child-care provider, experience their masculinity being questioned. Men who break the rules might be degraded and demoted to the status of women. A man who fails to live up to gender norms might be called names such as sissy, girlie, or gay, insinuating that he is like a woman or is homosexual and therefore inferior. These names highlight the power associated with traditional views of masculinity in society and the sanctions for stepping outside these ways of being male.

These two bottles of body wash are essentially the same product. However, the men's product is invigorating, uses sea minerals, and is in a dark bottle. The women's product is uplifting, has a cherry and peony scent, and is in a pink bottle. Why do companies advertise and package products differently for men and women? How do such products reinforce our ideas of gender?

Islandstock / Alamy Stock Photo

Gender plays out in all our social interactions. Think about the seemingly small issue of what men and women tend to drink at parties. Who would you expect to drink Hey Y'alls or coolers? What about beer? Jessica Streeter (2012) argues that even what we drink reinforces ideas of gender. She is particularly interested in craft beer. Craft beer, which comes from small-scale producers, is increasingly popular as drinkers look for options beyond the large-scale breweries such as Coors or Budweiser. Streeter claims that, in the craft beer scene, women and new drinkers are encouraged to try fruit beers, blonde ales, and wheat beers, but men are offered dark India pale ales (also called IPAs), aged stouts, and other high-alcohol beers. In other words, women and novices are offered light styles of beer. Bolder flavors, such as beers that are hoppy, bitter, or thick, are marketed to men, who are encouraged to advance beyond what are considered more feminine offerings.

You can see from this argument that even what we select to eat and drink is, in some ways, a gendered performance. When a woman says that she prefers fruit beers and a man says that he favors stouts, they are reporting their preferences. But their social environments shape these preferences, which reinforce dominant notions of masculinity and femininity. How and why do advertisers and producers reinforce these norms?

Methods in Depth: Learning Gender From Our Parents

How do we learn to perform our gender? One way is through seeing how our parents think about gender and model gender-appropriate behaviors. But which do you think is more important: how our parents think about gender (their gender ideology) or how they act out gender (their gender behavior)?

Methodology

Research by Hillary Paul Halpern and Maureen Perry-Jenkins (2016) examines these issues. They used a self-report survey of 109 dual-earner, working-class families in the United States. The parents were recruited through prenatal classes at hospitals in western Massachusetts.

The researchers surveyed the parents five times in the first year of parenthood and again 6 years later, when their children were just about to enter school. They also collected data from children when they were 6 years old.

Findings

The researchers found that mothers' and fathers' behaviors are better predictors of children's gender role attitudes than parents' ideology—in essence, it is what we do, not what we think, that shapes children's attitudes. They also found that mothers and fathers play different roles in their children's gender socialization. Mothers were the primary imparter of knowledge about feminine behaviors for girls and masculine behaviors for boys. But the gender ideology and gendered behavior of the mothers was not related to the children's gendered ideas about the opposite sex. The ideology of the fathers was a strong predictor of boys' stereotypes about girls but was not strongly related to the attitudes of girls (Halpern & Perry-Jenkins, 2016).

This study is novel in many ways. First, it focused on both gendered beliefs and gendered behaviors. The researchers measured gendered beliefs through a series of scales focusing on beliefs about gender roles, attitudes toward women generally, and ideas of mothers working outside the home. Gendered behaviors were measured based on questions about the gendered division of household labor, child care, and employment. It is very important to examine beliefs and behaviors separately. Although beliefs about gender equality are related to behaviors, they are not the same thing. Many people, for example, espouse gender-equal ideas but live in very gender-divided relationships. Measuring these two variables separately allows us to see their differing effects on children.

Second, you will note that both the beliefs and the behaviors about gender of the mothers and fathers were used as predictors of children's behaviors. This seems very reasonable, but it is an unusual research design. Past work has either completely overlooked fathers or used mothers' reports of fathers' behaviors. Why might it be important to look at attitudes and behaviors of both mothers and fathers? One reason is that the findings of this study show that fathers' and mothers' attitudes and beliefs are both important and they work in different ways in shaping children's ideology about gender. For this reason, it is important to study both fathers and mothers. In addition, past work that asks mothers about the beliefs of fathers is flawed. We cannot know the degree to which mothers are accurate in their knowledge and description of the attitudes of fathers.

A third interesting component of the study is that it was longitudinal, meaning that the researchers collected data at multiple points in time. It is often quite difficult to recall our attitudes or even behaviors from the past. If we asked the mothers and fathers of a 6-year-old child what they thought or did in the first year of their child's life, they might have trouble remembering details of their actions and their beliefs. In addition, when we collect data at multiple points in time we can use behavior or attitudes in the first period to predict behavior and attitudes in the second period. Although it is always difficult to get at causality, we can be sure that, at least temporally, the behavior or attitudes in the first period are not caused by the things in the second period.

Ethical Issues

This research collects data from children. In the same way that it was problematic to ask mothers about the attitudes of fathers, it is also problematic to rely on parents to describe the gendered beliefs of their children. Asking children about their own beliefs is an important step in more accurately capturing how children think about gender. Children were asked questions about gender using the Sex Roles Learning Inventory, a set of questions about their gendered beliefs. However, it is always important to consider ethical issues when doing research with children. Whenever a group is studied who may be vulnerable or less able to give informed consent, we want to make sure that we are especially careful to make the research the least obtrusive and stressful for the subjects.

GENDER AND INSTITUTIONS

Our ideas of sex and gender are socially constructed and created through interacting with agents of socialization (family, friends, peers) who encourage us to present our gender in particular ways. Gender and gender relations are also constantly reinforced through various institutions. Families, for example, sometimes give different amounts of attention, reward different behaviors, and teach different skills to boys and to girls. In this section we will look at how the institutions of sports, education, work, and politics reinforce gender distinctions in society.

Gender and Sports

Sports are a social institution. They allow people with a common interest to unite across racial, ethnic, and class distinctions. They also reinforce social norms and values such as hard work, teamwork, and obedience to authority. As Messner (1992, p. 8) writes, a sport is "not an expression of some biological human need, it is a social institution. Like other institutions, such as the economy, politics, and the family, the structure and values of sport emerge and change historically, largely as a result of struggles for power between groups of people." Sports are an influential institution in many societies. For example, the 2021 Super Bowl was watched by 96.4 million people (Florio, 2021). Many people are exposed to professional sports every day. The content of sports, however, includes more than simply the activity.

As with other institutions in society, sports are highly gendered. On the micro level, language used in sports is gendered, such as when we refer to defense*men*. Females and femininity can hold negative connotations in sports, such as when someone comments on a man's lack of athletic ability by saying, "He runs (or throws) like a girl." On the macro level, sports are also gender unequal. In 2021, Naomi Osaka was the first woman to appear on the Forbes list of the world's highest-paid athletes at 12th, with Serena Williams in the 28th spot (Forbes, 2021). The highest-paid athlete in the NBA, Stephen Curry, made more than $51 million in salary in the 2023 season (Spotrac.com, 2023a). By contrast, Jewell Loyd, the highest paid athlete in the WNBA, makes $234,936 per year in salary (Spotrac.com, 2023b). USA Soccer is another example of gender inequality in sports. Even though the women's team has been much more successful than the men's, the female players made about 40% of the salaries of their male counterparts (Close, 2016). The women's national soccer team took the team management to court to challenge this inequity and, in 2022, won their case and now, theoretically, will be paid the same amount as the male soccer players on the national team (Lenthang, 2022). In addition to the pay discrepancy, sports media is also dominated by coverage of male sports. In 2019 women's sports received only 5.4% of the network sports news coverage, essentially the same coverage received by women's sports in 1989 (Cooky et al., 2021).

In 2021, the Norwegian Women's Beach Handball team was fined for wearing "improper clothing." The women elected to wear spandex shorts instead of the mandated bikini bottoms shown in the picture above. Compare the women's clothing with the official men's uniform. What are the implications of these different standards for women's and men's athletic uniforms?

Xinhua / Alamy Stock Photo

Gender and Education

Gender is critically intertwined with the institution of education. We can see this in the curriculum we learn, the ways that male and female students are differentially streamed and rewarded, and the employment and income outcomes of our degrees across gender groups. Sociologist Michela Musto examines the relationship between gender and education in middle school. In the following article, consider how young girls and boys are encouraged to speak out in class (or not) and how this might impact how they learn. These processes happen differently depending on the racial or ethnic group of the child. Consider how gender and ethnicity interact in the school setting.

READING: "BRILLIANT OR BAD": THE GENDERED SOCIAL CONSTRUCTION OF EXCEPTIONALISM IN EARLY ADOLESCENCE

"Are boys better at school than girls?" I asked Daniel and Mason, two students I interviewed while conducting research at a racially diverse, suburban middle school in Los Angeles. Daniel, a multiracial White and Asian American boy, momentarily pondered my question before saying, "The average girl student is probably better than the average boy student. . . . But there's probably more best boy students than best girl students. There's probably about three super star boys like Jacob, RJ, and Curtis. . . . I can't think of three super smart girls." Mason, a White boy, nodded and chimed in, "I can think of really smart girls but not like *Jacob* smart."

The question of how gender shapes students' achievement is one of the most studied topics in educational sociology (Buchmann, DiPrete, and McDaniel 2008; Xie, Fang, and Shauman 2015). Research tends to align with Daniel's initial response, finding that girls outperform boys in most areas of education. Girls average higher grades (Buchmann et al. 2008), high school graduation rates (Snyder and Dillow 2012), and college enrollment rates (Buchmann and DiPrete 2006). These gendered achievement gaps have sparked talk of a "crisis" about boys' underachievement (Epstein 1998; Ringrose 2013), with pundits and journalists writing books titled *Why Boys Fail* (Whitmire 2010), *The War against Boys* (Sommers 2015), and *The End of Men* (Rosin 2012). As these titles suggest, popular discourses construct the traditional gender hierarchy—where boys receive greater amounts of power and privileges over girls—as reversed. Instead, boys are now perceived as the newly disadvantaged in education.

Despite popular conceptions, inequality disadvantaging girls and women persists (Armstrong and Hamilton 2013; Khan 2011; Martin 1998; Morris 2012; Pascoe 2007; Thorne 1993). Aligning with Daniel's and Mason's perceptions that only boys are "super stars," research consistently finds that gender status beliefs—or cultural expectations about traits girls and boys possess—associate boys with increased competency and social esteem (Charles and Grusky 2004; Correll 2004; Morris 2012; Ridgeway 2011; Thébaud and Charles 2018). From kindergarten through college, students perceive boys as more intelligent (Bian, Leslie, and Cimpian 2017; Grunspan et al. 2016), and children's television shows tend to depict men as geniuses (Long et al. 2010). Parents often perceive their sons as having higher IQs than their daughters (Furnham, Reeves, and Budhani 2002), and teachers are more likely to identify boys as gifted (Petersen 2013). In the workforce, men are more often described as geniuses when applying for academic positions or technology jobs (Correll et al. 2017; Dutt et al. 2016; Schmader, Whitehead, and Wysocki 2007), and women's participation rates are the lowest in academic fields where raw intelligence is considered integral to one's success, such as philosophy, math, and physics (Leslie et al. 2015).

Although gender status beliefs play a key role in limiting girls' and women's opportunities for advancement (Charles and Grusky 2004; Ridgeway 2011; Thébaud and Charles 2018), few sociological studies have identified how boys (and later men) come to be perceived as exceptionally intelligent. Instead, existing ethnographic research primarily focuses on students of color attending schools in low-income, urban neighborhoods—schools where educators' disciplinary practices often encourage students to perceive girls as academically superior to boys (Carter 2005; Ferguson 2000; Lopez 2003; Rios 2011). Without examining the flip-side of these inequalities—specifically, the processes shaping students' perceptions of privileged boys in suburban schools—scholars are left with an incomplete understanding of how school processes shape students' gender status beliefs.

The main contribution of this article is to identify the processes by which educators' differential responses to boys' rule-breaking by course level produced gender differences in students' perceptions of intelligence. To do so, I draw on two-and-a-half years of longitudinal ethnographic research and 196 semi-structured interviews conducted in a racially diverse, suburban middle school in Los Angeles. In higher-level courses, where affluent, White, and Asian American students were overrepresented, educators tolerated—and to some extent encouraged—boys' misbehavior. Because educators' leniency allowed 6th- and 7th-grade boys to repeatedly interrupt and challenge girls' opinions, boys learned early on how to monopolize classroom discussions. By the end of middle school, higher-level students perceived boys as more exceptionally intelligent than girls. However, a different configuration of gender relations emerged in the school's lower-level courses, where non-affluent Latinx students were overrepresented. In a setting where educators penalized boys' misbehavior, boys gradually disengaged. Rather than participating like they once had, many lower-level 8th-grade boys began spending class time sitting with their heads on their desks. Because educators' stricter disciplinary practices reduced the likelihood of boys interrupting girls in lower-level courses, girls had more opportunities to participate and become confident in their public speaking capabilities. Lower-level students finished middle school perceiving lower-level girls as smarter than lower-level boys, but not as exceptional.

This article's second contribution is to illustrate how race intersected with gender when shaping students' perceptions of intelligence. Educators in higher-level courses held Asian American boys to a higher standard of behavior, tending to discourage their non-academically oriented interruptions, despite tacitly encouraging similar interruptions from White boys. Because educators' disciplinary practices provided White boys more opportunities to demonstrate their social competency during classroom conversations, higher-level students gradually began to perceive White boys as more "well-rounded" than Asian American boys. However, in lower-level courses, educators reserved their harshest disciplinary practices for Latinx boys. Because educators' disciplinary practices repeatedly called Latinx boys' competency into question, students gradually began to perceive Latinx boys as the "dumbest" students at the school. Through this analysis, my findings contribute to sociological scholarship by providing a new understanding of how school processes associate affluent White boys with exceptionalism, thereby reproducing social inequalities in early adolescence.

Gender, Education, and Academic Exceptionalism

Gender inequality is embedded within multiple dimensions of relations (Connell 2009; Martin 2004; Messner 2000; Ridgeway 2011; West and Zimmerman 1987). At the structural level, masculinities and femininities are ranked in a societal-wide gender order, which is created and recreated through institutions, laws, policies, and hegemonic meanings (Connell 2009; Martin 2004; Ridgeway 2011; Schippers 2007). These structural relations provide a background frame for everyday life (Ridgeway 2011; West and Zimmerman 1987), encouraging individuals to interact in ways that reinforce perceptions of inherent male superiority. For example, gender status beliefs associating men with increased competency and social esteem are routinely created and recreated during adult interactions in workplaces (Charles and Grusky 2004; Ridgeway 2011). Men often ignore women's ideas, interrupt women when they are talking, and challenge women's suggestions (Schilt 2010), thus perpetuating beliefs that men are more intelligent than women.

Individuals, however, do not spontaneously begin interacting in ways that associate men with increased competency and social esteem in adulthood; hegemonic gender beliefs have their roots in childhood (Khan 2011; Martin 1998; Morris 2012; Musto 2014; Pascoe 2007; Thorne 1993). Existing research has identified numerous processes at the school- and classroom-level that create and reinforce students' beliefs in categorical and hierarchical gender differences. Teachers are often quicker to discipline girls than boys for running, talking loudly, interrupting, and violating dress codes (Gansen 2017; Jordan and Cowan 1995; Martin 1998; Sadker and Sadker 1995), thereby encouraging students to dress, speak, and move in differently gendered ways. Furthermore, the formal age separation, large number of students, and risk of heterosexual teasing can encourage students to separate into gendered friendship groups in settings such as lunch and recess (Thorne 1993). When interacting with their friends, boys often control larger amounts of space, more frequently invade girls' games and activities, and tease or sexually objectify girls (Gansen 2017; Martin 1998; Khan 2011; Pascoe 2007; Thorne 1993). Because educators often leave boys' behavior largely unaddressed (Khan 2011; Pascoe 2007; Thorne 1993), students' patterns of interactions play an important role in legitimizing beliefs that boys are inherently stronger, louder, and more authoritative than girls.

School processes also shape students' perceptions of girls' and boys' academic capabilities. Focusing primarily on students of color attending schools in low-income urban areas, existing research documents how educators' disciplinary practices can encourage students to perceive girls as academically superior to boys (Carter 2005; Ferguson 2000; Lopez 2003; Rios 2011). In these schools—where students tend to be Black and Latinx—educators often perceive boys more negatively than girls, racializing Black and Latinx boys as dangerous criminals or "thugs" (Ferguson 2000; Morris 2006; Rios 2011). Educators scrutinize boys' behaviors and subject boys who break classroom rules to harsh disciplinary practices (Ferguson 2000; Lewis and Diamond 2015; Ochoa 2013), which places Black and Latinx boys at an increased risk of missing classroom instructional time, being suspended or expelled, and dropping out (Gregory, Skiba, and Noguera 2010; Perry and Morris 2014). As a result, low-income boys of color average lower levels of academic achievement and are often perceived as academically inferior to their female counterparts (Buchmann et al. 2008; Carter 2005; Hatt 2012; Lopez 2003; Valenzuela 1999).

Few sociological studies, however, have examined students' gender status beliefs in suburban schools—schools where students tend to come from race- and class-privileged backgrounds and average higher levels of achievement (Buchmann et al. 2008; Legewie and DiPrete 2012; Penner and Paret 2008; Reardon et al. 2018). Such an omission leaves a crucial gap in gender and education scholarship because gender achievement gaps are much smaller—or favor boys—among affluent, White, and Asian American students (Colón and Sánchez 2010; Feliciano 2012; Legewie and DiPrete 2012; Penner and Paret 2008). In a suburban school, race- and class-privileged students may develop differently gendered expectations about girls' and boys' academic capabilities (Khan 2011; Morris 2012), ultimately helping to explain how students come to perceive boys as exceptional (Bian et al. 2017; Grunspan et al. 2016). Indeed, by taking a racially diverse, suburban school as its point of inquiry, this article develops a new theoretical understanding of how school processes shape students' gender beliefs. Unlike the gender dynamics previously documented, I demonstrate how educators' differential enforcement of school rules by course level can encourage students to perceive race- and class-privileged boys as more exceptionally intelligent than girls, thereby reproducing social inequalities in early adolescence.

Perceptions of Intelligence by Course Level

Perhaps because high school girls now complete more college preparatory and Advanced Placement courses than boys (Buchmann et al. 2008; Xie et al. 2015), gender remains largely unmarked in existing accounts of how academic course sequences shape perceptions of students' intelligence. Yet, considering that in kindergarten through college, students perceive boys as more exceptionally intelligent (Bian et al. 2017; Grunspan et al. 2016; Morris 2012), this omission results in an incomplete understanding of how school processes shape students' gender beliefs. Although girls are well-represented in higher-level courses, school processes may encourage students to perceive boys as exceptional. Consequently, this article asks: Do students' gender beliefs about intelligence and exceptionalism vary by course level? If so, what are the processes encouraging students to perceive girls and boys as having different dispositions toward school, and how do their beliefs differ by course level? Does race intersect with gender when shaping higher- and lower-level students' gender beliefs about intelligence and exceptionalism? If so, how?

To answer these questions, this article illustrates how educators' differential enforcement of school rules by course level contributed to gender-based differences in students' perceptions of intelligence. Within the lenient disciplinary environment in higher-level courses—where affluent, White, and Asian American students were overrepresented—students came to perceive boys as exceptionally intelligent. However, in the punitive disciplinary environment in lower-level courses—where students tended to be non-affluent and Latinx—students came to perceive girls as smarter than boys, but not as exceptional. Students' perceptions of exceptional intelligence were also racialized, with students assigning the most superlatives to White—but not Asian American or Latinx—boys' academic capabilities. By demonstrating how students' perceptions of intelligence varied by students' gender, course level, and race, this article contributes to gender and education research by providing a new theoretical understanding of how school processes reify social inequalities in early adolescence....

The Gendered Construction of Exceptionalism at MHMS

Michela: Are there any people who interrupt the teachers a lot?

    Ashley: Lucas, Noah . . .

    Samantha: Noah, yes!

    Ashley: Ben. Ms. Emerson will be in the middle of telling us what's going on, he'll be like, "Did you just say 'swag,' Ms. Emerson?"

    Samantha: Ms. Noble was saying she'll get a tattoo on her forehead that says, "Raise your hand." Because everyone just yells out.

    Michela: All the people you named were boys. Do girls ever interrupt teachers?

    Ashley: No, girls are really straightforward, they don't talk—

    Samantha: They raise their hand! [laughs]

    Ashley: And when a teacher says like, "Raise your hand," they understand this right away and like, raise their hand.

When conducting research in 6th-grade classrooms at MHMS, I repeatedly observed boys break classroom rules. Similar to the way boys import "warrior narratives" into kindergarten classroom activities (Jordan and Cowan 1995), 6th-grade boys engaged in activities symbolically associated with weapons, violence, or sports. When teachers provided students time to complete assignments, boys routinely wrestled with their friends or used a crumpled piece of paper to start an impromptu game of finger football. Boys also fidgeted in their seats, moved around the classroom without permission, and loudly drummed their hands or pencils on their desks. In higher- and lower-level academic settings alike, boys began middle school behaving in similar ways; there was no distinguishable difference in the frequency or type of misbehavior.

In what follows, I focus on the classroom rule 6th-grade boys most frequently disregarded: raising their hands and waiting to be called on before speaking. Instead, 6th-grade boys regularly interrupted teachers and classmates to blurt out comments, questions, or jokes. These interruptions occurred so frequently in Samantha's 6th-grade history class that her teacher threatened to tattoo the phrase "raise your hand" on her forehead. Two years later, however, I rarely observed 8th-grade boys shout out answers or make extemporaneous comments during class. Instead, in higher-level classes, primarily composed of affluent, White, and Asian American students, boys now raised their hands before speaking. However, boys—especially those who repeatedly interrupted as 6th- and 7th-graders—continued to monopolize speaking opportunities in higher-level classes. Two years of being pushed aside by interrupting boys had a different consequence for girls. Girls enrolled in the school's higher-level courses tended to finish middle school participating less frequently, and they described their speaking skills with less confidence than did boys. In lower-level classes, however, where non-affluent Latinx students were overrepresented, boys who routinely spoke out of turn as 6th- and 7th-graders had disengaged. Rather than participating as they once had, lower-level boys—especially those who repeatedly interrupted as 6th- and 7th-graders—now spent class time sitting slouched in their seats or with their heads on their desks. Instead, *girls* in lower-level courses were the ones who most frequently participated during classroom conversations and described themselves as confident public speakers.

Critical Reading Questions:

1. How did teachers respond to girls and boys who interrupted the class? Why does this different response matter for how boys and girls learned?

2. How was the teacher response to boys and girls different across racial and ethnic groups? How might this create or reinforce social inequality?

3. How does the earlier context of the 6th-grade classes, where boy students are more often allowed to interrupt while girl students are not, shape the classes of the students in the 8th and 9th grade? What are the outcomes of these different ways that teachers interact with boy and girl students?

4. This research shows that the subtle, and often unintended, ways that we treat different gender and ethnic groups can reinforce inequalities in society. Can you think of another example of where you, or anyone, might be unintendedly reinforcing an inequality? How could we change this?

Musto, M. (2019). "Brilliant or bad": The gendered social construction of exceptionalism in early adolescence. *American Sociological Review, 84*(3), 369–393.

Gender and Work

Another major institution of society that reinforces our conceptions of gender and gender inequality is the workforce. Over the past 70 years, women's labor force participation has dramatically increased. In 1948 only 29% of the labor force was made up of women. By 2020, women were 47% of all civilian workers in the United States (see Figure 6.2). This rise in the number of women in the workforce is the result of changing norms about the role of women

FIGURE 6.2 ■ Share of the Civilian Labor Force, by Sex, 1948–2020

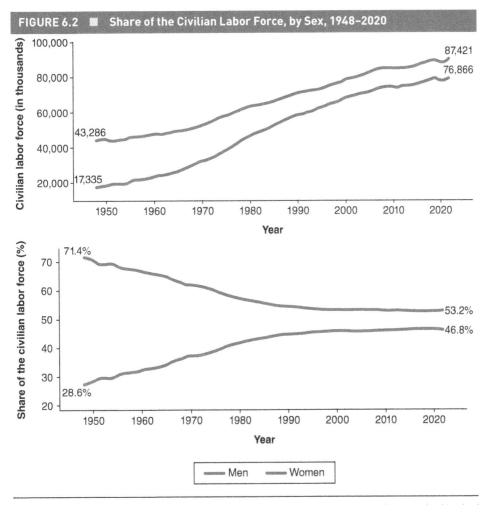

Source: U.S. Department of Labor. (n.d.). *Civilian labor force by sex.* https://www.dol.gov/agencies/wb/data/lfp/civilianlfbysex

in society, a greater need for dual income households, and increased rates of women obtaining higher education. Despite there currently being more women in the workforce than ever before, there remains a great deal of inequality in what men and women earn, the types of jobs they have, and the household tasks they do at home in addition to their paid labor.

The gap between the income of men and women has fluctuated over time. As Figure 6.3 indicates, in 1979 women made only 62% of what men earned. By 2021 this had increased to 83%. You will note, however, that by 2005 women had already increased their share of men's earnings to 81%. This number has remained fairly stagnant since that time and there has not been a notable reduction in inequality between men and women's earnings in the past 16 years.

FIGURE 6.3 ■ Women's Wages as a Percentage of Men's, 1979–2021

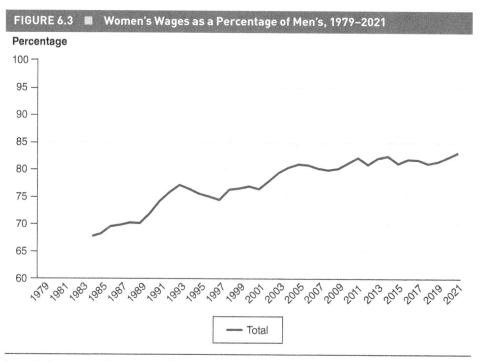

Source: U.S. Bureau of Labor Statistics. (2023). *Highlights of women's earnings in 2021.* https://www.bls.gov/opub/reports/womens-earnings/2021/home.htm

One reason for this discrepancy in men and women's earnings is that men and women tend to perform different kinds of jobs. In fact, both groups are disproportionately concentrated in a small number of occupations. The most common occupations for women are teachers, social workers, nurses, and service jobs, including food service. The most common occupations for men are supervisors or managers, manufacturing, law enforcement, and the trades (such as electrician or plumber; U.S. Department of Labor, 2018). Some jobs that men and women perform require less education, such as food service and manufacturing. However, the types of low-education jobs that men perform are usually better paid than those performed by women. This difference is, in part, explained by the higher rate of unionization in construction and manufacturing jobs than in food service or sales work.

How Work Is Gendered

There are two main ways that work is gendered. First, there is gender concentration among the people employed in some kinds of work or among students in some programs. We saw this gendering occur in certain occupations such as sales or manufacturing, which are female and male dominant, respectively. Second, work can also be imbued with gendered meaning and can be defined in gendered terms. For example, professions that people consider to be caring or nurturing tend to be seen as more feminine and so more appropriate for women. Take the difference between doctors and nurses: Nurses are expected to be more caring, whereas doctors (particularly specialists) are expected to focus on the science of medicine. Teaching is another good example. Elementary school teaching is associated with more nurturing, while university- or college-level teaching is often seen as a less caring job that is more focused on specific area-related expertise. Think about how many of your elementary school teachers were male and how many were female. Then do the same for your professors. You likely had more female teachers in elementary school and more male professors in university or college. Since university professors make more money and have a higher status than elementary school teachers, this inequality could be problematic.

The **feminization** of an occupational sphere occurs when a job, profession, or industry becomes dominated by or predominantly associated with women. Such feminized jobs are referred to as "pink collar" jobs. Examples of jobs that were previously mostly done by men but have been feminized include bank tellers, secretaries, teachers, and family doctors. The important point here is that a feminized occupation tends to lose prestige, wages, required skill levels, and opportunities for promotion. For example, in the early 1900s most clerical workers were men. Now, almost 95% of clerical workers and secretaries are women (U.S. Department of Labor, 2018). Meanwhile, the wages and possibilities for promotion in clerical and secretarial jobs have steadily declined.

You might be surprised to learn that clerical work was traditionally a man's job. The male bookkeeper's duties included accounting, note taking, and organizing. As companies grew, there was an increasingly large amount of clerical work to be done and businesses moved toward more efficient systems of managing such tasks. Instead of having one bookkeeper who would do a variety of challenging tasks, companies hired many more clerical staff to do smaller parts of the larger job, such as only typing or only answering the phone. This sort of assembly-line office work created very few opportunities for advancement. If all you did was answer the phone all day, how could you learn other tasks and get promoted?

In the early 1900s, the prevalent ideas regarding women's capabilities led to a growing belief that women were ideally suited for this type of narrow and repetitive work. The expectation was that women would work only until they married: If they continued to work past that point, their jobs would be secondary to their primary roles as mothers and wives. As William Leffingwell (1925, p. 116) explains,

> A woman is to be preferred for the secretarial position for she is not averse to doing minor tasks, work involving the handling of petty details, which would irk and irritate ambitious men, who usually feel that the work they are doing is of no importance if it can be performed by some person with a lower salary. Most such men are also anxious to get ahead and to be promoted from position to position, and consequently if there is much work of a detail character to be done, and they are expected to perform it, they will not remain satisfied and will probably seek a position elsewhere.

The Second Shift

Another concern when talking about the occupational inequality of men and women is the **double shift (second shift)** that women often perform. The double or second shift refers to individuals working outside the home for money and inside the home on unpaid, domestic tasks. In 1990, Arlie Hochschild and Anne Machung found that, in dual-earner heterosexual couples, women spent more hours per week on domestic labor (e.g., cleaning, cooking, and caring for children) than did men. This imbalance, they argued, is caused by our traditional expectation that women should perform domestic work regardless of their labor outside the home (Hochschild & Machung, 1990). A 2019 Gallup poll reveals that although allocation of household tasks has become more equitable since the 1990s, women still do the cleaning, laundry, and cooking more than 50% of the time (Brenan, 2020).

As illustrated in Figure 6.4, even among parents who work full time outside the home, women still perform more child care and household activities than men, on average. Women perform unpaid household and care work that averages 5.7 hours per day, compared with an average of 3.6 hours per day for men. This means that, on average, women are spending 37% more time on this type of unpaid domestic and care labor.

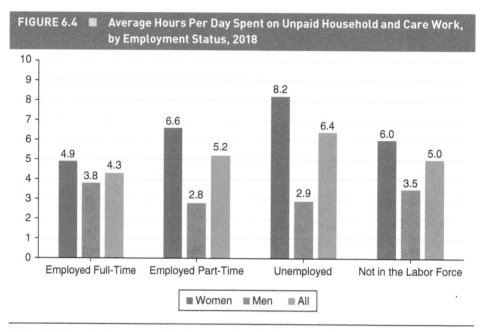

FIGURE 6.4   ■   Average Hours Per Day Spent on Unpaid Household and Care Work, by Employment Status, 2018

Notes: Aged 15 and older. Care work includes secondary child care as well as primary child and elder care. Secondary child care is considered as a separate activity and is counted independently even though it may be performed while doing housework or primary care work.

Source: Hess, C., Ahmed, T., and Hayes, J. (2020). *Providing unpaid household and care work in the United States: Uncovering inequality.* Figure 3, page 5. Washington, DC: Institute for Women's Policy. https://iwpr.org/wp-content/uploads/2020/01/IWPR-Providing-Unpaid-Household-and-Care-Work-in-the-United-States-Uncovering-Inequality.pdf

Gender inequality in the workforce is not only unfair; it is also costly. In fact, research shows that the United States could add $4.3 trillion to its overall economy by 2025 if women attained gender parity. In fact, every U.S. state and city could add at least 5% to its GDP in that period by advancing equity between men and women (Shakeri, 2017). How would this gender parity happen? The authors of the report from McKinsey Global Institute (MGI) argue that most of the growth in the economy as a whole comes from the increase in labor force participation—more people working outside the home. In order to increase this participation, more women need to enter the workforce, move from part-time to full-time work, and shift to more productive and higher paying industries. About 40% of the growth would come from more women entering the workforce, 30% can come from narrowing the gap between men and women who work part time and full time, and another 30% can come from changing the mix of sectors in which men and women work.

We might assume that the United States is a leader on gender inequality. However, according to the World Economic Forum (2021), the United States ranks 30th out of 156 countries on equality between men and women. This measure compares men's and women's outcomes in four main areas: economic participation and opportunity, educational attainment, health and survival, and political empowerment. The United States does relatively well on gender equality in economic participation and opportunity (30th) as well as educational attainments (36th) and political empowerment (37th). However, it does quite poorly comparatively in gender equality in health and survival (87th; World Economic Forum, 2021).

The report provides a series of recommendations for reducing gender inequality, particularly in the workforce. They suggest that companies should commit to diversity and emphasize its importance for the company as a whole and their profits. Companies should also set clear targets for representation of women and ethnic minorities and track their progress in reaching this equality. Workplaces should also have programs to mentor and promote women and minorities. And, companies should raise awareness about subconscious biases and actively try to make the workplace more inclusive.

Gender and Politics

The institution of politics is also affected by and affects gender. Although there has been much improvement in women's representation in government, women still make up only 27% of Congress and 30% of elected statewide leaders in the United States (Represent Women, 2022). When we compare this with other countries, the United States ranks 75th in the world in terms of women's representation in federal elected office: only 27% of all representatives in the United States are women (Represent Women, 2022), far behind countries such as Rwanda (57%), Cuba (53%), and Bolivia (52%). Most Western European countries also have much higher rates of representation for women, such as Sweden (44%), Finland (42%), and Norway (41%; Inter-Parliamentary Union, 2018). See Table 6.1 for the percentage of women who hold elected office in different regions.

TABLE 6.1 ■ Historical Comparisons of the Percentage of Women in Parliaments Across Regions, 1955–2022								
	1955	1965	1975	1985	1995	2005	2017[1]	2022
Scandinavia	10.4	9.3	16.1	27.5	34.4	38.2	41.7	44.7
OECD	3.6	4.0	5.5	8.6	12.8	22.7	25.2[2]	31.1
Eastern Europe	17.0	18.4	24.7	27.0	8.4	15.7		
Latin America	2.8	2.7	5.2	8.1	10.0	17.1	28.2[3]	29.2
Africa	1.0	3.2	5.3	8.0	9.8	16.3	23.8	25.9
Asia	5.2	5.3	2.8	5.6	8.8	15.3	19.7	20.7
Middle East	1.2	1.2	2.9	3.5	3.9	8.1	18.2	18.2

Note: 1. 2017 data from the Inter-Parliamentary Union. http://www.ipu.org/wmn-e/world.htm. 2. All European countries combined. 3. Includes North, Central, and South America.

Source: Kunovich, Sheri, Pamela Paxton, and Melanie M. Hughes. 2007. "Gender in Politics." *Annual Review of Sociology* 33: 263–84. http://digitalrepository.smu.edu/hum_sci_sociology_research/3; 2021 data from the Inter-Parliamentary Union, https://data.ipu.org/women-averages; 2017 data from the Inter-Parliamentary Union, http://www.ipu.org/wmn-e/world.htm.

Why are fewer women elected to political office in the United States? Many of the possible answers center on the organization of politics. For example, if political parties do not nominate women to be candidates in elections, people will not even have the option to vote for them. Because women are often excluded from informal party networks and do not have the connections to help them get nominated, they are less likely to be put on the ballot. They are also often unable to afford the expense of running for office. As previously discussed, women earn less money than men do; they also frequently lack a network of people who could financially support their campaigns. Finally, political office requires considerable travel time, evening and weekend meetings, and other demands that might conflict with family obligations. Although both men and women have these responsibilities, we learned in the preceding section that women tend to spend more hours a day doing household and child care tasks. Becoming involved in a political campaign and holding office, therefore, could create an additional burden for women (Kunovich et al., 2007).

Is it a problem that there are few women in elected positions in the United States? Research shows that having more women in government can be important both for the types of policies put forward and for the general perceptions of women's role in society. Although it is certainly true that both male and female political leaders can be concerned with issues of gender equality, women are much more likely to prioritize those issues and to put them on the political agenda (Kunovich et al., 2007). For example, women are more likely to raise discussion of policies related to child care, violence prevention, and pay equity in political debates. This does not mean that men do not care about these issues, only that they do not tend to be the top legislative priorities for men. It is important to note that women politicians certainly do not agree on solutions to these issues simply because they are women, but they are more likely to introduce these issues into the debate.

Having women as elected officials has also been shown to change the public's perceptions of women's roles and abilities as leaders. Female politicians provide role models for young women. In places where there are more women in politics, girls have higher self-esteem and a greater knowledge of and interest in politics than do girls in other places (Kunovich et al., 2007).

FEMINISM AND FEMINIST THEORY

Feminism is concerned with equality between women and men. It focuses on attaining that equality in politics, in the economic system, and through social and cultural change. Feminism exists as a set of ideologies and as groups of people who support these ideologies. These groups seek equality of opportunity for women in multiple areas, including education, the workplace, and the family. All people with these interests, both women and men, can be feminists.

Feminist theory focuses on how gender inequality comes about in society and how men's and women's gender roles are created and re-created in society. This theory has been influential in many social sciences and humanities disciplines, including sociology, anthropology, political science, history, philosophy, English, and women's studies. In addition, it is rooted in the feminist movement and political action. Many scholars of this movement talk about feminist activism as happening in three distinct periods, or waves.

First, Second, and Third Waves of Feminism

First-wave feminism began in the 19th century and was mostly centered in Canada, the United Kingdom, and the United States. This wave was focused on de jure inequalities, meaning inequalities that are part of the legal and political system. For example, women's rights to vote and to hold property were of primary interest to first-wave feminists.

Second-wave feminism began in the United States in the early 1960s and spread throughout Canada and Europe. Second-wave feminists broadened the movement beyond political and legal rights and sought social change on a wide range of issues, including equality in the workplace and reproductive rights. During this period women made widespread social gains and moved into a variety of professions and other areas of society that traditionally had been dominated by males, such as the media, sports, and the military. This wave was also concerned with violence against women, including sexual violence and spousal abuse. The women's movement was quite successful at making these issues mainstream, getting marital rape laws passed, and establishing rape crisis centers and shelters for women who have been victims of abuse.

Third-wave feminism began in the early 1990s and continues to the present. This wave, which is a more diverse group of women's movements, arose as a critique of the previous wave. Many activists believed that the second wave was controlled by a small group of White middle-class women and that it did not represent the diverse experiences of women of different races, ethnicities, religions, classes, and sexual orientations (Staggenborg, 2011).

Third-wave feminism challenges what it sees as the essentialist nature of second- wave's defi-nition of what it means to be a woman. This third wave has moved away from the focus on social and political rights. Instead, it tends to work in cultural arenas, for example challenging gender depictions in the media, sexist language, and gendered norms around sexuality.

At the 2014 MTV Video Music Awards, Beyoncé performed in front of a large sign that read, "Feminist." Some praised her performance as a political statement and argued that it raised feminism's profile among young women. Others were more critical of the word being used by a performer who often uses her sexuality to sell her music. Do you think that Beyoncé is a feminist? How does this performance fit into (or challenge) our ideas of what a feminist is?

Jason LaVeris/FilmMagic

Feminism is a collection of beliefs, values, identities, and ideologies that is incredibly diverse and constantly evolving. There are many different types of feminism that emerged over time with distinct ideas on how best to ensure equality and more progressive attitudes about gender.

Liberal feminism emerged in the 18th and 19th centuries as a direct response to a traditional culture that views women as "naturally" less physically and mentally capable than men. This was a core part of the first and second waves of feminism. These feminists argued that oppressive and discriminatory beliefs limited women's ability to work outside of the home or to acquire education. Liberal feminism is a direct a challenge to such beliefs, demanding the inclusion of women in society, particularly in the arenas of politics and the law. It seeks change through institutional means. For example, liberal feminists are concerned with issues such as the right to vote (the suffrage movement), repealing discriminatory laws, and ensuring policies are put in place to prevent sexual harassment in the workplace. These feminists work to change existing institutional arrangements to promote equality between the sexes.

Beginning in the 1960s, some feminists argued that women should not want to be accommodated and included in the existing patriarchal structure of society. Instead, these new radical feminists viewed current social institutions as so flawed that they could not be reformed and, instead, should be eliminated. In particular, radical feminists target the institutions of the family and church as well as ideologies that support traditional understandings of sexuality and reproduction. For example, radical feminists want to decouple sex from marriage (specifically between a man and a woman) and challenge restrictive norms around sexual behavior, particularly norms that have restricted how we understand women's sexuality.

Marxist-socialist feminists question both liberal and radical feminism. Marxist-socialist feminism believes that women cannot experience true liberation in existing institutions (liberal feminism) or through changes in cultural understandings of sex and sexuality alone (radical feminism). According to Marxist-socialist feminism, the main obstacle to women's liberation and equality is a class-based society where the powerful few absorb the wealth created by the many. And, class-based societies have their origins in private property, which has historically been linked to a small group of powerful men. Given this, radical feminists claim that it is capitalism itself that impedes women's liberation and equality and, only by overthrowing capitalism can there be gender equality.

Liberal, radical and Marxist-socialist feminism have all been critiqued for portraying an image of universal womanhood. But, not all women are the same—the everyday experiences of black queer women will be different from those of straight White women. Multicultural or intersectional feminism recognizes that women are not a homogenous group, and there are differences between women based on, for example, their race, class, ethnicity, sexual orientation, and religion. Intersectional feminism thus finds that a focus on sameness could be counterproductive and may not facilitate women's liberation but might act as an instrument of oppression. These forms of feminism characterize the third wave of this movement.

Getting to Know: Patricia Hill Collins (b. 1948)

- Her book, *Black Feminist Thought: Knowledge, Consciousness, and the Politics of Empowerment*, won the C. Wright Mills Award from the Society for the Study of Social Problems in 1990.

- Hill Collins can play the organ, trumpet, and piano.

- Collins was involved with community groups that supported cultural and educational programming for girls and women in Cincinnati.

- Collins was the director of the African American Center at Tufts University (1976–1980).

- She was the first African American president of the American Sociological Association in 2009.

- She received the American Sociological Association's W.E.B. Du Bois Career of Distinguished Scholarship Award in 2017.

Feminism has clearly gone through many iterations, or waves, over the centuries. And, feminists coming from different perspective have very different ideas about how we can create a more equal society. This ideology continues to evolve with the emergence of eco-feminism, trans-exclusionary radical feminism, fat feminism, and Indigenous feminism, which all shine a spotlight on different types of inequalities that inform our experiences in society.

"HeForShe" is a campaign that brings women and men together to address gender inequality. This campaign argues that gender inequality is bad for everyone—regardless of gender. What do you think about this campaign? What is the role of men in supporting feminism?

Pacific Press Media Production Corp. / Alamy Stock Photo

INTERSECTIONALITY

The concept of intersectionality—the study of how various dimensions of inequality can combine—is one product of feminism's third wave. Kimberlé Williams Crenshaw coined the term in 1989 and explains it with the following metaphor:

> Discrimination, like traffic through an intersection, may flow in one direction, and it may flow in another. If an accident happens in an intersection, it can be caused by cars traveling from any number of directions and, sometimes, from all of them. Similarly, if a Black woman is harmed because she is in an intersection, her injury could result from sex discrimination or race discrimination. But it is not always easy to reconstruct an accident. Sometimes the skid marks and the injuries simply indicate that they occurred simultaneously, frustrating efforts to determine which driver caused the harm. (Crenshaw, 1989, p. 149)

The theory came out of Crenshaw's research on work and discrimination in the 1980s. Crenshaw (1989) studied a group of Black women in the United States who had filed a workplace discrimination lawsuit. A round of layoffs at their workplace had resulted in all the Black women being laid off. The trial judge ruled against these women: He said that there was no gender discrimination because White women were not laid off and there was no racial discrimination because Black men were not laid off. Because the law saw only two types of discrimination (discrimination against women based on their sex or discrimination against racial minorities based on their race), there was no discrimination in this case.

These Black women and Crenshaw understood that the former's experience was rendered invisible by intersectionality. The fact that they were both Black and women made the discrimination invisible. The theory of intersectionality highlights how various dimensions of inequality can intersect with one another. For example, we have very different stereotypes about young people who use wheelchairs than we do about older people who use them. Perhaps we assume that young people were injured in a sports or car accident and that older people are in poor health. We also have different stereotypes regarding gay men and lesbian women because of their gender. Seeing the complicated ways that inequalities intersect is a prime feature of third-wave feminist theory.

SEXUALITY

Sexuality is feelings of sexual attraction and behaviors related to them. One important element of sexuality is sexual orientation, which involves whom people desire, with whom people want to have sexual relations, and with whom people have a sense of connectedness (Scott & Schwartz, 2008). Our ideas about sexuality have changed considerably over the past 100 years. In general, there is an increasing openness to diverse sexual behaviors and attitudes, which has led to changing norms surrounding sexuality. For example, Americans today tend to have sex younger and with more partners than was true in the past, and are more likely to engage in sexual activity outside of marriage than they were in the past. There is also an increasing acceptance of same-sex relationships.

The Kinsey Reports

The first systematic study of sex and sexuality was conducted by Alfred Kinsey in the 1940s. Kinsey's initial study interviewed 18,000 adults about their sexual behaviors, interests, and thoughts. Previously, we did not know much about these topics because no one had thought it appropriate (or interesting) to ask these questions. You can imagine how revolutionary (and shocking) this study was at the time!

Kinsey published *Sexual Behavior in the Human Male* in 1948 (Kinsey et al., 1948) and *Sexual Behavior in the Human Female* in 1953 (Kinsey, 1953), which together are known as the Kinsey Reports. The reports were highly controversial, but they became bestsellers and made Kinsey a celebrity. His work created a precedent for a legitimate study of human sexuality and laid the groundwork for a body of sexuality research in the social and biological sciences. His research showed that there was much more diversity in sexual desire and behavior than was previously thought. After realizing this huge diversity, Kinsey argued that people should not think of sexuality as either normal or abnormal. We should define what is normal by looking at what people are doing, not by ideas of morality. For example, if most people have sexual relations before marriage, Kinsey argued that that is normal, regardless of society's moral ideals about premarital sex.

Perhaps Kinsey's most famous contribution to the study of sexuality is his Heterosexual–Homosexual Rating Scale, a seven-point scale of sexual inclinations (see Figure 6.5). After thousands of interviews with men and women, Kinsey argued that people are not simply gay or straight, so we should not categorize people in this way. Instead, we should see that individuals have life histories that express different desires at different times. People can have homosexual or heterosexual desires and experiences to a greater or lesser degree, but desires and experiences are not always related.

FIGURE 6.5   ■   Kinsey's Heterosexual–Homosexual Rating Scale

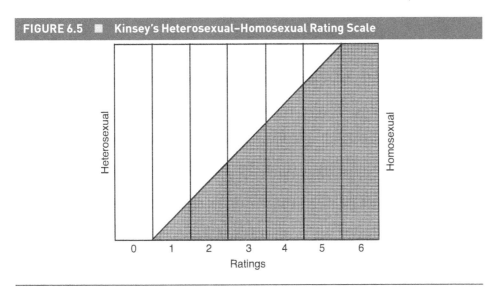

Kinsey's work also highlighted the importance of social context in shaping sexual desire and behaviors. For example, Kinsey and his colleagues (1948) found that men's sexual behaviors differed by their social class—men of higher social class tended to be more experimental than those of lower social class. Women's behavior differed by their age and their view of gender equality: Those who were older and who had a more liberal view of women's role in society were much more likely to experiment sexually and have more partners (Kinsey, 1953). Thus, Kinsey showed that what people do sexually is, at least in part, shaped by their characteristics, such as social class and age.

Sexual Attitudes and Behaviors Over Time

In the 1990s further research on sexual attitudes and behaviors found that Americans are moderately sexually conservative. Most people favor monogamy in sexual relationships both in principle and in practice. According to surveys, 93.7% of married persons had been monogamous over the year before the study compared with only 38% of single people. However, about 20–25% of men and 10–15% of women had had at least one extramarital affair during their marriage (Laumann et al., 1994). Surprisingly, this number seems to be declining: In 2000 only about 11% of men and women had had an extramarital affair (Treas & Gieden, 2000). If anything, this change shows a more traditional view of sexual relationships over time.

At the same time, there has been an increase in the percentage of people who identify as gay or lesbian. In the 1990s 9.1% of men and 4.3% of women say they have had a same-sex sexual experience since puberty, but only 1.4% of men and 2.8% of women reported that they identified as homosexual. In 2010, 7% of men and 7% of women identified as gay, lesbian, or bisexual (National Survey of Sexual Health and Behavior, 2010). The larger number of people identifying as gay, lesbian, and bisexual is, at least in part, a result of declining rates of homophobia in society. Homophobia is a set of negative attitudes and beliefs about individuals who are LGBTQ (lesbian, gay, bisexual, transgender, or queer/questioning) that can lead to negative behaviors, prejudice, or discrimination. Sometimes these negative attitudes can manifest into behaviors such as hate crimes. According to Dowden and Brennan (2012), 16% of hate crimes are based on sexual orientation, with 65% being violent in nature.

How can we measure feelings of homophobia? Figure 6.6 shows the percentage of people in various countries who say they would not like to live next door to someone who is gay. Rates in the United States are similar to those in a range of other countries, including Germany and Mexico. However, U.S. rates are much higher than in countries such as the Netherlands, Spain, and Sweden—about four times as high. These negative attitudes have declined in the United States, from 29.7% in 1990 to 12.7% in 2020 (and the number is presumably still decreasing).

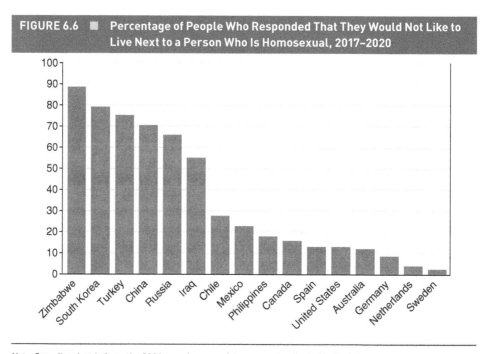

FIGURE 6.6 ■ **Percentage of People Who Responded That They Would Not Like to Live Next to a Person Who Is Homosexual, 2017–2020**

Note: Canadian data is from the 2006 wave because data were not collected in the later survey wave.

Source: World Values Survey, 2017–2020 wave, http://www.worldvaluessurvey.org/WVSOnline.jsp

Herek (2002) examines the factors that predict homophobic attitudes and finds that the most important predictor of more tolerant attitudes toward LGBTQ people is simply knowing someone who is in one of these groups. Having a personal connection with a person who is LGBTQ makes you significantly more likely to have a positive attitude toward individuals in these groups. In addition, people who have more education and higher incomes and who live in an urban setting are less likely to be homophobic. Finally, people with higher self-esteem tend to be more tolerant than those with lower self-esteem.

Heteronormative Ideals and Practices

Even though attitudes toward LGBTQ people are becoming more positive, we still live in a heteronormative society: Our social institutions, practices, and norms support an automatic assumption that other people are or should be heterosexual. For example, the poster in the photo shown here is an ad targeted to first-time home buyers. At the same time, it reinforces the idea that a family includes a woman, a man, and children. You might notice that, when you meet a person, he or she might assume that you are heterosexual. For example, if you purchase a bouquet of flowers, the florist might assume that it is for someone of the opposite sex.

Ads such as this one, however unintentional, present a heteronormative idea of the family. What heteronormative images have you seen lately?

Pictorial Press Ltd / Alamy Stock Photo

Heteronormativity is a social process evident in many institutional settings that we interact with across the lifespan. Starting when children are very young, they are engaged in a gendered process through which they learn norms and behaviors deemed appropriate for their gender. Children learn these norms and behaviors everywhere: from media, from their parents or other family members, and from their peers. A major location in which children are exposed to sexual socialization is the preschool classroom. Gansen (2017) conducted a 10-month observation of nine preschool classrooms and found that sexual socialization in these classrooms is often heteronormative, in that it assumes and expects children to express heterosexual behavior, treats such behavior as normal, and privileges it above nonheterosexual behavior.

Gansen (2017) found that teachers use various tactics to normalize heterosexuality. In her research, she observed that teachers often encourage children to express heterosexual behavior by acting upon their "crushes" on opposite-sex children, developing "relationships" with opposite-sex children, and to playing "house" or "family" with opposite-sex children. For instance, boys and girls who were friendly with each other were often said by teachers to be "boyfriend and girlfriend." Children who exhibited similar friendly behaviors toward same-sex children were seen as good friends rather than having this relationship interpreted romantically. At the same time, teachers discouraged and even censured behavior seen as inappropriate—either because it occurred between same-sex children or because it was seen as gender nonconforming. For example, although boys were allowed to engage in "potty humor" and discuss intimate body parts, girls were censured for doing the same.

In only two instances in more than 400 hours of observation did teachers acknowledge relationships or family forms that undermine heteronormativity: when two girls wanted to play "wedding" and marry each other, and when children wanted to marry their same-sex toys. Teachers allowed both of these games, but the scarcity of these examples and teachers' explicit encouragement of heterosexual forms of interactions between children demonstrates how, even at a very young age, heterosexuality is treated as normal, expected, and privileged.

These cultural norms follow us throughout our lives and are invoked in numerous situations, thus continuously reproducing heteronormativity. Celia Kitzinger's (2005) study of after-hour medical call centers in the UK illustrates this point. Kitzinger analyzed recordings of calls made to after-hour medical centers, where patients can speak to a doctor outside of their clinic's regular working hours. Calls are answered by whichever doctor happens to be on call at the time, not their regular family doctor, so the doctor they are speaking to often is not familiar with them or their personal history. Kitzinger found that in these calls doctors routinely make assumptions that reinforce heteronormativity. Doctors assume that callers live in a heterosexual household with their opposite-sex partner and their biological children. As a result, opposite-sex adults mentioned in the call are assumed to be callers' spouses; children mentioned in the call are assumed to be callers' biological children, for which they are legal guardians; if a child is unwell, it is assumed that care is provided by the mother; and the family is assumed to all share the same residence. These assumptions are made and invoked in conversations with callers even when callers explicitly state otherwise. Kitzinger note that doctors invoke these assumptions without the intent of privileging heterosexual relationships and families or a deliberate intent to discriminate against LGBTQ patients. They simply employed the categories they believed to be mundane, ordinary, and natural to facilitate their goals in the conversation, which were to ascertain the caller's medical situation and decide on a course of treatment. However, in doing so, doctors privileged heteronormativity and were unintentionally exclusionary toward patients who did not fit into this narrow norm.

These heteronormative sentiments could easily create a situation that makes homophobic attitudes more likely. Heteronormativity persists in our society, but there are also examples of increased tolerance and acceptance for a diversity of lifestyles. For example, American retailer JC Penney released an ad showing a family with two male parents (though the ad did spark some controversy). To avoid assumptions regarding sexual orientation, many individuals use the term *partner* to describe the person with whom they have an intimate relationship. These trends illustrate how our society is moving away from an automatic heteronormative assumption.

READING: FROM *THE INVENTION OF HETEROSEXUALITY*

Jonathan Ned Katz

Just as gender is socially constructed, so is sexuality. Our ideas about what is normal sexuality, how many groups of sexual orientations there are, and how to delineate sexual preferences is created and reinforced in our society as we interact with one another. These ideas are also historically contingent—they have not always been as they are now. In *The Invention of Heterosexuality*, Jonathan Ned Katz outlines how our modern ideas about heterosexuality and homosexuality are socially constructed and how they have changed. We think that heterosexuality is unchanging and universal; however, we create the categories of sexuality and then forget that we made them and see them as unchanging. Moreover, changes in these norms are tied to larger social, historical, economic, and political processes. In fact, heterosexuality is a modern invention.

Heterosexuality is old as procreation, ancient as the lust of Eve and Adam. That first lady and gentleman, we assume, perceived themselves, behaved, and felt just like today's hetero-sexuals. We suppose that heterosexuality is unchanging, universal, essential: ahistorical.

Contrary to that common sense conjecture, the concept of heterosexuality is only one particular historical way of perceiving, categorizing, and imagining the social relations of the sexes. Not ancient at all, the idea of heterosexuality is a modern invention, dating to the late nineteenth century. The heterosexual belief, with its metaphysical claim to eternity, has a particular, pivotal place in the social universe of the late nineteenth and twentieth centuries that it did not inhabit earlier. This essay traces the historical process by which the hetero-sexual idea was created as ahistorical and taken-for-granted. . . .

Contrary to our usual assumption, past Americans and other peoples named, perceived, and socially organized the bodies, lusts, and intercourse of the sexes in ways radically dif-ferent from the way we do. If we care to understand this vast past sexual diversity, we need to stop promiscuously projecting our own hetero and homo arrangement. Though lip ser-vice is often paid to the distorting, ethnocentric effect of such conceptual imperialism, the category heterosexuality continues to be applied uncritically as a universal analytical tool. Recognizing the time-bound and culturally specific character of the heterosexual category can help us begin to work toward a thoroughly historical view of sex. . . .

Before Heterosexuality: Early Victorian True Love, 1820–1860

In the early nineteenth-century United States, from about 1820 to 1860, the heterosexual did not exist. Middle-class white Americans idealized a True Womanhood, True Manhood, and True Love, all characterized by "purity"—the freedom from sensuality.[1] Presented mainly in literary and religious texts, this True Love was a fine romance with no lascivious kisses. This ideal contrasts strikingly with late nineteenth- and twentieth-century American incitements to a hetero sex.[2] . . .

The actors in this sexual economy were identified as manly men and womanly women and as procreators, not specifically as erotic beings or heterosexuals. Eros did not constitute the core of a heterosexual identity that inhered, democratically, in both men and women. True Women were defined by their distance from lust. True Men, though thought to live closer to carnality, and in less control of it, aspired to the same freedom from concupiscence.

Legitimate natural desire was for procreation and a proper manhood or womanhood; no heteroerotic desire was thought to be directed exclusively and naturally toward the other sex; lust in men was roving. The human body was thought of as a means toward procreation and production; penis and vagina were instruments of reproduction, not of pleasure. Human energy, thought of as a closed and severely limited system, was to be used in producing chil-dren and in work, not wasted in libidinous pleasures. . .

Late Victorian Sex-Love: 1860–1892

. . . In the late nineteenth-century United States, several social factors converged to cause the eroticizing of consciousness, behavior, emotion, and identity that became typical of the twentieth-century Western middle class. The transformation of the family from producer to consumer unit resulted in a change in family members' relation to their own bodies; from being an instrument primarily of work, the human body was integrated into a new economy, and began more commonly to be perceived as a means of consumption and pleasure. . . .

In the late nineteenth century, the erotic became the raw material for a new consumer culture. Newspapers, books, plays, and films touching on sex, "normal" and "abnormal," became available for a price. Restaurants, bars, and baths opened, catering to sexual con-sumers with cash. Late Victorian entrepreneurs of desire incited the proliferation of a new eroticism, a commoditized culture of pleasure.

In these same years, the rise in power and prestige of medical doctors allowed these upwardly mobile professionals to prescribe a healthy new sexuality. Medical men, in the name of science, defined a new ideal of male–female relationships that included, in women as well as men, an essential, necessary, normal eroticism. Doctors, who had earlier named and judged the sex-enjoying woman a "nymphomaniac," now began to label women's *lack* of sexual pleasure a mental disturbance, speaking critically, for example, of female "frigidity" and "anesthesia."[3]

By the 1880s, the rise of doctors as a professional group fostered the rise of a new medical model of Normal Love, replete with sexuality. The new Normal Woman and Man were endowed with a healthy libido. . . .

Heterosexuality: The First Years, 1892–1900

In the periodization of heterosexual American history suggested here, the years 1892 to 1900 represent "The First Years" of the heterosexual epoch, eight key years in which the idea of the heterosexual and homosexual were initially and tentatively formulated by US doctors. The earliest-known American use of the word *heterosexual* occurs in a medical journal article by Dr. James G. Kiernan of Chicago, read before the city's medical society on 7 March 1892 and published that May—portentous dates in sexual history.[4] But Dr. Kiernan's heterosexuals were definitely not exemplars of normality. Heterosexuals, said Kiernan, were defined by a mental condition, "psychical hermaphroditism." Its symptoms were "inclinations to both sexes." These heterodox sexuals also betrayed inclinations "to abnormal methods of gratification," that is, techniques to insure pleasure without procreation. . . .

Though Kiernan used the new words *heterosexual* and *homosexual,* an old procreative standard and a new gender norm coexisted uneasily in his thought. His word *heterosexual* defined a mixed person and compound urge, abnormal because they wantonly included procreative and non- procreative objectives, as well as same-sex and different-sex attractions.

. . . The idea of heterosexuality as the master sex from which all others deviated was (like the idea of the master race) deeply authoritarian. The doctors' normalization of a sex that was hetero proclaimed a new heterosexual separatism—an erotic apartheid that forcefully segregated the sex normals from the sex perverts. In 1901, in the comprehensive *Oxford English Dictionary, heterosexual* and *homosexual* had not yet made it.

The Distribution of the Heterosexual Mystique: 1900–1930

. . . In its earliest version, the twentieth-century heterosexual imperative usually continued to associate heterosexuality with a supposed human "need," "drive," or "instinct" for propagation, a procreant urge linked inexorably with carnal lust as it had not been earlier. In the early twentieth century, the falling birth rate, rising divorce rate, and "war of the sexes" of the middle class were matters of increasing public concern. Giving vent to heteroerotic emotions was thus praised as enhancing baby-making capacity, marital intimacy, and family stability. . . .

The first part of the new sex norm—hetero—referred to a basic gender divergence. The "oppositeness" of the sexes was alleged to be the basis for a universal, normal, erotic attraction between males and females. The stress on the sexes' "oppositeness," which harked back to the early nineteenth century, by no means simply registered biological differences of females and males. The early twentieth-century focus on physiological and gender dimorphism reflected the deep anxieties of men about the shifting work, social roles, and power of men over women, and about the ideals of womanhood and manhood The stress on gender difference was a conservative response to the changing social-sexual division of activity and feeling which gave rise to the independent "New Woman" of the 1880s and eroticized "Flapper" of the 1920s. . . .

The Heterosexual Steps Out: 1930–1945

In 1930, in *The New York Times,* heterosexuality first became a love that dared to speak its name. On 20 April of that year, the word *heterosexual* is first known to have appeared in *The New York Times Book Review.* There, a critic described the subject of André Gide's *The Immoralist* proceeding "from a heterosexual liaison to a homosexual one." The ability to slip between sexual categories was referred to casually as a rather unremarkable aspect of human possibility. . . .

In September the second reference to the hetero/homo dyad appeared in *The New York Times Book Review,* in a comment on Floyd Dell's *Love in the Machine Age.* This work revealed a prominent antipuritan of the 1930s using the dire threat of homosexuality as his rationale for greater heterosexual freedom. Young people, Dell said, should be "permitted to develop normally to heterosexual adulthood." . . .

Heterosexual Hegemony: 1945–1965

The "cult of domesticity" following World War II—the reassociation of women with the home, motherhood, and childcare; men with fatherhood and wage work outside the home—was a period in which the predominance of the hetero norm went almost unchallenged, an era of heterosexual hegemony. This was an age in which conservative mental-health professionals reasserted the old link between heterosexuality and procreation. In contrast, sex-liberals of the day strove, ultimately with success, to expand the heterosexual ideal to include within the boundaries of normality a wider-than-ever range of non-procreative, premarital, and extramarital behaviors. But sex-liberal reform actually helped to extend and secure the dominance of the heterosexual idea, as we shall see when we get to Kinsey. . . .

The idea of the feminine female and masculine male as prolific breeders was also reflected in the stress, specific to the late 1940s, on the homosexual as sad symbol of "sterility"—that particular loaded term appears incessantly in comments on homosex dating to the fecund forties.

In 1948, in *The New York Times Book Review,* sex liberalism was in ascendancy. Dr. Howard A. Rusk declared that Alfred Kinsey's just published report on *Sexual Behavior in the Human Male* had found "wide variations in sex concepts and behavior." This raised the question: "What is 'normal' and 'abnormal'?" In particular, the report had found that "homosexual experience is much more common than previously thought," and "there is often a mixture of both homo and hetero experience."[5] . . .

Kinsey also explicitly contested the idea of an absolute, either/or antithesis between hetero and homo persons. He denied that human beings "represent two discrete populations, heterosexual and homosexual." The world, he ordered, "is not to be divided into sheep and goats." The hetero/homo division was not nature's doing: "Only the human mind invents categories and tries to force facts into separated pigeon-holes. The living world is a continuum."[6]

With a wave of the taxonomist's hand, Kinsey dismissed the social and historical division of people into heteros and homos. His denial of heterosexual and homosexual personhood rejected the social reality and profound subjective force of a historically constructed tradition which, since 1892 in the United States, had cut the sexual population in two and helped to establish the social reality of a heterosexual and homosexual identity. . . .

Heterosexual History: Out of the Shadows

Because much stress has been placed here on heterosexuality as word and concept, it seems important to affirm that heterosexuality (and homosexuality) came into existence before it was named and thought about. The formulation of the heterosexual idea did not create a heterosexual experience or behavior; to suggest otherwise would be to ascribe determining power to labels and concepts. But the titling and envisioning of heterosexuality did play an important role in consolidating the construction of the heterosexual's social existence. Before the wide use of the word *heterosexual,* I suggest, women and men did not mutually lust with the same profound, sure sense of normalcy that followed the distribution of "heterosexual" as universal sanctifier.

According to this proposal, women and men make their own sexual histories. But they do not produce their sex lives just as they please. They make their sexualities within a particular mode of organization given by the past and altered by their changing desire, their present power and activity, and their vision of a better world. That hypothesis suggests a number of good reasons for the immediate inauguration of research on a historically specific heterosexuality.

Notes

1. Barbara Welter, "The Cult of True Womanhood: 1820–1860," *American Quarterly*, vol. 18 (Summer 1966); Welter's analysis is extended here to include True Men and True Love.
2. Some historians have recently told us to revise our idea of sexless Victorians: their experience and even their ideology, it is said, were more erotic than we previously thought. Despite the revisionists, I argue that "purity" was indeed the dominant, early Victorian, white middle-class standard. For the debate on Victorian sexuality see John D'Emilio and Estelle Freedman, *Intimate Matters: A History of Sexuality in America* (New York: Harper & Row, 1988), p. xii.
3. This reference to females reminds us that the invention of heterosexuality had vastly different impacts on the histories of women and men. It also differed in its impact on lesbians and heterosexual women, homosexual and heterosexual men, the middle class and working class, and on different religious, racial, national, and geographic groups.
4. Dr. James G. Kiernan, "Responsibility in Sexual Perversion," *Chicago Medical Recorder*, vol. 3 (May 1892), pp. 185–210.
5. Dr. Howard A. Rusk, *New York Times Book Review*, 4 January 1948, p. 3.
6. Alfred Kinsey, Wardell B. Pomeroy, Clyde E. Martin, *Sexual Behavior in the Human Male* (Philadelphia, W. B. Saunders, 1948), pp. 637, 639.

Reading Questions

1. What are the major periods in the development of the concept of heterosexuality?
2. How did social, historical, economic, and political changes shape the development of our current ideas about heterosexuality? For example, what role did doctors, wars, economic changes, and women's rights play?
3. The period covered in this article ends at 1965. List three main ways that our ideas about heterosexuality and homosexuality have changed since then.

Katz, J. N. (1990). The invention of heterosexuality. *Socialist Review, 20*, 7–34.

SUMMARY

In this chapter we examined the concepts of sex and gender. Sex is based on perceived biological and physical characteristics and is categorized into the main groups of male and female. Gender is based in cultural and social distinctions and exists along a continuum from masculine to feminine. Both gender and sex are socially constructed and created (and re-created) when we perform gender roles in our daily lives. We looked at gender in music to illustrate how the media and other institutions socialize us to perform our gender roles in particular ways. We discussed three major institutions of society that help to create and perpetuate gender distinctions and inequality: sports, the workplace, and politics. Feminist theory and the concept of intersectionality were introduced as ways to understand the importance of gender in our society. We ended this chapter by examining the changing ideas of sexuality in society. The LGBTQ movement has been important in fighting for political, cultural, and social acceptance of the diversity of sexual orientations in modern society. Homophobia has declined, but the generally heteronormative nature of our society remains.

FOR FURTHER READING

Butler, J. (1990). *Gender trouble: Feminism and the subversion of identity*, Routledge.

Collins, P. H. (2005). *Black sexual politics*, Routledge.

Foucault, M. (1998). *The will to knowledge. The history of sexuality, 1*. Penguin. (Original work published 1976)

Hochschild, A., & Machung, A. (1990). *The second shift*, Avon Books.

Kimmel, M. (2012). *The gendered society* (5th ed.). Oxford University Press.

Messner, M. A. (1997). *Politics of masculinities: Men in movements.*, Alta Mira Press.

Smith, D. E. (1987). *The everyday world as problematic: A feminist sociology*, Northeastern University Press.

GLOSSARY

costs of masculinity

double shift (second shift)

feminism

feminization

gender

gender roles

heteronormative

heterosexual–homosexual rating scale

homophobia

intersectionality

intersex people

Kinsey Reports

LGBTQ

performativity

sex

sexual orientation

sexuality

transgender (trans) umbrella

PART III

THE ROLE OF INSTITUTIONS

7 LANGUAGE, MEDIA, AND CULTURE

1. Describe the role of language and its connection to culture.

2. Explain how the media is an institution in society and its role in socialization.

3. Examine the role of corporate concentration in shaping the demographic and idea diversity of the media we consume.

4. Explain the concepts of new media and social media and illustrate how the rise of these new forms of media alter social interactions and society.

5. Critically assess the effects of media on society and how we can address some of the unintended consequences of unequal access to the media.

Sociology is centrally concerned with the role of institutions in our society, such as the family, the education system, or the government. We focus on the important ways that these institutions can shape us as individuals and alter society. However, we tend to see the institution of the media in a different way. When studying the media, the focus is on how individuals consume the media and the messages that it relays. We are less likely to think of the important implications this media, and our exposure to it, has on society. This chapter examines the role of the media in society. We assess how the mass media has developed and how changes in the media have fundamentally shaped society. We also consider how the ownership of the media and differential access to the media can shape what we see and the implications this has for our understanding of the world around us.

LANGUAGE

The media is fundamentally related to language. Both language and the media are constantly evolving to represent changes in culture. Each year new words are added to the dictionary to reflect these changes. In 2020, the words added to the Oxford English Dictionary included *cringe factor, gaslighter, stress eater, vaxxer,* and *vaccine hesitant* (Oxford English Dictionary, 2022). Do you know what all these words mean? Do you think your parents would? Are you surprised by any of these additions?

The world is filled with language; there are roughly 7,000 languages spoken around the world today. Sociologists have long been interested in language because, as Durkheim argued, every language "represents a certain articulation of thought" (cited in Traugott, 1978, p. 102). Languages differ significantly, not just in words but also in ways of making sense of the social world. Attempting to translate poetry or humor from one language to another is often problematic, and meanings can be lost in translation. It is not enough to simply translate the words—translators need to understand how both the language and culture work so the joke or poem will make sense in another language.

"Doomscrolling" is the urge to continuously scroll through negative news stories. This word became popular during the COVID-19 pandemic when people were spending more time than ever in their homes and on the Internet following the—often negative and alarming—news.

urbazon/iStockPhoto

The Sapir-Whorf Hypothesis

Durkheim's understanding of the connection between language and thought was partly influenced by the work of anthropologists who studied languages in North America. One such anthropologist, Edward Sapir (1884–1939), compared indigenous languages with the European languages with which he was more familiar. He thought that these languages were so dissimilar because they are based in cultures that understand the world in very different ways. Based on this idea, Sapir and Benjamin Whorf developed the Sapir-Whorf hypothesis, which argues that language impacts thought. Whorf (1956) describes this relationship in the following way:

> We dissect nature along lines laid down by our native language. The categories and types that we isolate from the world of phenomena we do not find there because they stare every observer in the face; on the contrary, the world is presented in a kaleidoscope flux of impressions which has to be organized by our minds—and this means largely by the linguistic systems of our minds. We cut nature up, organize it into concepts, and ascribe significances as we do, largely because we are parties to an agreement to organize it in this way—an agreement that holds throughout our speech community and is codified in the patterns of our language . . . all observers are not led by the same physical evidence to the same picture of the universe, unless their linguistic backgrounds are similar, or can in some way be calibrated. (pp. 212–214)

An example of the connection between language and thought is the use of honorifics (a linguistic means of conveying respect to a person). Honorifics are not often used in English. When you address another person—no matter if he is your best friend, grandparent, teacher, or the president—you use the word "you." The Spanish language, however, has multiple levels of formality based on sex, age, and education. In addition, when you initially meet someone or speak to someone older or to whom you owe respect, you often address them as *usted* (a formal or respectful form of "you"). You do not use this formal way of saying "you" for your friends, family members, and others with whom you have a more informal relationship. Many people who learn Spanish later in life find it hard to understand when they should use each term and, especially, when they can move from *usted* to more casual terms. When does your relationship transition into a more informal one? This question is not simply a linguistic issue; it is also related to a cultural understanding of whom you should respect and how relationships change.

The Korean language has seven levels of respect, which are used to mark the formality of the conversation as well as elements of the relationship between the speaker and the listener. For example, you can use noun or verb endings to indicate clearly that your conversation partner has a higher or lower status than you. With these language rules, you would speak to an older relative, your boss, or your teacher differently than you would to a younger person or your employee. These rules of speech are quite complicated but are very important. If you refer to someone too casually (or too impersonally), you could cause offense.

Sapir and Whorf would argue that these differences in the use of honorifics illustrate something about these cultures, and, in turn, the languages represent the cultures in which they are created. Because North American or English culture (i.e., places where English is spoken) tends to pride itself on individualism and equality, there is less need to differentiate people in language based on their status. In cultures that value the role of the collective, respect for authority, and hierarchy (such as the culture in Korea), the need to distinguish speakers based on their status and to defer to authorities is a cultural element that is built into the language.

Another way that the language reflects culture, and changes in that culture, is in the use of gendered terms. Our language is filled with gendered terms and there is a lot of discussion about the importance of gendered language. Does it matter if we use the term *mankind, chairman,* or *freshman* when we really mean "humankind," "chair," or "first-year student"? These terms are changing over time, illustrating the changing nature of our culture and changing ideas about men's and women's roles in society. We now, for example, refer to police officers (instead of policemen) or fire fighters (instead of firemen). The Sapir-Whorf hypothesis would argue that simply using these gender-neutral terms can change how we think about gender roles and thus make us more egalitarian.

Methods in Depth: News Coverage of Refugees

The media is clearly an important source for learning about the world around us. As such, it has considerable power to shape the ways that we see and understand social issues. Hoewe (2018) was interested in how the news media covers the topic of refugees and how that coverage influences what we, as viewers, think about this issue. In particular, she examines the media coverage of refugees affected by three major wars: wars in Syria, Afghanistan, and Iraq. She compares how the media uses the terms *immigrant* and *refugee* in this coverage. Immigrants, by definition, are people who leave their home country by choice, whereas refugees are people who leave when they are forced to do so due to persecution, political or civil unrest, or natural disaster. By using one term more than the other, the news media is shaping how we think about the people who have fled their homes because of civil unrest and, potentially, the ways that we think the United States should (or should not) welcome these people.

Methodology

This research uses content analysis, a research method that is based on the analysis of documents. These documents could be newspaper articles, tweets, Facebook posts, television advertisements, letters between historical figures, images, or many other documents. Through systematic analysis, we can understand the meanings of these documents and compare how these meanings change over time, across contexts, or in other ways. For example, you can design a study of how images of men's and women's bodies in advertisements have changed over time by analyzing magazine ads. Or, we could conduct a content analysis of the ways that slavery is covered in high school textbooks over time to assess changing ideas about race.

Findings

In this research, Hoewe (2018) uses content analysis to compare how U.S. and international newspapers use the terms *immigrant* and *refugee*. She finds that U.S. newspapers are much more likely to misuse or confuse the two terms, calling individuals who have fled the three war-torn countries immigrants when they are, by definition, refugees. She also found that, when the term *immigrant* was used, it was often paired with the term *terrorist* or *terrorism*. This pairing was much less likely when the term *refugee* was used. These findings are significant because the association of a group of people with terrorism tends to increase support for more restrictive policies toward the group, such as limiting their numbers in the United States, and more hostile attitudes toward them.

Data

Hoewe's (2018) research is based on content analysis of news stories published in four newspapers. Two of these newspapers are based in the United States—*The Washington Post* and *The New York Times*—and two are based in other countries—*Al Jazeera* (Qatar) and *The Daily Telegraph* (United Kingdom). She selected the newspapers based on both theoretical and practical reasons. Theoretically, she wanted to compare newspapers inside and outside the United States, so she picked two newspapers from each category. She also needed to find international newspapers that would have enough coverage of these issues. She selected *Al Jazeera* because it is headquartered in Qatar and focuses its coverage on the Middle East, guaranteeing a lot of coverage of those conflicts. *The Daily Telegraph* is a UK newspaper that has a substantial amount of international news coverage and an international audience. In addition, all four of these newspapers are considered very influential publications in their regions, meaning that their coverage and tone of coverage would be more likely to shape the opinions of people than smaller or more isolated newspapers. From a practical perspective, all these newspapers are published in English and are accessible through a large database called LexisNexis, which is available through many university libraries. This made the content accessible to the researcher.

Hoewe began by searching for all articles in these newspapers that had the term *refugee* or *immigrant* in the headline with mentions of the following countries in the story: Syria, Iraq, and Afghanistan. She collected all articles in the time frame of each conflict (Syrian Civil War—March 2011 to June 2016; War in Afghanistan—October 2001 to June 2016; and the conflicts in Iraq—March 2003 to June 2016). This resulted in 416 stories from *The Washington Post*, 542 stories from *The New York Times*, 578 stories from *Al Jazeera*, and 340 stories from *The Daily Telegraph*.

There are many ways that one could code articles in content analysis. Remember from Chapter 1 that there are qualitative and quantitative research methods in sociology. Quantitative methods use large amounts of data and focus on counting patterns. Qualitative methods use a smaller number of cases and focus on process and meaning. Traditionally, content analysis tended to be a more qualitative method—researchers read all the articles or documents on a topic and created codes for the main themes that they saw. In more recent research, some academics have chosen to combine this qualitative hand coding with quantitative computer-assisted coding. Computer software is very good at the quantitative elements of coding. For example, a computer can count the number of mentions of each word, such as "refugee" or "immigrant." And, it can be used to see how these two words appear in relation to other concepts, such as terrorism.

This computer-assisted coding is very useful. It allows the researcher to analyze a much larger body of articles—in this case, 1,876 articles. This is much more than a researcher could hand code. It is important to note, however, that the ways in which these stories talk about immigrants and refugees is not clear from this coding. It is much more difficult for computer-assisted software to code the tone used in the article. Hand coding could add to our understanding by examining meanings and tones in a more nuanced way.

MEDIA AND CULTURE

Media, the plural of the Latin word *medius* (middle), refers to the technological processes that facilitate communication between a sender and a receiver. **Mass media** sends a message from one source to many people. Modern society has many types of mass media, including radio, television, books, the Internet, movies, music, and magazines. Using a telephone or e-mailing is not normally understood to be mass media because the contents involve private communication between two people and are not intended for a large audience.

Media are important socializing agents in our society: They teach us about the norms and expectations for different people and situations. The significance of the media is, in part, a result of our very high level of exposure to it. According to a recent study, the average American adult watches more than 33 hours of television a week (Nielsen, 2021). Americans also spend an average of about 17 hours a week surfing the Internet on their phones (Nielsen, 2021). In addition, Americans spend considerable amounts of time listening to the radio and reading newspapers and magazines. In this section, we examine changes in the media and the important role the media plays in our society.

The Medium Is the Message

One of the most important scholars of media was Marshall McLuhan (1911–1980), a Canadian academic who worked at the University of Toronto and founded the Centre for Culture and Technology. McLuhan (1964) is most famous for the statement, "The medium is the message." He argued that the content of the medium, such as the words on an Internet news site, is not as important as the physical or psychological effects of that medium. Different media have different effects because of the form of their messages. These various forms alter how we experience the world, how we interact with others, and how we process and communicate information. For example, in print media our visual sense rules; in radio, our aural; in television, both. McLuhan argued that the medium's properties (not just the messages' content) affect us as individuals, as well as our social world. The media can shape and change us; as we develop new technologies, those technologies change us as a result.

Francois BIBAL/Gamma-Rapho via Getty Images

Getting to Know: Marshall McLuhan (1911–1980)

- McLuhan became internationally famous in the 1960s due to his expression "the medium is the message."

- He is often referred to as the man who predicted the Internet because of his concept of global village, which stated that electronic media would facilitate the global flow of information.

- He was good friends with the 15th Prime Minister of Canada, Pierre Trudeau, whom he described as "both emperor and clown."

- McLuhan appeared in a cameo as himself in the 1977 romantic comedy, *Annie Hall*.

- In 1970, McLuhan was appointed a Companion to the Order of Canada, the country's highest honor awarded to civilians for their outstanding achievements and lifetime contributions to humanity at large.

The development of the printing press illustrates how changing mediums can affect individuals and society. The printing press was invented in China in 1041, but the version developed by Gutenberg in 1450 in Europe was particularly efficient and easy to use. This new press led to the production of the first mass-produced Bible in 1455. Previously, monks copied Bibles by hand, which took a long time. Not surprisingly, copies were scarce and very expensive.

The invention of the printing press had significant (and, in some cases, unintended) effects on society. A major consequence was the challenge to the elite's ability to hoard information and knowledge. Before the printing press, only very wealthy and well-connected individuals had books. The printing press made it possible for more people to purchase books. It increased the number of books available, and in a relatively short period of time they were being mass-produced. When only monks transcribed books, it was easy for the powerful to control what was printed. The printing press effectively opened a massive communication channel, allowing many groups and interests to promote their messages. One of the first things printed on the printing press in Europe was Martin Luther's *The 95 Theses*—a list of complaints about the Catholic Church that led to the creation of Protestantism. This work certainly challenged the status quo.

The printing press also led to the rise of individualism. Individuals became less reliant on others (especially elites) for information. People gained more access to books, pamphlets, and newsletters on a wide variety of subjects. This shift effectively helped to democratize access to information on, for example, how to cure illnesses, build machines, or start a political movement. Moreover, literacy rates among different groups of people, including the poor, women, and children, improved.

How has technology changed during your life? Did you have access to any computer devices—such as a tablet or smartphone—when you were a child? How would you have grown up differently if you had or had not had access to these devices?

staticnak1983/iStockPhoto

The invention of the printing press was not simply a change in media: It fundamentally changed the nature of society. Centuries later, the rise of the Internet has done the same. The Internet further democratizes access to information and content. Anyone can now read an almost unlimited number of books, magazines, and newspapers online as well as watch videos, movies, and TV shows. However, as we will discuss later in this chapter, there is still inequality regarding who has access to and knowledge about using computers and the Internet.

CORPORATE CONCENTRATION AND THE MEDIA

One key concern with modern mass media is the extent to which it is controlled by a limited number of people. Recent decades have seen an increase in the corporate concentration of media ownership. In other words, the media is increasingly owned and controlled by fewer huge media corporations and conglomerates. The United States has a fairly high level of corporate concentration in the media. In 1983, 50 companies owned 90% of all media in the United States. By 2012, only 6 companies owned 90% of the U.S. media (Lutz, 2012). The concentration has increased even further since 2012. In television ownership, for example, a small group of five companies has been buying local TV stations and increasing their overall hold on television (Matsa, 2017). These five companies owned 179 stations in 2004 but had increased their ownership to 443 stations by 2016—meaning that 37% of all local television stations in the country are owned by five companies. Such concentration could lead to fewer viewpoints being expressed in the media. Certainly the situation in the United States is not the same as it would be if there were a single state-run newspaper, but how much competition is enough to ensure a free and independent press?

This pattern of media control has long historical roots. The town newspaper was once a family-owned business, as was the dairy, hardware store, and grocery store. Today, provision of these basic items is controlled by large firms—for example, News Corp (newspaper), Nestlé (dairy), Home Depot (hardware), and Publix (groceries). Family-owned businesses have not disappeared, but they are now far less powerful and face continual threat, whether from Walmart, Amazon, or other big-box stores or online retailers. It may not be significant that we all get our milk or our light bulbs from the same store. However, we may be more concerned that our news and, as a consequence, our information about the world, is filtered by a smaller and smaller group.

READING: FROM *THE POWER ELITE*

C. Wright Mills

The issue of corporate concentration is at the core of C. Wright Mills's *The Power Elite* (1956). In this book, Mills argues that the power elite, a group of leaders in the military, corporate, and political spheres of society, have interwoven and complementary interests. He also found an interchangeability of top positions within these three institutions. As a result, the most powerful people in each institution develops a class consciousness and a similar set of interests.

The Nature of the Power Elite

We study history, it has been said, to rid ourselves of it, and the history of the power elite is a clear case for which this maxim is correct. Like the tempo of American life in general, the long-term trends of the power structure have been greatly speeded up since World War II, and certain newer trends within and between the dominant institutions have also set the shape of the power elite. . . .

1. In so far as the structural clue to the power elite today lies in the political order, that clue is the decline of politics as genuine and public debate of alternative decisions—with nationally responsible and policy-coherent parties and with autonomous organizations connecting the lower and middle levels of power with the top levels of decision. America is now in considerable part more a formal political democracy than a democratic social structure, and even the formal political mechanics are weak.

The long-time tendency of business and government to become more intricately and deeply involved with each other has, in the fifth epoch, reached a new point of explicitness. The two cannot now be seen clearly as two distinct worlds. It is in terms of the executive agencies of the state that the rapprochement has proceeded most decisively. The growth of the executive branch of the government, with its agencies that patrol the complex economy, does not mean merely the "enlargement of government" as some sort of autonomous bureaucracy: it has meant the ascendancy of the corporation's man as a political eminence. . . .

2. In so far as the structural clue to the power elite today lies in the economic order, that clue is the fact that the economy is at once a permanent-war economy and a private-corporation economy. American capitalism is now in considerable part a military capitalism, and the most important relation of the big corporation to the state rests on the coincidence of interests between military and corporate needs, as defined by warlords and corporate rich. Within the elite as a whole, this coincidence of interest between the high military and the corporate chieftains strengthens both of them and further subordinates the role of the merely political men. Not politicians, but corporate executives, sit with the military and plan the organization of war effort. . . .

The power elite is composed of political, economic, and military men, but this instituted elite is frequently in some tension: it comes together only on certain coinciding points and only on certain occasions of "crisis": In the long peace of the nineteenth century, the military were not in the high councils of state, not of the political directorate, and neither were the economic men—they made raids upon the state but they did not join its directorate. During the thirties, the political man was ascendant. Now the military and the corporate men are in top positions.

Of the three types of circle that compose the power elite today, it is the military that has benefited the most in its enhanced power although the corporate circles have also become more explicitly entrenched in the more public decision-making circles. It is the professional politician that has lost the most, so much that in examining the events and decisions, one is tempted to speak of a political vacuum in which the corporate rich and the high warlord, in their coinciding interests, rule.

It should not be said that the three "take turns" in carrying the initiative, for the mechanics of the power elite are not often as deliberate as that would imply. At times, of course, it is—as when political men, thinking they can borrow the prestige of generals, find that they must pay for it, or, as when during big slumps, economic men feel the need of a politician at once safe and possessing vote appeal. Today all three are involved in virtually all widely ramifying decisions. Which of the three types seems to lead depends upon "the tasks of the period" as they, the elite, define them. Just now, these tasks center upon "defense" and international affairs. Accordingly, as we have seen, the military are ascendant in two senses: as personnel and as justifying ideology. That is why, just now, we can most easily specify the unity and the shape of the power elite in terms of the military ascendancy. . . .

Neither the idea of a "ruling class" nor of a simple monolithic rise of "bureaucratic politicians" nor of a "military clique" is adequate. The power elite today involves the often uneasy coincidence of economic, military, and political power.

The Composition of the Power Elite

Despite their social similarity and psychological affinities, the members of the power elite do not constitute a club having a permanent membership with fixed and formal boundaries. It is of the nature of the power elite that within it there is a good deal of shifting about, and that it thus does not consist of one small set of the same men in the same positions in the same hierarchies. Because men know each other personally does not mean that among them there is a unity of policy; and because they do not know each other personally does not mean that among them there is a disunity. The conception of the power elite does not rest, as I have repeatedly said, primarily upon personal friendship.

As the requirements of the top places in each of the major hierarchies become similar, the types of men occupying these roles at the top—by selection and by training in the jobs—become similar. This is no mere deduction from structure to personnel. That it is a fact is revealed by the heavy traffic that has been going on between the three structures, often in very intricate patterns. The chief executives, the warlords, and selected politicians came into contact with one another in an intimate, working way during World War II; after that war ended, they continued their associations, out of common beliefs, social congeniality, and coinciding interests. Noticeable proportions of top men from the military, the economic, and the political worlds have during the last 15 years occupied positions in one or both of the other worlds: between these higher circles there is an interchangeability of position, based formally upon the supposed transferability of "executive ability," based in substance upon the co-optation by cliques of insiders. As members of a power elite, many of those busy in this traffic have come to look upon "the government" as an umbrella under whose authority they do their work. . . .

Given the formal similarity of the three hierarchies in which the several members of the elite spend their working lives, given the ramifications of the decisions made in each upon the others, given the coincidence of interest that prevails among them at many points, and given the administrative vacuum of the American civilian state along with its enlargement of tasks—given these trends of structure, and adding to them the psychological affinities we have noted—we should indeed be surprised were we to find that men said to be skilled in administrative contacts and full of organizing ability would fail to do more than get in touch with one another. They have, of course, done much more than that: increasingly, they assume positions in one another's domains. . . .

These men are not necessarily familiar with every major arena of power. We refer to one man who moves in and between perhaps two circles— say the industrial and the military—and to another man who moves in the military and the political, and to a third who moves in the political as well as among opinion-makers. These in-between types most closely display our image of the power elite's structure and operation, even of behind-the-scenes operations. To the extent that there is any "invisible elite," these advisory and liaison types are its core. Even if—as I believe to be very likely—many of them are, at least in the first part of their careers, "agents" of the various elites rather than themselves elite, it is they who are most active in organizing the several top milieu into a structure of power and maintaining it. . . .

The Interests of the Power Elite

The conception of the power elite and of its unity rests upon the corresponding developments and the coincidence of interests among economic, political, and military organizations. It also rests upon the similarity of origin and outlook, and the social and personal intermingling of the top circles from each of these dominant hierarchies. This conjunction of institutional and psychological forces, in turn, is revealed by the heavy personnel traffic within and between the big three institutional orders, as well as by the rise of go-betweens as in the high- level lobbying. The conception of the power elite, accordingly, does *not* rest upon the assumption that American history since the origins of World War II must be understood as a secret plot, or as a great and coordinated conspiracy of the members of this elite. The conception rests upon quite impersonal grounds.

There is, however, little doubt that the American power elite—which contains, we are told, some of the greatest organizers in the world—has also planned and has plotted. The rise of the elite, as we have already made clear, was not and could not have been caused by a plot; and the tenability of the conception does not rest upon the existence of any secret or any publicly known organization. But, once the conjunction of structural trend and of the personal will to utilize it gave rise to the power elite, then plans and programs did occur to its members and indeed it is not possible to interpret many events and official policies of the fifth epoch without reference to the power elite. "There is a great difference," Richard Hofstadter has remarked, "between locating conspiracies in history and saying that history is, in effect, a conspiracy." . . .

So far as explicit organization—conspiratorial or not—is concerned, the power elite, by its very nature, is more likely to use existing organizations, working within and between them, than to set up explicit organizations whose membership is strictly limited to its own members. But if there is no machinery in existence to ensure, for example, that military and political factors will be balanced in decisions made, they will invent such machinery and use it, as with the National Security Council. Moreover, in a formally democratic polity, the aims and the powers of the various elements of this elite are further supported by an aspect of the permanent war economy: the assumption that the security of the nation supposedly rests upon great secrecy of plan and intent. Many higher events that would reveal the working of the power elite can be withheld from public knowledge under the guise of secrecy. With the wide secrecy covering their operations and decisions, the power elite can mask their intentions, operations, and further consolidation. Any secrecy that is imposed upon those in positions to observe high decision-makers clearly works for and not against the operations of the power elite.

There is accordingly reason to suspect—but by the nature of the case, no proof—that the power elite is not altogether "surfaced." There is nothing hidden about it, although its activities are not publicized. As an elite, it is not organized, although its members often know one another, seem quite naturally to work together, and share many organizations in common. There is nothing conspiratorial about it, although its decisions are often publicly unknown and its mode of operation manipulative rather than explicit.

Conclusion

The idea of the power elite rests upon and enables us to make sense of (1) the decisive institutional trends that characterize the structure of our epoch, in particular, the military ascendancy in a privately incorporated economy, and more broadly, the several coincidences of objective interests between economic, military, and political institutions; (2) the social similarities and the psychological affinities of the men who occupy the command posts of these structures, in particular the increased interchangeability of the top positions in each of them and the increased traffic between these orders in the careers of men of power; (3) the ramifications, to the point of virtual totality, of the kind of decisions that are made at the top, and the rise to power of a set of men who, by training and bent, are professional organizers of considerable force and who are unrestrained by democratic party training. . . .

As a result, the political directorate, the corporate rich, and the ascendant military have come together as the power elite, and the expanded and centralized hierarchies which they head have encroached upon the old balances and have now relegated them to the middle levels of power. Now the balancing society is a conception that pertains accurately to the middle levels, and on that level the balance has become more often an affair of entrenched provincial and nationally irresponsible forces and demands than a center of power and national decision.

Reading Questions

1. Who are the power elite? What are the three types of institutions that make up the power elite?

2. How do the interests of these three groups coincide and how do they conflict? How do they share commonalities?

3. Does Mills think that the power elite has control because of a conspiracy? How does the power elite continue to exist?

Mills, C. W. (1956). *The power elite*. Oxford University Press.

Consequences of Media Ownership

As mentioned in the previous section, corporate concentration in the media and other areas can limit the free exchange of ideas and the diversity of content we receive as media consumers. The two main types of media diversity that can be affected are idea diversity and demographic diversity.

Idea diversity refers to the range of viewpoints expressed in the media marketplace of ideas. Media conglomerates have the power to censor information according to their interests. In *Manufacturing Consent: The Political Economy of the Mass Media*, Noam Chomsky and Edward S. Herman (2002) argue that wealthy and powerful people control the mass media. Because the mass media are one of the primary means of socialization and persuasion in our society, elites are able to create news that reflects their own interests. Herman and Chomsky also argue that elites can use this media control to legitimize the class system and other inequalities in our society.

Demographic diversity refers to how the media represents and addresses the interests of a diversity of people from a variety of races, ethnicities, genders, sexual orientations, and classes. One might argue that a way to ensure demographically diverse content is to support demographically diverse ownership (Gamson & Latteier, 2004). Women hold the majority ownership of only 8% of commercial broadcast stations and persons belonging to a racial minority hold majority ownership in only 4% of commercial broadcast stations (Federal Communications Commission, 2021) This lack of diversity in ownership could limit the variety of characters and shows presented. However, it is possible that a homogeneous group of media owners could be showing a range of characters.

Never Have I Ever attempts to show demographic diversity both in front of and behind the camera. Is it important to depict diversity in television shows? Can this lead to more inclusiveness in society?

Universal Pictures Television / Album / Alamy Stock Photo

A study of the top 100 films of 2021 found that only 34% of the speaking roles in movies were female, a decline of 2% since 2020 (Lauzen, 2022). In these movies, characters who were from racialized communities accounted for only 39% of female and 35% of male speaking roles, and only 1.4% came from the LGBTQ community (Lauzen, 2022). Within the LGBTQ community, there were only 3 trans characters depicted on screen—a 6-year high—but these characters were inconsequential to the story and only amounted to a total of 2 minutes of screen time. In addition, only 2.3% of the characters in the top 100 grossing films of 2019 had a disability (Neff et al., 2021).

Minority representation is increasing somewhat in the media. In 2021, minorities reached proportionate representation for the first time in overall cast diversity in films. That year, 43.1% of actors in the top 252 movies were BIPOC. This is a large increase in representation compared to 10 years earlier, when only 20.7% of actors in the top-grossing films were BIPOC. Almost one third of the top performing movies in 2021 had majority-minority casts. This increase can be partly attributed to the rise of direct-to-streaming offerings at a time when traditional theaters were closed due to COVID (Littleton, 2022).

The news is another area where diversity is critical. Much of what we learn about the world comes from the news. But, who is telling these stories? Recent research in the United States shows that newsroom employees are more likely to be White and male than U.S. workers overall. However, this might be changing as younger newsroom employees show greater racial, ethnic and gender diversity than their older colleagues, according to a Pew Research Center analysis of U.S. Census Bureau data (Grieco, 2018). More than three-quarters (77%) of newsroom employees—those who work as reporters, editors, photographers, and videographers in the newspaper, broadcasting, and Internet publishing industries—are non-Hispanic Whites, according to the analysis of 2012–2016 American Community Survey data. That is true of 65% of U.S. workers in all occupations and industries combined. Newsroom employees are also more likely than all workers to be male. About 6 in 10 newsroom employees (61%) are men, compared with 53% of all workers. When combining race/ethnicity and gender, almost half (48%) of newsroom employees are non-Hispanic White men, compared with about a third (34%) of workers overall.

When we consider various dimensions of diversity together, 38% of the youngest newsroom employees are both non-Hispanic White and male. This is still a higher share than among workers overall (30%), but this 8-percentage-point gap is smaller than among older age groups. Newsroom employees age 50 and older are 17 percentage points more likely to be White men than all workers in the same age group, while those ages 30 to 49 are 15 points more likely (Grieco, 2018).

Why might it matter that the people researching and reporting the news come from a less diverse background than the population as a whole? First, we might expect that one's background could shape the types of stories that one is attracted to telling. In addition, the ways that stories are told could differ depending on the characteristics of the researchers and reporters. Finally, seeing more representation across racial, ethnic, and gender lines is beneficial for the home audience as it legitimizes different perspectives and experiences.

Another area where a lack of diversity has been highlighted is at the Academy Awards, also known as the Oscars. In 2016, after the list of Oscar nominees was released, there was a pronounced backlash. For the second year in a row, all 10 of the nominees in the four top acting categories were White actors. There was no racial or ethnic diversity in the best actress, best actor, best supporting actress, or best supporting actor categories. The reaction led to the #OscarsSoWhite campaign. Many actors and directors refused to attend the ceremony, and articles appeared in the media criticizing the Academy for its lack of diversity.

It seems unlikely that there were no Oscar-worthy performances from non-White actors during the year. So what explains the all-White list of nominees? One thing that is important to consider is the availability of roles for people of different ethnic backgrounds. In addition, it is important to consider how the process by which actors—and others—are nominated structures the types of people who are selected for awards. Only members of the Academy vote for the winner of the Academy awards, but how do you become a member? Two people who are already members must sponsor you, and then you must be approved by the Board of Governors (Academy of Motion Picture Arts and Sciences, 2017). Given that only 7% of the members of the Academy were non-White in 2016, it is not surprising that there was so little diversity in the actors nominated. We can imagine that a group that is 93% White is also more likely to nominate other White people to join the Academy, perpetuating the inequality over time.

The Academy responded to the #OscarsSoWhite campaign and committed to doubling the number of ethnic minorities in the Academy by 2020. If they met this target, there would still only be 14% racialized minorities in the Academy, far below their representation in the population (38% in the United States; Cox, 2017). Despite not yet reaching their targets or not yet reflecting the diversity that exists in the population, the drive toward equality has already yielded some results. In 2022, the Academy nominated five minority actors and directors, including Ariana DeBose (who won best supporting actor for *West Side Story*), Will Smith (who won best actor for *King Richard*), Jane Campion (who won best director for *The Power of the Dog*), Aunjanue Ellis (nominated for best actress for *King Richard*), and Ryusuke Hamaguchi (nominated for best director for *Drive My Car*). Although it is important to note the achievements of the movement #OscarsSoWhite, we should remain critical of the general lack of diversity in these types of awards and the ways that institutions perpetuate inequality over time.

NEW MEDIA AND SOCIAL MEDIA

The media environment has undergone widespread change over the past 20 to 30 years with the rise of new media. New media is accessible on demand, digital, interactive, and encourages user comments and feedback. Wikipedia combines several features of new media: it is digitally based, incorporates images and video links, and allows interactive and creative participation among users. Social media, a type of new media, allows the creation and online sharing of information in communities and networks. According to Kaplan and Haenlein (2010), social media technologies can be classified into six types: collaborative projects (e.g., Wikipedia), blogs and microblogs (e.g., Twitter), content communities (e.g., YouTube), social networking sites (e.g., Facebook), virtual game worlds (e.g., *Clash of Clans*), and virtual social worlds (e.g., Minecraft or *Second Life*). However, the boundaries between the different types of social media are increasingly blurred.

Social media is mainly used for social interaction. The high usage rates of these technologies indicate that they are filling important social functions for many people. In fact, many argue that technology is transforming how we engage with others and how we spend our time. More and more people are willing to make social connections and seek companionship through social media such as Tinder or Grindr. The Internet is also an effective way for users to connect with people across great distances, such as through Zoom or Facetime. Moreover, our expectations and norms about love, friendship, and identity are strongly informed by our use of social media. What it means to "friend" someone, for example, is very different in the Facebook era than it was 50 years ago.

We can see that social media has created many large-scale changes in the United States. The biggest change is in the scale of our social networks—we can interact with many more people than was possible in the past. Traditionally, our social networks were limited by our geography, but physical presence is no longer a precondition for establishing a friendship or social tie. Think about how you show friends your vacation photos. Twenty years ago, you would have met your friends in person, flipped through printed photos, and explained them. Doing this with all your Facebook or Instagram friends would take a long time. Now you can simply upload your photos to Facebook and add descriptions; your friends can view the photos at their leisure, increasing the photo sharing. Although you can certainly share your photos with a larger group of people, the quality of the interaction is possibly lower. Not all your Facebook friends will commit the half hour they might have spent looking at your photos in the past. Lots of people might "like" your photos, but the nature of their interest in your vacation is surely lower.

Social media also places fewer restrictions on your communication. Previously, the only way to get your message to a large group of people was to talk with them face to face (perhaps in a speech to a large crowd); otherwise, you could be censored. For example, if you write a letter to the editor of your local newspaper, the publication has the power to select (or not select) your letter for printing. If you want to air an advertisement on TV, the station could refuse your ad or require that you change its content. But with social media, you can distribute your message to a virtually unlimited number of people with very little censorship (at least in the United States). If you are upset with something the president or your governor does, you can post your opinions on Twitter or Facebook, where all your friends and followers can read it.

The Challenges of Social Media

There are obvious benefits to social media. However, we must not overestimate the diversity of social media networks. Although it might seem that we can have contact and communication with virtually anyone, we know that individuals tend to create online communities of people who share similar characteristics and opinions. It is not surprising that, just as in face-to-face friendships, we tend to seek out others online who are similar to us. As a result, we are exposed to a limited number of views. People who hold very different beliefs or perspectives than we do are unlikely to be in our online circle of friends. Perhaps you are part of a political or religious group online: These groups will likely only have other members who share your political or religious ideology, which could simply reinforce the opinions you already have instead of exposing you to new ideas and information.

Social media's ability to spread information about ourselves and others so easily has created concerns about a lack of privacy, which can be a particular problem for young people. One implication of this lack of privacy is the rise of cyberbullying. Cyberbullying is defined as the willful and repeated harm inflicted through the use of computers, cell phones, and other electronic devices (Cyberbullying Research Center, 2016b). One in three Internet users between the ages of 12 and 17 have been cyberbullied or cyberstalked (Cyberbullying Research Center, 2016a). This type of harassment online can lead to

Heidi Klum dumped a bucket filled with ice water over Tim Gunn's head at the Project Runway Season 13 finale to raise awareness of ALS. How can celebrity engagement in this type of campaign help increase awareness and lead to social change?

Taylor Hill/FilmMagic/Getty Images

serious consequences for victims, including depression, social withdrawal, and risk of suicide. It is very challenging to address cyberbullying and cyberstalking because of the hidden nature of the online world and the difficulty of identifying the perpetrators.

Social media clearly presents many challenges, but also exciting opportunities. The following reading, by Tom Chiang Jr, outlines some of these issues, including the spread of sensationalized content and misinformation. Read the following article and consider how social media can be best studied and, potentially, changed.

READING: SOCIAL MEDIA IN SOCIETY: A POSITIVE OR NEGATIVE FORCE?

Tom Chiang Jr.

I teach a college-level introductory sociology course where we discuss the *functional role* of mass media. Talcott Parsons' functional perspective espouses that society is comprised of interrelated parts in order to promote solidarity and stability. Therefore, the functional role of mass media is to teach and reinforce the norms, values, and belief systems of a society in order to further social solidarity. From a functional lens, social media, a type of mass media platform that facilitates the sharing of ideas, thoughts, and information between its users, which had been dismissed as a fad back in 2006, has had a functional, and arguably positive, effect on society in recent years by empowering its citizens toward solidarity through collective action. Social media is now a platform that brings social justice issues to the forefront of the American discourse, and arguably, has helped rectify persistent inequities. To this end, social media has been a place where social movements of different forms, and their messages of empowerment through collective action, are solidified.

One way that social media facilitates social movements' message of empowerment through collective action is through grassroots online fundraising. For example, as a result of a tweet tweeted during the early stages of the coronavirus outbreak, online donors donated money to people who had student-loan and past-due medical bills. Another method in which social media empowers its users toward collective activism is through the use of hashtags, which then could be retweeted on Twitter. For example, in the article #SayHerName: a case of intersectional social media activism, Melissa Brown and her colleagues argue that #SayHerName, which has been retweeted many times over, is used to raise consciousness about the deaths of Black women, especially Black transgender women. As the data from the article demonstrates, hashtags, such as #SayHerName, can be used to bring awareness, and, in turn, attempt to rectify systemic injustices that affect hyper marginalized groups whose lived experiences have often been neglected by mainstream media.

Despite these positive impacts of social media, a first-year student in my sociology course asked me if I believed that social media was harmful to modern society. Given the importance of this question, I wanted to dedicate some time to answering it here in detail.

General Societal Effects of Social Media: The Pervasive Nature of Social Media

While social media was considered as a passing trend by researchers just a little less than a decade ago, social media has proliferated into mainstream society. Data from Pew Research Center show that 5% of the American adult population used social media in 2005, as compared to 72% of the public today. They also found that as social media usage increases so does the user base. In 2005, the few who used social media in America were young adults, but the user rates among older adults have also increased in recent years. In addition to the change in age among users of social media, the daily usage of social media sites, such as

Facebook and Instagram, has also increased. Data from Pew Research Center show that roughly 75% of users visit Facebook and 60% of users visit Instagram at least once per day.

People use social media for different reasons beyond keeping connections with friends and relatives who live far away. Increasingly social media will be used to complete daily tasks, especially in the field of commerce. For example, as of 2019, Facebook is developing a cryptocurrency system called Libra, which, some argue, will soon go mainstream with help from major banks. This is not surprising as social media, such as Facebook, is already changing the way we pay. Currently, Facebook users can pay other users through Facebook messenger. In addition to commerce, people use social media to keep up with the latest developments in the United States and abroad. Social media, specifically, has made information more accessible to consumers. This is evident with Twitter, which is a social media platform where individuals and organizations can share ideas, thoughts, and information with their followers.

Negative Effects of Social Media on Society: Social Media and the Proliferation and Consumption of Sensationalized (Clickbait) Content

While social media can be a platform to empower its citizens toward collective action, *social media* has *also had a negative effect on society* in recent years *through the proliferation and consumption of sensationalized content*. In fact, in the article The Road to Digital Unfreedom: Three Painful Truths About Social Media, Ronald Delbert, a professor of political science at the University of Toronto, has argued that social media proliferates attention- grabbing, often emotionally-driven and divisive material, rather than multi-facetted content that present multiple viewpoints. What Delbert is describing here is often known as *clickbait*. The article Misleading Online Content: Recognizing Clickbait as "False News" defines clickbait as content whose main purpose is to *attract readers* in by *producing headlines* that are often *sensational* and *scandalous*.

It can be argued that social media websites proliferate clickbait because social media has become so pervasive in our society that we often turn to sites on social media to satisfy our impulsive curiosity to get more information about, and react to, shocking events that are unfolding before our eyes. In fact, a sensationalized article written about Malia Obama garnered *readership* from well-known celebrities and commentators, who then posted their equally provocative *reactions* on their social media pages for their followers to react to. Therefore, clickbait content is rampant on social media because it often exaggerates and scandalizes quotidian events, and turns these every-day events into the unspeakable, which satisfies our impulsive desire to get information about, and react to, the abominable. However, since clickbait content privileges itself on shocking content, rather than a principled approach to presenting pressing current issues, Delbert argues that the proliferation and the consumption of provocative content on social media is a breeding ground for individuals in positions of authority to create confusion and ignorance among the citizenry.

Perspective on Power: The Intersection Between Authority and Misinformation on Social Media

Steven Lukes, political theorist and the author of Power a Radical View, and Charles Lindbloom, the author of Policy Making Process, would *probably agree* with Ronald Delbert's view on the societal effects of social media. If we use Steven Lukes' perspective on power, which has its framework based on Karl Marx's conflict perspective, we find that *social media facilitates misinformation*. According to Steven Lukes, *individuals in positions of authority* can use *ideology to control the narrative* by exercising considerable control over what issues people choose to care about and the degree of which they care about these issues. According to Charles Lindbloom, *individuals in positions of authority* can also use *their power to divert attention and misinform the people* about their actual circumstances. Social media is *often used* as a means for individuals in positions of authority to *put out misinformation*. Misinforming the people, which, in turn, could lead to confusion and ignorance among its citizenry can *prove to be destructive*. This was on full display during the 2020 presidential election where Trump and his followers spread misinformation, *which, arguably, led to the insurrection on the Capitol in January*.

Teaching the Importance of Evidence Based Research: Fighting the Negative Societal Effects of Social Media

Given the current pandemic and the recent presidential election, my student's question points to a *bigger issue on how we fight the negative societal effects of social media*. While, Trump may be voted out of office, it is likely that there will be *other individuals* in positions of authority who will *spread misinformation* on social media which will affect the fabric of American democracy and future elections. I believe that *teaching college-aged students*, who, according to the Pew Research Center, are the primary users of social media, *the importance of evidence-based research* is a way to *fight misinformation* on social media.

The concept of evidence-based research, which is grounded in the field of healthcare, encourages us to use sound research, rather than opinion, to make decisions. In practice, evidence-based research means that we must *rely on reputable*, often peer-reviewed, studies published in scientific journals to *guide our decision making* process. In fact, a recent study conducted by Gordon Pennycook on fighting misinformation found that people with an *increase* in science knowledge and an inclination for *accuracy* had a better time *weeding out* false information about Covid-19 and had an inclination *not to share misinformation* on social media.

While evidence-based research is primarily discussed in the field of healthcare, it can be *applied to other disciplines*, especially in the *social sciences*. In addition to teaching the college level introductory sociology course, I teach a research methods course where I have students analyze secondary data to better understand what makes information both valid and reliable. Students in my research methods course are taught to recognize signs that the information they found can be systematically verified as a trustworthy source. They are taught the importance and the signs of peer reviewed and fact-checked research. Moreover, they are taught data science methodologies, such as the process of replication and using the right instrument to ensure validity, that advances verified, and trustworthy, knowledge. I use a simple example to illustrate my point on validity: you would not measure temperature using a ruler. I often ask my students if the research can be replicated and if the same or similar results can be generated. I also teach them about the importance of sample sizes, stressing that the larger the sample size the better.

As an applied sociologist, I put theory into practice. I have students in my research methods courses generate a research paper based on a review of peer-reviewed studies and data from the General Social Survey, a nationally representative database. On the whole, my students successfully complete the assignment. They are able to synthesize and use peer-reviewed studies and data from the General Social Survey to support their arguments. By making students apply their knowledge of evidence-based research, it is my hope that they will be able to rely on evidence-based research to critically analyze the truth about the articles they may come across on social media.

Conclusion: How Evidence-Based Research Can Make Social Media a Better Place

In sum, *what I wished I had said* in response to my student's question on social media and its negative effects *was that social media doesn't have to be harmful to modern society*. Social media can be a great place where we can show solidarity in times of need. While social media can be a place where misinformation is spread, we can teach current and future generations of college students the importance of evidence-based research practices as a means to *filter out* and *not share* misinformation on social media, which will hopefully make social media a better place.

Reading Questions

1. How does Chiang use the "functional perspective"—what we have called structural functionalism—to understand the role of the media (and social media)? Is this a useful theoretical perspective to use in this situation? Why or why not?
2. How is social media related to the consumption of sensationalized content? What are the impacts of this for individuals and society as a whole?
3. Does the use of social media support or undermine our ability to understand the world around us? How is it related to spreading misinformation and what are the potential implications of this?
4. How can research, such as sociological research, help us to better understand the role of social media in society? Can it be used to counter some of its negative effects?

Chiang, T., Jr. (2021, June 25). Social media in society: A positive or negative force? *Contexts: Society for the Public*. Retrieved June 12, 2023, from https://contexts.org/blog/social-media-in-society-a-positive-or-negative-force/

USING YOUR SOCIOLOGICAL IMAGINATION: REALITY AND THE METAVERSE

Technology companies have increasingly invested in a virtual world called "the metaverse." But, what is the metaverse? Although there is no consistent definition, the metaverse has been generally defined as a series of virtual reality worlds that continue to function even when the user leaves. The metaverse also includes both digital and physical worlds through platforms like gaming consoles, virtual reality headsets, and phones (Ravenscraft, 2022).

Meta, formerly known as Facebook, sees the metaverse as a future site for socializing and exercise (Ghaffary, 2021). Watch this video on the metaverse and answer the following questions: https://www.youtube.com/watch?v=rtLTZUaMSDQ

1. Describe the reporter's experience in the metaverse for 24 hours. What tasks does she do that you would usually do in person?
2. How might the metaverse facilitate social connection and building relationships? What kinds of activities would you like to do in the metaverse?
3. The reporter says that moderation will be an intense challenge for the metaverse after her experience at the virtual comedy club. What does she mean?
4. How might the metaverse facilitate cyberbullying and harassment? What could companies do to prevent this?

The Digital Divide

Internet use has increased over time. More than 90% of Americans use the Internet, a dramatic increase from the 50% who were online in 2000 (Pew Research Center, 2018). However, use of the Internet and other communication technologies is not equally distributed across all groups. The digital divide is the inequality between groups with regard to their access to information and communication technologies and to their use of such technologies. The divide within a country occurs between individuals, households, geographic areas, and socioeconomic levels. The divide between countries, referred to as the global digital divide, measures the gap between the digital access and use of technologies across countries.

Remote learning during the COVID-19 pandemic further exposed America's digital divide. Some students did not have access to digital devices and reliable Internet. How might differences in access to the Internet further educational inequalities after students returned to in-person learning?

triloks/iStockPhoto

Age is a major dimension of the digital divide in the United States. People between the ages of 18 and 49 are almost universally online, with 99% having access to the Internet. And, although 96% of people from age 50 to age 64 are also connected, connection rates among those over 65 are quite low. In fact, only 75% of seniors have access to the Internet (Pew Research Center, 2021).

There is also a strong urban/rural digital divide. Although 89% of people who live in urban centers in America are connected to the Internet, only 80% of those in rural areas are online (Vogels, 2021). This is in part due to the lower level of Internet connectivity in rural areas and the difficulty of accessing high-speed Internet outside urban centers.

Finally, and perhaps most significantly, there is a large digital divide between the richest and poorest Americans. Although 99% of Americans who earn more than $75,000 a year are connected to the Internet, only 86% of those making $30,000 or less have this access (Pew Research Center, 2021). This could be true, in part, because of the relationship between income and education. College graduates are almost universally connected (98%), whereas those with less than a high school diploma have only a 65% rate of Internet access (Pew Research Center, 2018).

As illustrated in Figure 7.1, the digital divide is much more extreme across countries. Although the United States, Europe, and Australia have almost universal access to computers and Internet technology (from 80–100% of all citizens), many areas of Africa and Asia have connection levels lower than 20%.

The digital divide has important consequences, both within the United States and around the world. First, it creates unequal access to information. For example, in countries with limited access, schools must rely on expensive books that quickly become outdated instead of using Internet resources that are cheaper and more current. Access to the Internet and computers can also enable people to learn computer skills that are useful for employment and job training. Second, Internet access is important for commerce. Businesses with online access can sell their products to a larger group of people. Consumers with Internet access can purchase a larger variety

FIGURE 7.1 ■ Population Using the Internet, 2020

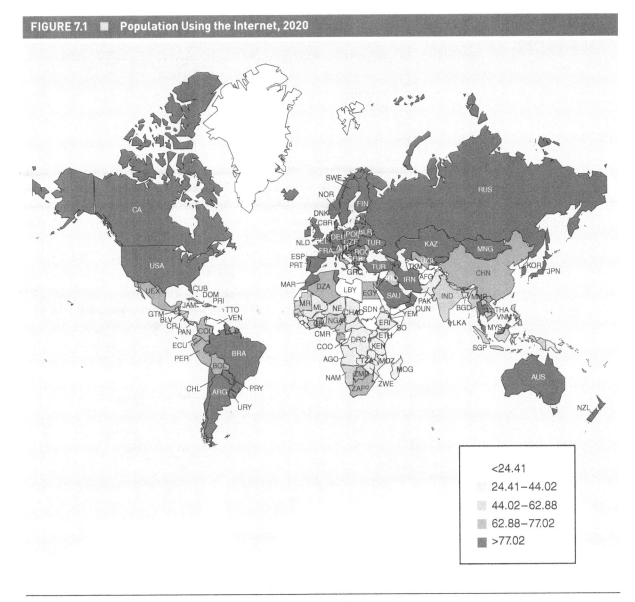

	<24.41
	24.41–44.02
	44.02–62.88
	62.88–77.02
	>77.02

Source: The World Bank, https://data.worldbank.org/indicator/IT.NET.USER.ZS? type=shaded&view=map

of products, usually for less money, than those who can access only local businesses. Third, the Internet can be an important social outlet for people. For certain groups of Americans, such as the elderly, people living in rural areas, and those who have lower incomes, the lack of access can reduce feelings of social connection with others. Finally, the Internet can provide important means of political organizing. Especially in countries with nondemocratic political regimes, the Internet can provide access to information that the government might censor. It can also provide a way of organizing people into activism.

How do we address these significant inequalities? One way is through organizations such as Close the Gap (2020), an international nonprofit organization that "aims to bridge the digital divide by offering high-quality, pre-owned computers donated by European companies to educational, medical, and social projects in developing and emerging countries." The organization also works with local groups to bring software and training to recipients.

MEDIA EFFECTS

The media has many important potential benefits. It helps to spread information, connects people, and is useful for education and trade. However, the vast spread of mass media also presents a number of challenges. Through media literacy and alternative media, we can all become more educated consumers of media messages.

Media Literacy

In light of the serious implications of the media in the socialization process, many critics have argued that we should increase media literacy in an effort to regain control over our media consumption. Media literacy is an educational tool that helps individuals analyze and evaluate the messages they receive from the media. It works to empower people to examine and think more critically about the media messages they receive.

Media literacy programs can take place in schools, online, or at community centers. Even a parent who watches television with his or her child and talks critically about what they are seeing engages in media literacy training. There are three main stages in media literacy education. First, you must become aware of your media diet—the media that you consume. It is obvious to think about the television shows that you watch, the radio that you listen to, or the Internet news you read. However, it is also important to consider the more incidental media to which you are exposed—billboards on the street, advertisements on Google, or radio in the background at a store.

The second stage is to learn specific skills of critical viewing, which requires you to analyze both what is shown on television and what is left out. Perhaps you notice that the TV shows you watch feature a lot of upper-class characters and that very few poor or homeless characters are depicted. Or perhaps you notice a lot of White lead characters but few characters from other racial or ethnic groups in the movies you watch.

Finally, media literacy pushes you to question what is behind the media and why certain messages are relayed while others are not. For example, TV shows might focus on upper-class characters because producers think that audience members will find them more interesting and compelling. But seeing so many upper-class characters also distorts our idea of how much money most people in society have, what regular jobs and careers are, and what we should aspire to be. Seeing so many extremely thin women or muscular men on television might distort our idea of beauty and a regular or normal body shape. This can have severe implications for individual self-esteem and lead to eating disorders and other health issues. By thinking critically about who produces the media for what purpose and who benefits from media images, we can better understand what we see. This comprehension can help individuals to be more critical about the media messages they receive.

Alternative Media

As we have discussed in this chapter, one major concern with media concentration is a potential decline in the diversity of perspectives available to consumers. One way to address this issue is alternative media, which provides "alternative information to the mainstream media in a given context, whether the mainstream media are commercial, publicly supported, or government-owned" (Atton, 2002). Blogs, podcasts, community- or student-run newspapers, public broadcasting radio and television stations, and pirate stations are examples of alternative media.

Alternative media is defined by four main characteristics. First, the message is not corporately controlled and is not based on a profit motive because alternative media is nonprofit. Second, the message's content tends to be antiestablishment, subversive, and change-centered. Third, alternative media is usually distributed in a creative way, focusing on being visually appealing and interesting. Finally, the relationship between the producer and consumer is fundamentally different in alternative media compared with traditional or corporate media. In the latter case, media is unidirectional—consumers simply receive the message, but they do not have the opportunity to shape it. Alternative media has a two-way relationship: Consumers can comment on and shape the media they consume. Alternative media, then, provides an interesting way to exert power and control over the media messages and content you receive.

USING YOUR SOCIOLOGICAL IMAGINATION
MISINFORMATION AND MEDIA LITERACY

Misinformation, or the spread of false information, has become a growing problem in the United States and around the world. How can we know whether information we see on the Internet or television is real? To distinguish real stories from fake ones, The Guardian Foundation suggests we ask ourselves the following questions:

1. Who is sharing the story? Are they trustworthy? Have you heard of them before?

2. Who else is reporting on this? What are they saying? Look out for fake news clue words (e.g., hoax, satire, fictitious, parody, fact-check, myth, false).

Now read the following stories. One of the stories is real and contains accurate information. The other story is fake and contains significant misrepresentations. See if you can spot the fake.

Article 1

15,000 Pounds of Delicious Hot Dog Filler Spill in Highway Crash: *Vice*
    https://www.vice.com/en/article/n7n8yw/15000-pounds-of-delicious-hot-dog-filler-spill-in-highway-crash

Article 2

Theme Parks in California Ban Screaming Because of COVID-19: *New York Post*
    https://nypost.com/2021/03/17/no-screaming-on-roller-coasters-under-californias-covid-19-plan/
    Now answer the questions below:

1. Which story do you think is true and which story do you think is fake? How did you arrive at this conclusion?
2. Make a list of news sources that you consider reliable. Why do you trust these sources? What kinds of practices do you think that reliable news sources should adhere to?
3. A friend sends you an article about a new pandemic spreading across the United States. Step by step, how do you decide whether the article is credible? What other sources could you consult to verify the article's contents?

Activity adapted and credited to The Guardian Foundation (2021). https://theguardianfoundation.org/programmes/behind-the-headlines/media-literacy-resources-send-students#fake-or-real-workshop

SUMMARY

Language is everywhere—without it you could not even read this book! We began this chapter by examining the importance of language and how language shapes thought and is shaped by culture. These connections were illustrated by examining racist terms in the English language. The chapter then discussed the mass media's role as a mode of communication. We looked at the evolution of the media, using Marshall McLuhan's famous idea that "the medium is the message," and we discussed the rise in corporate concentration and its effects on the diversity of ideas available to us as consumers of the media. C. Wright Mills's concept of the power elite illuminated how an increasingly small group of people holds power in the major political, military, and corporate institutions of society. This chapter also examined the rising importance of new media and social media, the digital divide, the need for media literacy, and alternative media.

FOR FURTHER READING

Chomsky, N., & Herman, E. S. (2002). *Manufacturing consent: The political economy of the mass media*, Pantheon Books.

McLuhan, M. (1964). *Understanding media: The extensions of man*, McGraw Hill.

Mills, C. W. (1956). *The power elite*, Oxford University Press.

Whorf, B. (1956). *Language, thought, and reality: Selected writings of Benjamin Lee Whorf*, MIT Press.

GLOSSARY

alternative media

corporate concentration

cyberbullying

demographic diversity

digital divide

honorifics

idea diversity

mass media

media

media literacy

the medium is the message

new media

power elite

Sapir-Whorf hypothesis

social media

8 THE FAMILY AND INTIMATE RELATIONSHIPS

LEARNING OBJECTIVES

1. Define the various forms of families and examine the different ways that they can be composed, including nuclear and extended families.

2. Assess the major changes that have occurred in marriage and families and the larger social causes of these changes.

3. Compare how the major sociological theories, particularly structural functionalism and conflict theory, study the family.

4. Assess the role of intimate relationships and the changing nature of dating in modern society.

One challenge that sociologists face is trying to make sense of things with which we are very familiar but might not have examined critically. As discussed in Chapter 1, Peter Berger (1963) argued that sociology helps us see the general in the particular and the strange in the familiar. Each of us has a lifetime of experiences in society, including experiences of a particular family context. From all these experiences, we begin to generalize about how families function. However, sometimes this familiarity can be a challenge; it can be quite difficult to study an institution such as the family because it is all around us. We also all have a very particular experience of family life—your family surely shares some features with your friends' families, but the families are probably different as well. If you compare your family with others you see on television, in the news, or in the larger community, you probably notice even starker differences.

In this chapter we will examine the family in a larger comparative perspective. We will also examine the intimate relationships that often form the foundation of families. How do we find and select mates and how might mate selection be changing over time? We will also assess the major changes that are happening to the family and the functions of the family in society. By taking a step back from our own experiences, we can begin to understand the role of intimate relationships and the family in society.

WHAT ARE FAMILIES?

A family is a group of people related by birth, affinity, or cohabitation. Families clearly differ radically from one another, and what people think of as a family has changed over time and differs across countries. In general, we think of an individual's family household as a group of people living together who share a relationship by blood, marriage, or legal adoption. Marriage is the legal union of two people. A nuclear family consists of two adults living with one or more children. An extended family moves beyond the nuclear family and consists of more than two generations who share the same residence.

USING YOUR SOCIOLOGICAL IMAGINATION
COMEDY AND THE TV FAMILY

Society has many stereotypes about men's and women's roles in romantic relationships and as parents. Think of the jokes you have heard about husbands and wives. Here are a few examples:

How many men does it take to change a roll of toilet paper? *Who knows? It hasn't happened yet!*

What do you instantly know about a well-dressed man? *His wife is good at picking out clothes.*

I married Miss Right. I just didn't know her first name was "Always."

I haven't spoken to my wife for 18 months: *I don't like to interrupt her.*

You might not have heard these specific (very bad) jokes. However, the general themes of these and similar jokes—that husbands and fathers are lazy and unable to do anything for themselves and that wives are bossy and nagging—are part of the overarching repertoire of how we understand men's and women's roles in relationships and families. You do not typically hear, for example, a joke about wives being lazy or men nagging.

Think about television shows such as Leave It to Beaver, The Brady Bunch, The Cosby Show, Roseanne, Gilmore Girls, Black-ish, This Is Us, Malcolm in the Middle, and Modern Family. (If you have not seen some of these shows, watch some clips on YouTube or read about the show on Wikipedia.) As you answer the following questions, keep in mind how jokes may be used to perpetuate and exaggerate stereotypes of gendered roles in the family.

1. How have depictions of the family changed? How did the earliest show on our list (*Leave It to Beaver*) depict the role of spouses and their relationship with their children? How does this show portray the functions of the family and the role of the family in society?

2. How did later shows (*The Brady Bunch*, *The Cosby Show*, and *Roseanne*) challenge some earlier depictions of the family? How are these challenges related to our changing ideas of gender norms and family relationships in society?

3. How do the most recent shows (*Gilmore Girls*, *Black-ish*, *This Is Us*, and *Modern Family*) further expand or change our perception of the role of spouses and parents in society? How do these shows reflect the times in which they are made? Are these positive reflections of the family today?

4. What shows do you watch that depict a positive view of the family and spousal relationships? What shows have negative depictions? What are the larger social implications of television shows presenting families in these ways?

The Changing Family

The American family is undergoing some widespread changes, as illustrated in Figure 8.1. These trends reflect a changing set of norms and expectations surrounding the family, particularly marriage and having children, in modern American society. Note the decline in the proportion of married households, from a high of about 78% in the early 1940s to less than 50% of all households today.

Andrew Cherlin (2004) argues that modern society is characterized by the deinstitutionalization of marriage, a process in which our understanding of the norms and rules surrounding marriage are changing, and people are increasingly questioning the role of marriage in their lives and in society (see also Cherlin, 2010). Cherlin argues that there are five main ways that marriage is becoming deinstitutionalized.

1. Fewer people are getting married because they are choosing to remain single or to cohabitate (i.e., same-sex or opposite-sex couples who live together without being legally married). Cohabitation gained popularity in the 1970s, and the rate of cohabitation has accelerated into the 21st century.

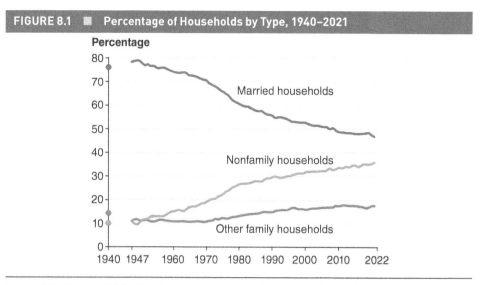

FIGURE 8.1   ■   Percentage of Households by Type, 1940–2021

Source: U.S. Census, 1940–2021, https://www.census.gov/content/dam/Census/library/visualizations/time-series/demo/families-and-households/hh-1.pdf

2. The roles of individuals in couples (married or not) have become increasingly questioned in modern society. The movement of women into the labor force in larger numbers has changed our conceptions about the way that labor should be divided within the home. We no longer simply assume that women will be homemakers and men will be breadwinners. Because there are more women working outside the home and more men staying home to raise children, the traditional gender roles in marriage are questioned. Our basic understanding of what men and women do in a relationship is blurring, leading to a lack of clarity about how marriages and the family work in modern society. This increased flexibility of gender roles in marriages can lead to a greater diversity of family arrangements, including the rise of one-parent families and same-sex marriages.

3. Norms about having children have also changed. In the past, it was socially acceptable to have children only within a marriage. Today, many people are single parents and many unmarried couples have children. Furthermore, more people choose to remain childless, even when married.

4. Divorce rates were at an all-time high in 1970 and have declined since this time. This is, in part, because there has been a declining rate of marriage since 1970. Divorce challenges the idea that individuals should remain married "till death do us part"— even if they are unhappy or the relationship is abusive. There is a general declining stigma associated with divorce and a waning of religious influences that traditionally prohibited this step.

5. There is a rising diversity in the forms of marriages in modern society. With the rise of marriages between couples from different ethnic, racial, religious, and class backgrounds, couples are becoming increasingly diverse (see Figure 8.2).

The number of mixed unions in the United States, in which partners belong to different racial groups, has increased over time. In 1960, less than 4% of couples were in mixed unions. There are a variety of reasons for this, including the fact that many states had laws restricting the

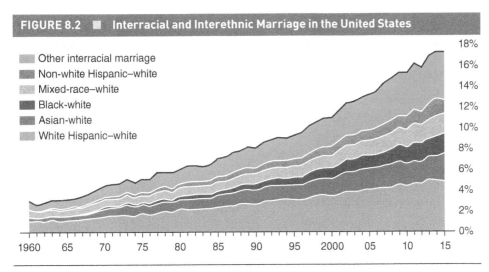

FIGURE 8.2 ■ Interracial and Interethnic Marriage in the United States

Legend:
- Other interracial marriage
- Non-white Hispanic–white
- Mixed-race–white
- Black-white
- Asian-white
- White Hispanic–white

Source: Chalabi, Mona. "What's behind the rise of interracial marriage in the US?" *The Guardian.* 21 February 2018.

rights of people from different racial groups to marry. In 1967, the U.S. Supreme Court struck down all state laws banning interracial marriage in the landmark decision of *Loving v. Virginia*. By 2017, 17% of marriages were between people from different racial groups. In fact, the number of mixed unions doubled between 2004 and 2019. The legalization of same-sex marriage in the United States, which was declared in the Supreme Court decision in *Obergefell v. Hodges* in 2015, further added to the diversity of the institution of marriage.

LARGER SOCIAL CHANGES THAT IMPACT THE FAMILY

Changes in marriage and families can be tied to many larger social changes. As we have already seen, the rise of women's rights is a major change in American society. This movement accounts for rising rates of college enrollment and graduation among women and increasing numbers of women in the paid workforce. These changes, in turn, are associated with lower rates of marriage, later age at the birth of a first child, and a higher divorce rate. Divorce, for example, is much more likely among women who work outside the home.

Our society is also becoming increasingly tolerant of diversity. This development partly explains the rise of marriages between people from different racial, ethnic, or religious backgrounds. This more-inclusive ideology in modern society was also a factor in the mobilization that led to legalizing same-sex marriage.

Another major change that has affected the family is the declining levels of religiosity in the United States and other Western nations, which was discussed in Chapter 1. Religions are generally strong supporters of a traditional view of marriage and childrearing. With the decline of religiosity in a society, we tend to see higher rates of cohabitation without marriage, more children raised by unmarried parents, and a rise in divorce rates.

Finally, modern society is characterized by a rising tide of individualism. Thus, we are more concerned with individual happiness and fulfillment than we were in the past. In the United States, most people select jobs and romantic partners based on their own interests and preferences. Young people usually resist the idea that they are simply expected to perform the same job as their parents or that their parents will select their mate for them. This surge in individualism occurred at the same time that religion's power over individuals was waning; both trends have radically altered our ideas about the nature of marriage.

The Changing Role of Marriage Over Time

Historically, marriage was seen as a way to bind larger families and communities. Institutional marriages have a collective focus; that is, they focus on how a marriage will solidify ties between families and communities and so benefit society. Think about how spouses were selected historically in royal families: No one cared whether a prince and princess from different countries liked one another or would fall in love. All that mattered was that the marriage would lead to a coalition between their countries. Institutional marriages are about the needs of society, not the individuals' need to be happy and fulfilled (Wilcox & Nock, 2006).

Over time, people began to think that marriages should be based on emotional bonds and sexual ties. Companionate marriages make a clear division of labor between breadwinner (usually the husband) and the homemaker (usually the wife). Husbands and wives are expected to be one another's companions. They are friends and confidants who need and rely on one another to perform the roles that they cannot. In companionate marriages, romantic love is very important (Wilcox & Nock, 2006). These relationships are based on the satisfaction of the couple, the family, and the roles the couple plays within the family.

Some couples choose to live apart together (LAT). This means that the couple has separate households but maintains a committed relationship. How do these couples embody individualized marriages?

mechichi/iStockPhoto

Lauer and Yodanis (2011) argue that we now live in a time of individualized marriages. These marriages are focused on each spouse's satisfaction and ability to develop and express his or her sense of self, happiness, and fulfillment. Individualized marriages tend to be more flexible than the other types described because they attempt to meet the varied needs of individual spouses. Despite these challenges to traditional ideas of marriage and the rise of individualized marriages, most people still get married at some point in their lives.

READING: FROM *GETTING MARRIED: THE PUBLIC NATURE OF OUR PRIVATE RELATIONSHIPS*

Carrie Yodanis and Sean Lauer

In the following chapter from *Getting Married*, Yodanis and Lauer unpack why people marry in modern society. They focus on how many explanations of why we marry are now very individualistic, focusing on the needs and desires of individuals instead of the social group. When you are reading this excerpt, consider how larger social structures and changes shape our very personal decisions about intimate relationships and marriage.

What About Love?

The social constraints encouraging us to marry are hard to see. We rarely think about them. Instead, we continue to think about marriage as a personal and private relationship. When people are asked why they got married, love is the number one reason given, with over 90 percent of married people saying that love is a very important reason for marriage.[1] But, as we will argue here, even love is not personal and private. Rather, it is the socially acceptable motive to give for marriage. It is part of the rules, expectations, and taken-for-granted assumptions of marriage.

Sociologists have argued that the motives people give for what they do are shaped by external expectations and constraints. And like behaviors themselves, certain motives are considered socially acceptable and expected. Only some motives are defined as legitimate for given situations and at certain points in time. Others are not. We use the acceptable motives to explain and justify our behaviors, regardless of our actual reasons for behavior, because when we do, our behavior is accepted.[2]

Today, individualized motives are socially acceptable in the United States.[3] Americans cherish the ability to act on their own as individuals— to succeed or fail on their own terms. Americans believe in individual choice and individual responsibility for the choices they make. Americans, as compared to people from other cultures, are more likely to believe that they have choice and control over their situations, even to the point of believing they have more choice than they actually have.[4] Researchers asked American and Japanese students to list all of the choices they made the day before. The American students reported that they made 50 percent more choices than the Japanese students reported, although their days were actually quite similar. During another study, Eastern European participants were asked to choose between seven sodas. The Eastern European participants responded that they had no choice—they were all soda. In comparison, Americans saw choice in objectively similar options. In products such as bottled water and makeup, we believe we have choice. In the end, however, "though we may feel steeped in variety, we actually have far fewer qualitatively different options than we realize."[5] Yet it is important for us to believe that we have choice in order to believe that we are acting as free individuals. As one author wrote in a book on sexual relationships,

> Of all the convictions that govern sexual conduct in the secular West, perhaps the most important is that there *are* no longer any rules. To suggest otherwise is to challenge the very fabric of how we perceive ourselves: as free, self-actualized individuals carving out our destinies from a sea of limitless options.[6]

Love is the primary socially acceptable motive for marriage. It is a motive that empha-sizes personal choice and freedom. People say they are marrying because they want to, because they are in love. But love is not merely a personal feeling. It is part of the rules and expectations of marriage. When people say that they are marrying because they are in love and are soul mates, the decision to marry and the quality of the marriage are accepted and unchallenged. Other motivations, particular those related to constraints, lead to questions and concerns. For example, these were the vows imagined by Dev, Aziz Ansari's character in his show, *Master of None*:

> Rachel, I'm . . . not 100% sure about this. Are you the one person that I'm supposed to be with forever? I don't f*cking know. And what's the other option? We break up? That seems shitty too. And I love you. I do . . . I don't know, I guess . . . getting married just is a safer bet at this point. [sighs] Sorry, I was just thinking about other paths my life could have taken.
>
> Dev, you're a great guy. You really are. But you're right. Are we supposed to be together forever? [inhales sharply] I don't know. And I've basically invested two of my prime years with you, so I should just go all in. That's just math. So let's do this. Quickly.
>
> Do you, Dev, take Rachel to be your partner in a possibly outdated institution in order to have a "normal" life? Are you ready to give up an idealistic search for a soul mate and try to make it work with Rachel so you can move forward with your life?
>
> I do.
>
> And do you, Rachel, promise to make a crazy eternal bond with this gentleman who you happen to be dating at this stage in your life when people normally get married?
>
> I do.
>
> I now pronounce you two people who might realize they've made an unfortunate mistake in about three years.[7]

Imagine if these were real vows at a wedding. The celebratory atmosphere of the wed-ding would quickly turn sour, and guests may regret giving gifts to the now perceived-to-be unhappy couple. In fact, it can even be considered fraud to marry without love. For example, it is illegal to marry someone for the purpose of immigrating to the country, and so immi-gration officers search for proof of love between partners before approving the visa of an immigrating spouse.[8]

When we use love as a motive for marriage and an explanation for when and whom we marry, we downplay or dismiss the constraints, rules, and expectations that shape our behavior. Instead, we emphasize individual choice. We marry because we are in love, we explain, not because marriage is required by the government and the church, or because of social pressure from your grandmother, or because of the risk and uncertainty of ending up 40 and not married. Instead, we claim it is all about love. Yet the rules, expectations, pres-sures, and constraints are still there, shaping and guiding what we do—even the motive we give for getting married.

In the book *Talk of Love,* a sociologist studied how couples talk about love. She found that people hold onto and discuss romantic notions of love despite the fact that they see these ideas as largely myths and unrealistic to their own marriages. The romantic love persists, the author concluded, because it helps us to act within the constraints of marriage, "recast-ing them as matters of individual volition."[9]

The mythic, romantic love, common in popular culture, is based on the idea that love is obvious and sure. It involves the idea that love can happen "at first sight," that there is "one true love" for everyone, that love can "conquer anything," and that love lasts and a couple can "live happily ever after." The concept of the "soul mate" is rooted in these ideas of romantic love.[10]

These ideas of romantic love persist, the author argued, because they parallel the rules and expectations of marriage and help us to make the otherwise overwhelming decision to marry. Marriage is a daunting thing to do. Think about it for a minute. You are supposed to select, from all of the people out there, only one person to marry. You are supposed to be married to this person for the rest of your life. Yet nearly everyone makes the decision to get married and about whom to marry in a relatively short period of their lives. People use cultural ideas of romantic love to make the decision and action of getting married easier. We tell ourselves that we know that we have successfully found our soul mate—our one true love. Our love will endure and will help us overcome challenges that come along, and we will be happy together for the rest of our lives. Telling ourselves these things, based on the notion of romantic love, helps us to enter marriage, with its requirements, in what would otherwise be an overwhelming act:

> The love myth answers that question, "What do I need to feel about someone in order to marry [commit myself to] him or her?" . . . In order to marry, individuals must develop certain cultural, psychological, and even cognitive equipment. They must be prepared to feel, or at least convince others that they feel, that one other person is the uniquely right "one."[11]

By this point, you may be thinking that sociologists aren't a romantic group of folks. We wouldn't say that, overall. Like everyone, sociologists feel and express love with intimate partners. They just also critically examine the context in which this love is felt and expressed. It may be best to describe sociologists as analytically romantic, which adds a whole new interesting dimension to love!

Notes

1. Pew Research Center 2010.
2. Mills 1959.
3. Bellah, Madsen, Sullivan, Swidler, and Tiption 1985; Cherlin 2009; Wuthnow 1991.
4. Iyengar 2010.
5. Iyengar 2010, p. 156.
6. Hills 2015, p. 57.
7. Master of None 2015.
8. Satzewich 2014.
9. Swidler 2001, p. 118.
10. Swidler 2001.
11. Swidler 2001, pp. 130–31.

Thinking About Change

In 1972, Jessie Bernard, a sociologist, predicted that the future of marriage would be a range of possible marriages. Anything would be possible, she wrote. Traditional marriages would continue, but they would exist alongside marriages which included

- No children
- More than two spouses
- Open sexual relationships
- A "free-wheeling" emphasis on spouses' individuality and independence, including partial commitment, maintaining separate households, and having "weekend marriages."
- "Temporary permanent" relationships, in which couples would outline how long the marriage would last and opt for an extension if desired.

In other words, Bernard predicted there would not be an established way to be married. Rather, people would be free to develop their relationships as they see fit and "tailor them to their circumstances and preferences."[1]

Social scientists, in a range of fields, have argued that essentially this future has arrived. For example, a psychologist wrote an interesting book, *The Paradox of Choice*, about the problems of having too much choice. His basic argument is that when people are faced with too many choices, they end up being dissatisfied with any choice they make or become unable to make a choice at all. He used a wide list of examples, including choice in salad dressing, phone plans, health care, and jam. He also highlighted relationships as an example of increasing choice. He wrote,

> In the past, the "default" options were so powerful, and dominant that few perceived themselves to be making choices. The anomalous few who departed from the pattern were seen as social renegades, subjects of gossip and speculation. These days, it's hard to figure out what kind of romantic choice would warrant such attention. Wherever we look, we see almost every imaginable arrangement of intimate relations. Today, all romantic possibilities are on the table; all choices are real.[2]

In other words, he concluded that there are no longer established ideas about how relationships "should" be and so people need to constantly make choices about what kind of relationship they want.

Even some sociologists have argued that people are free from social constraints in the modern world because social rules and expectations have weakened.[3] As a result, individuals can and indeed must figure out for themselves how best to organize their love lives and relationships. Now is the era of "do-it-yourself" biographies, they say. Anything is possible. Everything is acceptable. Again, the choices are unlimited. As one author noted,

> Of all the dreams today's young Westerners are sold about what our lives could look like, the biggest is that we have limitless opportunities, that we are free to pursue whatever work, relationships, and ways of being we like.[4]

Other sociologists have been critical of this idea.[5] Indeed, at its core, sociology focuses on how individuals can't and don't act completely independently of social forces. The sociological imagination involves understanding that an individual's experiences are shaped by the time and place within which their experiences occur. Put another way, there is a connection between private or individual troubles and public or social issues.[6] Take the example of marital problems and divorce rates. When a couple is constantly arguing, they experience that as a private problem. If divorce rates are high, however, that is a public issue. The marital problems of the couple and the divorce rate are linked. A couple who is constantly arguing may divorce, but only if they live in a time and place in which the social rules make divorce a possible and likely outcome of marital problems. Historically, there have been significant jumps in divorce rates right after laws were changed to make it easier to get a divorce. This does not mean that all of a sudden, once divorce laws changed, couples no longer got along. Rather, prior to changes in divorce laws, couples could argue all the time but could not divorce because getting a divorce was hard to do. External social forces shape what people do in their most private relationships. As we saw in this book, this holds true not just for marital troubles but for all kinds of marital behaviors, including selecting a partner, getting engaged, and having children.

We are not the first to make this point. Many others have made this same argument for a long time.[7] However, this point often gets lost in the emphasis on individual choice and freedom. As one author described it, the "shell" of marriage may have changed giving us, in theory, the potential to be more creative in our lives and relationships,

> yet the soul of marriage—its dreams, conscience, ethics, and rules— hasn't necessarily evolved to keep up. Instead we follow viscerally many of the same premises and orthodoxies as our parents, as if marriage is a Procrustean structure to which we must conform ourselves, rather than the other way around.[8]

People do decide how to act. But these decisions and actions never happen in isolation. Every person is surrounded by other people within a society, and people together create the social forces, processes, structures, rules, and expectations that are the contexts within which each individual person acts. Individuals have agency to act, but any action does not emerge purely from within an individual. Rather action is an outcome of the individual's interaction with the social world, including the rules, opportunities, and constraints that are built into a society. Individual action is never wholly determined by social structures, but at the same time, the individual, necessarily a part of society, can never act completely free of their social context. We are all actors acting within social contexts, which guide, shape, and limit our behaviors. Even when an individual goes against the social rules, breaks down social barriers, or leads a social movement to dramatic change, social rules still shape how they behave, including the need to react against the rules and expectations.

There are people who forge their own paths and are exceptions to the general patterns. This is certainly true today and has always been in the past. The book *Uncommon Arrangements*, for example, documents the creative living and loving arrangements of some couples between 1910 and 1939. These couples had open sexual relationships and same- and opposite-sex partners, welcomed friends and lovers into their families and households, had children with lovers, and lived oceans apart, often maintaining caring and loving relationships with each other all the while.[9]

Another book, *Spinster*, discusses two terms that described women who didn't marry more than 100 years ago. In 1895, the term "bachelor girl," discussed in a *Vogue* column of the same name, referred to a woman who lived alone and supported herself by getting an education and having a career. Around the same time, the term "new woman" also referred to independent, self-sufficient, and sexual women who were pursuing careers. As one man described in a letter to his mother in 1898,

> There is a girl in N.Y. who has been much more to me than any other girl I ever knew. We are not engaged and it is practically sure that we never shall be. She is a "new woman," ambitious and energetic, a hard worker . . . she has no idea of getting married, at any rate to me.[10]

There have always been people who have done things differently. Nonetheless, doing something different can require managing ongoing disapproval from family, neighbors, friends, coworkers, and strangers. And even if some individuals do not follow the social rules and expectations, the rules and expectations are likely to persist— constraining and shaping the behaviors of others—despite the actions of these individuals.

Social rules, expectations, and assumptions do change and evolve over time. Individuals create the rules and so they can change them. Marriage is not exactly the same as it was 100 years ago or 50 years ago. This is because the rules and expectations for how to have relationships shifted, as did patterns in marital behaviors.

Yet as the rules and expectations change, this does not mean that rules and expectations completely disappear. Instead, new rules and expectations replace old ones. Change does not mean anything goes. It means that something else goes.

We can think about our relationships following trends.[11] There are trends in nearly all parts of relationships. Dating trends change over time, including the order in which couples go to dinner and have sex. Even what a couple does on a date is shaped by trends. The age when people marry follows trends. And there are trends regarding how couples act in marriage. Having separate bedrooms, a practice that was recently called a new trend, is not new at all, but was practiced in the past. When we are living in a particular moment and place, with particular rules, we tend to follow these rules and be on trend. In another time or place, with different rules, we would follow those trends and behave differently.

It is often easy to get caught up in and fixate on the change, missing the larger picture. The story of change is exciting. Change can appear to be quite large and dramatic. It elicits shock and surprise, exciting news headlines, and juicy gossip.

But the story of change has two parts. The first part asks, what do people do differently? The second part asks, what most people continue to do? As we discussed earlier, people are marrying later today and are less likely to marry today than in the past, but the vast majority of people still marry at some point in their lives.[12] Interracial marriages are more common now than in past decades, but the vast majority of marriages are still between couples of the same racial background.[13] Cohabitation has increased dramatically since the 1970s, but the vast majority of couples in the United States are still married rather than cohabiting.[14] There is unquestionably change in marriage. Yet the majority of people continue to do things the same way.

Also, change over time is not always in a clear direction. Whether looking at the age of first marriage, the proportion of people who marry, or childlessness, change ebbs and flows over time. Behaviors increase and decrease, rates go up and down, practices go back and forth rather than going in a straight line toward a clear direction.[15] For example, women and men were *older* when they married in 1890 than they were in 1950.[16] *More* women and men *never* married in 1920 than in 1980.[17] Women born in 1910 were *more likely* to be childless than women born in 1960.[18]

Marriage is changing today, but marriage has always changed. For example, in what year do you think this statement was made? "A woman may now refuse to marry at all, and earn her own living in singleness." Answer: 1891.[19] In other words, more than 100 years ago, there was talk of change in the institution of marriage—change that actually seems a lot like the change we talk about now. In 100 years from now, what will we think of the quotes made about marriage today?

Notes

1. Bernard 1972, p. 302.
2. Schwartz 2004, pp. 38–9.
3. Beck and Beck-Gernsheim 2002; Cherlin 2004; Giddens 1992.
4. Hills 2015, p. 49.
5. Gross 2005; Jamieson 1999; Lauer and Yodanis 2010; Smart and Shipman 2004.
6. Mills 1959.
7. Baker 2014; Eekelaar 2007; Heaphy, Smart, and Einarsdottir 2013; Kingston 2004; Manfield and Collard 1988; Smith 1993; among many others, included those cited throughout this book.
8. Haag 2011, p. 100.
9. Roiphe 2007.
10. Bolick 2015, p. 100.
11. Aspers and Godart 2013.
12. Goldstein and Kenny 2001; Manning, Brown, and Payne 2014.
13. Rosenfeld 2007; Taylor, Wang, Parker, Passel, Patter, and Motel 2012.
14. U.S. Census Bureau 2014.
15. Yodanis and Lauer 2014.
16. Elliott, Krivickas, Brault, and Kreider 2012; Fitch and Ruggles 2000.
17. Elliott et al. 2012; Fitch and Ruggles 2000.
18. Kirmeyer and Hamilton 2011.
19. Campbell 1891; Smock 2004.

Reading Questions

1. What is the role of romantic love in modern relationships? How is this role related to our perceptions of individualism and individual choice in American society?

2. What sorts of constraints exist on our ability to form any kind of marriage or intimate relationship that we would like? Are there rules, expectations, or norms that limit our freedoms in these relationships?

3. How have the constraints on marriage and other intimate relationships changed over time and how do they differ across countries? What are the positive and negative implications of these changes?

4. How can we see problems within marriage (such as divorce, abuse, or other issues) as personal troubles or public issues? How does defining these problems as personal troubles or public issues change how we might want to deal with them?

Yodanis, C., & Lauer, S. (2017). *Getting married: The public nature of our private relationships*. Routledge. pp. 28–31 and 67–71.

THEORIZING THE FAMILY

Our ideas about the family depend, to a large extent, on the theoretical perspective we use to understand it. Two theoretical traditions used to explain the family's role in society are structural functionalism and conflict theory, theories that we discuss throughout this book. Each approach paints a very different picture of the family's role in and impact on modern society.

During the pandemic, some families combined to create pandemic "pods" or "bubbles," to socialize safely with members outside their households. How do these configurations challenge the nuclear family model?

Nes/iStockPhoto

Structural Functionalists and the Role of the Family

Structural functionalists focus on the functions of the family and the ways families can help create stability and order in society. From a structural functionalist perspective, the family performs a wide variety of important functions that fall into four main categories: reproduction, socialization, support, and regulation. In terms of reproduction, families help maintain the population by having and raising children. Families also care for children's physical and emotional needs. The essential process of socializing children into the larger culture and teaching them the norms and rules of society begins in the family. Families are also important because they can share resources. Parents support children when they are young and sometimes when they are adults; children often support parents in their old age. Families work to regulate behavior as well. For example, the family traditionally helps to control sexual behavior. This function might be declining as more people engage in sexual activity before and outside marriage.

Talcott Parsons was instrumental in developing structural functionalist theory in the 1950s and 1960s (Parsons & Bales, 1955). He argued that the nuclear family was very important (particularly for American society, where his research was based) because its structure frees individuals from the obligations of an extended family. The nuclear family gives individuals in family units the mobility needed in industrial society, where people often must move to a new town or across state lines to find work. It is much easier to move nuclear families because they do not involve the same close ties to extended families and the need to consider those family members in one's life plans. Parsons also argued that the nuclear family system works well to distinguish clearly between the expressive roles of women and the instrumental roles of men (Kimmel, 2011).

Getting to Know: Talcott Parsons (1902–1979)

- Parsons's interest in structural functional theory is often traced to his undergraduate coursework in biology, evolutionary theory, and physiology at Amherst College.

- Parsons published more than 10 books and as many as 100 essays during his lifetime.

- He was rarely satisfied with his own writing and would often significantly revise and extend his original ideas in subsequent drafts of his scholarship.

- In 1949 he served as president of the American Sociology Society (now the American Sociological Association).

The structural functionalist perspective on the family acknowledges the important functions the family performs for individuals and society. All societies are based on family units that provide important resources, support, and socialization for children. Clearly, family members are an important part of our lives—they provide care and company and help to mark important events such as holidays, weddings, and religious ceremonies. But what if you do not have a family? How can these functions be fulfilled when the number of people living alone, getting divorced, or migrating to other parts of the world is rising?

In Japan, companies are stepping in to help people deal with these new circumstances. In the early 1990s, the Japan Efficiency Corporation was "doing the booming business [of] renting families to the lonely," especially the elderly (Kubota, 2009). With the declining number of children per couple and the higher propensity of children to live far away from their aging parents, the elderly had fewer people to care for their physical and emotional needs. Office Agents, a Tokyo firm, offers friends and family for rent as event guests. They have about 1,000 such fake guests available for occasions such as weddings and funerals. The company reports that many brides and grooms do not even know which of their guests are real and which are rented. Perhaps most interestingly, the Hagemashi Tai agency rents temporary husbands to single mothers. Having a husband can be socially useful in many situations, such as in day care or elementary school admission interviews. Single mothers can even rent a "dad" to help children with homework, resolve issues with neighbors, or take children to events (Kubota, 2009).

USING YOUR SOCIOLOGICAL IMAGINATION
INCREASING OR DECREASING FERTILITY IN SWEDEN AND CHINA

We often hear about low fertility rates, the average number of children per woman over her lifetime, in many Western countries. These countries (including the United States) are below the replacement rate of fertility, meaning that people are not having enough children to replace the population. Other countries worry that their fertility rates are too high and face the difficult social problem of overpopulation. In some countries, such as in Sweden and China, the government has implemented policies to try to affect fertility rates.

Read the *OECD Observer* article on fertility in Sweden: http://oecdobserver.org/news/arc hivestory.php/aid/563/Can_governments_influence_population_ growth_.html

1. Why would the Swedish government, or any government, want to increase the fertility rate? What are the benefits of a higher fertility rate?

2. What specific policies have been enacted in Sweden to try to increase the fertility rate? Why might policymakers think that these measures would increase fertility?

3. How successful have these policies been at increasing fertility in Sweden? What are the other implications of these policies?

Now read this *New York Times* article about China's efforts to regulate its birth rate: http s://www.nytimes.com/2021/05/31/world/asia/china-three-child-policy.html

1. Why did China want to reduce its fertility rate in the 1980s? How can high fertility be a problem?

2. What specific policies were enacted by the Chinese government to try to limit fertility?

3. Why does the Chinese government now want to boost the fertility rate? Why might couples not want to have more children despite these efforts?

4. What social policies might be necessary to create a climate that encourages people to have children?

At a purely rational level, the idea of renting family members to serve particular social purposes makes sense, as it may be the most efficient way to fulfill the short-term goal of appearing to have family or friends. However, to many Americans, renting a family might seem odd and perhaps even offensive because it challenges our fundamental ideas about the nature of the relationship between family members. Do you see this trend catching on in the United States? Why or why not? How is it similar to, or different from, renting an escort to attend an event? What does it say about our emphasis on idealized notions of the nuclear family and the pressure to conform?

Critics of the structural functionalist perspective of the family argue that this theory overemphasizes the family's harmonious elements and tends to ignore the disharmony—such as the discord between parents and children, between siblings, and between spouses. Clearly, not everyone enjoys the functionality and stability of the family setting. This approach also focuses on the positive elements of the family, such as promoting and rationalizing the status quo. However, many social problems arise within families, such as abuse and mistreatment, that might be ignored by looking at only the functions of families.

Conflict Theory, Power, and the Family

Conflict theory offers a different lens on the family and its role in society. At its root, this approach is always concerned with the unequal distribution of resources between those with and those without power. Not surprisingly, conflict theorists do not see the family as the harmonious institution that structural functionalists do. Instead, they see the family as an arena for a wide variety of conflicts. For example, women and men have differing levels of power within the family, as do older and younger family members. Such conflicts are related to power within the family—who has it and how it is used.

Arguing from a conflict and feminist perspective, Randall Collins (1975) states that the family is an arena for gender conflict in which males have historically been more powerful. This causes discord between opposite-sex partners who struggle with their different roles in the relationship and the division of power and labor in the family unit. For example, many couples argue about who will do housework or control the finances.

Age-based conflict is also prevalent in the family. Parents have more power in the family than children do because of their greater access to resources. As children try to influence their parents' decisions or become autonomous, conflicts can arise. Although these conflicts can be benign, such as when children want to eat dessert and parents say no, they also can be much more serious, such as when parents abuse their children physically, emotionally, or sexually. This abuse is possible only because of the differential levels of power and resources in the family.

Conflict theorists note that a dire consequence of family power struggles is family violence, which is abuse, mistreatment, or neglect that a child or adult experiences from a family member, or from someone with whom they have an intimate relationship. Family violence can take the form of physical, sexual, emotional, and financial abuse of a spouse, child, or elder.

Family violence is a widespread problem around the world. According to the National Intimate Partner and Sexual Violence Survey collected by the Centers for Disease Control and Prevention (CDC), 1 in 4 women and 1 in 9 men have been victims of intimate partner violence. This includes sexual violence, physical violence, and/or stalking by a partner that resulted in injury, fear, or concern for safety. In addition, 1 in 4 women has experienced severe physical violence. This violence can be very serious; almost half of all female homicide victims are killed by a partner or former partner (CDC, 2017f).

How does a graphic like this work to highlight the diverse ways that family violence can occur and to expand how we understand family violence?

paci77/iStockPhoto

INTIMATE RELATIONSHIPS

The process of mate selection and dating creates the conditions for cohabitation, marriage, and families. Research shows that men and women tend to look for different features in spouses. This is, in part, because of gender stereotypes about how men and women should act and what role they should play in a relationship. These differences are also related to how we understand the marital (or spousal) relationship. Is that relationship one in which partners engage in very different roles, with one partner (often the woman) staying at home to raise children and the other partner (often the man) working? Or is it one of equal partners? Chapter 6 on gender and sexuality begins to explore some of these topics.

Intimate relationships are often founded on sexual ties and behaviors. And, the changing nature of these behaviors over time, including more people engaging in sexual relationships outside of marriage and with diverse partners, alters our ideas and expectations about both intimate relationships and families.

Methods in Depth: Surveying Hookup Culture Among Youths

Dating has changed in American society in the past 50 years. One of the ways that it has changed for some young people is with the rise of hookup culture. The term *hooking up* is based on the idea that emotional intimacy, commitment, and expectations of monogamy are no longer prerequisites for sexual encounters—it is a culture of more open attitudes toward casual sexual relationships outside of traditional monogamous dating. There is evidence that hooking up has become more common than traditional dating, with one study finding that emerging adults had nearly twice as many hookup partners as first dates in the preceding 2 years (Bradshaw et al., 2010). And most young adults (65–80%) reporting having hooked up in their lifetime (Aubrey & Smith, 2013).

Research Question

Some scholars have wondered about the effect of the rise of hooking up on individuals' choices and timing of marriage and attitudes toward marriage. James-Kangal, Weitbrecht, Trenel, and Whitton (2018) examined the association between engagement in casual sexual behavior (hooking up) and expectations for future committed relationships and marriage, as well as attitudes toward current relationships. The authors tested two competing hypotheses. On the one hand, the rise of hooking up could be an indication that young adults are no longer valuing relationships or marriage (the devaluing hypothesis). On the other hand, young adults could be delaying romantic commitments until they have achieved their personal and professional goals (the delayed timing hypothesis).

Methodology

This research is based on an online survey with questions about sexual behavior, beliefs about relationships, and expectations of marriage. It was conducted with undergraduate students between the age of 18 and 20 at a large Midwestern university ($n = 248$). The respondents were in a larger pool of students who had signed up to be part of studies at their university as part of their course credit. You may have such a situation at your college, where you can participate in research for course credit or money. There are many advantages to using students as research subjects. First, they are easily accessible if you are a professor on a college campus. Second, students are often very willing to participate for extra money or course credit.

Findings

The researchers found that hooking up was not associated with later expectations of marriage: People who hooked up more were just as likely to say that they wanted to marry at some point in their lives. This suggests that hooking up is a phase that many young people see themselves as moving out of when they enter their mid to late 20s (the delayed timing hypothesis). However, the authors also found that those who engaged in more hooking up had less-favorable attitudes about their current relationships.

Challenges

There are also important disadvantages to using students as research subjects. First, they are a very particular group that is, perhaps, not representative of the population as a whole. For example, they tend to be of similar ages, social classes, and less racially diverse than the U.S. population. This is less important for certain types of studies (e.g., a study of hand-eye coordination) but is very consequential for other types of research. The sample for this study was mostly female (72.6%) and White (78.0%). Women are much more likely to participate in this type of research. And, the fact that the sample was overwhelmingly White is probably a reflection of the college where the research was done, but it does not reflect the country, where only 62% of the population is White. In addition, 94.8% of the sample self-reported as heterosexual. This could have important consequences for the results. Finally, all the students in the sample are, obviously, students. This excludes those who do not attend college, who are more likely to marry earlier and who may have different attitudes about relationships. A sample of people beyond a college campus that is more diverse might yield different findings, and we want to keep that in mind when we consider this research.

Another major methodological consideration in this study are the challenges of researching sensitive topics. Asking someone about their sexual activity is sensitive. Many people would not want to answer these questions face to face. This is related to the issue of social desirability (which we discussed in the Methods in Depth section in Chapter 5). If a student is interviewed by a professor, for example, the student might underplay the extent of his casual sexual activity. However, if he is interviewed by another student his age, he might over-report how often he hooks up. The social pressure of face-to-face interviews is clearly not beneficial for this sort of research. To address this problem, the authors used an online survey so that respondents would feel less pressure to alter their responses to questions that they found sensitive.

Finally, this research asks respondents to think about whether they would like to marry by age 25 or 30; the findings are based on what respondents think they will do later in life. We do not actually know who does marry or when that happens. Research that is longitudinal (that follows respondents over time) could more accurately determine whether the students do marry and the timing of their later relationship choices. For example, a follow-up survey of respondents 10 years after graduation would provide a more accurate picture of their relationship trajectories.

READING: "ONE'S A CROWD"

Eric Klinenberg

This chapter focuses on the important role of the family in society. But, what about people who live alone? Living alone is a more common phenomenon now than ever before. What are the implications of living along for individuals and society? When reading this article, consider how the rising number of people living along alters our ideas about the role of family in society.

Neilson Barnard/Getty Images for the New York Times

More people live alone now than at any other time in history. In prosperous American cities—Atlanta, Denver, Seattle, San Francisco and Minneapolis—40 percent or more of all households contain a single occupant. In Manhattan and in Washington, nearly one in two households are occupied by a single person.

By international standards, these numbers are surprising— surprisingly low. In Paris, the city of lovers, more than half of all households contain single people, and in socialist Stockholm, the rate tops 60 percent.

The decision to live alone is common in diverse cultures whenever it is economically feasible. Although Americans pride themselves on their self-reliance and culture of individualism, Germany, France and Britain have a greater proportion of one-person households than the United States, as does Japan. Three of the nations with the fastest-growing populations of single people—China, India and Brazil—are also among those with the fastest growing economies.

The mere thought of living alone once sparked anxiety, dread and visions of loneliness. But those images are dated. Now the most privileged people on earth use their resources to separate from one another, to buy privacy and personal space.

Living alone comports with modern values. It promotes freedom, personal control and self-realization—all prized aspects of contemporary life.

It is less feared, too, for the crucial reason that living alone no longer suggests an isolated or less-social life. After interviewing more than 300 singletons (my term for people who live alone) during nearly a decade of research, I've concluded that living alone seems to encourage more, not less, social interaction.

Paradoxically, our species, so long defined by groups and by the nuclear family, has been able to embark on this experiment in solo living because global societies have become so interdependent. Dynamic markets, flourishing cities and open communications systems make modern autonomy more appealing; they give us the capacity to live alone but to engage with others when and how we want to and on our own terms.

In fact, living alone can make it easier to be social, because single people have more free time, absent family obligations, to engage in social activities.

Compared with their married counterparts, single people are more likely to spend time with friends and neighbors, go to restaurants and attend art classes and lectures. There is much research suggesting that single people get out more—and not only the younger ones.

Erin Cornwell, a sociologist at Cornell, analyzed results from the General Social Survey (which draws on a nationally representative sample of the United States population) from 2000 to 2008 and found that single people 35 and older were more likely than those who lived with a spouse or a romantic partner to spend a social evening with neighbors or friends. In 2008, her husband, Benjamin Cornwell (also a sociologist at Cornell), was lead author of "The Social Connectedness of Older Adults," a paper in the *American Sociological Review* that showed that single seniors had the same number of friends and core discussion partners as their married peers and were more likely to socialize with friends and neighbors.

Surveys, some by market research companies that study behavior for clients developing products and services, also indicate that married people with children are more likely than single people to hunker down at home. Those in large suburban homes often splinter into private rooms to be alone. The image of a modern family in a room together, each plugged into a separate reality, be it a smartphone, computer, video game or TV show has become a cultural cliché.

New communications technologies make living alone a social experience, so being home alone does not feel involuntary or like solitary confinement. The person alone at home can digitally navigate through a world of people, information and ideas. Internet use does not seem to cut people off from real friendships and connections.

The Pew Internet Personal Networks and Community Survey—a nationally representative survey of 2,512 American adults conducted in 2008 that was the first to examine how the Internet and cellphones affect our core social networks—shows that Web use can lead to more social life, rather than to less. "Social Isolation and New Technology," written by the Rutgers University communications scholar Keith Hampton, reveals that heavy users are more likely than others to have large and diverse social networks; more likely to visit parks, cafes and restaurants; and more likely to meet diverse people with different perspectives and beliefs.

Today five million people in the United States between ages 18 and 34 live alone, 10 times more than in 1950. But the largest number of single people are middle-aged; 15 million people between ages 35 and 64 live alone. Those who decide to live alone following a breakup or a divorce could choose to move in with roommates or family. But many of those I interviewed said they chose to live alone because they had found there was nothing worse than living with the wrong person.

In my interviews, older single people expressed a clear preference for living alone, which allowed them to retain their feelings of independence and integrity, and a clear aversion to moving in with friends or family or into a nursing home.

According to research by the Rutgers sociologist Deborah Carr, at 18 months after the death of a spouse, only one in four elderly men and one in six elderly women say they are interested in remarrying; one in three men and one in seven women are interested in dating someday; and only one in four men and one in 11 women are interested in dating immediately.

Most older widows, widowers and divorced people remake their lives as single people. A century ago, nearly 70 percent of elderly American widows lived with a child; today—thanks to Social Security, private pensions and wealth generated in the market—just 20 percent do. According to the U.C.L.A. economist Kathleen McGarry: "When they have more income and they have a choice of how to live, they choose to live alone. They buy their independence."

Some unhealthy old people do become dangerously isolated, as I learned when I researched my book about the hundreds of people who died alone in the 1995 Chicago heat wave, and they deserve more attention and support than we give them today. But the rise of aging alone is also a social achievement. The sustained health, wealth and vitality that so many people over age 65 enjoy allow them to maintain domestic independence far longer than previous generations did. What's new today is that the great majority of older widows, widowers and divorced people prefer living alone to their other options, and they're willing to spend more on housing and domestic help for the privilege. Some pundits predicted that rates of living alone would plummet because of the challenged economy: young people would move into their parents' basements; middle-aged adults would put off divorce or separation for financial reasons; the elderly would move in with their children rather than hold on to places of their own.

Thus far, however, there's little evidence that this has happened. True, more young adults have moved in with their parents because they cannot find good jobs; but the proportion of those between 20 and 29 who live alone went down only slightly, from 11.97 percent in 2007 to 10.94 percent in 2011. In the general population, living alone has become more common—in absolute and proportional terms. The latest census report estimates that more than 32 million Americans live alone today, up from million in 2000 and 31 million in 2010.

All signs suggest that living alone will become even more common in the future, at every stage of adulthood and in every place where people can afford a place of their own.

Reading Questions

1. How has the proportion of people living alone changed over time and how does that proportion differ across countries?
2. What is the effect of living alone? How do people who live alone differ from those who are married, according to the article? Do they differ in their number or strength of relationships?
3. How are these changes related to changes in technology in modern society?
4. How does the rise of single people change our idea of the role of the family in society?

Klinenberg, E. (2012, February 5). One's a crowd. *The New York Times*, SR4. https://www.nytimes.com/2012/02/05/opinion/sunday/living-alone-means-being-social.html

Arranged Marriages

In an arranged marriage a third party selects the bride and the groom. Parents or others might make the match without consulting their children. However, the children usually have some level of control over choosing among partners deemed appropriate by their parents. This type of marriage was common worldwide until the 18th century and remains prevalent in many areas, including parts of Asia, Africa, the Middle East, and Latin America. Arranged marriages also occur in the United States, particularly among some ethnic groups.

Our modern ideas about marriage, and the role of romantic love within it, seem inconsistent with arranged marriage. But research shows that these marriages might be more likely to develop into lasting love than previously thought (Bentley, 2011). According to research conducted by Robert Epstein (discussed in Bentley, 2011), individuals in arranged marriages tend to feel more in love over time, whereas individuals in non-arranged marriages (which would include most U.S. marriages) tend to feel less in love. Epstein interviewed 30 individuals in 22 marriages and found that, within 10 years, the self-rated satisfaction among individuals in arranged marriages was twice as high as it was for those in non-arranged marriages. There are many possible reasons for this finding: Arranged marriages are carefully planned and considered by families and communities, whereas non-arranged marriages can be spontaneous and may be less thought out. As a result, individuals in arranged marriages may be more likely to remain married, even if times are difficult, because they have the interests of their extended families to consider. Those in non-arranged marriages tend to be more focused on romantic love and can often overlook other critical compatibility issues. It is also possible, however, that those in arranged marriages might be more likely to report being in love because of different expectations. These different levels of reporting may not reflect true differences in feelings.

Epstein's research shows that, the more parents are involved in the selection process, the more successful the resulting marriage tends to be. Parents can help weed out potential mates with deal-breaker features—perhaps an incompatibility on values, the number of children they want, or where they want to live. Parents are also important because their support can help solidify the marriage. This support can come in the form of financial help for the wedding, for one or both spouses to attend school, for a home, or for help with children. Along with emotional support, this assistance can provide the resources needed to help single people transition into being married and, perhaps, into being parents. Arranged marriages provide an interesting counterpoint to most major trends in dating and families—including more individual choices in mate selection and flexibility within relationships. The existence of all these different forms of relationships highlights the rising diversity in relationships and families in modern society.

The matrimonial classified ad sections of Indian newspapers cover every aspect of life that is considered important in India—from religion, caste, profession, and family to dietary habits and skin complexion.

DSK/AFP via Getty Images

SUMMARY

This chapter critically examines the role of intimate relationships and the family in society. We began by talking about major changes in the family, including Andrew Cherlin's argument that modern society has seen a deinstitutionalization of marriage. This and other changes in the family are related to larger social processes, such as the rise of women's rights and individualism and the decline of religiosity. We also discuss how different theoretical perspectives, such as structural functionalism and conflict theory, help us to understand the family's role in society. We assess dating and intimate relationships, which often provide the foundation for families. The reading from Yodanis and Lauer examines the role of romantic love in marriages and how our ideas of the importance of love have changed over time. We end by discussing the larger patterns of dating and selecting mates and how these are changing in modern times, with serious implications for the family.

FOR FURTHER READING

Cherlin, A. J. (2004). The deinstitutionalization of marriage in America. *Journal of Marriage and the Family*, *66*, 848–861.

Engels, F. (1946). *The origin of the family, private property and the state*. *International*. (Original work published 1894)

Kimmel, M. (2012). *The gendered society* (5th ed.). Oxford University Press.

Lauer, S., & Yodanis, C. (2011). Individualized marriage and the integration of resources. *Journal of Marriage and the Family*, *73*, 669–683.

Parsons, T., & Bales, R. F. (1955). *Family socialization and interaction process*, Free Press.

GLOSSARY

arranged marriage

cohabitate

companionate marriage

deinstitutionalization of marriage

extended family

family

family household

family violence

fertility rates

individualized marriages

institutional marriage

marriage

nuclear family:

 **EDUCATION**

LEARNING OBJECTIVES

1. Critically assess the ways in which education has changed in the modern schooled society.

2. Compare the main functions of education, including socialization, selection, and legitimation.

3. Assess how the education system is related to maintaining and eliminating social inequality.

4. Explain the concepts of cultural and social capital and how they are related to education.

5. Compare education systems around the world and how funding is related to educational outcomes across countries.

You are probably very familiar with the institution of education. The average American youth spends 30% of each weekday in school. (The only other activity in which youth spend this much time is sleeping!) If you are the typical undergraduate student, you have been in the education system almost your whole life. Perhaps you started in preschool when you were 3 or 4 years old, moved through elementary and high school, and now attend a university or college. You might have also attended other classes outside school—perhaps piano, tennis, or Japanese lessons. Unless you took some time off between high school and postsecondary education, you probably cannot even remember a time when most of your waking hours were spent somewhere other than in school. And you are currently gaining even more schooling. Why did you make the decision to continue your education? What is the role of the education system in society?

THE SCHOOLED SOCIETY

Schooling and the education system have fundamentally changed in modern society. Scott Davies and Neil Guppy (2018) argue that we live in a schooled society. There are three main reasons for this. First, there is a growth in modern schooling. Today, there is mass postsecondary enrollment in the United States, with 44.3% of 18- to 24-year-olds enrolled in a college or university (OECD, 2021; see Figure 9.1).

Second, schooling has become increasingly integral to modern life. Individuals with a postsecondary degree earn higher incomes, on average, and are less likely to experience unemployment (Davies & Guppy, 2018). (We will discuss these important implications of education later in this chapter.) Whereas in the past many countries, including the United States, emphasized manual labor and resource extraction, in recent years governments have become more interested in education's role in improving national productivity, calling for a focus on the development of highly educated knowledge workers. These changes can be linked to the decline in the primary sector (where jobs did not usually require much education). Today, the government tries to encourage the growth of jobs that require higher education and often have more stability and better pay. The evolution of working conditions and employment sectors in the United States is discussed in more detail in Chapter 10.

Finally, the forms and functions of education are increasing and diversifying in our modern schooled society. Historically, schools focused on reading, writing, and basic math. Today, the education system is expected to teach these skills as well as a host of additional subjects, such as physical education, media literacy, drug and alcohol awareness, environmental responsibility, and sex education. Many view modern schools as solutions to a myriad of social problems and as a way to help people become well-rounded and socially responsible.

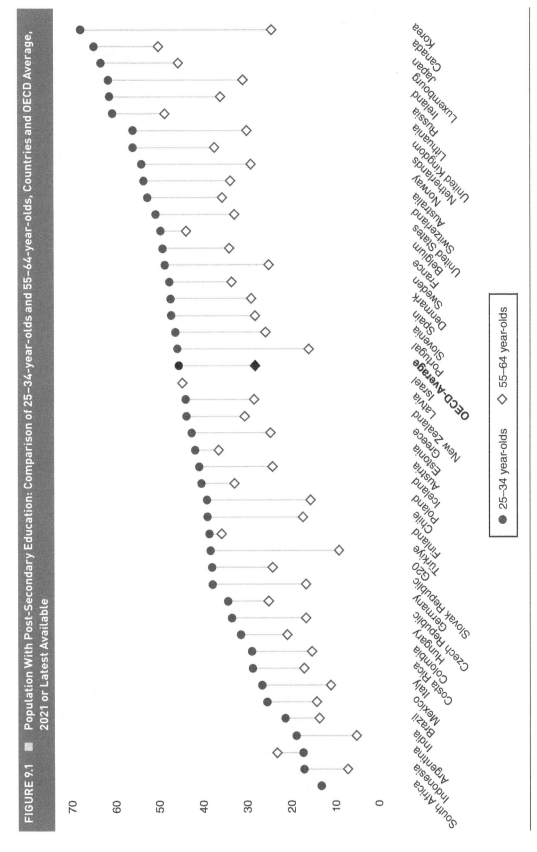

FIGURE 9.1 ■ Population With Post-Secondary Education: Comparison of 25–34-year-olds and 55–64-year-olds, Countries and OECD Average, 2021 or Latest Available

● 25–34 year-olds   ◇ 55–64 year-olds

Source: OECD (2021), Population with tertiary education (indicator). doi: 10.1787/0b8f90e9-en (Accessed on 06 May 2021).

THE FUNCTIONS OF EDUCATION

The education system has many functions. The obvious and intended ones, such as teaching students basic knowledge and skills, are known as manifest functions. Although learning to read, write, and do math are certainly important parts of education, sociologists also focus on other functions of education, some of which are less obvious. These functions fall into three broad categories: socialization of young people, selection of people into employment, and legitimation of certain types of knowledge and divisions in society. These functions are latent functions of the education system, functions that might not be obvious or intended. Durkheim, Marx, and Weber were all interested in these functions of education and saw them as integral to modern society. Let's explore how each of these sociologists understood education's role in society.

USING YOUR SOCIOLOGICAL IMAGINATION
HOW CAN WE MEASURE THE COLLEGE EXPERIENCE?

Colleges and universities are increasingly interested in comparing postsecondary institutions and the experiences of students on campus. How do we judge the best university, professor, or campus? How you answer this question depends on who you are within the institution (a university president, professor, or student) and what you think the role of a university should be in society.

Looking at online resources that attempt to quantify and compare universities and professors pushes us to think critically about what we value in a university education and how to best assess how well our school or professors educates us. Go online to access two measures of the university experience: the *New York Time's* Higher Education Rankings system of ranking American universities and colleges and Rate My Professors' criteria. After you have examined these sites, answer the following questions:

1. How do these organizations judge a school to be good? What criteria do they use? How do their criteria differ?
2. Based on the criteria of each measure, what are the most important aspects of universities and the role of universities in society?
3. Who makes each of these lists? On whose interests do each of these rankings focus?
4. Which ranking do you think is best? Which is worst? What would you include in the perfect ranking?
5. How could you use these rankings? What problems or unintended consequences could arise from measuring postsecondary education in these ways?

Socialization

Durkheim focused on the socializing role of the education system. The common theme in Durkheim's work is a fundamental concern with the functioning of society and what accounts for its solidarity and cohesion. These foci are the bases for structural functionalist theory generally and is the core of his interest in the education system.

Durkheim (1956) argued that universal education serves the needs of society in several ways. Tasked with providing individuals with training for life in broader society, schools convey basic knowledge and skills that will be useful for members of society. In addition, individuals need specialized training for the specific roles that they will occupy in life, such as an occupation. Durkheim argued that in the complex division of labor that characterizes modern society, education should be aligned with each person's future occupational aspirations; that is, teachers should learn how to teach and lawyers should learn how to practice the law.

The education system helps to socialize us for later employment. Learning to work cooperatively in groups is an important skill that could be useful after graduation.

GCSutter/iStockPhoto

Education also socializes children into the mainstream. Each society has unique needs; schools can provide the guidelines that help us fit into society. Education acts as the social glue that helps a highly differentiated society remain normatively coherent by offering a moral education, where young people learn the norms and values of their society and the importance of following these rules of behavior. Moral education is "the means by which society perpetually re-creates the conditions of its very existence" and schooling is about the "systematic socialization of the young generation" (Durkheim, 1956, pp. 123–124). Socialization occurs when children are rewarded—such as given grades and gold stars—for following the rules. This practice helps bring together children of different backgrounds by tying them into the cohesive whole of society.

Remember that Durkheim argued that there are two types of societies: those based on mechanical solidarity (everyone is similar) and those based on organic solidarity (people are dissimilar but interdependent). From a structural functionalist perspective, Durkheim saw religion as a source of moral guidance in societies based on mechanical solidarity. However, with the cultural diversity in modern society and waning of religion's influence on our daily lives, Durkheim claimed that education is the new way to morally integrate people into our modern society, which is based on organic solidarity.

Durkheim focused on the education system's part in training young people to fit into society and play the many roles expected of them. As a result, he saw the education system as an important part of how society reproduces itself. He explained that education "is only the image and reflection of society . . . it does not create it" (Durkheim, 1897/1951, p. 371). For Durkheim and others who focus on the socializing role of the education system, education plays a fundamental role in promoting social order and in creating stability in society.

Selection

A second major function of the education system is to select individuals by awarding badges of ability through sorting and differentially rewarding graduates by giving them grades and degrees (Davies & Guppy, 2018). Focusing on this element of the education system, Weber argued that schools are organized as bureaucracies and work to confer status and prestige.

Weber was interested in the rise of rationalization in society, particularly the development of bureaucracies in several different areas. (We will discuss this topic in more detail in the next chapter.) The education system—including your college—is filled with bureaucracies. There are many positive aspects of the bureaucratization of the education system. For example, universities are very efficient systems for producing degrees. It is clear what classes and grades students need to graduate, and many students earn degrees in 4 years. These educational bureaucracies also strive to be fair. Student numbers, not names, are often used on exams so that the professor or teaching assistant grades tests without regard to her opinion of the student.

Just as they are efficient at producing degrees, universities and colleges can be frustrating in the amount of red tape students need to go through to fulfill all the requirements. These requirements can limit your choice of classes—you need certain courses in a particular order to get your degree, regardless of your interests or abilities. They can also be very depersonalizing. The use of those student numbers, which is efficient and perhaps makes grading fairer, might make you feel as though you are not being treated as a unique individual.

A consequence of the rise of bureaucracies in society, including in the education system, is a growing need for individuals to have specialized certifications linked to specific occupations. Instead of providing a general education to all young people, modern society requires individuals to be trained in particular tasks, such as medicine, engineering, or social work. Weber highlighted how this specialization leads to an increasingly complicated set of certifications and degrees that can prevent certain people from entering a trade or profession. Although it makes sense for certain professionals to earn a specialized degree, the practice of certification also allows these individuals to gain significant control over entrance to their respective fields and to monopolize access to the elite positions and status.

Randall Collins (1979) called Weber's observation credentialing, the attestation of a qualification or competence issued to an individual by a party with authority to do so, such as a university. In this process, high-status groups maintain their social position by acquiring more education and educational credentials and keeping others out of these routes to upward mobility. Occupational groups have an obvious interest in making it difficult to enter their occupations (so students need a bachelor's degree before entering medical school or teaching college). By limiting the number of people who may practice in their area, groups within these occupations can reduce competition and keep their pay and job security high.

Getting to Know: Randall Collins (b. 1941)

- In his youth Randall enjoyed reading entire encyclopedias, works of literature, and comic books.

- Collins lived in Germany, Russia, and Uruguay as a child because his father was a diplomat for the U.S. State Department during the Cold War.

- He participated in the Free Speech movement and was once arrested due to his activism while a PhD student at the University of California, Berkeley.

- He wrote the novels *The Case of the Philosophers' Ring* (1979) and *Civil War Two* (2018).

Legitimation

The third major function of the education system is to legitimate certain kinds of knowledge and divisions in society. Karl Marx (Marx & Engels, 1964) noted the general tendency of dominant groups to attempt to subdue the masses. He argued that the education system is a part of this process by maintaining social inequality and preserving the power of capitalists who are already in control of society. This position is consistent with Marx's overall theory that society's dominant institutions (including schools, religions, and the state) support and reproduce the capitalist system. Thus, Marx argued that schools work to systematically reproduce class relations and the capitalist order with each new generation of students.

As we have learned from Marx earlier in this book, "the ruling ideas of each age have ever been the ideas of its ruling class" (Marx & Engels, 1964, p. 125). The ruling class diffuses its ideas throughout society in several ways, such as by setting the school curriculum. In formal education, a curriculum is the planned interaction of pupils with instructional content, materials, resources, and processes for evaluating the attainment of educational objectives (Adams & Adams, 2003). Phillip W. Jackson (1968) claimed that ideas are disseminated through both the official and what he called the hidden curriculum, the lessons that are not normally considered part of the academic program but that schools unintentionally or secondarily provide. Marx's work made a similar claim and he argued that, along with teaching social studies, English, and science, schools teach students to be submissive, docile, punctual, and hard working—all the traits that make for "good" workers in the capitalist system. In this way, education dulls the lower classes into obedient workers. Individual traits, such as punctuality, perseverance, and obedience, are rewarded with high grades and praise in school. For example, students are told to be quiet when the teacher is talking and to raise their hand when they would like to speak. The education system encourages and fosters this conformity to authority, which benefits the overarching interests of the society's powerful.

READING: "A MATTER OF DEGREES"

William Beaver

Education serves a variety of different roles in modern society. In "A Matter of Degrees," William Beaver examines the theories that sociologists use to explain how education functions. When reading this article, try to connect the theories Beaver discusses with the ideas of Durkheim, Weber, and Marx that we have learned about in this chapter. Consider your own schooling and how it fits within the different theories of education.

Americans value few things more than college degrees. Right now, 29 percent of adults over age 25 have a bachelor's or higher. That figure has more than doubled since the 1970s, and many within the educational establishment argue it will have to increase significantly for the United States to remain globally competitive.

The number of graduate degrees also continues to rise—masters' have doubled since 1980 and record numbers are enrolled in master's programs, a recent article in *The New York Times* reported.

In many ways these numbers aren't surprising. Early on, students learn that a college degree is the starting point to making it in American society. . . .

Media reports periodically reinforce such beliefs, reminding us that degree-holders have important income advantages. A recent news story in *The Washington Post* reported that in tough economic times, those with college degrees are much more likely to avoid lay-offs and maintain their incomes than those with high-school diplomas or less.

But what exactly do degrees do for people? The conventional wisdom holds that college graduates acquire skills that better prepare them for the world of work, which makes them more attractive to employers. Thus, students and parents are willing to pay the continually rising costs of higher education, assuming the pay-off will be worth it.

Although college graduates do have higher incomes, the reasons why, and our ever-increasing need to acquire educational credentials, are tied to larger social forces that sociologists have explored—forces that will continue to impact all those trying to climb the ladder of success.

The most popular view on the purpose of a college degree is known as the human capital model, which argues students attend college to acquire the knowledge and skills modern societies require, and that this allows them to obtain meaningful employment.

It's the model most students seem to accept, too. For example, surveys conducted by UCLA's Higher Education Research Institute found that 72 percent of college freshman cite "to get a better job" as the major reason for going to college.

However, if the human capital model is correct, it must be assumed students acquire skills in the classroom that are directly transferable to the job. One can certainly argue certain majors like accounting and computer science offer more skill-training than others, and research indicates that with these types of majors, employers do tend to hire on the basis of perceived skills.

The fact of the matter is, though, most college students don't major in areas that teach job skills. Some 22 percent of students currently major in business, but even within the business curriculum not all areas of study focus on acquiring specific skills. Moreover, many students continue to major in the social sciences and liberal arts, where there is little or no skill-training.

Along these lines, it would be logical to assume those possessing the necessary job skills, as indicated by their college major, would be more productive. Yet, the research that does exist on this idea suggests job productivity isn't significantly related to major. . . .

Why We Credential

Max Weber is credited with being the first sociologist to closely examine the function of degrees. He concluded educational credentials had much less to do with acquiring job skills than providing occupational and professional groups with a way of excluding certain individuals. The ability to exclude not only gives these groups power but helps ensure those hired will be loyal to the organization.

Weber's basic insights provided the foundation for modern credentialing theory, the most important work about which remains Randall Collins's *The Credentialed Society*. His detailed historical and social analysis supported Weber's contention that degrees allow certain occupational groups to exclude individuals, and that even business degrees seldom provide actual job training but do serve as indicators that a potential employee possesses the correct values that make compliance with organizational standards more likely.

There are always uncertainties about how new hires will adjust. The last thing most employers want is for them to "rock the boat," which could threaten stability within the organization. It's assumed individuals with the appropriate college degree will be more likely to fit in, but why? Part of the answer is self-selection. That is, students choose a college major that appeals to them, hoping to land a job and the start of a career, and hence are more than willing to conform. On the other hand, it's also likely that being exposed to a curriculum socializes students to acquire values associated with a profession. For years sociologists have investigated this so-called hidden curriculum.

For example, prospective managers are taught that their interests and the interests of workers are often in conflict and that their loyalties should be tied to management. Credentialing theorists have also suggested possessing the appropriate values is particularly important in higher-level positions, where individuals are often given more autonomy and are less likely to be closely monitored. So perhaps it isn't surprising that business researchers Nasrollah Ahadiat and Kenneth Smith discovered employers considered "professional conduct" the most important attribute when hiring accounting graduates.

Besides conformity and control, credentialing theory emphasizes that degrees also confer status on those who hold them. Along these lines, sociologist David K. Brown traced the development of the credentialing system to the late nineteenth century and the rise of large-scale bureaucratic organizations where individuals with management skills were needed.

It was assumed college graduates possessed the cognitive and verbal abilities good managers needed, which also reduced the uncertainty associated with hiring. Interestingly, studies do show college tends to increase cognitive abilities, so in many cases these assumptions weren't unfounded. Nonetheless, degrees provided a claim of competence or status that came to be taken for granted.

Thus credentials, as David Labaree points out in his book *How to Succeed in College Without Really Learning*, have exchange value because they allow students to obtain employment based largely on the status a degree confers. However, much less use value is apparent because the connection between degrees and actual job performance is questionable.

The Pay Gap

Many students pursue a degree to position themselves to earn a higher income, and it has been well established that college graduates earn more. In fact, four-year degree holders earn nearly 45 percent more per year than high-school graduates, according to the U.S. Census Bureau.

Indeed, the pay gap is one of the strongest arguments for the conventional wisdom of the human capital model, because it seems to demonstrate that employers are willing to pay for the skills college graduates possess. On the other hand, it's difficult to know exactly how much degrees are really worth because the most capable students go to college. As a result, there's no control group of equally capable, non-degree students available for comparison.

Nonetheless, credentialing theorists would agree that income and degrees are clearly related. Research by Ross Boylan found the largest gains in income occur soon after obtaining a degree. In this regard, reports from the Bureau of Labor Statistics show income gains for students are small unless they obtain a credential, even though students could certainly acquire job skills without earning a degree.

Consider that the median weekly income of individuals with some college but no degree in 2004 was $574, compared to $916 for those with a bachelor's. This suggests degrees do serve as status indicators. Just as important, Boylan found income gains experienced by degree holders are often relative. That is, as the number of people with degrees increase, degree holders take jobs formerly held by high-school graduates. Hence, the relative value of a degree actually increases because non-degree holders are forced into even lower-paying jobs.

One result, according to D. W. Livingstone in his book *The Education–Jobs Gap*, is that workers are often underemployed, because employers have increased the educational requirements for jobs whose basic content hasn't changed. Research by Stephen Vaisey discovered that nearly 55 percent of workers are overqualified, which has produced increasing levels of job dissatisfaction, to say nothing of the fact that workers are forced to pursue even higher, increasingly expensive credentials (which is particularly burdensome to lower income groups) if they want a chance to be hired.

This phenomenon has been termed "defensive credentialing," where students attend college to keep from losing ground to degree holders. As one student recently put it, "I don't like college much, but what kind of job can I get without a degree?" Similarly, as the number of bachelor's degrees climbs, more have pursued graduate degrees, hoping to gain some advantage. This also helps explain the increase in the number of master's degrees.

Credentialing and Higher Education

The role of higher education in a credentialing system seems obvious— to grant degrees to those who earn them. But there's still more involved. Although higher education certainly responds to the demands of industry and students for credentials, colleges haven't just been passive participants waiting for students to enroll. They've used the credentialing system to their advantage, having relied on demographic changes.

By the late 1970s, higher education faced a troubling reality. The education of the baby boom generation that had produced the so-called golden years of higher education, when enrollments tripled, was coming to an end. The last of the boomers would be graduating in a few years and the future looked grim. The Carnegie Council warned enrollments could decline by as much as 50 percent, while others predicted 30 percent of colleges might have to close or merge. To survive, they would have to recruit more students from a dwindling pool.

Hence, colleges began to enroll a more academically diverse group of students and recruit more women and minorities, many of whom represented first-generation college students. To a lesser extent, the situation was helped by the fact that more students were completing high school. According to the U.S. Department of Education, between 1972 and 1985 high-school completion rates increased by roughly 2.6 percent, and then climbed by about 3 percent by 1999.

Moreover, the curriculum, particularly at less prestigious institutions, was expanded and further vocationalized. In fact, W. Norton Grubb and Marvin Lazerson in their book *The Education Gospel and the Economic Power of Schooling* maintain that expansion in higher education has only occurred when more occupational majors have been added to the curriculum.

In the early 1970s, 58 percent of majors were considered occupational and by the late 1980s that figure had climbed to 65 percent. These types of degrees can be particularly appealing to first-generation college students, who often come from working- and lower-class backgrounds and want a degree that seems to improve their chances for employment and justifies the considerable investment.

New degree programs were often in subject areas that in the past hadn't required a bachelor's degree for employment. For example, females who might have needed a certificate or an associate degree to secure work as a secretary could now earn a four-year degree in office management. Such was also true for other areas, ranging from various medical technologies to the performing arts, which reinforced the credentialing system in two significant ways. First, a more diverse group of students earned degrees, many of whom might not have obtained them in the past. Second, by creating new majors, credentialing was expanded into vocational areas not traditionally associated with a four-year degree, while at the same time reinforcing the notion that a college degree imparts job skills. . . .

Recommended Resources

Ross D. Boylan. "The Effect of the Number of Diplomas on Their Value," *Sociology of Education* (1993) 66: 206–221. Shows how the relative value of college degrees has increased while their absolute value has not.

David K. Brown. *Degrees of Control: A Sociology of Educational Expansion and Occupational Credentialism* (Teachers College Press, 1995.) Documents the development of the credentialing system to the late nineteenth century and how it came to be assumed that degree holders had certain traits that made them more attractive to employers.

Randall Collins. *The Credentialed Society: An Historical Sociology of Education and Stratification* (Academic Press, 1979). A detailed historical account of the credentialing system and its implications for American society.

W. Norton Grubb and Marvin Lazerson. *The Education Gospel and the Economic Power of Schooling* (Harvard University Press, 2004). Discusses the rise of vocationalism and its continuing impacts on higher education.

D.W. Livingstone. *The Education–Jobs Gap: Underemployment or Economic Democracy* (Westview Press, 1998). Suggests workers are increasingly underemployed because the educational credentials required for jobs has risen even though the content of most jobs has not essentially changed.

Eric Margolis, ed. *The Hidden Curriculum in Higher Education* (Routledge, 2001). One of the first attempts to describe and analyze the hidden curriculum at colleges and universities.

Reading Questions

1. What evidence does Beaver use to support the human capital model? Does he find this theory convincing? Which classical theory (Durkheim's, Weber's, or Marx's) does this theory most closely resemble?
2. What classical theory discussed in this book is related to the screening and sorting theory? What evidence supports this theory and how accurate does Beaver think this theory is?
3. What is defensive credentialing?
4. Why has there been an expansion in the number and types of degrees?

Beaver, W. (2009). A matter of degrees. *Contexts, 8*(2), 22–26.

EDUCATION AND SOCIAL INEQUALITY

Americans pride themselves on living in a meritocracy, which is a society in which individuals achieve based on their personal merit. Although the United States has many features of a meritocracy, not all individuals are equally likely to succeed in our society. In the previous chapters we learned about the importance of social class, race, ethnicity, and gender in shaping people's opportunities. Despite the significance of these individual characteristics in shaping our lives, we are not simply passive agents who are doomed to certain kinds of lives. Many individuals who come from disadvantaged backgrounds achieve great things, and many people who come from positions of advantage do not have high-paying jobs or high-status degrees.

The education system is a centrally important institution in a meritocracy because it has the potential to level the playing field and provide equal opportunities for individuals to move up the social hierarchy through hard work. Yet all Western countries have a clear pattern of inequality that suggests that the educational system is not meritocratic. For example, children from lower-class families tend to do worse in the education system than those from higher-class backgrounds.

It is important to note that not all dimensions of inequality work as we might expect in the education system. For example, when it comes to gender inequality, we might guess that men would be advantaged in the education system. However, women tend to perform better than men within the education system, on average, and are more likely to earn degrees. In addition, some racialized groups perform better than the majority White population, although this trend varies across racial and ethnic groups.

Education and Social Class

The largest and most persistent inequality in educational outcomes is based on social class. The relationship between these two factors is persistent over time, robust across measures, and exists across country contexts. According to the Pell Institute (see Figure 9.2), Americans from families in the top 25% of earners have a 59% chance of getting a bachelor's degree by age 24, whereas those in the bottom 25% of earners have only a 15% chance of doing so.

FIGURE 9.2 ■ Bachelor's Degree Attainment by Age 24 by Family Income Quartile, 1970–2020

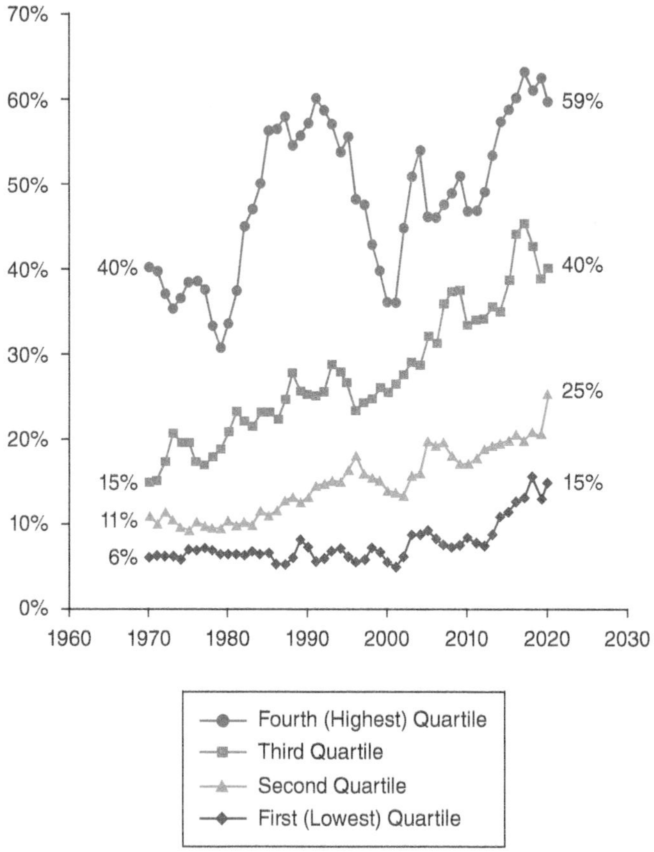

Source: Cahalan, M.W., Addison, et al. *Indicators of higher education equity in the United States: 2022 historical trend report.* Washington, DC: The Pell Institute. Council for Opportunity in Education (COE), and Alliance for Higher Education and Democracy of the University of Pennsylvania (PennAHEAD).

There are a variety of reasons that individuals from lower social class backgrounds are less likely to perform well in schools and achieve degrees. First, lower-class families might have differential expectations and values than upper-class families. Second, there could be differential association: Children from lower-class backgrounds are less likely than those from an upper-class background to have role models who were high achievers in school or who attended college. As a result, children from lower-class backgrounds lack the knowledge of how to work within the educational system (e.g., how to apply to college, what classes to take in high school to get into college). Differential preparation is another possible explanation. Children from families with more money are more likely to have access to private tutors, go on educational trips, have educational toys, and have books and newspapers in the home. These resources help to prepare them for school and to succeed in the educational system.

Social class is also important because it can help determine your position within the organization of a school. Tracking (also called streaming) is the practice of placing students with comparable skills or needs together. Tracking includes putting students in specific schools for high or low achievement, in specific classes such as enriched/advanced or applied/basic, or giving students harder or easier work within one class.

Tracking students into groups with similar skill levels has many advantages. It allows students to advance according to their ability, thus helping to preserve their interest and incentive to perform. Because bright students are not bored by the slower participation of others, they also are more likely to continue to engage in the class. Moreover, teachers can adapt their teaching styles and materials to the type of students in their classes and the abilities of these students. This approach can be beneficial to students because they will have material targeted to their ability level.

These purported advantages explain why tracking remains popular in schools in the United States and around the world. However, tracking also has some noteworthy disadvantages. The stigma attached to being assigned to the lower-ability group might discourage children labelled in this way from wanting to learn. This situation can create a self-fulfilling prophecy. Robert K. Merton (1949/1957/1968) coined this term in *Social Theory and Social Structure* and defined it in the following way: "The self-fulfilling prophecy is, in the beginning, a *false* definition of the situation evoking a new behavior which makes the original false conception come 'true.' This specious validity of the self-fulfilling prophecy perpetuates a reign of error. For the prophet will cite the actual course of events as proof that he was right from the very beginning" (Merton, 1949/1957/1968, p. 477, emphasis in original). In other words, a strongly held belief thought to be true (even if it is false) may have such a strong influence on a person that his actions ultimately make the belief come true. This idea might remind you of the Thomas principle (see Chapter 5). Both stress the importance of our perceptions of a situation and how, even if they are not based in reality, these perceptions can change our real experiences.

How do students who are expected to do better end up performing better, even when their ability is no greater than that of their peers? Barr and Dreeben (1983) looked at first-grade classes in which students were grouped by their reading ability at the beginning of the year. Students in higher-ability groups learned more new words and improved their reading skills more rapidly than students in the low-ability groups. Better readers were placed in high-ability groups at the beginning of the year; they received more instructional time, were exposed to more new words, and experienced a faster pace of instruction than students in the low-ability groups. In short, higher-performing students received more learning opportunities than lower-performing students. Consequently, the gap between high- and low-achieving students grew over the course of the year.

These experiments show the powerful effect of positive expectations. Many researchers and observers have generalized these findings to argue that there must be powerful negative effects of negative expectations. However, running an experiment with negative expectations would be unethical. Suppose you told teachers that certain students are slow learners. They might hold the pupils back or spend less time instructing them. Because we cannot test this directly, it is important to question whether the effect of the positive expectation experiments would hold true of students expected to perform poorly. Would it really hold students back in the same way that positive expectations can benefit students?

If all students are equally likely to make it into the high- and low-ability tracks and student placement is based solely on their ability, tracking would not reproduce inequalities. However, when students with the same test scores and grades are compared, students from higher-SES families are still more likely than low-SES students to be enrolled in high-track classes (Gamoran & Mare, 1989). Thus, the former are advantaged regardless of their ability and test scores; they are not only more likely to be prepared for school, but they are also more likely to be placed in the high-ability track, with all its benefits.

Separating students into high- and low-achieving streams can be very beneficial for students who are per-forming well. However, this practice can also stunt the later advancement of students who are placed in the less advanced classes.

SDI Productions/iStockPhoto

Annette Lareau's (2003) *Unequal Childhoods: Class, Race, and Family Life* addresses this issue. Through interviews and observations of 10 families, Lareau examined the factors that led to different educational outcomes across SES groups. First, parents who went to university are more knowledgeable regarding which classes are the best and most likely to prepare children for higher education. Parents with higher SES have the means to send their children to enrichment schools and to enroll them in extracurricular activities. Second, university-educated parents are better integrated into school networks—more often having the time to engage in Parent Teacher Associations or volunteer at the school—which gives them more information about the best (and worst) classes and teachers. Finally, these parents influence their children's class selection by encouraging them to challenge themselves and to think about the long-term consequences of their choices, such as which classes best prepare them for college.

Getting to Know: Annette Lareau (b. 1952)

- Lareau's interest in family, education, and social class was partially inspired by her mother's impoverished childhood and experiences with eviction.

- She worked as a full-time interviewer in San Francisco's city jail for 2 years following college to collect data to determine whether inmates could be released without bail.

- She enjoys gardening, reading novels, and attending baseball games and the opera.

Tracking seems to have serious benefits for some students at the cost of others. Students in the advanced classes do better, in part because they tend to be taught by more experienced teachers (Kelly, 2004). In fact, research shows that similar students will perform quite differ-ently if they are placed into a high or a low track. Being put into a low track will reduce student learning, while being in a high track will increase it, even if these students have similar abilities at the beginning. Tracking also has long-term implications. For example, high-tracked students are more likely to attend college. Tracking can create what is referred to as a cumulative disadvantage: The most advanced individuals are awarded the best opportunities, which increases inequality (DiPrete et al., 2006).

USING YOUR SOCIOLOGICAL IMAGINATION
CRITICALLY ANALYZING SCHOOL CURRICULUM

Every state outlines a specific curriculum for each grade in order to standardize what is taught to students across all the schools in the state. These curricula, along with the teaching resources on which they rely, are given to teachers at all levels to help them plan their classes. As we have learned in this chapter, the decisions of what will and will not be taught shapes what students learn and their worldview. Consequently, a curriculum is not neutral in its effect on students.

In this activity, we will explore the 10th-grade curriculum in your state. Search online for your state's curriculum. Then answer the following questions:

1. What topics and materials are covered that might not have been included 50 years ago?
2. What topics and materials might have been dropped from earlier curricula? What does this difference tell us about the changing ideas of education's role in modern society?
3. How does this curriculum tackle issues of social inequality? Looking at the specific subject areas and the additional resources on the Web page, how do the curriculum designers address gender, ethnic, and class inequality?
4. How does this curriculum address the value of diversity in American society? Where are ideas about diversity included in this curriculum?
5. How does this curriculum deal with other social issues, such as concerns about the environment or the changing importance of technology in society? Where do these concerns appear in the curriculum?

Methods in Depth: Testing the Self-Fulfilling Prophecy

The self-fulfilling prophecy is the idea that a false interpretation of a situation can lead to behaviors that cause this interpretation to become true. Robert Merton first coined the term. Decades of research in education has expanded upon Merton's original ideas. Education researchers believe that self-fulfilling prophecies follow a three-stage sequence: (1) teachers form inaccurate expectations (either higher or lower expectations) of their students; (2) inaccurate expectations result in differences in how teachers interact with students they expect to perform to higher and lower degrees; and (3) students respond to, and confirm, these different teacher expectations. In this sequence, the relationship between teacher expectations and student outcomes is mediated by how teachers interact, or behave toward, high and low expectancy students. But how do we study this empirically?

To determine how teacher expectations and behaviors shape student outcomes, researchers need to keep several considerations in mind. First, researchers need to ensure that teachers do not have prior knowledge of their students because this may bias their expectations. Second, researchers need to be able to measure student achievements over time—both at the start and end of a study—to ensure that teacher expectations and practices do, in fact, shape student outcomes. Third, in order to measure different teacher behaviors, researchers need to observe how teachers interact with their students in a classroom setting. Much of the research on this topic is limited because it does not address this three-stage process holistically, and more specifically because base-line student achievements are often not included. However, a study conducted by Sarah Gentrup and colleagues (2020) used a variety of methods to address these limitations to reveal how the self-fulfilling prophecy works among 1,026 first-grade students from 64 classrooms in Germany.

Methodology

The research took place over an entire school year and included three waves of data collection across two subjects: math and reading. The first wave of data collection occurred immediately following the beginning of the school year and included standardized achievement tests for both subjects as well as general cognitive ability tests; interviews with students; a survey of teachers about their expectations; and telephone interviews with the parents. The second wave occurred in the middle of the school year and included interviews with students in addition to video recordings of teacher-student interactions during math and reading lessons. The third and final wave occurred at the end of the school year. Just like the first wave, the third wave included standardized achievement tests on general cognitive, math, and reading abilities as well as a survey of teacher expectations.

Findings

Analysis of the data from teacher expectation surveys and student achievement scores across waves one and three reveal that teacher expectations were often inaccurate—they did not correctly reflect students' general cognitive abilities. Or, in the language of self-fulfilling prophecies, teachers held false interpretations about their students' academic abilities. More important, inaccurate teacher expectations significantly predicted end-of-year achievement: Inaccurately high teacher expectations led to greater student achievement in both math and reading while inaccurately low expectations were associated with lower achievement in reading classes only. After analyzing the video footage, they found that teacher-student interactions in the classroom did not substantially influence the relationship between teacher expectations and end-of-year student achievement. However, evidence of the self-fulfilling prophecy was found to exist: Inaccurate teacher expectations (whether higher or lower) significantly influenced student performance in the classroom.

Limitations

The use of interviews, surveys, standardized tests, and video recordings over the course of a school year provide invaluable insights on teacher expectations and student achievement. By testing students at the beginning and end of the school year, we can be more confident that teacher expectations do, in fact, shape student outcomes. However, the conclusions of this study are restricted to first-grade classrooms in Germany, and more research from different countries and grade levels is needed to ensure that these results have external validity.

Education and Gender

When we discuss inequality, we are sometimes tempted to think that certain groups are always disadvantaged. For example, we know that women tend to earn less money than men and are more likely to live in poverty. It therefore seems logical to assume that women, and other groups who are similarly disadvantaged, are disadvantaged in all realms of society, including education. Yet, as previously mentioned, American women currently tend to do better, on average, than men in the educational system (see Figure 9.3). For example, since

FIGURE 9.3 ■ Postsecondary Completion by Gender, 1980–2016

Women in the U.S. are outpacing men in college graduation

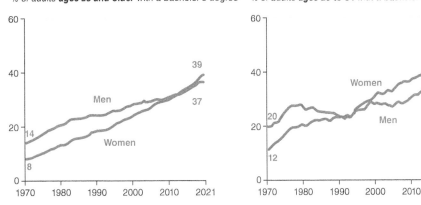

*% of adults **ages 25 and older** with a bachelor's degree*   *% of adults **ages 25 to 34** with a bachelor's degree*

Source: Data from National Center for Education Statistics, U.S. Department of Education.

the early 1990s, more women have earned degrees (both undergraduate and advanced) than have men in the United States.

How can we understand this gender reversal in educational outcomes? Since the 1960s, the women's movement has had many important impacts on American society. This movement was instrumental in gaining women more opportunities to enter higher education. Furthermore, women in the 1960s and 1970s were entering the workforce at higher rates than ever before and were becoming involved in more professional occupations that required more education.

The declining influence of religion, something we talked about in Chapter 1, changed our expectations about the need for men and women to marry and the timing and number of children couples had. With delayed marriages, a rise in the number of people choosing to remain single, and a decline in the number of children per couple, women had more time and ability to focus on higher education. The development of modern birth control methods, particularly the birth control pill, was also very important. The pill, first approved for contraceptive use in the United States in 1960, is used by more than 100 million women worldwide (Shader & Zonderman, 2006). The pill's creation and availability was a major development in women's engagement in the education system. Now that women could control when and how many children they had (at least to some extent), they could remain in education longer and pursue degrees with fewer interruptions.

Although women have made large gains in terms of attendance and completion of university degrees, women still earn less than men once they have completed school. In fact, women earn about 15% less than men early in their careers (Blau, 1998). The early income inequalities are particularly important because those inequalities tend to grow over time (Marini, 1989). One of the main reasons given for women earning less than men, even though they are more likely to earn a degree, is the different majors that women and men select. Men are overrepresented in majors such as sciences and engineering, which are more likely to lead to high-paying jobs. In addition, women are not able to translate their degrees into earnings the same way that men do.

READING: "THE NOT-SO-PINK IVORY TOWER"

Ann Mullen

Educational attainment varies widely by sex, race, and ethnic group. As we learned in Chapter 5, racial and ethnic groups have very different rates of high school and university graduation. However, as with gender, these inequalities do not always follow the general trends of discrimination that we observe in society. Ann Mullen discusses how men's and women's performances in higher education differ by social class and ethnicity. As you read Mullen's article, keep in mind the concept of intersectionality (introduced in Chapter 6).

Since 1982, women in the United States have been graduating from college at higher rates than men; they currently earn 57 percent of all bachelor's degrees. Some view this trend as a triumphant indicator of gender egalitarianism, while others sound the alarm about the supposed "male crisis" in higher education and the problem of increasingly "feminized" universities. . . .

Who's Getting Degrees

During the past 40 years, the gender distribution of bachelor's degrees reversed. In 1970, men earned 57 percent of all degrees; today, women do. This trend leads some to conclude that women are squeezing men out of higher education, and that women's success has led to men's decline. In fact, this zero-sum scenario is incorrect: the college-going rates for both men and women have increased substantially. Both genders are far more likely to graduate from college now than at any previous point in time. Women's increasing graduation rate isn't due to a decrease in the number of graduating male students, but to the fact that women's increases occurred faster than men's. Particularly between 1970 and 1990, as employment opportunities for women expanded, their college graduation rates grew more rapidly than did those of men.

The rates of growth for men and women have now equalized. Over the past decade, the number of degrees earned by both men and women actually increased by the identical rate of 38 percent. The U.S. Department of Education predicts that over the course of the next decade women's share of bachelor's degrees will rise by only one percentage point, to 58 percent of all degrees. In looking at these figures, we see that women's successes did not come at the expense of men, and that the gender gap is not growing uncontrollably. It has in fact stabilized, and has held steady for more than 10 years.

To fully assess the gender distribution of bachelor's degrees, we also need to look at what kinds of men and women graduate from college, and whether men and women of different racial, ethnic, and class backgrounds have the same chances of graduating. Among 25- to 29-year-olds, across all racial and ethnic groups, more women than men hold bachelor's degrees. The gap is just over 7 percent among whites and Hispanics, 6 percent among blacks, and about 10 percent for Asians.

But in terms of race and ethnicity, the gaps in college completion far exceed that of gender: 56 percent of Asians between 25 and 29 years old hold bachelor's degrees, compared to only 39 percent of whites, 20 percent of blacks, and nearly 13 percent of Hispanics. Both white and Asian men are far more likely than black or Hispanic students of either gender to earn a bachelor's degree. These racial gaps are actually larger now than they were in the 1960s: while students from all backgrounds are now more likely to graduate from college, the rates have increased more quickly for whites and Asians.

Social class continues to be the strongest predictor of who will attend and graduate from college—one that far outweighs the effects of either gender, or race and ethnicity. Surveys by the U.S. Department of Education show that 70 percent of high-school students from wealthy families will enter four-year colleges, compared to only 21 percent of their peers from low-income families. Gender differences also vary by social class background. According to education policy analyst Jackie King, for the wealthiest students, the gender gap actually favors men. (For families in the highest income quartile, men comprise 52 percent of college students, compared to 44 percent in the lowest income quartile, and 47 percent in the middle two quartiles). Age also plays a role: among adults 25 years and older, women are far more likely than men to return to college for a bachelor's degree. But among those 24 and under, women make up only 55 percent of all students, and the gender difference among enrollment rates for recent high-school graduates is small (41 percent of men and 44 percent of women).

In other words, women's overall advantage in earning college degrees is not shared equally among all women. White women, Asian women, and wealthy women outpace women from other backgrounds. Gender differences are largest among students 25 years and up, Asians, and low-income students. But differences in relation to class, race, and ethnicity greatly overshadow gender gaps in degree attainment.

Not at Caltech

In assessing gender equity in higher education, it's also necessary to take into account where men and women earn their degrees. While more women than men tend to graduate from college, women are disproportionately represented in less competitive institutions. Sociologist Jayne Baker and I found that women earned more than 60 percent of degrees in the least selective institutions, but only slightly more than half in the most selective institutions. Women's gains have been greatest at institutions with lower standardized test scores and higher acceptance rates, while men and women are roughly on par with each other at elite institutions. Women are also underrepresented at the top science and engineering institutions, like Caltech and MIT. So, while women may be in the majority overall, their integration into higher education has been uneven, and they are more likely to attend lower-status institutions.

Perhaps the most striking disparities are in the choice of college majors. In spite of their overall minority status, men still earn 83 percent of all degrees in engineering, 82 percent in computer and information sciences, 70 percent in philosophy, and 69 percent in economics. Women, on the other hand, continue to earn the lion's share of degrees in traditionally female-dominated fields: 77 percent in psychology, 80 percent in education, and 85 percent in nursing and other health professions. About a third of all men (or women) would have to change majors in order to achieve gender parity across majors today. This hasn't changed much in the last 25 years. (Through the 1970s and early 1980s, fields moved steadily toward becoming more integrated, but in the mid-1980s, this trend slowed and then stalled, shifting very little since then.)

Sociologists Paula England and Su Li found that most of the decrease in segregation came from the growth of gender-integrated fields, like business, and from the flow of women into previously male-dominated fields. Men are much less likely to move into female-dominated fields. They also found that women's entrance into predominantly male fields discourages later cohorts of men from choosing those fields. Women gain status and pay by entering predominantly male fields, while men lose out when they enter devalued, predominantly female fields of study.

Women and men are ostensibly free to select any field they wish, and they no longer face the blatant kinds of barriers to entry that have historically existed. But, other factors influence students' choices subtly, but powerfully. Sociologist Shelly Correll has done innovative experiments with undergraduate students that demonstrate how cultural beliefs about gender shape individuals' career aspirations. When exposed to the idea that men are better at certain tasks, male participants in the study rated their own abilities higher than the women, even though they were all given the same scores. These subjective assessments of their own competencies then influenced students' interest in related careers. Correll argues that widely shared cultural beliefs about gender and different kinds of competencies (like math and science) bias men's and women's perceptions of their own abilities, and their interest in pursuing these fields. She finds that men assess their own capabilities in math more generously than do women, which then encourages them to go into math and science fields. . . .

After College

Paradoxically, women's success in closing the gender gap in higher education has not closed the gender gaps in the labor market. Men and women still generally work in different kinds of jobs, and women still earn considerably less than men (even with the same levels of education). Occupational segregation remains high and the trend toward narrowing the gender gap in pay has slowed. Currently, young, college-educated, full-time working women can expect to earn only 80 percent of the salaries of men ($40,000 annually compared to $49,800), a ratio identical to that of 1995. In fact, women with bachelor's degrees earn the same as men with associate degrees. Some of this pay gap can be attributed to students' undergraduate fields of study. Engineering graduates, for example, earn about $55,000 annually in their first year after graduation, while education majors bring home only $30,500. However, even after taking into account fields of study, women still earn less than men.

These pay disparities suggest an economic rationale for women's vigorous pursuit of higher education. Not only do women need to acquire more education in order to earn the same salaries as men, they also receive higher returns on their educational investments. Education scholar Laura Perna has found that even though women's salaries are lower than men's, women enjoy a greater pay-off in graduating from college than men do. In the early years after graduating, a woman with a college degree will earn 55 percent more than a woman with a high-school degree. For men, that difference is only 17 percent. What's more, men with only a high-school education earn a third more than women do, and are more likely to find work in traditionally male blue-collar jobs that offer health care and other benefits—which are not available in the sales and service jobs typically held by women.

Though men with high-school educations enjoy higher salaries and better benefits than do women, they are also more vulnerable to unemployment. In general, the rates of unemployment are twice as high for high-school graduates as they are for college graduates. They are also slightly higher for men than for women at all educational levels below the bachelor's degree. According to data from a 2010 U.S. Census survey, the unemployment rate for high-school graduates was 11.3 percent for men versus 9 percent for women (compared to 4.8 percent and 4.7 percent, respectively, for those with at least a bachelor's degree), due in part to the effects of the recent recession on the manufacturing sector.

Along with offering access to better jobs, higher salaries, and less risk of unemployment, going to college offers a host of other advantages. College graduates live longer, healthier lives. They are less likely to smoke, drink too much, or suffer from anxiety, depression, obesity, and a variety of illnesses. They are more likely to vote, to volunteer, and to be civically engaged. Because of this broad array of social and economic benefits, we should be concerned about patterns of underrepresentation for any group.

Incomplete Integration

To some, the fact that women earn 57 percent of all degrees to men's 43 percent suggests the gender pendulum has swung too far. They claim that if the ratio still favored men, there would be widespread protest. But such claims fail to see the full picture: though women earn more degrees than men, the gender integration of higher education is far from complete. Men and women still diverge in the fields of study they choose, their experiences during college, and the kinds of jobs they get after graduating.

In the early 1970s, when men earned 57 percent of college degrees, women faced exclusion and discrimination in the labor market and earned less than two-thirds of what men earned. Many professions, and most positions of power and authority, were almost completely closed to women. While the ratio of college graduates now favors women, women are not benefiting from more education in ways that men did 40 years ago. In terms of the economic rewards of completing college, women are far from matching men, let alone outpacing them.

By paying exclusive attention to the gender ratio, we tend to overlook much more serious and enduring disparities of social class, race, and ethnicity. This lessens our ability to understand how gender advantages vary across groups. If there is a crisis of access to higher education, it is not so much a gender crisis, as one of race and class. Young black and Hispanic men and men from low-income families are among the most disadvantaged, but women from these groups also lag behind their white, Asian, and middle-class counterparts. Addressing the formidable racial and economic gaps in college access will improve low-income and minority men's chances far more than closing the gender gap would.

The higher proportion of degrees earned by women does not mean that higher education is feminizing, or that men are getting crowded out. It seems that if women hold an advantage in any area, even a relatively slim one, we jump to the conclusion that it indicates a catastrophe for men. In the case of access to college degrees, that's simply not true.

Recommended Resources

England, Paula, and Su Li. "Desegregation Stalled: The Changing Gender Composition of College Majors, 1971–2002," *Gender & Society* (2006), 20: 657–677. Reviews trends in the gender segregation of fields of study and the reasons behind shifts toward integration as well as the stalling of desegregation.

Sax, Linda J. *The Gender Gap in College: Maximizing the Developmental Potential of Women and Men* (Jossey-Bass, 2008). Examines the impact of college experiences, peer groups, and faculty on a comprehensive array of student outcomes.

U.S. Department of Education, National Center for Education Statistics, Institute of Education Sciences. (Washington DC, various years). *Digest of Education Statistics* and *The Condition of Education*. Comprehensive compendiums of education statistics, including a wide range of gender, race, ethnicity, and class indicators.

Reading Questions

1. How has the percentage of women and men earning degrees changed? What would you expect the situation to be in 10 years?
2. What is the role of race and ethnicity in the relationship between gender and degrees? Do all ethnic groups have the same gap between men and women in terms of the number of degrees earned?
3. What is the role of social class in the relationship between gender and degrees?
4. Why is it important to assess men's and women's majors when talking about inequality in education? How is the factor of majors related to the types of jobs that men and women perform?

Mullen, A. (2012). The not-so-pink ivory tower. *Contexts, 11*(4), 34–38.

EDUCATION, CULTURAL CAPITAL, AND SOCIAL CAPITAL

One reason that education can perpetuate social inequality, or conversely lead to social mobility, is its relationship to different forms of capital. When we think about capital, we tend to think about economic capital—things that have a monetary or exchange value (see Chapter 3). However, there are other kinds of capital, such as cultural and social capital; these resources can be acquired through the education system and can affect a person's chance of future success.

Cultural and Social Capital

Cultural capital is the noneconomic social assets that promote social mobility. For example, we can earn degrees, learn a more refined style of speech, or adopt elite social tastes, which can make us appear to belong to a higher social class than the one to which we were born. Pierre Bourdieu, who developed the concept, defines cultural capital as the cultural knowledge that we learn over the course of our lives that confers power and status (Bourdieu & Passeron, 1973).

Cultural capital consists of the behaviors, knowledge, and values that indicate a person's social class. For example, liking the theater and classical music is considered more sophisticated than liking action movies and heavy metal music. Some individuals or families are more likely to possess these "sophisticated" tastes and styles. In addition, this cultural capital is taught and institutionalized in the education system.

Getting to Know: Pierre Bourdieu (1930–2002)

- In 1955, Bourdieu was deployed to Algeria during its war of independence from France.

- In France, Bourdieu publicly supported a variety of causes including the 1995 railway worker strike and the 1996 sans papier (without papers) movement that organized against the government's expulsion of undocumented immigrants.

- His public commentary and book *Acts of Resistance: Against the Tyranny of the Market* (1999) made him a leading intellectual reference for social movements opposing neoliberalism and globalization.

- *Sociology Is a Martial Art* (2002) is a documentary about Pierre Bourdieu's life with footage capturing his lectures, meetings with students and researchers, and attendance at political rallies.

- In his documentary, Bourdieu states, "sociology is a martial art, a means of self-defense. Basically, you use it to defend yourself, without having the right to use it for unfair attacks."

Social capital is the collective value of all a person's social networks. It is about who you know and the norms of reciprocity that develop between people who know one another. Social capital is important because it can provide a wide variety of benefits. For example, having wide social networks can help foster trust among people, provide resources and information, and lead to cooperation. Both cultural and social capital can be acquired through the education system (Bourdieu & Passeron, 1990).

An example of social capital in education is the Greek system. Rushing a fraternity or sorority is a very common social activity in many American colleges. The networks afforded through membership in these communities help individuals expand their social capital and gain access to social circles that can influence their future success in work and other realms. For example, 85% of Fortune 500 CEOs have been in the Greek system, and the majority of U.S. presidents were once in fraternities (Konnikova, 2014).

According to Marx and other conflict theorists, the education system reflects the interests and experiences of the dominant class in society. Children from the dominant class in a society tend to do better in this system because they enter it with certain types of cultural and social skills that facilitate their progress. Children from the working class, however, must learn these skills in schools, which can slow down their progress in other areas of the curriculum. Marx also argued that even if children from the working class can learn the social and cultural skills that upper-class children naturally possess, these skills will never be natural for them. Teachers, principals, employers, and other children detect who innately possesses these social and cultural skills and tend to reward those students, perhaps by tracking them into advance placement classes or other special educational opportunities.

Omega Psi Phi fraternity performs at Gabrielle Union's "School Daze" birthday celebration Step Show at The Basement at The Edition Hotel on November 7, 2015 in Miami Beach, Florida.

Bobby Metelus/Getty Images

The Consequences of Degrees

A person's level of education has many important consequences. We have already indicated two of the most important effects: earning more money and being less likely to fall into unemployment (see Figure 9.4). However, these advantages are not equally felt by all groups of people. According to a 2021 study by Georgetown University, Black and Latino students need to get a master's to make the same amount of money as a White student with a bachelor's degree. Black workers with a high school diploma, associate's degree, or bachelor's degree earn lifetime medians of $1.4 million, $1.7 million, and $2.3 million, respectively—18%, 19%, and 21% less than the median for White workers with these same levels of education. Native American/Alaskan

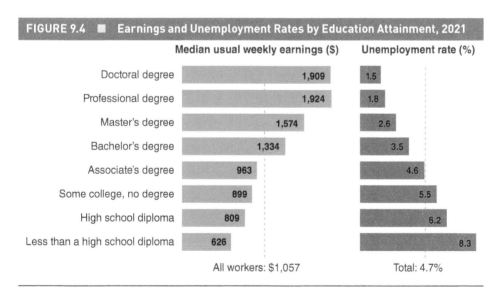

FIGURE 9.4 ■ Earnings and Unemployment Rates by Education Attainment, 2021

Education	Median usual weekly earnings ($)	Unemployment rate (%)
Doctoral degree	1,909	1.5
Professional degree	1,924	1.8
Master's degree	1,574	2.6
Bachelor's degree	1,334	3.5
Associate's degree	963	4.6
Some college, no degree	899	5.5
High school diploma	809	6.2
Less than a high school diploma	626	8.3
	All workers: $1,057	Total: 4.7%

Source: US Bureau of Labor Statistics. https://www.bls.gov/emp/chart-unemployment-earnings-education.htm

Native workers earn $2.2 million, which is 24% less than the median for White workers of their education levels (Carnevale et al., 2021).

Differences are also stark by gender. With a bachelor's degree, women on average earn $2.4 million over their lifetime while men earn $3.3 million. And, on average, women need a PhD to get more money than men with a bachelor's over the course of their lives (Center on Education and the Workforce, 2021).

EDUCATION AROUND THE WORLD

Education is an important institution in every country. However, the amount of money a country spends on the education system and the results from these expenditures differ significantly from one country to the next. Countries that spend a lot on education hope that this money will lead to better educational outcomes, such as higher achievement on international tests and higher graduation rates.

Table 9.1 shows the relationship between the amount of money a government spends on tertiary education (education after high school) and the percentage of the population ages 25–34 with a postsecondary degree. You can see that, in general, the more money a government spends on education, the higher its degree attainment rate. For example, the United States and the United Kingdom spend more on education and more of their young people have degrees than do Indonesia and Chile. However, this relationship is not universal. At $30,003 per student per year, the United States spends the most of all countries but has a rate of completion similar to that of France, which spends only about $16,114 per student.

TABLE 9.1 ■ Education Spending on Tertiary Education and Percentage of Population Aged 25–34 with Tertiary Education, 2019		
Country	**Education Spending (USD)**	**Percentage of People 25–34 with Tertiary Education**
Indonesia	$3,764.70	16.13
Chile	$8,405.90	33.73
Turkey	$8,900.70	35.33
Korea	$10,108.90	69.8
Brazil	$14,337.00	21.31
France	$16,144.80	48.05
Japan	$19,289.20	61.51
Australia	$20,344.20	52.48
United Kingdom	$26,320.10	51.81
United States	$30,003.20	50.38

Source: Adapted from OECD (2021a), Education spending (indicator). doi: 10.1787/ca274bac-en (Accessed on 19 May 2021) and OECD (2021b), Population with tertiary education (indicator). doi: 10.1787/0b8f90e9-en (Accessed on 19 May 2021)

Another exception is Korea, a remarkable success story in educational attainment. The country spends relatively little per student but has one of the highest rates of education completion in the world: 69.8% of Koreans between the ages of 25 and 34 have a university or college degree (van Damme, 2013). The Korean government spends only $10,108 per student but has a remarkably high rate of postsecondary educational attainment.

When considering inequality and education, we also want to consider how this inequality has been further exacerbated throughout the COVID-19 pandemic and how the impacts of the pandemic are not experienced equally among all social groups. This is particularly true for low-income university students. Research shows that they have experienced more negative effects of the pandemic than other groups.

New research from Arizona State University finds that for all students, the COVID-19 pandemic has led to negative academic and labor outcomes. For example, 50% of surveyed students reported spending less time studying, 40% lost a job, and 31% of working students witnessed a reduction in their wages. However, the effect is much stronger for low-income students than it is for their more affluent peers. Findings indicate that low-income students are 55% more likely to delay their graduation due to COVID-19, and they are 41% more likely to report that the pandemic has impacted their choice of major. Perhaps more striking is the fact that students expect the GPA gap to nearly double as a result of the pandemic. Evidence like this indicates that although the pandemic affects us all, we are not always experiencing it equally (Aucejo et al., 2020).

SUMMARY

The education system is one of modern society's central institutions and permeates many aspects of our day-to-day lives. This system works to socialize, select, and legitimize knowledge in our society. We have seen that not all individuals have equal access to or perform equally well in the education system. In this chapter, we have critically examined the role of this system in perpetuating, and potentially alleviating, social inequality, including the role of cultural and social capital in this relationship. We also discussed education around the world, comparing funding in various countries. There are widespread changes occurring in education in the United States and around the world that have important implications for educational outcomes across groups.

FOR FURTHER READING

Bourdieu, P., & Passeron, J.-C. (1990). *Reproduction in education, society, and culture* (2nd ed.). SAGE.

Coleman, J. (1990). *Foundations of social theory*, Harvard University Press.

Collins, R. (1979). *The credential society: A historical sociology of education and stratification*, Academic Press.

Davies, S., & Guppy, N. (2018). *The schooled society: An introduction to the sociology of education* (4th ed.). Oxford University Press.

Durkheim, É. (1956). *Education and sociology*, Free Press.

GLOSSARY

credentialing

cultural capital

curriculum

defensive credentialing

differential association

differential expectations

differential preparation

gender reversal in educational outcomes

hidden curriculum

human capital model

latent function

legitimation

manifest functions

schooled society

selection

self-fulfilling prophecy

social capital

tracking

Peter Treanor / Alamy Stock Photo

10 WORK AND RATIONALIZATION

LEARNING OBJECTIVES

1. Explain the rise of rationalization and the positive and negative consequences of this process for individuals and society.

2. Illustrate and apply the concepts of commodities and commodification.

3. Explain the changing division of labor in society and how this shapes social relationships and the individual worker.

4. Explain how precarious employment and the rise of emotional labor have changed the experience of labor in modern society.

Sociologists have long been interested in the changing nature of society. Max Weber, in particular, focused on the rise of rationality, the scientific understanding and processes oriented toward rational goals. He described how this new rationalized world contrasts with earlier faith-based societies, in which the world seemed unknowable and mystical. This chapter will focus on the process of rationalization in society. It will also look at the role of work and occupations in society and how work is becoming increasingly rationalized. We will examine several key changes in the American labor market, including the rise of scientific management, the rise in precarious employment, outsourcing, automation, and the prevalence of emotional labor.

THE RATIONALIZED WORLD

Weber (1965) argued that, prior to the Enlightenment (a movement in Europe in the late 17th and early 18th centuries, also known as the Age of Reason), we lived in an enchanted world. People had very little understanding of why natural events occurred—before the Enlightenment, people believed that the sun orbited around the earth. They explained droughts and plagues by claiming that the gods were angry or that Mother Nature was out of sync with people. The only way to solve these problems was to appease the gods, such as by performing a ritual or sacrifice.

The Enlightenment was an exciting intellectual movement: People embraced new ideas of science, logic, and reasoning, as well as the use of evidence to make sense of the world. This movement initiated new ways of understanding the natural and social worlds. People used to think that things fall to the ground because it was simply in their nature to do so. For example, the 7th-century Indian mathematician Brahmagupta argued that things fall toward the earth because the earth attracts them and that water flows downstream because it is in the nature of water to move. But through experiments and logic, we discovered gravity.

The Age of Reason also marked a decline in religion's role in society. Instead of looking to religious institutions and leaders to make sense of the world, people increasingly looked to science. For example, although the church tells us to have faith that humans were created in God's image because that is what the Bible says, Darwin argued that humans have evolved over millennia through the process of natural selection. This new way of seeing the world—through science and the principles of rationality—weakened the influence of religious authorities. Weber called this process the disenchantment of the world.

Rationalization

Rationalization is a way of solving problems based on four main factors: predictability, calculability, efficiency, and control. Predictability means that things can be repeated with the expectation of the same results. When a scientist does an experiment, for example, she will replicate it many times to make sure that the findings are correct. Calculability focuses on things that can be counted and quantified. In modern society, we tend to like to measure things with numbers and to compare things numerically—we assess runners' abilities by comparing their race times and academic ability by comparing grades, even though there are other, less quantifiable ways to measure these things. Rationality is also based on efficiency, the best means to a given end. For instance, it would be nonsensical to drive from Seattle to Miami through Mexico. The route might be more enjoyable, but it is not efficient because it would take longer and therefore would not fit with our modern principles of rationality. Finally, rationality is based on ideas of control and an enhanced certainty of outcomes, such as knowing exactly how long a trip will take by looking it up on Google maps, thus providing a basis for choosing how to undertake the task.

Rationalization has changed many aspects of society and permeates modern life. Living in such a world has many benefits. Most important, rational systems are very efficient. We can make many more products and run organizations more efficiently in a rationalized world. Rationalization and the rise of science also help us solve certain problems. When we thought that the plague was caused by bad humors or evil natures, we were ill-equipped to stop it. When we realized that vermin living in the city caused the plague, we could address the problem by improving sanitation. The Age of Reason allowed us to make sense of the world and afforded us some control over it. In this rationalized world, we tend to live longer and healthier lives, partly because of our understanding of science.

Despite these benefits, rationalization is not without its downsides. Weber (1965) argued that the process of disenchantment is also a process of disillusionment. As the world becomes less enchanted and less magical, it also becomes less meaningful for people. Part of what makes us human is our ability to be creative, emotional, and spontaneous. None of these qualities makes sense in a rationalized world. Creativity is absent from mass-produced consumer goods and the worker is unable to express individuality or make unique additions to the product. Spontaneity is taken away when we always look for the most efficient way to do things. In this way, the rise of rationality might be robbing us of our very humanity.

Rationalization in Modern Society

The prototype of rationalization in modern society is the bureaucracy. The word "bureaucracy" originated in 1789 and is based on the French root *bureau,* which means office or desk, and the Greek root *kratia*, which means power or rule. Bureaucracy, then, is the rule of the office or desk and is a machine made of humans. Bureaucracies rose to prominence as an organizational form in the 20th century. Examples in modern society include nonprofit organizations (e.g., many colleges, the YMCA or YWCA, and the United Nations [UN]) and for-profit companies (e.g., Starbucks, Microsoft, or Apple).

According to Weber (1965), bureaucracies have six core features:

1. Bureaucracies are based on hierarchically organized offices.

2. Bureaucracies have a vertical chain of command. Your college has professors who report to a chair who reports to a dean.

3. Bureaucracies have a clear, formal division of labor. In your college there are people who teach classes (professors), those who run the library (librarians), and those who clean and maintain the buildings (maintenance staff). The university could not run without these and many other individuals. However, these people do not switch from one task

Universities are bureaucracies. How does being a bureaucracy increase efficiency, predictability, calculability, and control? What are the potential positive and negative implications of this way of organizing higher education?

martinedoucet/iStockphoto.com

to the other. Instead, there is a clear separation of roles, with different people doing different tasks.

4. Bureaucracies are dominated by technical qualifications. Specific degrees and qualifications are needed to perform each job.

5. Bureaucracies have impersonal decision making. For example, all prospective students submit the same application that is judged without knowing the student's name or identifying features.

6. Bureaucracies are staffed by full-time, salaried employees.

READING: FROM *THE "MCDONALDIZATION" OF SOCIETY*

George Ritzer

A prototypical bureaucracy is the fast-food restaurant McDonald's. In the following excerpt, George Ritzer applies Weber's ideas about the rise of rationality to the emergence of fast-food restaurants and discusses how these establishments have affected society (a process he calls McDonaldization). Consider how this process of McDonaldization is happening all around you—at your college, at the grocery store, and at places you frequent in your leisure time.

A wide-ranging process of *rationalization* is occurring across American society and is having an increasingly powerful impact in many other parts of the world. It encompasses such disparate phenomena as fast-food restaurants, TV dinners, packaged tours, industrial robots, plea bargaining, and open-heart surgery on an assembly-line basis. As widespread and as important as these developments are, it is clear that we have barely begun a process that promises even more extraordinary changes (e.g. genetic engineering) in the years to come. We can think of rationalization as a historical process and rationality as the end result of that development. As an historical process, rationalization has distinctive roots in the Western world. Writing in the late nineteenth and early twentieth centuries, the great German sociologist Max Weber saw his society as the center of the ongoing process of rationalization and the bureaucracy as its paradigm case. The model of rationalization, at least in contemporary America, is no longer the bureaucracy, but might be better thought of as the fast-food restaurant. As a result, our concern here is with what might be termed the "McDonaldization of Society." While the fast-food restaurant is not the ultimate expression of rationality, it is the current exemplar for future developments in rationalization.

A society characterized by rationality is one which emphasizes *efficiency, predictability, calculability, substitution of non-human for human technology*, and *control over uncertainty*. In discussing the various dimensions of rationalization, we will be little concerned with the gains already made, and yet to be realized, by greater rationalization. These advantages are widely discussed in schools and in the mass media. In fact, we are in danger of being seduced by the innumerable advantages already offered, and promised in the future, by rationalization. The glitter of these accomplishments and promises has served to distract most people from the grave dangers posed by progressive rationalization. In other words, we are ultimately concerned here with the irrational consequences that often flow from rational systems. Thus, the second major theme of this essay might be termed "the irrationality of rationality."

In spite of the emphasis here on the problems posed by rationalization, this will not be one of those pleas for a return to a less rationalized way of life. Although there is certainly room for less rationalized pockets in a rational society, in most cases we cannot, and should not, try to reverse the process of rationalization. In our rush to critique rationalization we cannot ignore its many advantages (McDonald's does offer a lot of tasty food at relatively low cost). Furthermore, we should not romanticize the "noble" life of the pre-rational society with its many problems and disadvantages. We would not, in most cases, want to recreate a life beset by these problems, even if it was possible to do so. Instead, what we need [to] do is gain a better understanding of the process of rationalization so that we can come to exercise more and better control over it. . . .

Efficiency

The process of rationalization leads to a society in which a great deal of emphasis is placed on finding the best or optimum means to any given end. Whatever a group of people define as an end, and everything they so define, is to be pursued by attempting to find the best means to achieve the end. . . .

The modern American family, often with two wage earners, has little time to prepare elaborate meals. For the relatively few who still cook such meals, there is likely to be great reliance on cookbooks that make cooking from scratch much more efficient. However, such cooking is relatively rare today. Most families take as their objective quickly and easily prepared meals. To this end, much use is made of pre-packaged meals and frozen TV dinners.

For many modern families, the TV dinner is no longer efficient enough. To many people, eating out, particularly in a fast-food restaurant, is a far more efficient way of obtaining their meals. Fast-food restaurants capitalize on this by being organized so that diners are fed as efficiently as possible. They offer a limited, simple menu that can be cooked and served in an assembly-line fashion. The latest development in fast-food restaurants, the addition of drive-through windows, constitutes an effort to increase still further the efficiency of the dining experience. The family now can simply drive through, pick up its order, and eat it while driving to the next, undoubtedly efficiently organized, activity. The success of the fast-food restaurant has come full circle with frozen-food manufacturers now touting products for the home modeled after those served in fast-food restaurants.

Increasingly, efficiently organized food production and distribution systems lie at the base of the ability of people to eat their food efficiently at home, in the fast-food restaurant, or in their cars. Farms, groves, ranches, slaughterhouses, warehouses, transportation systems, and retailers are all oriented toward increasing efficiency. A notable example is chicken production where they are mass bred, force fed (often with many chemicals), slaughtered on an assembly line, iced or fast frozen and shipped to all parts of the country. Some may argue that such chickens do not taste as good as the fresh-killed, local variety, but their complaints are likely to be drowned in a flood of mass-produced chickens. . . .

The fast-food restaurant is certainly not the only place one can spend money. The center of spending is now the modern shopping center and the supermarket. These are organized in a highly efficient manner in order to aid business. Supermarkets have grown even more efficient recently with the advent of computer scanning devices which expedite the checkout process and, at the same time, make the work of stockpeople more efficient by eliminating the need to stamp prices on the items.

When our shoppers return home (in efficiently produced cars and on efficiently built roads) they are likely to enter apartments or suburban tract houses which have been efficiently constructed. Among other things, this means there is little or nothing to distinguish one apartment or house from many others. In constructing such dwellings, esthetic elements like trees or hills are likely to be leveled if they stand in the way of efficient construction. . . .

If the family is unhappy with the efficiency that pervades virtually every facet of daily life, it might seek relief in leisure-time activities that it may assume to be immune from the process of rationalization. However, even in these areas, the principles of efficiency are omnipresent. International travel is affordable for many only through organized tours that efficiently transport large groups of tourists from one site to another. The modern amusement park is often little more than a vast, elaborate people-moving machine designed to transport people through the park and its various attractions as efficiently as possible. Campgrounds, trout farms, sporting events, and night clubs are other examples of entertainment that have grown increasingly efficient. . . .

Predictability

A second component of rationalization involves the effort to ensure predictability from one place to another. In a rational society, people want to know what to expect when they enter a given setting or acquire some sort of commodity. They neither want nor expect surprises. They want to know that if they journey to another locale, the setting they enter or the commodity they buy will be essentially the same as the setting they entered or product they purchased earlier. Furthermore, people want to be sure that what they encounter is much like what they encountered at earlier times. In order to ensure predictability over time and place a rational society must emphasize such things as discipline, order, systemization, formalization, routine, consistency, and methodical operation. . . .

Fast-food restaurants rank very high on the dimension of predictability. In order to help ensure consistency, the fast-food restaurant offers only a limited menu. Predictable end-products are made possible by the use of similar raw materials, technologies, and preparation and serving techniques. Not only the food is predictable; the physical structures, the logo, the "ambience," and even the personnel are as well.

The food that is shipped to our homes and our fast-food restaurants is itself affected by the process of increasing predictability. Thus our favorite white bread is indistinguishable from one place to another. In fact, food producers have made great efforts to ensure such predictability. . . .

Other leisure-time activities have grown similarly predictable. Camping in the wild is loaded with uncertainties—bugs, bears, rain, cold, and the like. To make camping more predictable, organized grounds have sprung up around the country. Gone are many of the elements of unpredictability replaced by RVs, paved over parking lots, sanitized campsites, fences, and enclosed camp centers that provide laundry and food services, recreational activities, television, and video games. Sporting events, too, have in a variety of ways been made more predictable. The use of artificial turf in baseball makes for a more predictable bounce of a ball. . . .

Calculability or Quantity Rather Than Quality

It could easily be argued that the emphasis on quantifiable measures, on things that can be counted, is *the* most defining characteristic of a rational society. Quality is notoriously difficult to evaluate. How do we assess the quality of a hamburger, or a physician, or a student? Instead of even trying, in an increasing number of cases, a rational society seeks to develop a series of quantifiable measures that it takes as surrogates for quality. . . .

One of the most obvious examples in the university is the emphasis given to grades and cumulative grade point averages. With less and less contact between professor and student, there is little real effort to assess the quality of what students know, let alone the quality of their overall abilities. Instead, the sole measure of the quality of most college students is their grade in a given course and their grade point averages. Another blatant example is the emphasis on a variety of uniform exams such as SATs and GREs in which the essence of an applicant is reduced to a few simple scores and percentiles.

Within the educational institution, the importance of grades is well known, but somewhat less known is the way quantifiable factors have become an essential part of the process of evaluating college professors. For example, teaching ability is very hard to evaluate. Administrators have difficulty assessing teaching quality and thus substitute quantitative scores. Of course each score involves qualitative judgments, but this is conveniently ignored. Student opinion polls are taken and the scores are summed, averaged, and compared. Those who score well are deemed good teachers while those who don't are seen as poor teachers. There are many problems involved in relying on these scores such as the fact that easy teachers in "gut" courses may well obtain high ratings while rigorous teachers of difficult courses are likely to score poorly. . . .

Sports in general, and baseball in particular, are dominated by an emphasis on numbers. However, in sports there is a closer relationship between quantity and quality than in many other areas of life. The earned run average of a pitcher or the batting average of a batter are fairly good measures of the quality of their play. But even here a number of intangible qualities of play do not show up. For example, a player may be very valuable, even though his statistics are not particularly good, for his ability to make a clutch play, inspire his teammates, or be a leader. . . .

Politics offers a number of interesting examples of the substitution of quantitative for qualitative measures. Presidential candidates are obsessed by their ratings in the polls and often adjust what they say or do to what the pollsters tell them is likely to increase their ratings. Even sitting presidents (and other politicians) are highly attuned to the polls. The emphasis often seems to be on their impact on the polls of taking a specific political position rather than the qualities of that position. . . .

Substitution of Non-Human Technology

In spite of Herculean efforts, there are important limits to the ability to rationalize what human beings think and do. Seemingly no matter what one does, people still retain at least the ultimate capacity to think and act in a variety of unanticipated ways. Thus, in spite of great efforts to make human behavior more efficient, more predictable, more calculable, people continue to act in unforeseen ways. People continue to make home cooked meals from scratch, to camp in tents in the wild, to eat in old-fashioned diners, and to sabotage the assembly lines. Because of these realities, there is great interest among those who foster increasing rationality in using rational technologies to limit individual independence and ultimately to replace human beings with machines and other technologies that lack the ability to think and act in unpredictable ways.

McDonald's does not yet have robots to serve us food, but it does have teenagers whose ability to act autonomously is almost completely eliminated by techniques, procedures, routines, and machines. There are numerous examples of this including rules which prescribe all the things a counterperson should do in dealing with a customer as well as a large variety of technologies which determine the actions of workers such as drink dispensers which shut themselves off when the cup is full; buzzers, lights, and bells which indicate when food (e.g. French fries) is done; and cash registers which have the prices of each item programmed in. One of the latest attempts to constrain individual action is Denny's use of pre-measured packages of dehydrated food that are "cooked" simply by putting them under the hot water tap. Because of such tools and machines, as well as the elaborate rules dictating worker behavior, people often feel like they are dealing with human robots when they relate to the personnel of a fast-food restaurant. When human robots are found, mechanical robots cannot be far behind. Once people are reduced to a few robot-like actions, it is a relatively easy step to replace them with mechanical robots. Thus Burgerworld is reportedly opening a prototypical restaurant in which mechanical robots serve the food.

Much of the recent history of work, especially manual work, is a history of efforts to replace human technology with non-human technology. Scientific management was oriented to the development of an elaborate and rigid set of rules about how jobs were to be done. The workers were to blindly and obediently follow those rules and not to do the work the way they saw fit. The various skills needed to perform a task were carefully delineated and broken down into a series of routine steps that could be taught to all workers. The skills, in other words, were built into the routines rather than belonging to skilled craftspersons. Similar points can be made about the assembly line which is basically a set of non-human technologies that have the needed steps and skills built into them. The human worker is reduced to performing a limited number of simple, repetitive operations. However, the control of this technology over the individual worker is so great and omnipresent that individual workers have reacted negatively manifesting such things as tardiness, absenteeism, turnover, and even sabotage. We are now witnessing a new stage in this technological development with automated processes now totally replacing many workers with robots. With the coming of robots we have reached the ultimate stage in the replacement of human with non-human technology. . . .

Control

This leads us to the fifth major dimension of rationalization—control. Rational systems are oriented toward, and structured to expedite, control in a variety of senses. At the most general level, we can say that rational systems are set up to allow for greater control over the uncertainties of life—birth, death, food production and distribution, housing, religious salvation, and many, many others. More specifically, rational systems are oriented to gaining greater control over the major source of uncertainty in social life—other people. Among other things, this means control over subordinates by superiors and control of clients and customers by workers. . . .

At a more specific level, the rationalization of food preparation and serving at McDonald's gives it great control over its employees. The automobile assembly line has a similar impact. In fact, the vast majority of the structures of a rational society exert extraordinary control over the people who labor in them. But because of the limits that still exist on the degree of control that rational structures can exercise over individuals, many rationalizing employers are driven to seek to more fully rationalize their operations and totally eliminate the worker. The result is an automated, robot-like technology over which, barring some *2001* rebellion, there is almost total control.

In addition to control over employees, rational systems are also interested in controlling the customer/clients they serve. For example, the fast-food restaurant with its counter, the absence of waiters and waitresses, the limited seating, and the drive-through windows all tend to lead customers to do certain things and not to do others.

Irrationality of Rationality

Although not an inherent part of rationalization, the *irrationality of rationality* is a seemingly inevitable by-product of the process. We can think of the irrationality of rationality in several ways. At the most general level it can simply be seen as an overarching label for all the negative effects of rationalization. More specifically, it can be seen as the opposite of rationality, at least in some of its senses. For example, there are the inefficiencies and unpredictabilities that are often produced by seemingly rational systems. Thus, although bureaucracies are constructed to bring about greater efficiency in organizational work, the fact is that there are notorious inefficiencies such as the "red tape" associated with the operation of most bureaucracies. Or, take the example of the arms race in which a focus on quantifiable aspects of nuclear weapons may well have made the occurrence of nuclear war more, rather than less, unpredictable.

Of greatest importance, however, is the variety of negative effects that rational systems have on the individuals who live, work, and are served by them. We might say that *rational systems are not reasonable systems*. As we've already discussed, rationality brings with it great dehumanization as people are reduced to acting like robots. Among the dehumanizing aspects of a rational society are large lecture classes, computer letters, pray TV, work on the automobile assembly line, and dining at a fast-food restaurant. Rationalization also tends to bring with it disenchantment leaving much of our lives without any mystery or excitement. Production by a band craftsman is far more mysterious than an assembly-line technology where each worker does a single, very limited operation. Camping in an RV tends to suffer in comparison to the joys to be derived from camping in the wild. Overall a fully rational society would be a very bleak and uninteresting place.

In addition to being dehumanizing and disenchanting many rational systems which are supposedly constructed to help people, in the end often have very negative effects. Thus to produce massive amounts of food, producers are driven to rationalize food production in a number of ways including the use of more and more pesticides and artificial ingredients. While such rational technologies are capable of producing a lot of food, they often produce foods that are not as nourishing as their natural counterparts and, in some cases, include chemicals that may be harmful, dangerous, and even fatal. McDonald's seemingly rational way of feeding people quickly and cheaply has had many unforeseen and irrational consequences such as weight gain because of the highly caloric nature of the food, increased cholesterol levels, heightened blood pressure as a result of the high salt content of the food, and it has played a key role in the destruction of the family meal and perhaps ultimately the nuclear family. . . .

Reading Questions

1. How do McDonald's and other fast-food restaurants embody the ideas of rationalization?
2. What are the benefits of McDonaldization?
3. What are the problems with McDonaldization?
4. Ritzer outlines many other examples of things that have become McDonaldized in modern society, including camping, education, work, politics, and television. Take one of these examples and outline how it has become more predictable, calculable, efficient, and controlled.

Ritzer, G. (2011). *The McDonaldization of society.* SAGE.

Undoubtedly, the process of rationalization occurs in modern society. As Ritzer (2011) notes, we cannot and should not try to stop it. There are many important benefits to rationalization. For instance, it allows us to produce a wider range of goods and services and to make them available to a much larger portion of the population. These goods are convenient and less expensive alternatives to higher-priced customized goods. Rationalization also allows us to create goods of uniform quality and to provide a sense of familiarity and stability for the consumer.

Does this mean that everything in modern society is rationalized or McDonaldized? Ritzer (2011) argues that two main types of organizations are not. First, organizations that are traceable to an earlier premodern age, such as independent corner stores or garage sales, are not McDonaldized. Moreover, some businesses are in direct opposition to McDonaldized companies. People who do not want to stay at a Holiday Inn or other chain hotel can stay at a bed and breakfast, where they will receive personalized attention and a homemade breakfast from a friendly proprietor. If you do not want to go to the rationalized Starbucks, you can go to an independent coffee shop.

Getting to Know: George Ritzer (b. 1940)

- Ritzer's critique of corporations stems from growing up relatively poor and witnessing his father's treatment in low-status occupations.

- He spent a lot of time during his youth reading *The New York Times* and attending outdoor events and concerts.

- One notable but seemingly mundane event that influenced his intellectual life was visiting a McDonald's for the first time as a City College of New York student. He thought that the restaurant seemed out of place in an environment surrounded by distinct restaurants (and inspired his later work on McDonaldization!).

- After receiving his MBA from the University of Michigan, Ritzer participated in a series of failed interviews with General Electric (GE), during which both parties realized he was too pro-union for the company.

- For decades throughout his career, he began his 10–14 hour writing days at 4 a.m.

Negative Outcomes of Rationalization

Despite the existence of some nonrationalized parts of society, the general trend is toward increasing rationalization. Ritzer (2011) highlights how this trend can create what Weber referred to as the irrationality of rationality. On a general level, the irrationality of rationality is simply that rationalized systems can create negative outcomes. For example, the rationalized education system, in which you have a student number and are judged based on your grade point average, can be alienating and frustrating. Although it may be more fair to test each student with a standardized test, doing so ignores a student's individuality. It is also irrational to think that each student understands the material in the same way.

The irrationality of rationality can also be seen in the fact that rationalized systems are sometimes unreasonable, which leads to negative effects. As previously mentioned, bureaucracies involve a lot of red tape. Red tape is an excessive adherence to formal rules that hinders the functioning of organizations. Anyone who has filled out student loan forms has had first-hand experience with red tape. If you have ever worked on a committee such as your high school student council, think of the issues (such as decorations for a dance) that were long debated and that went through an unnecessarily tedious approval process that was disproportionate to its significance.

Here you see a group of kids at a lemonade stand that they have built. Because it is hand-made by the children (with the help of their parents!) it is unique.

viafilms/iStockPhoto

This lemonade stand kit rationalizes the process of making a lemonade stand. In the kit, you get a sales banner, price sign, and all the materials you need. It promises to help you "achieve your highest lemonade sales imaginable!" This is certainly more efficient than having children make their own sign or organize their own table. How does it reduce the creativity and diversity in the stands?

AP Photo/Reed Saxon

Returning to Ritzer's (2011) main example, it is easy to see that the rationalized system of McDonald's has negative consequences. For example, McDonald's (and other fast-food restaurants) produces huge amounts of waste, which is bad for the environment. It also produces food that, although cheap and plentiful, leads to obesity and other health problems.

The 2004 documentary *Super Size Me* (Spurlock, 2004) focuses on the negative health effects of McDonald's. The film follows Morgan Spurlock as he eats only McDonald's food for 30 days and experiences drastic changes to his physical and psychological well-being. Spurlock, then 32 years old, consumed an average of 5,000 calories a day. He gained 24.5 pounds, increased his body mass by 13%, and experienced mood swings and sexual dysfunction. It took only 30 days to gain the weight but 14 months to lose it.

One of the goals of McDonaldization is to make consumers' lives easier, yet rationalized systems also require consumers to do more of the labor originally assigned to workers. This practice allows corporations to save money on labor. For example, in most states consumers now pump their own gas, often have the option to go through a self-checkout line to buy groceries, and can bank online, all under the façade that it is more efficient for them to do so. However, this is also beneficial for the company, which no longer hires as many employees to work at their stores.

Another potential drawback of rationalization and McDonaldization is that it produces a focus on efficiency and calculability that spreads to all aspects of our lives. In a rationalized world, we are encouraged to see everything through the lens of rationalization. For example, we see things that previously were viewed as having no monetary value as having a price.

COMMODIFICATION

A commodity is a product that has some monetary value, is standardized, and is mass-produced by many different producers. Consumer goods, such as clothing, cars, and food, are commodities. Commodification is the transformation of what is normally a non-commodity into a commodity—that is, commodification assigns monetary value. Commodification refers to the process through which social relations are reduced to an exchange relationship, or, as Karl Marx (Marx & Engels, 1964) called it, callous cash payment. Marx focused on the commodification of the labor process, in which the real, material activity of labor by individual workers was transformed into abstract labor, meaning just another cost in the process of production. The cost of labor could be measured in terms of hours and dollars.

Modern society has many examples of commodification. When we bottle water, we take something that was not seen as a commodity (it was something everyone could get free) and make it into one (something that is bought and sold). There are now oxygen bars where you can buy oxygen. Imagine trying to explain to your grandparents that you spent money to buy oxygen. Other things that were never thought of as having a cash value are also now commodified. For example, human organs are bought and sold for transplant in some countries, and individuals who want children can pay a woman to be a surrogate mother for them. In a rationalized world, more and more realms of life are controlled by and valued with money.

This Las Vegas oxygen bar offers scented oxygen. Oxygen bars claim that extra oxygen to the brain might increase a person's mental performance—which could be useful at the casino! What is the effect of selling oxygen? How does it change the way we feel about it as something to which everyone should have access?

Kevork Djansezian/Getty Images

In modern society, culture can also be commodified. The process can reduce ideas, customs, and behaviors to items that can be bought and sold. When culture is commodified, it becomes mass-produced and can be removed from its original meaning and significance.

USING YOUR SOCIOLOGICAL IMAGINATION
THE COMMODIFICATION AND RATIONALIZATION OF THE HUMAN BODY

Early sociologists who considered the process of commodification focused mostly on how we commodify labor and goods. However, in modern society the process of commodification extends to almost all aspects of our lives, including the sale of reproductive materials like eggs and sperm. Researcher Renee Almeling (2007) set out to find out how social factors shape the way that people are recruited, screened, and compensated for their reproductive materials. Almeling interviewed staff at egg agencies and sperm banks to observe how these organizations sought out clients and decided the worth of their genetic materials. She found that egg agencies aimed to recruit altruistic women, who were less concerned with the money that they would receive from selling their eggs. By contrast, sperm banks expected their clients to be financially motivated and did not question why men would want to sell their sperm. Do these gendered standards for selling eggs and sperm still apply today?

Visit these websites and then answer the following questions:

https://www.shadygrovefertility.com/become-egg-donor/

https://www.cascadecryobank.com

1. What features do these websites emphasize in recruiting egg donors versus sperm donors? What qualities are the same and what qualities are different?
2. How much can someone make from selling eggs? How much can someone make from selling sperm? How are these amounts determined?
3. What social factors other than gender (race, ethnicity, disability, sexual orientation, etc.) could play a role in the commodification of reproductive material?
4. In some countries, egg and sperm donors are not paid. Do you think donation of reproductive materials should be compensated? Why or why not?

There are many examples of the commodification of culture. Asian American actress Awkwafina has been accused of using a stereotypical Black accent and mannerisms in her comedy. In 2019, Kim Kardashian released a line of body shaping underwear that she called Kimono. But after accusations of cultural appropriation, she changed the name to SKIMS. Native American symbols have long been appropriated and commodified. For example, sports teams such as the Cleveland Indians (now known as the Cleveland Guardians) and the Washington Redskins (now known as the Washington Commanders) were criticized for their racist and negative depictions of Indigenous people. The clothing company Urban Outfitters has also caused controversy due to its use of Navajo tribal patterns in its clothing designs. What do you think about the use of these symbols? Are there situations when it is acceptable to use symbols from another culture?

Katy Perry's geisha-inspired performance at the American Music Awards stirred controversy. Do you think that this is cultural appropriation? Should we be able to use cultural symbols that are borrowed in this way? Why or why not?

Kevin Winter/Getty Images

THE DIVISION OF LABOR IN SOCIETY

The question of what holds society together has long intrigued sociologists and other social scientists. As a structural functionalist, Émile Durkheim (1960) was interested in examining how things evolve to function as they do. His work focused on how the glue that holds society together has changed over time. We have moved from a time characterized by mechanical solidarity to one characterized by organic solidarity. As you will recall from Chapter 4, in a society exhibiting the former, cohesion and integration come from the fact that individuals are all the same. Small-scale traditional societies are based on mechanical solidarity. Think of a small village in 1500. Most people in that village would do similar sorts of jobs, would have the same level of education (which would probably be quite low), and would be from the same religious and ethnic group.

Modern and industrial societies, such as the United States, are characterized by organic solidarity. In these societies we are not tied together because we are so similar but rather because we are so different. People in modern societies are very diverse—they have different religious beliefs, come from different cultural traditions, and have different interests and values. However, we need one another because we are so specialized that we cannot survive without others who do different tasks.

For Durkheim, one of the major differences between societies based on mechanical solidarity and those based on organic solidarity is the extent to which these societies have a complex division of labor (the specialization of labor into specific and distinct tasks). Societies based on mechanical solidarity have very little division of labor—most people perform a variety of tasks to navigate their daily life. Everyone grows their own food, sews their own clothes, and makes their own candles.

A society based on organic solidarity has a much more complex division of labor, which has both advantages and disadvantages. If tasks are split into smaller and simpler units, we can hire cheaper unskilled labor to perform them. For example, if you no longer need to hire a tailor to design, measure, and sew your clothes but can have one person who only designs, one who only cuts material, and one who only sews, you can have people with fewer skills doing each task. Moreover, an individual worker is no longer instrumental to a whole factory. If your tailor quits, you are left with no means to get clothes. However, if the fabric cutter in a factory leaves, you can easily find another unskilled worker to do the job and the overall production is not seriously affected. It is also possible to use more machinery when the tasks are broken down: A machine can cut material, but it cannot do all the parts of production. A high degree of division of labor is therefore a very efficient and cheap way of making products.

Scientific Management

Frederick Taylor developed the principle of scientific management (Taylorism) within the manufacturing industries of the 1880s and 1890s. This theory applies scientific principles and methods to labor management and involves creating divisions in the labor process. He sought to rationalize work and make it more efficient by dividing it into smaller and smaller tasks. Henry Ford, the founder of the Ford Motor Company, helped to perfect these ideas of scientific management at the turn of the 19th century. Ford developed the modern method of mass production, in particular the assembly line. Although Ford's methods of scientific management were used to improve the speed and standardization of production in the automotive industry, his principles have been applied to many manufacturing processes and other workplaces (Bonanno, 2012).

Ford practiced two main principles of scientific management: the standardization of products and the use of specialized equipment. Using scientific management, products are not handmade or unique. Instead, they are made with machines using molds and models without the need for skilled craftspeople. This system of production relies on the use of specific machines and tools designed so that workers do not need specialized skills to work on the assembly line. A worker can easily be trained to do a small repetitive task and can be replaced without much difficulty (Beyon & Nichols, 2006).

Increased efficiency and productivity are the two main benefits to scientific management. However, the system also has many disadvantages. For example, Taylor (1947) found that the workers he studied often became dissatisfied with the work environment and angry at their treatment by management. This was partly because, under scientific management, the conception of work was separated from its execution. Managers—with the help of efficiency experts—decided how the work was to be done, while the workers were expected to do what they were told in an unthinking and uncreative manner. Because workers were asked to do only one or a few repetitive tasks, most of their skills and abilities (including the ability to think) were not used. In general, scientific management separates head work from hand work. Before Taylor and other innovators of scientific management, the skilled worker performed both head and hand work by exercising control and creativity at work: They decided how they worked and did the physical tasks of the work themselves. Taylor took the time to understand the head work that skilled workers were doing and then divided it into simpler, repetitive tasks that anyone could easily learn. As a result, workers had to do only easy and monotonous hand work.

The Ford Motor Company's assembly lines are a classic example of mass production. Such scientific management made it possible to create the Ford Model T, the first automobile that a wide range of consumers could afford.

ullstein bild / GRANGER

Automation

Scientific management practices had many far-reaching implications for how we work today. These systems of work led to automation, where control systems for operating equipment are run with minimal or reduced human activity. The benefit of automation is that it saves labor (and, as a result, money for business owners) and can help to improve the quality and precision of the labor process. However, it can also lead workers to lose their jobs and changes the nature of the work for those who remain on the assembly line—who now are just working with machines instead of with their fellow employees.

We see automation all around us. For example, companies are now working to create fully automated grocery stores. When you walk in, there would be no workers. Instead, a computer with facial recognition software welcomes you by name and directs you to the items that you are looking for. You select the items you want from a small area, since there are only samples in the store. You scan them yourself with your phone and then leave (with nothing in your bag). Robots in the back of the store put the items you have selected into a box and a driverless car delivers them to your home that day. You never interact with another person.

This experience is an extreme example of automation, the process of replacing human labor with mechanical labor. About half of all work activities globally have the technical potential to be automated, meaning that we currently have the technologies that would make it possible to use machines instead of workers. About 25% of work in the United States could be automated by 2030 (McKinsey Global Institute [MGI], 2017). However, not all jobs are equally at risk. Jobs that require higher levels of education are least likely to be automated. For example, jobs that require less than a high-school education, including taxi drivers and resource extraction such as mining and logging, are 55% automatable, whereas jobs that require bachelor's or graduate degrees, such as lawyers, doctors, and teachers, are only 22% automatable (MGI, 2017).

In Amazon's new "Just Walk Out" convenience stores, there are no cashiers. Instead, customers are tracked using automatic surveillance technology for their purchases. How does this type of store promote efficiency? What are some of the challenges that both the company and customers might encounter?

Frederic REGLAIN/Alamy Stock Photo

Companies are embracing automation because it saves money by paying fewer workers. Although the overall American economy could benefit from these technological advances, we must also prepare for the job losses and greater income inequality that could come from this automation. In order to deal with these problems, governments could spend money on education and skills training to help workers and businesses adjust to increased automation and job losses in certain industries.

Outsourcing is another major implication of scientific management. Because labor is divided into smaller and smaller components, companies can separate the production processes, which often involves moving their manufacturing division, telephone call center, or their entire business to other countries to save money.

In scientific management, the worker is merely a cog in the machine. In fact, Taylor (1947) had a negative view of the worker. When describing the average worker, he wrote,

> Now one of the very first requirements for a man . . . is that he shall be so stupid and so phlegmatic that he more nearly resembles in his mental make-up the ox than any other type He is so stupid that the word "percentage" has no meaning to him, and he must consequently be trained by a man more intelligent than himself into the habit of working in accordance with the laws of this science before he can be successful. (p. 59)

Henry Ford also did not have a positive view of workers. In his autobiography he explains that "repetitive labor—the doing of one thing over and over again and always in the same way—is a terrifying prospect to a certain kind of man. It is terrifying to me The average worker, I am sorry to say, wants a job in which he does not have to think" (Ford, 1922, p. 103).

Methods in Depth: Worker Productivity and the Hawthorne Effect

Methodology

The research process can lead to some surprising discoveries. This was the case in the famous Hawthorne studies. Elton Mayo, an Australian-born sociologist, was interested in how physical conditions increased or decreased worker productivity. He started with a study of lighting in the workplace (Mayo, 1946). Mayo divided the workers into two groups. One group had its lighting increased (the experimental group). He did not change the lighting for the other group (the control group). Mayo found that the group with more lighting was more productive than the control group. Clearly, more lighting led to more productivity! Then Mayo changed the working conditions again. Now he reduced the lighting for the workers in the experimental group (while keeping the lighting the same for the control group). The group with less lighting was more productive. Clearly, less lighting made workers more productive! In fact, in all cases of changed working conditions, the workers became more productive. By the time the research was completed and everything had been returned to the way it was before the research had begun, productivity at the factory was at its highest level. The conclusion: All changes increased productivity!

The researchers were initially puzzled by these findings: How was it possible that increased lighting and decreased lighting led to more productivity? Mayo realized that it was not the specific changes that caused the increased productivity of the workers. Instead, workers were responding to being studied: They were aware they were being observed and reacted by being more productive. When the lights went up, they worked harder knowing they were being observed. When the lights went down, they again worked harder knowing they were being observed. It was only the workers not being observed (those in the control group who always had the same level of regular lighting) who did not change their work output. Mayo called this the Hawthorne effect, named after the factories where the studies were conducted. The Hawthorne effect occurs when individuals modify their behaviors because they are aware they are being observed (Mayo, 1946).

Implications

Mayo and others concerned with worker productivity quickly appreciated the importance of the Hawthorne effect. It showed that it was not the changes in physical conditions that were affecting the workers' productivity (Mayo, 1949). Rather, it was the fact that someone was actually concerned about their workplace and their working conditions that led them to work harder. This finding could be useful for employers concerned with the happiness and productivity of their workplaces. Mayo argued that workers were often unhappy because they had been unable to find satisfactory outlets for expressing personal problems and dissatisfactions in their work life (Mayo, 1949). When employers showed more interest in their workers, workers were happier and more productive.

Applications

There have been many studies since this early research that have illustrated the power of the Hawthorne effect. It is very important to test research findings through repeated studies to see if they apply across different contexts and situations. Replicating research to test findings is a critical part of the scientific method used in sociology and other social sciences. Researchers interested in the sociology of health, for example, have conducted many studies of the Hawthorne effect and showed how it can be consistently seen across a variety of research settings (McCambridge et al., 2014). Researchers in many areas have taken the findings of the Hawthorne study into consideration when they do research (Muldoon, 2012). When studying individuals or groups, it is important to take into consideration how being observed could change a person's behavior. Even knowing one is being studied can change behavior simply because of the increased interest and attention from the researcher.

The Alienation of Labor

Marx, who spent his life examining the role of social class in society, feared the effect of these types of labor changes on the worker. He clearly notes that work in capitalism, using scientific management and rationalized techniques, is very productive (Marx & Engels, 1964). Under capitalism, we can create more goods faster than ever before. However, Marx also notes that capitalism is a problem because it distorts the process of work, something that should be creative and enjoyable for the worker.

This distortion occurs in four main ways.

1. Capitalism transforms a naturally social and collective activity into a process that is about pursuing one's own interests. Workers compete for jobs or promotions while capitalists try to maximize profits by exploiting workers.

2. In capitalism workers create wealth through their labor and the goods they produce, but they receive only a small portion of this money. If a person works faster or more productively, the additional profit (surplus) goes to the capitalist rather than to the worker.

3. As the division of labor in jobs increases, more surplus is created for capitalists. However, this change reduces the natural enjoyment of labor. Before the rise of factories, workers could labor in their own small cottage industries. A cobbler making shoes in his own family business has creative control over the process and the enjoyment of creating the whole product. In modern factories or other work settings, we all perform smaller portions of jobs that are less enjoyable. It is much less satisfying for you to add the sole to a hundred identical shoes in a factory than to make three beautiful unique pairs of shoes in your independent business.

4. According to Marx, capitalism distorts work because it separates the workers from the product they make, the production process, other workers, and themselves. Workers experience alienation, a feeling of isolation or detachment, from the product because

they have no creative control over what they make. They are alienated from the production process because they have no control over how they work—they do not create the assembly lines or stores in which they labor and do not have any control over how they make their products. They are alienated from other workers because they are separated from others on the assembly line and are forced to compete with the other workers. They are alienated from themselves because the process of work has become routine and exploitative.

These four ways in which the worker is alienated were, for Marx, the byproduct of capitalism. The rise of scientific management, spearheaded by people such as Taylor and Ford, furthered these problems.

CHANGES IN WORK IN THE UNITED STATES

The nature of work in the American economy has changed significantly over the past 100 years. One major change is in the types of jobs that workers perform and the economic sector in which they work. The goods-producing sector extracts or harvests resources and is engaged in construction and manufacturing. Activities associated with this sector include mining, forestry, farming, fishing, and manufacturing. This sector has seen a sharp decline, as shown in Table 10.1. Whereas 45% of the 1910 workforce was engaged in this type of work (most of them in the extraction of natural resources), only 14% of the 2021 workforce was employed in this sector, mostly in construction and manufacturing jobs (Bureau of Economic Analysis, 2021).

TABLE 10.1 ■ Employment by Major Industry Sector (Employment in Thousands of Jobs)			
Industry Sector	Employment, 2011	Employment, 2021	Employment, 2031
Total[1]	143,326.8	158,134.9	166,452.1
Nonagriculture wage and salary[2]	132,589.0	146,736.9	154,888.2
Goods-producing, excluding agriculture	17,999.6	20,279.5	20,408.6
Mining	739.2	519.6	583.4
Construction	5,533.4	7,413.3	7,618.0
Manufacturing	11,727.0	12,346.6	12,207.2
Services-providing, excluding special industries	114,589.4	126,457.4	134,479.7
Utilities	552.5	540.8	506.2
Wholesale trade	5,474.7	5,677.9	5,813.7
Retail trade	14,673.6	15,396.0	15,063.3
Transportation and warehousing	4,289.4	6,092.0	6,558.5
Information	2,673.3	2,831.4	3,041.2
Financial activities	7,696.6	8,777.0	9,113.2
Professional and business services	17,389.1	21,249.5	22,798.9

Industry Sector	Employment, 2011	Employment, 2021	Employment, 2031
Educational services	3,249.6	3,589.3	4,026.5
Health care and social assistance	17,068.8	20,084.0	22,694.0
Leisure and hospitality	13,352.6	14,100.8	16,024.2
Other services	6,082.7	6,114.1	6,641.4
Federal government	2,858.5	2,885.7	2,780.7
State and local government	19,228.0	19,118.9	19,417.9
Agriculture, forestry, fishing, and hunting[3]	**2,147.5**	**2,184.8**	**2,200.5**
Agriculture wage and salary	1,304.9	1,460.2	1,520.1
Agriculture self-employed	842.6	724.6	680.4
Nonagriculture self-employed	**8,590.3**	**9,213.2**	**9,363.4**

Footnotes:

[1] Employment data for wage and salary workers are from the BLS Current Employment Statistics survey, which counts jobs, whereas self-employed and agriculture, forestry, fishing, and hunting are from the Current Population Survey (household survey), which counts workers.

[2] Includes wage and salary data from the Current Employment Statistics survey, except private households, which is from the Current Populations Survey. Logging workers are excluded.

[3] Includes agriculture, forestry, fishing, and hunting data from the Current Population Survey, except logging, which is from Current Employment Statistics survey. Government wage and salary workers are excluded.

Source: Bureau of Economic Analysis. (2021). *National data: GDP and personal income.* https://apps.bea.gov/iTable/?req id=19&step=2&isuri=1&1921=survey

The service sector of the economy includes services to individuals and businesses. Retail sales, transportation and distribution, entertainment, the hospitality industry, tourism, banking, health care, and law are all part of this sector. The service sector is increasing rapidly in the United States—from about 52% of employees in 1910 to 86% in 2021 (Bureau Economic Analysis, 2021).

Service sector jobs tend to have lower wages than other occupations. This includes food service, food preparation, and cashiers. Americans working in goods-producing industries such as manufacturing earn, on average, $43,070 per year compared with those working in food preparation and serving-related occupations, who make on average $29,450 a year (Bureau of Labor Statistics [BLS], 2021). However, it is important to note that the service sector includes a great diversity in earnings. Some jobs, such as those in health care, teaching, and management, require high levels of education and training. These jobs tend to pay considerably more than those in manufacturing and other goods-producing jobs. Occupations within the service sector requiring less education, such as hospitality and retail services, tend to earn very low wages (BLS, 2018).

Precarious Employment

Service sector jobs vary considerably not only in their wages but also in their stability and potential for promotion. Government jobs, teaching, and business are considered good service jobs because of their higher pay, better job security, and more possibility for advancement. Service jobs in retail sales and food services tend to lack these advantages. This second set of jobs, sometimes called McJobs, constitute precarious employment. Precarious employment typically gives employers full control over their workers' labor process. Companies can hire and fire employees with ease and frequency because the kind of work they typically do makes them readily replaceable. Precarious employment is characterized by the three Ds—dirty, dangerous, and demeaning.

One of the major ways that jobs have changed is in workers' ability to advance. Neil Irwin, an investigative reporter, illustrates this in an in-depth article comparing the employment experiences of two women who worked as janitors at large companies. Marta Ramos works as a janitor at Apple headquarters today and Gail Evans worked as a janitor at Kodak in the 1980s. Marta makes $16.60 an hour, about the same as Gail did 35 years ago, adjusted for inflation. However, besides pay, their work experiences are very different (Irwin, 2017).

Gail Evans was a full-time employee of Kodak in the 1980s; because she was full time, she received 4 weeks of vacation a year, was reimbursed some tuition costs to go to college part time, and received a yearly bonus. When the facility she cleaned was shut down, the company found her another job cutting film. Once Gail had completed her college degree, she was promoted into a job in information technology (Irwin, 2017). Fewer than 10 years later, Gail Evans was the chief technology officer of the company—quite an advancement!

Marta Ramos cleans Apple headquarters but is not a direct employee of Apple. Apple hires Marta and others through another company. She does not receive any benefits, such as vacation, access to tuition reimbursement, or bonuses. If her job is no longer needed, she would not be moved to another job at Apple, and she has no possibility of advancing or being trained for different kinds of work. The only advancement possible for Marta is to become the team leader of a group of janitors, which would give her an hourly pay increase of $0.50 (Irwin, 2017). The experiences of these two women illustrates the ways in which changing labor practices, including outsourcing work and the rise of part-time and precarious employment, alters the experience of work for individuals and the possibility of advancement.

Many people who work in precarious employment are concerned with their working conditions. These workers are trying to organize into a union to bargain for better and more stable employment.

Andrew Lichtenstein/Corbis via Getty Images

Emotional Labor

Another challenge of service sector work is the need to engage in emotional labor (the emotional management done by workers and a process of commodifying emotional displays at work). Arlie Russell Hochschild (1983) defines the term as the result of work that involves direct contact with the public. Through this contact the employee is expected to not only provide the public with a product or service but also to make the customer feel a certain way. Employees are trained to do this by employers and, as a result, the employer controls the emotional responses of employees. Through the process of emotional labor, workers must control their own feelings to achieve the desired effect in others.

Getting to Know: Arlie Hochschild (b. 1940)

Michael Macor/The San Francisco Chronicle via Getty Images

- Hochschild's choice to pursue sociology partially stems from early childhood exposure to cultural differences while living abroad in Israel and Ghana.

- As a student at Swarthmore College, Hochschild was a member of the college's Political Action Group and Peace Corps Committee.

- Her book *Strangers in Their Own Land* (2016) inspired the musical comedy *One State, Two State/Red State, Blue State.*

- Her writing regularly appears in public forums such as *The New York Times, The Washington Post,* and *Harper's Magazine.*

Nurses, servers, and telemarketers, among others, must perform emotional labor. It is not enough that a nurse takes your blood; he must also chat and smile while doing it. A server is expected to welcome you warmly and treat you like a friend, and not just bring you your dinner. The service sector often requires workers to engage in emotional labor. Hochschild (1983) argues that this emotional labor leads service workers to become alienated from themselves and their own emotions in the workplace.

READING: "FEELING MANAGEMENT: FROM PRIVATE TO COMMERCIAL USES"

Arlie Russell Hochschild

In the following excerpt from the book *The Managed Heart: Commercialization of Human Feeling*, Hochschild (1983) looks at a variety of professions that engage in emotional labor. One of the best examples is a flight attendant. As you read about Hochschild's research on this job, think about the service work that you have done (e.g., in a restaurant, as a babysitter, as a camp counselor) and how you might have engaged in emotional labor in this job.

> If they could have turned every one of us into sweet quiet Southern belles with velvet voices like Rosalyn Carter, this is what they would want to stamp out on an assembly line.
>
> —Flight attendant, Delta Airlines

When rules about how to feel and how to express feeling are set by management, when workers have weaker rights to courtesy than customers do, when deep and surface acting are forms of labor to be sold, and when private capacities for empathy and warmth are put to corporate uses, what happens to the way a person relates to her feelings or to her face? When worked-up warmth becomes an instrument of service work, what can a person learn about herself from her feelings? And when a worker abandons her work smile, what kind of tie remains between her smile and her self?

Display is what is sold, but over the long run display comes to assume a certain relation to feeling. As enlightened management realizes, a separation of display and feeling is hard to keep up over long periods. A principle of *emotive dissonance*, analogous to the principle of cognitive dissonance, is at work. Maintaining a difference between feeling and feigning over the long run leads to strain. We try to reduce this strain by pulling the two closer together either by changing what we feel or by changing what we feign. When display is required by the job, it is usually feeling that has to change; and when conditions estrange us from our face, they sometimes estrange us from feeling as well.

Take the case of the flight attendant. Corporate logic in the airline industry creates a series of links between competition, market expansion, advertising, heightened passenger expectations about rights to display, and company demands for acting. When conditions allow this logic to work, the result is a successful transmutation of the private emotional system we have described. The old elements of emotional exchange— feeling rules, surface acting, and deep acting—are now arranged in a different way. Stanislavski's *if* moves from stage to airline cabin ("act as if the cabin were your own living room") as does the actor's use of emotion memory. Private use gives way to corporate use. . . .

Behind the Demand for Acting

"A market for emotional labor" is not a phrase that company employees use. Upper management talks about getting the best market share of the flying public. Advertising personnel talk about reaching that market. In-flight service supervisors talk about getting "positive attitude" and "professional service" from flight attendants, who in turn talk about "handling rates." Nevertheless, the efforts of these four groups, taken together, set up the sale of emotional labor. . . .

As competition grew from the 1930s through the early 1970s, the airlines expanded that visible role [with the customer]. Through the 1950s and 1960s the flight attendant became a main subject of airline advertising, the spearhead of market expansion.[1] The image they chose, among many possible ones, was that of a beautiful and smartly dressed Southern white woman, the supposed epitome of gracious manners and warm personal service.[2]

Because airline ads raise expectations, they subtly rewrite job descriptions and redefine roles. . . .

The ads promise service that is "human" and personal. The omnipresent smile suggests, first of all, that the flight attendant is friendly, helpful, and open to requests. But when words are added, the smile can be sexualized, as in "We really move our tails for you to make your every wish come true" (Continental), or "Fly me, you'll like it" (National). Such innuendos lend strength to the conventional fantasy that in the air, anything can happen. As one flight attendant put it: "You have married men with three kids getting on the plane and suddenly they feel anything goes. It's like they leave that reality on the ground, and you fit into their fantasy as some geisha girl. It happens over and over again." . . .

Behind the Supply of Acting: Selection

Even before an applicant for a flight attendant's job is interviewed, she is introduced to the rules of the game. Success will depend in part on whether she has a knack for perceiving the rules and taking them seriously. Applicants are urged to read a pre-interview pamphlet before coming in. In the 1979–1980 *Airline Guide to Stewardess and Steward Careers*, there is a section called "The Interview." Under the subheading "Appearance," the manual suggests that facial expressions should be "sincere" and "unaffected." One should have a "modest but friendly smile" and be "generally alert, attentive, not overly aggressive, but not reticent either." Under "Mannerisms," subheading "Friendliness," it is suggested that a success-ful candidate must be "outgoing but not effusive," "enthusiastic with calm and poise," and "vivacious but not effervescent." As the manual continues: "Maintaining eye contact with the interviewer demonstrates sincerity and confidence, but don't overdo it. Avoid cold or continu-ous staring." Training, it seems, begins even before recruitment. . . .

Different companies favor different variations of the ideal type of sociability. Veteran employees talk about differences in company personality as matter-of-factly as they talk about differences in uniform or shoe style. United Airlines, the consensus has it, is "the girl-next-door," the neighborhood babysitter grown up. Pan Am is upper class, sophisticated, and slightly reserved in its graciousness. PSA is brassy, fun-loving, and sexy. . . .

The trainees, it seemed to me, were also chosen for their ability to take stage directions about how to "project" an image. They were selected for being able to act well—that is, with-out showing the effort involved. They had to be able to appear at home on stage. . . .

Somewhat humbled and displaced, the worker was now prepared to identify with Delta. Delta was described as a brilliant financial success (which it is), an airline known for fine treatment of its personnel (also true, for the most part), a company with a history of the "per-sonal touch." Orientation talks described the company's beginnings as a family enterprise in the 1920s, when the founder, Collett Woolman, personally pinned an orchid on each new flight attendant. It was the flight attendant's job to represent the company proudly, and actu-ally identifying with the company would make that easier to do.

Training seemed to foster the sense that it was safe to feel dependent on the company. Temporarily rootless, the worker was encouraged to believe that this company of 36,000 employees operated as a "family." The head of the training center, a gentle, wise, authorita-tive figure in her fifties, appeared each morning in the auditorium; she was "mommy," the real authority on day-to-day problems. Her company superior, a slightly younger man, seemed to be "daddy." Other supervisors were introduced as concerned extensions of these initial train-ing parents. (The vast majority of trainees were between 19 and 22 years old.) As one speaker told the recruits: "Your supervisor is your friend. You can go to her and talk about anything, and I mean *anything*." The trainees were divided up into small groups; one class of 123 stu-dents (which included 3 males and 9 blacks) was divided into four subgroups, each yielding the more intimate ties of solidarity that were to be the prototype of later bonds at work. . . .

Beyond this, there were actual appeals to modify feeling states. The deepest appeal in the Delta training program was to the trainee's capacity to act as if the airplane cabin (where she works) were her home (where she doesn't work). Trainees were asked to think of a passenger *as if* he were a "personal guest in your living room." The workers' emotional memories of offering personal hospitality were called up and put to use, as Stanislavski would recom-mend. As one recent graduate put it:

You think how the new person resembles someone you know. *You see your sister's eyes in someone sitting at that seat.* That makes you want to put out for them. I like to think of the cabin as the living room of my own home. When someone drops in [at home], you may not know them, but you get something for them. You put that on a grand scale—thirty-six passengers per flight attendant—but *it's the same feeling.*

On the face of it, the analogy between home and airplane cabin unites different kinds of experiences and obscures what is different about them. It can unite the empathy of friend for friend with the empathy of worker for customer, because it assumes that empathy is the *same sort of feeling* in either case. Trainees wrote in their notebooks, "Adopt the passenger's point of view," and the understanding was that this could be done in the same way one adopts a friend's point of view. The analogy between home and cabin also joins the worker to her company; just as she naturally protects members of her own family, she will naturally defend the company. Impersonal relations are to be seen *as if* they were personal. Relations based on getting and giving money are to be seen *as if* they were relations free of money. The company brilliantly extends and uses its workers' basic human empathy, all the while maintaining that it is not interfering in their "personal" lives. . . .

Collective Emotional Labor

To thwart cynicism about the living room analogy, to catch it as it collapses in the face of other realizations, the company eye shifts to another field of emotion work—the field in which flight attendants interact with each other. This is a strategic point of entry for the company because if the company can influence how flight attendants deal with each other's feeling on the job, it can assure proper support for private emotion management.

As trainers well know, flight attendants typically work in teams of two and must work on fairly intimate terms with all others on the crew. In fact, workers commonly say the work simply cannot be done well unless they work well together. The reason for this is that the job is partly an "emotional tone" road show, and the proper tone is kept up in large part by friendly conversation, banter, and joking, as ice cubes, trays, and plastic cups are passed from aisle to aisle to the galley, down to the kitchen, and up again. Indeed, starting with the bus ride to the plane, by bantering back and forth the flight attendant does important relational work: she checks on people's moods, relaxes tension, and warms up ties so that each pair of individuals becomes a team. She also banters to keep herself in the right frame of mind. As one worker put it, "Oh, we banter a lot. It keeps you going. You last longer." . . .

Once established, team solidarity can have two effects. It can improve morale and thus improve service. But it can also become the basis for sharing grudges against the passengers or the company. Perhaps it is the second possibility that trainers meant to avoid when in Recurrent Training they offered examples of "bad" social emotion management. One teacher cautioned her students: "When you're angry with a passenger, don't head for the galley to blow off steam with another flight attendant." In the galley, the second flight attendant, instead of calming the angry worker down, may further rile her up; she may become an accomplice to the aggrieved worker. Then, as the instructor put it, "There'll be *two* of you hot to trot."

The message was, when you're angry, go to a teammate who will calm you down. Support for anger or a sense of grievance—regardless of what inspires it—is bad for service and bad for the company. Thus, the informal ways in which workers check on the legitimacy of a grievance or look for support in blowing off steam become points of entry for company "suggestions." . . .

Achieving the Transmutation

To the extent that emotion management actually works—so that Bloody Marys do not spill "by accident" on white pantsuits, and blowups occur in backstage offices instead of in airplane aisles—something like alchemy occurs. Civility and a general sense of well-being have been enhanced and emotional "pollution" controlled. Even when people are paid to be nice, it is hard for them to be nice at all times, and when their efforts succeed, it is a remarkable accomplishment.

What makes this accomplishment possible is a transmutation of three basic elements of emotional life: emotion work, feeling rules, and social exchange.

First, emotion work is no longer a private act but a public act, bought on the one hand and sold on the other. Those who direct emotion work are no longer the individuals themselves but are instead paid stage managers who select, train, and supervise others.

Second, feeling rules are no longer simply matters of personal discretion, negotiated with another person in private but are spelled out publicly—in the *Airline Guide to Stewardess and Steward Careers*, in the *World Airways Flight Manual*, in training programs, and in the discourse of supervisors at all levels.

Third, social exchange is forced into narrow channels; there may be hiding places along shore, but there is much less room for individual navigation of the emotional waters.

The whole system of emotional exchange in private life has as its ostensible purpose the welfare and pleasure of the people involved. When this emotional system is thrust into a commercial setting, it is transmuted. A profit motive is slipped in under acts of emotion management, under the rules that govern them, under the gift exchange. Who benefits now, and who pays? . . .

In relation to each issue, emotional labor poses a challenge to a person's sense of self. In each case, the problem was not one that would cause much concern among those who do not do emotional labor—the assembly line worker or the wallpaper machine operator, for example. In each case the issue of estrangement between what a person senses as her "true self" and her inner and outer acting becomes something to work out, to take a position on.

When a flight attendant feels that her smile is "not an indication of how she really feels," or when she feels that her deep or surface acting is not meaningful, it is a sign that she is straining to disguise the failure of a more general transmutation. It indicates that emotion work now performed on a commercial stage, with commercial directors and standardized props, is failing to involve the actors or convince the audience in a way that it once did.

When feelings are successfully commercialized, the worker does not feel phony or alien; she feels somehow satisfied in how personal her service actually was. Deep acting is a help in doing this, not a source of estrangement. But when commercialization of feeling as a general process collapses into its separate elements, display becomes hollow and emotional labor is withdrawn. The task becomes one of disguising the failed transmutation. In either case, whether proudly or resentfully, face and feelings have been used as instruments. An American Airlines worker said: "Do you know what they call us when we get sick? *Breakage*. How's that for a 'positive attitude'? Breakage is what they call people that go to the complaint service to cancel for illness." Or again, as a San Francisco base manager at United remarked ruefully: "And we call them bodies. Do we have enough 'bodies' for the flight?" Feeling can become an instrument, but whose instrument?

Notes

1. When an airline commands a market monopoly, as it is likely to do when it is owned by government, it does not need to compete for passengers by advertising friendly flight attendants. Many flight attendants told me that their counterparts on Lufthansa (the German national airline) and even more on El Al and Aeroflot (the Israeli and Russian national airlines) were notably lacking in assertive friendliness.

2. A black female flight attendant, who had been hired in the early 1970s when Delta faced an affirmative action suit, wondered aloud why blacks were not pictured in local Georgia advertising. She concluded: "They want that market, and that market doesn't include blacks. They go along with that." Although Delta's central offices are in Atlanta, which is predominantly black, few blacks worked for Delta in any capacity.

Reading Questions

1. Why do organizations want workers to perform emotional labor? What function does it serve?
2. What are the costs of emotional labor for the employee? How can the employee deal with these problems?
3. How does the performance of emotional labor relate to Goffman's dramaturgical perspective (see Chapter 2)?

Hochschild, A. R. (2009). Feeling management: From private to commercial uses. In *The managed heart: Commercialization of human feeling* (pp. 89–136). University of California Press.

USING YOUR SOCIOLOGICAL IMAGINATION
EMOTIONAL LABOR

Organizations in a variety of industries actively work to teach their employees how to engage in emotional labor. Watch the following video on empathy statements in customer service:

https://www.youtube.com/watch?v=YTtBh9AvTrY

1. What is the point of the video? How does it relate to the concept of emotional labor?
2. The video discusses the need to make the customer feel right, even if they are not. Why do the trainers believe that this is important? How could this cause problems for an employee?

The next set of questions relates to the video "Research Highlights: Managing Emotional Labour" by researchers at the University of Sidney. Watch this video at https://www.youtube.com/watch?v=Q2KoBk8cBs0

1. What are organizational display rules?
2. What is the difference between surface acting and deep acting? What are the costs of surface acting for the employee? How do these concepts relate to what you learned from Hochschild's article?
3. How does the video suggest that employees could be more satisfied at work? Do you think that this plan would work? Why or why not?
4. If you have had a service industry job such as a restaurant server or salesperson, how did you feel about performing emotional labor? Were you required to represent a certain type of identity as a representative of your company?
5. How do employees sometimes resist companies' attempts to force them to engage in emotional labor? Are these techniques effective? Why or why not?

SUMMARY

We began this chapter by learning about Weber's theory of rationalization in modern society and examining the rise of bureaucracies as a prototype of this process. George Ritzer built on Weber's theory by applying the idea of rationalization to the development of McDonald's and showing how much of modern society is becoming McDonaldized. One of the byproducts of this situation is the increasing commodification of many elements of our lives, from products and our labor to culture and love. We then turned to another major change in modern society, discussed by Durkheim: the increased division of labor over time. This division of labor is seen in processes of scientific management, developed by Taylor and Ford, and, according to Marx, can lead to feelings of alienation for workers. Finally, we discussed changes in work in the United States, including the rise of the service sector, precarious employment, and emotional labor.

FOR FURTHER READING

Hochschild, A. R. (1983). *The managed heart: Commercialization of human feeling*, University of California Press.

Marx, K., & Engels, F. (1964). *The communist manifesto*, Modern Reader Paperbacks.

Ritzer, G. (2011). *The McDonaldization of society: Into the digital age* (9th ed.). SAGE.

Weber, M. (1965). *The sociology of religion*, Methuen.

Weber, M. (1968). *Economy and society*, (pp. 2–4). Bedminster,1, Ch

GLOSSARY

alienation

automation

bureaucracy

commodification

commodity

disenchantment of the world

division of labor

emotional labor

goods-producing sector

irrationality of rationality

McDonaldization

outsourcing

precarious employment

rationalization

red tape

scientific management (Taylorism)

service sector

11 HEALTH

LEARNING OBJECTIVES

1. Explain the multifaceted nature of health, including how mental, social, and physical health are related.

2. Explain and apply the concept of the social determinants of health.

3. Describe the major dimensions of health inequality and explain how these inequalities occur.

4. Compare health care systems around the world and the consequences of different types of health systems.

We all want to be healthy, but what does that mean? According to the World Health Organization (WHO), health is "a state of complete physical, mental and social well-being" (WHO, 2017a). This definition of health encompasses more than the absence of physical illness. It also requires mental health and social connections with others. Let's consider each of these components of health.

Physical health is related to the functioning of the body. We can have physical illnesses that are short term or prolonged. Short-term illnesses include having a cold or the stomach flu, both of which typically last less than a week. Other physical health issues are more prolonged, such as arthritis. Physical illnesses can also be acute or chronic. Acute illnesses are severe and begin quickly, such as a heart attack. Chronic illnesses are slow to develop and are longer term, such as asthma. When we think of health, we often focus on physical health because physical illnesses and injuries can be easier than mental illnesses to see or diagnose.

Mental health is a state of "well-being in which every individual realizes his or her own potential, can cope with the normal stresses of life, can work productively and fruitfully, and is able to make a contribution to her or his community" (WHO, 2017a). Although it can be more difficult to see mental health issues, mental health is also critical to our functioning in society and our ability to enjoy happy and fruitful lives. Both physical and mental health can differ across individuals. What is normal mental or physical health for one person might not be the same for someone else. Just as some people have higher or lower blood pressure as part of the normal functioning of their bodies, people have different mental health. However, mental health issues are related to a person's ability to cope with the problems that come up in life.

The WHO's definition of health also focuses on social health. This is something that we do not tend to consider when thinking about whether someone is healthy or unhealthy. Sociologists who study health are very interested in how social connections inform our health. Considerable research shows that individuals who are more integrated with others and with institutions in their society tend to be healthier. Recall Durkheim's early study of suicide: He argued that one of the main predictors of death by suicide was a lack of social integration. Ever since the early days of our discipline, sociologists have recognized the critical importance of social integration to our health.

THE SOCIOLOGY OF HEALTH

It might surprise you to see a chapter in this sociology textbook dedicated to health. Don't medical doctors and health professionals usually conduct health research? Certainly, medical doctors are actively involved in researching health. However, their interests and perspectives on health are very different from the perspective of health sociologists. In a similar way, sociologists of education may study and understand education in ways that are different from how elementary or high school teachers address education. Taken together, these perspectives can complement each other and can help us to understand the various ways that health affects individuals and societies.

The Social Causes of Illness

Medical doctors tend to focus on the immediate causes of illness. For example, if you go to the doctor with the flu, she will ask whether you have been in contact with others who are sick. Then she will treat your flu with prescription drugs or bed rest. Sociologists take a different approach to the study of health: They focus on the social causes of disease within a population rather than on the immediate causes of an individual's illness. Why, for example, are some people much more likely to get the flu than others? Could it be that people living in buildings that are under-heated and under-insulated are more likely to get the flu? If this is the case, protecting people from the flu may require us to find ways to improve housing conditions. Health sociologists tend to look at larger social causes of health and illness and, as a result, to look for larger social solutions to health problems.

Sociologists are also interested in why different groups of people have different health outcomes—for example, poorer people tend to have much worse health than richer people. Why might this be? In order to address the health of a population, sociologists argue that we cannot simply prescribe medication: We must also find larger social solutions to health problems within a population.

The Sick Role

Sociologists have long been interested in health and how illness affects individuals. Talcott Parsons, one of the earliest structural functionalists, wrote about health and illness in his book

When a person is performing the sick role, they are usually not expected to perform their regular tasks, such as working. How has the rise in remote work during the pandemic challenged the sick role?

Eva-Katalin/iStockPhoto

The Social System (1951). As a structural functionalist, he was interested in how illness can disrupt the usual social cohesion that characterizes society. Remember, structural functionalists argue that society usually functions smoothly. However, illness can disrupt the regular order of society. How does illness do this? When a person is ill, he often cannot participate fully in society. Perhaps he cannot go to work, care for his children, or engage in other responsibilities. In this way, illness disrupts the normal patterns of social life.

Parsons (1951) was interested in how people who are ill work to minimize the disruptive impact of illness. Through socialization, we learn the sick role, which is a set of social expectations about how to act when we are sick. This role includes three main parts. First, the sick person is not held personally responsible for her poor health. We do not blame a person for being ill. Second, the sick person is entitled to certain rights and privileges, including a release from normal responsibilities. We allow and expect that a person who is ill will stay home from school or work. Third, the sick person is expected to take sensible steps to regain her health. We expect that a person who is ill will take medications prescribed by a physician and will rest until she is better. We would be surprised, and perhaps unhappy, if we found out that a person with an infectious disease was not taking prescribed antibiotics and was going to work. This behavior violates our expectation that the person who is ill is trying to get better.

This theory is a very useful way to think about how we expect people to act when they are ill. However, there have been critiques of this theory. First, when is a person allowed to take on the sick role? It is easy to see that if someone breaks her leg or gets the flu, she is excused from work or school. However, with illnesses that are less visible and/or more difficult to diagnose, such as depression or chronic fatigue, society is not always willing to let a person take on the sick role with all its privileges. Second, we want to consider who has the power to deem who is sick and who is not. When you are ill and will miss a test, for example, there is probably a group of people at your college who get to decide whether your illness is worthy of an excused absence and whether you will be allowed to take a makeup exam. We need to take into consideration who has the power to decide who counts as ill and who does not. Finally, we want to consider how our definition of the sick role has changed over time and differs across cultures. What did we previously consider an illness but no longer see in this way?

USING YOUR SOCIOLOGICAL IMAGINATION
THE FRESHMAN 15 AND BINGE DRINKING: HEALTH AS A PERSONAL TROUBLE OR PUBLIC ISSUE

Sociology is focused on connecting personal troubles and public issues. In many ways, a focus on the social determinants of health is a call to look at health as a public issue and not just a personal trouble. In this activity, consider two health-related issues that affect college students: the freshman 15 and binge drinking.

The "freshman 15" is a slang term that describes the fact that students often gain weight in their first year of college. How can we see the issue of weight gain in first-year students as a personal trouble and a public issue?

1. How can the freshman 15 be seen as a personal trouble? Consider how individual eating, drinking, and exercising habits contribute to weight gain.

2. How can the freshman 15 be seen as a public issue? Consider how food availability, the organization of student housing, class schedules, and other factors shape the sorts of decisions students make regarding food and exercise.

3. If we consider this issue to be a personal trouble, how can we address it? If we see this as a public issue, what sorts of solutions might we propose?

Binge drinking is another major issue on many college campuses. Binge drinking is defined as men consuming five drinks within 2 hours and women consuming four drinks within 2 hours. This drinking will, on average, increase blood alcohol level to 0.08 (CDC, 2017d). Binge drinking can be dangerous to a person's health. It can lead to increased risk of high blood pressure, stroke, heart disease, and liver failure. In addition, binge drinking is also associated with memory problems and alcohol dependence. Finally, binge drinking puts a person at a higher risk of engaging in, or being the victim of, violence (CDC, 2017d). With these serious concerns in mind, how can we see binge drinking as a personal trouble and a public issue?

1. How is binge drinking a personal trouble? What individual factors lead some people to engage in this behavior?

2. How is binge drinking a public issue? Why might it be more common on college campuses than in other places? Why are some dorms, campuses, or areas more likely to encourage binge drinking? What social factors are related to this behavior?

3. If binge drinking is a personal trouble, how can we deal with it? If binge drinking is a public issue, what sorts of solutions might we propose?

THE SOCIAL DETERMINANTS OF HEALTH

Sociologists focus on the larger social factors that shape our health, called the social determinants of health. In general, social determinants of health are the larger social factors that shape the quality of our lives. These include the conditions in which we are born and raised, as well as where we live and work. The factors are shaped by larger distributions of money and power at the local, national, and global levels. The social determinants of health are major factors in creating health disparities and unequal health conditions for people both within the United States and around the world.

Figure 11.1 illustrates the social determinants of health. If we begin at the center of the circle, we see the most immediate causes: our age, sex, and other genetic factors. Older people, for example, tend to be less healthy than younger people. The next set of factors that shape our health is individual lifestyle factors. For example, smoking can be very dangerous for your health. And, exercising and eating well can make you healthier and increase your life expectancy. We then consider social and community networks. Having close friends with whom you can discuss important issues and with whom you can relax and have fun is important for our mental well-being as well as our physical health.

The next set of factors includes a whole range of social determinants of health related to living and working conditions. For example, if you live in a community with a lot of air pollution, you may be more likely to develop asthma. If you live in a country with good health care services, and if you have greater access to these health services, you will, on average, be much healthier than if you lived in a country where those services are either not available or not accessible to everyone. As seen in Figure 11.1, other factors at this level include education and housing conditions.

The last set of factors is general socioeconomic, cultural, and environmental conditions. Individuals who live in countries that have a greater level of inequality between the rich and the poor tend to have poorer health (Pickett & Wilkinson, 2011). It is not simply that the poor are better off in societies that are more equitable. Interestingly, even rich people are better off in

FIGURE 11.1   ■   The Social Determinants of Health

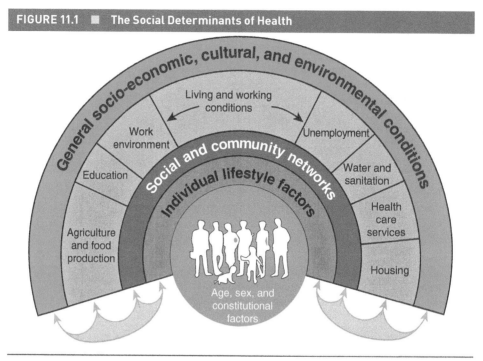

Source: Dahlgren, G., & Whitehead, M. (1991). *Policies and strategies to promote social equity in health.* Institute for Futures Studies, Stockholm, Sweden.

equitable societies. In more equitable societies, general health and welfare is better than in societies with more inequality. There are many reasons for this. For example, in more equitable societies there is less crime and violence, which benefits all people at all income levels. In addition, in more equitable societies there is less risk of falling into poverty, which reduces stress and anxiety for all people in a society.

As you can see from Figure 11.1 and our discussion of the social determinants of health, only the first circle—or perhaps the first two circles—are individual factors. Beyond that, there are a variety of larger social factors that shape the health of the lives that we lead.

Let's examine one particular disease and how we can better understand it through the lens of the social determinants of health. Tuberculosis (TB) is a disease caused by bacteria attacking the lungs. It is spread from infected to healthy people through coughing. We often think of TB as a disease that has been eradicated. However, TB is the 13th leading cause of death in the world and was the second leading infectious killer, after COVID-19, in 2020. If left untreated, TB leads to death in about 50% of cases (WHO, 2021).

India is the global epicenter of the TB epidemic (Mudur, 2021). There were 504,000 deaths from TB in India in 2020. This is about one-third of all deaths from TB in that year around the world (1.5 million; Mudur, 2021). TB is costly both in terms of human life and for the overall economy of India, costing India about $24 billion per year because the disease affects mostly people between the ages of 15 and 55. This age group represents a majority of the workforce, thus decreasing productivity and increasing unemployment.

India has worked to lower the high rates of TB infections. The Indian government has instituted several health programs that have been relatively effective. Despite the efficacy of these programs, they can be challenging for people to access. For example, many people must travel long distances to access care for TB, which is expensive. It is also expensive for individuals to

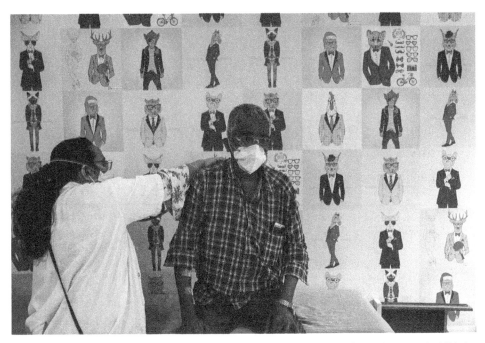

On March 22, 2022, Gautam Kamble, who is diagnosed with tuberculosis, goes through a routine test at the Médecins Sans Frontières (MSF) clinic, which treats people with drug-resistant tuberculosis, in Mumbai.

PUNIT PARANJPE/AFP via Getty Images

purchase the drugs that they need to deal with TB. Finally, there is a stigma associated with being diagnosed and labelled as a TB patient, which can negatively impact individuals and families who have the disease.

Although it is important to treat individuals with TB, health sociologists argue that we also need to look at the social and economic factors that lead to the high rates of TB. These researchers argue that "poverty sustains TB and TB ensures poverty" (Mehra, 2017). This is because TB is much more likely to spread in poor housing conditions. For example, the disease spreads rapidly in housing that is crowded and poorly ventilated. To deal with infectious diseases like TB, we must consider not only the individual factors that lead to transmission but also the larger social factors that lead some groups to be more at risk than others. Only by addressing larger social factors, like housing, access to care, and economic conditions, can we address these types of health concerns across communities and countries.

It can be challenging to consider health from a sociological perspective. We tend to think of a person's health as being mostly about their own genetics, behaviors, and choices. To understand the health of individuals and to start improving the health of a society we first need to understand how larger social conditions affect health.

Getting to Know: Michael Marmot (b. 1945)

- Marmot was knighted by Queen Elizabeth II in 2000 for his work on epidemiology and health inequalities.

- He is an advisor to the World Health Organization's director-general on matters related to the social determinants of health.

- He received the WHO Global Hero Award in 2015.

- He has received 18 honorary doctorates.

- He authored *Build Back Fairer: The COVID-19 Review* (2020) to center issues of equity in the UK government's Build Back Better pandemic recovery plan.

READING: FROM *THE HEALTH GAP: THE CHALLENGE OF AN UNEQUAL WORLD*

Michael Marmot

Michael Marmot is a health researcher and chair of the Commission on the Social Determinants of Health at the WHO. He has spent more than 30 years studying health and how social conditions can lead to very important health inequalities among people. In the following excerpt from his book *The Health Gap*, Marmot discusses some of his most important studies. Think about how these studies can help us to understand the larger social determinant of health and how this is related to unequal health outcomes across social groups.

As Japanese migrate across the Pacific, their rate of heart disease goes up and their rate of stroke goes down.[1] Would I like to work on this for my Berkeley PhD? Would I! It was a brilliant natural experiment. If you were trying to sort out genetic and environmental contributions to disease, here were people with, presumably, the same genetic endowment living in different environments. Japanese in Hawaii had higher rates of heart disease than those in Japan, Japanese in California higher rates than those in Hawaii, and white Americans higher rates still.

This was terrific. You couldn't have designed a better experiment to test the impact on health of 'environment', broadly conceived. Most likely, the changing rates of disease are telling us something about culture and way of life, linked to the environment. Simple hypothesis: Americanisation leads to heart disease, or Japanese culture protects from heart disease. But what does that mean in practice?

Conventional wisdom at the time was, and still is, that fatty diets are the culprit. Indeed, I have chaired committees saying just that.[2] Japanese-Americans had diets that were somewhat Americanised, with higher levels of fat than a traditional Japanese diet, and as a result had higher levels of plasma cholesterol than did Japanese in Japan.[3] Diet and high levels of cholesterol were likely to be playing a part in the higher rate of heart disease. What's more, the higher the level of plasma cholesterol, the higher the risk of heart disease. So much for the egg-package insert. It missed idea one. It grieves me to say it, but conventional wisdom is not *always* wrong.

Now for idea two. Japanese-Americans may be taller, fatter and more partial to hamburgers than Japanese in the old country, but their approach to family and friends resembles the more close-knit culture of Japan more than it does the more socially and geographically mobile culture of the US. That's interesting, but is it important for health? A Japanese-American social scientist with the very Japanese-American name of Scott Matsumoto had speculated that the cohesive nature of Japanese culture was a powerful mechanism for reducing stress.[4] Such a diminution could protect from heart disease. I particularly liked the idea of turning the study of stress on its head. Not looking at how being under pressure messes up the heart and blood vessels, but how people's social relationships were positive and supportive. We humans gossip and schmooze; apes groom. If, whether human or non-human primate, we support each other it changes hormonal profiles and may lower risk of heart attacks.

If this were true, I thought, then perhaps the Japanese in Hawaii had more opportunity to maintain their culture than the Japanese in California—hence the lower rate of heart disease in Hawaii. It seemed a reasonable speculation, but I had no test for it.

I had the data to test the hypothesis much more directly among the California Japanese. Men who were more involved with Japanese culture and had cohesive social relations should have lower rates of heart disease than those who were more acculturated—had adopted more of the American way of life. That is what I found. And this research result, perhaps, is where the egg cartons got their 'news'. The apparent protection from heart disease among the California men who were more 'Japanese' culturally and socially could *not* be explained by dietary patterns, nor by smoking, nor by blood pressure levels, nor by obesity. The culture effect was not a proxy for the usual suspects of diet and smoking.[5]

Two ideas then: conventional wisdom is correct, smoking and diet are important causes of heart disease; and, while correct, conventional wisdom is also limited—other things are going on. In the case of Japanese-Americans, it was the protective effect of being culturally Japanese.

Everything I will show you in this book conforms to that simple proposition— conventional wisdom is correct, but limited, when it comes to causes of disease. In rich countries, for example, we understand a good deal about why one individual gets sick and another does not: their habits of smoking, diet, drinking alcohol, physical inactivity, in addition to genetic makeup—we could call that conventional wisdom. But being emotionally abused by your spouse, having family troubles, being unlucky in love, being marginal in society, can all increase risk of disease; just as living in supportive, cohesive social groups can be protective. If we want to understand why health and disease are distributed the way they are, we have to understand these social causes; all the more so if we want to do something about it.

The British Civil Service changed my life. Not very romantic, a bit like being inspired by a chartered accountant. The measured pace and careful rhythms of Her Majesty's loyal servants had a profound effect on everything I did subsequently. Well, not quite the conservatism of the actual practices of the civil service, but the drama of the patterns of health that we found there. Inequality is central.

The civil service seems the very antithesis of dramatic. Please bear with me. You have been, let's say, invited to a meeting with a top-grade civil servant. It is a trial by hierarchy. You arrive at the building and someone is watching the door—he is part of the office support grades, as is the person who checks your bag and lets you through the security gate. A clerical assistant checks your name and calls up to the office on the fifth floor. A higher-grade clerical person comes to escort you upstairs, where a low-grade executive officer greets you. Two technical people, a doctor and a statistician, who will be joining the meeting, are already waiting. Then the great man's, or woman's, high-flying junior administrator says that Richard, or Fiona, will be ready shortly. Finally you are ushered in to the real deal where studied informality is now the rule. In the last ten minutes you have completed a journey up the civil service ranking ladder—takes some people a lifetime: office support grades, through clerical assistants, clerical officers, executive grades, professionals, junior administrators to, at the pinnacle, senior administrators. So far so boring: little different from a private insurance company.

The striking thing about this procession up the bureaucratic ladder is that health maps on to it, remarkably closely. Those at the bottom, the men at the door, have the worst health, on average. And so it goes. Each person we meet has worse health, and shorter life expectancy, than the next one a little higher up the ladder, but better health than the one lower down. Health is correlated with seniority. In our first study, 1978–1984, of mortality of civil servants (the Whitehall Study), who were all men unfortunately, men at the bottom had a mortality rate four times higher than the men at the top—they were four times more likely to die in a specific period of time. In between top and bottom, health improved steadily with rank.[6] This linking of social position with health—higher rank, better health—I call the social gradient in health. Investigating the causes of the gradient, teasing out the policy implications of such health inequalities, and advocating for change, have been at the centre of my activities since.

I arrived at Whitehall through a slightly circuitous route, intellectual as well as geographic.

You couldn't be interested in public health, or even just interested, and not aware that people in poor countries have high rates of illness and die younger compared with those in rich countries. Poverty damages health. What about poverty in rich countries? It was a niche interest in the US of the 1970s. After all, the USA thought of itself as a classless society, so there could not be differences between social classes in rates of health disease, right? Wrong—a piece of conventional wisdom that was completely wrong. The actual truth was handed around almost like Samizdat literature in the former Soviet Union in the form of a small number of papers, one of which was written by Len Syme and my colleague Lisa Berkman, now at Harvard.[7] People with social disadvantage did suffer worse health in the USA. It was, though, far from a mainstream preoccupation. Race and ethnicity were dominant concerns. Class and health was not a serious subject for study. Inequality and health was completely off the agenda, bar a few trailblazers, writing about the evils of capitalism.[8]

If there was a country on the planet that was aware of social class distinctions and had a tradition of studying social class differences in health, it was the United Kingdom. And if there was a place in Britain that excelled at social stratification it was the British Civil Service, familiarly known as Whitehall. . . .

Twice is a coincidence, three times a trend. In the 1970s I had done only two big studies, Japanese migrants and now Whitehall civil servants, and both had flown in the face of conventional wisdom. At the time, everyone 'knew' that people in top jobs had a high risk of heart attacks because of the stress they were under. Sir William Osler, great medical teacher from John Hopkins University and the University of Oxford, had, around 1920, described heart disease as being more common in men in high-status occupations. Osler fuelled the speculation that it was the stress of these jobs that was killing people.

We found the opposite. High-grade men had lower risk of dying from heart attacks, and most other causes of death, than everyone below them, and as I described earlier, it was a social gradient, progressively higher mortality going hand in hand with progressively lower grade of employment.

Further, conventional explanations did not work. True, smoking was more common as one descended the social ladder, but plasma cholesterol was marginally higher in the high grades, and the social gradient in obesity and high blood pressure was modest. Together, these conventional risk factors accounted for about a third of the social gradient in mortality.[9] Something else had to be going on. In that sense, it was similar to my studies of Japanese-Americans. The conventional risk factors mattered, but something else accounted for the different risks of disease between social groups. In the Japanese case we thought it was the stress-reducing effects of traditional Japanese culture.

You may think: stress in the civil service? Surely not! My colleagues Tores Theorell in Stockholm and Robert Karasek, the man who was eating eggs in Massachusetts, had elaborated a theory of work stress. It was not high demand that was stressful, but a combination of high demand and low control.[10] To describe it as a Eureka moment goes too far, but it did provide a potential explanation of the Whitehall findings. Whoever spread the rumour that it is more stressful at the top? People up there have more psychological demands, but they also have more control.

Control over your life loomed large as a hypothesis for why, in rich countries, people in higher social positions should have better health.

Endnotes

Gordon T. Further mortality experience among Japanese Americans. *Public Health Report.* 1967. 82: 973–84.

Committee on Medical Aspects of Food Policy. *Nutritional Aspects of Cardiovascular Disease.* London: HMSO. 1994. 1–186.

Marmot MG, Myme SL. Acculturation and CHD in Japanese-Americans. *American Journal of Epidemiology.* 1976. 104: 225–47.

Marmot MG, Shipley MJ, Rose G. Inequalities in death—specific explanations of a general pattern? *Lancet.* 984. 1 (8384): 1003–6.

Syme SL, Berkman LF. Social class, susceptibility, and sickness. *American Journal of Epidemiology.* 1976. 104: 1–8.

Navarro V. *Medicine under Capitalism*. Croom Helm, 1976.

Van Rossum CTM, Shipley MJ, Van de Mheen H, Grobbee DE, Marmot MG. Employment grade differences in cause specific mortality. A 25 year follow up of civil servants from the first Whitehall study. *Journal of Epidemiology and Community Health*. 2000: 54 (3): 178–84.

Karasek R, Reorell T. *Healthy Work: Stress, Productivity, and the Reconstruction of Working Life*. New York: Basic Books, 1990.

Navarro V. *Medicine under Capitalism*. Croom Helm, 1976.

Van Rossum CTM, Shipley MJ, Van de Mheen H, Grobbee DE, Marmot MG. Employment grade differences in cause specific mortality. A 25 year follow up of civil servants from the first Whitehall study. *Journal of Epidemiology and Community Health*. 2000: 54 (3): 178–84.

Reading Questions

1. What is the Whitehall study? What does it tell us about the relationship between social status and health?
2. Explain Marmot's study of men of Japanese descent in California and Japan. How does this study help us understand the complex ways culture shapes health outcomes?
3. Why should we be concerned with issues of health inequality? How can understanding these larger issues of health inequality help us to improve health?

Marmot, M. (2015). *The health gap: The challenge of an unequal world*. Bloomsbury, pp. 8–12 and 13–14.

HEALTH INEQUALITY

Americans are healthier today than ever before. Figure 11.2 shows life expectancy for American men and women over time. Americans born in 1960 were expected to live 70 years, on average. If you were born in 2020, you are expected to live to 79. This is a huge growth in life expectancy. There are many reasons why people are living longer. Many deadly diseases have been eradicated, including polio, scarlet fever, and diphtheria. Infant mortality has decreased, with many more children living past their first year of life. Better health technology and access to health care have also increased our life spans.

However, not everyone is benefiting equally from this general improvement in health. This is what the study of health disparities is all about. Health disparities are the differences in health status across groups that are the result of social, economic, or environmental conditions. For example, a person's social class, education, gender, and residence are very important predictors of how healthy he will be and how long he will live.

In order to consider these health disparities, we need to decide how to measure health. There are several different measures of health. First, we can measure life expectancy, the average number of years a population at some age can expect to live. Second, we can measure healthy life expectancy, a measure of the average number of healthy years one can expect to live if current patterns of death and illness remain the same. This means measuring how many years a person is expected to live without limitation of activity and free from chronic diseases. A third measure of health is to assess the number of physically and mentally unhealthy days an individual or group has per month. Finally, we can measure health by assessing chronic disease prevalence, which is a measure of how common chronic diseases such as asthma, cancer, or diabetes are across groups of people. With these different measures in mind, let's consider some of the most important health disparities.

FIGURE 11.2 ■ **Life Expectancy at Birth, 1960–2020, United States**

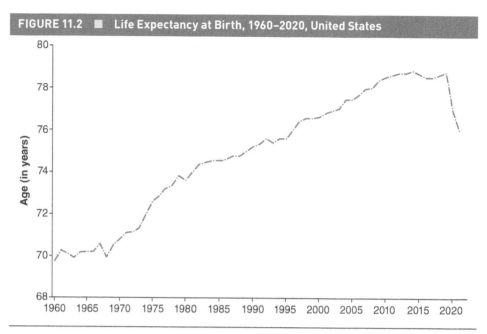

Sources: The World Bank. (2022). *Life expectancy at birth, total (years).* https://data.worldbank.org/indicator/SP.DYN.LE00.IN? locations=US

Class

Social class is a very important predictor of health. This should not be surprising, given what we have learned about the importance of social class generally. Social class shapes our socialization,

Many people live in areas where there is little access to fresh food, including fresh fruits and vegetables. How does this shape the health of people who live in areas with only fast food restaurants as options for food?

Richard Levine / Alamy Stock Photo

our educational opportunities and outcomes, and our jobs and work experiences. Given the power of social class across such a wide range of areas, it is not surprising that it is a critical component in shaping the quality and length of the lives that we lead.

There are strong health inequalities related to social class in the United States. A wide body of research links income inequality and health inequality, which is an increasing concern given the rising level of inequality between the richest and poorest Americans. For example, the life expectancy of the richest 1% of Americans is 15 years longer for men and 10 years longer for women than it is for the poorest 1% of Americans. This means that being in the poorest group of Americans will shorten your life about the same amount as being a lifetime smoker (Chokshi, 2018).

One way to think through these issues is to consider how social class affects our health over the course of our lives. Social class has a particularly pronounced effect on the health of children. Parents with more money can provide an environment and resources that foster children's good health. For example, they are more likely to be able to buy fresh food instead of less healthy prepackaged food. They also tend to have more time to cook for their children instead of having to rely on unhealthy fast food. Parents with more money are also more likely to live in neighborhoods with safe parks for children to spend time outside. Higher income is associated with better housing conditions, such as living in a home with good insulation and heating that is free from mold or vermin. Parents with more money are also more likely to have access to better medical care.

The effect of family income on the health of children increases over time (Case et al., 2002). For example, chronic conditions like asthma are less likely to occur in richer families. When they do occur, though, they are more likely to be kept under control because of better housing conditions, access to medical care, and other factors. Children living in poverty are also more likely to experience obesity or high levels of lead in their blood, both of which are serious risks to their long-term health (Chokshi, 2018).

Social class and area of residence are strongly connected. James Chesire from the University College London showed this in his analysis of life expectancy along the London subway line. As shown in Figure 11.3, where you are born even within a city has serious effects on your health. There is a 20-year gap in life expectancy between the richest areas of London, such as Oxford Circus, and the poorest areas of the city, such as Elephant & Castle. In some areas you can travel just two stops along the subway and find residents with life expectancies that are a full year shorter. In fact, if you travel 20 minutes on the Central subway line, the local life expectancy can vary by 12 years. This same difference in life expectancy exists between the UK and Guatemala. This important study illustrates how social conditions within even a small area can shape our health.

Global Health Inequality

In the same way that social class and income affect health within a country, the wealth of a country also affects the health of its citizens more generally. Not surprisingly, wealthier countries tend to have healthier populations. You can see in Figure 11.4 that increasing the GDP of a country from $5,000 to $15,000 is associated with a huge increase in the country's life expectancy. For example, Nigeria has a GDP of $5,238 and a life expectancy of 54 years, whereas China has a GDP of $13,102 and a life expectancy of 77 years. However, once a country is relatively wealthy, with a GDP of more than $14,000, there is very little effect of increased wealth on life expectancy. In fact, Costa Rica, with a GDP just above $14,000, has about the same life expectancy of 80 years as Taiwan, where the GDP is almost three times as high ($44,468).

FIGURE 11.3 ■ Life Expectancy at Each Subway Stop in London

This map shows the different life expectancies of children born near each subway stop in London. What larger factors explain how our neighborhood can shape our health?

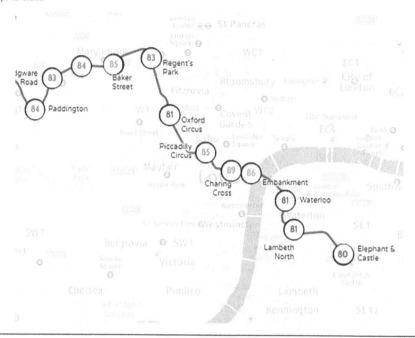

Source: From TubeCreature, "Lives on the Line." Created by Oliver O'Brien, UCL/CDRC. Data from Crown © & database right ONS, ORR, SDG, WDTK, OS, OSM & HERE.

Wealth matters, but being wealthy is not enough to guarantee longer lives. It is also the case that countries that are more equitable tend to have healthier populations. You can see from Figure 11.5 that countries with more equality (those with lower Gini coefficients) have citizens who live longer, on average. Take, for example, Iceland. That is the most equitable country on this chart and it also has the longest life expectancy.

Turkey, Argentina, and Mexico are quite inequitable, compared to the other countries in Figure 11.5. They also have much shorter life expectancies. It is important to note that the relationship between inequality and life expectancy plays a role even in rich countries. The United States is the richest of all the countries on this chart, but its life expectancy is only moderate. The high level of inequality within the United States is one of the main factors that account for the shorter lifespan in the county as a whole.

Education

Education is another important predictor of health. Clearly social class and education are related. As we have learned, people with more education tend to be in a higher social class and make more money. However, education is so important that it matters even apart from its relationship with income and class.

There are three main reasons why education is a key predictor of health. First, education is related to social class and income. And, as we learned in the last section, these are both very important predictors of good health. Second, education tends to improve our ability to understand health information. Information about healthy food is often complicated and ever

FIGURE 11.4 ■ Life Expectancy vs. GDP Per Capita, Selected Countries, 2018

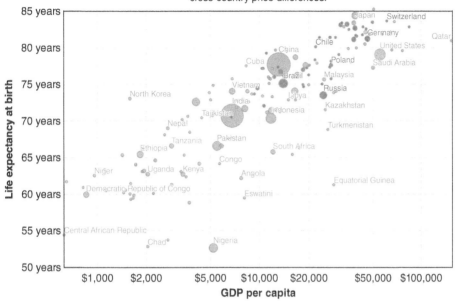

Source: Our World in Data. (2018). "Life Expectancy vs. GDP per capita, 2018." Retrieved from https://ourworldin data.org/grapher/life-expectancy-vs-gdp-per-capita

FIGURE 11.5 ■ Life Expectancy and Inequality, Selected Countries, 2019

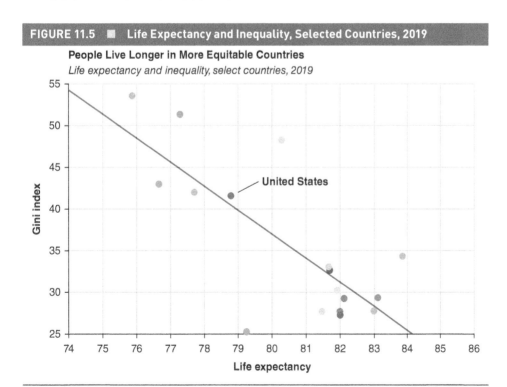

Source: Inequality.org. (n.d.). Inequality and health. Retrieved June 30, 2023, from https://inequality.org/facts/inequality-and-health/

changing. Should we eat fewer carbs or more whole-grain carbs? Should we consume less fat or more of certain types of fat? Having more education makes it more likely that you will both understand this information and, as a result, change your behaviors in healthy ways. Third, education increases your feelings of efficacy, the belief that you can change things around you. People who feel efficacious are more likely to change their health behaviors when needed and to advocate for their own health. For example, if you have a heart attack and your doctor tells you that you need to quit smoking, you have the choice to either try to change your behavior or to give up, believing that it is impossible to change your fate. In this example, those who believe they can change their behavior will have better health outcomes overall.

Much research has shown the positive effects of education on health. For example, those with more education are more likely to engage in preventive health behaviors, such as doing aerobic exercise and eating healthier food. Educated people are also less likely to engage in behaviors that are bad for their health, like smoking (Kenkel et al., 2006) or being overweight (Himes & Reynolds, 2005).

Race and Ethnicity

Race and ethnicity are also related to health outcomes in the United States. There are two core reasons for this. First, racism and discrimination affect the life experiences of racialized peoples. For example, racism and discrimination can shape both your access to the health care system and how you are treated when you are receiving care. Second, the relationship between race or ethnicity and health outcomes is, at least partly, shaped by social class. We know that many racialized groups have lower earnings and wealth than White Americans, on average. For this reason, the relationship between race or ethnicity and health outcomes is at least partly the result of the lower earnings and social class, on average, of racialized people in the United States.

There are many types of health disparities across racial and ethnic groups. For example, racial minorities tend to have higher rates of chronic disease and premature death compared to the rates among Whites. It is important to note, however, that this pattern is not universal. Some minority groups—most notably, Hispanic immigrants—have better health outcomes than Whites (Lara et al., 2005). This has been called the immigrant paradox and appears to diminish over time spent in the United States.

There has been some reduction in health disparities between White and racialized groups in the United States in the past 25 years. However, this is not because of health improvements among minorities. Instead, these diminishing inequalities are the result of declining health among Whites. Research suggests that the recent opioid epidemic, along with the rise of suicide and alcohol-related diseases, has contributed to the first increase in the national death rate in decades and to the unexpected recent decline in life expectancy for White females (Agency for Healthcare Research and Quality, 2016).

One way to see the persistence of health inequalities is to examine the different effect of the COVID-19 pandemic across racial and ethnic groups. As Figures 11.6, 11.7, and 11.8 show, death rates from COVID-19 were much higher among Native Americans than other groups. In fact, death rates among this community were 250 per 100,000, whereas they were only 150 per 100,000 among White and Latinx communities. Rates were also relatively high among Black and Pacific Islanders but quite low among Asians.

It is also important to note that hospitalization rates for COVID-19 also differed dramatically by racial and ethnic group, with Native Americans having the highest rate of

FIGURE 11.6 ■ COVID-19 Death Rates Are Higher for People of Color

Age-Adjusted U.S. deaths from Covid-19 per 100,000 people, by race, through October 22, 2022

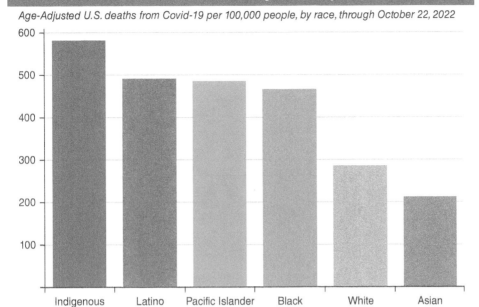

Source: Inequality.org (n.d.). *Inequality and health.* Retrieved June 30, 2023, from https://inequality.org/facts/inequality-and-health/

FIGURE 11.7 ■ COVID-19 Hospitalization Rates Are Higher for People of Color

Cumulative U.S. Covid-19 associated hospitalization rates, per 100,000 people, by race

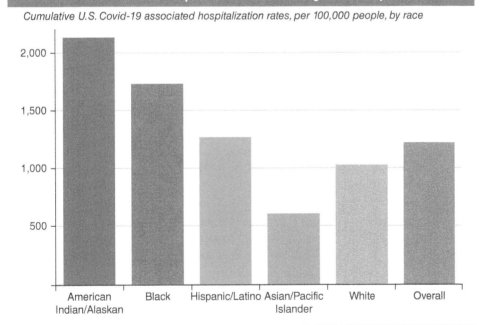

Source: Inequality.org. (n.d.). *Inequality and health.* Retrieved June 30, 2023, from https://inequality.org/facts/inequality-and-health/

FIGURE 11.8 ■ COVID-19 Hits Native, Latino, and Black Life Expectancy Hardest

U.S. life expectancy at birth by race, 2019–2021

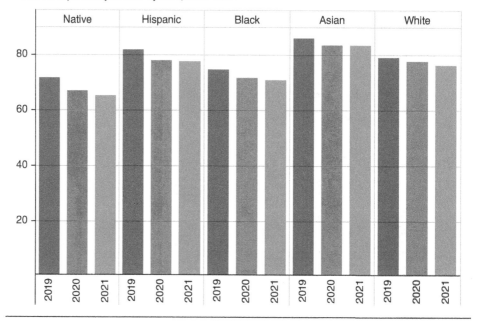

Source: Inequality.org. (n.d.). *Inequality and health.* Retrieved June 30, 2023, from https://inequality.org/facts/inequality-and-health/

hospitalization (at 1500 per 100,000 people). Black and Latino communities also had rates of hospitalization much higher than Whites. In fact, these higher hospitalization and death rates have dramatically impacted the overall life expectancy of all Americans, but this has been particularly pronounced among BIPOC communities. Life expectancy dropped 1.2 years for White Americans between 2019 and 2020, whereas Latinx communities have seen a 3.0 year drop and Black communities have seen a 2.9 year drop. This massive drop in overall life expectancy, and the differences across racial and ethnic groups, highlights the importance of examining health inequalities.

It is important to be cautious when analyzing data on health disparities for several reasons. First, data are often much better at capturing Black–White disparities, in part because of their large sample sizes. Other groups, however, are not studied in as much detail because the group sizes can be small. Moreover, heterogeneous groups may be folded together. For example, all Native American tribes are often grouped together, and Pacific Islanders and Asians are often considered as one group. These combined groups may mask large health differences within these populations (Bauer & Plescia, 2014). For Hispanics, an ethnic group with substantial heterogeneity by country of origin, many data sources report health outcomes for the entire population, despite evidence for within-group variation on important outcomes (Garcia et al., 2015). Relative to Black–White disparities, the literature examining disparities across other racial and ethnic populations is extremely limited. Considering the significant growth of minority populations in the United States, the insufficient knowledge base to date about the health conditions of several of these groups presents a serious challenge to understanding and addressing health disparities among specific populations.

Gender

Gender is strongly related to health. As most people know, women tend to live longer than men. We can see that this has been true over time in the United States. There are several reasons why women have longer life expectancies, on average. Even right at birth, baby girls are more likely to survive than baby boys. Then, in childhood, we socialize girls and boys in different ways. Boys are encouraged to be more aggressive and tend to engage in more risk-taking behavior. As a result, boys are three times as likely to die from accidents, four times as likely to die from suicide, and five times as likely to die from homicide (CDC, 2014).

The ways we socialize girls and boys has long-term effects. Men are much more likely to die from heart disease than women. Research has shown that one reason for this is because of our cultural definition of masculinity, which focuses on financial success and intense competition to achieve it, stifling emotions, and aggressive behavior. All these behaviors are what medical doctors call coronary-prone behavior that increases a person's risk of a heart attack (CDC, 2014).

An interesting puzzle when considering the relationship between gender and health is that, although women live longer than men, they tend to report poorer health. For example, women have higher rates of acute conditions and nonfatal chronic conditions, such as arthritis, osteoporosis, and depression. They spend 40% more days in bed sick each year and their activities are restricted because of health 25% more than men's activities. They visit the doctor more and have twice the number of surgeries per year than men (National Center for Health Statistics, 2003).

If women are in poorer health than men, why do they live longer? What explains this puzzle? First, it is possible that the relationship is in the exact opposite direction. The fact that women live longer is one reason they have poorer health. The longer you live, the more likely you are to make it to old age when most health problems occur. Because many more men die in childhood or early adulthood from things like accidents and violence, they are less likely to develop long-term chronic illnesses.

We should also consider how our traditional ideas of masculinity and femininity might shape how men and women use the medical system. For example, our ideas of masculinity encourage men to be tough and unemotional. This could be part of the reason why men are less likely to go to the doctor when they are ill or to take preventive measures to protect their health, such as going for annual checkups (Springer & Mouzon, 2011). This has important long-term consequences for men's health.

This advertisement for the movie *Black Widow* starring Scarlett Johansson was criticized for being overly photoshopped. In particular, the photo editors made her waist much smaller than it is in real life. What are the implications of this sort of extreme photoshopping?

Album / Alamy Stock Photo

Intersectionality in Health Inequalities

Obesity is a significant social problem in the United States and in many countries around the world. We measure overweight or obesity using the body mass index (BMI). A person can calculate her BMI by dividing her height (in meters) by the square of her weight (in kilograms). A healthy BMI is between 18.5 and 24.9. Individuals who have a BMI between 25 and 29.9 are categorized as overweight and those with a BMI more than 30 are labelled obese (National Heart, Lung, and Blood Institute, 2017). Obesity can be very serious for both children and adults. Being overweight as a child can have long-term effects throughout the life course. And, obesity in adults is linked with an increased risk of heart disease, high blood pressure, type 2 diabetes, and some cancers (National Institutes of Health, 2013).

Obesity has both individual and social causes. If it were simply a matter of biology, we would expect that the rates of obesity would be similar across groups and countries, and over time. However, the social problem of obesity is a relatively modern phenomenon that is common in only some countries. It is also stratified by social factors such as gender, age, social class, race, and ethnicity.

Let's begin by comparing obesity rates across countries. Figure 11.9 shows obesity rates across a selection of countries. Rates in the United States are relatively high. More than one-third of Americans are obese, according to BMI measures. By 2030 we project that almost half of Americans will be obese (see Figure 11.9). Rates are also quite high in Mexico and England. Rates of obesity are quite low in countries such as South Korea, Italy, and Switzerland. Although obesity rates differ widely across countries, it is important to note that they are increasing in all the countries in this figure over time.

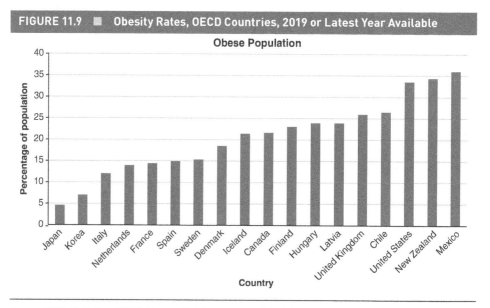

FIGURE 11.9 ■ Obesity Rates, OECD Countries, 2019 or Latest Year Available

Source: OECD Statistics. (2019). *Non-medical determinants of health: Body weight.* https://stats.oecd.org/index.aspx

Obesity is also highly variant across social groups. Obesity rates are highest for those with the lowest levels of education. In the United States, adults without a high school diploma have obesity rates of 36% compared with college graduates, who have obesity rates of 23%. Obesity is also related to social class. In general, having more money is associated with lower rates of obesity (CDC, 2018).

The relationship between obesity and social class has changed over time. It used to be that being thin was associated with poverty: Not having enough money to buy food and having to work in manual labor made you thin. Richer people could afford more and fattier foods, and they did not need to do physical labor to make money. In this context, being heavier was associated with wealth and luxury. Today, these relationships are the exact opposite in the United States and many countries. Cheaper food, like fast food, is much fattier than expensive food, such as organic produce and lean meats. People with more money are also more likely to have the resources to buy gym memberships and live in areas with parks for exercising. In this new context, having money is associated with thinness. These changes highlight the changing social construction of the healthy body and what type of body is desirable in a society.

Obesity is also related to age. Young people are much less likely to be overweight or obese. Those between the ages of 18 and 24 have the lowest rates of obesity (17%), whereas adults between the ages of 45 and 54 have rates of obesity more than twice as high (36%) (CDC, 2017a). There are many reasons for this: Young people often engage in more physical activity than older adults. For example, most schools require gym classes for all students, and young people, even after high school, are more likely to engage in sports and other physical leisure activities. Young people also do not tend to have the sorts of chronic or long-term health conditions that lead to being overweight or obese. However, obesity in young people in the United States is on the rise and is of great concern because of the long-term consequences.

Although individuals do make decisions about their eating habits and exercise, individual choices alone do not account for the rapid rise in obesity in the United States and around the world. There are many larger social reasons that account for the rising rates of obesity. For example, modern society tends to be very sedentary. Most people work in jobs that involve little physical activity. Professors, doctors, accountants, cashiers, and office workers sit down most of the workday. Think about your life as a student and the hours you spend sitting in lecture halls or in front of the computer working on assignments. Second, the rise of technology, such as television, computers, and smartphones, means that we spend more of our leisure time sitting. It also means that we can do a lot of things at home that used to involve a walk to the store because of online conveniences—such as ordering our groceries, making bank payments, and taking classes. Third, modern society is characterized by a constant feeling of being rushed. Because of this, we have less time to cook and make food at home. As a result, we rely more on packaged foods and fast foods, which are less healthy.

Once we see obesity as a public issue, and not simply as a personal problem, we can arrive at larger social solutions. For example, there are calls to bring more physical education into schools and to replace unhealthy foods in school cafeterias to address obesity among children. Does your campus offer soda machines or water fountains? Many cities are creating more parks and other facilities for people to exercise without paying for expensive gyms. And, some areas are passing laws that fast food restaurants must list the calorie counts of their foods, cannot use trans fats, or need to pay a tax on unhealthy foods they serve. These are all small parts of how we can, as a society, address the complex problem of rising obesity rates.

When considering the severity of the problem of obesity in our society, it is difficult to imagine why we would not want to take steps to ameliorate this problem. And, some solutions to the problem are very common sense. For example, asking schools to provide healthier lunches for students seems like an easy step to improve the health of children and reduce obesity. However, there are still many schools that provide unhealthy lunches for students. Why might this be? Given that no one would say that they are against children eating healthy food, how can we account for the fact that unhealthy food is still the norm in schools? To understand this, we need to consider the larger institutional factors that can, sometimes, impede social change.

READING: "BIG BUSINESS IN THE SCHOOL CAFETERIA"

Ivy Ken

School lunches are big business. In the following article, Ivy Ken discusses how school lunch programs have changed over time and how modern school lunch programs are associated with obesity among children. She also offers examples and suggestions of how these issues can be addressed by nonprofit organizations, community members, and governments. While you read this article, consider what your high school cafeteria offered to students. Was it healthy? Why do you think certain foods were (or were not) available?

Elementary school students in Washington, D.C., recently sat down to a meal of baked chicken drumsticks served with a whole-wheat roll, local braised kale, local potato salad, and a banana. It wasn't a special occasion. This was a typical school cafeteria lunch. The students loved it and there was very little "plate waste" because local legislation encourages schools here to conduct taste tests to find out how the students like the food prepared. The school—one of ten in my town where meals like this are served—also occasionally gets students involved in preparing the food and teaches them the importance of cooking without a lot of salt, fat, or sugar.

At most other schools in the United States, students are accustomed to options like pepperoni pizza, chocolate milk, and chicken nuggets. A recent investigation revealed that, unlike the simple but tasty drumsticks, the "chicken" part of chicken nuggets commonly served in school meals is actually made from 28 ingredients—not including the breading. Many of the agro-chemicals, hormones, antibiotics, and ingredients in food products like this have been linked to diabetes, cancer, food allergies, obesity, and other serious health concerns. The Centers for Disease Control report that the body-mass indexes of school-aged children have risen substantially over the last three decades, causing concern about an "obesity epidemic."

Architecture and the price of labor have a lot to do with the kind of food children eat at school. Federal legislation in the late 1940s provided funds for schools to install well-equipped and fully operational kitchens, but slashed budgets in the 1970s and '80s meant that school districts could not afford to hire the skilled workers to occupy them. Enter pre-packaged meals. By the 1990s, according to school food historian Janet Poppendieck, private food companies had made it easy for schools to purchase bulk "airplane meal packs" by providing schools with the freezers and ovens to accommodate them. No skilled on-site labor necessary, and no need to dip into the school's budget to finance and maintain real kitchen equipment. Just hire people to open the freezer, heat, and serve.

Today, over 7 billion meals are provided by the National School Lunch and School Breakfast Programs each year, which means that selling food products to schools is big business. Large food companies are eager to nurture this segment of the market. These same companies are also aware that sales of their products could be jeopardized by parents, students, and public health advocates who blame pre-packed, processed foods in schools with the rise in obesity and other food-related ills. To deflect this sales-shrinking public advocacy, several companies have formed "alliances" and "partnerships" that are engaged in coordinated public relations campaigns to send the message that they are working together to keep children and communities healthy.

What are we to make of the fact that corporations whose profits are tied up in mass levels of consumption claim to be leading the fight against unhealthy school diets and childhood obesity? . . .

Obesity is almost always framed in one of two ways: individualistically, as a choice; or medically, as a disease. But blaming our choices or our genes for a social problem obscures the important dynamics that influence what foods appear on the menu for us to choose from in the first place. This is especially true for schools, since the decision a third-grader makes between tater tots and French fries in the lunch line of an enclosed cafeteria could hardly be called a "choice."

Packaged for Profit

In order to make sense of having companies like Hershey and PepsiCo leading the push to fight childhood obesity, I carefully examined the "voluntary agreements" each company has made, scrutinized the speeches by the first lady and other prominent figures in support of these organizations, and analyzed the messages these organizations put out on their websites and in press releases, videos, conference programs, and related materials.

One traceable consequence of the Alliance and the Partnership's activities is that the reputation and profits of the food giants they partner with have been enhanced with only meager changes to the food products they produce and sell. The companies that have been marketing Funyuns and Mountain Dew to children for decades would not seem to be morally invested in fighting the "obesity crisis," but they have been swift to realize that when their market is threatened by community groups, legislation, and popular disapproval, the cover of the Alliance and the Partnership— including an A-list of public endorsements—serves as a powerful merger. The benefits to these companies include less public disapproval, as well as increased venues for easy marketing and distribution of their products. In return, they have only to make a voluntary commitment to offer or market slightly healthier products, especially to children.

And what of these commitments? On the Alliance website describing its "Healthy Schools Program," a company called Barrel O'Fun says it is a "family-owned company that believes in the environment, their employees and offers great tasting items that you want to serve to your students again and again." Barrel O'Fun has long made a product called Cheesey Puffs in which 85 percent of the calories come from fat. Because of its partnership with the Alliance, Barrel O'Fun now also makes a product called Jonny Rapp's Cheesy O's, which is specifically formulated to meet the federal government's new requirement that food sold in schools can contain no more than 35 percent of calories from fat. Cheesy O's meets the lower fat requirement, and also contains maltodextrin, disodium phosphate, Yellow 6, Yellow 5, and an unnamed "Artificial Flavor."

The Alliance and the Partnership have welcomed many companies like Barrel O'Fun that have created or modified their products to fit government requirements for schools. PepsiCo's FritoLay brand, for example, now makes RF Doritos (reduced fat) and Domino's now offers Smart Slice Cheezzzilla Pizza with 51 percent whole-wheat flour and "Lite" cheese. McCain makes Crispy Seasoned Bakeable Fries, which have been "par-fried," or fried at the manufacturing plant so they can simply be warmed on-site. ConAgra has a whole line of Max Snax, which, in the Totally Taco flavor, are "small triangular shapes made with two layers of quesadilla dough with Whole Grain, filled with beef, a blend of two cheeses and taco seasoned sauce."

Each of these products has been designed to just barely meet the government rules on what can be served in school meals (a pizza crust that is 51 percent whole-wheat, for example, is still 49 percent non-whole-wheat). But the major new federal legislation—the Healthy, Hunger-Free Kids Act of 2010—that prompted the creation of these products still allows snack products to have as much sugar as Cotton Candy Ice Cream and does not limit the amount of sugar in beverages like chocolate milk. The law does not stipulate that artificial colors, artificial flavors, artificial sweeteners, or other additives known to be harmful cannot be served, nor does it specify that food sources should be free of antibiotics, hormones, or pesticides. Some of the same companies that have partnered with the Alliance and the Partnership and received praise and endorsement from high-profile health advocates argued strongly against these additional restrictions.

This year the U.S. Department of Agriculture sent a memo to all state agencies to make them aware of an "important new tool" from the Alliance. The "Smart Snacks Product Calculator" on the Alliance's website helps food service directors determine which snacks comply with federal regulations. A related tool on the website, the "Product Navigator," provides easy access to "compliant" product listings and "streamlines the procurement process." Simple, fresh fruits and vegetables are not "products" so they are not included among the options. Rather, food service directors who seek help from the federal government are directed to the Alliance as a reliable source for finding and purchasing packaged products that meet the necessary requirements. The result for Alliance companies is a profitable and efficient distribution chain.

Community Partnerships Not Corporate Alliances

At a glance, the affiliation among corporate food giants within the Alliance for a Healthier Generation and the Partnership for a Healthier America is a problematic one. The reputation, marketing, and profits of corporate food producers have been greatly enhanced through this partnership, but the quality of the food students are consuming has improved only nominally. Nutritionists and advocates on staff at these organizations argue that it is better that these companies make some changes rather than no changes, and both organizations turn away companies that will not meet their terms. But the changes are paltry and amount to no more than an attempt to meet minimal government standards for school food. The real "health" indicators in this arrangement are large food companies' profit margins. More troubling still is the fact that these partnerships have conveyed legitimacy on corporate food giants just at a time when the public has come increasingly to question them.

We cannot rely on food companies to fix the problem of too much processed, unhealthy food on schools' menus. Instead, we have to depend on and contribute to our communities, and use tools like legislation, advocacy, and participation to ensure that students have access to good food. This is not as easy as using the free online procurement tools that feature products from the food industry, but our communities will be healthier for it in the long run.

Genuine school food reform requires partnerships with community groups like the Farm to School Network or the Edible Schoolyard Project aimed at creating an infrastructure for meals that contributes to the local economy, nurtures children's ecological literacy, and prioritizes children's health. Excellent models for this now exist. The meal of drumsticks and kale that I described in the opening illustration was prepared by chefs from a community organization called DC Central Kitchen, which provides a culinary job-training program for adults who have faced economic hardship and homelessness. This organization served over 4,200 from-scratch meals every day this year to students across ten schools in some of the city's poorest neighborhoods. They also paid their workers a living wage and made sure 30 percent of their food was purchased from local farms.

This all sounds expensive, but because students love the food and participate in the program, the model is sustainable enough to provide revenue to support the organization's other enterprises, such as providing meals to homeless shelters. It can be done. And it can be done without heavy reliance on pre-packed, additive-laden, obesity-related products manufactured for profit rather than for health. DC Central Kitchen works in schools that have operational kitchens, within a legislative environment that both mandates strict nutrition standards and provides monetary incentives for providing locally-grown, unprocessed foods, thanks to the advocacy of organizations like the Farm to School Network. Now those are real alliances for a healthy community.

Reading Questions

1. How can we think of childhood obesity as a personal trouble or a public issue?
2. How are companies, schools, parents, and children part of the solution to the issue of childhood obesity?
3. How can the government and public policy help create the conditions that would lead to healthier food in schools?

Ken, I. (2014). Big business in the school cafeteria. *Contexts, 13*(3), 84–87.

HEALTH CARE SYSTEMS

Health care is delivered through health care systems. Healthcare systems are the organizations of people, resources, and institutions that provide and deliver health care to a population. Health care systems differ in the extent to which they are funded and controlled by governments. On one end of the spectrum are systems called socialized medicine. In socialized medicine, the government owns and operates most medical facilities and employs most doctors. Both Britain and Sweden have socialized health care systems. On the other end of the spectrum are systems where individuals personally pay for their health care with no government assistance. In the middle ground are countries and systems where the government pays some portion of the cost of medical care or the cost for some people. The United States has this type of mixed system.

The U.S. Health Care System

The Patient Protection and Affordable Care Act (ACA) was enacted in the United States in 2010. It established a shared responsibility between government, employers, and individuals for ensuring that all Americans have access to affordable and good quality health insurance. The enactment of this law has led to a decrease in the number of Americans who are uninsured, from 9.1% in 2015 to 8.6% in 2016 (Commonwealth Fund, 2017). However, the health care system in the United States remains fragmented, especially when compared with other rich countries around the world (see Figure 11.10).

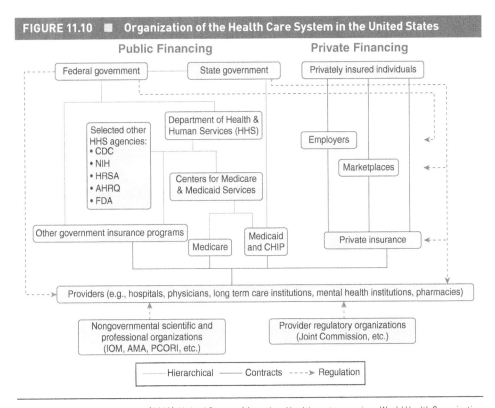

FIGURE 11.10 ■ Organization of the Health Care System in the United States

Source: Adapted from Rice et al. (2013). United States of America: Health system review. *World Health Organization, Health Systems in Transition, 15*(3), 27.

The government in the United States provides health care to certain segments of the population. The Centers for Medicare and Medicaid Services (CMS) administers Medicare, a federal and state program of health insurance for people 65 and older (as well as some people with disabilities), and Medicaid, a federal-state program for those with very low incomes. In 2020, 65% of U.S. residents received health coverage through private voluntary insurance, primarily through their employers. Public programs covered another 40% of the population (18% from Medicare, 18% from Medicaid, and 4% from military coverage). It should be noted that these estimates do not add to 100% as some people can receive coverage from multiple venues. Even with these coverages, 9% of Americans are uninsured (Congressional Research Services, 2022).

Health Policy

All health care systems are based on a set of health policies. Health policies are the decisions and actions that are undertaken to achieve specific health care goals within a health care system. These policies are much more specific than the overall health care system. For example, governments in many countries are attempting to tackle health problems such as drug use, obesity, smoking, and failure to vaccinate children. These specific policies are aimed at improving the health of the population.

One health care policy area that many governments are trying to tackle is related to the social problem of drug use and abuse, particularly opioid use. Opioids are drugs that include prescription pain relievers such as fentanyl and illegal drugs such as heroin. These drugs are very addictive and can lead to substance abuse problems, overdose, and even death. There has been a large increase in the number of overdoses and deaths from opioids in the past 5 years in the United States.

Fentanyl is a synthetic opiate pain reliever. It is legally prescribed to patients, often after surgery or to deal with severe pain or injury. It is a very effective drug because it is so potent. In fact, it is much more potent than heroin and about 100 times more potent than morphine. It is also very addictive. In fact, 70% of the 70,630 drug overdose deaths in 2019 involved opioids (CDC, 2022). Figure 11.11 shows the increase in overdose deaths between 1999 and

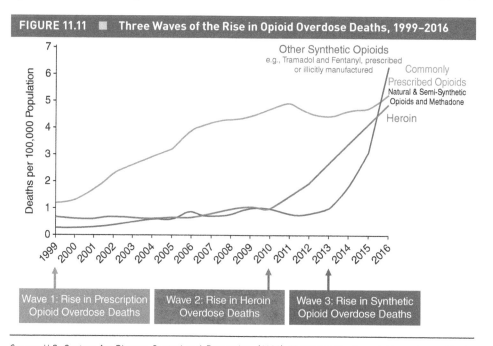

FIGURE 11.11 ■ Three Waves of the Rise in Opioid Overdose Deaths, 1999–2016

Source: U.S. Centers for Disease Control and Prevention. (2022). *Understanding the opioid overdose epidemic.* https://www.cdc.gov/opioids/basics/epidemic.html

2016. It shows the massive increase in overdose deaths and the critical role fentanyl plays in this increase.

Dealing with complex health issues such as drug addiction and overdoses is challenging. There are a variety of ways that health policy can try to address these issues. For example, many cities have created safe injection facilities (SIFs) to supervise the injection of illegal drugs and reduce overdoses. Drug treatment programs or education programs to discourage drug use are also important parts of reducing drug-related deaths.

Methods in Depth: Safe Supply, COVID-19, and Overdose Deaths

Deaths from drug overdoses are rising in the United States and around the world. The current overdose crisis is attributed to synthetic opioids (e.g., fentanyl), which are incredibly toxic and harmful. In the United States alone, this unprecedented drug poisoning crisis has resulted in the deaths of more than 70,000 Americans *a year* over the last several years (Bonn et al., 2021). One way that some areas are trying to reduce overdose deaths is through safe supply programs. Safe supply refers to the provision of regulated drugs that are typically only found in illegal markets. It is one harm reduction strategy that emerged in response to an increasingly toxic illegal drug supply.

Research Question

The emergence and persistence of the COVID-19 pandemic has increased efforts by advocates and some academics to scale up safe supply programs to reduce overdose deaths. The concern is that physical distancing measures require people to use drugs alone (preventing resuscitation if an overdose occurs) and that harm reduction or drug addiction treatment centers have a reduced capacity to keep people safe from COVID-19. The pandemic has also left homeless people who use drugs, and stay in congregate shelters, at risk of contracting COVID-19. If homeless people who use drugs acquire the infection and are told to isolate for 14 days, they are at risk of dying by overdose. In such scenarios, a safe supply program might be a risk mitigation strategy that can help prevent overdose deaths among COVID-19-positive homeless people who use drugs. How do we test this theory?

Challenges

Designing a study to test whether providing a safe supply of drugs and alcohol to COVID-19-infected homeless people improves health outcomes is fraught with methodological challenges.

Many of the traditional sociological methods would not be able to effectively assess how well this harm reduction strategy works. We could not, for example, conduct an experiment where some people have access to a safe supply and others to an illegal and likely toxic supply of drugs. This would be unethical because the people who do not have access to a safe supply would be at higher risk of overdose. It would also be difficult to conduct surveys or interviews on this topic because these surveys or interviews would be able to focus only on the experiences of health care professionals or people who use drugs and alcohol and might not be able to provide the objective data on death rates. It is also at risk of memory bias, since even those who work in these facilities may have a hard time remembering specific death rates over time.

Methodology

One way to assess how well this harm reduction strategy works is by retrospectively analyzing medical records of COVID-19-positive isolation shelter residents. This is just what Thomas Brothers and his multidisciplinary health care team (2022) did in their evaluation of an emergency safe supply drug and alcohol program among people experiencing homelessness who were required to isolate in government-funded hotels. In May 2021, a COVID-19 outbreak occurred in the congregate shelter system in Halifax, Nova Scotia, Canada. Due to the provincially mandated 14-day isolation policy, all residents in affected congregate shelters were relocated to hotels for the duration of their quarantine. The researchers used data from patient medical records, including prescriptions and progress notes from the health care team. In total, they analyzed the medical records of 77 hotel residents over a 25-day period.

Over this time, residents were prescribed numerous drugs (opioids, hydromorphone, benzodiazepines) as well as alcohol. Medical records revealed that an emergency safe supply of drugs and alcohol was associated with two positive health outcomes. First, mandated quarantine completion rates were high. Of the 77 residents, only 2 left against public health orders. Second, there were zero overdoses during the study period. Evidence from medical records indicates that the safe supply of drugs and alcohol is a successful risk mitigation and harm reduction strategy. However, the effectiveness of such programs cannot hinge on one study. Additional studies on the relationship between safe supply and health outcomes need to be conducted with different research designs to support stronger conclusions about the efficacy of this program.

Disability

A disability is any condition of the body or mind that makes it more difficult for a person to do certain activities and to interact with the world around them (CDC, 2017c). When thinking about disabilities, many disability rights activists argue for a people first philosophy, an approach that focuses on the individual and her abilities rather than on her limitations. This means using language such as "people with disabilities" rather than "the disabled." This focus on the person rather than the disability is very important because of the discrimination and stigma often faced by people with disabilities. Ableism is the term for discrimination against people who have a cognitive or physical disability on the basis of stereotypes about the limitations they may experience.

The study of disabilities is important to health sociology for several reasons. First, disabilities can be related to health inequalities. Disability can shape your access to the health care system and the kind of care that you receive. Second, countries have very different policies for addressing the various concerns of groups that experience disabilities. These policies can help individuals who have disabilities participate fully in society.

Most countries in the world have signed the United Nations (UN) Convention on the Rights of Persons with Disabilities (CRPD). This convention sets out a list of rights that people with disabilities have and how the state should work to protect these rights. In all, 164 countries have signed this convention, agreeing to enact its principles. The United States signed the convention and ratified it in 2009 (UN, 2016). This convention is, in part, modeled after the Americans with Disabilities Act (ADA) of 1990, which protects individuals with disabilities against discrimination in areas such as employment, public housing, and transportation (ADA, 2017).

The CRPD lists a set of rights for persons with disabilities. Countries that join in the convention promise to develop and carry out policies that help to protect the rights of people with disabilities and eliminate discrimination against them (Article 4). They also agree to fight stereotypes and prejudices and to promote awareness of the capabilities of persons with disabilities (Article 8). Another section of the convention focuses on creating legal recognition that all persons are equal before the law, to prohibit discrimination based on disability, and to guarantee equal legal protection (Article 5). The convention requires countries to eliminate barriers and to ensure that persons with disabilities can access their environment, transportation, and public services (Article 9). Countries also agree to ensure equal access to education (Article 24), equal rights to work and employment (Article 27), and equal participation in political life, including the right to vote (Article 29; UN, 2016).

USING YOUR SOCIOLOGICAL IMAGINATION
ACCESSIBILITY IN EVERYDAY LIFE

Twenty-six percent of all Americans report having a disability that limits their daily activity (CDC, 2017b). There is a wide diversity of types of disabilities that individuals have (see Figure 11.12). The United States has committed to the UN's Convention on the Rights of Persons with Disabilities, which requires the country to provide a society free from discrimination for people with disabilities and to facilitate work, education, and general integration for people with disabilities. Consider the different types of disabilities, such as physical and cognitive. How effectively are we creating an inclusive environment for people with these different types of disabilities?

FIGURE 11.12 ■ **Prevalence of Disabilities for Ages 18 and Older in the United States, 2020**

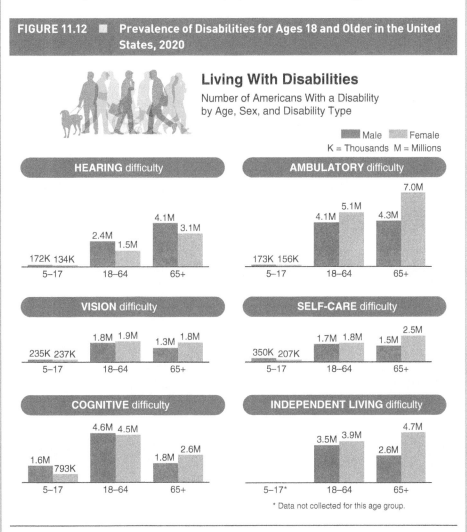

Living With Disabilities
Number of Americans With a Disability by Age, Sex, and Disability Type

■ Male   ■ Female
K = Thousands M = Millions

HEARING difficulty

	5–17	18–64	65+
Male	172K	2.4M	4.1M
Female	134K	1.5M	3.1M

AMBULATORY difficulty

	5–17	18–64	65+
Male	173K	4.1M	4.3M
Female	156K	5.1M	7.0M

VISION difficulty

	5–17	18–64	65+
Male	235K	1.8M	1.3M
Female	237K	1.9M	1.8M

SELF-CARE difficulty

	5–17	18–64	65+
Male	350K	1.7M	1.5M
Female	207K	1.8M	2.5M

COGNITIVE difficulty

	5–17	18–64	65+
Male	1.6M	4.6M	1.8M
Female	793K	4.5M	2.6M

INDEPENDENT LIVING difficulty

	5–17*	18–64	65+
Male		3.5M	2.6M
Female		3.9M	4.7M

* Data not collected for this age group.

Source: U.S. Census Bureau. (2021). *Living with disabilities.* https://www.census.gov/library/visualizations/2021/comm/living-with-disabilities.html

Consider your day and the different activities in which you engage—from waking up in the morning, driving or taking the bus to school, attending classes, socializing with your friends, to working at a job.

1. How accessible are these activities for individuals who have a physical disability, such as using a wheelchair or being sight impaired? Would some of these activities be challenging for people with a physical disability? How accessible are these activities for individuals who have a cognitive disability? Would some of these activities be challenging for people with a cognitive disability?

2. What has been done to make these activities more accessible to those with a physical or cognitive disability? What more could be done? How could we alter the environment to make it easier to go to class, take notes or engage in class sessions, travel to your school, or do other things?

3. What sort of resources are available on your campus to make it more inclusive for individuals with different sorts of disabilities? What other services do you think might be useful or important?

SUMMARY

This chapter begins by discussing the complex and multifaceted nature of health, which includes physical, mental, and social health. We examine the sociology of health and assess the ways that sociologists study health, particularly focusing on the social determinants of health. For example, the freshman 15 and binge drinking can be understood as health issues that are often related to larger social contexts. We assess the critical importance of health inequalities, particularly those based on social class, education, race and ethnicity, and gender. The reading by Michael Marmot also highlights these issues of health inequalities. We consider the role of health care systems and health policies for dealing with health issues within populations. This chapter ends with a discussion of disability in society and how disability can be related to both health inequalities and health policies.

FOR FURTHER READING

Davidson, A. (2014). *Social determinants of health: A comparative approach*, Oxford University Press.

Marmot, M. (2015). *The health gap: The challenge of an unequal world*, Bloomsbury.

Segal, A., & Fries, C. (2011). *Pursuing health and wellness: Healthy societies, healthy people*, Oxford University Press.

GLOSSARY

ableism

chronic disease prevalence

disability

health

health care systems

health disparities

health policies

healthy life expectancy

life expectancy

mental health

obesity

people first philosophy

sick role

social determinants of health

United Nations (UN) Convention on the Rights of Persons with Disabilities (CRPD)

12 GLOBALIZATION AND GLOBAL INEQUALITY

The world is more interconnected than ever before. This is, in part, because of the process of globalization. The implications of globalization are complicated: Whether we see it as promising or dangerous depends to a great extent on the theoretical lens we use to examine it. In this chapter we will discuss three core theories of globalization (modernization, world systems, and world society). We will also look at global inequality and examine how we can measure it, how it has changed, and how we can help alleviate it. Let's begin by defining globalization.

WHAT IS GLOBALIZATION?

We have all heard that we live in a globalized world. But what does this mean? What is globalization, how does it happen, and how does it affect the United States and other countries? Globalization is a process of increasing interconnectedness of people, products, ideas, and places. Globalization has several causes; for example, improvements in transportation systems and in communication and information technologies are particularly important factors that have led to increased globalization. These developments facilitate the easy movement of people, products, and ideas, which can lead to political, economic, social, and cultural integration.

Globalization increases interconnectedness in three main ways. First, material or physical connections increase. The movements of goods, people, and money across national borders are relatively fluid. These increased flows are facilitated by shared global infrastructure. For example, physical global infrastructure, such as international transportation and banking systems, are shared across countries and make increased interaction and the exchange of goods and money relatively easy. In addition, normative similarities such as trade agreements and friendly relations between countries develop from global infrastructure and make the movements of people and goods easier.

The importance of this physical interconnectedness is evident when we travel to different countries. Twenty-five years ago, people traveling from the United States to Europe had to take traveler's checks and exchange them for the currency of each country they visited (e.g., French francs, German marks, Italian lira). Now, we can all simply use our debit card at any bank in Europe and receive the local currency from an ATM, or we pay with our credit card at any store or restaurant. The international banking system has facilitated European travel, and the use of the euro, the common currency of many European countries, makes moving between nations easier than ever before. (No more converting currency in your head!)

Avocados are grown mostly in Mexico. However, we can buy them at any grocery store in America. The movement of products, such as these avocados, is a sign of the larger processes of globalization.

Second, globalization entails a spatiotemporal element; places that once felt very far away now feel much closer. We can get on a plane and be halfway around the world in a few hours or we can use technology such as Zoom or Facetime to talk to friends who live in other cities or countries. We could even take classes online during the pandemic from anywhere around the world. The impact of distant events also becomes more relevant to our day-to-day lives. Tsunamis or famines occurring in other countries seem more real to us because we can easily (and almost instantly) see pictures or videos of them. The 9/11 terrorist attacks in 2001 occurred around 9:00 a.m., yet many people did not hear about them until that afternoon or evening. Twenty years later in 2022, social media such as Twitter informed people of the invasion of the Ukraine as it happened.

This spatiotemporal convergence is the basis of theorist Marshall McLuhan's concept of the global village. We "got to know" McLuhan in Chapter 7 on language and the media. McLuhan argued that the ease of international communication has allowed us to form an increasingly interconnected and unified global community, where we can easily interact with and learn about faraway people and places. Through media such as the Internet, we can join Facebook groups or follow the Twitter accounts of people from other countries or continents and can easily connect with family and friends who live far away. We can learn about world events and share updates about our lives instantaneously. McLuhan believed that this increased shared interaction creates a greater global responsibility for social betterment through heightened awareness. For example, people from around the world re-tweeted #BlackLivesMatter in support of protests in the United States.

Finally, globalization has a cognitive element that involves the dissemination of ideas and culture throughout the world. This diffusion creates a situation in which cultural models can become increasingly similar across countries. If you have ever been in a remote location in another country and heard a Taylor Swift song on the radio or played Pokémon Go, you have witnessed the global dispersion of culture.

A positive example of the dissemination of cultural ideals is the spread of the concept of human rights. Most people would agree that individuals have the right to not suffer intentional and unwanted physical harm (unless provoked or legally necessary), to choose how to spend their time (within reasonable constraints), to have access to clean water and other resources necessary for survival, and to practice the religion of their choice. The first major human rights agreement, the International Declaration of Human Rights, was passed by the UN General Assembly in 1948. At that time, 48 countries signed the declaration, supporting the idea of human rights internationally. More recently, the UN passed the Convention on the Rights of Persons with Disabilities (CRPD) that was signed by 91 countries and ratified in 2008, which we discussed in Chapter 11. These two conventions illustrate the increased international support for the idea of human rights and the global spread of this cultural norm.

However, sharing ideas and cultural models is not always positive. Hearing a Billie Eilish song or seeing a Starbucks abroad would be a happy surprise to some but a disappointment to others. Other cultural ideals, such as consumerism and materialism, also spread from country to country. Bennett, Sharpe, Freeman, and Carson (2004) found that Western ideals of female beauty have significant reach, affecting many women and girls in other parts of the world. The researchers found that the rise in eating disorders in Ghana was partly explained by the low-weight girls' desire to conform to Western beauty standards. Other studies also report an increase in eating disorders among ethnic Fijian girls following the introduction of Western television. Weight concerns and anorexia became more common as exposure to Western media increased.

Many companies in the U.S. have changed their marketing in response to concerns from the civil rights movement, including Black Lives Matter. However, skin whitening creams, with their narrow ideals of beauty, are still popular in Asia. What do these creams say about the spread of Western ideals of beauty and how are they problematic?

Mark Azavedo/Alamy Stock Photo

UNDERSTANDING GLOBALIZATION

Globalization does not occur in only one direction—we are not simply becoming more globalized. Instead, it is a process that involves advances and regressions. The world is becoming more interconnected, but there are still times when countries or individuals become more isolationist, choosing to separate from larger international institutions. For example, a country might raise taxes on imported goods, restrict the amount of foreign content on television, or increase the barriers to immigration. Globalization is also not always a harmonious process. Not all individuals agree that becoming more interconnected is a good idea or is beneficial for all. For some countries, increased globalization can lead to a waning of culture, increased unemployment, and loss of autonomy over national services and resources. Academics, politicians, and the public continue to debate globalization's potential advantages and disadvantages, and concerned citizens and social movements encourage, contest, and challenge this process.

Globalization is a complicated process that can greatly affect individuals, communities, countries, and the world. How we understand globalization depends on our theoretical perspective. There are three main theories of globalization and global inequality in sociology: modernization theory, world systems theory, and world society theory. The following discussion examines these approaches and the ways these different theoretical lenses can help us to shed light on different aspects of globalization.

Modernization Theory

Modernization theory attempts to isolate the features that predict which societies will progress and develop. This theory argues that a society's internal features, including its economic, social, and cultural systems, can either help or hinder development. Modernization theory claims that countries are poor because they cling to traditional and inefficient attitudes, technologies, and institutions. In contrast, modern societies embrace industrial capitalism, advanced technologies, and modern institutions. With enough time and "correct" behaviors, all societies can become modernized and develop like Western societies.

Rostow's Stages of Economic Growth

Modernization theory encourages all countries to strive to modernize in the same way that Western Europe and North America did. This process requires that societies go through a set of established stages. W. W. Rostow (1991) describes these steps in his well-known book, *The Stages of Economic Growth: A Non-Communist Manifesto* (a play on the title of Marx and Engels's *Communist Manifesto*). Rostow argues that all societies start as traditional societies that emphasize the importance of history and tradition. He claims that traditional societies are static and rigid in that they have very little economic mobility and that they prioritize stability over change. They are based on subsistence agriculture (the growing of crops to feed the farmer's own livestock and family) or hunting and gathering. These societies, such as the feudal societies of medieval Europe, focus on spiritual richness but lack material abundance.

As the demand for raw materials increases, these traditional societies could not keep up. They were pushed to develop more-productive commercial agriculture and to create cash crops (crops to be sold instead of consumed by the producers). Widespread technological advances, including the development of irrigation systems and efficient transportation, led to increased productivity and the broader dissemination of goods. All these changes facilitated an increase in social mobility and put the previous social equilibrium, which had existed for centuries, in flux. This period is called the preconditions to takeoff (Rostow, 1991).

The second period is economic takeoff, during which manufacturing becomes more efficient and increases in size and scale. Because of this mass productivity, societies can produce goods for both domestic consumption and export. Markets emerge as people produce goods to trade with others for profit. This phase is also a time of rising individualism focused on individual material enrichment and can undermine family ties and time-honored norms and values.

Next, societies move toward technological maturity. In this period, all sectors of society become involved in market production, and international trade rises. Economies become increasingly diversified, and they produce and sell many different goods and services. This period is also associated with a great reduction in absolute poverty. Cities grow as people leave rural villages in search of jobs and economic opportunities in urban areas. The rise of individualism and an increased sense of efficacy generate social movements demanding greater political rights, for example to provide universal basic education and increase the rights of various groups, such as women and racial minorities.

The final period of development is mass consumption. The mass production that occurred in the last period stimulates this stage. People soon believe that they need the new diversity of products available and consume those goods accordingly. Because consumers now have more disposable income, they are able to consume more. American society currently is in this stage.

Poverty and Modernization Theory

Modernization theorists argue that, for most of human history, the world was poor. In fact, countries began moving out of poverty only a few centuries ago. From this perspective, it is the current affluence in some modern countries that is historically unusual. How have some countries been able to move out of poverty? During the Middle Ages a proliferation of colonialization and trade brought wealth to a growing share of people in Western Europe. The Industrial Revolution and the growth of capitalism also created vast new wealth. This affluence was initially concentrated in the hands of the few, but the industrial system was so productive that its benefits soon expanded to include a growing number of people. Today, middle-income countries in Latin America and Asia are also industrializing and becoming wealthier as a result.

If industrialization has such potential to reduce poverty, why isn't the whole world moving in this direction? Modernization theory points to tradition as the greatest barrier to development. It argues that traditional family values, gender roles, and cultural models can hinder the adoption of new technologies and procedures. For example, if a society believes that women should not work outside the home, there are fewer workers to produce goods or services. Not all societies seek new technology or embrace new methods of production; many people resist such advances because they see them as threats to their social and cultural systems and beliefs.

Black Friday and Cyber Monday are extreme examples of concentrated mass consumption. Retailers offer special deals to encourage the consumption of goods beyond basic needs. In 2021, U.S. consumers spent more than $9.9 billion on Black Friday alone. How does Black Friday illustrate the mass consumption that occurs in modern society?

STAN HONDA/AFP/Getty Images

Technology and Modernization Theory

Modernization theorists argue that traditional societies should embrace modern technologies and production methods. According to some modernization theorists, for example, a specific change that would help countries develop is to focus on cash crops of high-yield agricultural products. As mentioned earlier, traditional societies are based on subsistence farming, while more-developed countries sell cash crops for profit. Most farms in the United States and other developed countries currently practice monocropping, an economically efficient and profitable method of repeatedly growing one high-yield crop. Farmers using this technique purchase specialized equipment and design their fields and irrigation systems for the specific crop. By adopting this method, they can use the profits to purchase consumer goods and other products that could improve their lives. In theory, the process would lead to more economic productivity and to Rostow's period of economic takeoff.

Monocropping could increase short-term food production and lead to prosperity, but it also has certain disadvantages. Relying on cash crops can be volatile and unsustainable. Prices for major cash crops are set on a global scale, so nations, regions, or individual producers of these crops are at the market's mercy. Monocropping is also controversial because it has long-term environmental disadvantages. It can exhaust the soil, lead to the growth of parasites, and increase crop vulnerability to opportunistic insects and plants.

USING YOUR SOCIOLOGICAL IMAGINATION
THE ECOLOGICAL FOOTPRINT

We can get a sense of how much we impact the natural environment by calculating our eco-logical footprint—the amount of land and sea necessary to supply the resources a human population consumes and to process the waste it produces. We can use this information to estimate how much of the Earth (or how many Earths) it would take to support an individual or country if everybody followed a given way of life (Global Footprint Network, 2023).

Go to the website "What Is Your Ecological Footprint?" at https://www.footprintcalcula tor.org/home/en to access a test that calculates your ecological footprint. When you have completed the test, answer the following questions:

1. How many Earths would there need to be for everyone to live your lifestyle?
2. Where did most of your footprint come from—carbon, food, housing, or goods and services? Were you surprised by the areas where you had the largest and smallest footprints? If so, why?
3. How did your footprint compare with others from your country? Why is your footprint larger or smaller than the average American footprint?
4. What advice does the test give for reducing your footprint? What other methods could you use to reduce it? Consider which ways would be easiest and which would be hardest.

Now let's look at a bigger picture and compare ecological footprints in different parts of the world. Figure 12.1 shows the relationship between a country's footprint and its Human Development Index (HDI), a number that combines a variety of measures regarding the health and quality of life in a country (e.g., life expectancy, education, and income). Examine the figure and then answer the following questions.

5. Which regions have the largest ecological footprints and which have the smallest? How do the world's regions differ in their human development and in their ecological footprint?
6. How is a country's human development related to its ecological footprint? Why do you think this relationship exists?

FIGURE 12.1 ■ Human Welfare and Ecological Footprints Compared

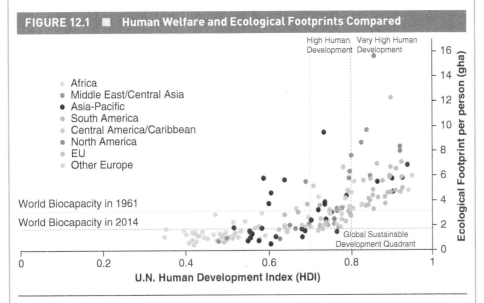

Sources: Lin, D.; Hanscom, L.; Murthy, A.; Galli, A.; Evans, M.; Neill, E.; Mancini, M.S.; Martindill, J.; Medouar, F.-Z.; Huang, S.; Wackernagel, M. Ecological Footprint Accounting for Countries: Updates and Results of the National Footprint Accounts, 2012–2018. Resources 2018, 7, 58. CC BY 4.0, https:// creativecommons.org/licenses/by/4.0/.

Solidarity and Modernization Theory

Modernization theory takes some of its ideas from Émile Durkheim (1960), who was interested in the social evolution of societies. He argued that, like organisms, societies progress through several stages: They start as a simple organism and evolve into something that is more complex.

Sociologists often focus on social problems, but Durkheim was more interested in how society functions efficiently, even when people have conflicting interests. In particular, he was interested in explaining social solidarity, a feeling of unity among people in a society. How do we explain this harmony? How has the foundation of such solidarity changed as societies have altered?

Durkheim argued that early societies were based on mechanical solidarity. Each unit (such as a family) provided for its own production and consumption needs, and subunits survived in isolation from one another. A family could live on a small subsistence farm, where it grew its own crops and made its own clothes, candles, and soap. In these societies, each unit could survive on its own—a family did not need to rely on anyone outside the family to make goods or provide services. However, these societies were held together by a shared sense of collective consciousness, the shared beliefs and sentiments that created solidarity among people. For example, most people in a village or town followed the same religion and thus had a shared set of beliefs about appropriate behaviors and attitudes.

Modern societies have changed. They tend to be made up of people who are different from one another. There is no common adherence to a collective conscience—people are from different religions, cultural traditions, or philosophies; this is especially true in a country as diverse as the United States. As a result, individuals are guided by distinct norms and values that could weaken the overall collective consciousness. However, modern societies also have an increased division of labor, with more people engaging in specialized tasks and activities. Some people are teachers, some farmers, others architects. Because different people perform different functions in society, no group can survive on its own. Farmers have food, but they probably cannot design their own houses or educate their children; they need architects and teachers, just as the architects and teachers need farmers to grow their food. These societies are based on organic solidarity: Because people are dissimilar and specialized, they depend on one another to provide what they cannot supply for themselves.

In many ways it is clear that we live in a society characterized by organic solidarity. However, the rise of technology could be undermining our dependency on one another (and the solidarity that this dependency can bring). In our daily lives we encounter numerous scenarios in which we use machines to perform a function instead of relying on another human. We bank online or use an ATM rather than wait in line for a teller, we get our own soft drink at a fast-food restaurant rather than wait for a cashier to serve us, and we even check out our own groceries at the supermarket. Even more complex tasks are being replaced by technological media. For example, we self-diagnose our ailments on WebMD rather than consult a doctor or purchase an online app to learn a language rather than take a course.

Modernization theory has been criticized on several different fronts. Some argue that it fails to recognize that rich nations industrialized from a position of global strength, by colonizing other countries and taking their resources. As a result, the countries that colonized early were able to accumulate wealth, while the colonized countries were exploited and became poorer. In other words, the European takeoff period was fueled by the resources (including natural resources and human resources in the form of slavery) taken from other countries. Colonization was hugely problematic at the time and is now an unrealistic (and undesirable) avenue for development. Furthermore, the idea that poor countries remain poor because of their "backward" ways or refusal to embrace technologies or progress suggests that all countries have the same resources and opportunities to develop, which is not the case.

Modernization theory is also criticized for being ethnocentric (judging other cultures by the standards of one's own). Many question whether it is fair to measure other countries against

Western standards or to assume that the Western mode of doing things is best. Western notions of development have led to many problems, such as environmental degradation and materialism. Is it, then, good to encourage other countries to become more like Western nations?

Methods in Depth: Building Consensus for Climate Action in Polarized Societies

Environmental problems, such as climate change, have serious implications for humans and the planet. They are also problems that are global in scale. We cannot solve these problems simply by working within our local communities or even nations. Although these issues are of critical importance and need to be addressed now, they can also often feel insurmountable. This is particularly true in the American context, where climate change is a highly charged and polarized issue. Research finds that Americans who value individual freedom, competition, and support traditional social hierarchies are often less concerned about climate change and the need for climate action than Americans who value equality and social solidarity (Rooney-Varga et al., 2021). Political polarization is thus a major challenge to consensus and science-based climate action.

Methodology

Juliette Rooney-Varga and her colleagues (2021) sought to understand how we can create consensus for global action on climate change across the ideological spectrum. The researchers deployed a unique set of methods to investigate this pressing problem. It included the use of a simulation (*World Climate*) which required participants to engage in a role-playing exercise simulating climate policy negotiations. More than 2,000 American participants, across 41 simulation sessions, role played as delegates to the United Nations. Participants were required to make collective decisions about issues such as emissions and land use to limit global warming to less than two degrees Celsius above preindustrial temperatures. The policies that participants settled on through negotiations were then entered into a computer program, C-ROADS, that models the climate system's response to the policies. If the stated policy solutions did not decrease global temperatures, they were encouraged to return to the negotiating table to develop better policies.

Because the researchers were interested in how people's ideologies might shape consensus building, they also included a pre/post survey design. Prior to the simulation, participants were asked about their political values, climate change knowledge, emotional responses to climate change, intent to learn more about climate change, and intent to engage in climate action. After the simulation, they were given the same set of survey questions, which allowed researchers to capture how the simulation changed—or did not change—their ideologies, knowledge, and intent to act. The researchers found that the simulation, which required people with different political values to work together, resulted in significant and substantial gains in knowledge of climate change, sense of urgency, and intent to act among *all* participants. More important, this change was stronger for those who tended to value individualism, competition, and traditional social hierarchies. And, these people showed a shift toward a more communitarian-egalitarian worldview by the end of the research.

Challenges

This work is critically important because it shows that when people are provided with the same scientific information and must work together, they are able to put aside political differences to address common challenges. However, because the sample for this research was not randomly selected or representative of the American population, it is difficult to say whether we would be able to replicate these findings. Still, it does provide hope that by participating in interactive role-play simulations, political polarization can be defused and encourage people to work together to tackle urgent global problems such as climate change.

World Systems Theory

World systems theory was developed by Immanuel Wallerstein (2011) as a critique of modernization theory. World systems theory highlights the inherent inequality that occurs through globalization and global development (see Figure 12.2). This theory understands globalization in a very different way than modernization theory does: It sees the world as a transnational division of labor between core, semi-periphery, and periphery countries.

- Core countries are the most powerful nations in the world. Their power is based on their economic diversification, high level of industrialization, high-skill labor, and focus on the manufacturing of goods instead of simply extracting raw resources for export. These nations dominate new technologies and industries and can exert significant economic and military influence over other countries. Core countries have been traditionally found in the northwest of Europe; however, Canada, Japan, and the United States are now part of the core.

- Periphery countries are the least powerful of the three types of countries. They are not economically diversified and are only minimally industrialized. These countries focus on extracting raw materials for export to core countries. Periphery nations, which are concentrated in Latin America and sub-Saharan Africa, are attractive to core countries' business interests because they tend to have lenient labor and environmental laws.

- Semi-periphery countries, such as Brazil, China, India, and South Africa, combine characteristics of the core and periphery. They are often countries moving toward industrialization and economic diversification. The United States was once a semi-periphery country, when its economy was focused on resource extraction with very low levels of industrialization.

FIGURE 12.2 ■ World Systems Theory Map

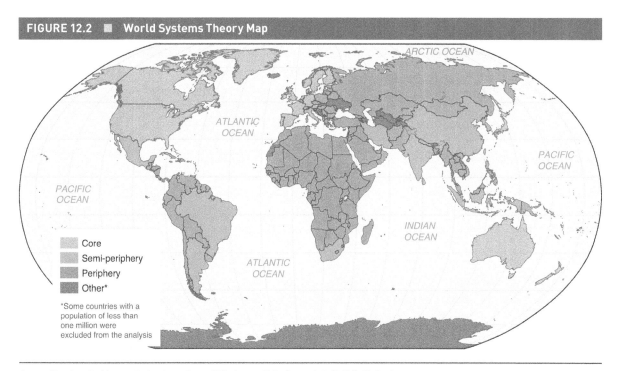

Legend:
- Core
- Semi-periphery
- Periphery
- Other*

*Some countries with a population of less than one million were excluded from the analysis

Source: Reprinted with permission from Scott, J.M., Carter, R.C., Drury, A.C. (2021). *IR: Seeking security, prosperity, and quality of life in a changing world.*, 4e. CQ Press.

As the example of the United States' shift from the periphery to the core highlights, countries can gain power over time. They can also lose power. Many countries, such as the Netherlands and the United Kingdom, had the distinction of being superpowers for a time. However, this status is hard to maintain.

World systems theory is based on Marxist principles. Think of the core countries as the capitalists. They benefit from the labor of the proletariat countries (the periphery) in several ways.

- First, companies in the core take the resources from the periphery countries, such as American companies buying oil from the Middle East.

- Second, they use the labor power of periphery countries and pay very low wages (which they cannot do in their own countries because of unions and labor laws). A classic example is companies such as Nike or Walmart, both American corporations, outsourcing their labor to Bangladesh or China, among other countries.

- Third, core countries pollute periphery countries and deplete their resources. Companies from the core might clear forests to make space for factories, which decreases air quality. Companies are also able to pollute more freely in periphery countries, which is prohibited in core countries by environmental protection laws.

- Finally, the capitalists in core countries sell the goods produced in the periphery to the workers in the periphery. These wealthy owners bring the resulting profits back to the core countries. In this way, poorer nations keep getting poorer and can never catch up economically.

According to world systems theorists, the unequal trade relations between the core and periphery countries create many problems for the periphery. Periphery countries are pressured to produce a small number of cash crops that are oriented to export. Modernization theorists, for example, encouraged periphery countries to move toward cash crops in order to develop. For example, these countries might be encouraged to produce coffee beans for export instead of fruits and vegetables, which could feed the local population. In addition, periphery countries are urged to extract natural resources in their raw formats and export them to core countries, where they are processed (e.g., mined stones set in rings or furniture built out of raw lumber) to make a profit. This process destroys the local environment in peripheral countries. It also creates low-wage and low-skill work in the periphery while moving the higher-wage and higher-skill work to the core.

USING YOUR SOCIOLOGICAL IMAGINATION
COMMODITY CHAINS AND GLOBAL INEQUALITY

Chances are that the clothing you wear, the computer you use, and the car or bus you take to school are made in countries other than the United States. Goods come to the United States through commodity chains, which gather resources, transform them into commodities, and distribute them to consumers. This process is a natural part of globalization.

Clelland (2014) traced the commodity chain of an Apple iPad. Clelland demonstrates Apple's profit from selling an iPad depends on exploitation of migratory Chinese workers. He writes:

> While China accounts for three-quarters of all direct labor costs, only 2 percent of the total gross profit margin ($223) stays in that country. Only 12 percent of the factory price is retained by waged workers, so Apple captures 4.5 times more of the surplus than its offshored iPad working class. (p. 89)

See Table 12.1 for a breakdown of the $150 profit captured by Apple in a single $499 iPad.

TABLE 12.1 ■ Flow of Bright Value in the iPad Commodity Chain, 2010–2011		
Activity	**A** **Cost in US$**	**B** **% Factory Price**
Retail Price	499	181.5
Wholesale Price	425	154.5
Factory Price	275	
Gross Profit Margin (GPM) (Total "value capture")	223	
Apple Gross Profit Margin (Design, Marketing, Chain Governance, Operating Profit)	150	54.5
Manufacturing GPM (Tiers 1 and 2)*	88	32.0
Taiwan	27	9.8
Korea	26	9.5
United States	23	8.4
European Union	5	1.8
Japan	4	1.4
China	3	1.1
Direct Labor to assemble iPads & to manufacture its	33	12.0
major component parts (Tiers 1 and 2) **	25	9.1
China	4	1.5
Korea	2	0.7
Taiwan	2	0.7
Philippines		
Material Inputs for Major Components	154	56.0

Notes: The model of the iPad examined is the 16GB Non-3G version (2010), the simplest, least expensive model. The starting point for the figures provided is a "teardown" by iSuppli Corporation (Rassweiler 2010) that identifies the major components, most suppliers, and the estimated costs. It is likely that these estimates are somewhat high, failing to take into account Apple's strong bargaining position (degree of monopoly) (EPT Newsletter 2010). Additional suppliers and component costs have been identified from teardowns, Wikipedia (2013) and internet searches. The gross margin of each supplier is available in annual reports and is reported by stock trader internet sites. The country shares of gross margin are the cumulative shares of the suppliers with headquarters located in that country. The country shares of direct labor are the cumulative shares allocated to actual production sites. Data in column A are derived from Kraemer, Linden and Dedrick (2010: Table 1) with adjustments for my revised list of iPad suppliers. Data in column B are calculated by dividing data in column A by the factory price ($275).

* Includes Singapore (less than 1%) represented in the rounded total.

** Includes Singapore (less than 1%). Numbers have been rounded.

Source: Clelland, D. A. (2014). The Core of the Apple: Degrees of Monopoly and Dark Value in Global Commodity Chains. *Journal of World-Systems Research, 20*(1), 82–111. Table 1, page 88 at: http://jwsr.pitt.edu/ojs/jwsr/article/view/564/656

For this activity, choose a product (a Starbucks coffee or a Nike shoe) and look at its manufacturing and delivery routes.

1. What stops (farms, factories, regions, countries) contribute to making the finished product? Use the Internet to research where your chosen product comes from and how it is made.

> **2.** Look at the CIA's *World Factbook* online (or access the direct link on this book's companion website) for information about the countries involved in making the product. Click on the economy, people, and government links to examine the conditions in these countries, including average life expectancy, infant mortality rate, unemployment rate, percentage of the population living below the poverty line, and inequality. With this information in mind, why do you think that your product was made in those countries? What is the implication of this process for global inequality?

Local industries in the periphery cannot compete with companies from the core. As a result, few local businesses develop in the periphery and workers must buy their processed goods from the core countries at high cost, creating more debt. For example, periphery countries sell inexpensive resources and raw materials to the core. To do so, they must buy expensive fertilizers, pesticides, and mechanical equipment from the core. This downward cycle leads the periphery to become poorer as the core becomes richer. Just as in Marx's theory, poor and rich countries depend on one another, but the benefits of their relationship are skewed toward the rich core countries.

World systems theory argues that resources flow from the periphery to the core and that ideas flow in the opposite direction. For example, the flow of news and entertainment media privileges the core's needs and interests. News about the core is reported everywhere in the periphery, while news about the periphery is rarely reported in the core. Thus, people in the periphery know a lot about processes and current events in core countries. Donald Trump's inauguration was reported all over the world, but news from other parts of the world is rarely covered in core media outlets. Events in the U.S., such as the Uvalde school shooting that killed 19 students and 2 teachers in Texas on May 24, 2022, are widely covered in the media around the world. Moments of silence for the victims were held around the world and the flag was lowered in Washington, DC. However, a mosque attack in Afghanistan on April 22 of the same year, which killed 31 people and wounded 87 more, received very little media coverage outside the country. This highlights the Western bias of our news. This lack of dialogue with non-Western countries perpetuates exploitation and global inequality, as those with the means to help create change (such as core country citizens) are usually unaware of events in the periphery.

Like all theories, world systems theory has been criticized. For example, many people note that foreign trade has assisted some countries or economies: Trade with rich countries has helped the economies of Hong Kong, Japan, and Singapore. Others also argue that, as modernization theory predicts, foreign investment stimulates growth, not economic decline. Furthermore, the ability of countries to move into the core counters the claim that globalization will lead to increased poverty in the periphery.

READING: "THE USES OF GLOBAL POVERTY: HOW ECONOMIC INEQUALITY BENEFITS THE WEST"

Daina Stukuls Eglitis

Daina Stukuls Eglitis asks why rich nations do not do more to reduce global poverty. This is a great question: Most people in core countries believe that global poverty is a significant social issue. However, global poverty continues and may even be worsening. How do we explain this trend? Eglitis argues that people in rich countries benefit from global poverty in

many ways. This argument is difficult to accept, especially for those who live in a rich country. As you read this excerpt, consider how you might benefit from global poverty.

Why don't rich nations do more to reduce the severe poverty that paralyzes much of the world? This selection argues that people in rich countries, including the United States, actually benefit from global poverty in a number of ways.

In the global village, there stand a wide variety of homes, from the stately mansion on the hill, to the modest abode blessed with electricity and running water, to the adequate but unheated (or uncooled) hut, to the flood-prone, tattered shanty cobbled together from gathered scrap. Those who live on the hill are aware of their neighbors, as their neighbors are aware of them. Most inhabitants of the global village recognize that wealth and the accompanying opportunities for education, health care, and consumption are not evenly divided and that a substantial gap exists between the more and less materially blessed populations. Not everyone agrees on why that is the case. . . .

What have been the responses of well-off states to this global class system with its extremes of wealth and poverty? Not surprisingly, perhaps, political rhetoric has consistently elevated the goal of spreading the prosperity enjoyed by the advanced industrial states of the West around the globe. . . .

If shared global prosperity was the goal, it seems safe to say that while there was some modest progress made in areas like Latin America, Eastern Europe, and parts of Asia, "we" did not really succeed, because the global wealth gap is still massive and growing. The rich countries remain rich, and the poor countries, for the most part, remain trapped in desperate, dire poverty. This has not changed. . . .

Western rhetoric, assistance programs, and advice seem to support the goal of global prosperity and its extension to the 1.3 billion who live on less than $1 per day and those millions or even billions more who eke out a sparse existence just above the threshold of absolute poverty. But the reality of prosperity has touched only a relative few countries, while the struggle to meet basic needs touches many more. Social indicators like the GNI PPP [gross national income purchasing power parity] highlight the differences we find in our village. But what explains them? Why does global poverty exist and persist? Why does a global class system with a thin layer of rich states and a broad strata of poor countries exist and persist? What explains why some villagers inhabit houses on the mount while others squat in mud huts below? Possible answers are many. This article explores one way of understanding the yawning gap between the planet's wealthiest and poorest states.

In 1971, sociologist Herbert Gans published an article entitled "The Uses of Poverty: The Poor Pay All."[1] In the article, Gans utilized a conservative theoretical perspective in sociology, functionalism, to inquire about the persistence of poverty in America. The functionalist perspective takes as its starting point the position that essentially all institutions and social phenomena that exist in society contribute in some manner to that society— that is, they are functional for society. If they did not contribute to the social order, the functionalists maintain, they would disappear. Using this perspective, functionalists may inquire about, for instance, the functions, both obvious and hidden (or manifest and latent, to use sociologist Robert Merton's terms), of institutions like the education system or the family or social phenomena like punishment for deviance. These social theorists assume that institutions or phenomena exist because they are functional, and hence their guiding question is, What function do they serve?

Gans posed a similar question about poverty, asking, What are the uses of poverty? Clearly, the notion that poverty is functional for society as a whole is ludicrous: Who would suggest that it is functional for those who endure economic deprivation? So Gans offered a modified functionalist analysis: " . . . instead of identifying functions for an entire social system, I shall identify them for the interest groups, socio-economic classes, and other population aggregates with shared values that 'inhabit' a social system. I suspect that in a modern heterogeneous society, few phenomena are functional or dysfunctional for the society as a whole, and that most result in benefits to some groups and costs to others."

Gans sought to explain the existence and persistence of poverty in modern, wealthy America by highlighting the way that the existence of poverty has benefits for the nonpoor— not just "evil" individuals like the loan shark or the slumlord, but for "normal" members of nonpoor classes. He identified 13 "uses" of poverty, including the notions that the existence of a poor class "ensures that society's 'dirty work' will be done," that "the poor buy goods others do not want and thus prolong the economic usefulness of such goods," and "the poor can be identified and punished as alleged or real deviants in order to uphold the legitimacy of conventional norms." He was not arguing that poverty is good. He was suggesting that understanding poverty's existence and persistence means recognizing that the poor have positive social and economic functions for the nonpoor. Thus, one would conclude that the elimination of poverty, while elevated as a societal goal, would be, in practice, costly to the nonpoor.

While Gans's theoretically based inquiry into poverty was focused on America's poor, the same question might be asked about the existence of global poverty: What are the "uses" of global poverty for the better-off countries of the world economic system? The purpose of such an inquiry would be, as it was in Gans's inquiry, not to use a functionalist analysis to legitimate poverty or the highly skewed distribution of wealth in the global system, but to contribute to a deeper understanding of why it continues to exist by explaining how its persistence confers benefits on well-off states and their inhabitants.

The argument is not that advanced states are consciously conspiring to keep the poor states destitute: well-off countries have historically sought to offer help to less developed countries. In reality, however, there are limited incentives for the better-off states to support the full industrial and technological (and even democratic) development of all the states in the global system. To the degree that the existence of a class of poor states is positively functional for wealthy states, we can begin to imagine why development and assistance programs that help ensure survival, but not prosperity, for poor populations are quite characteristic of Western policy.

This article notes 11 "uses" of global poverty. Global poverty is not, from this perspective, functional for the global community as a whole. The notion that the poverty of billions who live in economically marginal states is globally "useful" would be absurd. But it is not absurd to ask how the existence of a class of poor states serves wealthy states. In fact, asking such a question might contribute to a better understanding of the dual phenomena of global poverty and the global "class" system.

Point 1: The existence of global poverty helps ensure the wealth of affordable goods for Western consumers.

The cornucopia of decently priced goods of reasonable quality enjoyed by Western consumers is underpinned by the low-wage work done in low-income countries. The labels on the clothing you are wearing right now likely contain the familiar words "Made in China" or perhaps "Made in Pakistan." Your clothing is probably of reasonable quality, and you likely paid a reasonable (but not necessarily cheap) price for it.

The Western consumer of textiles such as off-the-rack clothing is a beneficiary of a globalized manufacturing process that has seen the movement of manufacturing to low-wage areas located in poor states that provide ready pools of workers needy enough to labor for a pittance. In China, the average hourly wage of apparel workers is about 23 cents. This benefits the consumer of that apparel. The worker herself (workers in this industry are usually female) derives less benefit: the average hourly wage needed to meet basic needs in China, according to Women's Edge, an advocacy group, is 87 cents.[2] . . .

Stories about low-wage workers in developing countries have, in recent years, emerged in the Western press and provoked some expressions of outrage and the formation of groups like United Students Against Sweatshops. These expressions have been small and limited. Imagine, however, the outrage if popular sports shoes, already pricey, climbed another $50 in cost as a result of manufacturers opting for well-paid, unionized labor. Or imagine if the price of a head of iceberg lettuce, America's favorite vegetable, suddenly doubled in price to $3.00. Which outrage would be more potent?

Point 2: The existence of global poverty benefits Western companies and shareholders in the form of increased profit margins.

Labor costs typically constitute a high percentage of a company's expenditures. By reducing labor costs, companies can both keep prices reasonable (which benefits, as noted, the consumer) and raise profit margins. Not surprisingly, then, companies are not likely to locate in—and are more likely to leave—locations where wages are relatively high. The use of poor female workers in the Third World is, in this respect, especially "beneficial" to companies. Women comprise about 80 per cent of workers in Export Processing Zones and are often paid 20 percent to 50 percent less than male counterparts. The less costly the workforce, the greater the opportunity for profit. Not coincidentally, countries with an ample supply of poor workers willing to work for miserable wages are also countries with lax safety and environmental regulations, which also keeps down the costs to the Western employer and pushes up the profits. Hence, companies benefit directly from the existence of economically deprived would-be workers willing (or not in a position to be unwilling) to work for paltry wages in potentially hazardous, or at least very unpleasant, conditions.

Point 3: The existence of global poverty fosters access to resources in poor states that are needed in or desired by the West.

Poor states may sell raw goods at low prices to Western states, which can transform the resource into a more valuable finished product. The position of the poor states in the world economy makes it less likely that they can derive the full benefit of the resources they possess for the government and people. The case of oil in resource-rich but desperately poor Nigeria is an example. Seven major foreign oil companies operate in Nigeria, all representing interests in wealthy states. The vast majority of benefits from Nigeria's oil has accrued not to the country's people, but to the companies (and consumers) of the wealthy states. . . .

Point 4: The existence of global poverty helps support Western medical advances.

The poor provide a pool of guinea pigs for the testing of medicines developed for use primarily in the West. The beneficiaries are not the poor themselves but Western consumers of advanced medicine (60 percent of profits are made in the United States, which leads the world in drug consumption) and the pharmaceutical companies, which stand astride a $350 billion (and growing) industry. A series of reports in *The Washington Post* in December 2000 documents the disturbing practice of conducting drug trials on ill inhabitants of poor states. For instance, an unapproved antibiotic was tested by a major pharmaceutical company on sick children during a meningitis epidemic in Nigeria. The country's lax regulatory oversight, the sense among some doctors that they could not object to experiment conditions for political or economic reasons, the dearth of alternative health-care options, combined with the desire of the company to rapidly prepare for the market a potential "blockbuster" drug underpinned a situation in which disease victims were treated as test subjects rather than patients. This case highlights the way that nonpoor states actually benefit from the existence of poor states with struggling, sick populations. . . .

Point 5: The existence of global poverty contributes to the advancement of Western economies and societies with the human capital of poor states.

Poorer states like India have become intellectual feeders of well-educated and bright individuals whose skills cannot be fully rewarded in less developed states. The magnetic draw of a better life in economies that amply reward their human capital pulls the brightest minds from their countries of origin, a process referred to as "brain drain." Advanced economies such as the United States and England are beneficiaries of brain drain. The United States has moved to take advantage of the pool of highly educated workers from the developing world. . . .

Point 6: The existence of global poverty may contribute to the pacification of the Western proletariat, or "Workers of the World, A Blue Light Special!"

To some degree, the broad availability of good, inexpensive merchandise may help obscure class divisions in the West, at least in the arena of consumption. It is clear that those with greater wealth can consume more high-quality goods, but low-end "designer" merchandise is accessible to the less well-off in cathedrals of consumption such as Wal-Mart. At K-Mart, for instance, Martha Stewart peddles her wares, intended to transform "homemaking chores . . . into what we like to call 'domestic art.'" Thanks in part to the low-wage workers in places like China, these goods are available to the unwashed masses (now washed by Martha's smart and cozy towels) as well as to better-situated homemakers. Consumption appears to be one of the great equalizers of modern society. (It is worth noting, though, that many members of the Western working class are also "victims" of global poverty, since many jobs have gone abroad to low-wage areas, leaving behind, for less educated workers, positions in the less remunerative and less secure service industry or leaving former industrial workers jobless.)

Point 7: Global poverty benefits the West because poor countries make optimal dumping grounds for goods that are dangerous, expired, or illegal.

Wealthy countries and their inhabitants may utilize poorer states as repositories for dangerous or unwanted material such as nuclear waste. The desperation of cash-strapped states benefits better-off countries, which might otherwise have difficulty ridding themselves of the dangerous by-products of their industrial and consumer economies. For instance, in December 2000, the Russian Parliament, in an initial vote on the issue, overwhelmingly supported the amendment of an environmental law to permit the importation of foreign nuclear waste. The alteration of the law was supported by the Atomic Ministry of the Russian Federation, which suggested that over the next decade, Russia might earn up to $21 billion from the importation of spent nuclear fuel from states like Japan, Germany, and South Korea. Likely repositories of the radioactive refuse are Mayak and Krasnoyarsk, already among the most contaminated sites on the planet. . . .

Point 8: The existence of global poverty provides jobs for specialists employed to assist, advise, and study the world's poor and to protect the "better-off" from them.

Within this group of specialists we find people in a variety of professions. There are those who are professional development workers, operating through organizations like the United States Agency for International Development (USAID). . . .

Academics in fields as diverse as economics, sociology, international affairs, political science, and anthropology study, write about, and "decipher" the lives of the poor and the condition of poor states. Texts on development, articles debating why poverty persists, and books from university presses are only some of the products of this research. Journalists and novelists can build careers around bringing colorful, compelling representations of the poor to the warm living rooms of literate, well-off consumers. Still others are charged with the task of protecting wealthy states from "invasions" of the poor: US border patrols, for instance, employ thousands to keep those seeking better fortunes out of US territory.

Point 9: Global poverty benefits inhabitants of wealthy countries, who can feel good about helping the global poor through charitable work and charitable giving.

From the celebrity-studded musical production "We are the World" to trick-or-treating for UNICEF, those who inhabit the wealthy corners of the world feel good about themselves for sharing their good fortune. The website of World Vision, a faith-based charity that offers the opportunity to sponsor poor children, features a speak-out area for contributors. On that site, a young sponsor wrote, "A few days ago I woke up early and turned the TV on . . . looking at those children made me realize I could help them. I thought if I have enough money to pay for the Internet, cellphone, and a couple of other things I didn't need, I said to myself, [then] why not give that money to people who need it instead of spending it all in (sic) luxury and things that are not really important. I immediately picked up the phone and called to sponsor a child! I am happy. I can help someone who needs it!"[3]

Apparently, we need not feel guilt about consuming many times what the unfortunate inhabitants of the world's poor states do if only we are willing to give up a few of our luxuries to help them. . . .

A related point is that the poor we see on television or hear about in news or music give those of us in wealthy countries the opportunity to feel good about ourselves, regardless of our position in the socio-economic structure of our own states. . . .

Point 10: The poverty of less developed states makes possible the massive flow of resources westward.

Imagine if large and largely poor countries like China, Nigeria, and India consumed at US rates. At present, Americans consume a tremendously disproportionate share of the world's resources. With their profligate use of all manner of resources, most notably fossil fuels, Americans are the greediest consumers of natural resources on the planet. On both an absolute and per capita basis, most world resources flow westward. Notably, a 4 October 2000 article in *The Seattle Times* reported that bicycles, long a characteristic and popular means of transport for Chinese commuters, are losing popularity: "Increasingly, young Chinese are not even bothering to learn to ride bikes, because growing wealth has unleashed a plethora of transportation choices, public and private."[4] The new transportation of choice is still largely public buses or private taxis: the Chinese have not yet graduated to mass private cars. But it is interesting to ponder whether there would be enough (affordable) oil for everyone if the Chinese, with their growing population and prosperity, became a country of two-vehicle families or developed a taste and market for gas-guzzling sports utility vehicles. In this case, the West likely benefits from the fact that few can afford (at least at present) to consume at the rate its people do.

Point 11: The poorer countries, which reproduce at rates higher than Western states, are useful scapegoats for real and potential global environmental threats.

What is the bigger environmental threat to our planet? Is it the rapid growth of the populations of developing states or the rapid consumption of resources by the much smaller populations of developed states? The overdevelopment of the West may well be the bigger threat, though the growth of populations in Third World countries, which is often linked to conditions of underdevelopment, such as a lack of birth control and the need to have "extra" children as a hedge against high child mortality rates, makes an attractive alternative explanation for those who would not wish to fault the SUV-driving, disposable-diaper using, BBQ-loving American consumer for threats to the global environment. While some Western policymakers express concern about the environmental threats emerging from rapid population growth or the use of "dirty" technology in developing states, there is comparably little serious attention given to the global threat presented by the profligate consumption by Western states. The poor divert attention from the environmental problems caused by Western overconsumption.

I have talked about 11 ways that the continued existence of global poverty benefits those who reside in wealthy states. The argument I have offered to explain the persistence of a strata of poor states and the yawning global gap highlights the idea that while global poverty (and the status quo) is beneficial to the wealthy West, serious steps to alleviate it will not be taken.

It is surely the case that poverty does not have to exist. But while we in the West derive the benefits and bonuses of these economic inequalities, it seems likely that our efforts to support, advise, and assist the less developed states will remain at levels that are financially and politically convenient and feasible, and will target survival rather than true prosperity for those outside our gated, privileged, greedy Western neighborhood. In Gans's words, "Phenomena like poverty can be eliminated only when they become dysfunctional for the affluent or powerful, or when the powerless can obtain enough power to change society."

Notes

Social Policy, July/August 1971.

Information on issues of trade and Chinese women is available at http:// www.womensedge.org. The information cited is from the April 2000 web issue of *Notes from the Edge*.

The charity's website address is http//www.worldvision.org.

The article is cited at the website of the Competitive Enterprise Institute: http://www.cei.org/CHNReader. asp? ID=1227.

Reading Questions

1. How does this article use ideas from structural functionalism (see Chapter 2)?
2. The article claims that global poverty benefits (is "functional" for) only some people in the world. Who benefits from global poverty and how?

3. How does this article use ideas from conflict theory (see Chapter 2)?

4. Of the 11 functions of global poverty outlined in this article, which three do you think are the most convincing or important? Which three are the least convincing or important? Give reasons to support your answers.

Eglitis, D. (2004). "The uses of global poverty: How economic inequality benefits the west." Reprinted by permission of the author.

World Society Theory

The third theory of globalization that we will examine is world society theory. John W. Meyer and colleagues (1997) developed this theory, which focuses on the importance of global institutions and cultural models in shaping the behavior of nations, organizations, and individuals. In contrast to world systems theory and modernization theory, the world society tradition focuses on global change as the consequence of emerging global institutions and a world culture.

World society theory argues that countries are becoming increasingly similar. These countries are moving toward a worldview that is consistent with Enlightenment ideals of progress, science, and human rights. As a result, both individuals and nation-states tend to adopt common cultural frames or perspectives, resulting in one world culture. Although this theory emphasizes the positive elements of globalization, such as the spread of ideals of human rights, science, and tolerance, it is important to note that negative ideas, such as consumerism, materialism, and violence, can also become common cultural frames.

World society theory is rooted in comparative education research conducted in the 1970s. Researchers noted that education systems in sub-Saharan Africa were surprisingly similar to the education systems in Western Europe and North America, despite the vast cultural, economic, and social differences in the societies. Theorists sought to explain these similarities by arguing that they resulted from some underlying assumptions about education. In this way, education systems were based on cultural models that spread across countries and provided blueprints for what a good education system should be, regardless of context (Meyer et al., 1997). International organizations are a very important part of the institutionalization of these cultural models and their spread from country to country.

Another cultural ideal that has spread in modernity is individualism and the importance of individual rights. At the end of World War II individuals and societies began to change their focus from the rights of groups (corporatism) to the rights of individuals (individualism). This shift led to many social changes. For example, the rise and spread of capitalist ideologies are based on an individual worker's (or capitalist's) ability to make a wage (or profit). Democracy is based on the idea of one person, one vote.

The world society framework can help us understand certain globalization processes. For example, Frank, Camp, and Boutcher (2010) examined the changing regulations of sex and sexuality (including laws about adultery, sodomy, child sexual abuse, and rape). They found that in the 60 years from 1945 to 2005, the criminal regulations of adultery and sodomy drastically diminished around the world, while those regarding rape and child sexual abuse expanded globally. During the period under study, 68% of the laws about adultery and 81% of those about sodomy lessened or eliminated state punishment for these acts. This change is in stark opposition to the laws about child sexual abuse and rape—85% of the laws about child sexual abuse and 98% of the laws about rape criminalized or increased the punishment for these two crimes (Frank et al., 2010).

Frank and colleagues (2010) suggest that we can understand these changes using world society theory. Early laws regulating sex and sexuality focused on the perceived needs of society, including the procreative functions of sex. Therefore, sexual activity that was procreative and could lead to legitimate heirs (e.g., children born from heterosexual sex between husbands and wives) was protected. Under this type of social focus, sexual activity that was nonprocreative (e.g., sodomy) or that undermined the family (adultery) was heavily regulated.

Today, laws about sexuality focus on protecting an individual's autonomy. As such, laws focus on an individual's right to consent to sexual activity. Rape and child sexual abuse laws are much more common now. These laws are based on the ideas of individual rights and the need for individual consent, which is absent in instances of rape and abuse. Other sexual acts, such as adultery and sodomy, are less of a concern in many societies, because they are seen to occur between consenting adults and to not violate a person's individual rights. Frank and colleagues (2010) argue that the rising regulation of rape and child sexual abuse (and the declining regulation of adultery and sodomy, both of which were previously illegal in most countries) indicates a widespread international change in norms about individualism.

American laws on marital rape are a case in point. Before 1979 there was no such thing as marital rape from a legal perspective in the United States. It was thought impossible for a man to rape his wife because rape was defined as an act that occurred outside marriage. Marital exemptions to rape laws focused on corporatist needs (e.g., the need of society to populate itself) over the individual rights of women to consent to sexual activity. The law was eventually changed to prioritize women's right to give or deny consent. In 1993, North Carolina was the final state to make marital rape illegal (Rothman, 2015).

GLOBAL INEQUALITY

In Chapter 3 we learned about income inequality in the United States. Income is unevenly distributed in the United States and, over time, the richest Americans have earned an increasingly larger share of all income made in the country. However, inequalities in income are even starker between countries. Modernization, world systems, and world society theories have different perspectives on the promise and pitfalls of globalization, but they all see these vast inequalities.

Between 1820 and 2020 global inequality increased fairly consistently. This increased inequality occurred because mean incomes were rising in Australia, North America, and Western Europe, whereas countries elsewhere, particularly China and India, had incomes that remained constant or declined (Bourguignon & Morrison, 2002). In the period between 1820 and 1912, the GDP of the United Kingdom went from $2,000 to $5,000. In the same period, the GDP of China decreased from $600 to $550. Thus, the Industrial Revolution sent one group of countries into great economic growth while leading the other group of countries to either stay where they were or to decline in income. This created vast inequality between countries and widened global inequality (Milanovic, 2016). Global inequality has declined slightly since about 2000. This is the result of increased income and earnings in Asia and a slowdown in the West (Milanovic, 2016).

One way to compare income inequality across countries systematically is with the Gini index, developed by the Italian sociologist Corrado Gini. This index measures income inequality on a scale of 0 to 1: 0 represents perfect equality in a society (all individuals in the society make the same income) and 1 represents the maximum level of inequality in a society (one person receives all the society's income). In other words, the lower the Gini index, the more equitable the country.

Figure 12.3 shows the Gini levels of most countries in the world. We can see that the United States is a relatively unequal society, with a Gini of 0.42 (OECD, 2016). The Scandinavian countries and many other nations in Western and Eastern Europe are more equitable (Slovenia is the most equitable society in the world, with a Gini index of 0.231). Countries in Africa and South and Central America are the most unequal countries. However, Africa has a huge amount of variability in terms of inequality—from the very high level in South Africa (the second-most unequal place in the world, with a Gini of 0.63) to the very low level in Ethiopia (0.33 Gini index).

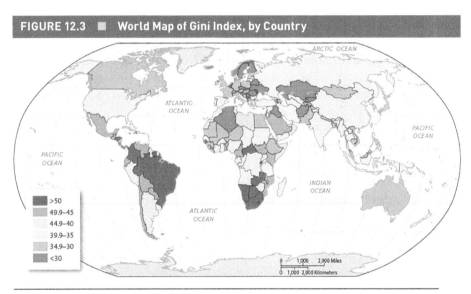

FIGURE 12.3 ■ World Map of Gini Index, by Country

Source: World Bank, CC BY 4.0, https://creativecommons.org/licenses/by/4.0/.

The Gini index measures inequality by comparing the incomes of the richest and the poorest in a society or across countries. However, we can also compare inequalities in health, education, employment, or a variety of other measures. Table 12.2 compares the wealth, inequality, health, and well-being outcomes, including infant mortality rate, for seven countries. These nations spend different amounts on health care and have different levels of inequality, as measured by their Gini indices.

People who live in countries with higher GDP (i.e., more wealth) generally have better health; they live longer and have lower infant mortality. In addition, governments in rich countries tend to spend more money on health care—Canada, Japan, Sweden, and the United States spend more than India, Mexico, and South Africa. However, more spending does not always buy better health. The United States spends more than 1.5 times as much per person on health care than do Canada and Japan, yet has a much shorter life expectancy than the other two countries (78.9 in the United States, compared with 82.4 in Canada and 84.6 in Japan).

One of the main reasons for these differences in life expectancies among rich countries is that wealthy countries differ significantly in terms of their levels of equality. The Gini indices in Table 12.2 indicate that the gap between the rich and the poor is greater in the United States than it is in Canada, Japan, or Sweden. In general, research shows that the higher the level of inequality in a country, the less healthy its population will be. A country's health care system also influences this relationship. Canada, Japan, and Sweden all have universal health care systems administered by their respective governments. The United States has a more mixed system

TABLE 12.2 ■ GDP, Health Spending, and Gini by Country

	Wealth and Inequality in Country			Health and Well-Being Outcomes	
	GDP per Capita (in thousands), 2021	Health spending as percentage of GDP, 2018	Gini Index, 2011–2017	Human Development Index, 2019	Life Expectancy, 2019
Sweden	58.98	10.9	28.8	0.945	82.8
Canada	49.22	10.8	33.3	0.929	82.4
United States	68.31	16.9	41.1	0.926	78.9
Japan	42.93	11.0	32.9	0.919	84.6
Mexico	9.25	5.4	36.8	0.779	75.1
South Africa	5.44	8.3	63.0	0.709	64.1
India	2.19	3.5	35.7	0.645	69.7

Source: Adapted from International Monetary Fund, 2021, GDP Per Capita, Current Prices (US dollars), https://www.imf.org/external/datamapper/NGDPDPC@WEO/OEMDC/ADVEC/WEOWORLD; Central Intelligence Agency, 2018, The World Factbook – Current Health Expenditure, cia.gov/the-world-factbook/field/current-health-expenditure; Central Intelligence Agency, 2021, The World Factbook – Gini Index coefficient, https://www.cia.gov/the-world-factbook/field/gini-index-coefficient-distribution-of-family-income; and United Nations Development Programme, 2020, "Table 1. Human Development Index and Its Components," Human Development Reports, http://hdr.undp.org/en/composite/HDI

(as described in Chapter 11). Access to health care is very different across groups of Americans. Another interesting comparison is between India and South Africa. People living in India are doing much better than people living in South Africa in terms of general well-being. Although South Africa has a GDP twice as high as India, South Africans live 5.6 fewer years on average, partly because of the extreme inequality in the country.

Inequality in a society can have serious and wide-reaching implications. Pickett and Wilkinson (2011; Wilkinson & Pickett, 2018) argue that more-equitable societies do better in a variety of ways than less-equitable ones. Furthermore, equitable societies are not simply better for those at the bottom of the social hierarchy. Because these societies function better overall, they are good for both the rich and poor within them. The researchers compiled information from 20 sets of data collected by the UN, the World Bank, the WHO, and the U.S. Census. They found, for example, that crime rates are closely tied to inequality: Violent crime tends to be much more prevalent in countries, regions, and cities with high levels of inequality. And, higher crime rates are bad for everyone in a society, regardless of their personal wealth.

Wilkinson and Pickett (2018) argue that everyone, not just the poor, is adversely affected by inequality. For example, Britain and the United States have relatively high levels of inequality and very high levels of mental health problems—25% of Britons and more than 25% of Americans report experiencing mental health problems in any given year. The relatively more equitable countries of Germany, Italy, Japan, and Sweden have far fewer mental health problems, with fewer than 10% of citizens per year reporting mental health issues. Inequality also leads to isolation and anxiety, experiences that are associated with mental illness. Thus, according to Wilkinson and Pickett, the structures of these unequal societies lead to higher levels of mental health problems for both the rich and the poor—problems that cannot be solved through individual mental health solutions because they are inextricably linked to the unequal nature of these societies.

USING YOUR SOCIOLOGICAL IMAGINATION
COVID-19 VACCINE INEQUITY

Inequality between, as well as within, countries has exacerbated the global COVID-19 pandemic. Wealthier countries have been accused of stockpiling excess doses of vaccines while less wealthy countries have not received access to initial vaccine doses. The United Nations reported in March 2022 that around 3% of people in low-income countries had received their first dose of the COVID-19 vaccine compared to more than 60% of people in high-income countries. By continent, Africa has the lowest vaccination rate, with around 25% of the population receiving their first vaccine dose by mid-2022 (Holder, 2022).

Look at the global COVID-19 vaccination trackers from the *New York Times* and the Our World in Data Project.

https://www.nytimes.com/interactive/2021/world/covid-vaccinations-tracker.html
https://ourworldindata.org/covid-vaccinations

1. Choose two countries that are geographically distant. For each country, what share of the population has been vaccinated for COVID-19 with at least one dose? What share has received 2 doses?

2. Now look at the "Vaccination rates by country income level" chart on the *New York Times* website. What patterns do you observe generally? Where do your countries belong on the income scale (low, lower middle, upper middle, high income)?

3. What is the COVAX program? How is this program working toward vaccine equity for lower income countries?

4. Look at the Our World in Data Project's table on vaccines donated to COVAX. Which countries have donated the most doses to COVAX? Now click the relative option box that measures vaccine donations relative to population size. Does this change which countries have donated the most doses?

These women in Bangladesh attend a microfinance training session. Microfinance attempts to address global poverty and inequality. Why might microfinancing be more effective at reducing poverty than traditional bank loans?

Thomas Imo/Photothek via Getty Images

The unequal nature of a society also has significant implications for how a country is able to weather the storm of a global pandemic. Figure 12.4 shows how 11 countries were able to respond to the COVID-19 pandemic, as measured by the number of deaths per million. In this case, the higher the number, the less countries were able to effectively control the pandemic. Over the time period analyzed, 8 of the 11 countries have not surpassed 10 deaths per million people. Such countries—including Canada, Sweden, and South Korea—also have more equitable societies and access to universal health care. The three countries with exceptionally high deaths per million people—United States, Mexico, and Brazil—are more inequitable, based on their Gini scores. These data support Wilkinson and Pickett's thesis that more equitable countries tend to perform better in a variety of areas and that equality is a benefit to all in a society, not just the poor.

FIGURE 12.4 ■ **More Equitable Societies Are Better Able to Control Pandemics**

Covid-19 deaths per million people, rolling 7-day average, August 1–September 15, 2020

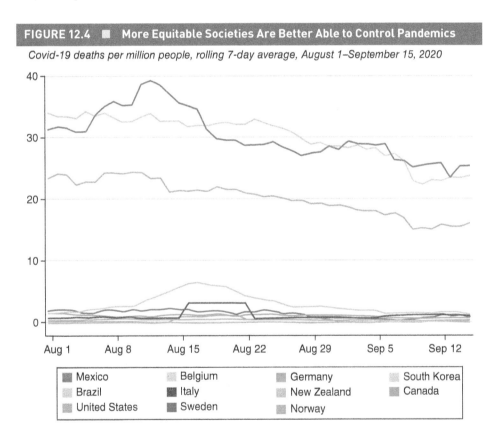

Source: Anderson, Sarah and Brian Wakamo. 2020. "Inequality and COVID-19 in 13 Charts." https://www.comm ondreams.org/views/2020/09/28/inequality-and-covid-19-13-charts.org/views/2020/09/28/inequality-and-cov id-19-13-charts

Global inequality is a serious problem that many individuals, organizations, countries, and international bodies have tried to solve. There are several ways to address global inequality. Three main strategies, which have been the focus of much international and domestic debate, are development assistance, debt relief, and microfinancing.

Development assistance is financial aid given by governments and some nongovernmental charitable agencies to support a country's economic, social, and political development. One of this strategy's primary goals is to reduce global poverty. In 2000 the UN developed a set of

Sustainable Development Goals. These are focused on eradicating poverty by 2030, increasing the spread of public schooling/work to stop drop outs, and continuing to stop the spread of HIV/AIDS. The UN's plan for tackling these problems centered on development assistance, a plan agreed to by all the world's countries and leading development institutions. This type of partnership has been relatively successful at dealing with some elements of global inequality.

The level of debt in some developing nations is a significant impediment to improving living conditions. Many developing countries and their citizens are burdened with insurmountable debts. Research has shown that for every $1 of aid that developing countries receive, they lose $24 in money leaving the country (Hickel, 2017). A country's debt works just like a personal credit card debt. Once the balance reaches a certain point, the monthly payments go toward the interest and it becomes impossible to pay off the principal. Activists and politicians from around the world have called for programs of debt relief, which would forgive portions of the debt that some countries owe.

The UN is actively working to reduce global poverty. Its Millennium Development Goals are one way that individuals and countries can come together to deal with the challenging social problem of global inequality.

Xinhua / Alamy Stock Photo

READING: "THE PROBLEM WITH FAIR TRADE COFFEE"

Nicki Lisa Cole and Keith Brown

In many ways, global poverty seems almost insurmountable. One new, innovative way of dealing with the problem is fair trade certification. The following article explains this strategy, its benefits, and some concerns regarding its practice. Do you use fair trade products, such as coffee?

Byron Corrales is known for growing some of the best coffee in Central America. His family-owned farm sits next to a nature reserve in a cloud forest north of Matagalpa, Nicaragua. Byron speaks poetically about his coffee: each morning he wakes and listens to his trees, trying to understand their needs. On his organic farm, Byron takes great efforts to reduce his oil consumption, lower his carbon footprint, and pay his employees a fair wage. He views himself as a socially conscious farmer and even sells some of his beans to Paul and Joan Katzeff, owners of Thanksgiving Coffee Company, longtime champions of the fair trade movement.

Corrales and the Katzeffs represent the core values of the fair trade movement. Corrales works meticulously to care for the local ecosystem and pay his workers fairly. The Katzeffs educate their consumers about fair trade's benefits and pay a premium for Corrales' coffee. Yet they all refuse to certify their coffee as "fair trade" with the largest certifier in the United States. They are part of a growing faction of small farmers and U.S. buyers of fair trade coffee who find themselves increasingly frustrated with the fair trade certification process.

While there is some diversity of opinion about what fair trade means, certification is designed to provide economic premiums for social and environmental investments—important for farmers who have historically received inadequate compensation for their crops. Recently some members of the global fair trade movement have become angry with Fair Trade USA, the organization that sets certification policy and licenses products for distribution in the United States. In January 2012, Fair Trade USA unilaterally altered their coffee sourcing policy to include not just cooperatives of small producers, but also large scale plantations. Under the slogan "Fair Trade for All," this new policy has changed the meaning of certification, and may negatively impact the very small-scale farmers fair trade was originally meant to protect.

We have interviewed fair trade store owners, coffeehouse managers and baristas, importers and exporters, coffee industry consultants, cooperative and movement leaders, farmers, artisans, and consumers. We have also conducted content analysis of fair trade advertisements and story displays, attended conferences around the United States, and lived alongside farmers in Nicaragua. Through this research, we came to learn how important fair trade certification is to small producers. We also learned that farmers' displeasure with Fair Trade USA's new policy reflects a long-standing tension between the founding values of the fair trade movement and profit-driven ethos of the fair trade market.

A Brief History of Fair Trade

European and American imports of textiles and handcrafts from war-torn and poverty-stricken communities around the world provided the foundation for today's fair trade system. In the mid-1980s, the concept was forever changed when coffee was folded into the fair trade model. At this time, a range of progressive entrepreneurs, including Paul Katzeff, began importing coffee from Nicaragua as an expression of support for Sandinista farmers. These Nicaraguan farmers were suffering from malnutrition and even starvation during the U.S.-imposed boycott of their country's goods. Over time, these seemingly disparate efforts—importing handicrafts, coffee, and other goods—coalesced into fair trade certification.

What Is Fair Trade Certified Coffee?

Fair trade certification guarantees that coffee producers are paid a stable, minimum price per pound for their product. Historically, this protection has been offered to small producers who are members of democratically organized cooperatives. These cooperatives give producers entry into a global market that is dominated by large transnational buyers.

The minimum price per pound is set by Fairtrade International, the umbrella organization that, until 2012, determined the global standards for fair trade criteria. The guaranteed minimum price creates economic stability for producers who would otherwise be at the whims of the volatile New York commodities market, which sets the international price for coffee. The New York "C" price can fluctuate widely, and was as low as 41 cents per pound in 2001.

Depending on how the coffee is processed prior to export, the fair trade minimum price is either $1.35 or $1.40 per pound, which includes a 20-cent per pound premium earmarked for development in producing communities. Because Fairtrade International sets a minimum price, coffee that is certified can be—and often is—sold for more. Sometimes a buyer pays more based on quality, and, when the New York price exceeds the fair trade minimum, the fair trade price increases to best it by 10 cents.

The fair trade system also provides small loans to producer groups to facilitate improved infrastructure for farms and communities. In the past, these benefits were available only to small producers affiliated with democratically organized cooperatives, since the movement was conceived to both increase access to the global market and protection from manipulative and exploitative buyers. Until recently, this was an important hallmark of fair trade certified coffee, as most of the world's coffee is grown by small-scale producers in remote areas. (To learn more about the coffee beans you consume, ask your local coffee vendor where their coffee is purchased, and on what terms.)

Independent labelling organizations such as Max Havelaar in the Netherlands (established in 1988) and TransFair in the U.S. (now Fair Trade USA, established in 1998) set national standards for fair trade certification. Fairtrade International (formerly Fairtrade Labeling Organizations International) was formed in 1997 as an umbrella organization to coordinate the various definitions of fair trade across national borders. These groups' dogged efforts provided legitimacy to the fair trade label and helped grow the movement throughout the late 1990s and early 2000s.

The tremendous growth of the fair trade coffee market has been beneficial to the many small farmers around the world. U.S. importers alone have paid over $61 million in premiums to producer cooperatives since 1998. It's neither a perfect system nor a solution to global poverty, but many lives have been improved through farmer and buyer participation in fair trade programs. However, on January 1, 2012, the fair trade movement underwent a significant change: Fair Trade USA implemented a new policy that would fold coffee produced on large-scale plantations into its certification system. Calling the change the "Fair Trade for All" policy, the organization claimed that including more types of farms would vastly increase the number of people served by the movement.

There is a long-standing tension between the founding values of the fair trade movement and the profit-driven ethos of the fair trade market.

This seemingly benevolent change stirred controversy within the specialty coffee industry. Many believe that it breaks with the founding goal of the movement—to empower small producers in the global market. To implement "Fair Trade for All," Fair Trade USA was forced to sever its ties with Fairtrade International. The global group felt the move to include large-scale, commercial farms was a betrayal of the core values of fair trade.

The Case for Fair Trade for All

In an open letter addressed to all fair trade supporters, Paul Rice, the founder and CEO of Fair Trade USA, cites three reasons for the change in his organization's policy. First, he claims that Fair Trade for All will reduce inconsistencies in the certification process. Some products, like bananas and tea grown on plantations, were already eligible for fair trade certification. By including coffee plantations, the certification process will be more consistent across products. Second, Rice wants to greatly increase consumer awareness about fair trade initiatives, further increasing the market for fair trade products. He believes consistency across all products will give consumers a clearer understanding of the overriding principles of fair trade.

Third, Rice argues that greater sales of fair trade products will help educate consumers about the plight of producers around the world. By his own estimate, a greater demand for fair trade will help an additional four million people gain access to fair trade benefits, including improved living conditions.

Rice believes that the new policy will extend benefits to not only farmers who own their land and are members of cooperatives, but also to tens of thousands of laborers who migrate seasonally to pick coffee. In Nicaragua, for instance, many coffee pickers are represented by the Association of Rural Workers, a large trade union that helps fight for better working conditions. Leaders of this organization told us that fair trade is just a "drop in the bucket" of the coffee market and that it offers no benefits to many coffee pickers who do not own their own land.

According to Fair Trade USA, laborers around the world would see improved wages and working conditions that currently only reach those farmers already fortunate enough to be landholders and cooperative members.

Backlash

At the Specialty Coffee Association of America's annual industry convention held in Portland, Oregon, in 2012, dissent was in the air. From baristas to buyers, roasters, coffee company owners, and producers, thousands assembled from around the world for the five-day meeting. As it followed so closely on the heels of Fair Trade USA's announcement of their new policy, the tension at the convention was palpable.

On the third morning, over a hundred people came together to discuss the future of fair trade in the United States. Through our own research, we've come to align ourselves with the critics present at this meeting. We find many flaws in "Fair Trade for All."

One of the most serious problems is that the supply for fair trade coffee currently outpaces demand. Today, only about 20 percent of the global supply of fair trade certified coffee is actually sold at the fair trade minimum price. As a result, many farmers work hard to meet fair trade certification's standards, but sell their coffee at the lower prices set on the commodities market.

Samuel Kamau, Executive Director of the African Fine Coffees Association, described how this disparity affects small producers when he spoke with Nicki at the convention: " . . . [W]e got so efficient in fair trade production, fair trade [buyers are] no longer interested in us. We over-produced fair trade certified coffee." Kamau explained that despite being members of certified fair trade cooperatives, many small producers are forced to sell their coffee with no guaranteed minimum price. It remains unclear to many within the fair trade movement why Fair Trade USA wants to increase the supply of fair trade coffee by including large plantations when demand, while growing, is still insufficient.

Aside from the supply and demand issue, the Fair Trade for All campaign mistakenly assumes that plantations will provide the same health, safety, and economic benefits for farmers as do cooperatives. Anthropologists and sociologists have been looking at this issue for the last decade and have shown that workers on fair trade plantations for products like tea and bananas do not receive the same benefits as farmers working in cooperatives.

Some see fair trade as a form of eco- or neo-colonialism.

Dana Geffner, Executive Director of the Fair World Project, a non-profit organization that promotes fair trade and produces a quarterly magazine, says that fair trade certification is ineffective for laborers on large plantations, and that it "often undermines in-country [labor] organizing efforts" by embedding the regulation of labor rights in a transnational market rather than domestic governmental structure. Richard Hyde of Twin Trading, a fair trade coffee importer based in the United Kingdom, pointed out that plantations have also been found to use intimidation tactics against worker organization and collective bargaining; by including them Fair Trade USA betrays the founding values of fair trade.

The Plight of Small Farmers

Some claim that Fair Trade for All will hinder the chances of small-scale farmers to make a living with coffee. Silvio Cerda, Coffee Director of CLAC (Latin American and Caribbean Network of Small Fair Trade Producers), spoke with Nicki about the new policy's implications: "In this situation, the small producer organizations will be competing under unequal conditions with big plantations and exporters. Because of the resources, technologies, and the economies of scale, the big plantations have lower costs in comparison to small producers."

Farmers have little voice within a system of trade that is supposed to provide them with social, economic, and environmental benefits.

Possibly the biggest problem with Fair Trade for All relates to governance. Many farmers feel betrayed: they were not included in the decision-making process at Fair Trade USA. Whereas producers hold a 50 percent stake in decision-making at Fairtrade International, they have little say in the U.S. organization. The bold, unilateral move is a dangerous precedent for how policy is decided at Fair Trade USA. When farmers have little voice within a system of trade that is supposed to provide them with social, economic, and environmental benefits, they become disillusioned. The policies meant to address their concerns and needs do not reflect their concerns and needs.

Other critics, including farmers like Byron, question the need for an outside organization to determine whether they are growing coffee "fairly." Some farmers, activists, and scholars have come to brand fair trade as a form of eco- or neo-colonialism. In order to access these "fair" markets, farmers must abide by a set of standards they did not create and cannot change. The majority of the voices we have heard from within the fair trade movement are disappointed at the concentration of power within Fair Trade USA. It doesn't seem, well, fair.

For all of these reasons, small producers and their advocates are frustrated and angry. These feelings bubbled to the surface at the Specialty Coffee Association of America forum when Paul Katzeff said that he felt betrayed by Fair Trade USA's leadership. When the translator struggled to find the Spanish word for "betrayal," a member of the audience shouted "*¡Traición!*" This elicited cheers, whistles, and raucous applause from the producers, importers, co-op leaders, and other movement allies. The moment illustrated the intensity of the anger and disappointment felt by many members of the movement.

What's Fair?

While the question of corporate participation has long been resolved, the issue of governance—how fair trade organizations are run and how fair trade policy will evolve—remains pressing. Though Fair Trade USA seems to stand nearly alone in its decision to fold plantations into the coffee certification system, the choice (motivated by the capitalist goal of growing the fair trade market, even though, at the moment, supply far exceeds demand) will have sweeping consequences for millions of small fair trade coffee farmers. Fair trade activists and scholars are also worried about the unilateral way in which Fair Trade USA implemented a sweeping new policy. It was a top-down decision in an organization that, ideally, should work in the opposite direction.

Here, Fair Trade USA ignored the vocal resistance of small producer organizations and movement members around the world. The governance issue is not just a question of how fair trade policy affects the livelihoods of small farmers, but also what the trusted "fair trade certified" label means to consumers. Previously, these virtuous little labels meant that small producers organized in democratically run cooperatives cultivated the coffee you purchased. Today, you cannot know for certain whether that coffee came from a small producer or from a large plantation controlled by a wealthy landowner.

This problem—that meanings of labels often change dramatically as the certification system behind them evolves—is not unique to fair trade. The dilution of the meaning of "organic" by large corporate farms is a case well-documented by Julie Guthman in her book *Agrarian Dreams: The Paradox of Organic Farming in California,* and it is aptly parsed by food scholar and activist Michael Pollan, who draws a distinction between "big organic" and "small organic." In the case of fair trade, the inclusion of large corporate buyers in the early 2000s grew the market significantly and funneled economic benefits to producers.

But for small growers, that growth came at a tremendous cost. The very movement that was founded to challenge the dominance of large transnational buyers in the coffee market is penalizing those who can least afford it: small farmers.

Reading Questions

1. What is fair trade certification? Why do farmers, buyers, and consumers look for this certification?
2. What institutions support fair trade? What institutions might undermine fair trade certification?

3. How does allowing large-scale producers of coffee to get fair trade certification change what it means to be fair trade? What are the positive and negative implications of this change to the certification process?

4. Do you consume fair trade products? Why or why not? What kinds of policies or campaigns could increase individual consumption of these types of products?

Cole, N. L., & Brown, K. (2014). The problem with fair trade coffee. *Contexts, 13*(1), 50–55.

SUMMARY

Sociologists are fundamentally concerned with inequality. In Chapter 3 we learned how social class and social status can create inequalities within a country. In this chapter we extended our focus to examine how inequality can arise between countries. Learning about how our world is becoming increasingly globalized can help us to understand how global inequality has arisen and how we can work to reduce it. The three theoretical lenses we covered in this chapter (modernization theory, world systems theory, and world society theory) understand globalization differently, but they all note the inequality resulting from this process. We also discussed ways to measure and compare global inequality, such as the Gini index and the HDI. We ended this chapter by exploring three ways to relieve global inequality: development assistance, debt relief, and microfinancing programs.

FOR FURTHER READING

Durkheim, É. (1960). *Division of labor in society*, Free Press.

Krücken, G., & Drori, G. S (Eds.). (2009). *World society: The writings of John W. Meyer.* Oxford University Press.

Martell, L. (2017). *The sociology of globalization* (2nd ed.). Polity Press.

Sassen, S. (2007). *A sociology of globalization*, Norton.

Wallerstein, I. (2011). *The modern world system*, University of California Press.

Wilkinson, R., & Pickett, K. (2010). *The spirit level: Why more equal societies almost always do better*, Bloomsbury.

GLOSSARY

cash crops

core countries

fair trade certification

Gini index

globalization

infant mortality rate

mechanical solidarity

microfinancing

modernization theory

monocropping

organic solidarity

periphery countries

semi-periphery countries

world society theory

world systems theory

SOCIAL CHANGE

Sandy Macys/Alamy Stock Photo

13 CHANGE THROUGH POLICY AND THE LAW

Throughout this book we have learned more about how our society works. We began by examining how we learn to fit into society through socialization, the ways we differentiate people and how doing so can lead to inequality, and the major social institutions and their roles. The final core area of sociology is the study of social change. For many students, learning about the inequality that exists in our society and how societal institutions often help to perpetuate that inequality can be frustrating. They ask, How can we change our society and make it more equal and just? How can we alter institutions to address important social problems? In this chapter and the next, we will learn about the major routes to social change.

HOW DOES SOCIETY REPRODUCE ITSELF?

We all want to change some things about society. Yet, for a variety of reasons, social change is very difficult and slow. We are all socialized to follow the rules and norms of society and to fit in. Those who question or resist the social order might be punished for their deviance. A child who will not listen to the teacher in class, who does not like to do the activities usually associated with her age group or gender, or who does not dress in a conventional way might be punished by being suspended, receiving poor grades, or being isolated or bullied by other children. Even later in life, we are rewarded for doing what we are supposed to—going to university, getting a "good" job, finding a partner, and raising a family. In general, we are taught not to question why things are as they are and to simply accept that the way our society is set up is the natural order. If formal laws and regulations are not enough to encourage us to conform, informal social sanctions such as exclusion and shaming ensure that we follow the rules.

Despite these disincentives, social change does happen. Social change, at a general level, is the transformation of culture and social institutions over time. Sometimes this change occurs quite quickly, such as by the invention of new computer technology that revolutionized how we interact with one another. At other times things happen more slowly, such as shifting gender norms (see Chapter 6). Social change can be intentional, such as when a law is passed to legalize marijuana or same-sex marriage. However, social change is often unintentional. The printing press, discussed in Chapter 7, was not invented to create social change, but that was its effect when it altered many facets of society and social interaction.

Finally, although we tend to think of many social changes as natural and inevitable, they were often quite contentious when they were happening. The women's suffrage movement required the dissolution of many informal norms about women's behavior, such as the idea that it was natural for women to remain within the domestic sphere and that they did not belong in

Protesters from the 2021 Glasgow climate summit, COP26, argue that the effects of climate change will be disproportionately felt by youth.

Peter Summers/Getty Images

the public sphere. The removal of formal laws restricting women's roles in public life brought about gradual social change. Women's suffrage, the legalization of marriage between people of different races, and the abolition of slavery seem like changes that everyone would have surely supported. However, these were very controversial proposals and many people fought vigorously against them.

One major way that social change can happen is through institutional channels, particularly through the state. The state provides an important arena for creating social change through elections, laws, and social policy. Social change can also occur outside the state's institutions, through cultural change or the work of social movements. This chapter focuses on state-based social change, and Chapter 14 examines social change outside the state.

To consider the general routes to social change, let's think about the expansion of LGBTQ rights. If you are interested in these rights and are working within the state, you could elect political leaders who are also concerned with LGBTQ rights—perhaps those who advocate for the passing of same-sex marriage laws or antidiscrimination laws. You could also challenge the legality of discriminating against gays and lesbians. The latter is, in fact, how same-sex marriage became legal in the United States in 2015. Gay couples argued in court that not being allowed to marry simply because of their sexual orientation was discriminatory.

The Supreme Court agreed, ruling that the fundamental right of same-sex couples to marry on the same terms and under the same conditions as opposite-sex couples is guaranteed in the Constitution. Another approach is to change the policies of government or government agencies. For example, at one time it was more difficult for gay and lesbian people to adopt children than it was for heterosexual people. Because of this, many states passed laws that adoption agencies could not use sexual orientation as a basis for determining who would be a good parent. This made it easier for gay couples to adopt.

THE RISE OF THE STATE

The state is a set of institutions that includes four components: political decision makers who are either elected or appointed, administrative units or bureaucracies, a judiciary or legal system, and security services such as police forces and armies. States are also attached to a geographic territory and maintain a monopoly and autonomy on rule-making, coercion, and violence within that territory. The state is, arguably, the most powerful institution in contemporary society. It is the only institution with the legal right to tax the population; to use violence through the police, military, and court systems; to permit or force you to kill by sending you to war; to legally imprison you; and, in some places, to kill you via capital punishment (Stanbridge & Ramos, 2012).

The state's right to use violence is considered justifiable because it works to maintain social order and to defend the nation's interests. As Max Weber famously said, the power of the state ultimately flows from its monopoly on the legitimate use of violence (Gerth & Mills, 1946). However, the state cannot wield these powers in any way it chooses. If people believe that the state uses violence in an illegitimate way, they can resist through civil unrest. The state can also be subject to sanctions from the international community and, eventually, experience a decline in state power.

The state is also powerful because it can set policies and laws governing your behavior—how you can buy or sell a car, rent a house, become licensed to work as a teacher or doctor, or whom you can marry. We permit the state to do these things because it provides us with services such as schools and roads, ensures a safe and orderly society, and protects our national interests (Stanbridge & Ramos, 2012).

States, like other institutions in society, change over time. The state emerged in its modern form between the 12th and 18th centuries in Western Europe. The three major explanations for

The state as an institution has changed over time. Despite these changes, many symbols of the state, such as flags, ceremonies, and traditions, often remain consistent over time.

Allison Bailey/NurPhoto via AP

this rise focus on the importance of the state for managing increasingly large territories, waging war, and controlling the economy. Let's examine each function in turn.

The Managerial Perspective

From 1100 to 1600 in Europe there was a rise of "political units persisting in time and fixed in space, the development of permanent, impersonal institutions, agreement on the need for an authority which can give final judgments, and the acceptance of the idea that this authority should receive the basic loyalty of its subjects" (Strayer, 1970, p. 10). As territories grew in geographic size and population, the state was needed to better manage and control these larger areas and groups of people. This managerial perspective focuses on the evolving practices relating to the recruitment, training, and employment of administrators needed to manage these new bureaucracies. The individual bureaucrats who occupy these offices are important because they convince the population that a central state can fulfill the needs and interests of the people, who often have intense local loyalties. It makes sense that individuals of this time would be much more connected to their local communities, which were filled with people they knew personally and who tended to be similar to them, instead of a distant, impersonal state. However, communities came to accept the obligations created by the individual bureaucrats through centralized state government.

The Militaristic Perspective

The state was also instituted to create a monopoly on the acceptable use of violence, particularly in relation to the ability to wage war. This militaristic perspective is related to Weber's earlier claim that the state is the only entity that can legitimately use violence within a territory. Early European states developed through war, particularly through conquering neighboring lands. The states with the better bureaucracies were more financially equipped to wage war because they were more efficient at taxation: They knew who lived where, the amount of property each person owned, and which of their activities could be taxed. In addition, knowing the population enabled these states to conscript soldiers more effectively.

From the beginning, the modern state was intended for war-making and was centrally concerned with establishing and maintaining its military might. Wars and who won them created the national boundaries in Europe and the original context of the state system (Poggi, 2004). As Charles Tilly (1985, p. 175) argues, "War made the state, and the state made war." His central claim is that the state is a protection racket—it trades security in exchange for revenues. Cooperation between people is difficult without a third party; citizens therefore cede to the state their rights to do whatever they want in return for a guarantee of protection.

As Tilly explains,

War-making, extraction, and capital accumulation interacted to shape European State making. Power holders did not undertake those three momentous tasks with the intention of creating national states— (centralized, differentiated, autonomous, extensive political organizations). Nor did they foresee that national states would emerge from war-making, extraction, and capital accumulation. . . Instead, they warred in order to check or overcome their competitors and thus to enjoy the advantages of power within a secure or expanding territory. To make more effective war, they attempted to locate more capital. In the short run, they might acquire that capital by conquest, by selling off their assets, or by coercing or dispossessing accumulators of capital. In the long run, the quest inevitably involved them in establishing regular access to capitalists who could supply and arrange credit and in imposing one form of regular taxation or another on the people and activities within their spheres of control. (Tilly, 1985, p. 172)

To have military might, states must engage in four activities: war-making (eliminating or neutralizing their rivals outside the territories), state-making (eliminating or neutralizing their rivals inside their territory), protection (eliminating or neutralizing their clients' enemies), and extraction (acquiring the means of carrying out the first three activities).

Getting to Know: Charles Tilly (1929–2008)

- Tilly published 51 books and authored more than 600 academic articles.

- He served in the Navy during the Korean War.

- Tilly failed his preliminary exam at Harvard because he forgot what time it was and did not show up.

- He worked at various universities, including Harvard, the University of Delaware, and the University of Toronto, before joining Columbia in 1996.

- He was a recipient of the American Sociological Association's W.E.B Du Bois Career of Distinguished Scholarship Award in 2005.

- He supervised more than 200 PhD dissertations over the span of his career.

The Economic Perspective

Finally, the state is the result of capitalist class struggle and works to regulate economic relations. This perspective is related to Marx's theories and can be termed the economic perspective, which argues that the state is needed to regulate economic interests and the clashing of these interests between groups in a capitalist society. Marx argued that the state usually resolves these conflicts by siding with capitalists (Marx & Engels, 1964). For Marx, the state—what he called the executive committee of the bourgeoisie—is just an extension of the dominant capitalist class.

From the economic perspective, the state manages economic relations to facilitate the work of capitalists. The formation of states allows for a power center to have an increasing reach. The state is able to standardize and secure relations between many individuals across wide spaces. This capacity is important for capitalism because it makes both the production and the exchange of goods easier and more calculable. The state also imposes rules of law about property, which helps in the exchange of goods and services between partners.

THE WELFARE STATE

To this point, our discussion of the state has highlighted its many important functions and its origins. However, this depiction emphasizes the negative things that the state can do (e.g., coerce you to pay taxes). Why do humans create states and why do we, as individuals, give states power even when we know that doing so restricts our individual freedoms? One of the main reasons has already been mentioned: The state offers many important benefits, such as education, clean water, and social services, that we cannot enjoy as isolated individuals. Without people joining to create these services, we would not all have access to these important resources.

These benefits are part of the welfare state, a type of state that performs three basic functions. It attempts to provide a minimum income for individuals; to reduce the potential economic insecurity that could come from events such as illness, old age, and unemployment; and to give the public a range of social services (Briggs, 2000). In a welfare state, the government plays a primary role in the promotion of its citizens' economic and social well-being. Such states also expand their bureaucracies to provide a variety of programs that reduce economic inequality in society (Peoples, 2012).

The 20th century saw the development of welfare states around the world. The expenditures of these states vary greatly (see Table 13.1). The countries of Europe, particularly France, Italy, Germany, and Sweden, have the highest spending on welfare programs as a percentage of their overall GDP. Spending on welfare programs is much lower in Turkey, Chile, and Mexico. It is in the mid-range in the United Kingdom, the United States, and Canada. We might expect that countries with higher GDPs would spend more on social welfare. Yet the group of countries that spend 24% or more of their GDPs on welfare have GDPs from $27,948 to $55,037, whereas the countries that spend between 10% and 20% have GDPs in a similar range, from $25,110 to $63,206. There does not seem to be a direct relationship between a county's overall GDP and its

TABLE 13.1 ■ Welfare Expenditures by Country, 2019–2020

Nation	Welfare Expenditure (% of GDP)	GDP per capita, PPP
France	31	46,999
Italy	28.2	41,902
Germany	25.9	54,844
Sweden	25.5	55,037
Spain	24.7	37,756
Greece	24	27,948
Japan	22.3	42,390
Poland	21.3	34,287
Slovenia	21.1	39,725
United Kingdom	20.6	46,482
United States	18.7	63,206
Canada	18	46,572
Iceland	17.4	53,616
Australia	16.7	53,316
Netherlands	16.1	59,266
South Korea	12.2	45,225
Turkey	12	27,235
Chile	11.4	25,110
Mexico	7.5	18,444

Note: *PPP = purchasing power parity.

Source: https://www.oecd.org/social/expenditure.htm; https://data.worldbank.org/indicator/NY.GDP.PCAP.PP.CD?year_high_desc=true

welfare spending. The United States is a case in point: It has the highest GDP of all the countries in the chart ($63,206) but spends relatively little on welfare expenditures (18.7%).

The Welfare State in the United States

A hundred years ago care for those in need, including health and welfare services, was provided at the local community level. Community groups and charities attempted to provide minimal social services. The United States was the only industrialized country that went into the Great Depression of the 1930s with no social insurance policies. During the Great Depression, the U.S. unemployment rate reached 24.9% at its highest point, and the federal government was under considerable pressure to become involved in dealing with this important social issue. This widespread unemployment and poverty created many social problems that touched many Americans. When these problems were seen as public issues instead of personal troubles (as C. Wright Mills explained), the government responded in the form of social programs. This was the origin of the American welfare state.

From 1933 to 1936, President Franklin D. Roosevelt instituted the New Deal, a series of programs and reforms that resulted in several social insurance policies and began to develop the welfare state in the United States. These programs included social relief programs and a federally sponsored retirement program. Congress passed the Social Security Act in 1935 and it came into effect in 1939. These social programs were very effective. Price Fisherback, Haines, and Kantor (2007) examined the impact of the New Deal in the 114 largest U.S. cities over time. They found that each additional $153,000 spent on these social programs (in 1935 dollars, or $2.2 million in 2018 dollars) was associated with a reduction of one infant death, one suicide, and 2.4 deaths from infectious disease. These are very real and consequential impacts of these policies.

The social welfare state slowly expanded over time until the 1990s, when widespread welfare reform was put in place. Before this time, welfare was considered an open-ended right, but welfare reform reconceptualized it as a finite program built to provide short-term cash assistance and to steer people quickly into jobs. This change in philosophy led to a massive restructuring of welfare programs and much more control of these programs being left to state governments. In many countries, including the United States, the welfare state has declined since the 1990s. Evidence includes less-generous benefits and more-rigorous eligibility tests (van den Berg et al., 2008). Many other countries around the world, including those in Europe, are retrenching their social welfare programs. Even countries with very strong and entrenched programs, such as Sweden, have decreased their social spending.

The Welfare State and Social Inequality

Social programs enacted through the welfare state are important for a variety of reasons. We have already mentioned that they are instrumental in dealing with and reducing inequality. A wide body of evidence shows the significant effects of welfare programs on inequality. For example, taxes and transfers reduce poverty considerably in most countries whose welfare spending constitutes at least a fifth of their GDP (Bradley et al., 2003; Kenworthy, 1999).

Most welfare states have notably lower poverty rates than they had before the implementation of welfare programs. Table 13.2 lists some countries and the percentage of their populations that lived under the absolute poverty line before and after welfare policies were enacted. Through the implementation of welfare policies, all the countries included cut their poverty rate by at least half. For example, the poverty rate in the United States fell from 21.0% to 11.7% after welfare policies were enacted.

TABLE 13.2 ■ Absolute Poverty Rate (Threshold Set at 40% of U.S. Median Household Income)		
Country	Prewelfare	Postwelfare
Australia	23.3	11.9
Belgium	26.8	6.0
Canada	22.5	6.5
Denmark	26.4	5.9
Finland	11.9	3.7
France	36.1	9.8
Germany	15.2	4.3
Italy	30.7	14.3
Netherlands	22.1	7.3
Norway	9.2	1.7
Sweden	23.7	5.8
Switzerland	12.5	3.8
United Kingdom	16.8	8.7
United States	21.0	11.7

Sources: Kenworthy, L. 1999. "Do Social-Welfare Policies Reduce Poverty? A Cross-National Assessment." *Social Forces* 77 (3): 1119–39; Bradley, D., E. Huber, S. Moller, F. Nielson, and J. D. Stephens. 2003. "Determinants of Relative Poverty in Advanced Capitalist Democracies." *American Sociological Review* 68 (3): 22–51.

Social Policy: Universal and Means-Tested Programs

Social programs in the welfare state can be categorized as either universal or means tested. Universal programs are available to all citizens, regardless of income or wealth. These programs tend to be very popular because everyone benefits equally. For example, people over a certain age are eligible to receive Social Security, and all children have access to a free public education. Because these programs are available to everyone, all citizens have a stake in seeing them continue and thrive. However, universal programs might not be the most efficient way to deal with issues such as poverty. Because some of the money allocated to Social Security goes to wealthy seniors who do not need these payments to protect them from poverty, we have less money for seniors who are living at or near the poverty line. In other words, payments to everyone create inefficiencies in the system by assisting people who are not at risk of living in poverty.

A means-tested program relies on a determination of whether an individual or family needs government assistance. In the United States, means tests are used for student finance (for postsecondary education), legal aid, and welfare (direct transfer payments to individuals to combat poverty). Compared to universal programs, means-tested programs are a more efficient way to address inequality. By simply giving more money to people who have less and giving no benefit to people who already have enough, you can reduce the gap between the rich and the poor.

Yet means-tested programs are often less popular than universal programs. The former tends to have less political support because they are seen to benefit only a small group of people.

In contrast, universal programs are viewed as something that all citizens share. Some people also argue that means-tested programs carry a stigma. For example, many schools, in cooperation with the U.S. Department of Agriculture, offer free or reduced-price lunch programs for students from low-income homes. Children who participate in this program might be teased by other students. To combat this social stigma, many schools make it difficult to tell which students get lunch for free and which pay.

Means-tested programs are also often criticized based on access issues. Means tests, particularly complicated ones, can make it difficult to access social programs. Sometimes individuals cannot easily decipher whether they qualify for different programs and under which conditions. The work required to verify that the tests are satisfied can increase administrative costs. Some argue that these costs can offset part of the savings from not giving the benefit universally.

Despite these drawbacks, means-tested programs such as Supplemental Security Income (SSI) can decrease inequality. Like Social Security, SSI is a pension benefit for seniors, but it is for only those who make below a certain income level. It is designed for the elderly (as well as for people who are blind or have other disabilities) and provides cash to meet basic needs for food, clothing, and shelter. Social Security and SSI have been instrumental at lowering poverty among seniors. Before these programs came into being in the late 1930s, poverty among the elderly was a staggering 40%. It now hovers around 10% (Romig, 2018). These programs have cut poverty among this age group by a quarter.

USING YOUR SOCIOLOGICAL IMAGINATION
REDUCING CHILD POVERTY

There have been many universal and means-tested programs aimed at alleviating poverty among seniors. Research shows that these programs have been very successful and poverty rates among seniors have been drastically reduced. In fact, seniors are now the age group least likely to live in poverty in the United States. Poverty is much higher for children under the age of 18. As seen in Figure 13.1, in recent years child poverty has been about twice the rate of poverty among seniors.

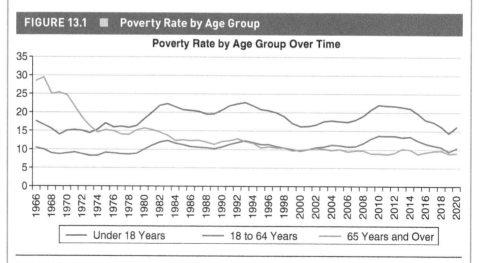

FIGURE 13.1 ■ Poverty Rate by Age Group

Poverty Rate by Age Group Over Time

Legend: Under 18 Years — 18 to 64 Years — 65 Years and Over

Source: United States Census Bureau https://www2.census.gov/programs-surveys/cps/tables/time-series/historical-poverty-people/hstpov3.xlsx

Child poverty is also much higher in the United States than it is in most other OECD countries (see Figure 13.2). The child poverty rate in the US is relatively high compared to the other countries in the chart, at more than 20%. The rates for many European countries, such as Iceland, Denmark, Finland, and Ireland, fall under 10%.

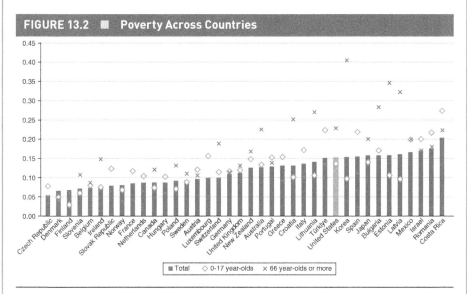

FIGURE 13.2 ■ Poverty Across Countries

■ Total   ◇ 0–17 year-olds   × 66 year-olds or more

Source: OECD (2023), Poverty rate (indicator). doi: 10.1787/0fe1315d-en (Accessed on 01 July 2023). https://data.oecd.org/inequality/poverty-rate.htm

There are several programs that are aimed at reducing poverty for children and families. For example, the Supplemental Nutrition Assistance Program (SNAP; formerly the Food Stamp Program) helps families, including children, to access food. The Earned Income Tax Credit (EITC) is a refundable tax credit for low- to moderate-income working people or couples, particularly those with children. There is also a Child Tax Credit (CTC), which lets a family reduce its federal income tax by up to $3,600 for each child under 6 and $3,000 for each child 6 to 16.

Begin this activity by researching one of these programs: SNAP, the EITC, or the CTC.

1. What is this program and how does it work? How can you access this benefit?
2. What are the positives and negatives of this program? How effective has it been in dealing with poverty among children?

   Now, please consider other ways that we could reduce poverty among children.

3. What other ways could we reduce poverty among children, beyond these federal government policies? Think of another social program that could be effective at targeting poverty in this group.
4. How could schools be a part of reducing child poverty or the effects of this poverty?
5. How could other community groups, such as community centers or nonprofit organizations (e.g., the YMCA or religious groups), help to reduce poverty or the effects of poverty for this group?

Methods in Depth: Assessing the Effectiveness of Means-Tested Social Programs

Social programs aimed at addressing poverty are expensive, and it is important to assess how effective they are at meeting their goals, particularly in addressing poverty among groups in which the rates are very high. Although much research has shown that divorce is an important determinant of poverty for both men and women, we know that the effect of divorce on poverty is much stronger for women than for men. One reason is that women are much more likely to have custody of children. This means that children also face dramatic declines in their well-being as a result of divorce. The loss of spousal earnings is partially offset by alimony, child support, welfare payments, and an increase in labor force participation of women. However, marital separation still significantly increases the odds of poor female-headed families. A study by Hauser, Burkhauser, Couch, and Ozturk (2016) found that pre-government income of the median woman fell by 25% 1 year after divorce. However, U.S. tax and transfer policies partially reversed these large drops, as the median reduction in post-government income was 18%. This means that government transfers, through welfare and other programs, reduced the income drop for women from 25% to only 18%. Despite the redistributive power of government policies, the median woman's economic well-being remained substantially lower (–18%) than that of the median man (–3%) 1 year after divorce.

Research Question

But how do social programs help to reduce poverty among divorced women, and which policies are most effective at doing this? Gulgun Bayaz Ozturk (2018) conducted a study to shed light on the antipoverty effects of increased welfare spending 5 years into the economic recovery (from 2009 to 2015) by examining the poverty experience of people living in families with a divorced or separated female head. More specifically, he examined the antipoverty effects of six social programs: SNAP; the National School Lunch Program (NSLP); the Special Supplemental Nutrition Program for Women, Infants, and Children (WIC); EITC; Temporary Assistance for Needy Families (TANF); and housing and energy assistance.

Methodology

To assess the impact of these various programs, Ozturk uses the Sen, Shorrocks, and Thon poverty index. This index allows you to see changes in three main parts of the poverty rate: incidence (how much there is), intensity (how deep the level of poverty is), and inequality (how much poverty differs among groups) over time. It is important to look at these measures separately. Doing so allows us to differentiate how many people are living in poverty from the experience of poverty (if you are living near the poverty line or in a situation where you have very little access to resources). He assesses the incidence, intensity, and inequality of poverty among single-woman-headed households over time as it relates to use of these six means-tested programs.

There are a few notable things about how Ozturk conducted this study. First, the focus of this study is income poverty. This means that he is only looking at people who have low incomes. This study does not consider asset poverty: Assets include things like home ownership or savings. Asset wealth can help a person or family avoid poverty if they lose a job or have other types of economic hardships. The study does not assess this type of wealth.

Second, the analysis is only focused on people living in families headed by females whose marital status is divorced or separated. This means that the author does not look at women who have never been married, even if they lead households with children. We might expect that women who have not had spouses would be in a worse economic situation on average because they would not have access to spousal support and might be less likely to have access to child support. By only looking at women who were married, he does not need to worry about the different experiences of women with and without spouses who might provide some sort of support.

Findings

Ozturk (2018) found that people living in divorced or separated female-headed households with children have the highest rate of poverty (25% in 2009 and 24% in 2015) among all demographic groups. He also found that large-scale programs such as SNAP and housing assistance generated the largest impact in lowering the incidence and intensity of poverty. In addition, he found that as programs such as tax credits and the school lunch program were eliminated, many more people fell into poverty. This research highlights the importance of these types of means-tested programs in helping groups that are most at risk of living in poverty.

REPARATION PROGRAMS

Social change within the state can happen in the form of social policies and programs. One such example is the use of reparations. In Chapter 3 we learned about restorative justice, in which offenders restore order by compensating or fixing the injustice caused by their crime. One part of restorative justice can be the payment of reparations. Reparation programs are measures taken by the state to redress gross and systematic violations of human rights or humanitarian law through some form of compensation or restitution to the victims. They are examples of social policies that deal with inequality and injustice on a societal level. Reparations serve two main functions. First, they take seriously and publicly recognize the suffering of victims. Second, they try to deal with this suffering by offering redress and compensation to

Foreign Ministers of Britain, the United States, Russia, France, and China meet to discuss the Five Power Conference on Reparation for Non-Repatriable Victims of Germany. These sorts of reparations are an important part of the process of making amends for large-scale human rights abuses.

Hulton-Deutsch Collection/CORBIS/Corbis via Getty Images

victims. This redress can be either symbolic, such as an apology, or material, such as monetary payments.

Reparations have been made to several groups, including Japanese Americans after their forced internment in World War II, Jewish people after the Holocaust, Black South Africans after apartheid, and, most recently, Indigenous people in Canada after the elimination of the residential school system and the compensation of victims of the Bosnian War. Consider how reparations are an example of a large-scale social policy aimed at addressing inequality and injustice in society.

Another prominent situation where reparations have been discussed is in relation to slavery in the United States. After the end of slavery, there were proposals about giving each freed slave 40 acres of land and a mule as reparation. This never happened and now creates a challenging situation whereby issues of restorative justice and social policy come together in the debate over how to deal with the injustice of slavery and the inequality that still results from it many generations later. The following reading considers inequality in the United States and its relationship to slavery and the role of reparations in addressing this inequality.

READING: FROM "THE CASE FOR REPARATIONS"

Ta-Nehisi Coats

[...] The lives of black Americans are better than they were half a century ago. The humiliation of whites only signs are gone. Rates of black poverty have decreased. Black teen-pregnancy rates are at record lows—and the gap between black and white teen-pregnancy rates has shrunk significantly. But such progress rests on a shaky foundation, and fault lines are everywhere. The income gap between black and white households is roughly the same today as it was in 1970. Patrick Sharkey, a sociologist at New York University, studied children born from 1955 through 1970 and found that 4 percent of whites and 62 percent of blacks across America had been raised in poor neighborhoods. A generation later, the same study showed, virtually nothing had changed. And whereas whites born into affluent neighborhoods tended to remain in affluent neighborhoods, blacks tended to fall out of them.

This is not surprising. Black families, regardless of income, are significantly less wealthy than white families. The Pew Research Center estimates that white households are worth roughly 20 times as much as black households, and that whereas only 15 percent of whites have zero or negative wealth, more than a third of blacks do. Effectively, the black family in America is working without a safety net. When financial calamity strikes—a medical emergency, divorce, job loss—the fall is precipitous.

And just as black families of all incomes remain handicapped by a lack of wealth, so too do they remain handicapped by their restricted choice of neighborhood. Black people with upper-middle-class incomes do not generally live in upper-middle-class neighborhoods. Sharkey's research shows that black families making $100,000 typically live in the kinds of neighborhoods inhabited by white families making $30,000. "Blacks and whites inhabit such different neighborhoods," Sharkey writes, "that it is not possible to compare the economic outcomes of black and white children."

A national real-estate association advised not to sell to "a colored man of means who was giving his children a college education."

The implications are chilling. As a rule, poor black people do not work their way out of the ghetto—and those who do often face the horror of watching their children and grandchildren tumble back.

Even seeming evidence of progress withers under harsh light. In 2012, the Manhattan Institute cheerily noted that segregation had declined since the 1960s. And yet African Americans still remained—by far—the most segregated ethnic group in the country.

With segregation, with the isolation of the injured and the robbed, comes the concentration of disadvantage. An unsegregated America might see poverty, and all its effects, spread across the country with no particular bias toward skin color. Instead, the concentration of poverty has been paired with a concentration of melanin. The resulting conflagration has been devastating.

[...] III. "We Inherit Our Ample Patrimony"

In 1783, the freedwoman Belinda Royall petitioned the commonwealth of Massachusetts for reparations. Belinda had been born in modern-day Ghana. She was kidnapped as a child and sold into slavery. She endured the Middle Passage and 50 years of enslavement at the hands of Isaac Royall and his son. But the junior Royall, a British loyalist, fled the country during the Revolution. Belinda, now free after half a century of labor, beseeched the nascent Massachusetts legislature:

> The face of your Petitioner, is now marked with the furrows of time, and her frame bending under the oppression of years, while she, by the Laws of the Land, is denied the employment of one morsel of that immense wealth, apart whereof hath been accumilated [sic] by her own industry, and the whole augmented by her servitude.
>
> WHEREFORE, casting herself at your feet if your honours, as to a body of men, formed for the extirpation of vassalage, for the reward of Virtue, and the just return of honest industry—she prays, that such allowance may be made her out of the Estate of Colonel Royall, as will prevent her, and her more infirm daughter, from misery in the greatest extreme, and scatter comfort over the short and downward path of their lives.

Belinda Royall was granted a pension of 15 pounds and 12 shillings, to be paid out of the estate of Isaac Royall—one of the earliest successful attempts to petition for reparations. At the time, black people in America had endured more than 150 years of enslavement, and the idea that they might be owed something in return was, if not the national consensus, at least not outrageous.

[...] Edward Coles, a protégé of Thomas Jefferson who became a slaveholder through inheritance, took many of his slaves north and granted them a plot of land in Illinois. John Randolph, a cousin of Jefferson's, willed that all his slaves be emancipated upon his death, and that all those older than 40 be given 10 acres of land. "I give and bequeath to all my slaves their freedom," Randolph wrote, "heartily regretting that I have been the owner of one."

[...] Broach the topic of reparations today and a barrage of questions inevitably follows: Who will be paid? How much will they be paid? Who will pay? But if the practicalities, not the justice, of reparations are the true sticking point, there has for some time been the beginnings of a solution. For the past 25 years, Congressman John Conyers Jr., who represents the Detroit area, has marked every session of Congress by introducing a bill calling for a congressional study of slavery and its lingering effects as well as recommendations for "appropriate remedies."

A country curious about how reparations might actually work has an easy solution in Conyers's bill, now called HR 40, the Commission to Study Reparation Proposals for African Americans Act. We would support this bill, submit the question to study, and then assess the possible solutions. But we are not interested.

[...] That HR 40 has never—under either Democrats or Republicans—made it to the House floor suggests our concerns are rooted not in the impracticality of reparations but in something more existential. If we conclude that the conditions in North Lawndale and black America are not inexplicable but are instead precisely what you'd expect of a community that for centuries has lived in America's crosshairs, then what are we to make of the world's oldest democracy?

The urge to use the moral force of the black struggle to address broader inequalities originates in both compassion and pragmatism. But it makes for ambiguous policy. Affirmative action's precise aims, for instance, have always proved elusive. Is it meant to make amends for the crimes heaped upon black people? Not according to the Supreme Court. In its 1978 ruling in *Regents of the University of California v. Bakke*, the Court rejected "societal discrimination" as "an amorphous concept of injury that may be ageless in its reach into the past." Is affirmative action meant to increase "diversity"? If so, it only tangentially relates to the specific problems of black people—the problem of what America has taken from them over several centuries.

This confusion about affirmative action's aims, along with our inability to face up to the particular history of white-imposed black disadvantage, dates back to the policy's origins. "There is no fixed and firm definition of affirmative action," an appointee in Johnson's Department of Labor declared. "Affirmative action is anything that you have to do to get results. But this does not necessarily include preferential treatment."

Yet America was built on the preferential treatment of white people—395 years of it. Vaguely endorsing a cuddly, feel-good diversity does very little to redress this.

Today, progressives are loath to invoke white supremacy as an explanation for anything. On a practical level, the hesitation comes from the dim view the Supreme Court has taken of the reforms of the 1960s. The Voting Rights Act has been gutted. The Fair Housing Act might well be next. Affirmative action is on its last legs. In substituting a broad class struggle for an anti-racist struggle, progressives hope to assemble a coalition by changing the subject.

The politics of racial evasion are seductive. But the record is mixed. Aid to Families With Dependent Children was originally written largely to exclude blacks—yet by the 1990s it was perceived as a giveaway to blacks. The Affordable Care Act makes no mention of race, but this did not keep Rush Limbaugh from denouncing it as reparations. Moreover, the act's expansion of Medicaid was effectively made optional, meaning that many poor blacks in the former Confederate states do not benefit from it. The Affordable Care Act, like Social Security, will eventually expand its reach to those left out; in the meantime, black people will be injured.

"All that it would take to sink a new WPA program would be some skillfully packaged footage of black men leaning on shovels smoking cigarettes," the sociologist Douglas S. Massey writes. "Papering over the issue of race makes for bad social theory, bad research, and bad public policy." To ignore the fact that one of the oldest republics in the world was erected on a foundation of white supremacy, to pretend that the problems of a dual society are the same as the problems of unregulated capitalism, is to cover the sin of national plunder with the sin of national lying. The lie ignores the fact that reducing American poverty and ending white supremacy are not the same. The lie ignores the fact that closing the "achievement gap" will do nothing to close the "injury gap," in which black college graduates still suffer higher unemployment rates than white college graduates, and black job applicants without criminal records enjoy roughly the same chance of getting hired as white applicants *with* criminal records.

X. "There Will Be No 'Reparations' From Germany"

We are not the first to be summoned to such a challenge.

In 1952, when West Germany began the process of making amends for the Holocaust, it did so under conditions that should be instructive to us. Resistance was violent. Very few Germans believed that Jews were entitled to anything. Only 5 percent of West Germans surveyed reported feeling guilty about the Holocaust, and only 29 percent believed that Jews were owed restitution from the German people.

"The rest," the historian Tony Judt wrote in his 2005 book, *Postwar*, "were divided between those (some two-fifths of respondents) who thought that only people 'who really committed something' were responsible and should pay, and those (21 percent) who thought 'that the Jews themselves were partly responsible for what happened to them during the Third Reich.'"

Germany's unwillingness to squarely face its history went beyond polls. Movies that suggested a societal responsibility for the Holocaust beyond Hitler were banned. "The German soldier fought bravely and honorably for his homeland," claimed President Eisenhower, endorsing the Teutonic national myth. Judt wrote, "Throughout the fifties West German officialdom encouraged a comfortable view of the German past in which the Wehrmacht was heroic, while Nazis were in a minority and properly punished."

Konrad Adenauer, the postwar German chancellor, was in favor of reparations, but his own party was divided, and he was able to get an agreement passed only with the votes of the Social Democratic opposition.

Among the Jews of Israel, reparations provoked violent and venomous reactions ranging from denunciation to assassination plots. On January 7, 1952, as the Knesset—the Israeli parliament—convened to discuss the prospect of a reparations agreement with West Germany, Menachem Begin, the future prime minister of Israel, stood in front of a large crowd, inveighing against the country that had plundered the lives, labor, and property of his people. Begin claimed that all Germans were Nazis and guilty of murder. His condemnations then spread to his own young state. He urged the crowd to stop paying taxes and claimed that the nascent Israeli nation characterized the fight over whether or not to accept reparations as a "war to the death." When alerted that the police watching the gathering were carrying tear gas, allegedly of German manufacture, Begin yelled, "The same gases that asphyxiated our parents!"

Begin then led the crowd in an oath to never forget the victims of the Shoah, lest "my right hand lose its cunning" and "my tongue cleave to the roof of my mouth." He took the crowd through the streets toward the Knesset. From the rooftops, police repelled the crowd with tear gas and smoke bombs. But the wind shifted, and the gas blew back toward the Knesset, billowing through windows shattered by rocks. In the chaos, Begin and Prime Minister David Ben-Gurion exchanged insults. Two hundred civilians and 140 police officers were wounded. Nearly 400 people were arrested. Knesset business was halted.

Begin then addressed the chamber with a fiery speech condemning the actions the legislature was about to take. "Today you arrested hundreds," he said. "Tomorrow you may arrest thousands. No matter, they will go, they will sit in prison. We will sit there with them. If necessary, we will be killed with them. But there will be no 'reparations' from Germany."

[...] Survivors of the Holocaust feared laundering the reputation of Germany with money, and mortgaging the memory of their dead. Beyond that, there was a taste for revenge. "My soul would be at rest if I knew there would be 6 million German dead to match the 6 million Jews," said Meir Dworzecki, who'd survived the concentration camps of Estonia.

[...] The reparations conversation set off a wave of bomb attempts by Israeli militants. One was aimed at the foreign ministry in Tel Aviv. Another was aimed at Chancellor Adenauer himself. And one was aimed at the port of Haifa, where the goods bought with reparations money were arriving. West Germany ultimately agreed to pay Israel 3.45 billion deutsche marks, or more than $7 billion in today's dollars. Individual reparations claims followed—for psychological trauma, for offense to Jewish honor, for halting law careers, for life insurance, for time spent in concentration camps. Seventeen percent of funds went toward purchasing ships. "By the end of 1961, these reparations vessels constituted two-thirds of the Israeli merchant fleet," writes the Israeli historian Tom Segev in his book *The Seventh Million*. "From 1953 to 1963, the reparations money funded about a third of the total investment in Israel's electrical system, which tripled its capacity, and nearly half the total investment in the railways."

Israel's GNP tripled during the 12 years of the agreement. The Bank of Israel attributed 15 percent of this growth, along with 45,000 jobs, to investments made with reparations money. But Segev argues that the impact went far beyond that. Reparations "had indisputable psychological and political importance," he writes.

Reparations could not make up for the murder perpetrated by the Nazis. But they did launch Germany's reckoning with itself, and perhaps provided a road map for how a great civilization might make itself worthy of the name.

Assessing the reparations agreement, David Ben-Gurion said:

For the first time in the history of relations between people, a precedent has been created by which a great State, as a result of moral pressure alone, takes it upon itself to pay compensation to the victims of the government that preceded it. For the first time in the history of a people that has been persecuted, oppressed, plundered and despoiled for hundreds of years in the countries of Europe, a persecutor and despoiler has been obliged to return part of his spoils and has even undertaken to make collective reparation as partial compensation for material losses.

Something more than moral pressure calls America to reparations. We cannot escape our history. All of our solutions to the great problems of health care, education, housing, and economic inequality are troubled by what must go unspoken. "The reason black people are so far behind now is not because of now," Clyde Ross told me. "It's because of then." In the early 2000s, Charles Ogletree went to Tulsa, Oklahoma, to meet with the survivors of the 1921 race riot that had devastated "Black Wall Street." The past was not the past to them. "It was amazing seeing these black women and men who were crippled, blind, in wheelchairs," Ogletree told me. "I had no idea who they were and why they wanted to see me. They said, 'We want you to represent us in this lawsuit.'"

A commission authorized by the Oklahoma legislature produced a report affirming that the riot, the knowledge of which had been suppressed for years, had happened. But the lawsuit ultimately failed, in 2004. Similar suits pushed against corporations such as Aetna (which insured slaves) and Lehman Brothers (whose co-founding partner owned them) also have thus far failed. These results are dispiriting, but the crime with which reparations activists charge the country implicates more than just a few towns or corporations. The crime indicts the American people themselves, at every level, and in nearly every configuration. A crime that implicates the entire American people deserves its hearing in the legislative body that represents them.

John Conyers's HR 40 is the vehicle for that hearing. No one can know what would come out of such a debate. Perhaps no number can fully capture the multi-century plunder of black people in America. Perhaps the number is so large that it can't be imagined, let alone calculated and dispensed. But I believe that wrestling publicly with these questions matters as much as—if not more than—the specific answers that might be produced. An America that asks what it owes its most vulnerable citizens is improved and humane. An America that looks away is ignoring not just the sins of the past but the sins of the present and the certain sins of the future. More important than any single check cut to any African American, the payment of reparations would represent America's maturation out of the childhood myth of its innocence into a wisdom worthy of its founders.

In 2010, Jacob S. Rugh, then a doctoral candidate at Princeton, and the sociologist Douglas S. Massey published a study of the recent foreclosure crisis. Among its drivers, they found an old foe: segregation. Black home buyers—even after controlling for factors like creditworthiness—were still more likely than white home buyers to be steered toward subprime loans. Decades of racist housing policies by the American government, along with decades of racist housing practices by American businesses, had conspired to concentrate African Americans in the same neighborhoods. As in North Lawndale half a century earlier, these neighborhoods were filled with people who had been cut off from mainstream financial institutions. When subprime lenders went looking for prey, they found black people waiting like ducks in a pen.

"Wells Fargo mortgage had an emerging-markets unit that specifically targeted black churches."

"High levels of segregation create a natural market for subprime lending," Rugh and Massey write, "and cause riskier mortgages, and thus foreclosures, to accumulate disproportionately in racially segregated cities' minority neighborhoods."

Plunder in the past made plunder in the present efficient. The banks of America understood this. In 2005, Wells Fargo promoted a series of Wealth Building Strategies seminars. Dubbing itself "the nation's leading originator of home loans to ethnic minority customers," the bank enrolled black public figures in an ostensible effort to educate blacks on building "generational wealth." But the "wealth building" seminars were a front for wealth theft. In

2010, the Justice Department filed a discrimination suit against Wells Fargo alleging that the bank had shunted blacks into predatory loans regardless of their creditworthiness. This was not magic or coincidence or misfortune. It was racism reifying itself. According to *The New York Times*, affidavits found loan officers referring to their black customers as "mud people" and to their subprime products as "ghetto loans."

"We just went right after them," Beth Jacobson, a former Wells Fargo loan officer, told *The Times*. "Wells Fargo mortgage had an emerging-markets unit that specifically targeted black churches because it figured church leaders had a lot of influence and could convince congregants to take out subprime loans."

In 2011, Bank of America agreed to pay $355 million to settle charges of discrimination against its Countrywide unit. The following year, Wells Fargo settled its discrimination suit for more than $175 million. But the damage had been done. In 2009, half the properties in Baltimore whose owners had been granted loans by Wells Fargo between 2005 and 2008 were vacant; 71 percent of these properties were in predominantly black neighborhoods.

Shahar Azran/WireImage/Getty Images

Reading Questions

1. How is the legacy of slavery related to modern inequalities experienced by Black Americans?
2. What is the history of reparations in the United States? What does the story of Belinda Royall teach us about the possibilities and challenges of reparations?
3. Compare the issue of reparations in Germany for the Holocaust and the Unites States for slavery. What can we learn by comparing these two cases?

Coates, T. (2014). The case for reparations. *The Atlantic*. https://www.theatlantic.com/magazine/archive/2014/06/the-case-for-reparations/361631/

HOW THE STATE INVOLVES THE PUBLIC

One of the primary ways that the state engages the public is through regular elections, a formal decision-making process in which eligible citizens select individuals for public office. Elections are a critical part of representative democracies such as the United States. The percentage of Americans who vote in elections saw a sharp increase from the late 1700s until the mid-1800s (see Figure 13.3). Voting rates have been relatively stagnant since the early 1900s.

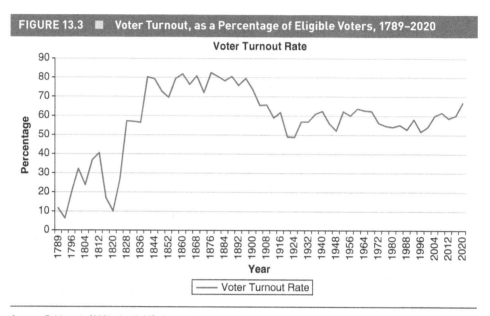

FIGURE 13.3 ■ **Voter Turnout, as a Percentage of Eligible Voters, 1789–2020**

Source: Fabina, J. (2021, April 29). *Despite Pandemic Challenges, 2020 Election Had Largest Increase in Voting Between Presidential Elections on Record;* Figure 2. Census.gov. Retrieved June 30, 2023, from https://www.censu s.gov/library/stories/2021/04/record-high-turnout-in-2020-general-election.html; US Elections Project: http://www.electproject.org/national-1789-present

Rates of voting differ greatly across groups of individuals. Voting is related to demographic characteristics, such as race and ethnicity. As shown in Figure 13.4, White non-Hispanics in the United States have the highest rates of voting, with more than 70% of people in this group going to the polls (File, 2017). Sixty-three percent of Black non-Hispanics voted in the 2020 presidential election, whereas only 54% of Hispanics did so (File, 2017).

Voting also differs across age groups. Young people are much less likely to vote than older people: 54% of people ages 18 to 29 vote, while about 73% of people over 65 do so (see Figure 13.5). It is important to note, however, that voting rates among the youngest group have been recently increasing.

Research on voter turnout indicates two main theories to explain changing voting patterns, the life-cycle effect and generational replacement. The life-cycle effect argues that fewer young people vote because of a variety of structural, social, and economic circumstances. As these young nonvoters age, they become more likely to vote. Several recent studies have pushed us to question this theory. For example, research finds that young people are less likely to engage than older people, but their willingness to participate appears to be declining over time (Barnes & Virgint, 2013).

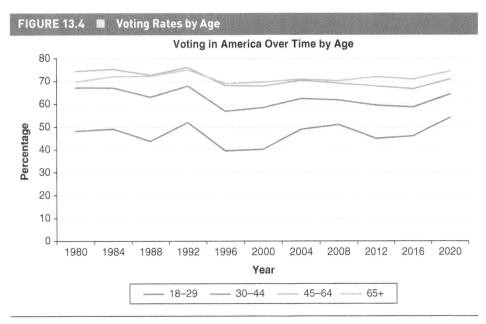

FIGURE 13.4 ■ Voting Rates by Age

Source: U.S. Census Bureau. *Data for 2020* https://www2.census.gov/programs-surveys/cps/tables/p20/585/ table01.xlsx; File, T. (2017, May 10). *Voting in America: A Look at the 2016 Presidential Election.* Census.gov. Retrieved June 30, 2023, from https://www.census.gov/newsroom/blogs/random-samplings/2017/05/voting_in_america. html

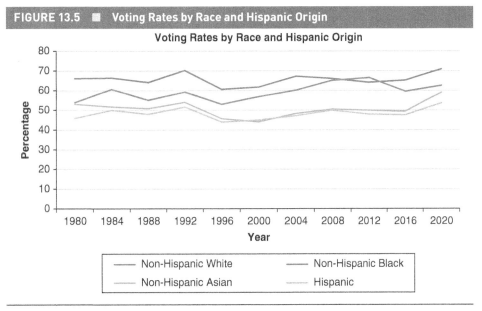

FIGURE 13.5 ■ Voting Rates by Race and Hispanic Origin

Source: Fabina, J. (2021, April 29). *Despite Pandemic Challenges, 2020 Election Had Largest Increase in Voting Between Presidential Elections on Record;* Figure 2. Census.gov. Retrieved June 30, 2023, from https://www. census.gov/library/stories/2021/04/record-high-turnout-in-2020-general-election.html; File, T. (2017, May 10). *Voting in America: A Look at the 2016 Presidential Election;* Figure 2. Census.gov. Retrieved June 30, 2023, from https://www.census.gov/newsroom/blogs/random-samplings/2017/05/voting_in_america.html

Generational replacement studies have grouped the electorate into approximate generations according to age and have tracked their voting propensities. These studies find that voters of the middle generations (born between 1945 and 1959) and those of the oldest generations (born before 1945) have a high propensity to vote. These generations are being replaced by younger generations (those born in 1960 or later) that have a lower propensity to engage in this way. Some of the studies' authors have proposed that this generational replacement could account for the decrease in voter turnout (Barnes & Virgint, 2013). If so, voting rates should continue to drop.

Blais and Loewen (2011) used census data to examine youth electoral engagement. They found that today's young people are better educated than young people of previous generations. Education is a very important predictor of a person's propensity to vote. Comparing young people between the ages of 18 and 24 who are students with those who are not shows that the former are 9% more likely to participate in politics. In addition to the importance of these sociodemographic factors, they found that interest in and information about politics have even greater effects on youth voting behavior. Why do you think that young people vote at a relatively low rate? What are the implications of low voting for society?

Challenges Facing the Modern State

Declines in voting rates in the United States and other countries challenge the government's ability to engage citizens. Many argue that these low voting levels are the result of the lower level of social capital and civic engagement in our society. Social capital is the social resources that individuals can draw on in making decisions and taking action (Coleman, 1990). This type of capital is based on people's social relations and their sense of underlying trust and confidence in one another.

Social capital is illustrated in the rotating credit associations that operate in Southeast Asia, West Africa, and the Caribbean, described by cultural anthropologist Clifford Geertz (1962). These associations are cooperative economic ventures. Individuals pool their resources and then rotate in drawing on the general fund of credit. The method provides people with a means to begin an economic enterprise; they are required to pay back into the pool from their earnings. These rotating credit associations require trust and cooperation among people and would be impossible without social capital. You would never contribute to the pool if you did not trust that you could take out money later when you needed it. We can also find examples of social trust and cooperation in other groups, particularly families. These feelings, which are at the heart of social capital, provide an important resource on which individuals can draw.

Robert D. Putnam and colleagues' (1993) influential study of regional government in Italy, *Making Democracy Work,* helped illustrate the importance of social capital. In the early 1970s, Italy created a system of 20 regional governments, which were all set up in the same way and had the same institutions. However, the citizens in some regions were more satisfied with their governments, and some governments were able to institute policies and function more effectively than others. The question was, "Why were some regional governments more effective than others?" Putnam and his colleagues worked to answer this question by comparing all 20 governments, using such sources as survey data of citizen engagement and participation. They found that wealth was not the most important predictor of regional success. Instead, governments tended to work more effectively and citizens were more satisfied and engaged in regions with strong civic traditions. Regions with more civicness—the fabric of values, norms, institutions, and associations—have higher levels of solidarity, mutual trust, and tolerance among citizens (Putnam et al., 1993). This greater social capital, in turn, made for more effective governance.

The Decline of Close Social Connections

We live in a time when people often feel very connected. Having a lot of Facebook friends or Twitter followers can make us feel integrated and tied to one another. However, recent research has shown that we might, in fact, be *less* connected than ever before. In fact, a third of Americans say that they have never even interacted with the person who lives next door to them. This is a big change from 40 years ago, when a third of neighbors socialized with the people next door more than twice a week (Poon, 2015).

The survey also asked respondents how many discussion partners (people with whom they discuss important issues) they have. The number for the average person has decreased from 2.9 to 2.1 since 1985. Almost half the population reports that they discuss important matters with only one other person or with no one at all. People who are very well connected, meaning they have more than four discussion partners, have decreased from one-third of the population to only one-fifth. And the number of people who have no one other than a spouse with whom to discuss their problems has increased by 50% over the past 30 years (McPherson et al., 2008).

One interesting trend to note is that highly educated people tend to have more confidants than those with less education. As Figure 13.6 shows, each additional year of education increases the number of discussion partners people have, on average. Highly educated people also have a smaller proportion of family in their networks than people with less education, which means

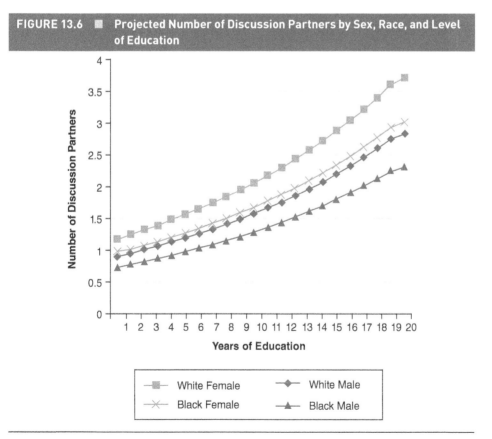

FIGURE 13.6 ■ Projected Number of Discussion Partners by Sex, Race, and Level of Education

that the former are more likely than others to be exposed to new perspectives by talking with someone outside their family circle.

The decline in the number of confidants is surprising considering the highly interconnected nature of modern society, including the widespread use of social media on the Internet. But some researchers argue that Internet use might interfere with communication in the home and neighborhood. Although the Internet can help us to interact with people across larger geographical areas, these looser ties might be replacing the stronger ones to confidants that we had in the past. For instance, we might be connected to a lot of people on Facebook, but these contacts are what sociologists call weak ties—friends of friends, or acquaintances. They might expose us to a greater range of information than close ties, but they are less likely to provide emotional support because we cannot rely on most of them when we are in need and cannot confide in them when we have a problem.

However, not everyone sees the creation of this wider net of weak ties as a negative. According to Veenhof and colleagues (2008), intense Internet users may be at least as socially engaged as nonusers. Their study found that, although high frequency Internet users have larger networks and more frequent interactions with friends and family, they tend to spend less in-person time and, of course, more time online. However, many frequent Internet users are civically and politically engaged, and they use the Internet for these types of activities.

In particular, the researchers examined how Internet use might be particularly important for certain groups of Americans. They found, for example, that recent immigrants are especially likely to use the Internet to maintain ties with family and friends in their country of origin and to integrate into larger American society. What are the differences between friends on Facebook and friends in real life? Why does it matter that we are replacing real-world friends with online friendships?

Technology during the COVID-19 pandemic was critical for helping people maintain social connections, like these young people having a games night online.

Tzido/iStockPhoto

READING: FROM "BOWLING ALONE: AMERICA'S DECLINING SOCIAL CAPITAL"

Robert D. Putnam

Angela Rowlings/MediaNews Group/Boston Herald via Getty Images

Putnam and others claim that voting rates are declining because of the decrease in social capital and civicness in modern society. Individuals are less likely to trust one another, less likely to participate together in social groups and organizations, and less likely to cooperate with one another. In the influential *Bowling Alone: The Collapse and Revival of American Community,* Putnam (2000) argues that American society has seen a decline in social capital and civic engagement, activities that address social issues. This change is particularly concerning because social capital and civic engagement are related to several positive social outcomes. For example, societies with high amounts of social capital tend to have lower levels of crime, healthier people, less poverty and unemployment, and many other benefits.

Many students of the new democracies that have emerged over the past decade and a half have emphasized the importance of a strong and active civil society to the consolidation of democracy. Especially with regard to the postcommunist countries, scholars and democratic activists alike have lamented the absence or obliteration of traditions of independent civic engagement and a widespread tendency toward passive reliance on the state. To those concerned with the weakness of civil societies in the developing or postcommunist world, the advanced Western democracies and above all the United States have typically been taken as models to be emulated. There is striking evidence, however, that the vibrancy of American civil society has notably declined over the past several decades. . . .

Researchers in such fields as education, urban poverty, unemployment, the control of crime and drug abuse, and even health have discovered that successful outcomes are more likely in civically engaged communities. Similarly, research on the varying economic attainments of different ethnic groups in the United States has demonstrated the importance of social bonds within each group. These results are consistent with research in a wide range of settings that demonstrates the vital importance of social networks for job placement and many other economic outcomes. . . .

The norms and networks of civic engagement also powerfully affect the performance of representative government. That, at least, was the central conclusion of my own 20-year, quasi-experimental study of subnational governments in different regions of Italy.[1] Although all these regional governments seemed identical on paper, their levels of effectiveness varied dramatically. Systematic inquiry showed that the quality of governance was determined by long-standing traditions of civic engagement (or its absence). Voter turnout, newspaper readership, membership in choral societies and football clubs—these were the hallmarks of a successful region. In fact, historical analysis suggested that these networks of organized reciprocity and civic solidarity, far from being an epiphenomenon of socio-economic modernization, were a precondition for it. . . .

Social scientists in several fields have recently suggested a common framework for understanding these phenomena, a framework that rests on the concept of social capital.[2] By analogy with notions of physical capital and human capital—tools and training that enhance individual productivity—"social capital" refers to features of social organization such as networks, norms, and social trust that facilitate coordination and co-operation for mutual benefit.

For a variety of reasons, life is easier in a community blessed with a substantial stock of social capital. In the first place, networks of civic engagement foster sturdy norms of generalized reciprocity and encourage the emergence of social trust. Such networks facilitate coordination and communication, amplify reputations, and thus allow dilemmas of collective action to be resolved. When economic and political negotiation is embedded in dense networks of social interaction, incentives for opportunism are reduced. At the same time, networks of civic engagement embody past success at collaboration, which can serve as a cultural template for future collaboration. Finally, dense networks of interaction probably broaden the participants' sense of self, developing the "I" into the "we," or (in the language of rational-choice theorists) enhancing the participants' "taste" for collective benefits.

I do not intend here to survey (much less contribute to) the development of the theory of social capital. Instead, I use the central premise of that rapidly growing body of work—that social connections and civic engagement pervasively influence our public life, as well as our private prospects—as the starting point for an empirical survey of trends in social capital in contemporary America. I concentrate here entirely on the American case, although the developments I portray may in some measure characterize many contemporary societies.

Whatever Happened to Civic Engagement?

We begin with familiar evidence on changing patterns of political participation, not least because it is immediately relevant to issues of democracy in the narrow sense. Consider the well-known decline in turnout in national elections over the last three decades. From a relative high point in the early 1960s, voter turnout had by 1990 declined by nearly a quarter; tens of millions of Americans had forsaken their parents' habitual readiness to engage in the simplest act of citizenship. Broadly similar trends also characterize participation in state and local elections.

It is not just the voting booth that has been increasingly deserted by Americans. A series of identical questions posed by the Roper Organization to national samples 10 times each year over the last two decades reveals that since 1973 the number of Americans who report that "in the past year" they have "attended a public meeting on town or school affairs" has fallen by more than a third (from 22 percent in 1973 to 13 percent in 1993). Similar (or even greater) relative declines are evident in responses to questions about attending a political rally or speech, serving on a committee of some local organization, and working for a political party. By almost every measure, Americans' direct engagement in politics and government has fallen steadily and sharply over the last generation, despite the fact that average levels of education—the best individual-level predictor of political participation—have risen sharply throughout this period. Every year over the last decade or two, millions more have withdrawn from the affairs of their communities.

Not coincidentally, Americans have also disengaged psychologically from politics and government over this era. The proportion of Americans who reply that they "trust the government in Washington" only "some of the time" or "almost never" has risen steadily from 30 percent in 1966 to 75 percent in 1992. . . .

Religious affiliation is by far the most common associational membership among Americans. Indeed, by many measures America continues to be . . . an astonishingly "churched" society. For example, the United States has more houses of worship per capita than any other nation on earth. Yet religious sentiment in America seems to be becoming somewhat less tied to institutions and more self-defined.

How have these complex crosscurrents played out over the last three or four decades in terms of Americans' engagement with organized religion? The general pattern is clear: the 1960s witnessed a significant drop in reported weekly churchgoing—from roughly 48 percent in the late 1950s to roughly 41 percent in the early 1970s. Since then, it has stagnated or (according to some surveys) declined still further. . . .

For many years, labor unions provided one of the most common organizational affiliations among American workers. Yet union membership has been falling for nearly four decades, with the steepest decline occurring between 1975 and 1985. . . .

Next, we turn to evidence on membership in (and volunteering for) civic and fraternal organizations. These data show some striking patterns. . . .

Evidence on "regular" (as opposed to occasional or "drop-by") volunteering is available from the Labor Department's Current Population Surveys of 1974 and 1989. These estimates suggest that serious volunteering declined by roughly one-sixth over these 15 years, from 24 percent of adults in 1974 to 20 percent in 1989. . . .

Fraternal organizations have also witnessed a substantial drop in membership during the 1980s and 1990s. Membership is down significantly in such groups as the Lions (off 12 percent since 1983), the Elks (off 18 percent since 1979), the Shriners (off 27 percent since 1979), the Jaycees (off 44 percent since 1979), and the Masons (down 39 percent since 1959). In sum, after expanding steadily throughout most of this century, many major civic organizations have experienced a sudden, substantial, and nearly simultaneous decline in membership over the last decade or two.

The most whimsical yet discomfiting bit of evidence of social disengagement in contemporary America that I have discovered is this: more Americans are bowling today than ever before, but bowling in organized leagues has plummeted in the last decade or so. Between 1980 and 1993 the total number of bowlers in America increased by 10 percent, while league bowling decreased by 40 percent. (Lest this be thought a wholly trivial example, I should note that nearly 80 million Americans went bowling at least once during 1993, *nearly a third more than voted in the 1994 congressional elections* and roughly the same number as claim to attend church regularly. Even after the 1980s' plunge in league bowling, nearly 3 percent of American adults regularly bowl in leagues.) The broader social significance, however, lies in the social interaction and even occasionally civic conversations over beer and pizza that solo bowlers forgo. Whether or not bowling beats balloting in the eyes of most Americans, bowling teams illustrate yet another vanishing form of social capital.

Countertrends

At this point, however, we must confront a serious counterargument. Perhaps the traditional forms of civic organization whose decay we have been tracing have been replaced by vibrant new organizations. For example, national environmental organizations (like the Sierra Club) and feminist groups (like the National Organization for Women) grew rapidly during the 1970s and 1980s and now count hundreds of thousands of dues-paying members. An even more dramatic example is the American Association of Retired Persons (AARP), which grew exponentially from 400,000 card-carrying members in 1960 to 33 million in 1993, becoming (after the Catholic Church) the largest private organization in the world. The national administrators of these organizations are among the most feared lobbyists in Washington, in large part because of their massive mailing lists of presumably loyal members.

These new mass-membership organizations are plainly of great political importance. From the point of view of social connectedness, however, they are sufficiently different from classic "secondary associations" that we need to invent a new label—perhaps "tertiary associations." For the vast majority of their members, the only act of membership consists in writing a check for dues or perhaps occasionally reading a newsletter. Few ever attend any meetings of such organizations, and most are unlikely ever (knowingly) to encounter any other member. The bond between any two members of the Sierra Club is less like the bond between any two members of a gardening club and more like the bond between any two Red Sox fans (or perhaps any two devoted Honda owners): they root for the same team and they share some of the same interests, but they are unaware of each other's existence. Their ties, in short, are to common symbols, common leaders, and perhaps common ideals, but not to one another. The theory of social capital argues that associational membership should, for example, increase social trust, but this prediction is much less straightforward with regard to membership in tertiary associations. From the point of view of social connectedness, the Environmental Defense Fund and a bowling league are just not in the same category. . . .

Within all educational categories, total associational membership declined significantly between 1967 and 1993. Among the college-educated, the average number of group memberships per person fell from 2.8 to 2.0 (a 26-percent decline); among high-school graduates, the number fell from 1.8 to 1.2 (32 percent); and among those with fewer than 12 years of education, the number fell from 1.4 to 1.1 (25 percent). In other words, at *all* educational (and hence social) levels of American society, and counting *all* sorts of group memberships, *the average number of associational memberships has fallen by about a fourth over the last quarter-century.* . . .

Americans are also less trusting. The proportion of Americans saying that most people can be trusted fell by more than a third between 1960, when 58 percent chose that alternative, and 1993, when only 37 percent did. The same trend is apparent in all educational groups; indeed, because social trust is also correlated with education and because educational levels have risen sharply, the overall decrease in social trust is even more apparent if we control for education.

Our discussion of trends in social connectedness and civic engagement has tacitly assumed that all the forms of social capital that we have discussed are themselves coherently correlated across individuals. This is in fact true. Members of associations are much more likely than nonmembers to participate in politics, to spend time with neighbors, to express social trust, and so on.

The close correlation between social trust and associational membership is true not only across time and across individuals, but also across countries. Evidence from the 1991 World Values Survey demonstrates the following:[3] . . .

Across the 35 countries in this survey, social trust and civic engagement are strongly correlated; the greater the density of associational membership in a society, the more trusting its citizens. Trust and engagement are two facets of the same underlying factor—social capital. . . .

Why Is US Social Capital Eroding?

As we have seen, something has happened in America in the last two or three decades to diminish civic engagement and social connectedness. What could that "something" be? Here are several possible explanations, along with some initial evidence on each. . . .

Mobility: The "re-potting" hypothesis. Numerous studies of organizational involvement have shown that residential stability and such related phenomena as homeownership are clearly associated with greater civic engagement. Mobility, like frequent re-potting of plants, tends to disrupt root systems, and it takes time for an uprooted individual to put down new roots. It seems plausible that the automobile, suburbanization, and the movement to the Sun Belt have reduced the social rootedness of the average American, but one fundamental difficulty with this hypothesis is apparent: the best evidence shows that residential stability and homeownership in America have risen modestly since 1965, and are surely higher now than during the 1950s, when civic engagement and social connectedness by our measures was definitely higher.

Other demographic transformations. A range of additional changes have transformed the American family since the 1960s—fewer marriages, more divorces, fewer children, lower real wages, and so on. Each of these changes might account for some of the slackening of civic engagement, since married, middle-class parents are generally more socially involved than other people. Moreover, the changes in scale that have swept over the American economy in these years—illustrated by the replacement of the corner grocery by the supermarket and now perhaps of the supermarket by electronic shopping at home, or the replacement of community-based enterprises by outposts of distant multinational firms—may perhaps have undermined the material and even physical basis for civic engagement.

The technological transformation of leisure. There is reason to believe that deep-seated technological trends are radically "privatizing" or "individualizing" our use of leisure time and thus disrupting many opportunities for social-capital formation. The most obvious and probably the most powerful instrument of this revolution is television. Time-budget studies in the 1960s showed that the growth in time spent watching television dwarfed all other changes in the way Americans passed their days and nights. Television has made our communities (or, rather, what we experience as our communities) wider and shallower. In the language of economics, electronic technology enables individual tastes to be satisfied more fully, but at the cost of the positive social externalities associated with more primitive forms of entertainment. The same logic applies to the replacement of vaudeville by the movies and now of movies by the VCR. The new "virtual reality" helmets that we will soon don to be entertained in total isolation are merely the latest extension of this trend. Is technology thus driving a wedge between our individual interests and our collective interests? It is a question that seems worth exploring more systematically.

Notes

Robert D. Putnam, *Making Democracy Work: Civic Traditions in Modern Italy* (Princeton: Princeton University Press, 1993).

James S. Coleman deserves primary credit for developing the "social capital" theoretical framework. See his "Social Capital in the Creation of Human Capital," *American Journal of Sociology* (Supplement) 94 (1988): S95–S120, as well as his *The Foundations of Social Theory* (Cambridge: Harvard University Press, 1990), 300–21. See also Mark Granovetter, "Economic Action and Social Structure: The Problem of Embeddedness," *American Journal of Sociology* 91 (1985): 481–510; Glenn C. Loury, "Why Should We Care about Group Inequality?" *Social Philosophy and Policy* 5 (1987): 249–71; and Robert D. Putnam, "The Prosperous Community: Social Capital and Public Life," *American Prospect* 13 (1993): 35–42. To my knowledge, the first scholar to use the term *social capital* in its current sense was Jane Jacobs, in *The Death and Life of Great American Cities* (New York: Random House, 1961), 138.

I am grateful to Ronald Inglehart, who directs this unique cross-national project, for sharing these highly useful data with me. See his "The Impact of Culture on Economic Development: Theory, Hypotheses, and Some Empirical Tests" (unpublished manuscript, University of Michigan, 1994).

Reading Questions

1. According to Putnam, what is social capital and why is it important?
2. How is bowling an example of declining civic engagement? What are some other pieces of evidence, aside from lower voting rates?
3. What are some of the arguments Putnam gives for the decreasing levels of social capital? What might he say about the rise of the Internet (e.g., social networking sites, online activism) for the development of social capital?

USING YOUR SOCIOLOGICAL IMAGINATION
COVID-19 STIMULUS CHECKS AND POVERTY

In 2020, the U.S. government distributed stimulus checks, a benefit of $1,200 to most eligible adults (Siegel Bernard & Lieber, 2021). The checks aimed to address unemployment and support the economy in the wake of the COVID-19 pandemic. The stimulus also provided an opportunity to study real-time effects of a large-scale social program. Would sending nearly 90 million Americans a payment of $1,200 reduce poverty? (Konish, 2022).

Read the analysis from the U.S. Census Bureau on the 2020 stimulus checks and poverty and answer the following questions.

https://www.census.gov/library/stories/2021/09/who-was-lifted-out-of-poverty-by
-stimulus-payments.html

1. Are the stimulus checks an example of a universal or means-tested program? To understand who qualified for the checks and why, read this FAQ from the *New York Times:* https://www.nytimes.com/article/coronavirus-stimulus-package-questions-ans wers.html
2. Look at the 2020 Supplemental Poverty Chart on the Census website. What welfare program was responsible for the greatest reduction in U.S. poverty? Which age group had the largest reduction in poverty due to this program? Why might this be the case?
3. How many people did the stimulus checks lift out of poverty? What age group had the largest reduction in poverty from the stimulus? How do these trends vary by race?
4. Look at the chart on child poverty rates by race and Hispanic origin. What racial groups had the largest reductions in child poverty after the stimulus? What other social programs in the U.S. aim to reduce child poverty?
5. After the initial wave of $1,200 checks in 2020, the government provided two more waves of COVID-19 recovery stimulus checks. Do you think the U.S. government should continue to provide stimulus checks? Why or why not?

SUMMARY

This chapter began by examining how society changes over time. Social change can happen either through the state, the focus of this chapter, or outside the state, the focus of Chapter 14. Because of the state's role in social change, we examined the rise of the state and its components. We then looked at the development of the welfare state, both in the United States and internationally. The welfare state provides many goods to citizens, particularly social programs. By examining both universal and means-tested programs, we assessed how government programs can reduce social inequality and deal with particular social issues, such as poverty among the elderly and children. We also explored the role of reparation programs as a means by which the state addresses social inequality. The chapter ended with a discussion of a key issue facing the modern state, the decline of social capital. This weaker connectedness among people can make it difficult for the state to engage citizens and effectively institute social change.

FOR FURTHER READING

Evans, P. B., Rueschemeyer, D., & Skocpol, T. (1985). *Bringing the state back in*, Cambridge University Press.

Inglehart, R. (1997). *Modernization and postmodernization: Cultural, economic and political change in 43 nations*, Princeton University Press.

Putnam, R. D., with, Leonardi., R, R. Y., & Nanetti, . (1993). *Making democracy work: Civic traditions in modern Italy*, Princeton University Press.

Stanbridge, K., & Ramos, H. (2012). *Seeing politics differently: A brief introduction to political sociology*, Oxford University Press.

Tilly, C. (1992). *Coercion, capital, and European states (1990–1992*, Basil Blackwell.

GLOSSARY

civic engagement

civicness

economic perspective

elections

generational replacement

life-cycle effect

managerial perspective

means-tested program

militaristic perspective

reparation programs

rotating credit associations

social change

Social Security

state

Supplemental Security Income (SSI)

universal program

welfare state

Alex Wong/Getty Images

SOCIAL MOVEMENTS

1. Define a social movement and explain its core components.

2. Explain the core theories of why people participate in social movements.

3. Describe how the media covers social movements and the role of framing, selection and description bias, and the protest paradigm in this process.

4. Define the multiple dimensions of social movement success, including acceptance and new advantages.

5. Apply the concept of public sociology to the research you have learned in this book and your class.

On May 25, 2020, George Floyd—a 46-year-old Black man—was arrested and pinned to the ground by a White police officer in Minneapolis after buying cigarettes with a counterfeit $20 bill. For 9 minutes and 29 seconds, George Floyd continuously pleaded, "I can't breathe" as the police officer kneeled on his neck before becoming unconscious and showing no signs of life. The murder of George Floyd, caught on video, went viral and reignited the Black Lives Matter movement. Thousands of protests were organized around the world during the months following this disturbing, but not uncommon, incident of police brutality. By July 2020, there had been more than 4,700 demonstrations organized in the United States, an average of 140 per day (Buchanan et al., 2020). In total, an estimated 15 to 26 million Americans marched in grief and anger, marking these protests as the largest in the country's history (Buchanan et al., 2020). George Floyd's murder, and the protests emerging because of it, sparked intense conversations about police brutality and anti-Black racism in American society and around the world.

In Chapter 13 we learned how social change can occur through the state. For example, we can elect leaders who will pass laws and policies that create social change. However, not all social change happens in this way. Sometimes social movements, such as Black Lives Matter, arise through other means without the state's active involvement. In this chapter we will learn about social movements, specifically how people begin to participate in them and how those movements can lead to social change.

SOCIAL MOVEMENTS

Social movements are sustained challenges to existing holders of power in the name of a wronged population. This population could be a group that believes that its rights have not been respected, such as women, LGBTQ people, ethnic minorities, immigrants, Native Americans, people with disabilities, the young, or the homeless. Their members engage in activities such as holding a protest in the street, occupying buildings, sending e-mails to political leaders, striking, and boycotting products. Through these actions the wronged population and/or sympathetic allies work to demonstrate that they are worthy of being listened to, united in their cause, numerous, and committed to social change (Tilly, 1995).

In many ways, social movements are similar to routine politics, such as elections. Groups use both means to gain public support for their opinions and interests. For example, a social movement organization might work to increase public support for restricting the use of oil

Worldwide protest against the war erupted after Russia invaded Ukraine in February of 2022.

Matysas Rehak/Alamy Stock Photo

pipelines. In election campaigns, political leaders sometimes discuss the merits or problems of oil pipelines; they try to convince the public that their perspective on this issue matches voters' opinion and therefore merits votes. In addition, the interests of social movement groups can be incorporated into party policy and government. For example, political parties might take up issues raised by the environmental movement, by saying they will pass laws that limit pollution or encourage the use of renewable energy. And the federal government has created large bureaucracies, such as the Environmental Protection Agency, to deal with these issues, often after much pressure from the environmental movement.

There are also important differences between elections and social movements. Elections and political parties are often run by powerful political insiders. Social movements, however, tend to represent the interests of outsiders who have less power. Elections are also routine, occurring at set times. Engagement in social movements is less predictable and involves different strategies depending on the situation. Participation in elections is also low cost, as going to the polls does not usually require risky behavior or a great amount of time. Participating in social movements requires more energy and commitment over time from members and activists.

The Five Main Components of Social Movements

According to Charles Tilly (1995), social movements require five main elements. They must involve a sustained challenge; engage power holders; act on behalf of a wronged population; participate in unauthorized action; and work to demonstrate worthiness, unity, numbers, and commitment. Let's examine each of these components separately.

Sustained Challenge

The first major component of a social movement is that it involves a sustained challenge. One protest event does not make a social movement. If there is a protest on your campus to reduce tuition fees but no other event ever materializes, it is not a social movement. However, once the issue of tuition fees is taken up by an organization such as Rise, a student organization in California fighting to cut tuition fees, and/or is the source of repeated protests, online campaigns, and media advertisements, it fulfills Tilly's first requirement. This sustained challenge involves repeated collective claims to power holders, which demonstrate to the public that the movement is committed to the issue at hand.

Engage Power Holders

Social movements tend to involve people with less power challenging those with more. For example, social movements can try to convince government leaders to change laws. Activists can also work to get business leaders to alter their practices, perhaps by paying their workers higher wages. Movements can encourage other institutions, such as religious institutions, the media, or schools, to change how they operate. For example, activists could call for the media to be more inclusive of people from various ethnic and racial backgrounds. In all these examples, social movements focus their actions on trying to get power holders to change elements of society with which they disagree.

Act on Behalf of Wronged Populations

We mentioned at the beginning of this section that social movements represent a wronged population. For example, the women's movement fights for the rights of women, including the right to vote, to get equal pay, and to be protected from physical and sexual violence. Civil rights movements fight for the rights of minority groups to have equal access to voting, for protection against violence from police and other powerholders, and for freedom from racial discrimination.

Young people protest against gun violence in schools and for the banning of assault weapons at the March for Our Lives in 2022.

Leigh Vogel/Getty Images for March For Our Lives

Movements consist of both the wronged population and conscience constituencies, other people who are sympathetic to the group's plight but who are not directly affected. Many men support groups such as Take Back the Night, a feminist organization that works to raise awareness of sexual assault against women. Many White people support Black Lives Matter. Conscience constituents do not directly benefit from the movement's success, yet they support the cause and efforts.

Participate in Unauthorized Action

To gain attention, social movements disrupt daily routines. Protesting clear-cut logging in the middle of an old growth forest far from any towns or cities will neither be seen by many people nor cause a disruption. As a result, it probably will not create social change. Conversely, the activists of the Greensboro sit-ins in 1960, a major action in the civil rights movement, protested in busy stores. Because of these disruptions, the sit-ins gained public attention and were instrumental in creating mass social change. In fact, they were a major reason that businesses in the South were desegregated. Social movement activists must engage in action that is outside regular politics—and not just vote or donate money to political parties. They must also protest, boycott, or do other unconventional activities to gain media and public attention.

Protest can take many forms and can occur across the political spectrum. One example of this is the anti-mask rallies that happened from 2020 to 2022 in the U.S. and in many other countries around the world. Americans' trust in government, doctors, and scientists increased in the first months of the COVID-19 pandemic. And, most Americans were quick to adopt mask-wearing at the urging of these officials. In fact, willingness to wear masks to protect against the spread of COVID-19 was very high across the political spectrum.

Activists challenged government mandates requiring people to wear masks and/or get vaccinated during the COVID-19 pandemic. How are these groups using traditional social movement tactics to challenge these mandates? How did they use rhetoric around freedom and bodily autonomy to support these claims?

Getty Images/NurPhoto

However, over time, there has come to be a political divide in the willingness of Americans to wear masks. By early June 2020, 76% of politically left Americans reported wearing masks as part of their regular routines, whereas only 53% of politically right Americans did so (Kramer, 2020).

Beginning in 2020, there were a series of protests against policies of mandatory mask-wearing across the country. Protesters gathered in cities across the country and argued that wearing masks should be voluntary and not mandated by the government. The rise of anti-mask, and later anti-vaccination, groups in the United States highlights how groups across the political spectrum use social movement strategies to try to achieve their goals. These strategies include protesting in the street and lobbying government officials. They also engage in framing activity—working to link wearing a mask to larger issues of freedom of choice or expression. It is clear that this framing is highly contested. The majority who support wearing masks and vaccinations argue that not wearing a mask (or not getting vaccinated) is not simply a matter of personal choice because it has serious implications for others (including allowing COVID-19 to continue to spread and putting others at risk). These framing debates can be seen across social movements as different sides work to sway public opinion on major social issues.

Work to Demonstrate WUNC

Finally, the strength of a social movement is based on the worthiness, unity, numbers, and commitment (WUNC) of its members. Worthiness is showing that your group or interests are worth listening to—that you are important enough to deserve the attention of the public and those in power. Endorsements from moral authorities, such as religious or community leaders, can show worthiness. Having the pope or Dalai Lama support your cause, for example, would demonstrate worthiness of a cause.

Groups exhibit unity by sharing similar values, interests, and goals. A group that seems fragmented will not be as strong as one that is united. Wearing the same shirts, having the same signs, or singing the same songs shows that the group belongs together and is unified in its cause. A group also needs to demonstrate that it has the support of many people. Leaders and the public will be much more likely to care about social issues if they are brought forth by a large group instead of by a small circle of friends.

A group can show its power in numbers by holding large public demonstrations that fill the streets, sending petitions with many signatures, or having many members in their organization. Finally, a group must show that members are committed to the cause. When members are willing to persist in costly or risky behavior, they show their commitment. For example, if your members are willing to be arrested, go to jail, or camp out in the cold for long periods, they are highly committed to the cause.

Tilly (1995) says that the strength of a social movement is the result of the formula W x U x N x C. If any of these numbers is zero, the movement will have no strength, even if it has a lot of the other three components. However, you can make up for less of one with more of another. If you do not have many people interested in your cause but the people in your group are highly committed, you might engage in a more radical tactic, such as having them chain themselves to a gate at city hall. Even though there are only 10 people at your event, you can still garner attention through this risky behavior. If many people are interested in your cause but not intensely committed to it, you might want to launch a Facebook campaign. People do not need to be very committed to a cause to "like" it; if you can get 1,000 people to respond, you can show that your issue is important.

READING: "SCHOOL STRIKE FOR CLIMATE": SOCIAL MEDIA AND THE INTERNATIONAL YOUTH PROTEST ON CLIMATE CHANGE

Shelley Boulianne, Mireille Lalancet, and David Ilkiw

Introduction

On March 15, 2019, approximately 1.4 million protesters worldwide joined the youth strike for climate change (Barclay & Amaria, 2019). The global climate strike was founded by Swedish teenager Greta Thunberg as a protest led by youth and younger generations to oppose past and current actions of older generations towards the environment. The strikes occurred over a series of Fridays, spanning more than one year, under the hashtag Fridays for Future. The March 15, 2019, event was the first time that the ongoing events drew more than 1 million protesters. Students went on strike and walked out of schools across the globe in order to draw attention to and encourage action on climate change. The strike continued into 2020; more youth protesters are taking to the streets in order to challenge governments and the media about the climate crisis. These protest initiatives followed similar grassroots-intensive blueprint used by other protest movements in recent years. This article examines 993 tweets with at least one #SchoolStrike4Climate hashtag. We examine the spatial markings of the tweets (local, national, global), which demonstrated a pattern of connecting local action to global processes. We also examine the functions of the tweets (information, opinion, mobilization, or attacks), which reflected both support and criticism of the movement. As observed with other movements, the most common function was to share information and the least common function was to mobilize citizens to take action.

This article thus sheds light on the dynamics of collective/connective action among younger segments of the public as well as other civil society actors. It also offers a perspective about how youth are using social media while protesting and what kinds of reactions their protest generates from other members of society. Social media platforms are transforming political engagement by offering agency through the ability to voice political views. This research is important as action on climate change requires a global response. Social media can fill a gap in institutional processes which are not currently designed to engage citizens in global policy decisions. Social media can be used to question, contest, and/or support decisions or actions of media, political, private or governmental organizations related to the climate crisis. The global climate strike reflects a trend in international protest events, which are connected through social media and other digital media tools.

Youth Activism

There is a widespread concern about youth political participation in democratic countries, especially with regard to voting (Grasso, 2016; Martin, 2012; Sloam, 2016). Far from being apathetic, young people are more involved in other forms of engagement. These forms are ad hoc, issue-oriented, non-electoral, and personalized (Sloam, 2016; Vromen, Loader, Xenos, & Bailo, 2016). However, this political activism could be used to influence government, as documented in the recent climate strikes (Pickard, 2019). In some countries, youth are more likely to engage in protest activities, but in other countries, there are minimal age differences or the patterns reflect generational political action repertoires (Grasso, 2016; Martin, 2012; Sloam, 2016). Pickard (2019) calls this activism "Do-It-Ourselves" politics, which uses a variety of tactics, including lifestyle choices, such as veganism and recycling, as well as climate strikes and non-violent direct action. Acting collectively is a key feature of this form of activism (Pickard, 2019).

Young people may use social media to express their political views. However, not all youth feel free to express their views online. Youth, as well as others, are reluctant to post their political views online, because of a fear of negative reactions or conflict, privacy concerns, and fear of posting something wrong (Bäck, Bäck, Fredén, & Gustafsson, 2019; Thorson, 2014; Vromen et al., 2016). Yet, social media remain as popular forums for political expression. This form of activism is often regarded as slacktivism, instead of being viewed as an activity along a continuum of participation (Dennis, 2019). Furthermore, a meta-analysis demonstrates that these online activities are correlated with offline activities (Boulianne & Theocharis, 2020). We expect to see youth using social media to express opinions, but we also expect to see others using social media to express opinions about youth and the global climate strike (Lievrouw, 2011; Pappacharissi, 2014). Digital media allows for political expression and this expression links individuals into a loosely organized network (Bennett & Segerberg, 2012). In other words, "identity reference is more derived through inclusive and diverse large-scale personal expression rather than through common group or ideological identification" (Bennett & Segerberg, 2012, p. 744). Thorson, Edgerly, Kligler-Vilenchik, Xu, and Wang (2016) illustrate this connective network in relation the 2014 People's Climate March.

Climate Change

The environmental movement has been described as the most influential and global movement of our time (Rootes, 2007). The nature of environmental issues requires a global lens, as environmental problems such as air pollution cannot be contained within political borders. Solutions require international collaboration involving governments and nonprofit organizations (Fisher & Green, 2004). Furthermore, efforts to conserve resources, such as wildlife, also require global interventions, as demonstrated by the World Wildlife Fund. Indeed, the environmental movement is distinctive as a movement, because of the global scale and need for international collaboration (Rootes, 2007).

A major focal point of the current environmental movement is climate change. Public opinion research shows that concern about climate change fluctuates over time with key events triggering increased concern (Ballew et al., 2019; Brulle, Carmichael, & Jenkins, 2012). Economic downturns, political elites, media coverage, availability of scientific information, weather changes, and activities of social movements/counter-movements have been considered as triggers for changing levels of concern about climate change (Benegal, 2018a; Brulle et al., 2012).

Concern about climate change is also marked by age, with young people more likely to express concern and believe in the anthropogenic origins of climate change (Arbuckle, 2017; Benegal, 2018a, 2018b; Hornsey, Harris, Bain, & Fielding, 2016). In the US, even among Republicans, younger people "worry" more about climate change, than their older counterparts (Republicans: 40% versus 28%, Democrats: 86% versus 78%; Ballew et al., 2019). Beyond the US, there are many studies documenting that young people are more concerned about climate change, compared to older people (Tobler, Visschers, & Siegrist, 2012). In addition, age distinguishes those who are merely concerned from those who are "concerned activists" in Germany (Metag, Füchslin, & Schäfer, 2017).

Hashtag Activism

The School Strike 4 Climate builds on existing movements and their use of social media, including the global Occupy movement (Theocharis, Lowe, van Deth, & Garcia-Albacete, 2015), Arab Spring, and Idle No More (Raynauld, Richez, & Boudreau Morris, 2017) as well as more youth-driven movements (see Raynauld, Lalancette, & Tourigny-Koné, 2016, 2019; Theocharis, 2012). In addition, the social media tactics can reflect practices from more national or localized movements, such as the Black Lives Matter (Freelon, McIllwain, & Clark, 2016) and Euromaidan (MacDuffee-Metzger & Tucker, 2017). These studies use hashtags to identify and analyze a discursive community around a particular topic. Jost et al. (2018) provide a summary of these movements.

These studies tend to find that Twitter is used largely for circulating information and rarely includes calls to action to engage in protest activities, following early work in this field (Theocharis et al., 2015). For example, using #Ferguson, LeFebvre and Armstrong (2018) find that only 4% of tweets were calls for peaceful action, 2% of tweets were calls for digital action, and less than 1% were calls for violent action. Freelon et al. (2016) offer a big picture of 40 million #BlackLivesMatter tweets, noting that invitations to participate were quite rare. Hodges and Stocking (2016) find that only 5% of tweets related to the Keystone XL pipeline involved a request to take action, such as signing a petition or protesting. In 2012, just 3% of tweets about the Quebec student strike were recorded as having a mobilization function (Raynauld et al., 2016). In contrast, Raynauld et al. (2017) find that 14% of #IdleNoMore tweets included details about mobilization. Following this line of research, we have similar expectations.

The infrequency of mobilization tweets is not indicative of the limited mobilization potential of social media, as studies of protesters find that social media use is a popular way to learn about a protest event (Fisher, 2019). Furthermore, many studies document a positive correlation between social media use and the likelihood of participation in protest (Boulianne, Koc-Michalska, & Bimber, 2020). Social media platforms were critical to mobilizing participation in the March for Science in 2017 (Boulianne et al., 2020) as well as for young people in Chile during the 2011 environmental protest (Scherman, Arriagada, & Valenzuela, 2015). There is a legacy of digital media being used to organize and mobilize participants in the environmental movement (Fisher & Boekkooi, 2010).

As mentioned, most of the studies analyzing tweets conclude that the primary objective is to share information about the movement (Jost et al., 2018; LeFebvre & Armstrong, 2018). Interviews with Black Lives Matter tweeters affirm that the motivation is to educate and raise awareness (Freelon et al., 2016). This information can be shared through links to traditional news sources and sharing photos of the event. Hyperlinks are popular in tweets, recognizing this core function (Jost et al., 2018; Merry, 2013; Pang & Law, 2017; Raynauld et al., 2016, 2017).

Moving research forward, we recognize that the environmental movement is very much a global movement and as such, social media may be used differently. Pang and Law (2017) offer a review of Twitter-based studies in relation to the environmental movement. They explore how the inclusion of hyperlinks in tweets impact retweet patterns related to #WorldEnvironmentDay, and examine how the use of visuals may persuade tweeters. Hodges and Stocking (2016) examine the Keystone XL pipeline Twitter discourse and find that supportive and oppositional groups make different uses of Twitter. Those who opposed the pipeline were more likely to interact with other Twitter users, share tweets about their views, and request donations (Hodges & Stocking, 2016). Merry (2013) studied environmental groups on Twitter in the aftermath of the BP oil spill, and finds that 90% of tweets contained hyperlinks. She concludes that Twitter offers a new venue for conflict expansion and poses a problem for environmental groups trying to control the narrative around the BP oil spill (Merry, 2013). Thorson et al. (2016) explore how hashtags are used in the People's Climate March in 2014. They argue that the use of hashtags creates "a digital space of shared attention for the climate change march" (Thorson et al., 2016, p. 4791). This shared space is important for global protest events.

The key challenge for environmental action is that it requires local action to a global problem. This can lead to free-rider problems or bystander effects, where no one takes action. Individual actions might be perceived as inconsequential, given the global and overwhelming nature of environmental problems. This can deter environmentally friendly practices, as well as reduce the incentive to participate in marches and demonstrations, a high-effort activity. In the case of protests, if everyone can enjoy the benefits of a successful protest, then why would a single individual decide to incur the costs of participation (Jost et al., 2018)? Social media are believed to reduce the costs of participation, because information about the location and turnout are easier to acquire (Jost et al., 2018).

At the institutional level, environmental political action also poses a challenge. Democratic institutions are tied to nation-states, which are bounded to geographically-defined constituencies. Governments are held accountable by citizens within their country. However, the failure to address climate change has impact on global citizens, not just those citizens within one's country. Yet, global citizens do not have access to the global leaders that make decisions about climate change policies. Indeed, some global citizens are more vulnerable than others to the impacts of climate change, but their country may not be equipped to adapt to climate change (Sarkodie & Strezov, 2019). For example, sub-Sahara Africa is often identified as a vulnerable region for climate change, but the governments in these countries have little control over the fate of global agreements on climate change (Sarkodie & Strezov, 2019). As such, it is important to understand the global dimension to this activism. People are protesting in the streets to raise awareness of this issue at the local level as well as the global level in an effort to encourage global political action.

Social media present an opportunity to voice one's concerns about climate change and the need for action, as well as document the discontent among citizens by posting pictures of the protest event. Social media users may connect their local events to global events. In doing so, they are documenting their and others' discontent so that local political leaders can view their events virtually through social media images. However, they are also documenting their and others' discontent for global leaders to take note. Indeed, the spatial markings of protest events across the globe suggest that there is a global community concerned about climate change. Seeing this global community through protest images might help encourage action on climate change. Global citizens cannot participate in elections to choose global political leaders, nor can they participate in referendums to support climate change agreements. Social media offer a substitute for lacking global governance structures. As such, we are interested in the extent to which social media posts reflect this local-global tension. Our research questions are as follows:

RQ1: What are the spatial markings of tweets (local, national, global) related to #SchoolStrike4Climate?

RQ2: What were the primary functions of tweets (information, opinion, mobilization, or blame) using #SchoolStrike4Climate?

Methods

5.1 Sample

In order to systematically study how Twitter was used during the protests, the researchers decided upon several criteria for the sample. The choice of hash tags was based on Twitter trending topics statistics on the day of the event (approximately noon, mountain standard time, on March 15, 2019). At that time, these hashtags were trending: #YouthClimateStrike (10.5K Tweets); #ClimateActionNow (7K Tweets), and #SchoolStrike4Climate (86.6K Tweets). #FridaysforFuture was also trending, but unfortunately was not included in our subsequent scraping efforts. Indeed, this discursive network was difficult to capture, as the hashtag was also tweeted as "FridayforFuture" (missing the "s") and sometimes 4 was used in lieu of "for." Nonetheless, this discourse was picked up through the use of multiple hashtags as many of our tweets included #FridaysforFuture and #SchoolStrike4Climate, as our findings demonstrate.

The data were scraped from Twitter using Netlytics (https://netlytic.org). Netlytics caps the scrapes per query at 1,000 (most recent) tweets. As such, we chose a series of hashtags to scrape data and staggered the data collection process over time, beginning on March 15 at 16h through to March 18 at 20h. These strategies allowed us to collect more than 35,000 tweets related to this event (tied to these various hashtags). We then turned our focus to the #SchoolStrike4Climate, because it contained the largest number of tweets (n 13,542). We narrowed the list by identifying the duplicates within the database. When identifying the distinctive tweets, we sorted these results from most to least frequent, then chose the most frequent/retweeted 1,000 from the 1,842. Focusing on popularity/retweets helps capture the most common messages circulating around this event and the youth participants. Netlytic does not scrape the retweet/like metrics for individual posts. To compensate for this weakness, we added the metrics of the tweets that we quote, using estimates gathered as of December 9, 2019.

5.2 Coding

The number of tweets coded reflects recent practices in this field when using human coders (Pang & Law, 2017; Raynauld et al., 2016, 2017, 2019). We coded 993 tweets into the following broad themes: spatial markings and function. Non-English tweets were translated using Google Translate and then coded. The diversity of languages and regions expressed in these tweets helped to gain a more global perspective in comparison to other hashtags. The codes were created in order to answer our research questions.

As per RQ1, we are interested in the physical location of the protest event. As mentioned, participants in the Student Strike 4 Climate may feel an increased need to ground the movement in physical locations, by posting locations to Twitter. In addition, this practice highlights the global-local challenges of action related to environmental issues. To study mentions of location, we created seven categories for spatial location: 1) local; 2) national; 3) global; 4) local and national; 5) local and global; 6) national and global; and a combination of 7) local, national, and global. The spatial locations were the most straightforward to code. We coded for any reference to a location: a city (or a key location in a city, such as Buckingham Palace), a country, a region, for example. There were no disagreement per se, rather sometimes a marker was missed and this information was corrected. However, the correction rate was less than 1%. Each coder could "correct" the coding and offer a rationale for the change.

For RQ2, we used an existing coding scheme from the GGI codebook, which was originally developed to study the 2012 Quebec Student Protest (Raynauld et al., 2016, 2019). From this coding rubric, we adapted the original categories of information tweets, opinion tweets, mobilization tweets, and attack or denunciation tweets to fit this new strike. In line with prior applications of this coding scheme, these categories were treated as mutually exclusive to one another; if a tweet was interpreted as having two or more elements of these categories, it became the responsibility of the coder to determine which category best encapsulated the contents of the tweet. Within each function, we highlight subthemes of tweets. We ordered the subthemes in terms of most frequent to least frequent, without providing exact numbers, because the intent is to establish relative patterns, rather than exact estimates, which would require a larger random sample or the entire population of tweets using this hashtag.

The categories of information tweets were: tweet documenting the protest, tweet about an issue or event related directly to the strike, news reports related to the strike, and tweet sharing climate/environmental information. As mentioned, we present subthemes ordered from most to least frequent.

The opinion tweets category was broken down into subcategories: opinion about protest, opinion about climate change, opinion about youth protesters, and opinion about youth in general.

Expanding upon Merry (2013) and Hodges and Stocking (2016), who differentiate between online and offline forms of activism, we adjusted the mobilization category to distinguish between offline and online mobilization. The first category applied to attempts for "traditional" offline forms of participation. Offline participation included activities like protesting, putting up flyers, and boycotting goods and industries. The second category was online mobilization requests, such as signing petitions and retweeting.

Findings

6.1 RQ1: Spatial Markings

We first wanted to see how location was mentioned in the tweets in order to understand the local–global dimension of this protest. The results showed that approximately 533 of 993 tweets mentioned a location (Table 1). Tweets that mentioned local protests were the most common (53.1%). Local tweets mentioned towns or cities, including London, New York City, Paris, Montreal,

TABLE 1. ■ Frequency and percent of spatial marking tweets.		
	Frequency	**Percent**
Spatial marking	533	53.7%
Local	283	53.1%
Global	98	18.4%
National	64	12%
Local and global	38	7.1%
Local and national	25	4.7%
National and global	11	2.1%
Local, national, and global	9	1.7%
Other	5	0.9%
No spatial markings	460	46.3%
Total	993	100%

Dublin, and Stockholm. They were followed by tweets mentioning the protest at a global scale (18.4%), including this tweet by Greta Thunberg:

> Tomorrow we school strike for the climate in 1769 places in 112 countries around the world. And counting. Everyone is welcome. Everyone is needed. Let's change history. And let's never stop for as long as it takes. #fridaysforfuture #schoolstrike4climate #climatestrike (9,751 Retweets; 27,679 Likes)

The framing of this tweet creates a cosmopolitan image of protest rather than an image of protests located in a single city or country.

Tweets also connected the protest to the national level (12%). These tweets referred to the countries in which the strikes occurred. Other tweets connected local cities to the global scale of the protest (7.1%) and also connected local protests to protests across a nation state (4.7%). Although these tweets create a similar cosmopolitan framing as tweets that framed the movement as global, it is worth noting that they were still attached to local and national spaces. There were relatively few tweets connecting local events to broader (national and global) events. These types of tweets would identify a specific city, the country, and link the event to the global events.

6.2 RQ2: Function of Tweets

The main focus of this research was to study the function of #SchoolStrike4Climate tweets. The function of each tweet was broken into four variables with corresponding subcategories connected to each of the four larger variables. The first variable tested was information tweets. Information tweets had the highest frequency of occurrence (52.3%; see Table 2). The next most popular category was opinion tweets (29%), followed by attack/blame tweets (13.6%). Finally, mobilization was not a popular function of tweets (4.8%). As mentioned, the

TABLE 2. ■ Frequency and percent of tweet function categories.		
Function Categories	**Frequency**	**Percentage**
Information Documentation tweet Tweet about an issue or event related directly to the strike News reports related to the strike Climate/environmental information tweet	519	52.3%

Function Categories	Frequency	Percentage
Opinion Opinion about the protest Opinion about climate change Opinion about youth protesters Opinion about youth	288	29.0%
Attack/blame Attack/blame at government Attack/blame at media organization	135	13.6%
Mobilization Online mobilization requests Offline mobilization requests	48	4.8%
Other (not about school strike or environment or youth or climate change)	3	0.3%
Total	993	100%

objective was not to establish precise estimates about the function of tweets, but to establish their relative frequency. As observed with other hashtag movements, information tweets were the most popular and mobilization the least popular.

In the next section, we take a qualitative look at how these functions were used to talk about the strike and the youth protesters and frame it/them in a positive or a negative light. We highlight subcategories for tweets that were most common within each of the function areas. The list of subcategories was ordered by frequency: The most frequently appearing subtheme in the dataset is listed first.

INFORMATION TWEETS

Information tweets documented the protest, an issue or event related directly to the strike, news reports related to the strike, and shared climate/environmental information. The most popular type of information tweet was documentation of the protest, but offering little other information (see Table 2). Documentation tweets provided little actual detail about the protest beyond documenting location and size. For example:

"Incredible!! Over one million students on school strike for the climate. #FridayForFuture #schoolstrike4climate" (581 Retweets; 1,390 Likes).

While there may be details lacking, this tweet conveys to the readers that over a million students are missing school in a global environmental protest. Even if documentation tweets did not convey a large quantity of information, their brevity might make them more accessible to readers. We might argue that sharing information about the strike can help bring attention to environmental issues since these tweets generally contained information like place and protest size. This tweet also exemplifies the ongoing issue with the Fridays for Future hashtag, which we mentioned in Section 5.1. This hashtag was difficult to track because sometimes "s" is not used in the hashtag.

We also see, albeit less frequently, tweets that convey information about the strike, news reports about the strike, and information about climate change or environment. Tweets included updates about the number of participants and number of countries reporting strikes, including this tweet, also from Greta Thunberg:

"According to https://t.co/pzYB6XuR6u we have already passed way over one million students on school strike today. Over 2000 places in 125 countries on all continents. And we have only just started! #fridaysforfuture #school strike4climate (picture from Prague, Czech Republic)" (6,401 Retweets; 18,688 Likes).

She also posted an update of this news:

"Over 1,4mn on #SchoolStrike4Climate yesterday according to latest update. 2083 places in 125 countries on all continents. "Biggest day of global climate action ever" says @350 And this isn't even the beginning. Because we have done our homework. #FridayForFuture Pic: Montreal, CAN" (6,841 Retweets; 20,063 Likes).

Both of the above tweets included references to local events (Prague, Montreal, respectively), but connected these local events to the larger global event. Despite the tweet originating from @GretaThunberg's account, we note that the Friday for Future hashtag is missing the "s" in the example above.

In addition, tweets contained news about the strike, such as this tweet which included a video of protesters scaling the barricades:

Police tried to close the entrance to The Mall leading to Buckingham Palace but they just keep on coming... #ExtinctionRebellion #climatestrike #schoolstrike4climate, @ LdnRebellion. #YouthStrike4Climate #FridaysForFuture @Strike4Youth @UKSCN1 @ ukycc (207 Retweets; 420 Likes).

Information tweets sometimes went beyond simple information about the strike and presented the larger consequences of climate change. In this example, a professor of climate science at Potsdam University tweeted about a *The New York Times* article summarizing the science behind climate change:

The 20 warmest years on record have all come in the past 22 years, essentially the lifetime of today's children and young adults. Great collection of images of #schoolstrike4climate #ClimateStrike from around the world! https://www.nytimes.com/2019/03/15/climate/climate-school-strikes.html#click=https://t.co/XQB2LmKYJL... #FridaysForFuture#Fridays4Future (89 Retweets; 164 Likes).

Overall, the most popular function of tweets was to share information about the event. In particular, information tweets focused on documenting the size and location of events, with tweets from Greta Thunberg receiving a large number of reactions (retweets, likes).

OPINION TWEETS

Opinion tweets were mostly related to opinions about the protest (Table 2). From these tweets, we see support as well as opposition to the climate strike. For example, this tweet was from the Global Warming Policy Forum and it was sharing a piece profiling a young girl who refused to go along with the strike:

Here's why I won't strike: One brave schoolgirl refuses to go along with the crowd and says climate strikers should "first go study economics." #schoolstrike4climate #ClimateStrike (416 Retweets; 811 Likes).

In contrast, we see another tweet in which an Australian TV host Lee Constable (2019) wrote:

When I was at school we knew climate change was happening and climate action wasn't. We didn't strike. I stayed at school like a good girl so I could go be a scientist and solve it. Now I've got these degrees and I just wish we'd striked. #Strike4Climate #school strike4climate. (418 Retweets; 1,867 Likes)

Additionally, opinion tweets were often about climate change. They stressed the severity of environmental issues like climate change and often used these issues to frame the School Strike 4 Climate as protecting the future of the world. Tweets made claims like "not having a choice." This tweet from Sky News included a link to an interview with a teenager:

"We do not have a choice, we have to act on climate now"— @deespeak says she is a big fan of @GretaThunberg and completely supports the #SchoolStrike4Climate movement. #DeepOceanLive For more, head here: https://t.co/mE2xz5s65c (25 Retweets; 66 Likes).

These tweets framed environmental issues as urgent and positioned the protesters as protagonists fighting for the future. They also bring an impression of urgency in relation to climate change.

The next most popular subcategory was tweeting about the youth protesters. In this example, the tweet was a meme with students using an extinguisher to stop a fire in the classroom, while the teacher is complaining that last week it was the climate strike and this week, a fire—students will do anything to skip school. The tweet was from a Swedish cartoonist:

The irresponsible climate activist youth of today! #climechange #climate #FridaysForFuture #earthstrike #extinctionrebellion #RebelForLife #ClimateCrisis #Environment #GreenNewDeal #ClimateAction #GretaThunberg #schoolstrike4climate #SchoolStrike #schoolstrikefor climate (588 Retweets; 1,679 Likes).

Opinions were also about youth. The "brave schoolgirl" story made a reappearance in a tweet but this time with the annotation from a different tweeter that reads "Some young people think for themselves, some just follow the herd #schoolstrike4climate" (154 Retweets; 407 Likes). As another example of negative opinions, a news report quoted the Australian Education Minister condemning the protest:

"Students leaving school during school hours (to protest) is not something to encourage, especially when they're being encouraged to do so by green political activists," says Education Minister @DanTehanWannon #SchoolStrike4Climate (55 Retweets; 78 Likes).

It was difficult to code whether the opinion tweets expressed support or criticism for the strike, especially when the tweet was not in English.

Attack/Blame Tweets

Tweets with the function of attacking and blaming were the third most popular category (see Table 2). Approximately, 13.6% of tweets blamed someone or an institution, as the most popular attack/blame tweet targeted the government and government officials. Attacks directed at the government were often based on past discontent with government inaction, and a lack of faith and distrust for future promises of government action. US President Donald Trump was often at the center of the attacks. Many tweets simply have @realDonaldTrump, the number of participants in the specific event, and the hashtag. However, other politicians, including those in the UK and Australia were specifically mentioned. For example, this post was retweeted during our data collection period. The tweet originated with the account @mac123_m, with 30,000 followers, and it criticized the UK's Tory government, specifically Michael Gove, and had a link to a *The Guardian* article:

The nine green policies killed off by the Tory govt. The Tories do not fight for the climate however much Michael Gove complains. Hope the young realise the way forward is with LAB & their radical green policies. #ClimateStrike #SchoolStrike4Climate. (227 Retweets; 180 Likes)

Attack/blame tweets were directed at media organizations, especially the BBC. This tweet was posted by a UK magazine, Little Green Space, praising one media outlet and criticizing another media outlet. The tweet included a link to *The Guardian* report:

Great reports from @guardian on today's global #SchoolStrike4Climate. Dear other UK media, including @BBCNews, there's a world beyond Brexit: PS give the 1000s of young people taking action the coverage they deserve and our planet needs. #FridayForFuture https://t.co/aGSKh1NSbS (95 Retweets; 177 Likes).

Again, we see that the hashtag for Friday for Future does not contain an "s," making this hashtag a difficult focal point for a discursive community around this event.

Mobilization

Mobilization tweets comprised the smallest category of tweet functions (4.8%; see Table 2). In these handful of tweets, online mobilization was more popular than offline mobilization. For example, Change.org UK posted an invitation to sign a petition with the fist-raised emoji, earth emoji, and the green heart emoji:

These students are fighting to save our planet Support their demand to declare a climate emergency here: https://t.co/9pGQBVfc6W #YouthStrike4Climate #SchoolStrike4Climate #climatestrike #climatechange #Youth4Climate #FridaysForFuture @GretaThunberg @Strike4Youth (95 Retweets; 147 Likes).

As for mobilization to offline activities, Amnesty International posted a tweet explaining why people should participate: "Here are 5 reasons students (& everyone else) should strike for climate. #SchoolStrike4Climate" (395 Retweets; 681 Likes). These types of tweets were quite infrequent, as observed with other studies.

Discussion

As observed with other protest events, information was the most popular function of tweets and mobilization was the least popular. As mentioned, we borrowed the coding approach from Quebec Student Strike (see Raynauld et al., 2016, 2019) and #IdleNoMore (see Raynauld et al., 2017). However, the results were largely the same. In all three studies, information tweets were the most frequent category recorded (see Table 3). Additionally, the percentage of opinion tweets and attack tweets were fairly similar. The biggest difference is that #IdleNoMore tweets called for more mobilization, but this movement is distinctive compared to other movements (Freelon et al., 2016; Hodges & Stocking, 2016; LeFebvre & Armstrong, 2018; Theocharis et al., 2015).

TABLE 3.   ■   Percent totals of function categories for #SchoolStrike4Climate, #ggi, and #IdleNoMore.

Function categories	#SchoolStrike4Climate (%)	#ggi (%) (Quebec student strike)	#IdleNoMore (%)
Information	52.3%	59%	52%
Opinion	29%	28%	16%
Attack	13.6%	10%	10%
Mobilization	4.8%	3%	21%

Based on the similarities, we suggest that the uses of the Twitter platform for protest events have stabilized and, for now, no new uses could be observed. We have contributed to this scholarship by examining the nuances within these broad function categories. We also highlight the role of Twitter in documenting the size of these events. We also document the various types of opinions shared on Twitter and nuances about who is blamed for the climate crisis. This discourse moves beyond diagnosing the problem of climate change into discussions about who is responsible for solutions. As it was the case for the 2014 People's Climate March, we also saw different types of stakeholders come together in order to discuss the climate crisis and they were connected through a common hashtag (Thorson et al., 2016).

Twitter as a platform was used by the leader of the School Strike 4 Climate, Greta Thunberg. Her tweets were widely circulated, liked, and commented upon. However, we do not know the extent to which youth, more generally, are using this platform. We did not analyze the users who were tweeting about the strike; instead, we focused on the content being circulated. This content focused on youth. Aside from Greta Thunberg's tweets, every tweet used as an example included a mention of "students," "youth," "young," and "school girl." These examples represent the larger database of tweets, which included many mentions of these concepts as well as many @GretaThunberg references. In the larger database of 13,542, the word "students" appeared 33,000 times and @GretaThunberg appeared 20,000 times. Further research might consider who is tweeting and whether youth are using this platform (or another one) to express their views about climate change and the need for collective action. This information is difficult to acquire from Twitter profiles, which rarely mention age and often do not include a picture. However, since there was a clear leader and focal point for this movement, future research might consider using @GretaThunberg as a central node and examine the pattern of retweets around this node. This research could test the "committed minorities" versus "critical periphery" dynamic suggested by Barberá et al. (2015).

Conflict of Interests

The authors declare no conflict of interests.

References

Arbuckle, M. B. (2017). The interaction of religion, political ideology and concern about climate change in the United States. *Society & Natural Resources, 30*(2), 177–194.

Bäck, E., Bäck, H., Fredén, A., & Gustafsson, N. (2019). A social safety net? Rejection sensitivity and political opinion sharing among young people in social media. *New Media & Society, 21*(2), 298–316.

Ballew, M. T., Leiserowitz, A., Roser-Renouf, C., Rosenthal, S. A., Kotcher, J. E., Marlon, J. R., . . . Maibach, E. W. (2019). Climate change in the American mind: Data, tools, and trends. *Environment: Science and Policy for Sustainable Development, 61*(3), 4–18.

Barberá, P., Wang, N., Bonneau, R., Jost, J. T., Nagler, J., Tucker, J., & González-Bailón, S. (2015). The critical periphery in the growth of social protests. *PloS One, 10*(11). https://dx.doi.org/10.1371%2Fjournal.pone.0143611

Barclay, E., & Amaria, K. (2019, March 17). Photos: Kids in 123 countries went on strike to protect the climate. *Vox*. Retrieved from https://www.vox.com/energy-and-environment/2019/3/15/18267156/youth-climate-strike-march-15-photos

Benegal, S. D. (2018a). The impact of unemployment and economic risk perceptions on attitudes towards anthropogenic climate change. *Journal of Environmental Studies and Sciences, 8*(3), 300–311.

Benegal, S. D. (2018b). The spillover of race and racial attitudes into public opinion about climate change. *Environmental Politics, 27*(4), 733–756.

Bennett, W. L., & Segerberg, A. (2012). The logic of connective action: Digital media and the personalization of contentious politics. *Information, Communication & Society, 15*(5), 739–768.

Boulianne, S., Koc-Michalska, K., & Bimber, B. (2020). Mobilizing media: Comparing TV and social media effects on protest mobilization. *Information, Communication & Society*. Advance online publication. https://doi.org/10.1080/1369118X.2020.1713847

Boulianne, S., & Theocharis, Y. (2020). Young people, digital media and engagement: A meta-analysis of research. *Social Science Computer Review, 38*(2), 111–127.

Brulle, R. J., Carmichael, J., & Jenkins, J. C. (2012). Shifting public opinion on climate change: An empirical assessment of factors influencing concern over climate change in the U.S., 2002–2010. *Climatic Change, 114*(2), 169–188.

Dennis, J. (2019). *Beyond slacktivism: Political participation on social media*. Cham: Palgrave Macmillan.

Fisher, D. (2019). *American resistance: From the women's march to the blue wave*. New York, NY: Columbia University Press.

Fisher, D. R., & Boekkooi, M. (2010). Mobilizing friends and strangers: Understanding the role of the Internet in the step it up day of action. *Information Communication & Society, 13*(2), 193–208.

Fisher, D. R., & Green, J. F. (2004). Understanding disenfranchisement: Civil society and developing countries' influence and participation in global governance for sustainable development. *Global Environmental Politics, 4*(3), 65–84.

Freelon, D., McIllwain, C. D., & Clark, M. D. (2016). *Beyond the hashtags: #Ferguson, #Blacklivesmatter, and the online struggle for offline justice*. Washington, DC: Center

For Media & Social Impact. Retrieved from https://cmsimpact.org/resource/beyond-hashtags-ferguson-blacklivesmatter-online-struggle-offline-justice

Grasso, M. T. (2016). *Generations, political participation and social change in Western Europe.* London: Routledge.

Hodges, H. E., & Stocking, G. (2016). A pipeline of tweets: Environmental movements' use of Twitter in response to the keystone XL pipeline. *Environmental Politics, 25*(2), 223–247.

Hornsey, M. J., Harris, E. A., Bain, P. G., & Fielding, K. S. (2016). Meta-analyses of the determinants and outcomes of belief in climate change. *Nature Climate Change, 6*(6), 622–627.

Jost, J. T., Barberá, P., Bonneau, R., Langer, M., Metzger, M., Nagler, J., . . . Tucker, J. A. (2018). How social media facilitates political protest: Information, motivation, and social networks. *Advances in Political Psychology, 39*(Suppl. 1), 85–118.

LeFebvre, R. K., & Armstrong, C. (2018). Grievance-based social movement mobilization in the #Ferguson Twitter storm. *New Media & Society, 20*(1), 8–28.

Lievrouw, L. A. (2011). *Alternative and activist new media.* Malden, MA: Polity Press.

MacDuffee-Metzger, M., & Tucker, J. A. (2017). Social media and Euromaidan: A review essay. *Slavic Review, 76*(1), 169–191.

Martin, A. J. (2012). *Young people and politics: Political engagement in the Anglo-American democracies.* New York, NY: Routledge.

Merry, M. K. (2013). Tweeting for a cause: Microblogging and environmental advocacy. *Policy & Internet, 5*(3), 304–327.

Metag, J., Füchslin, T., & Schäfer, M. S. (2017). Global warming's five Germanys: A typology of Germans' views on climate change and patterns of media use and information. *Public Understanding of Science, 26*(4), 434–451.

Pang, N., & Law, P. (2017). Retweeting #WorldEnvironmentDay: A study of content features and visual rhetoric in an environmental movement. *Computers in Human Behavior, 69,* 54–61.

Pappacharissi, Z. (2014). *Affective publics: Sentiment, technology, and politics.* Oxford: Oxford University Press.

Pickard, S. (2019). Young environmental activists are doing it themselves. *Political Insight, 10*(4), 4–7.

Raynauld, V., Lalancette, M., & Tourigny-Koné, S. (2016). Political protest 2.0: Social media and the 2012 student strike in the province of Quebec, Canada. *French Politics, 14*(1), 1–29.

Raynauld, V., Lalancette, M., & Tourigny-Koné, S. (2019). Rethinking digital activism as it unfolds: Twitter-based contention during the 2012 Quebec student strike. In M. Lalancette, V. Raynauld, & E. Crandal (Eds.), *What's trending in Canadian politics? Understanding transformations in power, media, and the public sphere* (pp. 44–62). Vancouver: UBC Press.

Raynauld, V., Richez, E., & Boudreau, M. K. (2017). Canada is #IdleNoMore: Exploring dynamics of Indigenous political and civic protest in the twitter-verse. *Information, Communication & Society, 21*(4), 626–642.

Rohlinger, D., & Bunnage, L. (2017). Did the Tea Party movement fuel the Trump-train? The role of social media in activist persistence and political change in the 21st Century. *Social Media + Society, 3*(2). https://doi.org/10.1177%2F2056305117706786

Rootes, C. (2007). Environmental movements. In D. Snow, S. A. Soule, & H. Kriesi (Eds.), *Blackwell companion to social movements* (pp. 608–640). Oxford: Blackwell Publishing.

Sarkodie, S. A., & Strezov, V. (2019). Economic, social and governance adaptation readiness for mitigation of climate change vulnerability: Evidence from 192 countries. *Science of the Total Environment, 656*, 150–164.

Scherman, A., Arriagada, A., & Valenzuela, S. (2015). Student and environmental protests in Chile: The role of social media. *Politics, 35*(2), 151–171.

Sloam, J. (2016). Diversity and voice: The political participation of young people in the European Union. *British Journal of Politics & International Relations, 18*(3), 521–537.

Theocharis, Y. (2012). Cuts, tweets, solidarity and mobilisation: How the internet shaped the student occupations. *Parliamentary Affairs, 65*(1), 162–194.

Theocharis, Y., Lowe, W., van Deth, J. W., & Garcia-Albacete, G. (2015). Using Twitter to mobilize protest action: Online mobilization pattern and action repertoires in the Occupy Wall Street, Indignados, and Aganaktismenoi movements. *Information, Communication & Society, 18*(2), 202–220.

Thorson, K. (2014). Facing an uncertain reception: Young citizens and political interaction on Facebook. *Information, Communication & Society, 17*(2), 203–216.

Thorson, K., Edgerly, S., Kligler-Vilenchik, N., Xu, Y., & Wang, L. (2016). Seeking visibility in a big tent: Digital communication and the people's climate march. *International Journal of Communication, 10*, 4784–4806.

Tobler, C., Visschers, V. H. M., & Siegrist, M. (2012). Consumers' knowledge about climate change. *Climatic Change, 114*(2), 189–209.

Vromen, A., Loader, B. D., Xenos, M. A., & Bailo, F. (2016). Everyday making through Facebook engagement: Young citizens' political interactions in Australia, the United Kingdom and the United States. *Political Studies, 64*(3), 513–533.

About the Authors

Shelley Boulianne is an associate professor in sociology at MacEwan University, Canada. She earned her PhD in sociology from the University of Wisconsin-Madison. She conducts research on media use and public opinion, as well as civic and political engagement, using meta-analysis techniques, experiments, and surveys. She has published in many journals, including *New Media & Society, Information, Communication & Society, Political Communication*, and *Communication Research*.

Mireille Lalancette is full professor of political communication at Université du Québec à Trois-Rivières. She conducts research on social media and political actors from politicians to interest groups and citizens. She is interested in mediatization of politics as well as gender and politics questions. She is also the editor of *What's #Trending in Canadian Politics? Understanding Transformations in Power, Media, and the Public Sphere* (Vancouver: UBC Press, with V. Raynauld and E. Crandall). Her work has been published in Canadian and international research publications.

David Ilkiw is an undergraduate student in the honours sociology program at MacEwan University, Canada. His honours thesis explores the formation of collective memory in news publications.

Reading Questions

1. Why is social media important for social movements? In what contexts is it most important?

2. What are the different kinds of tweets that the researchers found online? What different purposes do they serve for the movement?

3. How is social media important for the environmental movement? Is this related to the international character of this movement? How might these findings be applied to other movements or settings?

Boulianne, S., Lalancette, M., & Ilkiw, D. (2020). "School Strike 4 Climate": Social media and the international youth protest on climate change. *Media and Communication, 8*(2), 208–218. https://doi.org/10.17645/mac.v8i2.2768

This article is part of the issue "Youth Digital Participation: Opportunities, Challenges, Contexts, and What's at Stake" edited by Neta Kligler-Vilenchik (Hebrew University of Jerusalem, Israel) and Ioana Literat (Teachers College, Columbia University, USA).

The Collective Action Problem

Early work on social movements argued that participation is irrational. If you think about the costs and benefits of participating, it is clear that the former are relatively high and the latter relatively low. The costs of participating include finding information about a cause, a group involved in that cause, and an event that the group is putting on. In addition, you need to spend the time and energy to go to the protest event, sign the petition, or boycott the product. All these activities are costly in terms of time and energy. If you believe that there is a relatively small chance that you will help the group be successful, perhaps it does not make sense to participate in social movements.

This sort of reasoning is very familiar. Everyone has heard the argument that people do not vote because they believe that it will not make a difference. Even if they care about the cause, people might not go to a protest because they think that their individual participation will not contribute to the group's success. This perspective, first articulated by Mancur Olson (1965), is called the collective action problem (free-rider problem). Olson argued that people tend to avoid participating in collective action (e.g., social movements) because they still benefit from whatever is gained whether or not they contribute to the cause. Therefore, collective action is unlikely to occur even when large groups of people have common interests.

Social movements often fight for public goods, things that are nonexcludable (one person cannot reasonably prevent another from consuming the good) and nonrivalrous (one person's consumption of the good does not affect another's). Clean air is a public good that illustrates the collective action problem. Environmental activists lobby the government to pass laws restricting pollution and they boycott companies that pollute. If these tactics are successful, we will have cleaner air. Once the air is cleaner, I (as an environmental activist) cannot stop you (a free rider) from breathing my clean air, even though you never went to any of my protest events to fight for it. Voting rights is another example of a public good. Once women had the right to vote, all women—those who fought for it and those who did nothing—enjoyed this right.

Olson's argument makes some intuitive sense, but it also poses some important problems. If everyone sat at home and waited for others to push for social change, nothing would ever happen. (You need someone fighting for clean air and voting rights!) Also, if Olson's theory is true, how do we explain all the social movement events and campaigns that have occurred? Are all social movements simply irrational people getting together? The next section considers the variety of reasons why someone might join a social movement.

TRENDS IN SOCIAL MOVEMENT PARTICIPATION

Many people participate in social movements, and they do so in various ways. Some are members of social movement organizations. Others never join groups but go to social movement events, such as protests or marches. Still others simply do things that support social movement causes. For example, composting or biking to school both support the environmental movement.

These different methods of engaging in social movements vary along two main dimensions that have already been introduced: the risk associated with the activity and the cost of engaging (Corrigall-Brown, 2013). Most activism in the United States is not particularly risky. For example, usually there is little danger in attending a peaceful protest or signing a petition. Some American activists do participate in risky activities, such as occupying a building, which can lead to jail time or social stigma. Engaging in social movement activities in other contexts (particularly in nondemocratic countries) can be quite dangerous. Participation can also be more or less costly, in terms of how difficult the activity is for an individual. If you need to travel a far distance or take time away from work or school to engage, the activity has a higher cost than other, easier activities.

Risk and cost are usually related. Signing a petition is both low risk and low cost. Camping out at an anti-pipeline protest for weeks is both risky (in that you could be arrested) and costly (in terms of time and energy). However, quitting your job to volunteer for Greenpeace is costly but not very risky. Attending a protest event in a country that does not permit protest is not very costly (does not take a lot of time) but is extremely risky (could lead to a jail sentence).

Using World Values Survey data, Figure 14.1 compares three social movement activities: protesting, signing a petition, and boycotting a product. Protesting is the most contentious of these activities, although it is legal in all the countries surveyed (the survey does not ask about protest participation in countries where it is illegal, such as in China). Boycotting is the least contentious of the three acts because it requires only that you avoid doing something. For example, if you are concerned with sweatshop labor, you might avoid buying clothing from companies that use sweatshops. If you are an advocate of animal rights, you might avoid buying products from companies that engage in animal testing.

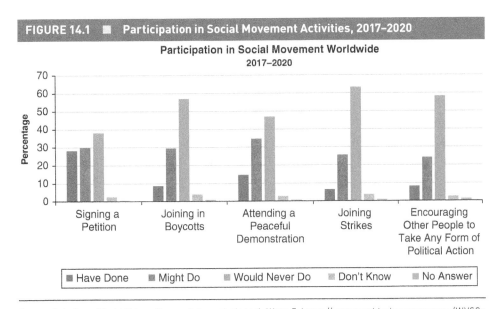

FIGURE 14.1 ■ Participation in Social Movement Activities, 2017–2020

Source: Data from World Values Survey data analysis tool, Wave 7. https://www.worldvaluessurvey.org/WVSOnline.jsp.

You can see from Figure 14.1 that people are more likely to sign a petition or boycott a product than attend a protest event. And, they are also usually more apt to sign a petition than boycott a product. This is partly because signing a petition is a one-time activity while boycotting requires a sustained commitment not to buy something.

Americans are active in social movements. However, this is because they are very likely to have signed a petition (70%). Americans are not very likely to engage in protest, with only 17% having done so, compared with a high of 41% in France, 32% in Germany, and 26% in Canada (see Table 14.1).

TABLE 14.1   ■   Participation in Social Movement Activities by Country, 2017–2020

Country	Protested (%)	Signed a Petition (%)	Boycotted a Product (%)
France	40.8	63.7	17.8
Germany	31.7	60.7	10.1
Canada*	26	73	24
Netherlands	15.5	51.4	10.1
Australia	18.8	75.5	16
Nigeria	18.5	7.4	4.5
India*	18.4	13.7	12.9
United States	16.6	59.7	21.1
United Kingdom	16.4	68.4	15.6
Mexico	9.1	11.3	3.2
Zimbabwe	8.6	8.7	9.7
Japan	5.8	50.8	1.8
Turkey	6.5	8.2	4.2

Source: World Values Survey Wave 7 (2017–2020), Online Data Analysis, https://www.worldvaluessurvey.org/WVSOnline.jsp

* Data unavailable for 2017–2020. Values listed here are drawn from World Values Survey, Wave 6 (2010–2014), https://www.worldvaluessurvey.org/WVSOnline.jsp

Over the past 50 years, the character of protest in modern industrial democracies, such as the United States, has changed radically. Since the 1960s and 1970s the frequency of protest events and the levels of individual participation in protest activity have increased (Meyer & Tarrow, 1998). In the United States the percentage of people who have attended a demonstration has increased, from 11% in 1975 to 17% in 2020 (World Values Survey, 2020; see Table 14.1). Over the last quarter of the 20th century, most advanced industrialized democracies saw a rise in protest participation (Inglehart, 1997; Norris, 2002).

Explaining Social Movement Participation

The survival and success of social movements is based on the participation of individuals. What predicts who will participate in a social movement? What leads certain individuals to participate in social movements while others do not? Participation requires four main elements: ideology, resources, biographical availability, and social ties and identity.

Ideology

Individuals need to be committed to the goals of a movement to participate (Klandermans, 1997). However, not all individuals who believe in a cause become activists. Regardless, ideological commitment is important because it makes people at least cognitively available to participate in a movement.

Ideology is also a very significant part of why many people participate in protests. We usually think of a protest as something in which liberals engage. Research supports this argument, showing that those on the left are more apt than those on the right to attend protests (Dalton et al., 2010). However, protest is clearly no longer just for people on the political left. The prominence of conservative movements in the United States has brought people from across the political spectrum into social movements.

Religious ideologies are also important predictors of engagement. Religious beliefs can motivate individuals to come together to create social change. Belonging to and participating in a religious institution can lead individuals to develop social networks, political knowledge, and resources. Such factors make these individuals more prone to join social movements than those not tied to religious institutions (Diani, 2004; McAdam, 1986).

However, ideology alone is not enough to predict engagement. Individuals must also believe that their participation will yield results. This sense of efficacy is the belief that one is capable of the specific behaviors required to produce a desired outcome in a given situation (Gecas, 2000). Individuals who are efficacious are self-confident and believe that they can produce the changes in the world that they desire. Not surprisingly, these individuals are more likely to participate in protest activities (Rosenstone & Hansen, 1993).

Resources

Along with ideologies, individuals must have the resources that enable them to engage in social movements. For example, individuals with more money are much more apt to protest than people with less money. This difference is not because those with more money believe more strongly in social movement goals but because money helps individuals to translate their beliefs into action. The importance of resources was first highlighted in resource mobilization theory.

SES is one of the most important predictors of an individual's propensity to protest (Verba et al., 1995). Individuals with high SES tend to have other resources, such as free time and certain skills that enable them to participate in social movements. As a result, they are more likely than other people to engage in groups of all kinds, including social movement organizations (see also Rosenstone & Hansen, 1993).

Other nonfinancial resources, such as education and political knowledge, also predict engagement (Wilkes, 2004). Putnam's (2000) work on political participation and general group membership finds that political knowledge is a "critical precondition for active forms of participation" (p. 35) and that those who know more about politics are more disposed to engage in protest.

Biographical Availability

When individuals have biographical availability to participate in social movements, they have the opportunity to convert their ideology and resources into action (Beyerlein & Hipp, 2006). Life changes make some individuals more available and others less available to participate. For example, if you are married or have children, you might be less inclined to attend protests because you have less free time to engage, and you might be more fearful of the risks of participation (McAdam, 1986, p. 70). Students are often considered particularly biographically available because many do not have spouses, children, full-time jobs, or other constraints on their time (Wiltfang & McAdam, 1991). Older people are also frequently biographically available because they are usually retired and do not have children living at home (Nepstad & Smith, 1999).

Social Ties and Identity

Having social ties to other activists is another central component of participating in social movements. If you have many close friends who are active in social movements, you are much more likely to join (McAdam, 1986).

One of the main reasons that social ties are so important is that they can help create identities that facilitate and encourage social movement engagement. Identities are the names that people give to themselves and others in the course of social interaction (Snow, 2001). Some sociologists argue that a collective identity, a sense of "we-ness" that comes from shared attributes or experiences among a group (Melucci et al., 1989), is a prerequisite for collective action (Klandermans & de Weerd, 2000). By participating in social movements, individuals begin to change their identities, sometimes adopting an activist identity (Taylor & Raeburn, 1995).

Political Context/Critical Events

Social movement participation is also shaped by the context in which it happens. Some contexts are more facilitative to the growth of social movement mobilization than others. The importance of political context was first highlighted in political process theory. These facilitative contexts are called free spaces; they are the small-scale settings within a community or movement that are removed from the direct control of dominant groups, are voluntary, and generate the cultural challenge that precedes or accompanies political mobilization (Polletta, 1999). These free spaces protect activists from those in power who might oppose them. Student lounges, union halls, and neighborhood groups are examples of free spaces (Fantasia & Hirsch, 1995). In his research on Beijing's pro-democracy student movement, Zhao (1999) conducted 70 interviews with student activists. He found that free spaces were critical to the movement's success. Universities acted as safe places that allowed students to meet and organize. More recent work focuses on how online venues can be free spaces where individuals and groups can organize anonymously and away from public view. However, in countries where the government monitors or censors the Internet, online venues do not provide free spaces.

Consequences of Participation

Participating in a social movement or protest activities can have long-term transformative effects for individuals. A group of studies (e.g., Whalen & Flacks, 1989) that interviewed people who were active in the social movements of the 1960s found that participating in protest had important consequences for the later lives of individuals. Activists tended to maintain the same ideology over the course of their lives and to remain politically active. There were many interesting personal consequences to their participation as well. Former activists are concentrated in teaching and other helping professions; have lower incomes; are more likely to have divorced, married later, or remained single; and are more apt to have experienced an episodic or nontraditional work history than nonactivists (Giugni, 2004).

Methods in Depth: How Can Activism Change You?

Social movements can have important implications for society. They can change laws or policies, alter the culture of a society, and change the nature of communities. Engagement can also change the activists themselves. However, studying *how* one might (or might not) be changed by activism is difficult. Simply asking someone whether they are different after engaging would not work well for several reasons. First, it is often difficult to remember with clarity how you were before you did something, such as participated in activism. In addition, change can happen slowly and be hard to notice. Finally, how are we to know what we would have been like without experiences of activism? If I work as a social worker later in life, how can I know whether this career choice is a result of my activism or simply the job I would have had with or without engaging?

Doug McAdam (1988) examined these questions in his study of Freedom Summer, a critical campaign in the civil rights movement. In the summer of 1964, a group of mostly White college students traveled from elite universities in the North to Mississippi to work with the Congress of Racial Equality and the Student Non-Violent Coordinating Committee (SNCC) on two projects. First, they registered African Americans to vote. Although voting was, of course, legal for African Americans at the time, voting rates among Blacks in Mississippi were very low. There was intense and violent voter suppression and it was very risky for African Americans to register to vote or go to the polls. And, even if they did so, their votes were often not counted for arbitrary and racist reasons. Second, the volunteers worked in Freedom Schools, which were schools that helped to address the massive inequality in spending and facilities for White and Black students in the state. By all accounts, this was a transformative experience for the volunteers. They experienced massive levels of violence and aggression from law enforcement and many Whites in Mississippi. At the same time, they met and developed intense friendships with fellow volunteers and the Black community; many say those friendships transformed their lives.

The challenge is how to compare people who were involved in activism with those who were not. If we simply look at how the volunteers who were involved in Freedom Summer differed before and after engagement, we cannot know for sure that the volunteering is what changed them. This was also a time of massive social change in American society. If our volunteers became more liberal in their ideology, was this because of Freedom Summer or just the general change at the time that was altering many young people's ideologies?

Methodology

To make a more systematic comparison, one would need to find people who were similar to the volunteers before engagement but who did not have the experience of Freedom Summer. McAdam (1988) had been doing archival research for an earlier book and was looking through documents on the U.S. civil rights movements in libraries and archives when he came across a surprising discovery—the original five-page applications to the Freedom Summer project filled out before volunteers went to Mississippi. And, most important, these applications included both the people who went to Mississippi to volunteer as well as 300 people who applied to the program and were accepted, but did not end up going for various reasons (a group he calls "no-shows"). These data created a natural experiment—McAdam could compare the volunteers with those who were similar before the summer but did not volunteer. This would allow him to see how volunteering for the summer in the civil rights movement shaped the lives of those who participated.

McAdam sought to follow up with the volunteers and the no-shows to see how activism had (or had not) shaped their lives. It is very difficult to find people 20 years after they leave university. McAdam had two primary ways of locating the applicants. First, applicants had to list their university on the form. McAdam then went to the alumni organizations of each university to find people after graduation. This method enabled McAdam to locate 49% of the applicants. Second, applicants had to list the name and address of their parents on the application. McAdam was able to locate an additional 11% of applicants through their parents. He used a variety of other ways to contact the remaining applicants, including asking people for their friends' addresses (also listed on the application). In total, he was able to contact 73% of the no-shows and 53% of the volunteers 20 years after Freedom Summer.

McAdam sent a survey to all the volunteers and no-shows. The survey data enabled him to say, in a more representative way, how the volunteers and no-shows differed over time. He also interviewed 80 people (40 volunteers and 40 no-shows). The interviews enabled him to understand how engagement in activism changed individuals. As he explains in the foreword to his book, after the interviews

> I came away with a much clearer sense of what Freedom Summer had meant to the volunteers and how it had shaped their lives in ways that clearly distinguished them from the no-shows. The somewhat superficial differences between the two groups that had been apparent in their questionnaire responses came alive in conversation. (McAdam, 1988, pp. 9–10)

Implications

This research demonstrates how engagement in Freedom Summer had transformative effects for the volunteers. It shifted their ideologies and opened their eyes to racial discrimination and inequality. It also shaped their later life choices. For example, many more of the volunteers chose professions that were linked to their overarching interest in social justice—such as working as social workers, teachers, or in the law. These activists were also the foundation for a whole set of movements that came in the 1970s and 1980s, including the women's movement, antiwar movements, the free speech movement, and others. This work highlights the ways that engaging in activism can change both individuals and society.

THE MEDIA AND SOCIAL MOVEMENTS

Most of what we learn about social movement causes and campaigns comes from the media, which frames the work of movements and activists. Frames are ways of interpreting the world that enable individuals to understand and label occurrences in their daily lives. There are simply too many things happening in the world: We need frames to condense the world into a smaller set of ideas designed to attract and mobilize potential participants. The process of framing is about selecting certain parts of the world to emphasize and others to deemphasize. Think of a photograph. When you take a picture, you capture some of what is happening, but some elements are left out. In the same way, a frame focuses on some aspects of reality to promote an interpretation of an event or issue. Activists use frames to inspire and legitimate social movement activity. The media might pick up these frames and make them available to the public.

Frames have three key parts: diagnostic, prognostic, and motivational. First, social movement and activists diagnose the problem. In terms of the environmental movement, a group could argue that environmental problems are the result of weak laws that do not prevent or restrict pollution. Second, a social movement tries to propose a solution to the problem. If we think that the government's environmental laws are too weak, the prognosis is that we should lobby the government to pass firmer legislation. Third, social movement activists encourage individuals to do something to solve the problem. Perhaps we should start a petition, go to a protest event in Washington, DC, or create a Facebook page for environmental protection. A different group might argue that individual consumers cause environmental problems by buying too much stuff and using too many resources (diagnosis). It might suggest that consumers should buy less or recycle/reduce/reuse (prognosis) and campaign to encourage recycling (motivation). Even though both groups are interested in protecting the environment, their different diagnostic frames lead to different solutions and calls to action.

Selection and Description Bias

One way for the public to be exposed to social movements' frames is by attending their events or going to social movement organizations' websites. We can also learn of social movement activities and causes through media coverage of protests and campaigns. Because so many events occur every day, the media must select which are the most important to cover. Many social movement groups stage events that receive no coverage at all.

Black Lives Matter supporters rally to bring attention to police brutality against the Black community.

Elsa/Getty Images

Protesters attended a rally at the White House on January 6, 2021 in an attempt to overturn the results of the U.S. presidential election.

Samuel Corum/Getty Images

Media editors must pick a limited number of events to observe and report because there is only so much space in the paper, on the website, or in the broadcast. Selection bias involves media editors' choices of a small number of protest events from a much larger pool. Media agendas can influence this selection, independent of an event's characteristics. Apart from event size, objective matters such as the form of the protest or its timing will determine whether an event is reported in the mass media (Smith et al., 2001).

Events are more likely to be reported if their substantive focus can be used to illustrate an issue that is already on the media's radar. A group concerned with gun control has a better chance of getting media attention after a large-scale incident of gun violence. Such issue attention cycles are the specific times when the public is more apt to become concerned about a problem and attempt to solve it. Once the public realizes the cost of addressing a problem, however, enthusiasm for solutions often dampens. Eventually, the decline in public interest is followed by (as Staggenborg says) a post-problem phase.

Once a group has secured media coverage (which is no small feat), activists become concerned with description bias, or how they and their actions are depicted. We can make sense of how the media selects what to cover and how they frame that coverage in a variety of ways. These explanations are generally based on either organizational or ideological models (Smith et al., 2001).

The Organizational Models of the Media

From the perspective of organizational models of media coverage, the media act as gatekeepers. These gatekeepers do not just choose the most important events to cover. Instead, they also give more coverage to events that are seen to be changing. For example, in the last chapter we learned about the very serious problem of child poverty in the United States. Attracting coverage for this issue is difficult because it is relatively stagnant over time (i.e., the rates remain high and unchanging). Why would the media cover child poverty today or tomorrow instead of something that is considered more current? For social movement activists to get this issue covered, they must connect it to some event or matter that is seen to be increasing, spreading, or intensifying to make it sufficiently interesting. A UN report stating that child poverty in the United States is higher than most other Western countries or a story of a particular child and his plight can capture the public's interest and therefore draw media attention to the larger issue.

Economics also shape what is covered in the media. Newspapers, television stations, and news websites are experiencing budget cuts. Consequently, editors tend to favor generalist reporters rather than specialists. Generalists can write a story on transit today, education tomorrow, and health the next day, which eliminates the need to have a different reporter (who might not have anything to cover on a given day) for each area. Generalists are less expensive and more efficient to hire; however, by their very nature, they do not know as much about each area that they cover because they are required to move from one to another. As a result, they are more reliant on official government sources for information. A reporter who covers a transit strike, the education system, and Department of Motor Vehicles wait lines can call up a government contact and get a quote to include in the article on any of these topics. She is less apt to contact social movement activists or others (such as bus drivers, teachers, or workers) because she lacks contacts in all these different areas. This means that the news is more likely to represent the interests and perspectives of officials and those in power than of challengers.

The organizational perspective does not argue that journalists and editors conspire against coverage of social movements and other critical groups. Reporters and editors want to get the best and most accurate story out to the public. The structure and organization of news collection simply makes it so that reporters write and editors choose stories that tend to support the status quo and undermine activists.

The Ideological Model of Media Coverage

The ideological model of media coverage argues that there is a more concerted effort on the part of the media, political, and corporate elites to control the information in the news. This model says that broader structures of power relations in society affect the portrayal of social movements and protest. Such structures lead to increased privatization, commercialization, and concentration of ownership, which severely limits the range of ideas conveyed in the media (see Chapter 7).

The media profits from selling advertising; therefore, it tends to cover issues that will get the most attention, regardless of their importance. Articles about Kim Kardashian or Jennifer Lopez dating someone new are not really important, but they attract many readers. As a result, the news outlet can charge more for advertisements. Publishing sensational stories to draw the public's attention is also the basis of the saying, "If it bleeds, it leads." News coverage of crime often focuses on particularly gruesome murders. Such articles frequently appear on the front page or as the top item on a broadcast or website and include dramatic photographs of the accused killer or innocent victim. Even though the overall crime rate in the United States is declining, coverage that emphasizes these dramatic crimes is selected because it attracts attention and makes money for the news outlet.

Because of the importance of advertising revenue, journalists must be very aware of advertisers' interests. Thus, from the perspective of the ideological model, the media works to reproduce broader power relationships. For example, it tends to focus on individual responsibility for social problems and neglect social causes. Instead of reporting on the overall reasons that crime rates are higher in some areas or groups, the media tends to center on one individual criminal or victim. This approach encourages a shallow understanding of these issues and discourages the critical engagement of audiences.

As our discussion has indicated, media framing is important because the media plays a powerful role in educating the public about social issues. It sends signals about who is legitimate and sympathetic and to whom we should listen. Consequently, the media can affect public opinion and government policy. In terms of social movements, the media coverage of protests generally tends to be limited and, when it does occur, negative. These findings are consistent with both the organizational and ideological perspectives: the media tends to emphasize the views of officials at the expense of those of activists and other challengers. It also tends to center on individual-level explanations instead of the social explanations most movements try to convey. In addition, because the media tries to attract attention and emphasize drama to increase circulation and revenue, they tend to focus on the violence, the drama, and the unusual at a protest event. The specific way that the media tends to cover protest events is known as the protest paradigm (McLeod & Hertog, 1999). Together, these elements lead to the delegitimization, marginalization, and even demonization of protesters.

USING YOUR SOCIOLOGICAL IMAGINATION
MEDIA IMAGES OF PROTEST

To see how the media depicts protest events, let's look at two examples: Black Lives Matter and the Women's Marches of 2017. Donald Trump was inaugurated on January 20, 2017. The very next day, activists came together in at least 408 marches to express their unhappiness with the new president and his agenda (Women's March, 2017). These marches were unprecedented in size, bringing together between 3.3 and 5.3 million people across the United States, or about 1.0 to 1.6% of the U.S. population (Chenoweth, 2017). Allied marches took place in at least 168 events outside of the United States, bringing an additional

2 to 3 million participants to the cause (Women's March, 2017). And, although these events were predominantly populated by women, they brought together a wide diversity of activists interested in a variety of issues, including women's rights, reproductive rights, immigrant rights, civil rights, LGBTQ rights, the environment, government accountability, workers' rights, and more. Go online and find images of the Women's Marches.

1. How do the images represent the protesters? Do the photos reflect a positive or negative view of this group? How is the relationship between protesters and police or other authorities shown?
2. Why would these images have been selected for publication? Answer this question using the organizational model and then the ideological model.

Black Lives Matter is an activist movement resisting violence and systemic racism toward Black people. It was started in 2013, after the acquittal of George Zimmerman in the shooting death of Black teen Trayvon Martin. Trayvon was an unarmed 17-year-old walking home when Zimmerman shot and killed him. The hashtag #BlackLivesMatter was first used after Zimmerman's acquittal but gained further prominence following the deaths of two more young Black men, Michael Brown in Ferguson, Missouri and Eric Garner in New York City. The movement has held many protest events across the country and around the world. Black Lives Matter has expanded over time into a national organization with more than 30 chapters. This movement works to affirm the humanity, contributions, and resilience of the Black community.

1. Look online for images of the Black Lives Matter protests. How are the protesters depicted in these images? How are officials depicted (if they are shown)?
2. Why were these images selected? How do they relate to the organizational or ideological theories of the media? Do these images support or challenge the idea of the protest paradigm?
3. Are the depictions of protesters and officials the same or different than they were for the Women's Marches? If so, why?

SUCCESS IN SOCIAL MOVEMENTS

Social movement groups often call for large-scale social changes. A women's group that calls for equality between the sexes will find that it is difficult to achieve the goal. How can full equality be attained? If men and women make the same salaries, is that equality? What about access to education or depictions in the media? When groups have large and broad goals, it is frequently difficult to determine whether they have been successful. Moreover, groups with a variety of goals tend to achieve only some of those goals.

Another reason that it is difficult to measure success is that politicians, business leaders, and others in power are often reluctant to admit being influenced by social movement groups. Leaders might believe that doing so makes them seem weak and easily swayed by public opinion. They often do not want to encourage more protests or campaigns. It is certainly more difficult to govern a very active and engaged population than one that sits at home and only comes out to vote once every 4 years. With these issues in mind, how can we measure social movement success?

William Gamson (1990) has created a typology of outcomes for social movements. He examines two markers of social movement success. First, groups are looking for acceptance and to be seen as a valid spokesperson for a legitimate set of concerns. Second, groups are looking for new advantages like laws, policies, or other gains. We can see that these two dimensions may overlap, but this is not always the case. In fact, when we combine these two dimensions, we arrive at four distinct outcomes.

If a group gets full acceptance and many new advantages, this is full response. This is exactly what a challenger wants—to be seen as a legitimate spokesperson and to get the law or policy that you want. The other end of the spectrum is when you get no acceptance or new advantages. In this situation, your group is in collapse—you have not won anything and may not survive as a group. The final two combinations are more complex. If you get full acceptance but no new advantages, this could be a case of cooptation. Perhaps the government senses that public opinion is on your side, so they allow your group to sit on government boards without giving your group the policies or laws they seek. Or, if there is no acceptance but many new advantages, this could be a case of preemption. The government could quickly respond to your policy requests but undermine the existence of your group (Gamson, 1990). Measuring social movement success is a challenge because all these outcomes are ideal types: No group will fall neatly into any of these boxes. However, this work highlights the complex factors involved in measuring whether social movements have won.

Getting to Know: William Gamson (1934–2021)

- Gamson contracted scarlet fever at age 6 or 7 and had to remain at home for six months, during which his passion for making games developed.

- He organized and led what is believed to be the first anti-Vietnam War teach-in while a professor at the University of Michigan in 1965.

- Gamson organized faculty and led a hunger strike in protest of the University of Michigan's involvement in military research.

- He co-created The Global Justice Game, which is a seven-module game intended to train activists and teach undergraduates about globalization issues.

- He was president of the American Sociological Association in 1994.

- He was a recipient of the American Sociological Association's W.E.B Du Bois Career of Distinguished Scholarship Award in 2012.

READING: "THE MEANING OF SUCCESS FROM THE STRATEGY OF SOCIAL PROTEST"

William Gamson

In order to think more systematically about social movement success, William Gamson has created a typology of the outcomes of social movements. Read this classic piece and consider what it takes to be successful as a social movement. Have recent movements, such as Black Lives Matter, Me Too, anti-mask rallies, rallies against the war in the Ukraine, or protests in support of gun control measures, been successful?

Success is an elusive idea. What of the group whose leaders are honored or rewarded while their supposed beneficiaries linger in the same cheerless state as before? Is such a group more or less successful than another challenger whose leaders are vilified and imprisoned even as their program is eagerly implemented by their oppressor? Is a group a failure if it collapses with no legacy save inspiration to a generation that will soon take up the same cause with more tangible results? And what do we conclude about a group that accomplishes exactly what it set out to achieve and then finds its victory empty of real meaning for its presumed beneficiaries? Finally, we must add to these questions the further complications of groups with multiple antagonists and multiple areas of concern. They may achieve some results with some targets and little or nothing with others.

It is useful to think of success as a set of outcomes, recognizing that a given challenging group may receive different scores on equally valid, different measures of outcome. These outcomes fall into two basic clusters: one concerned with the fate of the challenging group as an organization and one with the distribution of new advantages to the group's beneficiary. The central issue in the first cluster focuses on the acceptance of a challenging group by its antagonists as a valid spokesman for a legitimate set of interests. The central issue in the second cluster focuses on whether the group's beneficiary gains new advantages during the challenge and its aftermath.

Both of these outcome clusters require elaboration, but, for the moment, consider each as if it were a single, dichotomous variable. Assume a group that has a single antagonist and a single act which they wish this antagonist to perform—for example, a reform group which desires a particular piece of national legislation. We ask of such a group, did its antagonist accept it as a valid spokesman for the constituency that it was attempting to mobilize or did it deny such acceptance? Secondly, did the group gain the advantages it sought—for example, the passage of the legislation that it desired?

By combining these two questions, as in Table 14.2, we acquire four possible outcomes: full response, co-optation, preemption, and collapse. The full response and collapse categories are relatively unambiguous successes and failures—in the one case the achievement of both acceptance and new advantages, in the other, the achievement of neither. The remainder are mixed categories: co-optation is the term used for acceptance without new advantages and preemption for new advantages without acceptance.

TABLE 14.2 ■ Outcome of Resolved Challenges			
		Acceptance	
		Full	None
New Advantages	Many	Full response	Preemption
	None	Co-optation	Collapse

Table 14.2 is the paradigm for handling outcomes of challenging groups, but it requires additional complexity before it can be used to handle as diverse a set of groups as the 53 represented here. Acceptance must be given a special meaning for revolutionary groups, for example, which seek not a nod of recognition from an antagonist but its destruction and replacement. Similarly, new "advantages" are not always easy to define. We must deal with cases in which a group seeks, for example, relatively intangible value changes, shifts in the scope of authority, or a change in procedures as well as the simpler case of material benefits for a well-defined group.

The Endpoint of a Challenge

The outcome measures used refer to "ultimate" outcome, to the state of the group at the end of its challenge. A given group might achieve significant new advantages at one point without receiving acceptance, but we would not consider that preemption had occurred as long as it continued to press an active challenge. Only when it eventually collapsed or ceased activity would we classify its outcome as preemption. Or, if it eventually won acceptance, its outcome would be full response instead. Similarly, the new advantages might be withdrawn and the group brutally crushed, making "collapse" the appropriate outcome. Thus, during its period of challenge, a group might appear to be in one or another cell of the figure at different times, but the outcome measures only consider its location at the end.

A challenge period is considered over when one of the following occurs:

1. The challenging group ceases to exist as a formal entity. It may officially dissolve, declaring itself no longer in existence. Or, it may merge with another group, ceasing to maintain a separate identity. Note, however, that a group does not cease to exist by merely changing its name to refurbish its public image. Operationally, we consider that two names represent the same challenging group if and only if:

    a. The major goals, purposes, and functions of the two groups are the same.
    b. The constituency remains the same.
    c. The average challenging group member and potential member would agree that the new-name group is essentially the old group relabelled.

2. The challenging group, while not formally dissolving, ceases mobilization and influence activity. A five-year period of inactivity is considered sufficient to specify the end of the challenge. If, after such a dormant period, the group becomes active again, it is considered a new challenging group in spite of its organizational continuity with the old challenger. This occurred, in fact, with two of the 53 challengers in the sample. In each case the period of dormancy was quite a bit longer than the required five years, and, in one case, the geographical location of activity was different as well.

Marking the end of a challenge is more difficult with groups that continue to exist and be active. The line between being a challenging group and an established interest group is not always sharp. The essential difference lies in how institutionalized a conflict relationship exists between the group and its antagonists. When this conflict becomes regulated and waged under some standard operating procedures, the challenge period is over. Operationally, this can be dated from the point at which the group is accepted. Hence, for continuing groups, the challenge period is over when:

3. The challenging group's major antagonists accept the group as a valid spokesman for its constituency and deal with it as such. In the case of unions, this is indicated by formal recognition of the union as a bargaining agent for the employees. In other cases, the act of acceptance is less clear, and, even in the case of unions, different companies extend recognition at different times. Issues such as these are dealt with in the discussion of measures of acceptance below.

With continuing groups, then, there is some inevitable arbitrariness in dating the end of a challenge. The compiler was instructed to err, in ambiguous cases, on the side of a later date. Thus, where acute conflict continues to exist between the group and important antagonists, the challenge is not considered over even when some other antagonists may have begun to deal with the challenger in a routinized way. Furthermore, by extending the challenge period, we include new benefits that might be excluded by using a premature termination date.

Measuring Outcomes

Acceptance

Did the relationship between the challenging group and its antagonists change from the beginning to the end of the challenge? Although more than 75 percent of the groups here are more complicated, we will begin the discussion of this question with the simplest case of a group with a single antagonist. This antagonist necessarily begins with a relationship of active or passive hostility toward the challenging group or, at best, indifference. Acceptance involves a change from hostility or indifference to a more positive relationship.[1]

There are four indicators of this more positive relationship:

1. Consultation. This must involve some degree of initiative by the antagonist. For example, if a legislative body has opened hearings on a matter of importance to the challenging group, the antagonist might invite representatives of the group to testify. On the other hand, if the group asks to testify and is permitted, this would not by itself be considered

consultation. Similarly, if the antagonist issues a subpoena to force the group to testify, no consultation would be coded because the group is not being treated in such an instance as a legitimate spokesman for a constituency.

2. **Negotiations.** If the antagonist is willing to enter into negotiations with the group on a continuing basis, not simply at the height of a particular crisis, this also implies acceptance of the group as a spokesman for a constituency. To be coded as acceptance, the negotiations must imply that the antagonist is dealing with the challenging group's negotiators as representatives of a constituency. The outcome of the negotiations is not relevant here; the two parties may fail to reach an acceptable settlement. But the mere fact of a continuing negotiating relationship implies acceptance.

3. **Formal recognition.** This form of acceptance is characterized by the antagonist making explicit, typically in writing, that it recognizes the challenging group as a legitimate spokesman for a designated constituency. This is the functional equivalent of diplomatic recognition of a government in international politics. Nothing needs to be implied about general mutuality of interests or approval of the challenging group and its actions.

4. **Inclusion.** This form of acceptance is characterized by the inclusion of challenging group leaders or members in positions of status or authority in the antagonist's organizational structure. It is essential, however, that the included challenging group members maintain their status, formally or informally, as group members. If serving in the antagonist's organization requires repudiating membership in the challenging group as a condition of office, it is not coded as acceptance through inclusion. . . .

New Advantages

Did the potential beneficiaries of the challenging group receive what the group sought for them? No assumption is made that the challenging group necessarily caused the benefits. We asked only whether desired results were forthcoming, for whatever reason, during and immediately after the period of challenge. . . .

How is the achievement of new advantages actually measured? First, consider the simplest case of a group with a single goal or area of concern. Four perceptions of goal achievement were coded: the perception of degree of achievement (1) by historians, (2) by the challenging group, and by its antagonist, and (4) the challenging group's level of satisfaction with its achievement at the end of the challenge. In many cases, we were unable to get sufficient information on one or more of these perceptions, in which case we coded what we could. The codes covered changes both during the period of the challenge and in the following 15 years.[2]

Since many groups had multiple goals and since sources sometimes disagreed on how well the goals were achieved, each group had multiple measures of new advantages. To reduce this complexity for analysis, a summary measure was essential. We ended up using the following four categories:

1. Twenty groups (38 percent) received no new advantages. These groups had minuses and zeroes on all clusters.

2. Twenty-six groups (49 percent) received new advantages. These groups had at least one positive field (i.e., pluses, no more than two zeroes, and no minuses) in a majority of their areas of concern. In other words, on most of their goals, these groups received a positive response on at least one major aspect.

3. Four groups (7 percent) received peripheral advantages. These were groups that had some positive fields but did not meet the full definition of a group receiving new advantages.

4. Three groups (6 percent) received equivocal advantages. These were groups with mixed fields (some pluses and some minuses concerning the same goal). In other words, these were groups on which disagreement existed among different observers on whether goals had been realized or not.

The seven groups in the last two categories will be combined with the no-advantage group for analysis purposes. Table 14.3 shows the distribution of the 53 groups in the four

TABLE 14.3 ■ Outcomes for the Sample of Challenging Groups Based on Summary Measure of Acceptance and New Advantages		Minimal Acceptance Relationship	
		Yes	**No**
New Advantages	Yes	Full response = 20 38%	Preemption = 6 11%
	No (or equivocal and peripheral)	Co-optation = 5 9%	Collapse = 22 42%
		n = 53	

[1]If acceptance existed from the very beginning, the group would not qualify as a challenging group.

[2]Since most groups had multiple goals and multiple areas of concern within each goal cluster, a challenger's goal achievement was covered by a code consisting of many columns. We first broke goals down into specific clusters for separate evaluation. Then, for each cluster, we gave a challenger a plus for each source (that is, an historian, challenging group, or antagonist) who agreed that at least half of the relevant targets had responded in the desired fashion. We recorded a minus when a source asserted that less than half of the targets responded as desired or the group was no more satisfied at the end of the challenge than when it began. If there was insufficient information on the perceptions of one or another source, a zero was recorded.

outcome categories described above. In many analyses, we will examine each summary measure separately as we explore the relative influence of some variable of interest on these different measures of outcome. Henceforth, when I use the term "success," it will refer to either or both outcome measures in those contexts in which there is no need to differentiate between them.

Reading Questions

1. What are the different ways that social movements can achieve success? What is the difference between acceptance and new advantage?
2. Gamson outlines four main outcomes that social movement groups can achieve: full response, cooptation, preemption, and collapse. Explain what he means by each of these terms.
3. According to Gamson, when do social movement challenges end? Is a social movement ever really over?

Gamson, W. (1975). The meaning of social movement success. In *The strategy of social protest*. The Dorsey Press. Reprinted with permission from William Gamson.

PUBLIC SOCIOLOGY AND USING OUR SOCIOLOGICAL IMAGINATION

Recently, there have been calls for sociologists to engage more with the public and to bring sociological ideas to the larger community. Public sociology, a term introduced by Herbert Gans in 1988, uses the sociological imagination to engage with wider audiences outside traditional academic circles. Promoters of public sociology have sought to encourage sociologists to engage with social issues in explicitly public and political ways. This movement uses the theories and findings of sociology in debates about not just what is or what has been in society but also what could be.

USING YOUR SOCIOLOGICAL IMAGINATION
PATRICIA HILL COLLINS AND SOCIAL CHANGE

Patricia Hill Collins, an important feminist scholar, has long been concerned with her work's impact on different communities of people. She and many other sociologists hope that their work and a sociological understanding of the world can be used to improve society. Collins (2013) discusses intellectual activism and how it can help us use our sociological imagination to improve society and the lives of individuals. This idea is similar to public sociology. She argues that, as sociologists, we should both speak truth to power and speak truth to people. The former uses the power of ideas to confront existing power relations in order to change the foundations of social hierarchy—the less powerful take on the ideas and practices of the powerful and often are armed solely with their ideas. The latter means talking to the masses and is based on the idea that sociologists should communicate how sociological knowledge can help improve individuals' daily lives (Collins, 2013).

Think about the things that we have learned in this book and in your sociology class.

1. How can sociology students engage in these activities? Is it possible to be a public sociology student? Why or why not?
2. Take one of the main theories or research findings that you have learned in this book. How could you use this information to engage in public sociology?
3. Who would you want to know about your public sociology research? How would you try to get this information to them? How could it create social change and a more equitable world?

SUMMARY

In this final chapter, we have examined social change as it can occur through social movements. We began by learning about the core features of social movements. The collective action problem helped us to understand why we might not expect individuals to engage in social movements. Despite this problem, American participation is relatively high and is increasing. Therefore, it is important to know why some individuals take part in protest and social movement events. We discussed the media's importance in social movements, particularly regarding issues of selection and description bias. We also considered how to measure success for social movements. We ended this chapter, and this book, by thinking about public sociology and intellectual activism.

FOR FURTHER READING

Klandermans, B. (1997). *The social psychology of protest*, Blackwell.

McAdam, D. (1988). *Freedom summer*, Oxford University Press.

McCarthy, J., & Zald, M. (1973). *The trend of social movements in America: Professionalization and resource mobilization*, General Learning Press.

Meyer, D. S., & Tarrow, S (Eds.). (1998). *The social movement society: Contentious politics for a new century.* Rowman and Littlefield.

Staggenborg, S., & Ramos, H. (2016). *Social movements* (3rd ed.). Oxford University Press.

GLOSSARY

acceptance

biographical availability

boycotting

collective action problem (free-rider problem)

commitment

conscience constituencies

description bias

efficacy

frames

free spaces

identities

ideological model of media coverage

issue attention cycles

new advantages

organizational models of media coverage

petitions

protest

protest paradigm

public goods

public sociology

selection bias

social movement

worthiness, unity, numbers, and commitment (WUNC)

APPENDIX 1: READINGS IN *IMAGINING SOCIETY*

Original readings by classic sociologists and modern researchers illustrate how concepts and ideas have their origins in the work of our founding sociologists. Most important, the excerpts show how the concepts of our discipline are being applied.

In Vantage, these readings are presented as assignable activities with multiple choice and short answer questions.

Chapter	Topic	Reading	Page	Summary
1	The Sociological Imagination	*The Sociological Imagination* (C. Wright Mills)		Classic reading in which Mills encourages us to use our sociological imagination by (1) seeing the link between personal troubles and public issues and (2) connecting our personal biography with the history of society.
		"Body Ritual Among Nacirema" (Horace Miner)		Classic reading in which Miner describes the "exotic" behaviors of a group of people who are actually just "Americans" (Nacirema backwards is American). This highlights how sociologists should critically examine elements of their own society.
2	Socialization and Social Interaction	"Review of Albert Schaeffle" (Émile Durkheim)		An early article by Durkheim in which he outlines the core of his theory of society, focusing on how society is more than just a collection of individuals and how society can shape the individuals within it.
		The Presentation of Self (Erving Goffman)		Classic reading in which Goffman outlines his dramaturgical model for understanding social interaction by comparing it to acting in a play.
3	Deviance, Law, and Crime	"On Being Sane in Insane Places" (D. L. Rosenhan)		Classic study of labeling theory. Non-mentally ill people check themselves into a mental institution and then see how long it takes for them to be released as "healthy." This takes a surprising length of time and illustrates the power of labeling.
		"The Body of the Condemned" (Michel Foucault)		This excerpt from the classic book by Foucault examines how our ideas of punishment have evolved. Early punishment focused on the body (through physical torture) and modern punishments, which are no less inhumane, focus on punishing the mind or soul (through solitary confinement).

(Continued)

(*Continued*)

Chapter	Topic	Reading	Page	Summary
4	Social Stratification and Social Class	"Manifesto of the Communist Party" (Karl Marx and Friedrich Engels)		Classic Marx and Engels reading that outlines their theory of class conflict and calls for social change.
		Race, Gender, and New Essential Workers During COVID-19 (Nicole Pangborn and Christopher Rea)		In this reading, Pangborn and Rea examine the rise of a new class of essential workers during the COVID-19 pandemic, which include grocery workers and service staff. They examine what types of workers can work at home or must interact with the public. Through this analysis, we can see how inequality creates more dangerous and precarious conditions for a new group of workers.
5	Race and Ethnicity	Middle Eastern and North African Americans May Not Be Perceived, nor Perceive Themselves, to Be White (Neda Magbouleh, Ariel Schachter, and Rene Flores)		This article assesses how people understand their ethnicity, focusing particularly on how those with Middle Eastern and North African (MENA) backgrounds categorize themselves and are categorized by others. These processes shine a light on the social construction of racial and ethnic categories and how they can be contested over time and across groups.
		Imagined Communities (Benedict Anderson)		A classic reading that outlines how nations are imagined communities—too large for us to know one another but connected by larger ideologies and feelings of communion.
6	Gender at the Intersections	"Brilliant or Bad": The Gendered Social Construction of Exceptionalism in Early Adolescence (Michela Musto)		In this article, Musto examines how young people from different racial, ethnic, and gender backgrounds are engaged with in the classroom. Through assessing how "disruptive" students from different backgrounds are rewarded or punished for this behavior, we can see one way whereby inequality is created and reinforced in the education system.
		The Invention of Heterosexuality (Jonathan Ned Katz)		A historical analysis that unpacks the concept of heterosexuality and shows that we have not always identified gender and sexuality in the same ways we do today. This article also examines how larger social changes, such as wars, depressions, and political upheavals, change our ideas of "normal" and "healthy" sexuality.

Chapter	Topic	Reading	Page	Summary
7	Language, Media, and Culture	*The Power Elite* (C. Wright Mills)		A classic reading in which Mills outlines how a set of individuals, the power elite, come together from multiple institutions in society and share similar interests and ideologies.
		Social Media in Society: A Positive or Negative Force? (Tom Chiang, Jr.)		This article examines the role of social media in society and assesses its benefits for society as well as its negative consequences for both individuals and social groups.
8	The Family and Intimate Relationships	*Getting Married: The Public Nature of Our Private Relationships* (Carrie Yodanis and Sean Lauer)		Yodanis and Lauer unpack why people marry in modern society. They focus on how many explanations of why we marry are now very individualistic, focusing on the needs and desires of individuals instead of the social group as a whole.
		"One's a Crowd" (Erik Klinenberg)		Klinenberg explores how living alone is a more common phenomenon now than ever before. What are the implications of living alone for individuals and society?
9	Eduation	"A Matter of Degrees" (William Beaver)		Beaver outlines the many functions of education in modern society, such as sorting and selecting people into jobs and credentialing.
		"The Not-So-Pink Ivory Tower" (Ann Mullen)		This article examines gender equity in education and the different outcomes of education for male and female graduates.
10	Work and Rationalization	*The McDonaldization of Society* (George Ritzer)		A classic reading that focuses on how our modern society is being increasingly rationalized (as Weber predicted) by comparing it to the super-rationalized McDonald's.
		"Feeling Management: From Private to Commercial Uses" (Arlie Hochschild)		Hochschild's study of emotional labor in the workforce, particularly looking at emotional labor conducted by flight attendants who not only need to serve meals and keep passengers safe but also display a happy and pleasant facial expression while doing it.

(Continued)

(*Continued*)

Chapter	Topic	Reading	Page	Summary
11	Health	*The Health Gap* (Michael Marmot)		Marmot outlines some of his key studies of health inequality and how larger social determinants of health shape the length and health of the lives we lead.
		"Big Business in the School Cafeteria" (Ivy Ken)		Ivy Ken discusses how school lunch programs have changed over time and how modern school lunch programs are associated with obesity among children. She also offers examples and suggestions of how these issues can be addressed by nonprofit organizations, community members, and governments.
12	Globalization and Global Inequality	"The Uses of Global Poverty: How Economic Inequality Benefits the West" (Daina Stukuls Eglitis)		Eglitis outlines a series of ways in which rich Western countries benefit from global poverty. For example, we can scapegoat poor countries for environmental problems and use their cheap labor to make inexpensive products for Western consumers.
		"The Problem With Fair Trade Coffee" (Nicki Lisa Cole and Keith Brown)		An article that explains fair trade certification as a solution to global poverty, its benefits, and some concerns regarding the practice.
13	Change Through Policy and the Law	"The Case for Reparations" (Ta-Nehisi Coats)		In this article, Coats examines the long history of racial inequality in the United States. This article also engages in the complex debate around the idea of reparations for slavery in the United States.
		"Bowling Alone: America's Declining Social Capital" (Robert D. Putnam)		A classic reading outlining the decline of social capital in modern American society and its causes.
14	Social Movements	"School Strike for Climate": Social Media and the International Youth Protest on Climate Change (Shelley Boulianne, Mireille Lalancette, and David Ilkiw)		An examination of the Youth Protest on Climate Change, particularly the role of social media in mobilizing this movement. The role of youth activists is central to this article and the movement as a whole.
		"The Meaning of Success" (William Gamson)		A classic reading outlining the various ways that social movements can be successful through gaining acceptance and new advantages for their constituents.

APPENDIX 2: METHODS IN *IMAGINING SOCIETY*

Each chapter introduces students to all the major qualitative and quantitative methods used by sociologists to better understand the family, race, gender, education, health, and other areas.

Method	Section	Reading
Survey	Methods in Depth: Learning Gender From Our Parents—Hillary Paul Halpern & Maureen Perry-Jenkins (Chapter 6)	
	Methods in Depth: Surveying Hookup Culture Among Youths—James-Kangal, Weitbrecht, Trenel, & Whitton (Chapter 8)	
	Methods in Depth: Testing the Self-Fulfilling Prophecy—Sarah Gentrup, et al. (Chapter 9)	
	Methods in Depth: Assessing the Effectiveness of Means-Tested Social Programs—Gulgun Bayaz Ozturk (Chapter 13)	
	Methods in Depth: How Can Activism Change You?—Doug McAdam (Chapter 14)	
Experiment	Prejudice and Discrimination—Muzafer Sherif (Chapter 5)	"On Being Sane in Insane Places" by D. L. Rosenhan (Chapter 3)
	Methods in Depth: Testing the Self-Fulfilling Prophecy—Sarah Gentrup et al. (Chapter 9)	*The Health Gap: The Challenge of An Unequal World* by Michael Marmot (Chapter 11)
	Methods in Depth: Building Consensus for Climate Action in Polarized Societies—Juliette Rooney-Varga et al. (Chapter 12)	
Interviews	Methods in Depth: The Socialization of Women in the Hate Movement—Kathleen Blee (Chapter 2)	"One's a Crowd" by Eric Klinenberg (Chapter 8)
	Methods in Depth: Big Data, Predictive Policing and Surveillance—Sarah Brayne (Chapter 3)	"Brilliant or Bad: The Gendered Social Construction of Exceptionalism in Early Adolescence" by Michela Musto (Chapter 6)
	Methods in Depth: *Women Without Class* by Julie Bettis (Chapter 4)	
	The Kinsey Reports—Alfred Kinsey (Chapter 6)	"Feeling Management: From Private to Commercial Uses" by Arlie Hochschild (Chapter 10)
	Methods in Depth: Testing the Self-Fulfilling Prophecy—Sarah Gentrup et al. (Chapter 9)	
	Methods in Depth: How Can Activism Change You?—Doug McAdam (Chapter 14)	
Participant Observation	Methods in Depth: The Socialization of Women in the Hate Movement—Kathleen Blee (Chapter 2)	"Brilliant or Bad: The Gendered Social Construction of Exceptionalism in Early Adolescence" by Michela Musto (Chapter 6)
	Aging and Socialization—Margaret Mead (Chapter 2)	
	Social Explanations of Deviance and Crime—Elijah Anderson (Chapter 3)	
	Methods in Depth: Big Data, Predictive Policing and Surveillance—Sarah Brayne (Chapter 3)	
	Methods in Depth: *Women Without Class* by Julie Bettis (Chapter 4)	

(Continued)

(*Continued*)

Method	Section	Reading
Content Analysis/ Document Analysis	Methods in Depth: The Socialization of Women in the Hate Movement—Kathleen Blee (Chapter 2)	Race, Gender, and New Essential Workers During COVID-19 by Nicole Pangborn and Christopher Rea (Chapter 4)
	Methods in Depth: Racial Stereotypes and Voting—Seth Stephens-Davidowitz (Chapter 5)	"The Not-So-Pink Ivory Tower" by Ann Mullen (Chapter 9)
	Methods in Depth: News Coverage of Refugees—Jennifer Hoewe (Chapter 7)	
	Methods in Depth: Safe Supply, COVID-19, and Overdose Deaths—Thomas Brothers et al. (Chapter 11)	

GLOSSARY

ableism: A term for discrimination against a person with a cognitive or physical disability based on stereotypes about their limitations.

acceptance: According to W. Gamson, a measure of social movement success in which a movement is considered a valid representative for a legitimate set of interests.

achievement-based stratification system: A system that ranks individuals based on their accomplishments.

agents of socialization: The various societal groups that help us learn to become members of society. Examples are family, peer groups, the education system, mass media, and religion.

alienation: Generally, the separation of things that naturally belong together. According to Marx, workers become alienated from the products they make, the process of production, other workers, and themselves.

alternative media: Media that is non-profit, antiestablishment, and creative and is based on a two-way relationship between the producer and the consumer.

anticipatory socialization: The process in which individuals rehearse potential roles that they may take on in the future.

arranged marriage: A marital union in which a third party selects the bride and groom. Arranged marriage was common in certain cultures and areas throughout history and remains so in South Asia, Africa, the Middle East, Latin America, Southeast Asia, and parts of East Asia.

ascription-based stratification system: A system that ranks individuals based on a person's ascribed features (e.g., race or sex).

authoritarian personality: Adorno's term for a personality that is more likely to develop prejudicial attitudes. People with this type of personality tend to see the world in terms of good and evil and strictly follow rules and orders.

automation: The operation of equipment with minimal or reduced human intervention.

biographical availability: A main predictor of social movement engagement. Individuals with fewer responsibilities and constraints, such as young people, students, single people, and those without children, are more likely to have the time, energy, and inclination to engage in contentious political activity.

bourgeoisie (capitalist): One of the two primary classes in Marx's theory. The bourgeoisie are the owners of the means of production.

boycotting: The refusal to buy or use products to punish or protest a company.

breaching experiments: Experiments that intentionally break a social rule or norm to reveal the common work done by individuals to maintain social order in day-to-day life.

bureaucracy: Literally, the rule of the office or desk. Bureaucracy is an organizational form that predominates in modern society and focuses on rationality. Weber described bureaucracies as human machines.

cash crops: Crops that are sold for profit. This type of agriculture contrasts with subsistence farming, in which farmers grow crops for their own consumption.

census: The systematic collecting and recording of information about members of a given population.

chronic disease prevalence: A measure of the health of a population that assesses how common chronic diseases are within a group.

civic engagement: The individual and collective actions designed to identify and address issues of public concern. The decline of civic engagement is the core concern of Robert D. Putnam's work.

civicness: Putnam's term for the values, norms, institutions, and associations that allow and foster civic commitment, solidarity, mutual trust, and tolerance.

class consciousness: An awareness of what is in the best interests of one's class. Marx argued that this awareness is an important precondition for organizing into a class for itself and advocating for class interests.

classes: Groups of people who play different roles in the production system.

class struggle: The conflict between those who own the means of production (bourgeoisie) and those who own only their labor power (workers).

cohabitate: The state of a heterosexual or homosexual couple living together and having a sexual relationship without being legally married.

collective action problem (free-rider problem): The idea, posited by Olson, that people tend to avoid participating in collective action (e.g., social movements) because they will benefit from whatever is gained whether or not they contribute to the cause.

commitment: Being dedicated to a cause or activity.

commodification: The process of reducing social relations to an exchange relationship (i.e., assigning them with a monetary value).

commodity: An item of value and uniform quality produced in large quantities by many producers. Consumer goods, such as clothing, cars, and food, are commodities.

companionate marriage: A marriage based on the satisfaction of the couple, the family, and the different roles each person plays in the family. Companionate marriages include a clear division of labor between the breadwinner (usually the husband) and the homemaker (usually the wife). Husbands and wives are seen as friends and confidants who need and rely on one another to perform the roles that the other cannot.

conflict theory: The idea that human behavior and social relations result from the underlying conflicts that arise from the power differences between competing groups in society.

conscience constituencies: A sympathetic ally who is outside the wronged population represented by the social movement.

consensus crimes: Deviant acts that are illegal, perceived to be very harmful to society, and have a high level of public agreement regarding their severity. Murder and sexual assault are examples of consensus crimes.

contact theory: Allport's theory that increasing contact between antagonistic groups can reduce prejudice, lead to a growing recognition of similarities, and alter stereotypes about the other group.

content analysis: A research method that is based on the analysis of documents.

control theory: Hirschi's theory that weak social control contributes to an individual engaging in deviant or criminal acts. Weak controls can be the result of having few social connections and relationships.

core countries: The most economically diversified, wealthy, and powerful nations in the world. Core countries are highly industrialized and tend to produce manufactured goods rather than extract raw materials for export.

corporate concentration: The extent to which an industry, such as the media, is increasingly owned and controlled by a small number of large corporations and conglomerates.

costs of masculinity: Messner's concept that there are rules to masculinity and what men can be and do. For example, masculinity is defined by external success: Men must avoid everything feminine and are expected to be aggressive and show little emotion.

counterculture: A group, such as an anti-consumerist organization, that rejects certain elements of the dominant culture.

credentialing: Collins's term to describe an authority, such as a university, issuing a qualification or competence to an individual. This practice is used to exclude some people from certain jobs or opportunities.

critical race theory: A theory used to explain the role of racism and racial inequality in society that focuses on how race and racism is structurally embedded in our society.

cultural capital: Bourdieu's term for the nonfinancial social assets that promote social mobility. For example, individuals can gain degrees, learn a more refined style of speech, or adopt elite social tastes, which can make them appear to belong to a higher social class than the one they were born into.

culture: A system of behavior, beliefs, knowledge, practices, values, and materials that shape how people act and the physical elements of society.

curriculum: The standardized content, materials, resources, and processes used to teach students. Each U.S. state outlines a specific curriculum for each grade.

cyberbullying: The use of technology, such as the Internet, to deliberately harass, intimidate, or threaten a person.

cycle of poverty: The causes and elements of poverty that trap people in poverty and that require outside intervention.

defensive credentialing: The process of attending college or university and/or enrolling in graduate and professional programs to avoid losing job opportunities to degree holders and to gain an advantage in employment.

deinstitutionalization of marriage: The term used by Cherlin to describe the weakening of social norms concerning marriage and people's resulting doubt of their actions, and those of others, within this institution.

demographic diversity: The extent to which the media represents and addresses the interests of people from a variety of races, ethnicities, genders, and classes.

dependent variables: A variable that is affected by other variables.

description bias: In terms of social movements, the media's positive or negative depiction of a protest event or activist.

deterrence: The process of dissuading someone from committing future wrongdoings by making the cost of punishment outweigh the benefit of the offense. The idea assumes that individuals conduct a rational cost-benefit analysis before committing a crime.

deviance: The act of breaking a social norm.

differential association: The idea that children from a lower social class are less likely than children from a higher class to have role models who have achieved at school or attended university. As a result, these children lack the knowledge of how to work within the system and are less successful in it.

differential expectations: The different values and outlooks that families have, based on their social class. The different education expectations of low-income and high-income families could explain why individuals from the former are less likely to perform well in school or earn high school diplomas or postsecondary degrees than people from the latter.

differential preparation: The various ways that individuals can be prepared for an aspect of society, depending on their social class. For example, children from families with more money probably have more access to private tutors, educational trips, educational toys, and books and newspapers than children from poorer families. These resources help to prepare them for school and to succeed in the educational system.

digital divide: An inequality between groups' ability to access, use, or learn about information and communication technologies. Within countries, this term refers to inequalities between individuals, households, and geographic areas at different socioeconomic levels. The global digital divide examines the gap in digital access across countries.

disability: A mental or physical condition that limits a person's daily activities.

discrimination: The unfair treatment of an individual based on his actual or perceived membership in a certain group or category.

disenchantment of the world: The term used by Weber to describe the change from explaining phenomenon through magical or otherworldly forces to using rational thought and science.

division of labor: A focus of Durkheim's work, the specialization of cooperating individuals who perform specific tasks and roles.

dominant culture: The culture that, through its political and economic power, is able to impose its values, beliefs, and behaviors on a given society.

double shift (second shift): Hochschild's concept that women in heterosexual dual-income households often spend significantly more time on household tasks and caring work than their partners do, in addition to their work in the paid workforce.

dramaturgical perspective: Goffman's theory that social life is like a stage and individuals are actors on it, performing roles for others.

economic perspective: Based on Marxist theory, the argument that the state is needed to regulate economic interests and the clashing of those interests between groups. Marx argued that the state usually resolves these conflicts by siding with capitalists.

efficacy: The belief that one is capable of the specific behaviors required to produce a desired outcome in a given situation. Efficacy is an important predictor of social movement engagement.

elections: A formal decision-making process in which eligible citizens select individuals for public office.

emotional labor: Work, especially in the service sector, that requires emotional performances from employees. This labor is commodified and controlled by management.

essentialism: The theory that some essential element makes a person part of a race or ethnic group. From this perspective, ethnic groups and nationalities are based on biological factors (similar appearance, skin color, or eye color) and territorial location (region or country).

ethnicity: The shared language, religion, customs, and history of a group. The core difference between race and ethnicity is that race is based on perceived biological traits and ethnicity is based on cultural differences.

experiments: A process that allows researchers to examine a specific factor's effect on individual behavior by comparing two groups: the experimental (which is exposed to the factor) and the control (which is not exposed to it).

extended family: Two or more generations of a family living in the same household or near one another; often contrasted with the nuclear family.

fair trade certification: An official certification that tells consumers that a product is produced in a way that is consistent with principles of ethical fair trade.

false consciousness: A willingness among the working class to support ideologies that are advantageous to the ruling class but disadvantageous to working-class interests. Marx argued that false consciousness is part of the reason that the working class does not unite and overthrow the capitalist system.

family: A group of people who are related by birth, affinity, or cohabitation.

family household: A residential unit of people who are related by blood, marriage, or adoption.

family violence: Any abuse, mistreatment, or neglect in which the victim and perpetrator are related or have an intimate relationship. Types of family violence include physical, sexual, emotional, and financial abuse.

feminism: The various movements and ideologies that seek to define, confirm, and protect equal political, economic, and social rights for women. Feminism is sometimes understood historically as occurring over three waves of activism.

feminization: The process of a job, profession, or industry being dominated by or predominantly associated with women (e.g., nurses, secretaries, teachers, and family doctors).

fertility rates: The average number of children born to a woman over her lifetime.

frames: Interpretation schemes that enable individuals to understand and label occurrences in their daily lives. Framing comprises three parts: diagnostic, prognostic, and motivational.

free spaces: The small-scale settings of a community or movement that are outside dominant groups' direct control, are voluntary, and create the cultural challenge preceding or accompanying political mobilization. Social movements need free spaces so that activists can have some protection from authorities.

gender: A social concept that includes all social patterns associated with being male or female and that ranges from masculine to feminine. Gender focuses on differences that are social and cultural, not biological.

gender reversal in educational outcomes: The trend, which seems to have stabilized, of more women than men obtaining postsecondary degrees. In the past, men were much more likely than women to attend and graduate from university or college.

gender roles: The behaviors and mannerisms that people learn as being appropriate to their respective genders and that are reinforced by cultural norms.

gender socialization: The process of learning how to behave consistently with society's gender rules and norms.

general deterrence: A type of deterrence that makes examples of deviants to discourage others from committing crimes.

generational replacement: A main theory in voter turnout research that seeks to explain declining voting rates by examining how the emergence of new generations of voters (who vote less often) are replacing older generations of voters (who vote more often).

Gini index: A measure used to compare income inequality across countries. The index ranges from zero (perfect equality) to one (total inequality).

globalization: A process of increasing interconnectedness of people, products, ideas, and places. It has three major dimensions: physical, spatiotemporal, and cognitive.

goods-producing sector: The economic sector that manufactures finished goods. Metalwork, automobile production, textile production, and engineering industries are part of this sector.

health: A state of physical, mental, and social well-being.

health care systems: The organizations of people, resources, and institutions that provide and deliver health care to a population.

health disparities: The differences in health status linked to social, economic, or environmental conditions.

health policies: The decisions and actions that are undertaken to achieve specific health care goals.

healthy life expectancy: The average number of healthy years one can expect to live if current trends remain.

heteronormative: The social institutions, practices, and norms that support the assumption that people are or should be heterosexual.

heterosexual–homosexual rating scale: Kinsey's seven-point scale of sexual inclinations. Instead of thinking of people as either gay or straight, Kinsey argued that people simply have life histories that express different desires. People can have homosexual or heterosexual desires to a greater or lesser degree and homosexual or heterosexual experiences to a greater or lesser degree, but these desires and experiences are not always related.

hidden curriculum: Marx's term for lessons that are not normally considered part of the academic curriculum and that schools unintentionally or secondarily provide. These lessons teach students to be submissive, punctual, and hard working—all the traits that make "good" workers in the capitalist system.

high culture: The culture of the elite. Those who are not exposed to high culture may find it difficult to appreciate it. High culture is often juxtaposed with popular culture, which is the culture of the majority.

homophily: The propensity of individuals to make friendships and other social ties with people who share their characteristics, such as race, class, or religious beliefs.

homophobia: The negative attitudes and feelings, ranging from antipathy to hatred, toward homosexuality or people who identify as or are perceived to be LGBTQ.

honorifics: A form of address or reference that shows esteem or respect for a person.

human capital model: The argument, related to Durkheim's theory, that schools are organized largely to nurture productive skills needed in the economy.

hypotheses: Testable propositions about society.

idea diversity: The diversity of viewpoints expressed in the media.

identities: The names that people give to themselves and others in the course of social interaction. Identity is central to social movement participation as both a cause and an outcome of engagement.

ideological model of media coverage: The perspective that media, political, and corporate elites make a concerted effort to control the information released through the media. This model argues that broader structures of power relations in society affect the portrayal of social movements and protest.

ideology: A system of conscious and unconscious ideas that shape a person's or group's objectives, expectations, and actions. Marx argues that a society's dominant ideologies come from the dominant class and serve to perpetuate the capitalist system.

imagined communities: Anderson's term to describe members of a nation that feel a sense of community even though they will never know most of their fellow members.

immigration: The movement of people around the world.

independent variables: A variable that affects other variables.

individualized marriages: A marriage that focuses on the individual's satisfaction and ability to develop and express a sense of self. These marriages are more flexible than other types because they attempt to meet the varied needs of each spouse.

infant mortality rate: A common measure of health in a country. This rate reflects the number of deaths in the first year of a child's life, per 1,000 live births.

institutional marriage: A marriage that is less concerned with whether spouses are in love or are good companions to each another and more focused on how the marriage solidifies family and community ties and benefits society.

intergenerational income elasticity: The statistical relationship between a parent's and a child's economic standings; the higher the elasticity, the less social mobility a society offers. When there is a high level of intergenerational income elasticity, childhood upbringing plays a larger role than individual talents and capabilities in predicting later income.

intersectionality: Crenshaw's term for the study of how various dimensions of inequality can combine.

intersex people: People who are born with both male and female sexual organs.

interviewing: A qualitative research technique whereby a researcher asks questions, records the subjects' answers, and then analyzes the responses.

invisible knapsack: A term coined by McIntosh; an unseen collection of unearned assets that White people use in their daily lives but about which they are expected to remain oblivious.

irrationality of rationality: Weber's concept that rationalized systems can create negative outcomes.

issue attention cycles: The specific times when the public is more apt to become concerned about a problem and attempt to solve it.

Kinsey Reports: The name given to Kinsey and colleagues' two books on human sexuality, *Sexual Behavior in the Human Male* (Kinsey et al., 1948) and *Sexual Behavior in the Human Female* (Kinsey, 1953).

labelling theory: Becker's theory on how we label and think about individuals who engage in deviance. Becker argues that the important element is not the behavior but the label of being deviant, which can create a deviant or criminal identity and produce a self- fulfilling prophecy that leads to more deviance.

latent function: Unintended function.

learning theory: Developed by Sutherland, who argued that different environments or social milieu, such as a jail, provide opportunities to learn to engage in crime. This theory claims that we are socialized into deviance and criminality through learning from others.

legitimation: A major function of the education system, aimed at legitimating certain kinds of knowledge and divisions in society. This process is consistent with Marx's conflict theory.

lesser crimes: Acts of deviance that are illegal; their perceived harmfulness and severity of public response are moderate, however. An example of a lesser crime is speeding.

LGBTQ: Lesbian, gay, bisexual, transgender, or queer/questioning.

life-cycle effect: A main theory in voter turnout research that seeks to explain turnout by illustrating that there is usually an increase in the propensity to vote as people age.

life expectancy: The average number of years a population at some age can expect to live.

looking-glass self: Cooley's theory that we refine our sense of self over time by considering how others react to us.

lumpenproletariat: The lowest layer of the working class, according to Marx; includes criminals and the chronically unemployed.

macro-level theories: Theories that focus on large-scale issues and large groups of people.

managerial perspective: One of the major lenses used to understand the rise of the state. This perspective argues that the state was established to politically administer increasingly large territories more effectively.

manifest functions: Obvious and intended functions.

marriage: The legal union of two people in an intimate relationship.

mass media: A message that originates from one source but is intended for many people.

McDonaldization: Ritzer's term to describe the movement from traditional to rational methods of thought. Where Weber used the model of the bureaucracy to represent this change, Ritzer sees the fast-food restaurant as representing this transformation.

means-tested program: A type of social program that bases eligibility for government assistance on whether an individual or family possesses the means to do without that help.

mechanical solidarity: The type of solidarity that involves societies being held together by similarities among people. Durkheim argued that, in early societies, people shared a collective consciousness that created solidarity, even though each unit (such as a family) provided for its own production and consumption needs and subunits could survive in isolation from one another.

media: The technological processes facilitating communication between a sender and a receiver.

media literacy: The framework used to access, analyze, and evaluate media messages and thus create an understanding of the media's role in society.

mental health: A measure of the state of well-being in which one can realize one's potential, cope with the normal stresses of life, work productively, and make a contribution to one's community.

meritocracy: The idea that people will achieve based on their own merit.

microfinancing: A system of offering financial services to individuals who are not served by the traditional financial system. These services provide small amounts of start-up capital to assist people with their entrepreneurial projects and thus help lift individuals, families, and communities out of poverty.

micro-level theories: Theories that focus on relationships between individuals and groups.

militaristic perspective: One of the main lenses used to understand the rise of the state. From this perspective, the state was instituted to create a monopoly on the legitimate use of violence, particularly in relation to the ability to wage war.

mode of production: The system that a society uses to make things.

modernization theory: One of the main theories of globalization; it contends that countries are poor because they cling to traditional and inefficient attitudes, technologies, and institutions. Modern societies embrace industrial capitalism, modern technologies, and modern institutions. This theory predicts that, given enough time and with the correct behaviors, all societies can become modernized and develop like Western societies.

monocropping: The agricultural practice of producing high yields by growing a single crop on the same land each year. Corn, soybeans, and wheat are three common monocrops.

multiculturalism: Based on the idea of pluralism, support for having various cultural or ethnic groups in a society; the belief that conflict is a central feature of societies and that ethnicity is an essential aspect of individual identity and group behavior.

nation: A group of people united based on shared language, ethnicity, or history.

nation-state: A group of people who share a physical territory and government.

new advantages: According to W. Gamson, a measure of social movement success in which a group gains benefits, such as a new policy or law, during a challenge and its aftermath.

new media: On-demand access to content, interactive user feedback, and creative contribution on any digital device. New media technologies are digital and interactive and can be manipulated, networked, and compressed.

normality of crime: Durkheim's argument that crime is necessary, functional, and even good for a society. According to Durkheim, all societies have crime and deviance, which allow groups to define and clarify their collective beliefs.

norms: Social expectations that guide behavior.

nuclear family: A family consisting of two adults living with one or more children.

obesity: A body mass index (BMI) of 30.0 or more.

organic solidarity: The type of solidarity formed by people who are quite different. Durkheim argued that modern societies tend to lack adherence to a collective conscience. What holds these societies together, despite the differences among people, is that people need one another because they are so specialized.

organizational models of media coverage: The perspective that the media acts as a gatekeeper that determines what events are newsworthy and, because of the way it is set up, tends to rely on official sources and generalist journalists, leading to a particular type of coverage of protest.

outsourcing: Contracting work, usually manufacturing or supporting processes, to another country.

parole: The supervised early release of a prisoner for good behavior, among other reasons. Parolees work with a parole officer to adjust to life outside prison and to ensure that they do not violate the conditions of their release. If they do, their parole can be revoked and they can be sent back to prison.

participant observation (ethnography): A qualitative research method in which a researcher attempts to deeply understand a given group of individuals and their practices by becoming intensively involved with them over an extended period.

parties: In Weber's theory, organizations that attempt to influence social action and focus on achieving some political goal.

patriarchy: The system of male domination in society.

people first philosophy: An approach that focuses on the on the individual and on the individual's abilities rather than limitations.

performativity: Judith Butler's term to describe the repeated rituals that create and sustain gender through performance.

periphery countries: The world's least economically diversified and industrialized nations. These countries focus on a single type of economic activity, usually extracting and exporting raw materials to core countries.

personal troubles: Problems that we face as individuals.

petite bourgeoisie: Small-scale capitalists, such as shopkeepers and managers.

petitions: Formal written requests, typically signed by many people, appealing to authority with respect to a particular cause.

popular (or low) culture: The culture of the majority or the masses; often juxtaposed with high culture, the culture of the elite.

poverty: A condition in which material or cultural resources are lacking. Relative poverty describes the deprivation of some people in relation to those who have more; absolute poverty is a life-threatening deprivation of resources.

poverty threshold: The minimum level of income deemed adequate in a given country.

power: According to Weber, the chance that a person or group can realize its own will in a communal action, even against the resistance of others participating in the same action. The idea is based on a person's or group's economic class, social status, and party.

power elite: C. Wright Mills's name for the interwoven interests of society's military, corporate, and political leaders.

precarious employment: Employment in dead-end, low-paying, and insecure jobs; sometimes called McJobs. In precarious employment, employers have full control over the labor process. Employers can hire and fire employees with ease and frequency because the kind of work makes them readily replaceable.

prejudice: A negative attitude toward someone, based solely on that individual's membership in a particular group.

primary deviance: In labelling theory, early acts of deviance. Isolated acts of primary deviance rarely lead to the successful application of a deviant label.

primary socialization: The earliest stage of socialization, in which we learn how to be a member of society and what attitudes, values, and actions are culturally and socially appropriate.

prison industrial complex: The large number of people, including bureaucrats, politicians, and prison employees, who have a vested interest in the existence and further expansion of the prison system.

probation: A community release that can be granted to individuals who have been convicted of lesser crimes. Probation entails supervision and certain conditions, such as being involved in and completing a substance abuse program. If the offender does not adhere to these conditions or is re-arrested, the probation can be revoked.

proletariat (worker): One of the two primary classes in Marx's theory. Proletariats own only their capacity to labor, which they must sell to the capitalist.

property: Any resource that can be used to produce things of value and to generate wealth. In Marxist theory, property is owned by the capitalist.

protest: An organized and public demonstration against an event, policy, or action.

protest paradigm: The way that the media tends to cover protest events, which works to delegitimate and marginalize protesters and focuses on the spectacle by highlighting sensational details such as violence, visible drama, and deviant or strange behavior.

public goods: Goods that are nonexcludable (a person cannot reasonably prevent another from consuming the good) and nonrivalrous (a person's consumption of the good does not affect another's). Clean air is an example of a public good.

public issues: Social problems that a society faces.

public sociology: A sociological approach that attempts to interact with audiences outside academia by encouraging sociologists to engage publicly and politically with issues concerning public policy, political activism, and the institutions of civil society.

punishment: The penalty (e.g., denial of certain privileges, abilities, or rights) inflicted on someone for committing a transgression. In criminal law, a judge and/or jury decide punishments.

qualitative research: A set of research techniques, including interviews and participant observation, in which the researcher intensely studies a small number of cases. This research tends to focus on process questions, including how and why certain things happen, and to look at how actions affect individuals and groups.

quantitative research: A set of research techniques that focus on things that can be counted, examine how variables relate to one another, and test relationships with statistical models. This type of research explores what, where, when, how often, and how long social phenomena occur.

race: A social distinction based on perceived physical or biological characteristics.

racism: The systematic belief that races have characteristics or abilities that make them inferior or superior to others. Racism is present at every level of society.

rationalization: According to Weber, rationalization and rationality are ways of solving problems by focusing on the optimal means toward an end. The process is based on predictability, calculability, efficiency, and control.

realistic conflict theory: Based on the work of Bobo, the theory that prejudice originates from social groups competing over valued resources or opportunities.

recidivism rates: The rate at which individuals recommit crimes after an initial and/or subsequent offense.

red tape: An excessive adherence to formal rules that hinders the functioning of organizations.

rehabilitation: The attempt to reform (or heal) an offender so she will not reoffend.

religiosity: A measure of how religious a person is, based on attendance at religious services or intensity of belief, among other criteria.

reparation programs: Measures taken by the state to redress gross and systematic human rights violations through some form of compensation or restitution to the victims. Governments enact these programs to deal with injustices on a societal level.

research questions: The first stage of research. Research questions focus on the relationship between two variables.

resocialization: The process in which individuals take on new roles and discard former behaviors, attitudes, and values.

restoration: An aspect of restorative justice that requires offenders to accept their guilt and to restore the moral order by compensating or fixing the injustice they caused.

retribution: Based on "an eye for an eye," punishment that makes offenders undergo suffering that is comparable to the suffering they have inflicted.

roles: The associated behaviors, beliefs, and norms that individuals perform and/or display in social situations.

rotating credit associations: An example of social capital, a cooperative association that operates in Southeastern Asian societies, among others. In these organizations, people pool their resources and then take turns drawing on the general fund of credit.

Sapir-Whorf hypothesis: Developed by Edward Sapir and Benjamin Whorf, the idea that language influences thought.

schooled society: A term used by Davies and Guppy to describe the education system in modern society, particularly how mass education has expanded from elementary to high schools and to high postsecondary enrollment, how schooling has become increasingly integral to modern life, and how the forms and functions of education are increasing and diversifying.

scientific management (Taylorism): The application of scientific principles and methods to the management of labor. These practices were popularized by Frederick Taylor to rationalize work and make it more efficient by dividing it into increasingly smaller tasks.

secondary deviance: In labelling theory, deviant acts that persist, become more common, and eventually cause people to organize their lives and identities around their deviant status.

secondary socialization: The second stage of socialization, in which people learn the appropriate behaviors and attitudes of a smaller group (a subculture) within larger society.

secularization: A process whereby society moves away from religious explanations, institutions, and values to secular explanations.

selection: A major function of the education system; sorting, differentially rewarding, and certifying graduates of elementary, secondary, and postsecondary schools. According to Weber, schools use this function to confer status and prestige.

selection bias: In regard to the media and social movements, the gatekeepers' (editors') choice to report on a small number of protest events. Media agendas can influence this selection, independent of the events' characteristics.

self-fulfilling prophecy: Defined by Merton as a strongly held belief that a person thinks of as true, regardless of whether it actually is, which so influences the person that his reactions ultimately fulfill the expectation.

semi-periphery countries: Countries that are moving toward industrialization and a more diversified economy. During this transition, these countries are not usually dominant in international trade.

service sector: The sector of the economy that provides services to individuals and businesses. Retail sales, transportation and distribution, entertainment, the hospitality industry, tourism, banking, health care, and law are all part of this sector.

sex: A biological identity that is based on physical or biological differences and that can be divided into the main categories of male and female.

sexuality: Feelings of sexual attraction and behaviors related to them.

sexual orientation: A person's sexual identity, expressed in terms of whom a person desires, wants to have sex with,

and feels a sense of connectedness with.

sick role: Based on the work of Talcott Parsons, the patterns of behavior that a sick person adopts to minimize the disruptive impact of illness.

significant others: Key individuals, such as parents, whom young children imitate and model themselves after in the process of socialization.

social capital: From the work of Bourdieu, Coleman, and Putnam, the collective value of all social networks. Social capital is about whom you know and the norms of reciprocity that develop among people who know one another.

social change: The alteration of culture and social institutions over time.

social construction: According to Berger and Luckman, a process that involves two steps: (1) People categorize experience and then act on the basis of those classifications. (2) People eventually forget the social origins of the categories and begin to see them as natural and unchangeable.

social desirability bias: People who are the subject of research tend to behave or answer in ways that make them appear favorably to researchers.

social determinants of health: The larger social factors that shape the kind of lives we lead and the health of those lives.

social facts: Larger structures of society and norms that shape individuals' actions.

social inequality: The result of social differences that have consequences for individuals. This inequality shapes the rights individuals enjoy, their opportunities, and the privileges that they can exercise in society.

social institutions: The norms, values, and rules of conduct that structure human interactions.

socialization: The lifelong process of developing a sense of identity and self, as well as of inheriting and transmitting norms, customs, and ideologies that

provide the skills and habits required to participate in society.

social media: Websites and other means that allow users to create, share, and/or exchange information and ideas.

social mobility: The upward or downward movement in a stratification system, such as the class system. Social mobility can be intergenerational (between generations) or intragenerational (within a single generation).

social movement: An organized and sustained challenge to existing power holders on behalf of a wronged population.

Social Security: An earned social program for people over a certain age; created to alleviate poverty among seniors in the United States. Eligibility depends on lifetime earnings (or disability or other factors).

societal protection: An element of punishment that protects members of a society from harm. For example, we can limit a person's ability to commit crimes by incarcerating him or her.

society: Human groupings that are based in a defined geographic area and share common institutions.

socioeconomic status (SES): A measure of a person's or family's income, educational attainment, and occupational prestige that is used to determine one's social and economic position in relation to the position of others.

sociological imagination: A worldview that sees the connections between our individual lives (and our personal troubles) and the larger society in which we live (and its public issues).

sociology: The systematic study of human society.

specific deterrence: A type of deterrence that aims to discourage the specific individual by convincing him that engaging in crime does not benefit him.

stages of role-taking: Outlined by George Herbert Mead, the four stages that occur in socialization and teach people to take the role of the other. The stages are preparatory, role-taking, game, and taking the perspective of the generalized other.

state: A set of institutions that include four groups of people: political decision makers, who can be either elected or appointed; administrative units or bureaucracies; a judiciary or legal system; and security services. States are attached to a geographic territory and maintain a monopoly on rule-making, coercion, and violence within that area.

status groups: Weber's term for a group that is based on social honor or prestige and that has a style of life. The word "honor" refers to any distinction, respect, or esteem that is accorded to an individual by others.

strain theory: Merton's theory that some individuals experience a poor fit between cultural goals and opportunities for success. For example, these individuals might want to earn enough money to support themselves but cannot get a well-paying job. Thus, they may turn to illegitimate means (e.g., crime) to make money.

structural functionalism: A theory that, by looking at how societal structures or institutions work together to create consensus and social cohesion, focuses on explaining how society functions effectively.

subcultural theory: A theory that focuses on the role of culture in crime. Cohen argues that gangs and other criminal organizations are subcultures with norms and values that are different from the larger culture.

subcultures: A group within a society that differs from the larger culture in attitudes, customs, or practices, but does not necessarily oppose it.

Supplemental Security Income (SSI): A federally funded means-tested program that provides cash to meet basic needs for seniors, the blind, and those with other disabilities who are below a certain income level.

surplus value: In Marx's theory, the new value created by workers that is in excess of their own labor cost and is available to be appropriated by the capitalist. This value is the amount of money that the capitalist keeps after paying the worker's wages.

survey research: A major tool of quantitative research that involves learning about people's characteristics, attitudes, or behaviors by having several members of a large group complete a questionnaire.

symbolic ethnicity: Waters's term for the individualistic type of ethnicity that some people can adopt with little social cost.

symbolic interactionism: A theory that argues that meanings do not naturally attach to things. Instead, we derive meaning from and understand our society and our role in it through interacting with other people.

the medium is the message: Marshall McLuhan's famous statement that argues that the content of the medium is less important than the physical or psychological effects of that medium.

theory: A way to explain different aspects of society and to create hypotheses.

Thomas principle: Thomas and Thomas's theory that, if we define a situation as real, it is real in its consequences.

tracking: The placing of students with those of similar skills or needs, such as in specific classes or groups within a class.

trade union density: The percentage of a population's wage earners who are members of a union.

transgender (trans) umbrella: A term used to encompass the variety of different sexual expressions in modern society.

types of suicide: According to Durkheim, suicide has four variations that differ based on the level of integration or regulation in society. The types are egoistic (low integration), altruistic (high integration), anomic (low regulation), and fatalistic (high regulation).

Uniform Crime Reporting (UCR) Program: Created by the FBI in 1929 to collect information on murder and manslaughter, forcible rape, robbery, aggravated assault, burglary, larceny-theft, motor vehicle theft, arson, and human trafficking.

unions: Organizations of employees who work together to negotiate a variety of common matters, such as benefits, pay, hiring and firing processes, and working conditions.

United Nations (UN) Convention on the Rights of Persons with Disabilities (CRPD): A UN convention that sets out a list of rights that people with disabilities have and how the state should work to protect these rights.

universal program: A type of social program available to all citizens, regardless of income or wealth. Social Security is an example of a universal program in the United States.

variable: A construct that can take on different values. Examples include age, gender, height, or nationality.

wealth inequality: Inequality in the total amount of assets across individuals or household, including property, stocks, and pensions.

welfare state: A system in which the state provides a range of social services, including a minimum income and economic security.

white-collar crime: A type of crime that occurs in a work setting and is motivated by monetary gain, but does not involve intentional or direct acts of violence.

world society theory: A main theory of globalization that emphasizes the significance of institutions and culture in forming the structure and behavior of nation-states, organizations, and individuals worldwide. This theory seeks to explain global change (especially the dispersion of Western policies) as due to the post–World War II emergence of global institutions and international organizations, as well as an increasingly shared world culture.

world systems theory: A main theory of globalization that views the world as a transnational division of labor; it classifies countries as core, semi-periphery, or periphery.

worthiness, unity, numbers, and commitment (WUNC): According to Tilly, the criteria that determine the strength of a social movement.

REFERENCES

CHAPTER 1

Berger, P. (1963). *Invitation to sociology.* Doubleday.

Berman, E. (2015, July 15). *How the G.I. Bill changed the face of higher education in America. Time.* Retrieved from http://time.com/3915231/student-veterans

Bibby, R. (2011). *Beyond the gods and back: Religion's demise and rise and why it matters.* Project Canada Books.

Charon, J. M. (2012). *Ten questions: A sociological perspective.* Wadsworth.

Collins, R. (1992). *Sociological insight: An introduction to non-obvious sociology* (2nd ed.). Oxford University Press.

Collins, R. (1994). *Four sociological traditions: Selected readings.* Oxford University Press.

Durkheim, É. (1951). *Suicide: A study in sociology.* Free Press. (Original work published 1897)

Durkheim, É. (1960). *The division of labor in society.* Free Press. (Original work published 1893)

Durkheim, É. (1982). S. Lukes (Ed.), *The rules of the sociological method.* Free Press. (Original work published 1895)

Durkheim, É. (2008). *The elementary forms of religious life.* Oxford Paperbacks. (Original work published 1912)

Gallup. (2021). *Religion.* https://news.gallup.com/poll/1690/Religion.aspx

Garfinkel, H. (1991). *Studies in ethnomethodology.* Polity Press.

Grabb, E. (2006). *Theories of social inequality* (5th ed.). Nelson.

Mills, C. W. (2000). *The sociological imagination.* Oxford University Press. (Original work published 1959)

National Catholic Register. (2022, February 11). *Vatican: Number of Catholics worldwide rose by 16 million in 2020.* https://www.ncregister.com/cna/vatican-number-of-catholics-worldwide-rose-by-16-million-in-2020-b1zvp6f1

Seidman, S. (2008). *Contested knowledge: Social theory today.* Wiley-Blackwell.

Shrider, E. A., Kollar, M., Chen, F., & Semega, J. (2021, September 14). *Income and poverty in the United States: 2020.* United States Census Bureau https://www.census.gov/library/publications/2021/demo/p60-273.html

Smith, D. (1987). *The everyday world as problematic: A feminist sociology.* Northeastern University.

Tucker, R. C (Ed.). (1978). *The Marx-Engels reader.* Norton.

U.S. Department of Labor. (2020). *Median annual earnings by sex, race and Hispanic ethnicity* https://www.dol.gov/agencies/wb/data/earnings/median-annual-sex-race-hispanic-ethnicity

CHAPTER 2

Blumer, H. (1969). *Symbolic interactionism: Perspective and method,* Prentice-Hall.

Blee, K. (2003). *Inside organized racism,* University of California Press.

Cooley, C. H. (1902). *Human nature and the social order,* Scribner.

Deschamps, T. (2020, July 16). *Women's participation in labour force reaches lowest level in 3 decades due to COVID-19: RBC. CBC News.* https://www.cbc.ca/news/canada/toronto/women-employment-canada-covid-19-1.5652788

Dollar, C. (2017, May 5). *My (so called) Instagram life. New York Times.* Retrieved from https://www.nytimes.com/2017/05/05/style/modern-love-my-so-called-instagram-life.html

Ebaugh, H. R. F. (1988). *Becoming an ex: The process of role exit,* University of Chicago Press.

Fry, R., Passel, J. S., & Cohn, D. (2020, September 4). *A majority of young adults in the U.S. live with their parents for the first time since the Great Depression. Pew Research Center.* https://www.pewresearch.org/fact-tank/2020/09/04/a-majority-of-young-adults-in-the-u-s-live-with-their-parents-for-the-first-time-since-the-great-depression/

Furstenberg, F. F., Jr., Kenned., S., McLoyd, V. C., Rumbaut, R. G., & Settersten, R. A., Jr. (2004). Growing up is harder to do. *Contexts, 3*(3), 33–41.

Goffman, E. (1959). *The presentation of self in everyday life,* Anchor Books.

Hall, G. S. (1904). *Adolescence: Its psychology and its relation to physiology, anthropology, sociology, sex, crime, religion, and education,* Prentice-Hall.

Kohn, M. L. (1959). Social class and parental values. *American Journal of Sociology, 64*(4), 337–351.

Mather, M., Jacobsen, L. A., & Pollard, K. M. (2015). Aging in the United States. *Population Bulletin, 70*(2). Retrieved from http://www.prb.org/pdf16/aging-us-population-bulletin.pdf

Mead, G. H. (1934). *Mind, self, and society,* University of Chicago Press.

Mead, M. (1928). *Coming of age in Samoa,* W. Morrow.

Mintz, S. (2004). *Huck's raft: A history of American childhood,* Belknap Press.

Parsons, T. (1955). *Family, socialization, and interaction process,* Free Press.

Rousseau, J-J. (2011). Discourse on the origin of inequality. In *The basic political writings* (D. A. Cress. In, Trans.). (2nd ed.).

Seidman, S. (2008). *Contested knowledge: Social theory today*, Wiley-Blackwell.

Smith, D. (1987). *The everyday world as problematic: A feminist sociology*, Northeastern University.

Southern Poverty Law Center. (2021). *In 2021, we tracked 733 hate groups across the U.S* https://www.splcenter.org/hate-map

CHAPTER 3

Anderson, E. (1999). *Code of the street: Decency, violence, and the moral life of the inner city*, Norton.

Aronson, J., & Aronson, E (Eds.). (2011). *Readings about the social animal*. Worth.

Bazemore, G., & Umbreit, M. (2001, February). *Comparison of four restorative conferencing models. Juvenile Justice Bulletin*. Retrieved from https://www.ncjrs.gov/pdffiles1/ojjdp/184738.pdf

Becker, H. (1963). *Outsiders: Studies in the sociology of deviance*, Free Press.

Berger, P., & Luckmann, T. (1966). *The social construction of reality: A treatise in the sociology of knowledge*, Anchor Books.

Brayne, S. (2017). Big data surveillance: The case of policing. *American Sociological Review, 82*(5), 977–1008.

Centers for Disease Control and Prevention (CSC). (2020). *Leading Causes of Death Reports, 1981–2020. [Data set]*. https://wisqars.cdc.gov/fatal-leading

Cohen, S. (2011). *Folk devils and moral panic*, Routledge.

Collins, R. (1992). *Sociological insight: An introduction to non-obvious sociology* (2nd ed.). Oxford University Press.

Durkheim, É. (1982). S. Lukes (Ed.), *The rules of the sociological method*. Free Press.

Fair, H., & Walmsley, R. (2021). *World prison population list* (13th ed.). World Prison Brief. https://www.prisonstudies.org/sites/default/files/resources/downloads/world_prison_population_list_13th_edition.pdf

Federal Register. (2013, March 18). *Annual determination of average cost of incarceration*. Retrieved from https://www.federalregister.gov/documents/2013/03/18/2013-06139/ annual-determination-of-average-cost-of- incarceration

Foucault, M. (1995). *Discipline and punish: The birth of the prison*, Vintage.

Gramlich, J. (2022, February 3). *What the data says about gun deaths in the U.S. Pew Research Center*. https://www.pewresearch.org/fact-tank/2022/02/03/what-the-data-says-about-gun-deaths-in-the-u-s/

Heath, B. (2014, November 18). *Racial gap in US arrest rates: Staggering disparity. USA Today*. Retrieved from https://www.usatoday.com/story/news/nation/2014/11/18/ferguson-black-arrest- rates/19043207/

Hirschi, T. (2004). Self-control and crime. In R. F. Baumeister & K. D. Vohs (Eds.), *The handbook of self-regulation research, theory, and application* (pp. 537–552).

Jensen, E., Jones, N., Rabe, M., Pratt, B., Medina, L., Orozco, K., & Spell, L. (2021, August 12). *The chance that two people chosen at random are of different race or ethnicity groups has increased since 2010*. United States Census Bureau https://www.census.gov/library/stories/2021/08/2020-united-states-population-more-racially-ethnically-diverse-than-2010.html

Kyckelhahn, T. (2015). *Justice expenditure and employment extracts, 2012. Bureau of Justice Statistics, U.S. Department of Justice*. Retrieved from http://www.bjs.gov/index.cfm

Merton, R. K. (1949/1957/1968). *Social theory and social structure*, Free Press.

Milgram, S. (1963). Behavioral study of obedience. *Journal of Abnormal and Social Psychology, 67*, 371–378.

National Institute of Justice. (2018). *Recidivism*. Retrieved from https://www.nij.gov/topics/corrections/recidivism/ Pages/welcome.aspx

Pager, D. (2007). *Marked: Race, crime, and finding work in an era of mass incarceration*, University of Chicago Press.

Paternoster, R. (2007). Capital punishment. In G. Ritzer, J. M. Ryan, & B. Thorn (Eds.), *The Blackwell encyclopedia of sociology* (Vol. 2, pp. 385–388). Blackwell.

Pittman, T. P., Nykiforuk, C. I., Mignone, J., Mandhane, P. J., Becker, A. B., & Kozyrskyj, A. L. (2012). The association between community stressors and asthma prevalence of school children in Winnipeg, Canada. *International Journal of Environmental Research and Public Health, 9*(2), 579–595.

Public Broadcasting Service. (2018). *Juvenile vs. adult justice*. Retrieved from https://www.pbs.org/wgbh/pages/frontline/shows/juvenile/stats/ juvvsadult.html

Rogers, S., & Chalabi, M. (2013, December 13). *Death penalty statistics, country by country. The Guardian*. Retrieved from http://www.theguardian.com/news/datablog/2011/mar/29/death-penalty-countries-world

The Sentencing Project. (2021). *Fact sheet: Trends in U.S. corrections*. https://www.sentencingproject.org/app/uploads/2022/08/Trends-in-US-Corrections.pdf

Slevin, P. (2005, July 26). *Prison experts see opportunity for improvement. Washington Post*. Retrieved from www.washingtonpost.com/wpdyn/content/ article/2005/07/25/AR2005072501484.html

Sutherland, E. H. (1947). *Criminology* (4th ed.). Lippincott.

Swaine, J., & McCarthy, C. (2017, January 8). *Young black men again faced highest rate of US police killings in 2016. The Guardian*. Retrieved from https://www.theguardian.com/us-news/2017/jan/08/the-counted-police-killings-2016-young-black-men

U.S. Department of Justice. (2014, September). *The nation's two crime measures*. Retrieved from https://www.bjs.gov/content/pub/pdf/ntcm_2014.pdf

USA Facts. (2022). *How much do states spend on prisons?* https://usafacts.org/articles/how-much-do-states-spend-on-prisons/

Uniform Crime Reporting (UCR) Program. (2019). *Crime in the United States, Table 43: Arrests by race and ethnicity,*

2019. [Data set]. https://ucr.fbi.gov/crime-in-the-u.s/2019/crime-in-the-u.s.-2019/topic-pages/tables/table-43

Zimbardo, P. G., Maslach, C., & Haney, C. (1999). Reflections on the Stanford prison experiment: Genesis, transformations, consequences. In T. Blass (Ed.), *Obedience to authority: Current perspectives on the Milgram paradigm* (pp. 193–237). Lawrence Erlbaum Associates

CHAPTER 4

Bettis, J. (2014). *Women without class*, University of California Press.

Byrne, R. (2006). *The secret*, Atria Books.

Gerth, H. H., & Mills, C. W (Eds.). (1946). *From Max Weber: Essays in sociology*. Oxford University Press.

Hollander, J. A., & Einwohner, R. L. (2004). Conceptualizing resistance. *Sociological Forum*, 19(4), 533–540.

Kochhar, R., & Sechopoulos, S. (2022, April 20). *How the American middle class has changed in the past five decades. Pew Research Center*. https://www.pewresearch.org/fact-tank/2022/04/20/how-the-american-middle-class-has-changed-in-the-past-five-decades/

Luscombe, R. (2017, May 8). Life expectancy gap between rich and poor U.S. regions is "more than 20 years.". *The Guardian*, gap-rich-poor-us-regions-more-than-20- year. Retrieved from https://www.theguardian.com/ inequality/2017/may/08/life-expectancy-

Marx, K. (1907). *The eighteenth Brumaire of Louis Bonaparte*, Charles H. Kerr.

Marx, K. (1975). Critique of Hegel's doctrine of state. In *Karl Marx: Early writings* (R. Livingstone. In & G. Benton, Trans.). (pp. 57–198). Vintage.

Marx, K. (2000). *Das kapital. Regenery*. (Original work published 1867)

Marx, K., & Engels, F. (1848). Manifesto of the communist party. In K. Marx & F. Engels (Eds.), *Marx/Engels selected works* (Vol. 1, pp. 21–65). Progress.

Marx, K., & Engels, F (Eds.). (2004). *Theses on Feuerbach*. Progress Press. (Original work published 1888)

Northwestern Mutual. (2018, September 25). *Nearly half of Americans think the middle class is shrinking and one third believe it will disappear entirely*. https://news.northwesternmutual.com/2018-09-25-Nearly-half-of-Americans-think-the-middle-class-is-shrinking-and-one-third-believe-it-will-disappear-entirely

Pew Trusts. (2015). *Economic mobility in the United States*. Retrieved from http://www.pewtrusts.org/~/media/assets/2015/07/fsm-irs- report_artfinal.pdf

Scutti, S. (2017, May 9). *Life expectancy differs by 20 years between some U.S. counties. CNN*. Retrieved from https://www.cnn.com/2017/05/08/health/life-expectancy- by-county-study/index.html

Shimer, W. A. (1946). Review of *From Max Weber. The American Scholar*. 15

Social Security Administration. (2018). *Social security history*. Retrieved from https://www.ssa.gov/ history/50mm2.html

Weber, M. (1958)*The Protestant ethic and the spirit of capitalism*, Scribner,Original work published 1905

CHAPTER 5

Adorno, T. W., Frenkel-Brunswik, E., Levinson, D. J., & Sanford, R. N. (1950). *The authoritarian personality*, Harper and Row.

Allport, G. W. (1954). *The nature of prejudice*, Perseus.

Berger, P., & Luckmann, T. (1966). *The social construction of reality: A treatise in the sociology of knowledge*, Anchor Books.

Bobo, L. (1983). Whites' opposition to busing: Symbolic racism or realistic group conflict? *Journal of Personality and Social Psychology*, 45(6), 1196–1210.

Cazenave, N. A., & Maddern, D. A. (1999). Defending the white race: White male faculty opposition to a white racism course. *Race and Society*, 2, 25–50.

Davis, H. B. (1967). *Nationalism and socialism: Marxist and labor theories of nationalism to 1917*, Monthly Review Press.

Delgado, R., & Stefancic, J. (2001). *Critical race theory: An introduction*, New York University Press.

Du Bois, W. E. B. (1899). *The Philadelphia Negro*, Cosimo.

Du Bois, W. E. B. (1903). *The souls of black folks*, A. C. McClurg.

Du Bois, W. E. B. (2002). *The Negro*, Humanity Books,Original work published 1915

FBI. (2021). *Hate crime in the United States incident analysis. [Data set]*. https://crime-data-explorer.fr.cloud.gov/pages/explorer/crime/hate-crime

Gover, A. R., Harper, S. B., & Langton, L. (2020). Anti-Asian hate crime during the COVID-19 pandemic: Exploring the reproduction of inequality. *American Journal of Criminal Justice*, 45, 647–667.

Lee, B. Y. (2020, June 24). *Trump once again calls Covid-19 Coronavirus the 'Kung Flu'. Forbes*. https://www.forbes.com/sites/brucelee/2020/06/24/trump-once-again-calls-covid-19-coronavirus-the-kung-flu/?sh=687c1e2a1f59

Lewis, D. L. (1993). *W. E. B. Du Bois: Biography of a race 1986–1919.*, Henry Holt.

Malkin, B. (2015, July 21). *Rachel Dolezal making a living braiding hair. The Telegraph*. Retrieved from https://www.telegraph.co.uk/news/worldnews/ north america/usa/11752577/Rachel-Dolezal-I-am-black-and-I-havent-deceived-anyone.html

Marcus, M. B. (2017, April 5). *Doctor salary survey reveals big pay gap for some. CBS News*. https://www.cbsnews.com/news/doctor-salaries-compensation-survey-reveals-big-race-gender-pay-gap/

McIntosh, P. (1988). *White privilege and male privilege: A personal account of coming to see correspondences through work in women's studies. Working Paper 189*. Center for Research on Women.

Migrant Integration Policy Index. (2019). *Overall score (with health), 2019* https://mipex.eu/play/

Morris, A. (2015). *The scholar denied: W. E. B. Du Bois and the birth of modern sociology*, University of California Press.

Roy, W. G. (2001). *Making societies*, Pine Forge Press.

Ruetschlin, C., & Asante-Muhammad, D. (2015). *The retail race divide: How the retail industry is perpetuating racial inequality in the 21st century. Demos*. https://www.demos.org/research/retail-race-divide-how-retail-industry-perpetuating-racial-inequality-21st-century

Sherif, M., Harvey, O. J., White, B. J., Hood, W., & Sherif, C. W. (1961). *Intergroup conflict and cooperation: The robbers cave experiment*, University Book Exchange.

Stephens-Davidowitz, S. (2014). The cost of racial animus on a black candidate: Evidence using Google search data. *Journal of Public Economics, 118*, 26–40.

Stop, AAPI Hate Coalition. (2021). *Stop AAPI Hate national report*. https://stopaapihate.org/wp-content/uploads/2022/03/22-SAH-NationalReport-3.1.22-v9.pdf

Thomas, W. I., & Thomas, D. S. (1928). *The child in America*, Knopf.

U.S. Department of Homeland Security. (2020). *Yearbook of Immigration Statistics 2020*. https://www.dhs.gov/immigration-statistics/yearbook/2020

U.S. Department of State. (2018). *Chinese immigration and the Chinese exclusions acts*. Retrieved from https://history.state.gov/milestones/1866-1898/chinese-immigration

Viala-Gaudefroy, J., & Lindaman, D. (2020, April 21). *Donald Trump's 'Chinese virus': The politics of naming. The Conversation*. https://theconversation.com/donald-trumps-chinese-virus-the-politics-of-naming-136796

Wells, S. (2002). *The journey of man: A genetic odyssey*, Princeton University Press.

Yam, K. (2020, March 31). *Asian Americans are least likely to report hate incidents, new research shows. NBC News* https://www.nbcnews.com/news/asian-america/asian-americans-are-least-likely-report-hate-incidents-new-research-n1262607

CHAPTER 6

Aschwanden, C. (2016, June 28). *The Olympics are still struggling to define gender. FiveThirtyEight*, New York. Retrieved from https://fivethirtyeight.com/features/the-olympics-are-still-struggling-to-define-gender/

Brenan, M. (2020). *Women still handle main household tasks in U.S. Gallup*. https://news.gallup.com/poll/283979/women-handle-main-household-tasks.aspx

Butler, J. (1990). *Gender trouble: Feminism and the subversion of identity*, Routledge.

Close, K. (2016, March 31). *Here's how poorly female soccer players are paid compared to men. Time*. Retrieved from http://time.com/money/4277843/us-womens-soccer-equal-pay/

Cooky, C., Council, L. D., & Messner, M. (2021). One and done: The long eclipse of women's televised sports, 1989–2019. *Communication & Sport, 9*(1), 347–371.

Crenshaw, K. W. (1989). Demarginalizing the intersection of race and sex: A black feminist critique of antidiscrimination doctrine, feminist theory and antiracist politics. *University of Chicago Legal Forum*, 139–167.

Dowden, C., & Brennan, S. (2012, April 12). *Police-reported hate crime in Canada, 2010. Juristat*. Retrieved from http://www.statcan.gc.ca/pub/85-002-x/2012001/article/11635-eng.pdf

Fausto-Sterling, A. (2000). *Sexing the body: Gender politics and the construction of sexuality*, Basic Books.

Florio, M. (2021, February 9). *Super Bowl viewership drops sharply from last year. NBC Sports*. https://profootballtalk.nbcsports.com/2021/02/09/super-bowl-viewership-drops-sharply-from-last-year/

Forbes. (2021). *The world's highest-paid athletes*. Retrieved September 14, 2022, from https://www.forbes.com/athletes/list/

Gansen, H. M. (2017). Reproducing (and disrupting) heteronormativity: Gendered sexual socialization in preschool classrooms. *Sociology of Education, 90*(3), 255–272.

Goffman, E. (1959). *The presentation of self in everyday life*, Anchor Books.

Halpern, H. P., & Perry-Jenkins, M. (2016). Parents' gender ideology and gendered behavior as predictors of children's gender-role attitudes: A longitudinal exploration. *Sex Roles, 74*, 527–542.

Herek, G. M. (2002). Heterosexuals' attitudes toward bisexual men and women in the United States. *Journal of Sex Research, 39*(4), 264–274.

Hochschild, A., & Machung, A. (1990). *The second shift*, Avon Books.

Inter-Parliamentary Union. (2018). *Women in parliament world classification*. Retrieved from http://archive.ipu.org/wmn-e/classif.htm

Kimmel, M. (2011). *The gendered society*, Oxford University Press.

Kinsey, A. C. (1953). *Sexual behavior in the human female*, W. B. Saunders.

Kinsey, A. C., Pomeroy, W. B., & Martin, C. E. (1948). *Sexual behavior in the human male*, B. Saunders.

Kitzinger, C. (2005). Heteronormativity in action: Reproducing the heterosexual nuclear family in after-hours medical calls. *Social Problems, 52*(4), 477–498.

Kunovich, S., Paxton, P., & Hughes, M. M. (2007). Gender in politics. *Annual Review of Sociology, 33*, 263–284.

Laumann, E. O., Gagnon, J. H., Michael, R. T., & Michaels, S. (1994). *The social organization of sexuality*, University of Chicago Press.

Leffingwell, W. (1925). *Office management: Principles and practice*, A. W. Shaw.

Lenthang, M. (2022, February 22). *U.S. soccer and women soccer stars settle* equal pay lawsuit for $24 million. NBC News. https://www.nbcnews.com/news/us-news/us-soccer-women-soccer-stars-settle-equal-pay-lawsuit-24-million-rcna17138

Lorber, J. (1994). Paradoxes of gender, Yale University Press.

Messner, M. A. (1992). Power at play: Sports and the problem of masculinity, Beacon Press.

Messner, M. A. (1997). Politics of masculinities: Men in movements, AltaMira Press.

National Survey of Sexual Health and Behavior. (2010). Special issue: Findings from the National Survey of Sexual Health and Behavior, Centre for Sexual Health Promotion, Indiana University. Journal of Sexual Medicine, 7(5), 243–373.

Represent, Women. (2022). By the numbers. https://www.representwomen.org/current-women-representation#us_overview

Scott, B. M., & Schwartz, M. A. (2008). Sociology: Making sense of the social world, Allyn and Bacon.

Shakeri, S. (2017). Reducing Canada's workplace gender gap would add $150 billion to GDP. Huffington Post. Retrieved from https://www.huffingtonpost.ca/2017/06/29/reducing-canadas-workplace-gender-gap-would-add-150-billion-to_a_23008616/

Spotrac.com. (2023a). 2023 NBA cap hit rankings. [Data set]. https://www.spotrac.com/nba/rankings/

Spotrac.com. (2023b). 2023 WNBA cap hit rankings. [Data set]. https://www.spotrac.com/wnba/rankings/

Staggenborg, S. (2011). Social movements (2nd ed.). Oxford University Press.

Streeter, J. (2012). Gentlemen prefer stouts. Contexts, 11(3), 5.

Treas, J., & Gieden, D. (2000). Sexual infidelity among married and cohabiting Americans. Journal of Marriage and the Family, 62(1), 48–60.

U.S. Department of Labor. (2018). Traditional and nontraditional occupations. Retrieved from https://www.dol.gov/wb/stats/nontra_traditional_occupations.htm

World Economic Forum. (2021). Global gender gap report 2021: Insight report https://www3.weforum.org/docs/WEF_GGGR_2021.pdf

CHAPTER 7

Academy of Motion Picture Arts and Sciences. (2017). Academy membership. Retrieved from http://www.oscars.org/about/join-academy

Atton, C. (2002). Alternative media, Sage.

Chomsky, N., & Herman, E. S. (2002). Manufacturing consent: The political economy of the mass media, Pantheon Books.

Close the Gap. (2020). Our mission. https://www.close-the-gap.org/who-we-are

Cox, D. (2017, February 25). Did #OscarsSoWhite work? Looking beyond Hollywood's diversity drought. The Guardian. Retrieved from https://www.theguardian.com/film/2017/feb/25/did-oscars-so-white-work-looking-beyond-the-diversity-drought-in-hollywood

Cyberbullying Research Center. (2016a). Cyberbullying data. Retrieved from https://cyberbullying.org/statistics

Cyberbullying Research Center. (2016b). Cyberbullying data: Identification, prevention, and response. Retrieved from https://cyberbullying.org/Cyberbullying-Identification-Prevention-Response.pdf

Federal Communications Commission. (2021, September). Fifth report on ownership of broadcast stations. https://docs.fcc.gov/public/attachments/DA-21-1101A1.pdf

Gamson, J., & Latteier, P. (2004). Do media monsters devour diversity? Contexts, 3(3), 26–31.

Ghaffary, S. (2021, November 24). Why you should care about Facebook's big push into the metaverse. Vox. https://www.vox.com/recode/22799665/facebook-metaverse-meta-zuckerberg-oculus-vr-ar

Grieco, E. (2018, November 2). Newsroom employees are less diverse than U.S. workers overall. Pew Research Center. https://www.pewresearch.org/fact-tank/2018/11/02/newsroom-employees-are-less-diverse-than-u-s-workers-overall/

Hoewe, J. (2018). Coverage of a crisis: The effect of international news portrayals of refugees and misuse of the term immigrant. American Behavioral Scientist, 62(4), 478–492.

Kaplan, A. M., & Haenlein, M. (2010). Users of the world, unite! The challenges and opportunities of social media. Business Horizons, 53(1), 59–68.

Lauzen, M. M. (2022). It's a man's (celluloid) world, even in a pandemic year: Portrayals of female characters in the top U.S. films of 2021. Center for the Study of Women in Television & Film https://womenintvfilm.sdsu.edu/wp-content/uploads/2022/03/2021-Its-a-Mans-Celluloid-World-Report.pdf

Littleton, C. (2022, March 24). How BIPOC audiences drive moviegoing: UCLA Hollywood diversity report. Variety. https://variety.com/2022/film/news/movies-ucla-hollywood-diversity-report-1235213215/

Lutz, A. (2012, June 14). These 6 media corporations control 90% of the media in America. Business Insider, corporations-control-90-of-the-media-in-america-2012-6. Retrieved from http://www.businessinsider.com/these-6-

Matsa, K. E. (2017, May 11). Buying spree brings more local TV stations to fewer big companies. Pew Research Center. Retrieved from http://www.pewresearch.org/fact-tank/2017/05/11/buying-spree-brings-more-local-tv-stations-to-fewer-big-companies/

McLuhan, M. (1964). Understanding media: The extensions of man, McGraw-Hill.

Mills, C. W. (1956). The power elite, Oxford University Press.

Neff, K., Smith, S., & Pieper, K. (2021). Inequality across 1,500 popular films: Examining gender and race/ethnicity of leads/co-leads from 2007 to 2021. https://assets.uscannenberg.org/docs/aii-s

tudy-inequality-popular-films-20220 311.pdf

Nielsen. (2021). *The Nielsen total audience report: Advertising across today's media*. https://www.nielsen.com/insights/2021/total-audience-advertising-across-todays-media/

Oxford English Dictionary. (2022). *Updates*. https://www.oed.com/information/updates

Pew Research Center. (2018). *Internet/ broadband fact sheet*. Retrieved from http://www.pewinternet.org/fact-sheet/internet-broadband/

Pew Research Center. (2021). *Internet use by age. [Data set]*. https://www.pewresearch.org/internet/chart/internet-use-by-age/

Ravenscraft, E. (2022, April 25). *What is the Metaverse, exactly? Wired*. https://www.wired.com/story/what-is-the-metaverse/

Traugott, M (Ed.). (1978). *Émile Durkheim: On institutional analysis*. University of Chicago Press.

Vogels, E. (2021). *Some digital divides persist between rural, urban and suburban America. Pew Research Center*. https://www.pewresearch.org/short-reads/2021/08/19/some-digital-divides-persist-between-rural-urban-and-suburban-america/

Whorf, B. (1956). *Language, thought, and reality: Selected writings of Benjamin Lee Whorf*, MIT Press

CHAPTER 8

Aubrey, J. S., & Smith, S. E. (2013). Development and validation of the endorsement of the hookup culture index. *Journal of Sex Research, 50*(5), 435–448.

Bentley, P. (2011, March 4). *Why an arranged marriage is more likely to develop into lasting love. Daily Mail*. Retrieved from http://www.dailymail.co.uk/news/article-1363176/Why-arranged-marriage-likely-develop-lasting-love.html

Berger, P. (1963). *Invitation to sociology*, Doubleday.

Bradshaw, C., Kahn, A. S., & Saville, B. K. (2010). To hook up or date: Which gender benefits? *Sex Roles, 62*(9–10), 661–669.

Centers for Disease Control and Prevention (CDC). (2017f). *Violence prevention*. Retrieved from https://www.cdc.gov/violenceprevention/nisvs/infographic.html

Cherlin, A. J. (2004). The deinstitutionalization of marriage in America. *Journal of Marriage and the Family, 66*, 848–861.

Cherlin, A. J. (2010). *The marriage-go-round: The state of marriage and the family in America today*, Vintage.

Collins, R. (1975). *Conflict society: Towards an explanatory science*, Academic Press.

James-Kangal, N., Weitbrecht, E. M., Trenel, E. F., & Whitton, S. W. (2018). Hooking up and emerging adults' relationship attitudes and expectations. *Sexuality and Culture, 22*(3), 706–723.

Kimmel, M. (2011). *The gendered society*, Oxford University Press.

Kubota, Y. (2009, June 8). *Tokyo firm rents fake family, friends for weddings. Reuters*. Retrieved from https://www.reuters.com/article/us-japan-weddings/tokyo-firm-rents-fake-family-friends-for-weddings-idUSTRE5571IY20090608

Lauer, S., & Yodanis, C. (2011). Individualized marriage and the integration of resources. *Journal of Marriage and the Family, 73*, 669–683.

Parsons, T., & Bales, R. F. (1955). *Family, socialization, and interaction process*, Free Press.

Wilcox, W. B., & Nock, S. L. (2006). What's love got to do with it? Equality, equity, commitment and women's marital quality. *Social Forces, 84*(3), 1321–1345

CHAPTER 9

Adams, K. L., & Adams, D. E. (2003). *Urban education: A reference handbook*, ABC-CLIO.

Aucejo, E. M., French, J., Araya, M. P. U., & Zafar, B. (2020). The impact of COVID-19 on student experiences and expectations: Evidence from a survey. *Journal of Public Economics, 191*, 104271.

Barr, R., & Dreeben, R. (1983). *How schools work*, University of Chicago Press.

Blau, F. D. (1998). Trends in the well-being of American women, 1970–1995. *Journal of Economic Literature, 36*, 112–165.

Bourdieu, P., & Passeron, J. C. (1973). Cultural reproduction and social reproduction. In R. Brown (Ed.), *Knowledge, education and cultural change* (pp. 71–112).

Bourdieu, P., & Passeron, J. C. (1990). *Reproduction in education, society and culture* (2nd ed.). SAGE.

Carnivale, A., Cheah, B., & Wenzinger, E. (2021). *The college payoff. Center on Education and the Workforce*. https://cew.georgetown.edu/wp-content/uploads/cew-college_payoff_2021-fr.pdf

Collins, R. (1979). *The credential society: An historical sociology of education and stratification*, Academic Press.

Davies, S., & Guppy, N. (2018). *The schooled society: An introduction to the sociology of education*, Oxford University Press.

DiPrete, T. A., Eirich, G. M., Cook, K. S., & Massey, D. S. (2006). Cumulative advantage as a mechanism for inequality: A review of theoretical and empirical developments. *Annual Review of Sociology, 32*, 271–297.

Durkheim, É. (1951). *Suicide: A study in sociology*, Free Press, Original work published 1897

Durkheim, É. (1956). *Education and sociology*, Free Press.

Gamoran, A., & Mare, R. (1989). Secondary school tracking and educational inequality: Compensation, reinforcement, or neutrality. *American Journal of Sociology, 94*, 1146–1183.

Gentrup, S., Lorenz, G., Kristen, C., & Kogan, I. (2020). Self-fulfilling prophecies in the classroom: Teacher expectations, teacher feedback and student achievement. *Learning and Instruction*, 66, 1–17.

Jackson, P. W. (1968). *Life in classrooms*, Holt Reinhart and Winston.

Kelly, W (Ed.). (2004). *Fanning the flames: Fans and consumer culture in contemporary Japan*. State University of New York.

Konnikova, M. (2014). *18 U.S. presidents were in college fraternities. The Atlantic.* Retrieved from https://www.theatlantic.com/education/archive/2014/02/18-us-presidents-were-in-college-fraternities/283997/

Lareau, A. (2003). *Unequal childhoods: Class, race, and family life*, University of California Press.

Marini, M. M. (1989). Sex differences in earnings in the United States. *Annual Review of Sociology*, 15, 343–380.

Marx, K., & Engels, F. (1964). *The communist manifesto*, Modern Reader Paperbacks.

Merton, R. K. (1949). *Social theory and social structure*, Free Press.

Organization for Economic Co-operation and Development (OECD). (2021). *Population with tertiary education*. https://data.oecd.org/eduatt/population-with-tertiary-education.htm

Shader, L., & Zonderman, J. (2006). *Birth control pills*, Infobased.

van Damme, D. (2013). *Educational outcomes. OECD Reports* Retrieved from https://www.oecd.org/newsroom/achieving-sustainable-development-goal-for-education-by-2030-will-be-major-challenge-for-all-countries.htm

CHAPTER 10

Almeling, R. (2007). Selling genes, selling gender: Egg agencies, sperm banks, and the medical market in genetic material. *American Sociological Review*, 72(3), 319–340.

Beyon, H., & Nichols, T (Eds.). (2006). *The Fordism of Ford and modern management: Fordism and post-Fordism.* Elgar.

Bonanno, A. (2012). Fordism post Fordism. In G. Ritzer (Ed.), *The Wiley-Blackwell encyclopedia of globalization* (pp. 680– 684). Wiley-Blackwell.

Bureau of Economic Analysis. (2021). *National data: GDP and personal income.* https://apps.bea.gov/iTable/?reqid=19&step=2&isuri=1&1921=survey

Bureau of Labor Statistics (BLS). (2018). *Employment and wages by occupation. Economic Daily.* Retrieved from https://www.bls.gov/opub/ted/2018/employment-and-wages-by-occupation-may-2017.htm

Bureau of Labor Statistics (BLS). (2021). *Employment by major industry sector. [Data set].* https://www.bls.gov/emp/tables/employment-by-major-industry-sector.htm

Durkheim, É. (1960). *The division of labour in society*, Free Press.

Ford, H. (1922). *My life and work*, Doubleday.

Hochschild, A. R. (1983). *The managed heart: Commercialization of human feeling*, University of California Press.

Irwin, N. (2017, September 3). *To understand rising inequality, consider the janitors at two top companies, then and now. New York Times.* Retrieved from https://www.nytimes.com/2017/09/03/upshot/to-understand-rising-inequality-consider-the-janitors-at-two-top-companies-then-and-now.html

Marx, K., & Engels, F. (1964). *The communist manifesto*, Modern Reader Paperbacks.

Mayo, E. (1946). *The human problems of an industrial civilization* (2nd ed.). Harvard University Press.

Mayo, E. (1949). *The social problems of an industrial civilization*, Routledge.

McCambridge, J., Witton, J., & Elbourne, D. R. (2014). Systematic review of the Hawthorne effect: New concepts are needed to study research participation effects. *Journal of Clinical Epidemiology*, 67(3), 267–277.

McKinsey Global Institute (MGI). (2017). *Jobs lost, jobs gained: Workforce transitions in a time of automation.* Retrieved from https://www.mckinsey.com/~/media/BAB489A30B724BECB5DEDC41E9BB9FAC.ashx

Muldoon, J. (2012). The Hawthorne legacy: A reassessment of the impact of the Hawthorne studies on management scholarship, 1930–1958. *Journal of Management History*, 18(1), 105–119.

Ritzer, G. (2011). *The McDonaldization of society* (6th ed.). SAGE.

Spurlock, M. (2004). *Super size me* [Film]. Columbia TriStar Home Entertainment.

Taylor, F. W. (1947). *The principles of scientific management*, Harper & Row.

Weber, M. (1965). *The sociology of religion*, Methuen

CHAPTER 11

Agency for Healthcare Research and Quality. (2016). *National health quality and disparity report.* Retrieved from https://www.ahrq.gov/sites/default/files/wysiwyg/research/findings/nhqrdr/nhqdr16/2016qdr.pdf

Americans with Disabilities Act (ADA). (2017). *Information and technical assistance on the Americans with disabilities act.* Retrieved from https://www.ada.gov/

Bauer, U. E., & Plescia, M. (2014). Addressing disparities in the health of American Indian and Alaska native people: The importance of improved public health data. *American Journal of Public Health*, S255–S257. 104 Suppl 3(S3)

Bonn, M., Palayew, A., Bartlett, S., Brothers, T. D., Touesnard, N., & Tyndall, M. (2021). "The times they are a-changin'": addressing common misconceptions about the role of safe supply in North America's overdose crisis. *Journal of Studies on Alcohol and Drugs*, 82(1), 158–160.

Brothers, T. D., Leaman, M., Bonn, M., Lewer, D., Atkinson, J., Fraser, J., Gillis, A., Gniewek, M., Hawker, L., Hayman, H., Jorna, P., Martell, D., O'Donnell, T., Rivers-Bowerman, H., & Genge, L. (2022). Evaluation of an emergency safe supply drugs and managed alcohol program in COVID-19 isolation hotel shelters for people experiencing homelessness. *Drug and Alcohol Dependence, 235,* 1–9.

Case, A., Lubotsky, D., & Paxson, C. (2002). Economic status and health in childhood: The origins of the gradient. *American Economic Review, 92*(5), 1308–1334.

Centers for Disease Control and Prevention (CDC). (2014). *Suicide and self-inflicted injury.* Retrieved from https://www.cdc.go/nchs/fastats/suicide.htm

Centers for Disease Control and Prevention (CDC). (2017a). *Adult obesity prevalence maps.* Retrieved from https://www.cdc.gov/obesity/data/ prevalence-maps.html

Centers for Disease Control and Prevention (CDC). (2017b). *Disability impacts all of us.* Retrieved from https://www.cdc.gov/ncbddd/disabilityandhealth/ infographic-disability-impacts-all.html

Centers for Disease Control and Prevention (CDC). (2017c). *Disability overview.* Retrieved from https://www.cdc.gov/ncbddd/disabilityandhealth/disability.html

Centers for Disease Control and Prevention (CDC). (2017d). *Fact sheets: Binge drinking.* Retrieved from https://www.cdc.gov/alcohol/fact-sheets/ binge-drinking.htm

Centers for Disease Control and Prevention (CDC). (2018). *Adult obesity facts.* Retrieved from https://www.cdc.gov/obesity/data/adult.html

Centers for Disease Control and Prevention (CDC). (2022). *Death rate maps & graphs.* https://www.cdc.gov/drugoverdose/deaths/index.html

Chokshi, D. A. (2018, April 3). *Income, poverty, and health inequality. JAMA Forum.* Retrieved from https://jamanetwork.com/ journals/jama/fullarticle/2677433

Commonwealth Fund. (2017). *International health care system profiles.* Retrieved from https://international.commonwealthfund.org/countries/united_states/

Congressional Research Service. (2022). *U.S. health care coverage and spending.* https://sgp.fas.org/crs/misc/IF10830.pdf

Garcia, D., Betancourt, G., & Scaccabarrozzi, L. (2015). *The state of HIV/AIDS among Hispanics/Latinos in the U.S. and Puerto Rico.* Latino Commission on AIDS.

Himes, C. L., & Reynolds, S. L. (2005). The changing relationship between obesity and educational status. *Gender Issues, 22*(2), 45–57.

Kenkel, D. S., Lillard, D. R., & Mathios, A. D. (2006). *The roles of high school completion and GED receipt in smoking and obesity.* National Bureau of Economic Research.

Lara, M., Gamboa, C., Kahramanian, M. I., Morales, L. S., & Bautista, D. E. (2005). *Acculturation and Latino health in the United States: A review of the literature and its sociopolitical context.* RAND Corporation.

Mehra, C. (2017). *India cannot eliminate TB by 2017 without also tackling poverty and under nutrition. Huffington Post.* Retrieved from http://www.huffingtonpost.in/ chapal-mehra/india-cannot-eliminate-tb-by-2025-without-also-tackling-poverty_a_22116851/

Mudur, G. S. (2021, October 15). *Tuberculosis killed 504,000 people in India in 2020: WHO. The Telegraph Online.* https://www.telegraphindia.com/india/tuberculosis-killed-504000-people-in-india-in-2020-who/cid/1834644

National Center for Health Statistics. (2003). *Health, United States, 2003.*

National Heart, Lung, and Blood Institute. (2017). *Calculate your body mass index.* Retrieved from https://www.nhlbi.nih.gov/health/educational/lose_wt/BMI/ bmicalc.htm

National Institutes of Health. (2013). *Why obesity is a health problem.* Retrieved from https://www.nhlbi.nih.gov/ health/educational/wecan/healthy-weight-basics/obesity.htm

Parsons, T. (1951). *The social system,* Routledge and Kegan Paul.

Pickett, K., & Wilkinson, R. (2011). *The spirit level: Why greater equality makes societies stronger,* Bloomsbury.

Springer, K., & Mouzon, D. M. (2011). Macho men and preventative health care: Implications for older men in different social classes. *Journal of Health and Social Behavior, 52*(2), 212–227.

United Nations (UN). (2016). *Convention on the Rights of Persons with Disabilities.* Retrieved from https://www.un.org/development/desa/ disabilities/convention-on-the-rights-of-persons-with-disabilities.html

World Health Organization (WHO). (2017a). *Constitution of WHO: Principles.* Retrieved from http://www.who.int/about/mission/en/

World Health Organization (WHO). (2021, October 14). *Tuberculosis: Key facts* https://www.who.int/news-room/fact-sheets/detail/tuberculosis

CHAPTER 12

Bennett, D., Sharpe, M., Freeman, C., & Carson, A. (2004). Anorexia nervosa among female secondary school students in Ghana. *British Journal of Psychiatry, 185*(4), 312–317.

Bourguignon, F., & Morrison, C. (2002). Inequality among world citizens: 1820–1992. *American Economic Review, 92*(4), 727–744.

Clelland, D. A. (2014). The core of the apple: Degrees of monopoly and dark value in global commodity chains. *Journal of World-System Research, 20*(1), 82–111.

Durkheim, É. (1960). *The division of labour in society,* Free Press.

Frank, D. J., Camp, B. J., & Boutcher, S. A. (2010). Worldwide trends in the criminal regulation of sex, 1945 to 2005. *American Sociological Review, 75*(6), 867–893.

Global Footprint Network. (2023). *Ecological footprint.* www.footprintnetwork.org

Hickel, J. (2017, January 14). *Aid in reverse: How poor countries develop rich countries. The Guardian.* https://www.theguardian.com/global-development-professionals-network/2017/jan/14/aid-in-reverse-how-poor-countries-develop-rich-countries

Holder, J. (2022, September 4). *Tracking coronavirus vaccinations around the world. The New York Times*. Retrieved September 4, 2022 from https://www.nytimes.com/interactive/2021/world/covid-vaccinations-tracker.html

Meyer, J. W., Boli, J., Thomas, G. M., & Ramirez, F. O. (1997). World society and the nation-state. *American Journal of Sociology, 103*(1), 144–181.

Milanovic, B. (2016). *Global inequality: A new approach for the age of globalization*, Harvard University Press.

Organisation for Economic Co-operation and Development (OECD). (2016). *World development indicators: Gini*. Retrieved from http://databank.worldbank.org/data/ reports.aspx?source=2&series=SI.POV. GINI&country=

Pickett, K., & Wilkinson, R. (2011). *The spirit level: Why greater equality makes societies stronger*, Bloomsbury.

Rooney-Varga, J. N., Hensel, M., McCarthy, C., McNeal, K., Norfles, N., Rath, K., Schnell, A. H., & Sterman, J. D. (2021). Building consensus for ambitious climate action through the World Climate simulation. *Earth's Future, 9*(12), 1–16.

Rostow, W. W. (1991). *The stages of economic growth: A non-communist manifesto*, Cambridge University Press.

Rothman, L. (2015, July 28). *When spousal rape first became a crime in the U.S. Time*. Retrieved from http://time.com/3975175/ spousal-rape-case-history/

Wallerstein, I. (2011). *The modern world system*, University of California Press.

Wilkinson, R., & Pickett, K. (2018). *The inner level: How more equal societies reduce stress, restore sanity and improve everyone's well-being*, Allen Lane

CHAPTER 13

Barnes, A., & Virgint, E. (2010). *Youth voter turnout in Canada. Pub.*Library of Parliament.

Blais, A., & Loewen, P. (2011, January). *Youth electoral engagement in Canada*. Working Paper Series. Elections Canada.

Bradley, D., Huber, E., Moller, S., Nielson, F., & Stephens, J. D. (2003). Determinants of relative poverty in advanced capitalist democracies. *American Sociological Review, 68*(3), 22–51.

Briggs, A. (2000). The welfare state in a historical perspective. In C. Pierson & F. G. Castles (Eds.), *The welfare state reader* (pp. 1–31). Polity Press.

Coleman, J. S. (1990). *Foundations of social theory*, Belknap Press.

File, T. (2017). *Voting in America: A look at the 2016 presidential election*. U.S. Census Bureau. Retrieved from https://www.census.gov/newsroom/blogs/random-samplings/2017/05/voting_in_america.html

Fisherback, P., Haines, M. R., & Kantor, S. (2007). Births, deaths, and the New Deal relief during the great depression. *Review of Economics and Statistics, 89*(1), 1–14.

Geertz, C. (1962). The rotating credit association: A middle rung in development. *Economic Development and Cultural Change, 10*, 240–263.

Gerth, H. H., & Mills, C. W (Eds.). (1946). *From Max Weber: Essays in sociology*. Oxford University Press.

Hauser, R., Burkhauser, R. V., Couch, K., & Ozturk, G. B. (2016). *Wife or frau, women still do worse: A comparison of men and women in the United States and Germany after union dissolutions in the 1990s and 2000s. Working Paper 2016-39, Department of Economics, University of Connecticut, Storrs.* https://ideas.repec.org/p/uct/ uconnp/2016-39.html

Kenworthy, L. (1999). Do social-welfare policies reduce poverty? A cross-national assessment. *Social Forces, 77*(3), 1119–1139.

Konish, L. (2022, June 11). *How effective were those stimulus checks? Some argue the money may have fueled inflation. CNBC.* https://www.cnbc.com/2022/06/11/the-pandemic-stimulus-checks-were-a-big-experiment-did-it-work.html

Marx, K., & Engels, F. (1964). *The communist manifesto*, Modern Reader Paperbacks.

McPherson, M., Smith-Lovin, L., & Brashears, M. (2008). The ties that bind are fraying. *Contexts, 7*(3), 32–60.

Ozturk, G. B. (2018). Anti-poverty effects on in-kind transfers among divorced or separated women in the United States. *Poverty and Public Policy, 10*(1), 57–80.

Peoples, C. D. (2012). Welfare state. In G. Ritzer (Ed.), *The Wiley-Blackwell encyclopedia of globalization* (pp. 2218–2221). Wiley-Blackwell.

Poggi, G. (2004). Formation and form: Theories of state formation. In K. Nash & A. Scott (Eds.), *The Blackwell companion to political sociology* (pp. 95–106). Blackwell.

Poon, L. (2015, August 19). *Why won''t you be my neighbor? Bloomberg*. https://www.bloomberg.com/news/articles/2015-08-19/why-americans-are-less-likely-to-interact-with-their-neighbors-than-ever-before

Putnam, R. D. (2000). *Bowling alone: The collapse and revival of American community*, Simon & Schuster.

Putnam, R. D., Leonardi, R., & Nanetti, R. Y. (1993). *Making democracy work: Civic traditions in modern Italy*, Princeton University Press.

Romig, K. (2018, November 5). *Social security lifts more Americans above poverty than any other program. Center on Budget and Policy Priorities.* Retrieved from https://www.cbpp.org/research/social-security/social-security-keeps-22-million-americans-out-of-poverty-a-state-by-state

Siegel Bernard, T., & Lieber, R. (2021, June 2). *F.A.Q. on stimulus checks, unemployment and the coronavirus plan. The New York Times.* https://www.nytimes.com/article/coronavirus-stimulus-package-questions-answers.html

Stanbridge, K., & Ramos, H. (2012). *Seeing politics differently: A brief introduction to political sociology*, Oxford University Press.

Strayer, J. R. (1970). *On the medieval origins of the modern state*, Princeton University Press.

Tilly, C. (1985). War making and state making as organized crime. In P. Evans, D. Rueschemeyer, & T. Skocpol (Eds.), *Bringing the state back in* (pp. 169–187). Cambridge University Press.

van den Berg, A., von Restorff, C-H., Parent, D., & Masi, A. (2008). From unemployment to employment insurance: Towards transitional labour markets in Canada. In R. J. A. Muffels (Ed.), *Flexibility and employment security in Europe: Labour markets in transition* (pp. 308–335). Edward Elgar.

Veenhof, B., Wellman, B., Quell, C., & Hogan, B. (2008). *How Canadians' use of the internet affects social life and civic participation. Catalogue 56F0004M*— no. 016 Retrieved from http://www.statcan.gc.ca/ pub/56f0004m/56f0004m2008016-eng.htm

CHAPTER 14

Beyerlein, K., & Hipp, J. R. (2006). A two-stage model for a two-stage process: How biographical availability matters for social movement mobilization. *Mobilization*, 11, 299–320.

Buchanan, L., Bui, Q., & Patel, J. K. (2020, July 3). *Black Lives Matter may be the largest movement in U.S. history. The New York Times.* https://www.nytimes.com/interactive/2020/07/03/us/george-floyd-protests-crowd-size.html

Chenoweth, E. (2017, February 7). *This is what we learned by counting the women's marches. Washington Post.* Retrieved from https://www.washingtonpost.com/news/monkey-cage/wp/2017/02/07/this-is-what-we-learned-by-counting-the-womens-marches

Collins, P. H. (2013). Truth-telling and intellectual activism. *Contexts*, 12(1), 36–41.

Corrigall-Brown, C. (2013). Participation in social movements. In D. A. Snow, D. della Porta, B. Klandermans, & D. McAdam (Eds.), *The Wiley-Blackwell encyclopedia of social and political movements.* Wiley-Blackwell.

Dalton, R. J., Van Sickle, A., & Weldon, S. (2010). The individual-institutional nexus of protest behaviour. *British Journal of Political Science*, 40, 51–73.

Diani, M. (2004). Networks and participation. In D. A. Snow, S. A. Soule, & H. Kreisi (Eds.), *The Blackwell companion to social movements* (pp. 339–359). Blackwell.

Fantasia, R., & Hirsch, E. L. (1995). Culture in rebellion: The appropriation and transformation of the veil in the Algerian revolution. In H. Johnston & B. Klandermans (Eds.), *Social movements and culture* (pp. 144–162). University of Minnesota Press.

Gamson, W. (1990). *The strategy of social protest* (2nd ed.). Wadsworth.

Gecas, V. (2000). Value identities, self-motives, and social movements. In S. Stryker, T. J. Owens, & R. W. White (Eds.), *Self, identity, and social movements* (pp. 93–109). University of Minnesota Press.

Giugni, M. G. (2004). Personal and biographical consequences. In D. A. Snow, S. A. Soule, & H. Kriesi (Eds.), *The Blackwell companion to social movements* (pp. 489–507). Blackwell.

Inglehart, R. (1997). *Modernization and postmodernization: Cultural, economic and political change in 43 nations*, Princeton University Press.

Klandermans, B. (1997). *The social psychology of protest*, Blackwell.

Klandermans, B., & de Weerd, M. (2000). Group identification and political protest. In S. Stryker, T. J. Owens, & R. W. White (Eds.), *Self, identity, and social movements* (pp. 68–90). University of Minnesota Press.

Kramer, S. (2020, August 27). *More Americans say they are regularly wearing masks in stores and other businesses. Pew Research Center.* https://www.pewresearch.org/fact-tank/2020/08/27/more-americans-say-they-are-regularly-wearing-masks-in-stores-and-other-businesses/

McAdam, D. (1986). Recruitment to high-risk activism: The case of freedom summer. *American Journal of Sociology*, 92, 64–90.

McAdam, D. (1988). *Freedom summer*, Oxford University Press.

McLeod, D. M., & Hertog, J. K. (1999). Social control, social change and the mass media's role in the regulation of protest groups. In D. Demers & K. Viswanath (Eds.), *Mass media, social control and social change: A macrosocial perspective* (pp. 300–305). Iowa State University Press.

Melucci, A., Keane, J., & Mier, P. (1989). *Nomads of the present: Social movements and individual needs in contemporary society*, Temple University Press.

Meyer, D. S., & Tarrow, S (Eds.). (1998). *The social movement society: Contentious politics for a new century.* Rowan and Littlefield.

Nepstad, S. E., & Smith, C. (1999). Rethinking recruitment to high-risk/cost activism: The case of the Nicaragua exchange. *Mobilization*, 4, 25–40.

Norris, P. (2002). *Democratic phoenix: Reinventing political activism*, Cambridge University Press.

Olson, M. (1965). *The logic of collective action: Public goods and the theory of groups*, Harvard University Press.

Polletta, F. (1999). "Free spaces" in collective action. *Theory and Society*, 28, 1–38.

Putnam, R. D. (2000). *Bowling alone: The collapse and revival of American community*, Simon & Schuster.

Rosenstone, S. J., & Hansen, J. M. (1993). *Mobilization, participation, and democracy in America*, Macmillan.

Smith, J., McCarthy, J. D., McPhail, C., & Angustyn, B. (2001). From protest to agenda building: Description bias in media coverage of protest events in Washington, DC. *Social Forces*, 79(4), 1397–1423.

Snow, D. A. (2001). Collective identity and expressive forms. In N. J. Smelser & P. B. Blates (Eds.), *The international encyclopedia of the social and behavioral sciences.* Elsenier Selpin.

Taylor, V., & Raeburn, N. C. (1995). Identity politics as high-risk activism: Career consequences for lesbian, gay, and bisexual sociologists. *Social Problems*, 42, 252–273.

Tilly, C. (1995). *Political identities. [Working paper]. Center for Advanced Study in the Behavioral Sciences.* Stanford University. Retrieved from https://www.ciaonet.org/catalog

Verba, S., Schlozman, K. L., & Brady, H. E. (1995). *Voice and equality: Civic voluntarism in American politics*, Harvard University Press.

Whalen, J., & Flacks, R. (1989). *Beyond the barricades: The sixties generation grows up*, Temple University Press.

Wilkes, R. (2004). First nation politics: Deprivation, resources, and participation in collective action. *Sociological Inquiry*, *74*, 570–589.

Wiltfang, G. L., & McAdam, D. (1991). The costs and risks of social activism: A study of sanctuary movement activism. *Social Forces*, *69*, 987–1010.

Women's, March. (2017). *Sister marches*. Retrieved from https://www.womensmarch.com/annual-report

World Value Survey. (2020). *World Value Survey Wave 7: 2017-2020. [Data set]*. https://www.worldvaluessurvey.org/WVSOnline.jsp

Zhao, Dingxin. (1999). State legitimacy, state policy, and the development of the 1989 Beijing student movement. *Asian Perspective*, *23*, 245–84

INDEX